Mujūn

Libertinism in Mediaeval Muslim Society and Literature

by

Zoltan Szombathy

Gibb Memorial Trust

2013

Published by

The E. J. W. Gibb Memorial Trust

ISBN 978-0-906094-61-7

A CIP record for this book is available from the British Library

Further details of the E. J. Gibb Memorial Trust and its publications
are available at the Trust's website

www.gibbtrust.org

Printed in Great Britain by
Short Run Press
Exeter

Contents

Acknowledgements v

Introduction ix

1. NORMS AND VALUES IN MEDIAEVAL MUSLIM SOCIETY 1
   1. Ideals and Actual Behaviour 1
   2. Some Enduring Values in Mediaeval Muslim Society 12
   3. A Preliminary Definition of *Mujūn* 34

2. THE MOTIFS OF *MUJŪN*: RELIGION 43
   1. An Omnipresent Religious Culture 45
   2. Quran and *Ḥadīths* 47
   3. The Stuff of a Sound Education: Religious Disciplines, Theology, and Islamic History 75
   4. The Religious Obligations 85
   5. Images of Afterlife 97
   6. Hyperboles in Praise Poetry 102
   7. Genuine *Mujūn*: A Provisional Summary 105

3. THE MOTIFS OF *MUJŪN*: DECENCY AND PROPRIETY 113
   1. Breaches of the Norms of Proper Conduct 115
   2. Images of Sexuality 129
   3. Stylistic Features: Punning, Double Entendre, Obscenity, and Parody 140

4. THE RECEPTION OF *MUJŪN* 155
   1. The Reception of *Mujūn* 159
   2. Sanctions and Rewards 215
   3. Regional Differences in the Reception of *Mujūn* 237

5. *MUJŪN*, VALUES AND NORMS 247
   1. *Mujūn* vis-à-vis Dominant Values 248
   2. The Sociology of *Mujūn* 284

Acknowledgements

The following chapters are the result of a research project that I have been pursuing for almost a decade. Throughout all these years I benefited from the expertise of a good many colleagues in various ways, as well as from the generosity of several institutions that provided invaluable financial support for various phases of my research. It would be futile to try to do justice to all of those who helped me in one way or another, and therefore this short note of gratitude must begin with a general thank you to everyone who did in any form, shape or manner. A general message, then, to all supporters, well-wishers and donors of this project: your help is much appreciated. However, some of my benefactors deserve special mention here for their precious advice and stimulating ideas, or their hospitality, or their monetary support.

To put pecuniary matters first. During the years of study culminating in this book I spent a total of half a year doing research at the library of the Instituto de Lenguas y Culturas del Mediterráneo y Oriente Próximo (formerly Instituto de Filología) of the Centro de Ciencias Humanas y Sociales (Consejo Superior de Investigaciones Científicas) in Madrid, as well as three months at the Institute for Advanced Studies in the Humanities in Edinburgh. Both institutions provided an ideal environment for concentrating on a major research project, as well as much-needed access to excellent library holdings and a lively scholarly community always ready with thought-provoking discussions. I absolutely relished my stays at those institutions, and feel a genuine debt for the opportunity. That is equally true of the Institute for Advanced Study at Princeton, where I spent an agreeable and productive year as a member in 2008–2009. True to the intentions and the spirit of its founders and its past generations of outstanding scholars, the institute awards its members with the luxury, rare in today's world, of not having to be distracted by any concerns from the research to be pursued. To be the beneficiary of such support is a privilege which I keenly feel and am happy to acknowledge here. My membership at the Institute for Advanced Study was made possible by the generous sponsorship of the Friends of the Institute for Advanced Study, while the Andrew W. Mellon Foundation provided the financial means of my fellowship periods at Madrid and Edinburgh. It is a pleasant obligation to acknowledge the support I received from these enlightened sponsors of learning and scientific endeavours. For the first three years of my research project I was also the recipient of a Bolyai Scholarship financed by the Hungarian Academy of Sciences; which, to put it simply, made the difference during that period between being able to dedicate myself to the project or being forced by economic circumstances to abandon it. Last but not least, when I had difficulty covering the expenses of a final linguistic check of the prose of this manuscript, the Avicenna Institute of Middle Eastern Studies (Piliscsaba, Hungary) came to the rescue. I am grateful for this important support that arrived just at the moment it was needed. Qui donne vite, donne deux fois, and therefore special thanks to Eva Jeremiás and Miklós Maróth.

In addition to providing calm and pleasant surroundings conducive to working on my research project, the above-mentioned institutes also privileged me with the acquaintance of a number of scholars who gave me a warm welcome and were willing to share their valuable expertise in the field of premodern Muslim culture and society. Many thanks to Patricia Crone, Maribel Fierro, Mercedes García-Arenal, Carole Hillenbrand, and Fernando Rodríguez Mediano. I am also grateful to a host of other scholars who, in the course of the long years of my research project on mujūn, lent their time and attention to discussing one aspect or another of the subject with me and offered valuable corrections and commentary. I would like to express my special gratitude to András Hámori, as well as to Saber el Adly, Abdessamad Belhaj, István Hajnal and Tamás Iványi. Furthermore, István Hajnal was unsparing of his time, a precious commodity given his many responsibilities, to help me with interlibrary loans. Many thanks for that too. I also had the luck of being invited by Beatrice Gruendler to give a seminar on my research to graduate students at Yale University in the autumn of 2008; I find I quite benefited from the insightful comments and questions of the audience there. Being aware that the text of this essay is anything but light reading, I owe very special thanks to the those colleagues who were kind enough to accord their time to reading all or parts of the first draft of my manuscript. I know what a burden I placed on their shoulders when casually asking them to have a so-called quick look into the text. I owe them all a great debt for their patience and goodwill, and especially for the truly helpful comments I received. Many thanks, then, to Patricia Crone, Maribel Fierro, Hilary Kilpatrick, James Montgomery, and Geert Jan van Gelder, to put their names in alphabetical order, which curiously happens to correspond roughly to the chronological order of their respective comments on the text. If, despite having benefited from the valuable advice and suggestions of so many learned colleagues, I have persisted in some erroneous views and interpretations, as I probably have, it goes without saying that the responsibility for all errors is entirely mine.

But whatever the number and gravity of the remaining inaccuracies and flaws in this essay, the manuscript now goes to press. That it finally does is due to the practical advice I received from several persons, which greatly facilitated my way through the publication process. I am particularly grateful to István Ormos, Iván Szántó, Khaled El Rouayheb, James Montgomery, and Eva Mayer. John Child read the manuscript to correct grammatical and stylistic errors. Special thanks to Sam McLeod for her patience and careful work in producing this volume. Above all, I feel privileged by the decision of the Gibb Memorial Trust to accept this volume for publication as part of the Gibb Memorial Series.

As ever, my warmest gratitude must go to my family, and to my kind-hearted parents in particular. Their love is the greatest support, and the greatest reward, one can wish for.

Introduction

This book is about an aspect of mediaeval Arabic culture and literature known in Arabic as *mujūn* (roughly, libertinism, licentiousness, frivolity, indecency, profligacy, shamelessness, impertinence', etc.), a concept that students of mediaeval Arabic texts will, upon closer inspection, find rather hard to define. Yet despite the difficulty of defining the concept, it is familiar in its rough outlines to those with an interest in Arabic literature. Whatever it may have meant in its different contexts, from about the early Abbasid period *mujūn* is a recurrent term and a widespread phenomenon in mediaeval Arabic literature, and if the testimony of written sources is to be trusted, it was also common in real life. It is some aspects of this phenomenon that the following chapters seek to explore.

One thing this essay does not aspire to do is offer an analysis of *mujūn* or interpret texts having *mujūn* content[1] from a literary point of view. The stylistic features of the works and the tropes therein are not the concern of this study, neither is a close reading of particular libertine texts *qua* literature one of its goals. It is an undertaking that I possess neither the proficiency nor the willingness to do; but we are fortunate in that experts of mediaeval Arabic literature have analysed a host of works that could be classified under the general heading of *mujūn* – poems of Abū Nuwās readily come to mind – and therefore various literary aspects of *mujūn* have been the objects of serious research.[2] The main concern of this book, however, lies elsewhere. It is the social implications and the social background of *mujūn* that we will focus on; in other words, this book is an attempt to learn what the popularity of *mujūn* during a certain period of the mediaeval Middle East can tell us about the society and the culture that produced such works. Strictly speaking, this is not a study of *mujūn* literature, but of the society in which such literature flourished, and especially the values and norms of that society. It is a study of the *mājin* (the man who does or writes *mujūn*) rather than of *mujūn* in itself.

As will be shown, people who produced, cultivated and enjoyed *mujūn* were a quite special bunch, the product of the specific cultural and social circumstances of a certain period of Middle Eastern history. However, the texts they left behind live

[1] For convenience and brevity, I will henceforward use the shorthand '*mujūn* literature' for such texts throughout the book. However, it has to be borne in mind that, as will be obvious, *mujūn* might crop up in all manner of literary texts as well as in a person's conduct; and whatever *mujūn* is, it is certainly not a definite literary genre.

[2] A particularly insightful study of *mujūn* as literature is Meisami 1993.

on, and people in our times, including contemporary Muslims in countless countries, continue to interact with and relate to these works in varying ways. Some may find these texts amusing, funny and entertaining, while the same works may strike others as insipid, boring, and also, not infrequently, as repetitive. Some, whether Muslim or non-Muslim, may feel unease and embarrassment at what often still appear to be indecent, irreverent or even outrageous texts depending on one's sensibility, tolerance level and indeed sense of humour. This cannot but pose a difficulty to the researcher whose intention is not to offend readers but to analyse a cultural phenomenon in as neutral a manner as possible. My intention being the latter rather than the former, it was necessary to give some thought to how to address a number of sensitive issues, such as the frequent occurrence of explicit obscenities and taboo words in the texts I studied, or the ubiquity of joking with Islamic religious concepts that could and can be taken as either innocuous or scandalous depending on the recipient's disposition and mood. As for jocular uses of religious motifs, it will be observed that it was mostly produced by believing Muslims, and there is little of it that could be described as hostile or truly offensive to someone having a minimal sense of humour. I have, therefore, decided that if mediaeval Muslims, including most *ʿulamāʾ*, could clearly perceive how innocuous it all was, there is no reason to contradict their implicit (and sometimes explicit) opinion, or to expect less sagacity from contemporary readers. With obscenities, the case is somewhat different: although I did not for a moment entertain the notion of bowdlerising the texts or sanitising their style, I did consider the idea of using abbreviated forms of words like 'fuck' and 'prick'. However, even that degree of coyness would be inappropriate in a work on *mujūn*. Although *mujūn* rarely degenerates into a sort of pure *Schmutzliteratur* – even if exceptions do exist – many mediaeval Muslim authors are anything but priggish when it comes to employing swearwords in their writing. Had I neutralised the directness of such vulgarities, it would have constituted a positive distortion of the texts. A few texts that were truly revolting to my own taste I have preferred not to quote, relegating them to the status of a reference in footnote – anyone is free to consult the sources.

Although this book's primary goal is to offer an interpretation of a literary phenomenon, *mujūn*, as a product of a particular social setting and its prevailing notions of what is and is not proper and reputable, it is not until the last two chapters that we really begin that interpretative attempt. As will presently be argued, the very notion of *mujūn* can be so vague, and so hard to grasp in a few words, that a long overview and categorisation of the relevant literary material is indispensable which will occupy as much as two whole chapters of this study. Firstly however, some of the most fundamental assumptions of mediaeval Middle Eastern society regarding prestige and social value will be briefly discussed. In examining prevailing values, we will not be detained by the powerful and pervasive commitment among mediaeval

Muslims to Islam and its elementary moral precepts, however relevant this fact is to a study of *mujūn*, because not only is it fairly obvious but its countless manifestations have been the subject of plenty of valuable research. Instead, the first chapter will focus on such oppository concepts as the 'élite' versus the 'commoners', serious versus humorous subjects, the city versus the countryside, and the written versus the vernacular language. In a sense, an attempt is made here to roughly outline the conceptual framework in which mediaeval Muslims viewed issues of value, respectability, propriety, and to be sure also that of *mujūn*. After this sketch, an initial glance at the semantics of the term *mujūn* follows, which rounds off the first chapter. As already noted, the next two chapters are devoted in their entirety to the compilation of an inventory of the varied motifs of *mujūn* in literature so as to define this elusive term by way of an accumulation of concrete examples. The second chapter, in particular, surveys the literary motifs of *mujūn* inasmuch as they touch on the subject of religion (mostly Islam, but occasionally also Christianity, Judaism and Zoroastrianism). In most cases, these motifs are characterised by a frivolous approach to religious tenets and precepts. The following chapter examines those motifs of *mujūn* that seem to refer to religious themes only indirectly if at all, playing instead with accepted norms of propriety in behaviour and speech, respectability, and deference to the political authorities and the cultural élite. After the completion of this survey of the miscellaneous corpus of literary motifs classifiable as *mujūn*, it will be time to gauge, to the extent that it is possible, the reception of this kind of literary material in the various subgroups of mediaeval Middle Eastern society, inevitably focusing on the reactions of the educated élite, especially those connected to the rulers' courts. Whether or not the powers that be tolerated, or possibly even encouraged, the production of *mujūn* works sheds much light on the way prevailing norms informed actual behaviour and on the limits of this influence. As the features of mediaeval Muslim society, as with all large-scale societies, were of course far from uniform over time and space, a study of the reception of *mujūn* must address another important question, to wit: was there any particular region and historical period with which *mujūn* can be associated either exclusively or to a great extent? The discussion of this issue completes the fourth chapter of this essay, to be followed by the final chapter, in which an interpretation of *mujūn* literature *qua* social phenomenon is finally proposed. In this interpretation my intention will be to find a plausible explanation for what appears to be a striking discrepancy in the attitudes of élite and common folk alike: despite an obviously widespread and, presumably, honest attachment to dominant values and norms (within the domains of religion, common decorum and decency, as well as politics) that to a large extent seem to have cut across class boundaries, one cannot fail to observe the equally widespread popularity of a literary posture that deliberately disregarded, or rather flouted, the very same values and norms. What is more, *mujūn* was very often enjoyed and produced by otherwise very respectable individuals of unquestionably high status, indeed its appreciation was an important part of the *mentalité* of the political and scholarly (and indeed some of the religious) élite of urban Muslim society for centuries.[3] The focus of the last chapter is therefore the mechanisms of the co-existence within mediaeval Arabic society of conflicting yet equally cherished values and norms.

This book owes a lot to the insights and methods of quite a number of cultural anthropologists and sociologists. In fact, the very structuring of the chapters, as justified in the preceding paragraphs, serves an additional purpose that has to do with a fundamental dilemma in anthropological research. I am referring to the ever-present danger of the anthropologist forcing a false interpretation on the data that is not borne out by the fieldwork data and which would be utterly unrecognisable to the informants themselves. Of course, the same problem attends every act of interpretation and is ultimately irresolvable, but it tends to be especially acute in anthropology, and has proven to be a major headache in studying *mujūn* owing to the scarcity and ambiguity of data with regard to many aspects of this phenomenon. (The reception of *mujūn* among the lower classes is one issue which reduces the researcher to doing a lot of guesswork and facing frustration.) As a partial solution, it seemed advisable to separate data from interpretation to the greatest possible extent, so as to offer the reader the opportunity to arrive at a different conclusion altogether or disagree on any particular detail of interpretation. This, I hope, is facilitated by the fact that Chapters Two and Three contain a minimal amount of analysis in favour of a bare presentation of much source material. (Even though the classification of *mujūn* motifs may, in itself, be regarded as an analytic framework superimposed upon the data, something that just cannot be avoided.) It is in Chapters One and Five, on the other hand, that most of my own interpretive input (and correspondingly, alas, most of the errors) are to be found. The fourth chapter also contains a lot of speculation; however, I sought to bring in a lot of supporting data, and to indicate clearly where data are so scant as to allow but a surmise.

It is partly for the same purpose – that of helping the reader make a distinction between what the data inescapably suggest and what I think they do – that a lot of primary source material is cited throughout the book. These excerpts are taken from larger texts and appear in translation rather than in the original; however wherever

[3] By using the term 'mentality' – popularised in anthropology by Lévy-Bruhl's misguided concept of *mentalité primitive* – I do not wish to imply the existence of an immutable 'Arab character' or 'Muslim way of thinking', notions as ridiculous as they are devoid of substance and meaning. On such usages, see Lloyd 1990: 1–2, 5, 13, 140. The 'mentality' of the élite referred to above is meant to describe a general attitude or outlook that appears to have characterised most members of the urban élite in a certain period of Middle Eastern history as a result of very specific cultural and social influences. Nothing immutable there.

the original wording has special significance or is not entirely clear it is given in parentheses. If this study is a work of historical anthropology, which I intend it to be, then it is probably not a bad idea to let the voice of 'informants' – in the event, mostly mediaeval Muslim littérateurs and savants with their highly specific biases and prejudices – express their own viewpoints. Some cultural anthropologists have suggested that one of the most appropriate ways to gain a better understanding of a foreign society is by paying attention to the many concrete (spoken or written) expressions of the controversies going on within that society. In this approach, which I find very useful, it is through the observation and analysis of a community's own discourse that its value system, worldview, and basic assumptions can best be grasped.[4] Further there is an additional reason justifying the practice of copious citation. *Mujūn* can sometimes be fairly entertaining even to a contemporary reader, an observation some of the excerpts may help illustrate.

[4] See Sherzer 1987: 297, 302, 305–6; and also cf. Douglas 1970: 11; and von Hees 2007: 22–3. On the importance of concrete examples for an anthropological analysis of underlying values and structures, see Eickelman 1989: 231.

1

Norms and Values in Mediaeval Muslim Society

> "The poor boy continually thought of the better class of his fellow-students, and tried to model his conduct on what he thought was theirs. 'They', he said to himself, 'eat a beefsteak? Never.' But they most of them ate one now and again, unless it was a mutton chop that tempted them. And they used him for a model much as he did them. 'He', they would say to themselves, 'eat a mutton chop? Never'..."
>
> Samuel Butler: *Erewhon*

1. Ideals and Actual Behaviour

This section of the essay bears directly on the issue of the nature of values and norms, a subject with a relevance far beyond the study of mediaeval Muslim society. It will be worthwhile then, to lend some attention to the concepts of 'value and norm' before having a look into the impact of certain normative concepts on the cultural ideals – and to an extent also on the patterns of behaviour – of the mediaeval Middle East.

An important difference between the conventional understanding of 'norms' and 'values' – one which is obviously a matter of degree rather than of kind – concerns the sanctioning of failure to conform. According to this view, norms may be understood as rules the transgression of which will often result in social penalties, not necessarily 'official' and systematic but noticeable. On the other hand, values being less concrete and their transgression less clear-cut, sanctions are less likely to follow.[1] However, the suggestion that non-conformity to norms must bring penalties and stigmatisation has been shown to be problematic.[2] There are other – and in my opinion more felicitous – ways to understand the two concepts and distinguish them from each other. To start with, norms are more specific (and more tied to behaviour) than values are: values are generalities that have more to do with the shared goals and ideals of a community than with the actual ways of attaining them. It follows,

---

[1] Clinard 1965: 9.

[2] Cf. Testé 2003: 18–9, 30, 31 [note 6].

then, that people sharing roughly the same values may well disagree on quite a lot of norms.[3] In other words, "values are rooted in human motivation [...] as it adapts to social requirements", whereas "norms actualize values".[4]

Certain behaviours may be described as normative in either a descriptive (statistical) or a prescriptive sense: in the former case, normative is what is actually observed to be most frequent and done by the majority; in the latter, normative is what most people accept would be desirable and ideal but may mostly fail to do. Of these two possible meanings of a 'norm', I opt for the prescriptive one. Understood this way, norms are not necessarily those patterns of behaviour that are statistically predominant. It is far from unusual that members of a society should show near-total consensus regarding certain forms of behaviour being normative, all the while failing to apply those norms in their actual conduct. (This is a very important point which will be taken for granted throughout the course of this study of *mujūn*.) In fact, when the term 'norm' is used in a descriptive sense to refer to those practices that are observed to be most common, it all but becomes synonymous with a host of other words like 'customs', 'traditions', 'ways', and so on, and therefore has little analytical value.[5]

For our present purpose, the most important observation is the fact, as just pointed out, that a norm need not be statistically predominant to fully qualify as a norm and have a palpable impact on both élite and popular culture. The reader is asked to remember this principle in order to avoid unnecessary objections to considering ideals obviously limited in application to be norms. For praying five times a day to be a valid norm of behaviour for Muslims, it is completely irrelevant whether the majority of people (or of adults, or adult males) did actually pray five times a day. What matters is whether the majority accepted it as a desirable pattern of behaviour that people should ideally conform to (but perhaps do not in practice, because of their human shortcomings). It is the – often only tacit – approval of the majority that makes a norm a norm (and distinguishes it from a mere 'rule').[6]

Of written texts in Arabic from the mediaeval period that could help us identify norms and ideals, there is certainly no shortage. Problems tend to arise when one would explore the actual situation, that is to say the extent to which those norms actually informed everyday behaviour. The primacy of ideals over the actual state of affairs for most mediaeval Arabic writers is a tendency all too familiar to students of Arabic: books tend to portray ideals, and authors appear to have had little interest

[3] For more on differentating values from norms, cf. Dubois 2003: 3, 9–10. For more on the nature of social values, cf. Sherif 1936: 113, 117, 128.

[4] Dubois, Beauvois 2003: 237.

[5] Nevertheless, there are sociologists using the term 'norm' in this descriptive or statistical sense. For a more detailed discussion of the question, see Dubois 2003: 1–2, 5; and Dubois, Beauvois 2003: 236.

[6] Dubois 2003: 2.

in the departures for any purpose other than with an eye to 'correct' the supposedly myriad faults of the ignorant. Thus, the first and most important difficulty in the course of an analysis of practically any aspect of mediaeval Middle Eastern culture is the adequate assessment, treatment and use of the sources. More often than not, the difficulty has little to do with the scarcity of sources – although that may also happen, as this study's repeated plaints about the lamentably fragmentary data on the provenance of literary motifs, for instance, will amply demonstrate. In plenty of subjects, however, the researcher does have a multitude of primary sources to rely on. Still, it is definitely injudicious to rush to rely on those sources before reflecting on a number of important points. First, as perhaps all traditional literacy, mediaeval Arabic literature and scholarship was the exclusive preserve of, and was produced by, a relatively small class of the general population, the educated urban élite[7], which poses considerable problems. Perhaps not all, but certainly the vast majority, of the sources at our disposal express the views, preferences and biases of the political and religious élite.[8] Not surprisingly, all but excluded are the voices of such social groups as the urban poor, and more generally the uneducated 'commoners' (*ʿāmma*) of the cities, let alone the rural peasantry, who despite their having always constituted the bulk of the population of the Middle East are for all practical purposes absent from the sources.[9] Likewise, reliable information on the lives of women – as opposed to ideological content – is difficult to come by in most sources, a state of affairs only partly attributable to factors of prestige and honour: sexual segregation may often have meant that men were barred from knowledge of most female concerns.[10] As Roy Mottahedeh pointed out, many aspects of mediaeval Arab society will remain unknown to us simply because the chroniclers deemed it beneath a scholar's dignity to record the concerns and dealings among themselves of mere lowly commoners.[11] For instance, valuable data are relatively scarce on the religious beliefs and practices of the uneducated masses,

---

[7] In some societies, linguistic reasons – namely a situation of diglossia, involving two distinct versions of Arabic in all Arabic-speaking lands, Latin and different vernaculars in early mediaeval Europe, or colonial 'official' languages (perpetuated by postcolonial élites) and local tongues in contemporary Africa – could exacerbate the monopoly of a certain social group over writing and 'high' culture. On this factor in the mediaeval Arab world, see for instance Rubiera Mata 1992: 45; and also cf. Sadan 1998: 3–4; Shoshan 1991: 75.

[8] Michael Cook comments on the existence and effect of such a bias in his study of the Islamic concept of 'commanding right and forbidding wrong' (*al-amr bi-l-maʿrūf wa-l-nahy ʿan al-munkar*), see Cook 2000: 487–8, 495.

[9] Berkey 2001: 11. Interestingly – and not quite incidentally – modern anthropological research on the Middle East also tends to neglect what is in fact the vast majority of the population, the agriculturists. See Eickelman 1989: 55–6.

[10] In traditional Middle Eastern societies, men have tended to know less about the social sphere of women than vice versa; see Abu-Lughod 1989: 294.

[11] Mottahedeh 1980: 108, 130. Also see Crone, Moreh 2000: 170.

with the possible exception of Sufism.[12] This maximises the value for the historian and the anthropologist of certain authors (and certain historical periods). For example, al-Jāḥiẓ (d. 255/869) does display a lively interest in the life and customs of the lower classes; and the Buyid period saw an increased curiosity among intellectuals about the common people (or perhaps rather the marginal and deviant elements among them and the underclass), if only for its entertainment value.[13] The virtual absence in the sources of the social reality of the mass of the population poses a serious dilemma to the contemporary researcher, that of making a hard choice between reducing his or her attention to the study of the élite and/or cultural ideals and expectations, or else facing, paradoxically, a severe shortage of useful source material despite the impressive number of extant primary sources. This might partly explain a conspicuous division of tasks in contemporary research on the Middle East: scholars at Middle Eastern Studies departments tend to focus on written texts produced by mediaeval urban literate élites, while ethnologists and anthropologists concentrate on the orally transmitted culture of contemporary (illiterate or semi-literate) rural communities to the almost total exclusion of written sources, even those formative of the customs of the communities concerned.[14] The result is a serious disconnect between both the research methods and the subject-matter of 'traditional' Middle Eastern studies and anthropology, with relatively few of the findings of either field finding their way into the other, apart from a handful of commendable exceptions in both fields.[15]

As will be obvious, the élitist bias has a direct – and quite negative – impact on this book's argument, in particular on the possibility of analysing the attitudes to *mujūn* of the lower orders, making any substantial findings, indeed anything beyond patchy impressions, virtually impracticable.

---

[12] Shoshan 1993: 10–1.

[13] On the interests of al-Jāḥiẓ, see ʿAwīs 1977: 53–63. As for the writers of the Buyid era, it is instructive, for instance, to peruse the list of informants given by the eminent author al-Qāḍī al-Tanūkhī (329/940–384/994). Even allowing for exaggeration and rhetoric, the list is very impressive, including as it does rulers, secretaries, jurisprudents, copyists, teachers, peasants, preachers, Sufis, Quran reciters, vagabonds, criminals, alcoholics, singers, dancers, homosexual prostitutes, libertines, beggars, pearl divers, swimmers, sailors, and so forth. See al-Tanūkhī, *Nishwār* I, 2–7.

[14] The reason is often simply a lack of familiarity with, and interest in, Classical Arabic. It is worth citing the succinct and appropriately ironic assessment of an anthropologist who did extensive fieldwork in an Egyptian community: "Like the people they have commonly studied, anthropologists have tended to be nonliterate. This means they have neither access to archives and texts that might illuminate what they are seeing nor interest in the complex role of texts in the communities they study." See Abu-Lughod 1989: 296. This less than desirable state of affairs seems to have gradually been changing for the better recently; on which see for instance Ibrahim 1994: 4; and cf. von Hees 2007: 24–7 on themes of historical anthropology in the field of Arabic and Islamic Studies.

[15] On this issue, see Lindholm 1995: 805–6 as well as Hartung 2007: 131; and some tangentially pertinent observations in Haeri 2000: 76–7.

Besides the inevitable élitist bias of the sources, an additional and closely related problem is that they also tend to reflect the *ideals* of the higher classes, *an idealised image of actual conditions*, rather than the social reality. One aspect of the cultural landscape that is rarely reflected in Arabic written sources in more than a cursory way is the variety of Islamic culture and its numerous local versions – understandably perhaps, as Muslim scholars tended to view such variety as a sign of decadence and imperfection – while the uniform and normative elements of Islam (whether actually predominant or advocated as ideals) are emphasised, probably far beyond their actual impact.[16] Thus, when collecting data from the sources, it is advisable to be constantly alert to "the peculiarly idealistic quality of much medieval Islamic legal and polemical writing", to use the apt phrase of Jonathan Berkey,[17] an observation that in my view has a broader validity, even beyond the confines of law and polemics. The problem is that (still according to Berkey) "[...] separating the imagined from the real can be a difficult task for the historian of medieval Islamic societies" because the existence of a written religious tradition enjoying unquestionable prestige "enabled the discourse to construct the very reality which it sought to describe".[18] Nor is the problem restricted to the study of mediaeval texts. Curiously enough, it is also familiar to anthropologists doing fieldwork, who will often receive answers not meant to deceive yet highly deceptive nevertheless owing to the tendency of informants to present normative patterns of behaviour as the actual way people behave. The idealised *Weltanschauung* of the Muslim religious élite, characterised by a strong prescriptive tendency, is not seriously questioned by the rest of the population, and it ends up influencing the work of Western scholars to a great degree, even specialists of disciplines with a heavy emphasis on the careful accumulation of empirical data such as sociology and anthropology.[19] To quote the opinion of a renowned expert of the anthropology of the contemporary Middle East:

> Western scholars often reproduced very exactly a particular "native" view of Muslim and Middle Eastern societies, especially the views of the Muslim learned elite as articulated in their own writings. It can be argued that the attitude of the Muslim elite toward the "lower orders" could often be as disparaging and self-serving as the writings of any colonialist. Further, if prior orientalist views of the Middle East can be criticized as too text-oriented, this fault is shared with the representations of medieval (and contemporary) Muslim society held by the learned Muslim elite itself.[20]

---

16 Bulliet 1972: 17.

17 Berkey 1995: 43.

18 Berkey 1995: 44.

19 On this point, cf. el-Zein 1977: 243. The same problems attend the study of Muslim societies beyond the Arabic-speaking Middle East; see for instance Hirsch 1998: 45.

20 Eickelman 1989: 47.

As we have noted above, not every Muslim scholar lacked an interest in the everyday culture of the people, even the lower classes. The name of al-Jāḥiẓ is a powerful reminder that interest in bookish élite concerns like theology and jurisprudence was not incompatible with interest in the mundane facts of the actual lifestyles of the masses. A sufficiently broad-minded scholar such as al-Jāḥiẓ could cultivate both types of subjects, but it must be added that the breadth of al-Jāḥiẓ's interests is extraordinary rather than typical among mediaeval Muslim intellectuals.

Certain types of sources yield more useful information than others. For example, collections of stories (*akhbār*) about littérateurs and other great personalities contain much fiction and were heavily edited by those who recorded them, yet with due care they can be utilised as "a literary refraction of contemporary circumstances".[21] Likewise, *fatwā* collections often provide felicitous insights into both real-life problems (usually briefly outlined in the inquiry section of a *fatwā*) and the scholars' proposed solutions to them, more or less reasonable as the case might be, depending on the particular scholar's personality and way of thinking. However, even *fatwā* collections tend to contain a good deal of obviously contrived, artificial problems (perhaps invented by the mufti himself, perhaps by some of his colleagues) serving as starting-points to discuss legal niceties, so caution is advisable when using them as a source of real-life cases.[22] Ironically, a particularly valuable type of source can be books dedicated to the eradication of reprehensible customs (sing. *bidʿa*, lit. 'innovations' because perceived in the ideology of Muslim scholars as later accretions to the original, authentic ways of the Muslim community). The ultimate prescriptive scholarly genre, this type of work nevertheless often describes and thus preserves from oblivion the very customs it seeks to root out, including not only practices of the higher classes but often those of the ignorant *ʿāmma* (the uneducated masses) too. Other types of writings, like *fiqh* manuals, are almost entirely prescriptive – indeed, explicitly so – and have little descriptive value other than as repositories of the scholars' theoretical stances. (This is not to say that their prescriptions and proscriptions were necessarily disregarded in practice – simply that it is impossible to ascertain it on the basis of such works alone.) Just how impractical and unrealistic some mediaeval scholars – indeed even highly intelligent and thoughtful men – could be when writing in the 'prescriptive mode' is illustrated by the following example,

---

[21] Gruendler 2005a: 59. Also see Gruendler 2005b: 96–7; Cooperson 2005: 69. Patricia Crone and Samuel Moreh point out that some of the material in literary sources – they are concerned with supposed graffiti – "are of the type where it is irrelevant whether they are factually true or not because the facts they contain are trivial while their messages are true to life". See Crone, Moreh 2000: 8.

[22] I have drawn on quite a number of *fatwā* collections, mainly for the purpose of learning about Muslim jurists' views on the legality or otherwise of various literary themes and motifs, a topic I discuss in Chapter Four of this book. In a few instances, they have also provided me with accounts of real-life events and dilemmas.

which I have chosen precisely for its glaring absurdity. It is a scholarly reaction to the widespread and long-established Shiʿite custom of cursing the Umayyad caliph Yazīd I (r. 60/680–64/683), regarded as the arch-villain responsible for the killing of the imam al-Ḥusayn, whom Shiʿites venerate and Sunnites also hold in respect. Without making it clear that the issue is in fact a popular custom among a considerable part of the Muslim population, the great Shāfiʿite author Abū Ḥāmid al-Ghazālī (d. 505/1111) advises that the explicit cursing of Yazīd ought to be suspended until clear evidence is forthcoming of his legal responsibility for the killing, and this formula should be used instead: "May the murderer of the imam al-Ḥusayn – if [the former] died before repenting his sin – be cursed by God!"[23] Needless to say, the recommended formula is unlikely ever to have caught on with the Muslim populace, Shiʿite or Sunnite.

Some examples will help illustrate the way mediaeval Arabic works tend to portray normative behaviour as recognised and articulated by the learned élite – and are thus good sources if dominant norms are to be explored – while they are little concerned with actual behaviour, which may often have departed considerably from both the tacit norms and the explicit prescriptions of élite writings. The reader is reminded of the observation, made in the beginning paragraphs of this chapter, that for a behaviour or cultural pattern to be an effective norm, it need not be statistically predominant, general perceptions of its being a norm being quite sufficient. The first example is the issue of women's dress and modesty. The rule that women must cover all parts of their body other than their faces and hands when outsiders are present is commonplace in written sources, where it is presented as a universal feature of Muslim societies. There is no denying that it was an ideal; the extent to which it really was applied in daily life is quite another matter. In fact, in many communities it appears to have remained a theoretical regulation with little impact on actual attire, owing to regional differences as well as limited material means. Edward Lane, for instance, reports in the late 13th/19th century that the dress of quite a few rural women in Egypt still consisted of "a narrow strip of rag bound round the hips".[24] Any number of examples could be adduced to show the same substantial divergence between scholarly theory and popular practice. Abraham Marcus has convincingly shown, on the basis of a large number of concrete cases,

[23] al-Ghazālī, *Iḥyāʾ* II, 156–7. For a number of comparably reasonable recommendations for linguistic usage, see op.cit. II, 202–4.

[24] Lane 1895: 59. Cf. Banton 1969: 81. Even quite recently, the male inhabitants of the South Iraqi marshlands (*Maʿdān*) would often go stark naked, or almost naked, when doing their daily work in the reeds, a far cry from the principles of male attire to be found in the written sources. Furthermore, in many villages almost all *Maʿdān* men were uncircumcised in spite of their being Muslims. See Thesiger 1967: 36, 106. However, in this context the huge differences between the customs of rural and urban communities cannot be disregarded as a crucial factor. (I am grateful to Tamás Iványi for calling my attention to this consideration.) Still, the point is that written sources claim to present universally applicable 'Islamic' regulations of dress, yet divergent local varieties did and do exist.

the limited applicability of cultural ideals in housing patterns and the protection of privacy in 12th/18th-century Aleppo.[25] The ideal norms and legal prescriptions of Muslim authors regarding wine-drinking were, as well known, diametrically opposed to the actual behaviour of a lot of people in the cities, especially those who could afford the price of the forbidden beverage, and the same observation can be made about other activities definitely proscribed by religious rules.[26]

It will be worthwhile to be more precise and examine in more detail the highly inconsistent and variable ways in which a reasonably unambiguous norm both affected and failed to affect behaviour. The norm I am referring to is the practically unanimous condemnation of illicit sex, notably fornication and sodomy, and the perception that these practices are a depravity. While it will be argued in Chapter Three of this book that literary depictions of fornication (*zinā*) and sodomy (*liwāṭ*) – let alone the actual practice of these activities – were definitely perceived as conscious breaches of elementary norms, and therefore representative of *mujūn*, it should not be inferred that such literary motifs and such acts were infrequent in mediaeval Muslim cities. In fact, quite to the contrary. Extramarital affairs with slave-girls, prostitutes, and married or unmarried free women seem to have been commonplace in the urban society that produced *mujūn* literature. For someone desirous of finding potential partners for illicit sex (like a libertine intellectual), the spaces of a mediaeval Muslim city, the exigencies of a sophisticated lifestyle, and the web of social relations offered myriad opportunities, including, ironically, the excuse of attending religious gatherings and ceremonies.[27]

On the other hand, the undeniable abundance of opportunities to transgress the norms of sexual propriety in no way diminished the validity of those norms for most people, and indeed made most members of the political and economic elite all the more resolute to stress traditional Bedouin – and religious – attitudes and roles within their own families, especially the imperative for a honourable man to control the activities of his dependents and womenfolk, whom he must make sure remained in strict seclusion from all prying eyes. For men of high status, ensuring

25 Marcus 1986: 165.

26 For the situation in mediaeval Damascus, see Pouzet 1991: 361–3. Further examples include the issues of begging and politics. Written sources emphasise that begging in mosques is forbidden, but in fact it was common practice; see Bosworth 1976: I, 15–6. On the wide divergence of political ideals and theory from actual political practice in traditional Muslim society; see Lapidus 1975: 364, 368–9 (and for an articulation of the commonly held but quite mistaken view, see for instance Gellner 1981: 1–2).

27 For a glimpse into the lamentably loose morals of the youth (and the mature) of both sexes, and their subterfuges to elude vigilantes of morals, see al-Tanūkhī, *Nishwār* III, 228–9; al-Shayzarī, *Nihāya* 109–10; Ibn Bassām, *Nihāya* 211–2; and also see al-Ibshīhī, *Mustaṭraf* 438; al-Tawḥīdī, *Imtāʿ* 196. If one trusts the testimony of Snouck Hurgronje, in late 13th/19th-century Mecca it was common for women to carry on extramarital affairs; see Snouck Hurgronje 1931: 92.

the morals of their female dependents was an absolute obligation, a matter of honour. Attitudes to sexuality and the relations between the two sexes could radically differ from one social subgroup to another, and individual differences introduced a further factor of variability. The Buyid period was hardly a repressive one as far as sexual mores are concerned – in fact, it was arguably in this period that *mujūn* reached its apogee in terms of popularity and cultural impact as well as extravagance – yet the following account must alert us to the simultaneous existence of a wholly traditional, even prudish set of assumptions that governed the daily behaviour of many rich and powerful people. The excerpt is a story recounted by the *qāḍī* Abū ʿUmar about the falsity of the image of the rich jeweller Ibn al-Jaṣṣāṣ (d. 315/927–8) as a halfwit:

> A few days ago, I was visiting him in his home to pay respect. There was a huge tent erected in his courtyard, and we sat down next to it to talk. Then suddenly there came the audible sound of sandals scuffing behind the canvas of the tent, whereupon [Ibn al-Jaṣṣāṣ] shouted: "Servant, bring here the woman who's just passed behind the tent!" A black maidservant was brought forth, whom he asked what business she had had being there. She replied: "I've come to the servant in order to tell him I'd finished cooking and to ask permission to bring the food." [Ibn al-Jaṣṣāṣ] told her she could leave and go back to her work. I realised that his intention was to indicate to me that those shuffling sounds had come from a black female [servant] of no consequence, not from a female relative of his or anyone whom he was obligated to guard (*laysat min ḥuramihi wa-lā mimman yaṣūnuhu*), and thus did he ensure I should not think such a [dishonourable] thing about his womenfolk. How could this man be [thought of as] a nitwit?[28]

The attitudes on display in this story are a far cry from the general laxity and frivolity of the urban society of the Buyid age. The somewhat contradictory testimony of all the above data must serve as a cautionary note against presuming any direct correlation between dominant norms and the actual behaviour of the majority of the population. Normative behaviour is not made less normative by the failure of the multitudes to live up to the exacting expectations, as long as the majority does accept those norms as the ideal patterns of conduct.

The situation was equally confusing as regards homosexuality,[29] concerning which the norms accepted by the majority might often diverge considerably from the actual behaviour of the same people, while in some cases conduct might also be in conformity with norms to a surprising extent. The norm could not be clearer:

---

[28] al-Tanūkhī, *Nishwār* I, 36.

[29] This term, which I use only for convenience and brevity, is highly misleading when used in reference to the premodern Middle East. What is in contemporary western culture called homosexuality – even there a relatively recent concept – corresponds to a number of disparate terms in Arabic (including *liwāṭ*, 'sodomy' or 'anal intercourse') that, prior to the twentieth century, were simply not perceived as forming one single category. See El-Rouayheb 2005, esp. pp. 5–6 for a brief summary of the problem.

homoerotic lust is dangerous and must never be indulged; sodomy is an abomination, a sin and a crime. Anal sexual congress between two persons of the same sex is under all circumstances illicit and subject to punishment. This was the unanimous opinion of all Muslim jurists, which also corresponded to the popular assessment of the phenomenon.[30] Somewhat confusing is the fact that the *ʿulamāʾ* apparently regarded homoerotic longing – more specifically, desire for adolescent boys – as a perfectly natural, inherent instinct in adult men. However, inherent though it might be, they never considered it innocent or harmless; it is precisely because of its perils that it must be kept in check by avoiding all situations of temptation.[31] Obviously, this conception of homosexuality is very negative, and the resulting norm could be phrased thus: it is degrading for a respectable man to give in to homoerotic temptations, and it is a grave sin to engage in sodomy. (All these observations should be understood to refer to the active role in a homosexual act; the passive role was regarded as infinitely worse, an unspeakable disgrace ruining a man's reputation, not just a sin in the religious sense.) That said, the existence of the norm, again, does not mean statistical preponderance: the behaviour of a significant part of the urban population hardly appears to have conformed to the largely uncontested norm. Homosexual sex – especially with slave-boys and other low-status youngsters – was widely available in Middle Eastern cities, nor was it uncommon for men to try to seduce adolescents or buy and keep slave-boys for sexual gratification.[32] Many of

[30] It is superfluous to cite legal works on this point – all of them condemn homosexuality in no uncertain terms; disagreements are limited to details of the suitable punishment and similar issues. There is a considerable number of *ḥadīths* denouncing sodomy and warning against lusting for boys; popular proverbs also express comparable sentiments. See for instance al-Ṭabarsī, *Makārim* 232, 238; al-Rāghib, *Muḥāḍarāt* III, 473; Westermarck 1930: 86–7. Also cf. Mezziane 2008: 279–80.

[31] Schmidtke 1999: 260. Many works of jurisprudence stress the necessity for an adult man to refrain from staring at, sitting in the company of, shaking hands with, embracing, or kissing the cheek of a beautiful boy, a stringency totally analogous to that applicable to the issue of acceptable behaviour with women. Some works might go further, declaring it objectionable for a father to let his son, provided the latter has good looks, go to dubious places or all-male company. Some religious scholars apparently made extreme precautionary measures to avoid homosexual temptations; Abū Ḥanīfa (d. 150/767) in particular is said to have confined a young and too attractive disciple to a seat behind his back so as to avoid looking at the youngster's face. See Ibn Baydakīn, *Lumaʿ* I, 85, 116, 237–8, 282; and also al-Shayzarī, *Nihāya* 104; Ibn al-Jawzī, *Talbīs* 266 ["*wa-matā iddaʿā l-insān annahu lā tathūru shahwatuhu...*" etc.], 274–6; al-Nawawī, *Fatāwī* 104–5; al-Anṭākī, *Tazyīn* 331–2; al-Tanūkhī, *Nishwār* III, 46.

[32] Homosexuality was especially prevalent among Sufis, as well as in the communities of young men existing in virtually every major Iraqi city and town (*fityān, shuṭṭār*) whose activities might at times border on criminality. See al-Jāḥiẓ, *Ḥayawān* I, 93–4; Ibn al-Jawzī, *Talbīs* 264–74. For a modern reader (whether Western or Middle Eastern) the advice of a father to his son about the respective merits of certain boys as objects of infatuation sounds extremely weird, showing as it does the extent to which such relationships were taken for granted in mediaeval Middle Eastern cities in certain historical periods. See al-Thaʿālibī, *Tatimma* I, 33–4; and also cf. al-Thaʿālibī, *Yatīma* I, 380–1, where the accompanying poem is ascribed to a different author.) Similarly instructive is a poem by al-Ṭāhir

the *ghilmān* (boy-servants, young male slaves; sing. *ghulām*) in the service of rich and powerful persons were essentially catamites. In fact, it has been argued that the prevalence of homosexual relationships was initially confined to the upper classes, from which it gradually spread 'downwards' to the masses.[33] Even if it is difficult to establish the history of the spread of such practices in mediaeval Middle Eastern society, the weight of anecdotal evidence culled from literary sources seems to confirm that homosexuality was indeed common – albeit discretion was always observed – in the ranks of the political and intellectual elite from the early Abbasid era onwards.[34] Outside those circles who could afford to buy attractive slave-boys, a lot of city dwellers would seek the services of boy prostitutes and effeminate men (sing. *mukhannath*) that seem to have been numerous in bigger cities. Being the greatest metropolis of the Middle East, Baghdad in particular drew a lot of people who would earn their livelihood in this fashion.[35]

al-Jazarī about a gorgeously handsome young man called Ibn Shibl; see al-Bākharzī, *Dumya* I, 154–5. Some cities – notably Mosul – had a reputation as hotbeds of homosexual activity, although it is difficult to see it as anything but a hostile stereotype with little factual basis. See Yāqūt, *Buldān* V, 224. Lesbian relationships were not uncommon either, albeit for obvious reasons they must have been less visible than male homosexuality. See for instance al-Jāḥiẓ, *Ḥayawān* I, 419. On the remarkable ubiquity of homosexual affairs in 19th-century Mecca (apparently comparable to the situation in mediaeval Iraqi cities), see Snouck Hurgronje 1931: 44, 51.

33 Shoshan 1991: 89–90.

34 A pertinent example is the jocular, friendly rapport of the caliph al-Maʾmūn (r. 198/813–218/833) with the chief *qāḍī* Yaḥyā b. Aktham, a notorious pederast. According to an account that leaked through the indiscretion of a favourite slave-boy of the caliph, when no-one else was present they would feel free to discuss and joke about boys (*khalā bihi l-Maʾmūn laylatan ʿalā l-mudāʿaba wa-l-muṭāyaba wa-l-mujārāt fī maydān al-ghilmān*). See al-Thaʿālibī, *Laṭāʾif* 63; al-Thaʿālibī, *Thimār* I, 272; and also see al-Tawḥīdī, *Baṣāʾir* II(iv), 128 [in this text, the same witticism is attributed to a woman: "*al-ṭīn idhā ḥalā tashaqqaqa*"]. For further examples, see al-Iṣfahānī, *Aghānī* XX, 57–8 [the Abbasid caliph al-Amīn on his slave-boy]; al-Thaʿālibī, *Yatīma* I, 89–90 [the emir Abū l-ʿAshāʾir on his feelings for a slave-boy]; II, 265–6 [comments of the vizier al-Ṣābī on his black slave-boy]; Ibn Saʿīd, *Ghuṣūn* 22–3 [the jesting words in a private setting of an Ayyūbid ruler of Egypt]. – The considerable notoriety of the chief judge Yaḥyā b. Aktham as an incorrigible homosexual might be due to some frivolous witticisms (notably a mock religious argument for the legitimacy of preferring boys) which he dropped in conversation and which became famous, although it is equally possible that the sayings were falsely attributed to him because he already was known for his penchant for boys. On Yaḥyā b. Aktham as a proverbial homosexual, see for instance al-Thaʿālibī, *Laṭāʾif* 62–3; al-Thaʿālibī, *Thimār* I, 271; and also cf. Ibn al-Muʿtazz, *Ṭabaqāt* 180 ["*Qāḍin yarā l-khulda fī l-zinā...*" etc.]; al-Thaʿālibī, *Yatīma* IV, 238 ["... *min sharṭi Yaḥyā bni Akthami*"]; al-Thaʿālibī, *Thimār* I, 273–4; al-Rāghib, *Muḥāḍarāt* III, 474 ["... *bi-dīni l-shaykhi Yaḥyā ʾbni Akthamin*"]; al-Tawḥīdī, Baṣāʾir V(ix), 180 ["... *yuʿarriḍu bi-Yaḥyā b. Aktham*"].

35 In the first century of Islamic history, some governors would periodically arrest and punish the 'effeminates' living under their jurisdiction; see for instance al-Iṣfahānī, *Aghānī* III, 30–1; and for some *ḥadīths* unequivocally condemning effeminacy in men, see al-Ṭabarsī, *Makārim* 118, 238. Even later on, legal sources advised that barbers must not shave the beards of *mukhannath* men and teenage boys, and adolescent boys known to be passive homosexuals, exactly like promiscuous women, must

In any case, conformity to the norm of shunning all exposure to homoerotic temptations was clearly far from universal in actual behaviour. However, one important indication of the continuing dominance of the norm, for all the departure from it in practice, was the necessity of being discreet about homosexual affairs. (Libertines did not, of course, observe discretion in this matter, outrage being their objective, but that subject will be discussed in a later chapter.) Talk about sex with boys was a suitable subject only within groups of intimate and trustworthy friends, if at all.

Popular attitudes to extramarital sex and homosexual affairs show the extent to which a norm could be commonly disregarded in practice by many and yet regarded as valid by the vast majority. The possibility of such a discrepancy between ideals and conduct is an important element of the social background of *mujūn*, as are the values to be discussed in the following sections of this chapter.

2. Some Enduring Values in Mediaeval Muslim Society

In the remainder of this chapter a number of opposites, having to do with the values of mediaeval Muslim society, will be briefly discussed. These pairs of concepts cannot accurately be called norms, representing as they do a much broader category, that of general principles, judgements, perspectives, or attitudes, from which more concrete norms were derived. In fact, when properly formulated they can be identified as 'values', as in the section heading. For instance, the superiority of serious,

be banished from their hometown. See for instance al-Shayzarī, *Nihāya* 88, 110. However, by the time of Abū Nuwās (late 2nd/8th c.), young male prostitutes sold their services more or less openly in the Bāb al-Ṭāq quarter, and they plucked their facial hair to make themselves more sought after. See Abū Hiffān, *Akhbār* 69; al-Jāḥiẓ, *Rasā'il* I(ii), 122–3. The ubiquity of this trade in Baghdad is the point of an anecdote in which a boy working as a prostitute in Baghdad is summoned home to *Ḥimṣ* by his mother to start working in the mill owned by their family. Writes the boy in response: "Mum, an arse in Iraq is worth more than a mill in *Ḥimṣ*." See al-Rāghib, *Muḥāḍarāt* III, 479 (and also see op.cit. III, 495–6). Effeminate men in mediaeval Baghdad were apparently so indiscreet about their vice that they would often address one another as 'my sister' (*ukhtī*) and use the feminine gender in talking among themselves; see for instance Ibn al-Jawzī, *Ẓirāf* 136. (Among the effeminates of early Medina, this peculiarity is also attested but seems to have been uncommon; see Rowson 1991: 689, note 138.) The vernacular of Baghdad used the term *kāghān* for boy prostitutes, while Damascenes called them *mikhnāth*; see Bosworth 1976: I, 38–9. In other historical periods and other geographical regions, boy prostitutes have been known by different names like *khawal* or *gink* (Egypt), *khanīth* (Oman), *dhakar binta* (Souther Iraq), *shoga* (coastal Kenya), etc. See Lane 1895: 376–7; Wikan 1977: 304–7; Feuerstein, al-Marzooq 1978: 665; Eickelman 1989: 188–9; Thesiger 1967: 46; Shepherd 1978a: 133; Shepherd 1978b: 665. Male prostitution in cities should not be confused, however, with the occasional instance of institutionalised homosexuality in some rural settings, such as the custom of Berber tribesmen living around Seṭīf (Algeria) to offer their sons, as a gesture of extreme hospitality, to their male guests to spend the night with. See Ibn Ḥawqal, *Ṣūra* 93; al-Idrīsī, *Nuzha* III, 269–70.

dignified behaviour over jesting can be said to have been a dominant (and enduring) value in mediaeval Muslim culture, one which was rarely questioned, even allowing for the occasional dissenting – or rather just more balanced – voice among intellectuals. Likewise, the undervaluing of villages, the 'common folk', and the vernacular tongues vis-à-vis the cities, the 'élite' and written Classical Arabic, respectively, is virtually a constant in mediaeval Muslim attitudes to their own culture and society. However, as we will have occasion to observe, such general judgements (or values) cannot be automatically translated into norms.[36] Norms are far more concrete. An example might be the norm that 'it is preferable to behave solemnly in a situation when one is dealing with subordinates in order to enhance one's own prestige', which is a manifestation of the value that says that serious discourse is superior to humour. Another example of a norm derived from the same value might be the idea that 'one must not (or should not) make irreverent jokes about the Prophet Muḥammad'. (Actual, explicitly formulated norms can be found, for instance, in *fiqh* manuals.) Whereas the general values tended to be questioned by few people, more concrete norms were often less fully agreed upon and subject to debate, mainly within the scholarly class. Further as noted above, norms might be accepted in principle yet not applied in practice. An individual might honestly uphold the validity of a norm and still utterly fail to conform to it in his conduct. This point bears repeating because it has great significance for the analysis of the social context in which *mujūn* could flourish.

The following sections discuss Muslim perceptions of the relative value of certain contrasting phenomena of culture, society or language. In some cases, such perceptions did directly affect social realities and were in their turn affected by social relations. For example, the prevalent élite disdain towards the common people (*ʿāmma*) certainly had an impact on the attitudes of the powerful and wealthy to the masses, while it was nourished by the huge social and economic distance between the higher and lower classes. In other cases, the connection of values to behaviour was more indirect: the greater prestige of serious discourse vis-à-vis jesting apparently did not result in a universal (or even widespread) shunning of jocular talk, humorous texts, anecdotes and frivolous entertainment, as we will have ample occasion to demonstrate.

2.1 Seriousness and Humour

This pair of opposites is the most relevant one for the purposes of this study. Its importance stems from the close association of *mujūn* with jesting and humour, a

[36] Cf. Dubois 2003: 3–4.

subject to be discussed in detail in the final chapter.[37] For the time being, it is only the relative prestige of 'serious' and 'humorous' utterances and texts in mediaeval Muslim society that will be investigated. It is to be noted that judgements on the two types of discourse and their relative value are also necessarily judgements on the persons who employ them; in other words, a positive or negative assessment of humorous discourse must also reflect on a man who is known for his penchant for joking.

Whereas attitudes to jesting varied even among the religious élite, with some members of this social group showing more indulgence than others, the view that 'serious' discourse, as well as the topics pertaining to that discourse, are superior to mere jesting and that it is preferable for a respectable man to focus his attention on 'serious' matters was rarely if ever contested. Humour, although permissible under certain conditions, was regarded as something of a diversion from more worthy pursuits even in the best of circumstances. This explains the unmistakably defensive and polemical tone of passages arguing for the permissibility and many advantages of humour in several works of belles-lettres. The following excerpt from a work on condemnable customs makes fine distinctions within the general category of jesting, yet displays a characteristic wariness about and mistrust of humour, which it considers to be a potential source of moral hazard. Note that according to the author humour is at best permissible:

> Know that a little jesting – provided it contains only truth – is permissible (*mubāḥ*); however, [too] much of it is undesirable (*lā yuḥmadu*), for whoever indulges in it will leave the path of the men of goodness, religion and uprightness. Still, it is not a sin to do so (*lā yaʾthamu l-fāʿil*), nor is it a misdemeanour (*junāḥ*), since jesting does have a basis in the *sharīʿa* as shown by several reliable *ḥadīths*. Some kinds [of jesting] are permissible, some disapproved, some prohibited, and some will turn the perpetrator into an unbeliever. We will specify all of these in their proper place if God wills, replete with explications. Jesting a lot is disapproved (*yukrahu*), because [it will cause] the heart to be hard, because it is a waste of time and of the duration [of one's life], and because it runs counter to [the message of] *ḥadīths*. And whoever lies while joking has fallen into a reprehensible innovation (*bidʿa*) and a shameful act. [...] As the Prophet said: "I may joke [at times], yet I tell but the truth."[38]

[37] The most detailed and in-depth analysis of mediaeval Muslim attitudes to humour and laughter is Ammann 1993.

[38] Ibn Baydakīn, *Lumaʿ* I, 176. On the opprobrious types of jesting, see op.cit. I, 176–90. Also see al-Ghazālī, *Iḥyāʾ* II, 159–63, where the celebrated Shāfiʿite author stresses the perils of 'excessive' jesting, whatever that definition may mean. For similar wisdom on the harmfulness of joking, see for instance Ibn Mufliḥ, *Ādāb* II, 180–1. Also cf. some brief observations in Pellat 1963: 356, and especially Ammann 1993: 74–84. As will be shown below, the disapproval of jesting and mirth was often cast in the form of *ḥadīths*, as was the contrary view as well. For a collection of such *ḥadīths* condemning

The author of this passage goes on to warn the reader of the manifold dangers and disadvantages of joking and laughter, making it amply clear where his sympathies lie:

> Too much laughter indicates that the man [doing so] is stupid, and it also hardens the heart. Now, you must know that whoever jokes and laughs a lot is exposed to bad temptations (*maftūn*). And laughing without pleasure is a kind of insanity. It is narrated that [the ascetic] al-Fuḍayl b. ʿIyāḍ [d. 187/803] never laughed in his whole life, except in the moment of the death of his son ʿAlī, and when asked [about the reason of such a confounding act], he said: "God wanted something [to happen], so I wanted it too."[39]

In this context, it is noteworthy that quite a few ʿulamāʾ, indeed whole schools of law, apparently regarded laughter as potentially polluting in the ritual sense. At least that is the impression created by the insistence of those scholars that loud laughter (*qahqaha*) during prayer invalidates the prayer and ends the state of purity, necessitating a renewed ritual ablution.[40] A text even quotes the distinguished religious scholar al-Awzāʿī (d. 157/773) equating, in the course of a homily, minor and major sins (as mentioned in Quran 18:49) with smiling and laughter respectively, an interpretation also attributed to Ibn ʿAbbās (d. 68/687).[41] Another indication of the suspect status of joking in the eyes of religious scholars is the recommendation of some Muslim jurists that appointees to the position of judge (*qāḍī*) should avoid laughter and jesting.[42]

The source of the passage quoted above is a work which offers us an overview of pastimes *sharīʿa*-minded scholars tended to consider to be a frivolous waste of time, hence best discouraged and suppressed. As quite a few of the activities condemned have continued to enjoy great popularity in the everyday culture of the Muslim Middle East up to these days, these passages are also a powerful reminder of the limits of the actual influence of many religious scholars' bookish preoccupations. For instance, one finds on the 'blacklist' two of the most popular parlour games of

---

joking, see for instance al-Ibshīhī, *Mustaṭraf* 528 (E.g. "Joking is a gradual [triumph] of Satan and a teasing of sinful desires.")

[39] Ibn Baydakīn, *Lumaʿ* I, 181.

[40] This was the opinion of the jurists of al-Kūfa, and possibly the Ibāḍites, the Ḥanafites, and the Ḥanbalites too, while the Mālikites disagreed. (According to other sources, repeating the prayer might be enough, without need of a renewed ablution.) All opinions are supported by *ḥadīths*. See Ibn Juzayy, *Qawānīn* 30; Ibn ʿAqīl, *Tadhkira* 64; Ibn Baraka, *Jāmiʿ* I, 327, 595; al-Marwazī, *Ikhtilāf* 114–5; and Ammann 1993: 69–73.

[41] al-Thaʿālibī, *Iqtibās* I, 201; al-Haytamī, *Zawājir* II, 22; and also see Ammann 1993: 36.

[42] E.g. Ibn Juzayy, *Qawānīn* 300–1. (The advice may also have to do with the desire that a judge should not get too friendly with litigants lest his impartiality should suffer. However, the Ḥanafī jurist Naṣr al-Samarqandī (d. 375/985–6) explicitly states that the judge must not laugh or jest because it "destroys the solemnity of the session [*yudhhibu bi-mahābat al-majlis*]"; see al-Samarqandī, *Fatāwā* 385.)

the Middle East, chess (*shiṭranj*) and backgammon (*nard* or *nardashīr*), as well as the controversial pastimes of singing, dancing and instrumental music.[43]

A recurrent theme of mediaeval Islamic writing is the need of a strong distrust of the urges and instincts of the soul (expressed by the Arabic noun *hawā*, a term with markedly negative connotations), which must ideally be suppressed and kept in check by constant introspective vigilance based on religious precepts.[44] For many *ʿulamāʾ*, this meant suspicion of all activities that brought all too evident pleasure and gratification. This outlook had obvious consequences for the enjoyment of humour – a very delectable activity by most people's standards – by making it somewhat suspect and thus liable to a lot of moral scrutiny regarding the innocence, or otherwise, of the pleasure caused by jokes and laughter.

A related but distinct issue was that of 'wasting time', which in the broad interpretation of many religious savants meant any entertainment, just about any activity not lucrative economically or religious in purpose. Such pastimes they considered to be unnecessary and even harmful distractions from pious concerns and activities. The category of what could be viewed as a waste of time is astonishingly spacious – the treatment of any not strictly religious subject such as narratives of travels and most genres of belles-lettres might qualify (not to speak of humorous anecdotes and frivolous poetry).[45] A term often used in this context by *sharīʿa*-minded authors is *laghw*, 'empty talk, prattle, twaddle'. It is interesting that one even encounters this deep-seated attitude in folk culture; indeed it is sometimes even displayed by people who habitually engage in, and enjoy, various forms of humour and frivolity, a rather schizophrenic condition.[46]

---

43 Ibn Baydakīn, *Lumaʿ* I, 101–12, 76; and on the issue of music also cf. al-Ibshīhī, *Mustaṭraf* 420–1 (and Lane 1895: 351 for views on music and dance in 19th-century Egypt). On the scant impact of the mediaeval scholars' proscriptions, see Rescher 1919: 14. The dislike of music and dance was often linked to the condemnation of 'unorthodox' Sufi ceremonies, while parlour games could become targets of the savants' ire for two primary reasons: first, on account of their being perceived as ways of 'wasting time' (on which issue more in the main text), and second, because they might be combined with gambling, which is strictly forbidden in Islam. These factors explains the vehemence of such verdicts (presented in the usual garb, that of *ḥadīths*) as "Whoever plays backgammon defies God and His prophet", "Whoever plays backgammon is as if he immersed his hand in swines' flesh and blood", and so on. See Ibn Baydakīn, *Lumaʿ* I, 110; and also al-Khaṭīb, *Kifāya* 139 about chess.

44 The notion is common in practically all genres of mediaeval Arabic writing; for a typical treatment, see Ibn ʿĀṣim, *Janna* I, 132–3.

45 E.g. al-Ghazālī, *Iḥyāʾ* II, 140–1.

46 Ibrahim 1994: 7. This admirable anthropological study also cites (p. 71) the words of an informant defining the pietistic conception of 'empty talk' as succinctly as an aphorism: it is *every* kind of human utterance except "God says, the Prophet says (*qāl Allāh, qāl al-rasūl*)", viz. the Quran and the *ḥadīths*. Also revealing is the traditional opening formula of folktales ('empty talk' *par excellence*) among the Sudanese Rubāṭāb: "They say – and may God protect us from the evil of 'we say' and 'they say' (*qālū wa-yakfīnā Allāh sharr qulnā wa-qālū*)"; see ibid. 76. Similar attitudes are evident in quite a few Moroccan proverbs; see Westermarck 1930: 277.

While this suspicion of all manifestations of humour and frivolity, very broadly defined, tended to be articulated most systematically in the writings of the *ʿulamāʾ*, one would be mistaken to suppose that other sectors of the educated class did not affirm the prestige of serious discourse. (In fact – although I will not pursue the question any further – it may well be that the preference for seriousness had more to do with the Bedouin tribal ethos than with religion despite the ostensibly religious language employed to express it.) Any number of recorded remarks and explicit statements by political leaders as well as littérateurs evince fairly pervasive negative attitudes to humour and jocundity, at least on the normative level. For example, Mundhir b. Saʿīd al-Ballūṭī, whom the Cordoban ruler ʿAbd al-Raḥmān al-Nāṣir (r. 300–50/912–61) appointed to the post of chief judge of the city, was a deeply religious man yet fond of jesting, and Yāqūt reports that this cheerful disposition made some people who did not know him well think ill of him (*fa-rubbamā sāʾa ẓann man lā yaʿrifuhu bihi li-duʿābatihi*).[47] The impression is that cheerfulness was, perhaps subconsciously, associated with godlessness. The same sentiment is apparent in the reported behaviour of the dreaded governor of Iraq under the Umayyads, al-Ḥajjāj b. Yūsuf al-Thaqafī (d. 95/714). This ruthless man had the habit, certainly not unparalleled, of asking God's forgiveness every time he had been unable to control himself and had burst out laughing.[48] Of course, al-Ḥajjāj was a state functionary of extraordinarily high status and immense power, with all the attendant need to maintain a solemn and awe-inspiring mien. It is noteworthy, then, that his presumable attitudes to jesting were not unlike those of many littérateurs whose social standing definitely did not necessitate the same constant show of grandeur. Here is the Egyptian anthologist Shihāb al-Dīn al-Ibshīhī (d. 850/1446–7) expounding his evaluation of humour: "[...] jesting destroys dignity, removes honour (*yudhhibu bi-māʾ al-wajh*), breeds hatred, spoils the sweetness of belief and love (*yudhhibu bi-ḥalāwat al-īmān wa-l-wudd*), tarnishes the learning of a religious expert (*faqīh*), emboldens the ignorant, deadens the heart, alienates from God, and spawns silliness and humiliation." The author also adds that whoever is "afflicted in a gathering with [having to listen to] joking" should ask God's forgiveness after his interlocutors have left, advice reminiscent of al-Ḥajjāj's habit mentioned above.[49] Similar views

[47] Yāqūt, *Udabāʾ* VI, 2721.

[48] al-Ibshīhī, *Mustaṭraf* 58. Charles Pellat notes that although dignified behaviour characterised by self-control and seriousness had virtually unquestioned prestige in the early Islamic period, it did not entail an explicit disapproval of jesting. See Pellat 1963: 354–5.

[49] al-Ibshīhī, *Mustaṭraf* 133. Part of the above quotation is echoed by a mediaeval Arabic proverb, according to which "too much laughter destroys dignity (*kathrat al-ḍaḥik tudhhib al-hayba*)"; see al-Maydānī, *Amthāl* II, 205; and for more on this notion, see Ammann 1993: 170–3. That joking breeds hatred is also expressed in the dictum that "joking is one of the two forms of vituperation (*al-mizāḥ aḥad al-sibābayn*)"; see al-Ṣūlī, *Adab* 74. Abū Ḥāmid al-Ghazālī sought to derive the very noun *mizāḥ* (joking) from the supposed tendency of joking to drive man away from the truth. (Or from God? The

are expressed in another, much earlier work, which is dedicated to the discussion of elegance, wit and good manners, a subject having little to do with either religion or politics:

> You must know that some of the distinguishing marks of cultured, well-informed, intelligent, honourable and sophisticated men (*al-udabā' wa-ahl al-ma'rifa wa-l-'uqalā' wa-dhawī l-murū'a wa-l-ẓurafā'*) is that they do not speak too much needlessly, consider joking and playfulness to be beneath their dignity, and avoid stooping to vulgar silliness (*sakhāfa*) and boisterous jokes and banter. That is because [too] much jesting is humiliating and degrading for a man; it ends all respectability, destroys brotherly feelings, and emboldens the lowly and vile against a noble freeman.[50]

While it is problematic to regard al-Washshā' as the spokesman for the cultured, refined urbanites of the high Abbasid era, whose collective wisdom he pretends to articulate (*v.i.*), it is beyond dispute that the political and cultural élite did tend to pay at least lip service to the idea that humorous topics (*hazl*), however delectable and attractive, are vastly inferior in significance and value to 'serious' concerns (*jidd*). The exact meaning of the latter term is somewhat hard to define, but it would generally encompass all that was really worthy of the attention of a respectable adult man including, but not limited to, religion and political affairs. As a rule of thumb, it can be said that the more unequivocally a topic or activity was perceived as belonging to the public sphere and being the privilege of grown-up men (as opposed to women and minors), the more it tended to be considered 'serious'. 'Serious' things included warfare, business and industry, law, and most certainly religion; 'unserious' ones, amorous and sentimental affairs, amusing anecdotes, and most certainly all kinds of jesting and frivolity.[51] In a telling verse, the aristocratic poet Abū Firās al-Ḥamdānī

Arabic original reads "*azāḥa ṣāḥibahu 'an al-ḥaqq*", and of course *al-Ḥaqq* is one of God's names. If this translation is preferred, the idea closely parallels a phrase in al-Ibshīhī's passage). Though a patently false etymology, it is nevertheless a telling error. See al-Ghazālī, *Iḥyā'* II, 160.

[50] al-Washshā', *Muwashshā* 21. This passage can be found under the heading 'Chapter about the Interdiction of Bantering with Friends and Joking with Mates' (*bāb al-nahy 'an mumāzaḥat al-akhillā' wa-l-nahy 'an mufākahat al-awiddā'*). A striking and surely significant feature of al-Washshā''s argument is the preponderance of proofs and literary evidence taken from the pre-Islamic and early Islamic periods to support his thesis (see op.cit. 21–3), which must raise serious doubts as to the extent to which this famous work can be considered as truly expressing the views of the majority of the sophisticates of Baghdad and other cities. In the last chapter, I will have occasion to discuss this question; suffice it here to say that the weight of this and other evidence, some of it already presented above, clearly shows that al-Washshā' was far from alone to harbour and give voice to such negative feelings about joking and humour, even though it was not necessarily a majority opinion among the *ẓurafā'*.

[51] It is interesting to note that this division appears to affect the difficulty of conducting anthropological research into certain topics in the Middle East; the favoured subjects of anthropological fieldworkers being largely 'serious' ones. On this tendency, see Abu-Lughod 1999: 30–1.

(320/932–357/968) disavows having anything to do with poetic genres he finds beneath his dignity; his list includes not only panegyrics and lampoons – neither of which would have been fitting for a man of his position – but also *mujūn* and all sorts of frivolity (*laʿib*).[52] The same distinction of worthy and unworthy concerns is elaborated at length in the following prose text; here the author's verdict is certainly coloured by his pride in his own métier, but the overall preference of 'serious' concerns he definitely shares with countless other Middle Eastern intellectuals:

> Prose [...] is nobler [than poetry] and closer to the ways of rulers and the powerful. Its cultivators are more eminent and their gatherings more august: the generations of secretaries have always been, and still are, above those of poets; for secretaries, who are the spokesmen of kings, correspond about [such matters as] the levying of taxes, the protection of a borderland, the development of a region (ʿimārat bilād), the remedying of corruption (*iṣlāḥ fasād*), the encouragement of jihad, polemics against a [deviant] faction (*iḥtijāj ʿalā fiʾa*), calling for concord and preventing discord, congratulations on a [royal] award, condolences at a tragedy, *and a host of similarly momentous matters and grand affairs [...]. Their high importance is commensurate with the high affairs that they are involved in and deal with* [emphasis added]. Poets, however, are only interested in, and occupied with, such topics and concerns as the description of [a tribe's] camping-grounds and the traces thereof, reminiscences of a homeland, yearning for one's passions, rhapsodising about women, or else requests and the solicitation of gifts, [as in] praise-poems and invective poetry. It is because of the low prestige of poetry that prophets have taken care to abstain from it and rulers have looked down upon it.[53]

A note of clarification is necessary here. The assertion made forcefully in this passage – that poetry (or at any rate most of its genres) is to be considered an unserious, and therefore trivial and unimportant, sort of discourse – is not atypical, and this view contributed to the remarkable ambiguity of the poet's position in Arabic culture. On the other hand, the prestige of poetry – of certain genres anyway – seems to have been quite variable over the history of Middle Eastern culture, and in a lot of rural and nomadic communities it is exactly poetry that was regarded as the most solemn and respectable mode of communication, the 'talk of men' *par excellence*. It is reasonable to suppose that the esteem in which poetry would be held had much to do with its locally predominant genres and subject-matter; thus the urban poetry of the Abbasid period could more easily be seen as frivolous and inconsequential than say, the tribal *qaṣīdas* of many Arabian communities.[54] An

---

[52] Abū Firās, *Dīwān* 29.

[53] al-Thaʿālibī, *Nathr* 7–8. In support of his thesis, the author proceeds to adduce some anecdotal evidence all of which serves to exemplify practically identical attitudes. – In another work, a fictitious secretary boasts of the superiority of his post over that of the boon-companion, citing among other proofs the serious nature of his job and the unserious concerns of a boon-companion ("*wa-anā li-l-jidd wa-anta li-l-hazl*"). See Kushājim, *Adab* 3.

[54] In recent centuries, the society of the northern part of the Arabian Peninsula viewed poems and

added factor affecting the varying local estimations of poetry might be the virtually universal tendency of societies to ascribe higher cultural value to those written genres and modes of discourse that are monopolised by the élite and to depreciate those that the élite shares with the lower orders.[55]

To conclude the discussion of the pervasive distinction between topics worthy and unworthy of a man's attention respectively, the following passage shows the way such principles could manifest themselves and affect behaviour in concrete situations:

> One day, when [the Abbasid caliph] al-Ma'mūn was talking, Isḥāq b. Ibrāhīm al-Muṣʿabī laughed at something. [The caliph] said: "Isḥāq, I've considered you suitable for [heading] my police force, and then you open your mouth in laughter? [Here, servants,] take away his insignia and his sword!" And he added: "You'd sooner make a suitable [companion] for a drinking party (*anta bi-majlis al-sharāb ashbah*). Put a scarf on his shoulders!" To this [Isḥāq] replied: "Forgive my blunder, oh Commander of the Faithful!" The caliph said he forgave him. [Isḥāq] would never laugh again.[56]

2.2 Elite and Commoners

The silence of the sources about the customs and affairs of the common people is a silence pregnant with significance. The scarcity of data in mediaeval Arabic works on the *ʿāmma* (the uneducated commoners) is in itself a powerful indication of the opinion of the cultural and political élite about the importance of the lower classes;

---

the explanatory stories attached to them (*sawālif*) as the 'talk of real men' (*kalām al-rijāl*), in contradistinction to folk tales, mostly favoured by women and children and consequently dismissed as trivial chatter. See Sowayan 1985: 125. In the southernmost corner of the peninsula, in the Yemeni highlands, similar attitudes have continued to prevail: poetry, unlike any kind of jesting, is thought to be a 'serious' mode of discourse worthy of men; as far as verse is concerned, the more 'serious' (that is to say political) a poem's theme, the more highly valued it is. It is usually only in their youth that poets compose love poetry, which they tend to dismiss when growing older even if it is a particularly masterful poem, because of the subject-matter being less than sufficiently serious. See Caton 1990: 27, 48, 53. Among the Arabic-speaking nomads of Mauritania, even 'serious' poetry used to be viewed with suspicion and regarded as silly and unbecoming, and such attitudes have only slowly dissipated; see Uld Abbāh 1987: 34–5. As for folk tales, the Rubāṭāb of Northern Sudan also regard them as an utterly discreditable pastime for a real man – one informant used the Quranic phrase *habā'un manthūr*, 'scattered dust', to characterise the genre. See Ibrahim 1994: 41–2.

55 On this tendency, see Foley 1997: 427–9.

56 Ibn Riḍwān, *Shuhub* 350–1. It is quite conceivable, of course, that the caliph took offence because he suspected Isḥāq of laughing at his expense. However, the text conspicuously fails even to hint at such a motive, whereas one would reasonably expect some comment had such a motive been at play. It seems more probable to me that what vexed the caliph was simply the lack of solemnity so unfitting for an important discussion – at any rate, that is the explanation he offered to explain his annoyance.

but we need not rely solely on such indirect evidence. A considerable number of passages and remarks attest to the attitudes of the élite towards whom they perceived as inferior in intellect as well as social (and often moral) standing – the ignorant masses. Indeed, disparagement of the *ʿāmma* is something of a topos in mediaeval Arabic writing, which it could hardly have come to be if the view had not been widespread and dominant amongst the higher classes. A significant, and probably decisive, part of the educated élite harboured a very negative attitude to the customs and everyday culture of the common people, limiting their commentary about the latter to occasional censure and perhaps diatribes.[57] In the opposition of the somewhat ill-defined concepts of *khāṣṣa* ('élite') and *ʿāmma* ('common people'), there was no ambiguity about the relative value of each.

I have called the concepts ill-defined, for the most fundamental problem with these categories is the very definition of what elements of the population they may comprise in any given context. The criteria of classifying someone as belonging to the *ʿāmma* or the *khāṣṣa*, respectively, are not always clear-cut. Which sectors of society constituted the 'élite' is not a straightforward issue, the categories appearing to have had a shifting and fluid meaning. Wealth is an obvious candidate for a criterion to decide membership in the *khāṣṣa*, but unfortunately the problem seems to be more complex.[58] A passage in Yāqūt's biographical dictionary mentions "a certain rich commoner (*baʿḍ al-ʿāmma al-muthrīn*)" in late 6th/12th-century Baghdad.[59] It appears that in some social contexts even a fabulously wealthy merchant might not qualify as a worthy member of the 'élite' (*khāṣṣa*). Consider the words of a certain Abū Manṣūr al-Sājī in reply to an invitation to a dinner by a son of the caliph al-Rāḍī (r. 322/934–329/940): "I am a common man, maladroit at eating in the presence of royalty (*anā rajul sūqī lā uḥsinu muʾākalat al-mulūk*)."[60] Another text also indicates that good table manners could make or break a man's status as a member of the élite: a rich wholesale dealer in textiles decides to leave the house of a customer when a big bowl of assorted fruits is served, only to receive this reproach: "What kind of common manners are these (*mā hādhā l-khulq al-ʿāmmī*)? Do sit down!"[61] The limited role of material prosperity

[57] Shoshan 1993: 67. This tendency is closely connected with the religious issue of the dichotomy of *sunna* (the ideological construct of an 'untainted tradition' of the Prophet) and *bidʿa* ('innovation', a reprehensible departure from the *sunna*), on which see Berkey 1995: 40; Gellner 1981: 5.

[58] See for instance Mottahedeh 1980: 115, 122. In some communities, a combined monopoly on wealth and learning created and defined a highly exclusive local élite; see Bulliet 1972: 14, 26, 57.

[59] Yāqūt, *Udabāʾ* IV, 1756.

[60] al-Thaʿālibī, *Laṭāʾif* 31.

[61] al-Ibshīhī, *Mustaṭraf* 196. See also Miskawayh, *Tajārib* I, 376 ["... *wa-ʿalimtu annahu tājir ʿāmmī*"]. It is worth noting that traders, for all their affluence, were often considered to be uneducated, witless bores and thus undesirable company at dinners, soirées and other social occasions. A poetic expression of this perception can be observed in the following four verses: "I was drinking in the company of traders, which I intend to have been a farewell to any occasion of its kind. / One [trader]

in ensuring élite status is also evident in anecdotes that portray certain rich merchants as the quintessential uncultured, uncouth oaf.[62] It is safe to state, then, that wealth alone was insufficient – at any rate in certain regions and historical periods – to elevate someone to the ranks of the *khāṣṣa* in its proper sense. It appears that erudition and knowledge, including the fundamental quality of literacy, constituted a much more decisive factor. On the other hand, it is distinctly improbable that any ruler or political leader, be he never so benighted and unlettered, would ever be classified as belonging to the 'common people', or *ʿāmma.* (This is not mere hypothetical hair-splitting – unlettered and ignorant individuals did rise to the position of ruler from time to time.) Like wealth, learning is not an absolute criterion to delineate the 'élite'. That literacy in itself did not mean entrance to the 'élite' is demonstrated by the following characterisation of the littérateur Ibn Abī Ṭāhir Ṭayfūr (d. 280/893): "[he] was [initially] a teacher at a Quranic school, a commoner (*ʿāmmī*), but later rose to the élite (*takhaṣṣaṣa*)".[63] Even higher learning beyond the level of knowing how to read and write was not a sure qualification for élite status. Yāqūt says in the biography of a grammarian called al-Thamānīnī (d. 442/1050–1) that 'the élite of the people' (*khawāṣṣ al-nās*) studied grammar from another scholar of that time, al-Asadī, while only 'the commoners' (*ʿumūmuhum*) frequented the lectures of al-Thamānīnī. Clearly, in some contexts one could be learned and a commoner at the same time.[64] In recent centuries the usual understanding of the term *khāṣṣa* in North African towns and cities was the holders of political and military power (in Algiers, the Janissaries in particular), excluding the religious scholars and dignitaries.[65] Surprisingly, it seems that in some historical contexts even the real or putative descendants of the Prophet Muḥammad would not necessarily qualify as part of the 'élite' despite the immense prestige of their lineage.[66]

---

says, 'How many deals I've concluded, giving the ell its due length'. / Another says, 'I have all sorts of [merchandise] but I neither sell nor buy [at the moment]'. / Never make them your boon-companions, for their presence will give you a headache." See al-Ibshīhī, *Mustaṭraf* 476.

62 In a later chapter, we will discuss the assigning of this role to Ibn al-Jaṣṣāṣ, one of the wealthiest jewellers of the Buyid period period, about whom a passage has already been cited above. See for instance al-Tanūkhī, *Nishwār* I, 29–30.

63 Yāqūt, *Udabāʾ* I, 283.

64 Yāqūt, *Udabāʾ* V, 2091.

65 Stambouli, Zghal 1976: 15–6, and also 16–7 on the local interpretation of the concept of 'common people'.

66 Such a conclusion is suggested by the following phrase of the qāḍī al-Tanūkhī (329/940–384/994): "the young [miscreants] of the Hāshimite family and other commoners (*aḥdāth al-Hāshimiyyīn wa-ghayruhum min al-ʿāmma*)"; see al-Tanūkhī, *Nishwār* I, 88. On the other hand, also cf. Mottahedeh 1980: 122. The Ḥanafī jurist Abū l-Layth Naṣr al-Samarqandī (d. 375/985–6) contrasts the term *ʿawāmm* (the plural of *ʿāmma*) to the combined categories of the Prophet's descendants (*ashrāf*), rulers and dignitaries (*al-salāṭīn wa-l-aʿlām*), jurisprudents (*al-fuqahāʾ*), and 'people of middling status' (*al-awsāṭ*); see al-Samarqandī, *Fatāwā* 261.

When all is said and done, it is perhaps reasonable to presume that the exact meaning of the terms 'élite' and 'commoners' depended to a great extent on the person using the words. With a modicum of cynicism, but not unreasonably, the term 'common people' could be defined as 'everyone beneath the likes of the speaker in rank, prestige and/or learning'. This approach might make it easier to understand the pejorative use of the term *ʿāmma* by an illiterate Bedouin – presumably to refer to a category not including himself – in a text from the Buyid era.[67] In the same period, the Twelver (Imāmī) Shiʿites would customarily apply the same label to the Sunnis.[68] Around the end of the Buyid period, the famous author al-Khaṭīb al-Baghdādī (d. 463/1071) distinguishes commoners and an élite *within* the scholarly class (*ahl al-ʿilm*), apparently equating the former with the more pietistic type of scholars.[69] Thus the particular circumstance in which the concept of 'élite' was being used seems to have greatly affected the sense it carried, allowing for a great deal of flexibility. In fact, this looseness of the signification of the words *khāṣṣa* and *ʿāmma* is by no means unique to mediaeval Arabic-speaking society; a possible parallel is the difficulty, much discussed in contemporary ethnography, of defining 'popular culture'.[70]

Whatever the exact connotations of the concept of *ʿāmma*, popularity among the common folk was apparently no concern of the majority of political leaders like rulers, viziers and governors. The opinion of the wider public – basically, the urban masses – simply did not matter. Indeed, the rare observation that a certain political leader was very popular with the commoners tends not to be meant as flattering. For instance, the vizier of the caliph al-Muqtafī (r. 530/1136–555/1160), Abū Shujāʿ al-Rūdhrāwarī is said to have been dismissed from his post and put under house arrest precisely because he sought popularity among the *ʿāmma* by ostentatiously walking instead of riding to the great mosque on Friday and shaking hands with the throngs of plebeians greeting him (gestures strangely reminiscent of the dishonest, crafty populism of presidential candidates during U.S. elections).[71] In an earlier

---

[67] The Bedouin makes the axiomatic assertion that "avoidance of acts [characteristic] of the common people is part of perfect manly virtue (*ijtināb afʿāl al-ʿāmma min al-murūʾa al-tāmma*)", from which it seems safe to deduce that he does not consider himself a commoner. See al-Tawḥīdī, *Baṣāʾir* III(vi), 58. A modern Druze folk song from Syria refers to the 'élite of the world' (*khwaṣṣ al-ʿālam*), a phrase translated by the collector as 'les hommes de bien' or 'les particuliers parmi les gens [...] c'est-à-dire: les notables, les meilleurs'. See Jargy 1970: 154–5, 156 [note 3].

[68] Kraemer 1986: 65; and for an example of such a usage, see Yāqūt, *Udabāʾ* VI, 2441 ["*dufina laylan khawfan min al-ʿāmma li-annahu yuttaham bi-l-tashayyuʿ*"]. On the meaning of the term 'élite' in Iraq under the Abbasids, also see al-Alūsī 1987: 65. On the huge and rapid transformations of the social stratification of Iraq in the early Abbasid era, see Pellat 1953: 224–5.

[69] Yāqūt, *Udabāʾ* II, 627–8.

[70] E.g. Shoshan 1993: 6–7.

[71] al-Iṣbahānī, *Kharīda* I(i), 78.

period, under al-Muqtadir (r. 295/908–320/932), comparable displays of populism by the vizier Abū ʿAlī al-Khāqānī, who would habitually pray in the mosques of the common people, also elicited nothing but contempt in the ranks of the political élite.[72] The following passage in al-Tawḥīdī's vilificatory book on the celebrated vizier and author al-Ṣāḥib b. ʿAbbād, seeking to expose yet another sordid detail about the latter's character, depicts a disgraceful habit of associating with the *ʿāmma*:

> From time to time he would wrap a turban around his head, passing it under his chin as well, and spread a long thin shawl (*ṭaylasān*) over it [to complete his typical religious scholar's attire]. Then he would set about discussing [theological issues] with the commoners – greengrocers, bakers, sellers of second-hand clothes, shoemakers – in the Darī [dialect of Persian] or that of al-Rayy, or some other tongue. All the while he would think that he was doing some important thing, spreading correct beliefs and boosting religion...[73]

Scornful attitudes to and explicit derision of the ʿā*mma* is something of a constant in the culture of the mediaeval Middle Eastern élite. To give substance to this observation, it will be instructive to survey the relevant views of a number of Abbasid caliphs as reported in the available sources. The second ruler of the dynasty, al-Manṣūr (r. 136/754–158/775) proudly claimed being totally indifferent to the opinions of the commoners about his reign.[74] His son and successor al-Mahdī (r. 158/775–169/785) gave instructions to his majordomo to allot as limited a part of audience time as possible to the commoners, so that they should have minimal opportunity to tire the caliph with their complaints.[75] Al-Mahdī's son, Hārūn al-Rashīd (r. 170/786–193/809), must have harboured similar feelings towards the masses as his predecessors had before him, judging by a remark he reportedly made when inviting his vizier to an early morning walk: "Come, let's inhale the air of al-Ḥīra before it is polluted by the breath of the common people."[76] One of the sons of this caliph, al-Maʾmūn (r. 198/813–218/833) summarised his assessment of the worth of the lower classes in these words: "The common people are lowly, artisans are scoundrels, traders are misers, and secretaries lord it over the the people (*al-sūqa suffal wa-l-ṣunnāʿ andhāl wa-l-tujjār bukhalāʾ wa-l-kuttāb mulūk ʿalā l-nās*)."[77] While this is a fairly unequivocal

[72] Miskawayh, *Tajārib* I, 24. Occasionally, however, even caliphs could be forced to take account, albeit grudgingly, of the mood of the masses; see for instance al-Alūsī 1987: 79.

[73] al-Tawḥīdī, *Akhlāq* 144.

[74] al-Ṭabarī, *Tārīkh* V, 1647; Ibn Simāk, *Zaharāt* 58.

[75] "*[...] wa-ʾjʿal li-l-ʿāmma waqtan idhā waṣalū aʿjalahum ḍīquhu ʿan al-talabbuth wa-l-tamakkuth*"; see al-Bayhaqī, *Maḥāsin* 188.

[76] al-Thaʿālibī, *Khāṣṣ* 50–1.

[77] al-Bayhaqī, *Maḥāsin* 128. After this passage the author, in an admirably objective spirit, points out that there is little justification for the élite's disdain of physical work and 'lowly' jobs as some of the most respectable personalities of early Islamic history, like the caliph Abū Bakr (r. 11/632–13/634) and the great jurisprudent Abū Ḥanīfa (d. 150/767) earned their living from manual work.

statement, an interesting account shows a high dignitary in al-Ma'mūn's court calling the caliph's attention to the expediency of at least a little sensitivity to the opinions of the masses. However, the narrator of the story – the Muʿtazilī theologian Thumāma b. Ashras (d. 213/828–9) – agreed with the caliph and advised an utter disregard for popular concerns:

> Al-Ma'mūn made a firm decision to have [the Umayyad caliph] Muʿāwiya cursed [publicly, in deference to Shiʿite sectarian custom], and have a letter/book (*kitāb*) written to denounce the latter. However, [the chief *qāḍī*] Yaḥyā b. Aktham advised him against such an act, saying: "Oh Commander of the Faithful, the common people (*al-ʿāmma*), especially the Khurāsānians, will not tolerate it. You cannot be sure that they will not become alienated and turn against you irremediably, the consequences of which would be unpredictable. The right thing for you to do is to leave people to their own beliefs, and refrain from showing which religious group you favour. This is more expedient politically, its consequences are safer, and it is also more prudent." [The caliph] accepted [Yaḥyā's] opinion. When I entered his hall, he said to me: "Thumāma, you know what we were about to do with regard to Muʿāwiya, but we now heard a contrary opinion which is more useful for the management of state affairs, and more conducive to perpetual praise among the commoners (*abqā dhikran fī l-ʿāmma*)." Then he told me that Yaḥyā b. Aktham had forewarned him, suggesting that the common people would be hostile to such a policy. I said: "Commander of the Faithful, do the commoners have as high a standing in your eyes as in Yaḥyā's? By God, if you sent a single man with a black [banner] on his shoulder [to indicate his allegiance to the Abbasids] and a staff in his hand, he could drive here ten thousand of them at once. By God, oh Commander of the Faithful: God the Most High is not content with equating them [viz. the common people] with a herd of livestock but says they go even more astray [than animals]: '*Or deemest thou that most of them hear or understand? They are but as the cattle; nay, they are further astray from the way.*' [...]"[78]

An incident involving the caliph al-Muʿtaḍid (r. 279/892–289/902) and his boon-companions again attests to an enduring and pervasive attitude of contempt towards the lower classes. The caliph is said to have interrupted a drinking session with a number of courtiers when some police informer brought a report of an insolent, slightly seditious political remark made by a cotton carder in one of the poorer quarters of Baghdad. When the miserable artisan was brought before the caliph, he pleaded his commoner's status and concomitant ignorance to minimise the consequences of his crime ("*anā rajul sūqī lā aʿrifu illā l-ghazl wa-l-quṭn wa-mukhāṭabat al-nisāʾ wa-l-ʿāmma*"). It is even more revealing that after the man was humiliated and duly thrown out of the palace, the caliph's boon-companions pointed

[78] al-Bayhaqī, *Maḥāsin* 170–1. The citation is from Quran 25:44, where the words refer to the unbelievers, not the common people.

out that the ruler need not waste his time with a mere 'dog of a plebeian' (*kalb min al-sūqa*), the commoners' opinions and grudges having no importance whatsoever.[79] Incidentally, giving the *ʿāmma* a cold shoulder and turning a deaf ear to their concerns did not prevent extremely harsh, ruthless reactions to any disturbance by the commoners; indeed, the plebeian mobs who took part in the recurring urban riots of the Buyid era were typically punished far more severely than any participants of élite status.[80]

As evident from some of the previous examples, the reigning caliph was never alone in despising the lower classes. The very negative stereotypes with reference to the commoners might even creep into the text of works of jurisprudence, despite the egalitarian ethic of Islam. For instance, the Shiʿite jurist Abū Jaʿfar al-Ṭūsī (d. 460/1067) advises against associating in any way with 'lowly people', craftsmen and manual workers, and Kurds (viz. uncouth hillsfolk).[81] Moreover, religious scholars generally considered the common people to be unworthy, and incapable, of being taught the finer points of religious learning, and the opinion that efforts to educate the *ʿāmma* are not only futile but possibly even harmful was widely accepted among intellectuals. (This seems to highlight the role of the educational factor in the definition of *khāṣṣa* versus *ʿāmma*.) The commoner's intellect being quite unable to grasp the real meaning of theological, legal and sectarian arguments, such debates must be kept out of his reach. The reader is reminded here of the charge of populism against the vizier al-Ṣāḥib b. ʿAbbād in al-Tawḥīdī's book-length denunciation of him, as quoted above. What al-Tawḥīdī holds against the vizier with particular emphasis is the toleration, indeed encouragement, of mere commoners' participating in debates on religious subjects. While this is somewhat anecdotal evidence, other sources are more explicit in this respect:

---

[79] al-Tanūkhī, *Nishwār* I, 326–8.

[80] For instance, consider the aftermath of the riots between the Alids and Abbasids during the viziership of al-Muhallabī, and especially his way of dealing with the participants in al-Tanūkhī, *Nishwār* I, 86–8. One wonders if the apparent hostility of some authors to the phenomenon of the so-called *futuwwa* (urban youths' groups engaging in various activities) may not be due in part to the participation of commoners in such groups. These coteries of 'young men' (*fityān*, *aḥdāth*) might in some cases be content with living and carousing together, while in other circumstances they formed veritable urban militias that could have a decisive role in rebellions and riots (in which case they would often be referred to as *ʿayyārūn*, 'vagabonds, idlers, loafers'). See for instance Cahen 1958–9: II, 29–30, 32–3; and for a brief description of the lifestyle of a concrete coterie of *fityān* in 8th/14th-century Anatolia, see Ibn Baṭṭūṭa, *Riḥla* 166–7. Thus the connotations and the social background of the concept of *futuwwa* were variable; however, its close association with the common folk seems to have been more or less constant. See al-Alūsī 1987: 91–7; Mottahedeh 1980: 157; Bulliet 1972: 44; Shoshan 1991: 98–9; Cahen 1958–9: II, 47. (Groups of the *futuwwa* type did not exist in all regions of the mediaeval Islamic world; for example, they were probably unknown in North Africa; see Stambouli, Zghal 1976: 10.) For a Ḥanafite author's markedly negative appraisal of *futuwwa*, see Ibn Baydakīn, *Lumaʿ* I, 113–24.

[81] al-Ṭūsī, *Nihāya* II, 377.

> A commoner (*al-ʿāmmī*) will eagerly plunge into the [religious] sciences, for Satan whispers to him: "You belong among the learned, the most eminent." [...] Every mortal sin that he may commit is less sure to lead to his perdition than is his embarking upon discussing [religious] scholarship, especially [the theological issue of] God and His attributes. The task of the common folk is to do the religious duties, believe in whatever is in the Quran and accept whatever the prophets have said, without further research. Their inquiring about anything beyond the religious duties is impertinence on their part, which will earn them God's displeasure and expose them to the peril of unbelief. It is like the hostlers in charge of the riding animals inquiring about the secrets of kings – such men must be punished. Anyone who inquires about a difficult discipline without his intellect being up to the task is blameworthy as well as a commoner.[82]

Similar views are reflected in the following excerpt from the book of the Ḥanbalite author Ibn al-Jawzī (d. 597/1201) on the semi-educated popular preachers known in Arabic as *quṣṣāṣ*:

> [...] They will then address the ignorant commoners who are as numerous as livestock. Far from having any objection to what [the *quṣṣāṣ*] say and lecture on, [the common people] will say: "Thus spake the great scholar (*ʿālim*)..." For in the eyes of the commoners a great scholar is anyone who happens to ascend the pulpit.[83]

Intellectuals who did not belong to the category of '*ulamā'*' could be no less dismissive of the commoners' mental capacities and general worth. One encounters similar views in works of *belles-lettres*. Here is some counsel regarding correct attitudes to the commoners from a 9th/15th-century *adab* collection: "Do not sit in the company of commoners, but should you [find it unavoidable to] do so, then the adequate conduct is to take no part in their conversation, give no ear to their empty nonsense, and ignore all the improper words they utter (*lā tujālis al-ʿāmma, fa-in faʿalta fa-ādāb dhālik tark al-khawḍ fī ḥadīthihim wa-qillat al-iṣghāʾ ilā arājīfihim wa-l-taghāful ʿammā yajrī min sūʾ alfāẓihim*)."[84] Whatever the impact of such recommendations, the 'empty nonsense' of the common people could catch the attention of the educated classes by way of entertainment, as evidenced by many intellectuals' fondness of anecdotes and jokes about the incredible levels of ignorance among plebeians.[85] Moreover, various authors expressed their contempt for the

---

[82] al-Ghazālī, *Iḥyāʾ* II, 204. In the subsequent paragraphs, the author is even more unequivocal: commoners *must* be barred from any discussion of religious issues ("*yajibu qamʿuhum wa-manʿuhum*").

[83] Ibn al-Jawzī, *Quṣṣāṣ* 318.

[84] al-Ibshīhī, *Mustaṭraf* 133 (and cf. the words of Sahl al-Tustarī in al-Ghazālī, *Iḥyāʾ* I, 111). A much earlier source also advises the genteel and refined to avoid spending time in the company of craftsmen and other commoners; see al-Washshāʾ, *Muwashshā* 222; and also cf. al-Khaṭīb, *Kifāya* 139.

[85] E.g. a grossly ignorant man supposes that Abū Turāb (the famous nickname of ʿAlī b. Abī Ṭālib)

ʿāmma in quite explicit ways. The following passage, recorded as a funny anecdote, makes the point clearly enough:

> It was narrated by ʿUthmān al-Warrāq ['the Copyist']: "Once I saw [the famous poet] al-ʿAttābī eating bread in the street near to the Bāb al-Shām [city gate of Baghdad]. I asked him how come he felt no embarrassment [to do such a lowly thing].[86] He replied: "Why, if we happened to be in a building full of cattle, do you think you'd feel embarrassed or ashamed to eat under their gaze?" I said I would not. He said: "Now you wait a bit, I'll show you that these [people] are all cattle." He stood up and started to preach and pray until a large crowd gathered around him, then he told them: "It's been transmitted to us by several [authorities] that whoever is able to reach the tip of his nose with his tongue won't enter Hell." There was no one there who would not keep shoving out his tongue towards the tip of his nose, to see if it would reach there. When [the crowd] had dispersed, al-ʿAttābī said to me: "Haven't I told you they're all cattle?"[87]

The great traveller and historian Abū l-Ḥasan ʿAlī al-Masʿūdī (d. 346/957) offers a more serious outline of what is essentially the same stereotype, the impressionability and naïveté of the commoners:

> It is characteristic of the commoners to make men unfit for leadership their leaders, to regard lowly men as eminent, and to call the ignorant learned. They become followers of whoever appears to them first, without discriminating between a superior man and an inferior one, merit and defect, having no ability to tell truth and falsity apart. [...] Just observe the common folk whenever they assemble and congregate: you will never see them [in any other condition] but flocking round a bear-leader or a trainer of apes beating his drum, or hankering for amusement and play, or watching a deceitful swindler and charlatan, or listening to a lying folk preacher, or gathering around a criminal being thrashed or standing around someone being crucified. Someone croaks at them and they will follow him; [an admonition] is roared at them and they will not heed it.

is the name of some brigand; a commoner leaving for the Meccan pilgrimage thinks that a voice will speak to him from the Kaʿba sanctuary; and so on; see al-Masʿūdī, *Murūj* II, 29–31. Some scholars sought to derive the very word *ʿāmma* ('common people') from the noun *ʿamā* ('blindness'), a perfectly untenable etymology from a linguistic point of view but a very revealing mistake nevertheless. See Ibn Makkī, *Tathqīf* 371.

86 Eating in the street in plain view of passersby was considered – at any rate, in polite society – to be a sign of extremely vulgar, plebeian manners. As a *ḥadīth* puts it, "eating in the bazaar is lowly behaviour (*al-akl fī l-sūq danāʾa*)"; see al-Ṭabarsī, *Makārim* 149; and also (replete with full *isnād*) in al-Washshāʾ, *Muwashshā* 220–1. Also cf. al-Khaṭīb, *Kifāya* 139. Similar norms of polite conduct have been reported from modern Omani society; see Wikan 1977: 307.

87 al-Iṣfahānī, *Aghānī* XIII, 128. (Note that the test of the masses' ignorance is their inability to recognise a mock sermon for the absurd caricature it is.) Another story – whose protagonist is a fanatical Khārijite in lieu of al-ʿAttābī – has a very similar plot and draws roughly the same conclusion; see al-Bayhaqī, *Maḥāsin* 171–2. Abū Ḥāmid al-Ghazālī's great work on religious ethics also stresses, with pronounced disapproval, the common folk's pliability: "they follow every croaking voice and are driven along by every wind." See al-Ghazālī, *Iḥyāʾ* I, 97.

> They take no action to suppress wrong, and do not do what is right. They have no qualms about treating a righteous man in the same way as they do a reprobate, a believer like an unbeliever...[88]

The negative prejudices of intellectuals – religious and 'secular' dignitaries alike – did not end here. In the final chapter of this book, the Arabic concept of *ẓarf* ('refinement, sophistication', and 'wit, humour') will be discussed at some length, but one observation that is worth making here is that this concept, not surprisingly, was widely considered to be the very antithesis of the perceived nature of the common people. This view manifested itself in various ways: elegant love affairs were thought to be above the station of mere commoners; the cultured urbanites of Abbasid society refused to consume certain types of food, drink and fruit that the common people were fond of ("*wa-huwa ʿindahum min akl al-ʿawāmm*", "*idh huwa min sharāb al-ʿāmma wa-l-raʿāʿ wa-shurb al-sūqa wa-l-atbāʿ*" being typical justifications for such a refusal); and so forth.[89]

In addition to the overall depreciation of the *ʿāmma*, the performers of certain crafts and trades were subject to extra derision, perhaps as almost proverbial embodiments of the unrefined qualities of the common folk. Weavers (sing. *ḥāʾik*) had an occupation thought to be extraordinarily humble, one fit for simpletons only, a stereotype attested by a host of disdainful remarks, stories and expressions in the sources.[90] Apparently, a greengrocer could also be viewed as the quintessential commoner, the ultimate bumpkin; this seems to be the point of a remark by a man of high status who justified his refusal to participate in the Friday communal prayer in these words: "I am afraid of being jostled about by greengrocers (*akhshā an yuzāḥimanī l-baqqālūn*)."[91]

2.3 City and Countryside

It could be argued that urban attitudes towards the rural population – especially agriculturists of every description – were but a variation on the theme of despising the common folk. Islamic high culture being the product of great metropolises which served as natural foci of literacy and sophisticated cultural activities such as the

[88] al-Masʿūdī, *Murūj* II, 31–2.

[89] al-Washshāʾ, *Muwashshā* 159–60, 191, 194, 196; Ghazi 1959: 61–2. (Dietary anathemas among the sophisticated included such common items as all kinds of fruit with a hard stone, the alcoholic beverage called *dūshāb*, meat broth with bread, and jerked meat.)

[90] For a number of jokes about the stereotyped idiocy of weavers, see al-Tawḥīdī, *Baṣāʾir* II(iv), 138–9; and also see al-Jāḥiẓ, *Rasāʾil* I(ii), 128. Also note the wording of a dismissive comment by a chief secretary in the Buyid administration about the written work of a colleague: "It is weaving, not writing... (*hādhihi ḥiyāka laysat kitāba*)"; see al-Tanūkhī, *Nishwār* I, 48. The negative stereotypes about weavers still survive in contemporary Iraq; see al-Wardī 1965: 158–9.

[91] al-Ibshīhī, *Mustaṭraf* 140.

pursuit of religious sciences, literature, courtly etiquette, and the luxuries of civilisation, it was inevitable that the villagers of the countryside should appear infinitely ignorant and backward in contrast to the brilliance of the cities. I will have occasion in the last chapter of this book to lend some attention to the question of the sharp differences between the metropolitan culture of Iraq and the relative cultural poverty of the peripheries. Therefore it is sufficient here to note the contrast of city and countryside as an important notion of mediaeval Arabic culture, and observe that quite unequal value was ascribed to one and the other. Needless to add that the city evoked very positive connotations, whereas the countryside was routinely associated with backwardness and ignorance, a pair of concepts that may well be virtually universal wherever a 'high', literate culture exists alongside the folklore of village-dwelling, illiterate cultivators.

The low prestige ascribed by city dwellers to peasants and their oral culture being a nearly universal phenomenon, it will not be necessary to let it detain us; I will limit the discussion of these attitudes to a number of characteristic glimpses into the relevant views of the mediaeval Arabic-speaking élite. A very telling example comes from the Umayyad period, the time when a celebrated Meccan singer called al-Gharīḍ, fearful of the governor of his city, had to flee Mecca and move to a safe distance. He settled in the land of the ʿAkk tribe, in the remote Red Sea coast of the Yemen. He is quoted in a source describing his new surroundings in the following disdainful words: "How could I feel well while living amongst folks who, seeing me carry my lute, will say: 'Hey you there, is this back of a camel-saddle for sale (*yā hanāh a-tabīʿ ākhirat al-raḥl*)'?"[92] Admittedly, the coastal lands (*Tihāma*) of Yemen are about as remote geographically, and as different culturally, from the urban centres of the Hijaz and Iraq as any region within the Middle East could be, but rural places nearer the metropolitan centres of Arabic culture would still be objects of contemptuous commentary by the educated classes. Well-known is the stereotype of the *sawādī* (peasants of the agricultural lands of Iraq, especially around and to the south of Baghdad) as the ultimate bumpkin, an uncouth ignoramus.[93] Besides *sawādī*, other slightly or strongly pejorative terms were also current to denote the peasants of the countryside; one such term is *nabaṭī*, which is strictly speaking an ethnic designation meaning 'Nabatean' but soon came to be a rather derogatory label with the approximate sense of 'yokel'.[94] It is on this connotation that the following joke is based, in which the 'Nabatean' – the stereotypical boor

[92] al-Iṣfahānī, *Aghānī* II, 392.

[93] For a famous literary treatment of the theme, see al-Hamadhānī, *Maqāmāt* 70–3. Also cf. al-Nuwayrī, *Nihāya* I(i), 283 ["*wa-qāla Bukhtīshūʿ tisʿa lā takhlū min tisʿa (...) wa-sawādī min jahl*"].

[94] Pellat 1953: 22. Cf. al-Muqaddasī, *Taqāsīm* 128 ["*fa-ammā l-Baṭāʾiḥ fa-nabaṭ, lā lisān wa-lā ʿaql*"].

– is contrasted to both Persians (as representatives of an ancient urban culture) and Bedouins (noble savages of the desert as it were):

> A king had three wives: a Persian, an Arab, and a Nabatean. One night he said to his Persian wife: "What time is it?" She said: "It's early dawn." He asked her how she knew, and she replied: "I can smell the scent of the sweet basil." Another night, [the king] asked his Arab wife what time it was, and she said: "It's early dawn." He asked her how she knew, and she replied: "I feel the coldness of my [golden] anklets." Another night, [the king] asked his Nabatean wife what time it was, and she said: "It's early dawn." He asked her how she knew, and she replied: "I want [to do] *that* again."[95]

2.4 The Written and the Spoken Language

There is neither room nor much need for discussing in any real depth the linguistic situation in the mediaeval Middle East, a subject that is complex enough to justify separate studies; yet it will be worthwhile mentioning some aspects of the problem, insofar as it is relevant to our present concerns. The idea of the existence, already in the early Abbasid period, of a considerable divergence between the spoken and the written language seems reasonable. Classical Arabic was for all practical purposes a different tongue, both in its grammar and vocabulary, from the spoken dialects of Arabic, and of course the linguistic duality was even more marked in the largely Persian-speaking cities of Iran and Central Asia, where classical Arabic continued to be used as the primary language of writing (especially in science and religion) even after the emergence of modern Persian as a written, literary language. As in the modern Arab world, the two versions of Arabic were thought to be suitable for different social situations, and were accordingly perceived by Arabic speakers, less as two *versions* but rather as two *levels* of Arabic, which means that the prestige of classical Arabic was, and still is, far superior to that of any dialect.[96] It is hardly surprising that classical Arabic, whose prestige rested not simply on its adequacy for the purpose of writing but also on the resultant factor of its being the sole medium

---

95 al-Tawḥīdī, *Baṣāʾir* II(iv), 102. Mediaeval Arabic jokes about the vulgarity and gracelessness of the Nabateans are an obvious parallel to modern Egyptian jokes about the inhabitants of Upper Egypt (the *Ṣaʿāyda*), which also highlight the supposed ignorance and village manners of the target group. That some ethnic groups or subgroups should be portrayed in jokes as the embodiment of stupidity and uncouthness is attested in a host of cultures beyond the Arab world as well. See Davies 1987: 40–1, 45.

96 I am oversimplifying here for the sake of brevity, leaving aside the issue of Middle Arabic, a widespread 'intermediate' version of written Arabic that shows quite a few dialectal features. On this, see Lentin 2005–9. I thank Hilary Kilpatrick both for calling my attention to the need to, at the very least, acknowledge the existence of a linguistic situation far more complex than a simple diglossia, and for providing me with a copy of the relevant entry in the Encyclopedia of Arabic Language and Linguistics.

of the Quran, all the religious disciplines and all solemn stately functions, should have been considered the highest possible means of communication. Although, as will be argued in the next and subsequent chapters, even illiterate people would be exposed to classical Arabic on a regular basis – through such channels as Friday sermons, public homilies, official speeches, Quran recitations at various *rites de passage*, and of course prayers – it is reasonable to suppose that most people's ability to understand it, let alone the skill of actively using it, was rather limited. The fact that his lack of the requisite linguistic skills precluded even the remotest possibility of a commoner's participation in the serious study of the Quran, the religious sciences, and the business of politics, must have contributed to the extremely low esteem accorded to the *ʿāmma*, discussed in detail above.

Classical Arabic for writing, the spoken language for the conduct of mundane affairs – this neat division is expectable and largely valid, but in reality the boundaries could often be somewhat blurred. It is certainly rare that one would encounter the occasional dialectal phrase in a written Arabic text from the mediaeval period, and when one does, it is invariably intended to bring some stylistic effect to the passage, usually a humorous one. The purpose of inserting a dialectal word or two into a classical Arabic text is mostly to illustrate the linguistic clumsiness and barbarism of the common folk, either as a warning to those who know better or, more typically, as a source of fun. One constant in all such passages is that the vernacular is never devoid of negative value in comparison with classical Arabic, and is treated as a mongrel, a distortion of written Arabic – in essence, a sign of ignorance and pedestrianism.[97] Both dialectal words and quasi-vernacular syntax appear to have been occasionally used in writing with the expectation, nay certainty, of their creating an instantly grotesque effect, as in a passage by Ibrāhīm b. Muḥammad al-Bayhaqī (fl. early 4th/10th c.) about the poetic aspirations of a Turkish military leader under al-Muʿtaṣim (r. 218/833–227/842), which probably recreates an anecdote widely circulating in his time. Based as it is on the peculiarly distorted and almost dialectal grammar of the poem's Arabic, the funny flavour of the verses is impossible to render in English; let it suffice to say that the vulgarity of the language of the couplet is paralleled by the banality of its topic, viz. an accident that befell a borrowed

[97] Such a view of the relationship of the dialects and Classical Arabic is still common among Arabic speakers. Many urban dwellers of contemporary Yemen regard tribal poetry as a deformed and inferior version of classical Arabic verse, an attitude that exists in other parts of the Arab world too; see for instance Caton 1990: 47; Jargy 1970: 28–9. What is more, the dialects are considered by many in the Arab countries to be the primary obstacle to 'progress' and 'development' (whatever is meant by these terms). Interestingly, however, the same charge is sometimes made against the use of written, Classical Arabic; with about the same degree of rationality. And of course, the dialects are often identified by Arabic-speaking ideologues as simply a hurdle in the way of Arab unity. On the whole issue, see Haeri 2000: 63–4; and on the relationship of language and political hegemony in general, cf. Hymes 1974: 433.

hunting-dog: "The dog you took right you gave back with a broken leg; / Give back a good one like the dog you took (*al-kalb akhatta jayyidun maksūra rijli jibta; / rudda jayyidun kamā kalbun kunta akhatta*)."[98] The perception that dialectal forms are simply primitive, and thus also grotesque and humorous, is similarly manifest in a sarcastic story about a singer of great local renown in a Syrian town and his dialectal (read primitive and inconsequential) songs.[99] In life as much as in literature, an all too obvious inability to use more refined and elegant language than the common dialect could be an invitation for scorn and mockery.[100]

An important consequence of such attitudes is in evidence in Arabic literature. The spoken Arabic of mediaeval Middle Eastern cities must have been as rich in puns, witty phrases, humour and lyricism as modern Arabic dialects are, but written Arabic texts are largely oblivious of or indifferent to the value of the oral culture of the common people. (One important, if only partial, exception is literary *mujūn*, which – as will be argued in this book – often shows adaptations and even direct borrowings from the spoken language.) A Maghrebi rhetorician of the 8th/14th century even formulates the explicit principle of the advisability of shunning all phrases and words widely known and used by the common folk (*al-mubtadhal fī alsun al-ʿāmma*), adding that the littérateurs of North Africa, more conservative as they tend to be than their eastern colleagues, make a point of avoiding readily comprehensible linguistic items, which by definition cannot form part of a beautiful style.[101] However most intellectuals of the eastern lands would not disagree with this assessment. Consider for instance the opinion of Jalāl al-Dīn Muḥammad al-Qazwīnī (d. 739/1338–9), who states that metaphors understood and used by the unlettered speakers of the vernacular (*istiʿāra ʿāmmiyya*) are indisputably inferior to those that are exclusively used in the written language (*istiʿāra khāṣṣiyya*), or in his own eloquent and revealing wording, "those that can only be grasped by such a man as has elevated himself above the common people (*allatī lā yaẓfaru bihā illā man irtafaʿa ʿan ṭabaqat al-ʿāmma*)."[102] Another littérateur claims that the elegant,

[98] al-Bayhaqī, *Maḥāsin* 478.

[99] E.g. "*Sillōru fī l-qidri waylī ʿalō*" etc.; see the story in al-Iṣfahānī, *Aghānī* I, 63–4. Another example is a joke from the Abbasid period based on the laughable attempt of an illiterate commoner, who does not know classical Arabic, to quote the Quran; see al-Tawḥīdī, *Baṣāʾir* II(iv), 74. Also see the barbarous language of a respectable-looking but laughably ignorant old man in Yāqūt, *Udabāʾ* I, 224. Apparently, the verbatim citation of the dialectal grammar of the caliph al-Muqtadir's servants (*fa-yaqūlū mā jāshi*, 'they say he isn't come yet') also serves to add humour to the account in al-Tanūkhī, *Nishwār* III, 189. However, it must be noted in this context that the spotless classical Arabic of many mediaeval literary sources in fact underwent a process of standardisation by editors; see Lentin 2005–9: 216–7.

[100] E.g. Yāqūt, *Udabāʾ* V, 2243.

[101] al-Shāṭibī, *Ifādāt* 157–8.

[102] al-Qazwīnī, *Īḍāḥ* V, 69. The low status of the dialects – and its consequent invisibility in the

well-educated and urbane people of his time insisted on avoiding a lot of perfectly everyday phrases ("*mimmā kathura ʾstiʿmāluhu fī khiṭāb al-ʿawāmm*") even in speech, because they considered them too vulgar for a polished man. Whether or not factually accurate, the statement does hint at negative attitudes to the everyday language.[103] Nor are these the only instances of a scholar's affectation of distance from the diction of mere commoners: the great linguist known as al-Akhfash al-Awsaṭ (d. 215/830–1 or 221/835–6) is said to have proscribed to his students the use of three of the commonest vernacular words, without which the Iraqi dialect would hardly have been viable.[104]

In sum, the evidence gives substance to the intuition that the contempt shown by members of the cultural and political élite towards the lower classes also manifested itself at the linguistic level, with the language of the commoners being, on the one hand, almost totally excluded from writing, and on the other hand used for sarcastic and humorous purposes whenever any dialectal locutions happened to be featured in a written text. The language of everyday conversation, despite its being used by practically everyone of all social classes for ordinary communication, was seen in the dominant normative system as a grotesque distortion of the sublime language of the Quran, classical Arabic.

3. A Preliminary Definition of *Mujūn*

In almost all the previous contrasting pairs, *mujūn* can be shown to lean towards the non-normative end of the value scale, or at least to occupy an ambiguous position in between the extremes. However, this observation must be strictly limited to the *contents of mujūn literature*. It is not the producers and cultivators of *mujūn* but its content – its subject-matter, motifs and conventions – that link it to the negative end of the value scale. *Mujūn* as written literature tended to be produced by educated and often high-ranking and respected men, genuine intellectuals who also often happened to be state functionaries and courtiers. These people were thus as firmly a part of the *khāṣṣa* as anyone. Furthermore, they lived in great cities, not the countryside; as polished intellectuals they typically had great ability in using classical

mediaeval sources – still affects attitudes among Arabic speakers today, so that stating that so-and-so 'does not know Arabic' even though he is fluent in an Arabic dialect sounds quite natural and reasonable even when the verdict itself is uttered in a dialect, as it usually will. See Haeri 2000: 65.

103 al-Washshāʾ, *Muwashshā* 194. It is to be noted, however, that the unmistakable prudery and priggishness of this author often puts him at variance with the majority of his learned contemporaries, and makes him a less than reliable authority in many respects; see Szombathy 2006.

104 To wit, *bass* ('only', 'well, now'), *ham* ('also, too'), and *bakht* ('luck, fortune'). See al-Tawḥīdī, *Baṣāʾir* III(vi), 179.

Arabic; and they had no problem in pursuing 'serious' concerns and being taken seriously: their oeuvres would mostly include a lot of 'serious' works in addition to *mujūn*, and most of them had respectable positions in society. The subject-matter of *mujūn* works is quite another matter, however.

To begin with the opposition of humour to seriousness. It will be observed that *mujūn* is almost by definition humorous, or at least not wholly serious. As for commoners versus the élite, *mujūn* in the form that has been handed down to our time was exclusively produced by the élite, but its subject-matter as well as its protagonists often link it to the common people and their culture, habits and manners: anecdotal literature features such figures as uncouth Bedouins, sodomites and boy prostitutes, beggars, insane men, half-educated Quran readers, and many other representatives of the urban poor; the plot of *mujūn* poems often takes place in such venues as lowly taverns run by Christians and Jews; and so on. As for dialects and classical Arabic: *mujūn* texts are one of the few types of literature in which one will find the occasional application of vernacular linguistic items in 'high' literature. The contrasting pair of city versus countryside, however, places the themes of *mujūn* in the more prestigious sphere, since as with mediaeval Arabic literature in general it admittedly has little to do with, and little if any interest in, rural culture; it is a quintessentially and characteristically urban – nay metropolitan – cultural product, a tendency barely affected by the fact that its protagonists may sometimes be uncouth rural folk like Nabatean peasants, Bedouins, Daylamī hillsfolk, and so on.

That said, one should not jump to rapid conclusions from the often low-prestige subject-matter of *mujūn*. The relationship of *mujūn* to widely accepted societal values and dominant norms being explored in more detail in the final chapter, we will now turn our attention to the import of the very term, *mujūn*, and its connotations for Arabic speakers in the mediaeval Middle Eastern cities. As has been observed in the Introduction, the concept of *mujūn* is almost impossible to render in English with one single term, a difficulty that is hinted at by the fact that two whole chapters in this work are dedicated to the concrete and detailed illustration of what is meant when Arabic authors talk of *mujūn*. Someone made an indecent remark, and the source that recorded the words by way of an anecdote branded it *mujūn*. A wine-poem, especially if it incorporated vivid depictions of debauchery, was prone to be described as *mujūn*. Blasphemy in poetry – or for that matter, in ordinary conversation – would often, but not in every case, be perceived as constituting *mujūn* of the grossest variety, as would obscenities occurring in written texts. The concept of *mujūn* was apparently spacious enough to extend even to the disrespectful treatment of the ancient Arabic poetic heritage, usually in the form of parodistic motifs. At first sight, there is little to unify these instances of *mujūn*, apart from the fact that they all appear somehow to run against usual norms of conduct and decorous literary expression, as the case might be. However, claiming prophet-hood is even more offensive to ordinary Muslim sensibilities, yet certainly no one would have identified it as *mujūn* (unless it was in the form of a joke). The same is true of a host of other breaches of dominant societal norms like gratuitous affronts to the honour of respected persons, the wilful neglect of prayers, disobedience to one's parents, or corruption and false testimony, none of which would be called *mujūn* by any mediaeval Muslim. Norm-breaking and *mujūn* were not synonymous concepts.

To complicate matters, *mujūn* might in some cases manifest itself in behaviour, and in other cases in literature. The literary depiction of a pattern of behaviour perceived as *mujūn* would as a rule also pass for *mujūn*,[105] and while the opposite is also often true, the connection is by no means automatic. For example, the frivolous depiction in literary works of adultery (*zinā*) – and especially wine-and-orgy poems – was usually given the name of *mujūn*, committing adultery (or simply drinking wine) in real life was definitely not, except in special circumstances. Furthermore, it cannot be automatically presumed in all cases that any poet or writer who posed as a libertine in his works, or assumed the literary persona of a libertine, was in fact a norm-breaker and libertine in real life.[106] In fact, a lot of them might actually lead quite sedate and unobjectionable lives. This issue takes us to the old controversies about the degree of the 'sincerity' of Arabic literature in general (including the literature of *mujūn*), a debate which I will argue is wholly futile and misleading. I will take up the topic of the relationship of *mujūn* in a person's life and his works in the last two chapters of this book. Let it suffice here to observe that it would be wholly artificial and unwise to draw a strict line between *mujūn*-as-literature and *mujūn*-as-behaviour: mediaeval Arabic sources never make such a distinction, which suggests that to mediaeval Arabic intellectuals the two manifestations of *mujūn* were felt to be essentially the same thing. This leads one to conclude that *mujūn* must have been perceived as an underlying attitude that could express itself in various ways, in daily behaviour as well as in literary composition.

As far as its literary expression is concerned, it has already been observed that one thing *mujūn* is not is a separate literary genre. Despite a handful of exceptions, it is rare that mediaeval Arabic literary works should be dedicated entirely to *mujūn*; the student of the subject typically finds such material scattered over the whole text of longer anthologies and *adab* collections, or else in specific chapters on frivolity and indecent themes within larger works, such as the eighteenth night in Abū Ḥayyān

[105] Unless the topic is treated in a scholarly manner and in explicitly condemnatory terms, as, for instance, in the genre of anti-*bidʿa* treatises.

[106] Rowson 1998: 547.

al-Tawḥīdī's *Kitāb al-imtāʿ wa-l-muʾānasa* or a section on *mujūn* in many a poet's *dīwān.*[107] For the present study, it proved worthwhile to peruse all manner of genres – poetic anthologies, collections of anecdotes, *adab* works, encyclopaedias, biographical dictionaries, and so on – to gather literary material classifiable and often explicitly classified in the sources as *mujūn.* This study will focus on the literary manifestations of *mujūn* for a simple reason: there is far more of this kind of material than of accounts telling of the everyday behaviour and occasional antics of libertines. This is deceptive, though, as it could easily reflect a function of the means of transmission: a lot of oral material was simply never recorded, much has been lost, and Arabic literature has a strong prescriptive bias. In fact, because speech is by definition fleeting – as the ancient Romans observed, *verba volant, scripta manent* – it was probably easier to engage in outrageous *mujūn* in the oral context of friendly gatherings than in writings. Also, much of *mujūn* was confined to the private sphere, and was never meant for publication. (Even when written down, for instance in the form of short notes or teasing exchanges of letters between friends.) Solitary *mujūn* is something of a contradiction, as I will argue, but this does not preclude a healthy caution on the part of libertines to keep their antics of *épater la société* to a reasonably safe part of the society, namely their own circle of friends. (More about this in Chapters Four and Five.)

Mujūn might manifest itself in a person's behaviour in the form of a scandalous, brazen disregard for ordinary norms of decency and religiosity (e.g. shameless and overt drinking – here the adjectives are as important as the noun!), or else in the form of outrageous or improper remarks made in everyday contexts. That said, a neat classification is again unjustified and misleading. It is reasonable to suppose that most libertines would be as ready to drop unfettered remarks and utterances as to behave improperly, so making a rigid distinction would be unnatural and unwarranted at best. Ultimately, all of these were labelled as the same thing – *mujūn.*

Because the following chapters tend to present *mujūn* in its literary version, I will offer here a sample of frivolous remarks that appear to have actually been made by historical personages. To be sure, the reason we know of them is that they were recorded – owing to their perceived originality or wit – in some written source, which also makes them literary texts of a sort. Because of the editing involved in recording such remarks, it is nearly hopeless to approach these accounts "as though fact and fiction are like wheat and chaff that must be winnowed", to borrow Robert

[107] The existence of a section headed *mujūniyyāt* within each of the two extant recensions of the poetry of Abū Nuwās is the main reason Rowson labels *mujūn* a genre (see Rowson 1998: 547), a generalised conclusion I quite disagree with. While *mujūn* was a speciality of Abū Nuwās which more than deserved a separate section, the term had a wider application to describe the contents of a bewildering variety of literary texts (prose as well as poetry) that were seen as being in some way or another 'indecent'.

Hoyland's phrase.[108] The historicity of any given story is typically suspect when it comes to *mujūn*; often one is dealing with pure fiction masquerading as a historical account (*khabar*), a not uncommon occurrence in mediaeval Arabic writings. A number of ostensibly non-fictional accounts, with historical personages as their protagonists, are clearly simply jokes in which the choice of a protagonist was either haphazard or dictated by stereotypical images of the historical personage in question.[109] For instance Abū Nuwās, notorious as he was for his penchant for boys and his disregard for ordinary norms, was a natural choice for protagonist for jokes featuring homosexuality and licentiousness. Still, it is quite realistic to assume that literary motifs were very often spawned by memorable utterances made by historical persons.[110]

Regardless of such technicalities, the bottom line is that there are quite a few remarks and quips recorded in our sources that appear to be non-fictional, yet manifest the same attitudes that one finds in obviously fictional *mujūn* texts. Cynicism towards religion – it must be emphasised: not outright rejection or hostility, just cynicism and flippancy – is one of those attitudes. As noted above, an extremely *outré* remark dropped among friends, or at any rate in the absence of actively hostile individuals, could pass without any repercussions other than a roaring fit of laughter, while a piece of writing accessible to personal adversaries as well as friends would be more of a risk. It is ironic that the popularity of *mujūn*-type wit would often land fleeting remarks on the pages of manuscripts. Consider the following comment by the famed statesman Abū Sahl b. Nawbakht on the ideas and propositions of the great mystic al-Ḥallāj (244/857–309/922). Aggrieved by his receding hairline and greying beard, the harbingers of old age, Abū Sahl reacted to the mystic's religious views thus: "If [al-Ḥallāj] can bring back my hair and turn my beard black again without the benefit of dyeing, I'll believe in anything he preaches. If he wants me to, I'll witness that he's the envoy (*bāb*) of the Imam; or if he prefers, that he's the Imam himself; if he prefers, I'll witness that he's the Prophet; and if he prefers, that

[108] Hoyland 2006: 19.

[109] Ulrich Marzolph points out that lots of Arabic jokes and anecdotes were actually part of an ancient all-Mediterranean heritage of humorous stories, of which Islamicate cultures served as a sort of relay station. See Marzolph 1992: I, 22, 54.

[110] This I will seek to demonstrate in more than one concrete case over the following chapters, but to illustrate the point I am making, here is a passage about a libertine poet of Tunis called ʿAbd al-Raḥmān al-Firāsī (d. 408/1017–8): "One day he was sitting in the company of the sheikh of Tunis, who was libertinism personified (*kāna nihāya fī l-mujūn*). A man passing by asked directions to the house of Ibn ʿAbdūn, to which the sheikh replied: 'There, the beautiful one where your prick gets erect.' [Probably a vicious allusion to ʿAbdūn's womenfolk in addition to the house's attractiveness.] Al-Firāsī said: 'By God, I'll turn it into a verse, for I've never heard such a poetic conceit (*maʿnā*).' And there and then he recited:'If you wish to know correctly the house of him who is claimed to descend from ʿAbdūna, / Just go, and when your prick sees it, it will stand on guard, since the door is still before it.'" See al-Kutubī, *Fawāt* II, 291.

he's God."[111] A similarly outrageous statement was made by the infamous blind poet Bashshār b. Burd (d. 167–8/784–5), noted both for his acerbic and irascible temper and his nonchalance about religious norms. As will be discussed in the next chapter, comparing the Quran – a work of divine origin in Muslim thought – to a human linguistic product cuts to the very heart of Islamic dogma and is thus an extremely improper poetic motif, although a very popular one in a form diluted with the use of conditional clauses and similar devices. No such reservation is observable in Bashshār's comment on the performance of a proficient singing-girl, which he declared was better than Chapter 59 of the Quran ("*hādhā [...] aḥsan min sūrat al-Ḥashr*").[112] Yet another example of spoken *mujūn* – which, not incidentally, closely resembles a known poetic motif – occurs in the biography of ʿAlī b. ʿAbdallāh al-Nāshiʾ (d. 365/975), a poet and theologian famous for his libertinism and homosexuality as well as his ready wit. The story is narrated by a friend of al-Nāshiʾ:

> He had a black slave-girl serving him. One day he visited his sister's house together with me, and he saw a small black boy there. He asked [his sister]: "Who's this?" She did not say a word, but he insisted, so she said [at last]: "He's the son of Bishāra [your servant-girl]." He asked: "Who's the father?" She replied: "That's why I kept silent." So he called for the slave-girl, and asked her: "Who's this boy's father?" She said: "He's got no father..." And he said: "[Let's] salute, then, Jesus Christ – peace be upon him!"[113]

Retorts to pious admonitions, even if a related phenomenon in some respects, constitute a category unto themselves. Of the various types of irreverent utterances, these sarcastic replies were one of the most widespread, despite the fact that they caused palpable distress and resentment amongst religious scholars. (This is reflected in the often lengthy and detailed fulminations on this topic in many *fiqh* works, about which more will be said in Chapter Four.) Also, despite the fact that such retorts are clearly in opposition to the fundamental Islamic concept of *al-amr bi-l-maʿrūf wa-l-nahy ʿan al-munkar* ('commanding right and forbidding wrong'), hence they were a serious and blatant breach of a widely accepted norm. An example of such retorts is an audacious answer reportedly given by the libertine poet Salm al-Khāsir (3rd/9th c.) (whose very sobriquet is attributed to a display of atrocious disregard for Islamic norms) to the pious reprimands of his acquaintances: "Why, no one's ever curried favour with Satan the way I have; I've managed completely to satisfy him."[114]

---

111 al-Tanūkhī, *Nishwār* I, 162.

112 al-Iṣfahānī, *Aghānī* III, 208. Another famous poet, Abū l-ʿAtāhiya (d. 210/825 or 211/826), was accused of having made a similar remark, and he very nearly got in serious trouble because of it, but this may well have been a malicious slander made up by his enemies and rivals. See ibid. IV, 38.

113 Yāqūt, *Udabāʾ* IV, 1785.

114 Ibn al-Muʿtazz, *Ṭabaqāt* 40.

So much about possible examples of real-life libertinism; and now back to the issue of defining the term *mujūn* itself. If one is to find a workable definition of it, consulting a mediaeval Arabic dictionary is an inevitable and helpful first step, yet it is ultimately not a solution to a problem of un-translatability that is rooted in culture rather than in semantics. That *mujūn* is a sort of attitude, or a sort of behaviour manifesting that attitude, is evident. Given the grammatical structure of Arabic, it is easy and customary to derive both a verbal form (*majana*, *tamājana* and similar verbs, meaning 'to display *mujūn*', 'to be characterised by *mujūn*', 'to behave in a way characteristic of *mujūn*') and an active participle or adjective, *mājin* ('one who has or displays *mujūn*'), from the same root. According to mediaeval Arab lexicographers, the root itself (*m-j-n*) has the primary meaning of hardness, callousness, from which they derived the figurative (and better-known) meaning that is the object of our study. *Mājin*, as the great lexicographer Ibn Manẓūr (d. 711/1311–2) explains, is a term applicable to a person who has a callous face and lacks all sense of shame and modesty ("*li-ṣalābat wajhihi wa-qillat ḥayāʾihi* "). An important ingredient in the meaning of *mujūn*, often mentioned by linguists, is a complete disconcern for one's reputation, an aspect recurring in more than one wording. As Abū Manṣūr Muḥammad al-Azharī (d. 370/980) puts it in his *Tahdhīb*, *mujūn* equals "not caring about what you have done and what others say to you" (*wa-l-majāna allā yubāliya mā ṣanaʿa wa-mā qīla lahu*). According to Ibn Sīda (d. 458/1066), a *mājin* man is one who is unconcerned about both his own and other people's words ("*alladhī lā yubālī bi-mā qāla wa-lā mā qīla lahu*"). More unambiguous still is the following definition: "A *mājin* is for the Arabs a person who commits ugly deeds leading to perdition, and scandalous and dishonourable acts, and no man's reproach and rebukes will stop him (*wa-l-mājin ʿinda l-ʿarab alladhī yartakibu l-maqābiḥ al-murdiya wa-l-faḍāʾiḥ al-mukhziya wa-lā yamuḍḍuhu ʿadhl ʿādhilihi wa-lā taqrīʿ man yuqarriʿuhu*)". But this persistence in scandalous conduct and notoriety is somewhat tempered by another constant, integral aspect of *mujūn*, namely its tendency to be not entirely serious in tone, and its close association with humour and jest. One derivative of the root *m-j-n* is defined quite simply as 'the mixing of seriousness with jesting (*khalṭ al-jidd bi-l-hazl*)'.[115] Another word about a *mājin*'s indifference to his reputation. This attitude has special significance, because there exist a host of terms in Arabic – with various connotations and shades of meaning, and often with strong religious overtones – that serve to describe disgraceful, immoral, unlawful or prohibited conduct, but none of those is synonymous with *mujūn*: for instance, *fisq*, *fujūr*, *fāḥisha*, *maʿṣiya*, *tahattuk*, *faḍīḥa*,

[115] Ibn Manẓūr, *Lisān* VI, 19; and also cf. Ibn al-Jawzī, *Ẓirāf* 27 and Ibn Makkī, *Tathqīf* 359. The all-important connection between *mujūn* and humour will be one of the crucial topics of the last chapter of this book.

and so forth.[116] One conspicuous difference between *mujūn* and the rest is precisely the element of intentionality. While all of the aforementioned terms describe serious breaches of societal norms, the scandal and the damage to the perpetrator's honour usually result from the exposure of an act (or activity) that was meant to be kept secret; by contrast, *mujūn* is meant to be scandalous by the person performing the act. *Mujūn* refers to deliberate, perhaps even ostentatious norm-breaking; the rest of the terms to the discovery of discreditable conduct. Unlike ordinary misconduct and breaches of norms, *mujūn* is done consciously and often – although not always – quite overtly; there is not a trace of surreptitious delinquency about it. *Mujūn* is in this sense a studied, mindful transgression of societal norms, which makes it a particularly good source of insight for anthropologists, sociologists and historians of culture.

For the time being we can settle on a rudimentary working definition of *mujūn* that integrates two important aspects: on the one hand a decided disregard for the usual norms of honourable behaviour and the abandonment of striving for social prestige and standing[117], and on the other a jestful, tongue-in-cheek attitude. Still, it is hard to be brief when it comes to defining *mujūn* in terms familiar to a Westerner. Here is an attempt, by no means unsuccessful, by Joel Kraemer: "[...] debauchery and frivolousness, libertinism, drinking, and sexual licentiousness [...] an exotic blend of the raffiné and recherché along with coarseness and vulgarity: poetry and wine along with scatological humor."[118] Note how it reads more like a list than a definition, and note the use of the adjective 'exotic' (presumably from a Western point of view), both of which offer a clue to a feasible way of treating *mujūn*: as a cultural phenomenon with no real parallel outside the Islamic world that is easier to approach through inventorying its different aspects, as it were, than by forcing a brief definition upon it. It is such an 'inventory' that the following sections of this book attempt to make.

A word on my terminology in reference to the main object of my research is in order before moving on to the next chapter. Given the vague semantics of *mujūn*, I will have no qualms about using a number of terms throughout my text fairly

---

[116] Cf. Ibn Manẓūr, *Lisān* V, 129, 94–5, 96, 136; IV, 357; VI, 303.

[117] On the features of the Mediterranean honour code, which corresponds in a remarkable measure to mediaeval Arabic concepts of honour, see Herzfeld 1980: 339–41.

[118] Kraemer 1986: 15. Everett K. Rowson defines *mujūn* in a similar way, as an amalgam of roughly the same elements as listed by Kraemer; see Rowson 1998: 546. Abdelwahab Bouhdiba also devotes a whole paragraph to defining *mujūn* and, besides other things, emphasises the combination of indecency and humour; see Bouhdiba (2004): 127. In an article on the place of jesting in the Shiʿite élite culture of modern Iraq, we find the term *mujūn* translated into German as *Obszönitäten*, which is certainly far too restrictive, and so is *Possenreißerei* (Ludwig Ammann's way of rendering *mujūn*, which elsewhere he expands to "schamlose Possen- und Zotenreißerei"). See Walther 2002: 511; Ammann 1993: 30–1, 212.

vaguely, and sometimes interchangeably, to render various aspects of *mujūn*: libertinism, licentiousness, frivolity, irreverence, shamelessness, and so on. The reader is asked not to give any of these terms too tight and specific a sense. In addition, wherever I see fit, I will feel free to retain the original Arabic term *mujūn*.[119]

[119] The terminology for certain genres of prose texts in which *mujūn* typically appears – often referred to variously as anecdotes, jokes – is also problematic, so much so that Ulrich Marzolph, the greatest authority on these texts, chose to give preference to the more scholastic term *humoristische Kurzprosa*. See Marzolph 1992: I, 25–8. Distinctions between genres being less of a concern in this book, I will freely use the terms 'joke' and 'anecdote' and ask the reader again to be aware of the potential imprecision of these usages.

2

The Motifs of *Mujūn*: Religion

In the preceding chapter my goal was to offer an overview, albeit sketchy, of some of the declared norms and values of mediaeval Middle Eastern urban culture, more precisely the values that informed literary and everyday forms of speech and writing. Having done that, it is time to turn our attention to clarifying what one means by the ill-defined terms 'frivolity' and 'libertinism' – as well as the Arabic *mujūn* – and show the concrete manifestations of the florescence of such attitudes in a certain period of mediaeval Arabic literature and everyday culture. Although I do not intend this study to be a systematic treatment of licentious literature *qua* literature in mediaeval Islamic culture, any further discussion of the phenomenon, no matter how little concerned with literary theory in the strict sense, will have to incorporate at least a brief survey of the most common motifs of those literary products that would have been recognised by a mediaeval Arabic speaker as representing *mujūn*. This is what the next two chapters are concerned with. As will be apparent from the quickest of glances, some of the products of urban culture and literature treated below are spectacularly, and at times even shockingly, contrary to the fundamental values and norms discussed in the previous chapter. As I have already remarked, this apparent opposition has been the fundamental question that I have posed to myself for this study, one to which I hope to be able to provide some answer in the final chapter of this work.

Although most of my examples have clearly originated in the literate, educated, sophisticated literary circles of the period – an unsurprising fact given the authorship of most of the written heritage of the mediaeval period – I have come to embrace the idea that *mujūn* in its broad sense was far from being the exclusive preserve of this literate, refined and polished class of intellectuals. Quite a few examples reflect attitudes of *mujūn* (either explicitly described as such in the sources or readily recognisable as related to literary manifestations of *mujūn*) displayed in the oral culture of the common folk, the urban masses. As I will argue throughout, the relative scarcity of such material seems to me to result from the elitist focus of the written sources rather than from an actual dearth of *mujūn* material in oral culture.

Wherever possible, I have taken pains to detect the relationship of *mujūn* motifs in 'high' culture, especially prose and poetry in classical Arabic, and in oral, 'low' culture respectively; furthermore in a limited number of cases it has been possible to trace literary motifs to oral sources on the authority of explicit references to such a process found in anthologies and such similar sources. In most cases, however, this has unsurprisingly proven to be unattainable because of the lack of relevant data.

The arrangement of the literary material in the next two chapters is thematic. Literary motifs considered mildly or grossly licentious – wherein one can usually point to particular norms transgressed – will be reviewed with an eye to identifying what made them offensive to ordinary sensibilities. That an anthropological study of the flagrant flouting of norms in literature should arrange the data on the basis of content instead of form, with a focus on social aspects rather than according to purely literary criteria, is perhaps not only excusable but rather natural.

In what follows, I have opted for a somewhat artificial arrangement for presenting my inventory of *mujūn* motifs. This is purely for reasons of convenience – my own convenience I might add – and the arrangement that I have chosen would certainly have been unrecognisable to a mediaeval Arabic speaker, someone who was an insider to the culture I am studying. This, I am aware, raises serious problems of forcing an alien explanatory framework upon my subject-matter, but a close study of literary motifs having been far from my primary concern, the arrangement I have chosen will perhaps not unduly distort my source material.

No less problematic is the division of norms (and literary themes) in mediaeval Arabic culture into 'religious' and 'secular'. This is obviously a division forced upon the material, one which would have sounded odd to a mediaeval Muslim. As the validity of the *sharīʿa* would theoretically encompass all aspects of human life – as a quick look into practically any *fiqh* manual will make clear – the phenomena I discuss separately as having to do with ('secular') concerns of propriety and decency would also appear religious in some sense to a mediaeval Muslim. An obvious example would be such transgressions as wine-drinking and drunkenness, not to speak of homosexuality and other forms of sexual deviance, insulting a legitimate ruler or a man of honour and authority, and so on. Even unbecoming topics (such as the description of fleas and lice) had some relationship to religious law – through the issue of a man's reliability or otherwise as a witness in court – as will be made clear in its place (in Chapter Four). That said, these caveats will have made it clear that I do not wish to imply that the framework I am using here is internal to the culture that I am studying.

1. An Omnipresent Religious Culture

Religious concepts, prescriptions and taboos form the first, and easily the most important, category of norms that all but invited the libertines to flout them. Motifs of *mujūn* that can be broadly defined as transgressing religious sensibilities, treating as they do various aspects of religion in a humorous or frivolous manner, will be discussed in the present chapter, while more 'secular' imperatives and taboos, and the ways in which they were flouted by the mediaeval *mājin* intellectual, will be relegated to the next section of my study.

It might be thought slightly surprising but is, upon reflection, in fact far from being so that religion and religious concepts should play such a prominent role in *mujūn* literature. The central role of religion in the cultural makeup of a mediaeval man could hardly be exaggerated, and that holds equally true for the Middle East. Islam was a constant source of inspiration and pride for most mediaeval Muslims; religion informed the whole lifestyle of a Muslim, from their everyday life to *rites de passage* to festivities. Religion in its various manifestations was omnipresent in the lives of men from the cradle to the grave, including not only occasions specifically recognised as having an obvious religious significance (such as the times of prayer or the month of fasting) but also the most mundane activities. Examples of cultural events serving as avenues through which religious ideas and attitudes seeped into the consciousness of all people abound, and it will suffice to mention a few of these that spring to mind. Such are the religious festivities like the month of Ramadan and the two great religious holidays (*ʿīd*), as well as – from a later period – the Prophet's birthday (*al-mawlid*); the ceremonies connected with rites of passage within a human life (like birth, circumcision, marriage and death), all of which were full of elements and customs derived from Islamic *fiqh* even in rural communities; the traditional schooling system, based as it was on an elementary level devoted to the memorisation of the Quran's text (the *kuttāb* or 'Quranic school'[1]) and an advanced level largely made up of studying various religious disciplines (the *madrasa*); the recurring, quotidian religious obligation that prayer represented – generally accepted to be compulsory in principle even if not necessarily fulfilled in practice. Finally, one might even mention such easily overlooked factors as the countless phrases of everyday speech which make references to Islamic tenets, concepts and rituals (from the ubiquitous *in shāʾa ʾllāh* to less frequently used expressions), there being no reason to doubt that the use of such phrases was no less widespread in the mediaeval period than in today's Arab world.

[1] On the role and importance of the Quranic school and the methods of instruction applied therein, cf. Messick 1993: 79; Snouck Hurgronje 1931: 115–6.

As far as values and norms are concerned, it is fair to say that probably the most enduring and most firmly established element of the value system of Muslim Arab society has been the high value attached to adherence to Islam as a religion as well as various constituent elements that make someone a Muslim. Regardless of whether one actually carried out all, or indeed any, of the obligations theoretically incumbent upon every adult Muslim, there seems to have been a great extent of cultural and emotional identification with Islam, and any questioning of the basic dogmas, tenets and values of Islam seems to have been the exception rather than the rule. Adherence to Islam, and pride in belonging to the *umma*, were the norm in both a prescriptive and a descriptive sense. (By a prescriptive norm is meant the expected 'right thing to do', whereas a norm in the descriptive sense is simply what is statistically, observably predominant). What a given individual actually meant by the simple term 'Islam' is a different kettle of fish, and it certainly varied not only from community to community and from individual to individual but also from situation to situation. However, this issue is not our primary concern here. What is important for the purpose of this discussion is that the founding texts of religious lore (especially the Quran and various redactions of *ḥadīths*), as well as the most elementary prescriptions of Islam, were always viewed and treated respectfully by the vast majority of Muslims, a veneration and deference there is no reason to regard as mere dishonest conformism. It is, then, accurate to state that respect for Islam, in very general terms, was one of the most important and powerful norms of mediaeval Muslim society; and that Islam had an unparalleled, truly formative impact on the culture of that society.

In view of this one may observe, with considerable puzzlement, that religion is also one of the most copious sources, if not *the* main source, of themes and motifs appearing in jesting, humorous, frivolous and often outright irreverent literary texts and everyday discourse. The paradox, however, is only apparent. Consider the omnipresence of religion in its many manifestations, already discussed above, in the everyday culture of Muslims, and it will be a logical conclusion that it must also be reflected in less serious aspects of that culture. Humour and frivolity are chiefly concerned with issues and themes that are relevant to most people's lives – otherwise they would be the exclusive preserve of highly educated literati. Having established that religion had an immediate relevance in most affairs of a mediaeval Muslim's life, it is logical that it could not have left any aspect of literature, *mujūn* included, unaffected. Be that as it may, the empirical observation that *mujūn* is full of imagery and themes taken from the Islamic religion is uncontestable. It is to this imagery that we shall turn our attention in the following pages.

2. Quran and *Ḥadīths*

2.1 Uses of Motifs Borrowed from the Quran

For Muslims, the Quran's text is the epitome of eloquence and linguistic beauty. It is this general idea that has been developed into the more theoretical notion of *iʿjāz al-Qurʾān*, the inimitability of the Quran. Inimitable it may be, but borrowing expressions, and citing phrases or whole utterances from it was always a common practice among Muslims, not surprisingly if one considers the fact that every literate Muslim's first exposure to writing and 'high style' necessarily began with becoming acquainted with the Quran's text, and was tied to the challenge of memorising portions of it, and in many cases its entirety. All over the Islamic world, there have always been people who, as a result of assiduous study, came to know the whole Quran by heart, *ḥāfiẓ* being the technical term that denotes such a person. The elegant, literary style of classical Arabic regarded the Quran not only as the highest standard of eloquence but as a desirable source of quotations and borrowed phrases, as well as of imagery paraphrased by way of new words. That the Quran was a veritable fountainhead of linguistic embellishments for Arabic littérateurs no student of Arabic mediaeval literature can possibly fail to observe. It is less readily apparent, however – for a paucity of sources – that the spoken language of Arabs is also likely to have always abounded in expressions borrowed from the Quran. We have only sporadic data hinting at this phenomenon – something that I shall return to discussing at a later point – but those hints suggest that a lot of such linguistic usages existed at some point but have been irrevocably lost.

Little though we may know about the actual exposure of the illiterate urban masses to the Quran's text, we do know that most literate poets and writers, who by definition would compose their works in Classical Arabic, must have known the sacred book intimately and often also had at least a passable knowledge of the religious sciences. In this respect, the most frivolous *mājin* was no exception as long as he was literate and well-educated, as most were. The all but emblematic Abū Nuwās, libertine extraordinaire, is typical in that. Thanks to his thorough studies in Basra and Kūfa in his adolescence and youth, he was well-versed in various branches of religious scholarship – even if no great devotee thereof – such as jurisprudence, law, theology, and last but not least, Quranic exegesis and *ḥadīth* scholarship.[2]

Borrowings from the Quran's text have typically tended to serve the purpose of embellishing an otherwise plainer text. Given that the Quran is the ultimate epitome of linguistic perfection, it was not unreasonable to use parts of it to elevate other,

---

[2] See Ibn al-Muʿtazz, *Ṭabaqāt* 91; and cf. Ibn Manẓūr, *Akhbār* 6; Abū Hiffān, *Akhbār* 38 ["*mā aḥad abṣar minka bi-taṣārīf al-kalām wa-l-adyān...*"]. Also see [JAL Symposium] 1994: 132; Montgomery 1996: 115.

merely human texts to a higher plane. The vast majority of such borrowings can be found within the context of unexceptionable, perfectly serious literary texts. Although, predictably, some hair-splitting debates did occur as to the admissibility of borrowing words and expressions from the Quran with the aim of embellishing a mere literary text, objection to such a practice seems to have been the exception rather than the rule even among religious scholars. The general attitude to borrowing from the Quran for impeccably 'serious' purposes – such as the decorating of sermons and pious prose texts – was one of approval; the ornamentation of 'serious' literary prose texts was still viewed with general acceptance; and while the incorporation of Quranic phrases into 'serious' poems was somewhat ambiguously regarded, it was still widely accepted by religious authorities.

The practice of incorporating Quranic passages into literary texts – whether prose or poetry – was termed in Arabic as *iqtibās*; and the same word could also refer to similar borrowings from the *ḥadīths* (about which later on). In manuals on Arabic rhetoric, *iqtibās* was often recognised as one of the rhetorical tools aimed at ornamenting literary style. *Iqtibās* might involve the use of the borrowed phrase in its original sense, but equally or more often one finds Quranic phrases applied in literary works in a sense different to their original meaning in the Quranic context.[3] Indeed, al-Suyūṭī (d. 911/1505), in the text of a legal opinion, even defines *iqtibās* as "the use of the Quran's words" in various literary and everyday contexts "in a sense different from that intended in the Quran" (*istiʿmāl alfāẓ al-Qurʾān [...] murādan bihā ghayr al-maʿnā ʾlladhī urīdat bihi fī l-Qurʾān*).[4] As I have indicated, *iqtibās* is as frequent in prose as it is in poetry, and it occurs across a variety of genres of mediaeval Arabic literature, not excluding the less serious, and sometimes quite jesting, types of texts. (This point I will take up below.) The very ubiquity of the practice is an unequivocal indication of the popularity thereof among the literate class.[5] A poetical practice closely related to *iqtibās* is that known as *ʿaqd*, or

---

[3] Ibn Ḥijja, *Khizāna* IV, 359.

[4] al-Suyūṭī, *Ḥāwī* I, 248.

[5] E.g. Ibn Ḥijja, *Khizāna* IV, 357–401; al-Qazwīnī, *Īḍāḥ* VI, 137–40; al-Jurjānī, *Ishārāt* 315–6; al-Thaʿālibī, *Thimār* I, 373–4; II, 860–1; al-Thaʿālibī, *Yatīma* II, 209, 279; al-Thaʿālibī, *Tatimma* I, 35, 135; II, 75; al-Thaʿālibī, *Nathr* 31; al-Bākharzī, *Dumya* II, 779, 795, 869, 1162, 1198–9, 1313, 1314, 1350, 1373, 1403, 1458; al-Ḥillī, *Sharḥ* 326–7; al-Ibshīhī, *Mustaṭraf* 490, 492; al-Shāṭibī, *Ifādāt* 115, 125; al-Jurjānī, *Wasāṭa* 80; Ibn Rashīq, *Qurāḍa* 14; al-Qalqashandī, *Ṣubḥ* I, 194–7; and a varied and fine sample in English translation in Zubaidi 1983: 322–39. In a later period (11th/17th c.), one finds two authors incorporating the titles of various Quranic chapters into the letters of their correspondence by way of *iqtibās*, in such a manner as to demonstrate their virtuoso mastery of Arabic yet make it sound perfectly natural in the context, not a small feat. See Ibn Maʿṣūm, *Sulāfa* 409, 474–5. For a number of similar but much earlier examples (from the Buyid period), see al-Tanūkhī, *Nishwār* VII, 254, where the editor fails to note that the text of the vizier's letter is in fact a quotation from the Quran. – In fact, webs of intertextual references to the Quran and outright quotations from it could at times be woven extraordinarily dense in a poem, a density and sophistication apparently much relished by

'versification', a literary exercise involving, instead of verbatim quotation, the slight modification of a passage to turn it into rhymed and metred lines. (Incidentally, the opposite practice, *ḥall* or 'prosification', was also widespread as an exercise of literary skills, but it obviously does not concern the Quran's text, which is not poetry.)[6] The use of *iqtibās* as a purely playful activity, an intellectual exercise aimed at developing and at the same time demonstrating one's poetic skills, seems to have been fairly widely accepted as a sort of poetic game in the polished circles of Abbasid society. When an accomplished or aspiring poet wished to hone his skills at composing verses, he might choose a passage from the Quran that had caught his attention in the mosque or in the street and try to fit it into a line of poetry in a creative and novel way. Alternatively, a group of intellectuals might challenge one another to compose a short poem with a set theme, rhyme and metre, stipulating that it should also incorporate a given Quranic verse. Whoever came up with a satisfactory poem in the shortest time would win the contest.[7]

In fact, one could even argue that citations from the Quran were for all practical purposes *de rigueur*, or at the very least quite common, in certain genres of prose and poetry like sermons, pious poems (the genre of *zuhdiyyāt*), and the opening, dedicatory paragraphs of most serious treatises regardless of their topic. Furthermore, there are few if any genres of written literature in which the reader will not come across at least occasional examples of *iqtibās*.

Some expressions of the Quran – similarly to phrases from the Bible in Western Christian culture – have come to be quasi-proverbs, recurring in myriad written literary texts as well as, in many cases, in the spoken language. One such phrase is a difficult expression of the Quran (105:3), *ṭayr abābīl* ("birds in flight"), which describes a flock of birds that were thought to have destroyed, in some mysterious manner, the Abyssinians laying siege to pre-Islamic Mecca. This phrase appears in such widely dispersed linguistic contexts as the classical Arabic poetry of the Abbasid period, modern Iraqi folk poetry and the spoken Arabic dialect of the region around Lake Chad.[8] Another frequent borrowing from the Quran is the use, to convey the

---

mediaeval Muslim culturati but hopelessly beyond the immediate grasp of a modern Western reader (especially in translation). For sensitive analyses of such webs of meaning in some of Abū Nuwās's poems, see [JAL Symposium] 1994: 123–31; and also Montgomery 1996: 122–3; Zubaidi 1983: 327–9. On the issue of *iqtibās*, and for further examples from the poerty of Abū Nuwās, see Sanni 1998: 141–3, 163–7.

[6] See for instance al-Qazwīnī, *Īḍāḥ* VI, 144–6; al-Jurjānī, *Ishārāt* 319; and on *ʿaqd* and *ḥall* in general, cf. Sanni 1998.

[7] E.g. Ibn al-Muʿtazz, *Ṭabaqāt* 94; and Abū Hiffān, *Akhbār* 68.

[8] For examples, see Ibn al-Kattānī, *Tashbīhāt* 277; Ibn Rashīq, *Qurāḍa* 36; Sanni 1998: 60–1; Jargy 1970: 222–3; and Howard 1921: 22–3, 95. (Jargy seems to be unaware that the expression originates from the Quran, or else he deems it unworthy of note, as he simply omits to translate the second part of the phrase, opting for the simple solution 'les oiseaux' instead.)

notion of narrowness, uncomfortableness, constraint and impenetrability, of the phrase *samm al-khiyāṭ* ("the eye of the needle"), which is as much of an impediment for a camel to pass through in the Quran (7:40) as it is in the Bible.[9]

A phrase appearing in the penultimate *sūra* of the Quran (113:4) and referring to an ancient Arabian magical custom (*al-naffāthāt fī l-ʿuqad*, "the women who blow on knots") recurs in a lot of poems and prose texts, sometimes in a slightly modified form to fit into the grammar and the context, as a hackneyed metaphor for overawing linguistic expression, or a style that captivates the reader's or hearer's heart and mind.[10] Some Quranic phrases easily lent themselves for use in a lot of poetic contexts, and thus became recycled, as it were, again and again by a host of poets. Such is the case of an expression occurring in Quran 8:42 and 8:44, which reads *li-yaqḍiya ʾllāhu amran kāna mafʿūlan* ("that God might determine a matter that was done"), words that we find woven into the text of quite a few mediaeval Arabic poems.[11] A remarkable fact to note is that, while the Quran's language is markedly different from any of the Arabic dialects also in its grammar, even dialectal poetry did make use of verbatim *iqtibās* from the Quran in a few cases, albeit of course incomparably less frequently than Classical Arabic poetry. This is all the more interesting in view of the fact that, at least in theory, it was thought to be a gross mistake for a dialectal poem to apply classical case endings, which are one of the compulsory and defining features of the Quranic diction.[12]

The list of borrowings from the Quran that became stock phrases in Arabic literature and, not infrequently, in spoken language as well, could be expanded almost at will. However, serious uses of such quotations not being our primary concern, let the above examples (and some more that I add in footnote) suffice here to demonstrate the point that I wish to make: a great number of phrases and expressions taken from the Quran's verses all but began a life of their own as fixed metaphors and tropes of other kinds, comfortably ornamenting even texts that had no direct relationship with religious themes and topics.[13] The ubiquity of this

[9] E.g. al-Thaʿālibī, *Thimār* II, 669, 675; al-Thaʿālibī, *Khāṣṣ* 49; Ibn Diḥya, *Muṭrib* 218; al-Zawzanī, *Ḥamāsa* II, 116; Kushājim, *Adab* 34; al-Tawḥīdī, *Baṣāʾir* I (ii), 146; al-Tawḥīdī [attr.], *Risāla* 230; Ibn Maʿṣūm, *Sulāfa* 7.

[10] E.g. al-Iṣfahānī, *Aghānī* VII, 210; al-Thaʿālibī, *Yatīma* II, 117; IV, 101, 367; al-Bākharzī, *Dumya* II, 753; Ibn Diḥya, *Muṭrib* 96; Ibn Maʿṣūm, *Sulāfa* 194.

[11] E.g. al-Bākharzī, *Dumya* I, 349–50; II, 1033; al-Iṣbahānī, *Kharīda* I(ii), 85; Ibn al-Khaṭīb, *Jaysh* 81.

[12] On this issue, see al-Ḥillī, *ʿĀṭil* 89.

[13] For a more expert discussion of this phenomenon, cf. Ben Cheneb 1922: 9; and Sanni 1998: 5–6. For a (by far not comprehensive) list of Quranic phrases used more or less proverbially in the mediaeval Arabic-speaking Middle East, see al-Ibshīhī, *Mustaṭraf* 34; al-Thaʿālibī, *Iʿjāz* 14–5. – A number of further examples of the literary (and in some cases also everyday) utilisation of a number of well-known Quranic expressions: 1. *ʿazzaznā bi-thālithin* ('We sent a third as reinforcement'; Quran 36:14) in al-Thaʿālibī, *Tatimma* I, 112; Ibn Diḥya, *Muṭrib* 238; Ibn Maʿṣūm, *Sulāfa* 208. 2. *ḥammālatu*

secularised use of short Quranic passages, I suspect, was instrumental in paving the way towards more unconventional and 'daring' uses of the same material.

Moral guidance and aesthetic pleasure were not the only purposes of quoting from the Quran. Humorous, frivolous, or simply unserious uses of *iqtibās* were in fact as widespread as the serious kind.[14] To emphasise the point as it ought to be, one is even justified to state that the most important single textual source for the frivolous humour of the period was the Quran. This is an observation hard to avoid making if one looks into the literary anthologies of the high Abbasid and Buyid periods (and onwards too, especially in the Seljuk period); these anthologies – and here both the serious and the frivolous sections thereof are meant to be included – literally teem with word-for-word quotations from the Quran, as well as direct and subtle allusions, irresistibly funny or somewhat stale references, to the stories and figures of the Quran.

This last statement has to be qualified somewhat. Of course, it is well nigh impossible for a modern Western (or, for that matter, modern Muslim) reader to

l-ḥatabi ('the carrier of the firewood'; Quran 111:4) in al-Iṣfahānī, *Aghānī* I, 397; al-Thaʿālibī, *Thimār* I, 468; Ibn Maʿṣūm, *Sulāfa* 231. 3. *qul huwa ʾllāhu aḥadun* ('Say: He is God, One'; Quran 112:1) in al-Thaʿālibī, *Laṭāʾif* 114; al-Ḥillī, *ʿĀṭil* 89, 146 [both of these examples occur in vernacular poems from the mediaeval period]; Wagner 2008: 69 [a love poem attributed to Abū Nuwās]; Sonneck 1904: II, 59 [a North African dialectal poem]. 4. *fuʾādu ummi Mūsā* ('the heart of Moses' mother', used as as a metaphor for emptiness or vacuity; Quran 28:10) in al-Tanūkhī, Nishwār II, 167; IV, 197. 5. *aqrabu [...] min ḥabli l-warīdi* ('nearer than the jugular vein'; Quran 50:16) in al-Thaʿālibī, *Thimār* I, 519; al-Thaʿālibī, *Yatīma* I, 112; al-Bākharzī, *Dumya* I, 666; al-Tawḥīdī, *Baṣāʾir* I(i), 82; al-Ibshīhī, *Mustaṭraf* 512 [in a vernacular poem]; al-Ḥillī, *ʿĀṭil* 179 [in a vernacular poem]. 6. *mazzaqnāhum kulla mumazzaqin* ('We tore them utterly to pieces'; Quran 34:19) in al-Ibshīhī, *Mustaṭraf* 457. 7. *baytu l-ʿankabūti* ('the house of the spider', used as a metaphor for frailty and thinness; Quran 29:41) in al-Thaʿālibī, *Thimār* II, 635–6; al-Thaʿālibī, *Yatīma* III, 118; al-Bākharzī, *Dumya* I, 611. 8. *ṣabrun jamīlun* ('sweet patience'; Quran 12:18) in al-Jurjānī, *Wasāṭa* 229–30; Ibn Saʿīd, *Muqtaṭaf* 231 [in a vernacular poem]. 9. *al-waswās al-khannās* ('the slinking whisperer', terms describing Satan in Quran 114:4) in Abū Nuwās, *Dīwān* V, 193; Ibn Saʿīd, *Rāyāt* 57; Ibn Saʿīd, *Muqtaṭaf* 242 [in a vernacular poem]. 10. *inna baʿḍa l-ẓanni ithmun* ('some suspicion is a sin'; Quran 49:12) in al-Iṣfahānī, *Aghānī* XVIII, 163; al-Iṣbahānī, *Kharīda* I(ii), 328. – Although at this point I will not be detained by the issue of the literary uses of portions of certain *ḥadīths*, it is worthy of note already that *ḥadīths* were handled by poets and prose writers in much the same way as, albeit definitely less frequently and less systematically than, Quranic phrases. As I will devote a separate section of this chapter to this question, here I will confine myself to mentioning a few perfectly serious, 'respectable' literary borrowings from *ḥadīths*. See for instance al-Yaḥṣubī, *Ilmāʿ* 66–7 [*ka-l-naqsh fī l-ḥajar*, 'as an engraving on a rock']; al-Washshāʾ, *Muwashshā* 41 [*al-arwāḥ ajnād mujannada*, 'souls are an army of recruits']; 46–8 [*zur ghibban tazdad ḥubban*, 'make your visits rare and far between to make yourself much liked'].

[14] For some preliminary examples of humorous *iqtibās*, see van Gelder 2002-3: 14–6. Ulrich Marzolph observes that in a huge corpus of jocular texts (consisting of 5,600 items) he researched, only some 3 percent involve the Quran; see Marzolph 2000: 286. My impressions of the *mujūn* material I studied would suggest a much higher proportion, and Marzolph himself goes on to say that, in any case, the importance of the Quran as a source and subject of jestful literature far outweighs that modest-looking percentage.

judge just what passed for funny among educated urban Muslims in the mediaeval period unless there is an explicit discussion of it with regard to any given joke, remark or poem. It is equally natural that there is no reason to doubt that tastes in this matter varied among mediaeval Muslims as much as they do today. An added stumbling-block for the modern scholar is the very distance, in temporal, cultural, and in many cases also in geographical terms, from the milieu that produced the *mujūn* literature under scrutiny. Interpreting these texts, based as they are on stylistic or semantic juggling with the texts of the Quran or certain *ḥadīths*, is hindered by the modern reader's – especially a Westerner's – presumably less thorough familiarity with these fundamental texts, for the funny element in such humour is provided by one's sudden realisation of the quotational nature of a passage and the inappropriateness of its application in the new context. This provides for the feeling of 'the penny having dropped', and it is simply not the same experience as searching Quranic and *ḥadīth* concordances and establishing, after a careful search, that the suspicious-looking passage does indeed come from the Quran or a *ḥadīth*. Immediacy and instantaneousness are essential in appreciating wit like this. The non-insider is irremediably at a disadvantage in trying to appreciate these jokes and poems, for to perceive their humour fully requires a thorough familiarity with the sources of the quotations and a quick recognition of just why their application in those particular contexts is inventive and bizarre.[15] This is the reason I will consistently do my best to avoid judgements as to whether any particular poem or joke is funny or stale in any sense other than its being presumably invented first by that particular author or else already conventional. The subject of the conventionalisation of *mujūn* motifs, a very important question, will be taken up at more length in Chapter Five. For the moment, it is the degree of familiarity with Quranic phrases and imagery among mediaeval intellectuals with which I shall be concerned.

The stories of the Quran and many of its narrative and linguistic motifs were absorbed by the minds of even the simple folk – let alone the highly educated class – to the extent of some words and phrases calling forth an all but automatic, knee-jerk association with the relevant story in the Quran. It is hard to notice how reflex-like it is for mediaeval Muslim intellectuals to associate the word *ʿaṣā* ('staff, rod, stick') with the Quranic legend of the encounter of Pharaoh and Moses, during which the prophet's staff, turned by him into a serpent, devours the rods of the Egyptian sorcerers similarly transfigured.[16] The motif of Moses' all-devouring, victorious rod appears in a lot of anecdotes, jokes and jesting poems; among other

[15] Cf. Marzolph 2000: 485.

[16] E.g. al-Tawḥīdī, *Baṣāʾir* II(iii), 162–3. The reflex appears still to exist among contemporary Arab intellectuals; see for instance Walther 2002: 509–10.

things it would serve as a metaphor for gluttonous gobbling, a swift and utter victory, and (not surprisingly given the shape of a staff) even for sexual intercourse.[17] In an obviously popular joke, a famous libertine of the early Abbasid period called Abū l-Ḥārith Jummayn (2nd/8th c.) is quoted in a source to have praised the luxurious sweetmeat *fālūdhaj* (a paste based on honey and flour): "Had Moses presented himself to Pharaoh with a portion of *fālūdhaj*, he would have managed to turn him into a believer, but instead he would insist on holding a staff!"[18]

It is a total automatism, an all but total predictability instead of a mere convention, that certain words or concepts would evoke the names of pertinent Quranic – and of course often Biblical – prophets. Thus 'patience' and 'perseverance' would almost inevitably be mentioned in juxtaposition with the name of Job, as would 'ancestry' with Adam, 'beauty' with Joseph, 'grief' or 'sadness' with Jacob, 'sonority', 'melody' and 'singing' with David, 'wisdom' or 'sagacity' with Solomon or Luqmān, 'sleep', 'slumber' and 'cave' with the mysterious Seven Sleepers (*Aṣḥāb al-Kahf* or *Aṣḥāb al-Raqīm*), 'gobbling' with Jonah and the whale (if, that is, not with the staff of Moses...), and so on.[19] One of the most memorable miracles of Jesus being the resurrection of a dead man, it is not surprising to find quite a few Arabic poets of the mediaeval period using this image too in a jesting way, often sarcastically contrasting it to the actions of someone who is only capable of performing the exact opposite, inadvertently causing a person to die, like an ignorant quack doctor or a *femme fatale* (or indeed, typically, a *garçon fatal*).[20]

---

[17] al-Thaʿālibī, *Thimār* I, 85, 114–7; al-Bākharzī, *Dumya* II, 1170; al-Ibshīhī, *Mustaṭraf* 192, 245; Abū Nuwās, *Dīwān* I, 232 and Abū Hiffān, *Akhbār* 32; al-Maqrīzī, *Khiṭaṭ* I, 85–6; Ibn al-Kattānī, *Tashbīhāt* 252; al-Rāghib, *Muḥāḍarāt* III, 508; al-Iṣbahānī, *Kharīda* II(i), 328, 330; al-Thaʿālibī, *Yatīma* II, 209, 273, 286; III, 271; IV, 102, 111; al-Thaʿālibī, *Iqtibās* I, 170–1; al-Thaʿālibī, *Tatimma* I, 69; II, 25. (In the last example, notice the use of the motif even in a poem in Persian.)

[18] Ibn al-Jawzī, *Ẓirāf* 137; al-Tawḥīdī, *Baṣāʾir* III(v), 76; al-Ibshīhī, *Mustaṭraf* 189.

[19] E.g. [for Adam:] al-Thaʿālibī, *Iqtibās* I, 143–8; al-Thaʿālibī, *Thimār* I, 97–8; al-Thaʿālibī, *Tatimma* I, 142; al-Tawḥīdī [attr.], *Risāla* 111. [Joseph:] al-Thaʿālibī, *Thimār* I, 112–3; al-Bākharzī, *Dumya* I, 682; al-Iṣbahānī, *Kharīda* I(i), 59, 158; al-Tanūkhī, *Nishwār* VIII, 57; al-Ibshīhī, *Mustaṭraf* 493; Ibn Diḥya, *Muṭrib* 75; Ibn al-Khaṭīb, *Jaysh* 10, 13, 78; al-Ḥillī, *ʿĀṭil* 45, 106; al-Ḥillī, *Dīwān* 483. [David:] al-Thaʿālibī, *Thimār* I, 123–4; Ibn al-Kattānī, *Tashbīhāt* 108; Ibn Saʿīd, *Muqtaṭaf* 102. [Job:] al-Thaʿālibī, *Thimār* I, 121; al-Thaʿālibī, *Yatīma* II, 20; al-Bākharzī, *Dumya* II, 1225; al-Tawḥīdī [attr.], *Risāla* 187; Ibn Maʿṣūm, *Sulāfa* 160. [Jacob:] al-Tanūkhī, *Nishwār* VII, 83; al-Tawḥīdī [attr.], *Risāla* 130, 187; al-Iṣbahānī, *Kharīda* I(i), 212; al-Ibshīhī, *Mustaṭraf* 171; Ibn Diḥya, *Muṭrib* 75; Ibn al-Khaṭīb, *Jaysh* 89; al-Ḥillī, *Dīwān* 483; al-Ḥillī, *ʿĀṭil* 45; Ibn Maʿṣūm, *Sulāfa* 425. [The Seven Sleepers:] al-Thaʿālibī, *Thimār* I, 165–6; Ibn Diḥya, *Muṭrib* 49; Ibn al-Kattānī, *Tashbīhāt* 276; al-Hamadhānī, *Maqāmāt* 123; and for the best summary of the subject, see Jourdan 1983. [Jonah and the whale:] al-Thaʿālibī, *Thimār* I, 121; al-Ibshīhī, *Mustaṭraf* 192; Ibn al-Kattānī, *Tashbīhāt* 277. The metaphors connected with the persons of Jacob, Jonah and Job live on in modern Arabic (dialectal) folk poetry too, see for instance al-Khāqānī 1381/1962: I, 39; Jargy 1970: 67, 219, 243; Sonneck 1904: II, 114. It is perhaps not unreasonable to suppose that such an influence on folk culture may be projected back to the mediaeval period too.

[20] E.g. al-Thaʿālibī, *Yatīma* I 286–7; II, 182; al-Ḥillī, *Dīwān* 642; Ibn Maʿṣūm, *Sulāfa* 189; and

It is a recurrent motif in lampoons to describe a person's obnoxiousness by claiming that had Adam had the prescience to anticipate this particular descendant of his, he would have preferred to castrate himself; while in praise poetry one encounters the motif that a person is so exceedingly generous as though Adam had entrusted him in his will with the care of all his descendants.[21] Protest against what one felt was excessive or disproportionate punishment was sometimes expressed with an allusion to the story of the Quranic prophet Ṣāliḥ. According to the Quran, having repeatedly warned in vain the sinful locals to reform themselves, Ṣāliḥ had to face yet another gratuitous iniquity when his she-camel was slaughtered, a last straw which brought down God's wrath on the sinners. It is this story that is reflected in the witty popular phrase pointing out the slightness of some misdeed: "I haven't slaughtered the she-camel."[22]

The metamorphosis of the staff into a snake was not the only element in Moses' story in the Quran that was taken up by poets fishing for witty applications of Quranic imagery. Another motif originating in that story evokes the image of the Hebrews wandering in the Sinai desert and growing impatient and dissatisfied despite God's gift of manna and quails to support them[23], and as usual, the literary uses involve the placement of this image in contexts very dissimilar to the original Quranic one. The following famous verse by Abū Nuwās, for instance, makes it a parallel to a promiscuous woman:

> I have come to complain to her heart of [the pain of] my love, only to find my way blocked by congestion.
> O you woman, who will not be content with one lover, not even with a thousand lovers a year!
> I suspect you must be a descendant of Moses' people, who could not endure a [single unchanging] diet.[24]

also cf. al-Thaʿālibī, *Thimār* I, 117, 129–30; al-Thaʿālibī, *Tatimma* I, 66; al-Bākharzī, *Dumya* II, 897; al-Jurjānī, *Wasāṭa* 149, 263; Ibn Diḥya, *Muṭrib* 16; Ibn al-Khaṭīb, *Jaysh* 74; al-Ṣafadī, *Tawshīḥ* 43. Jesus's miraculous deed of resurrecting a dead man may have been a lively image in the popular imagination too. A frivolous anecdote makes a slave-girl say exasperatedly to a man who has just proven to be hopelessly impotent in bed: "My master, I have no business doing anything here, but Jesus may." See al-Tawḥīdī, *Baṣāʾir* I(ii), 35. (This may be either a scholarly joke employing a slave-girl for a protagonist, or the recording of a popular joke based on a widely used ironic saying.) A mediaeval Arabic proverb described someone who keeps lecturing others more knowledgeable than him in the following manner: "So-and-So plays the doctor before Jesus" (*Fulān yataṭabbabu ʿalā ʿĪsā b. Maryam*); see al-Thaʿālibī, *Thimār* I, 129.

21 E.g. al-Tawḥīdī [attr.], *Risāla* 75; Ibn al-Kattānī, *Tashbīhāt* 248; al-Thaʿālibī, *Yatīma* IV, 111.

22 See al-Thaʿālibī, *Thimār* I, 107; and al-Bayhaqī, *Maḥāsin* 637–8. One finds a poem from the Buyid period making use of this phrase in an extremely vulgar context ("Do you suppose it was my prick that killed the she-camel?"), a vulgarity that had already been used in one of Abū Nuwās's poems. See al-Thaʿālibī, *Yatīma* III, 119; and Abū Nuwās, *Dīwān* V, 118.

23 Quran 2:61; and for brief exegetical notes, cf. al-Bayḍāwī, *Tafsīr* I, 64–5.

24 Abū Nuwās, *Dīwān* II, 83; al-Ibshīhī, *Mustaṭraf* 430. The same poem in a slightly different

It is to be remarked that a phrase appearing in the verse ("*lā yaṣbirūna ʿalā ṭaʿāmin*") came to be used in the vernacular of Iraqi towns as a proverb; although it is equally possible that in fact it is in the spoken language that it originated and that Abū Nuwās actually borrowed the motif from it.[25]

Two cases are particularly instructive, demonstrating as they do that utilising the Quran's motifs and themes was an almost automatic first choice for an intellectual desirous of coming up with a witticism. Although both cases took place outside the narrower geographical focus of this book – their respective scenes having been the Maghreb and Egypt – there is little reason to presume that the Arabic-speaking East would have had attitudes dramatically different in this respect. The first of the two stories shows the North African Zīrid ruler al-Muʿizz b. Bādīs (r. 406/1016–454/1062) asking two poets of exceptional renown, Ibn Sharaf (d. 460/1067) and Ibn Rashīq (390/1000–463/1070–1 [or 456/1063–4]), to compose poems eulogising the down on a woman's leg, apparently with the aim of offering the resulting poems as a gift to one of his wives. The two poets are supposed to have composed their poems independently of each other – and with two poets in the same court being inevitable rivals to an extent, this seems quite likely to have been the case – they both fell back on the use of Quranic imagery, more specifically the figure of Bilqīs, the beautiful queen of Sheba, whose long garments hid a pair of hairy legs according to the legend.[26] In the second story, a concubine of the Ayyūbid ruler al-ʿAzīz b. Salāḥ al-Dīn (r. 589/1193–595/1198) paints the likenesses of a snake and a scorpion respectively on each of her cheeks by way of amusement, using a sort of fragrant dyestuff; and the ruler is pleased with the somewhat vapid idea so much that he commands various court poets to memorialise the odd spectacle in verse. It must be emphasised that the Quran has no passages of obvious and direct relevance to any element of this entertaining sight, and yet all the poets, to a man, adorned their poems with playful uses of imagery taken from the Quran: two of them had recourse to the Quranic story of Moses, while a third packed his verse with references to the Seven Sleepers, Moses and Abraham.[27] The reader is reminded here of the practice among Arabic poets of versifying given passages from the Quran by way of either

version and unattributed to its author: al-Washshāʾ, *Muwashshā* 170. Other poets also utilised the theme; see Ibn Qutayba, *Shiʿr* 423; al-Thaʿālibī, *Thimār* I, 118. Also see Sanni 1998: 127–8.

25 See al-Maydānī, *Amthāl* II, 306, where the phrase is classified as a proverb of the *muwalladūn.*

26 Ibn Diḥya, *Muṭrib* 68–9. For some further literary motifs containing references to the personality and story of Bilqīs as she appears in the Quran, see al-Thaʿālibī, *Thimār* I, 474–5; al-Bākharzī, *Dumya* II, 1234; Ibn al-Kattānī, *Tashbīhāt* 69; Ibn al-Khaṭīb, *Jaysh* 74; al-Ṣafadī, *Tawshīḥ* 41. The figure of Bilqīs appears in modern Arabic folk poetry too; see for instance Jargy 1970: 299–300. (The author of this collection mistranslates the Quranic motif of the hoopoe, and then proceeds to misinterpret its significance. The hoopoe, as is well known, is a prominent feature of the story of Solomon and the Queen of Sheba in the Muslim tradition.)

27 Ibn Saʿīd, *Ghuṣūn* 14, 23–4, 130.

diversion or friendly competition, and then the almost instinctive use of the Quran's phrases and imagery to pack a poem with wit poses no puzzle at all.

There seems, then, to have been no sense of guilt attached to the use of Quranic phrases and imagery in nonreligious contexts in literature; in fact it was a perfectly everyday practice in mediaeval Arabic poetry. In particular, a lot of amorous poems exploited the potential conceits inherent in the correspondence of the beloved person's (as it happens, mostly boy's) name to that of a Quranic prophet. In the words of a widely read early 9th/15th-century Egyptian compilation of *adab* material, "if you would take stock of [the use of] this theme, you would need several volumes..." (*wa-law tatabbaʿta hādhā l-maʿnā la-ʾḥtajta ilā mujalladāt*).[28] Nor were the stories of the prophets the only kind of Quranic theme put to light-hearted literary uses; poets would often allude to just about any well-known image, expression or motif from the Quran. Thus, a Quranic phrase describing a vision of the moon splitting in two ("the moon is split", Quran 54:1) is transferred to a playful verse depicting the sorry sight of a boy's beautiful cheek gashed by a stone cast at him (it will be remembered that the moon is a clichéd metaphor for beauty in the Arabic language).[29]

Indeed, the high level of familiarity among Muslim intellectuals with the Quran's text ensured that one did not even have actually to quote a passage from the Quran to create a witty effect in literature, a key word being perfectly sufficient to produce an instant awareness of the relevant passage from the Quran. In other words, in the context of a humorous poem or a joke, a mere single word might easily make the penny drop with an educated audience. A fairly representative example follows, which can be found in a poem describing a humourless bore (*thaqīl*; literally 'heavy'), a favourite target of many a lampoon in the high Abbasid period and onwards. The relevant verse, which according to the celebrated anthologist Abū Manṣūr al-Thaʿālibī (d. 429/1038) is "the most eloquent line ever composed in this theme" (*ablagh mā qīla fī maʿnāhu*), tells of a bore who is such a heavy burden for the Earth to bear as if God had added an eighth layer to the seven that are thought to comprise the Earth. Of course, the verse alludes to a Quranic passage, namely 65:12 which states that God has created Earth to consist of seven layers.[30] In one case from the Buyid

[28] al-Ibshīhī, *Mustaṭraf* 302 (and examples of the conceit in ibid. 300–1). Predictably, the figure of Moses features prominently among the poetic motifs in the love poetry of the famous Sevillan poet, Ibn Sahl (d. 649/1251), a convert from Judaism. For an in-depth discussion of his uses of Moses's figure (often playing on the fact that the object of his affections was also called Mūsā, Arabic for Moses, which is precisely the phenomenon described above), see Schippers 2001.

[29] Ibn Diḥya, *Muṭrib* 101; Ibn Saʿīd, *Rāyāt* 210.

[30] al-Thaʿālibī, *Yatīma* I, 290; al-Thaʿālibī, *Nathr* 115; al-Zawzanī, *Ḥamāsa* II, 160. For further examples of brief allusions to certain Quranic passages as a poetic device, see al-Bākharzī, *Dumya* I, 433–4 ["*...ʿanā bihi l-mathala l-maḍrūba fī sūrati l-Naḥlī*"; allusion to Quran 16:76]; al-Thaʿālibī, *Thimār* I, 106 [*tuḥfat Ibrāhīm* and *tuḥfat Maryam*; allusions to Quran 11:69 and 19:25 respectively],

period, admittedly not typical, even the mere mention of the number of the Quranic verse alluded to ("... *ʿalā ʿishrīna min sūrati l-Kahfi*"; allusion to Quran 18:20) appears to have sufficed for the same purpose.[31] The phenomenon of these highly condensed and erudite allusions to some passage in the Quran naturally takes us to our next point, which I have already discussed briefly above: the evocation of some episode or figure of the Quran in prose, poetry or even speech without a specific textual reference, which, inasmuch as a literary device, was termed *talmīḥ* in mediaeval Arabic literary theory.[32]

That highly erudite, literate people should find no difficulty in instantaneously identifying certain words or phrases as Quranic and associating them with their original context is hardly surprising. That less educated people, possibly even illiterates, should also use motifs borrowed from the Quran is not so self-evident, but it does seem to have been common in everyday speech. It did not necessarily involve direct quotations from the holy book, which is rather easy to understand given the low level, if any, of the education that the people in question had received, but urban common people would certainly be familiar with some of the images of the Quran, which they were often exposed to in Friday sermons, the gatherings of street preachers (*quṣṣāṣ*), and suchlike situations. The motifs that even the ordinary folk came to know made their way into everyday speech usages, turning these themes into "things that are used aplenty in prose and poetry on the tongues of the elite and the common people alike" (*ashyāʾ [...] yakthuru fī l-nathr wa-l-naẓm ʿalā alsun al-khāṣṣa wa-l-ʿāmma ʾstiʿmāluhā*).[33]

---

560 ["*law kāna fī zaman Banī Isrāʾīl wa-nazalat āyat al-Baqara mā dhabaḥū ghayrahu*"; allusion to Quran 2:69]; al-Washshāʾ, *Muwashshā* 245 ["*Anā mawlā li-ahli hal...*"; allusion to Quran 76:1]; Ibn Diḥya, *Muṭrib* 221 ["*...ayna minki maqālu ʾllāhi fī l-lamamī*"; allusion to Quran 53:32]; al-Shāṭibī, *Ifādāt* 116 ["*wa-qad sabaqa l-Kitābū*"; allusion to Quran 8:68].

31 al-Zawzanī, *Ḥamāsa* II, 156.

32 See al-Qazwīnī, *Īḍāḥ* VI, 147; al-Jurjānī, *Ishārāt* 320.

33 al-Thaʿālibī, *Thimār* I, 50. This author also offers a list of such expressions alluding to the Quran's stories, including *ghurāb Nūḥ* (Noah's raven), *nār Ibrāhīm* (Abraham's fire), *dhiʾb Yūsuf* (the wolf [alleged to have eaten] Joseph), *ʿaṣā Mūsā* (Moses's staff; the literary uses of which I have already touched upon briefly), *khātam Sulaymān* (Solomon's seal), etc. The author of an oft-quoted lampoon manages to cram no less than three such images into one single verse line: "Whoever hopes for a gift from these people must possess three attributes: / He must own the hidden treasures of Qārūn, live as long as Noah, and have the patience of Job." See al-Bayhaqī, *Maḥāsin* 292; al-Thaʿālibī, *Thimār* I, 102; al-Thaʿālibī, *Nathr* 54. In the celebrated Baghdadian Epistle, a document offering some glimpses into the speech style of Buyid-era Baghdad, a fast-talking wit, on the pretext of commenting on a roast goat kid, makes a jesting overview of virtually every animal in the Quran (perhaps as potential roasts?), including the ram slaughtered by Abraham as a substitute for his son, the sacrificial cow of the Children of Israel, the whale that swallowed Jonah, the Golden Calf (*ʿijl al-Sāmirī*, 'the Samaritan's calf'). See al-Tawḥīdī [attr.], *Risāla* 294. (Not incidentally, modern Arabian dialectal poetry still makes frequent use of the Quran's motifs; see Sowayan 1985: 172.) – For further examples of the almost proverbial uses in both prose and poetry of motifs borrowed from the Quran, see Ibn al-Muʿtazz,

A lot of data in the sources bears evidence of the ubiquity of such usages in everyday speech in any number of contexts. In view of the elitist focus of the sources, it is natural that one finds most – but not all – of such data quoting educated people using such turns of speech, but this in my view is largely a function of the authors' attitudes.

For instance, a minor poet of the Buyid period known as Abū l-Faraj al-Babbaghā' (early 5th/11th c.) is cited to have poured his rage onto the radical Ismāʿīlite sect of the Carmathians, which he apparently despised, in the following words: "May God give power over them to the flood of Noah['s time], the gale [that destroyed the people] of ʿĀd, the rocks [that destroyed the people] of Lot, the lightning [that exterminated the people] of Thamūd!» (*sallaṭa 'llāh ʿalayhim ṭūfān Nūḥ wa-rīḥ ʿĀd wa-ḥijārat Lūṭ wa-ṣāʿiqat Thamūd*).[34] Another mediaeval littérateur uses the following florid phrases in complaining of the excessive parsimony of his patron, who is too

Ṭabaqāt 192 [Hārūt and Mārūt]; al-Jāḥiẓ, *Ḥayawān* I, 402 [Noah's longevity, the riches of Qārūn]; II, 8 and 13 [Solomon and the speech of the ants]; al-Thaʿālibī, *Thimār* I, 98–100 [Noah's Ark]; 103-4 [Abraham's ordeal in the fire], 109–11 [the shirt of Joseph], 117 [the burning bush], 119 [Eliah's wanderings], 140–1 and 376 [Hārūt and Mārūt], 163–4 [Hāmān], 470 [Joseph and the Egyptian women]; II, 820 [Abraham's ordeal in the fire]; al-Thaʿālibī, *Yatīma* I, 58 [the crossing of the Red Sea], 229 [Moses and Pharaoh], 303 [the Flood]; III, 48 [Luqmān], 342 [Abraham's ordeal in the fire], 418 [Noah's Ark]; IV, 307 [Joseph and the wolf]; al-Thaʿālibī, *Tatimma* I, 7 [Joseph and Potiphar's wife], 74 [Hārūt and Mārūt], 83 [Solomon, Noah]; II, 59 [the Flood]; al-Thaʿālibī, *Laṭā'if* 47 [the shirt of Joseph, Jacob's blindness, Job]; al-Thaʿālibī, *Iʿjāz* 248 [Joseph and his brothers]; al-Tanūkhī, *Nishwār* II, 260 [the crossing of the Red Sea]; al-Tawḥīdī [attr.], *Risāla* 76 [Noah and the dove sent as a scout], 189 [Hāmān's hubris], 273 [the story of Jacob and Joseph], 330 [Luqmān's longevity and the seven vultures], 375–6 [Hāmān, Nimrod and Pharaoh]; al-Iṣfahānī, *Aghānī* I, 159 [Hāmān and Pharaoh], 247 [Hārūt and Mārūt]; al-Tawḥīdī, *Baṣā'ir* I(i), 210 [Joseph's dream]; III(v), 134 [Solomon and the hoopoe], 197 [the vicissitudes of Joseph]; IV(vii), 200 [Hāmān]; al-Bākharzī, *Dumya* I, 41 [blood on the shirt of Joseph], 287 [Hārūt], 317 [Joseph and the Egyptian women], 531 [the shirt of Joseph]; II, 807 [the seal of Solomon], 907 and 1156 [Noah's Ark], 968 [Solomon and the hoopoe], 1323 [Moses and the Midianites], 1390 [the sorrow of Jacob]; Ibn al-Jawzī, *Ẓirāf* 35 [Solomon and the hoopoe in the context of a joke], 109 [Qārūn], 143 [the Golden Calf], 144 [Moses and Eliah]; al-Iṣbahānī, *Kharīda* I(i), 189 [Moses and Pharaoh], 205 [Joseph in Egypt]; al-Ibshīhī, *Mustaṭraf* 270 [Joseph in Egypt], 273–4 [Moses on Mount Sinai], 383 [Abraham's readiness to sacrifice his son], 474 [Hārūt]; Ibn Diḥya, *Muṭrib* 36 [Abraham's ordeal in the fire], 65 [Noah's Ark, Jesus walking on the water], 75 [Hārūt], 199 [the crossing of the Red Sea, Abraham's ordeal in the fire]; Ibn Saʿīd, *Ghuṣūn* 103 [Noah's Ark]; Ibn Saʿīd, *Muqtaṭaf* 105 [Moses and Eliah]; Ibn Saʿīd, *Rāyāt* 91 [Moses on Mount Sinai], 115 [Moses and Eliah], 133 [the crossing of the Red Sea, Abraham's ordeal in the fire]; al-Jurjānī, *Wasāṭa* 128 [Moses on Mount Sinai], 145 [the shirt of Joseph]; Ibn al-Kattānī, *Tashbīhāt* 111 [Hārūt], 150 [Joshua], 177 [the crossing of the Red Sea], 217 [Abraham's ordeal in the fire], 225 and 278 [Moses on Mount Sinai], 264 [Hāmān and Pharaoh], 289 [Joseph and Jacob]; al-Ḥillī, *ʿĀṭil* 139 [Moses and Pharaoh], 156 [Joseph in Egypt], 175 [Moses on Mount Sinai]; Ḥusāmzāde, *Risāla* 19 [the shirt of Joseph, Jacob's blindness]; Ibn Maʿṣūm, *Sulāfa* 298–9 [the burning bush, *nār Mūsā*].

34 al-Thaʿālibī, *Laṭā'if* 61; al-Thaʿālibī, *Thimār* I, 162. Every one of these phrases is a reference to a respective well-known Quranic story; for some literary uses of the same, see for instance Ibn al-Kattānī, *Tashbīhāt* 222. For a reference to these stories in a mediaeval Arabic popular saying, see al-Maydānī, *Amthāl* II, 305.

niggardly even to present him with a gift of a set or two of clothes: "If Jacob came to him accompanied by all the prophets as intercessors and all the angels as guarantors and asked him to lend one single needle so that he should be able to sew the shirt of his son Joseph torn at the back [by Potiphar's wife], he would not be willing to lend it to him; let alone his clothing me!"[35] The sight of the remarkable obesity of the famous – and infamous – poet of the early Abbasid period, Bashshār b. Burd (d. 167–8/784–5) occasioned the following sarcastic remark by an acquaintance, who was of course making a reference to the story of ʿĀd in the Quran: "I have the impression that even if God sent every gale with which He destroyed the peoples of ancient times, it could not budge you from your place."[36] The next example shows that such expressions were not unknown in al-Andalus either. In the second *sūra* of the Quran (2:69), one finds the description of a cow "of a shining yellow complexion, delighting the eye", which the Jews offer as a sacrifice to God. It is to this image that the Granadan poetess Nazhūn alluded when, catching sight of her famous fellow-poet Ibn Quzmān (d. 555/1160) wrapped in a bright yellow garment, she remarked: "You are looking quite like the cow of the Children of Israel, except for the fact that you do not delight the eye."[37] Another example from the Iberian Peninsula demonstrates that in addition to direct references to a given passage of the Quran, allusions might also be made to the more ornate popular legends based on a short Quranic story; such remarks may appear rather cryptic to the modern reader but must have been perfectly comprehensible to their original recipients.[38]

Uneducated people must also, at least occasionally, have used such references to the Quran's stories. The uncouth Daylamī warlord Mardāwīj (d. 323/935), the founder of the Ziyārid dynasty, called himself and his troops 'Solomon and the genies', an allusion to the Quranic depiction of the complete obedience of the jinns to the orders of Solomon and their serving as part of his cohorts (Quran 27:17 and 34:12–3).[39] The Quranic stories of the prophets were the basis not only of such phrases in the mediaeval Arabic spoken language but also of jokes; and indeed some better-known passages of the Quran seem to have been utilised as explanations – perhaps less than entirely serious – for certain popular prejudices.[40]

---

[35] al-Thaʿālibī, *Laṭāʾif* 86; al-Thaʿālibī, *Iqtibās* I, 161; al-Ibshīhī, *Mustaṭraf* 184. A different version of the story – with far more concrete details on the protagonists and the context – is in Yāqūt, *Udabāʾ* III, 1306. This verbal flourish was apparently much appreciated as a show of wit, judging from the fact that later on it was transformed into poetry too; see al-Thaʿālibī, *Thimār* I, 110; al-Zawzanī, *Ḥamāsa* II, 138.

[36] al-Iṣfahānī, *Aghānī* III, 212.

[37] Ibn Saʿīd, *Rāyāt* 159.

[38] See an abstruse remark by the Cordovan poet Muʾmin b. Saʿīd ("Incorpórate, Dāwūd, que ya te he concebido lo que habías pedido") and a very plausible interpretation thereof in Molina 2003: 218–21.

[39] Miskawayh, *Tajārib* I, 162.

[40] See for instance al-Jāḥiẓ, *Ḥayawān* I, 82; al-Maqrīzī, *Khiṭaṭ* I, 87.

2.2 Quranic Motifs in Mujūn

The fact that the boundaries of *mujūn* were probably quite fluid and open to interpretation, depending on individual indulgence or piety, has already been remarked upon. This is the reason that some of the examples of unserious borrowing from the Quran quoted in the preceding section might probably pass for *mujūn* in the view of some people, while the examples to be given in this chapter under the heading *mujūn* would perhaps not necessarily qualify as such for more lenient souls. However, following is a selection that I feel would be readily recognised as representative of *mujūn* for a sufficiently large number of mediaeval Muslim intellectuals to allow treating them within such a category here. This is not to insist that any of my readers may not be fully justified to deny such a description to any of the individual examples listed below. This section does not aspire to do more than offer an impressionistic picture of how Quranic phrases and themes were treated in *mujūn* literature, and thus through cumulative evidence help form a notion of one aspect of *mujūn* among many.

The uses of Quranic themes in *mujūn* literature – be it in verse, written prose literature, or jokes and everyday speech – can be categorised as belonging to one of two basic types. The first, and probably the more widespread, of the two is that in which the witty effect is provided by the deliberate misinterpretation or misapplication of the purport of a passage from the holy book.[41] What this involves is the placement of a Quranic verse in a context in which it is logically and semantically quite inappropriate but which nevertheless can, by a forced or crooked logic, be associated with the verse in question. (For instance, by *double entendre.*) In the other kind of *mujūn* motifs based on the Quran, the passage tends to retain its original purport, but it is quoted in a context highly incongruous with the elevated style of the holy text. (For instance, when ignoramuses cite the Quran to justify some petty business of theirs.) The effect of a contrast between the lofty feeling inevitably evoked by the holy text and the banal circumstances – and sometimes an added low linguistic register – into which it is put is usually very powerful and immediate, hence the popularity of this kind of *mujūn* motif. In fact, this type of motif exploits one of the most frequent sources of humour in general, namely the juxtaposition of extremely disparate linguistic elements in which the humorous effect is dependent upon the sudden realisation by the audience of the tension between the two registers.[42] In one of the two types, a misinterpretation of the Quranic passage is the crucial element, in the other a misplacement thereof. What

[41] This type of humour was in fact as frequent in the Christian and Jewish traditions as among Muslims; see Rosenthal 1956: 29.

[42] In this context, it is instructive to consult the discussion of the concept of *code consistency* in Irvine 1979: 777.

the two types of motifs have in common is the inappropriate, out-of-context use of Quranic quotations.

Between them these two types of Quranic motifs in Arabic frivolous literature constitute a substantial part of what passed for *mujūn* in the mediaeval period. Innumerable poems, anecdotes, jokes, and recorded spoken witticisms are based on this device. Indeed, it appears even in Persian *mujūn*, including the very frivolous works of ʿUbayd-i Zākānī.[43] The importance and sheer ubiquity of this motif makes it indispensable to discuss the topic at some length and offer some typical examples, although the fact that most Western readers, even specialists in Arabic Studies, will not be nearly as familiar with the Quran's text as the average mediaeval Arab intellectual makes it fairly hard to appreciate the wit of such jokes, dependent as it is on quick recognition. The very different cultural background also makes the appreciation of such humour by a Western reader somewhat arduous. The awkwardness of the situation when the point of a joke has to be explained results from the fact that a joke needing explanation is not powerful and not funny; in fact, for all practical purposes, it ceases to be a joke at all. With this in mind, the following selection of illustrative examples was made on utilitarian considerations and owes perhaps more to their being relatively translatable than to any other virtue they might have.

First, I will cite a number of prose texts, some of which may originally have been witty remarks made by certain individuals and then recounted by others and recorded, while some are undoubtedly simply jokes presented as actual encounters between historical personalities. (Whereas it is in most cases impossible to decide with certainty, it is really not a crucial question for my present purpose here; however, I will have more to say about the protagonists of *mujūn* anecdotes and jokes in a later section of this book.) To begin, the following texts are less than obviously historical, and indeed all but the first one are in my view distinctly unlikely to recount utterances by any actual living person:

> Al-Aṣmaʿī[44] was one of those who made a funny reference to [the Quranic story of] God's friend [i.e. Abraham] (*mimman mallaḥa fī l-tamthīl bi-khalīl Allāh*). When a very close friend of his asked him for a loan, he said: "Of course, with great pleasure, but please do put my heart at rest with a pawn that has many times the value of [the loan] you are asking for." The other said: "Come, Abū Saʿīd, don't you trust me?" To which [al-Aṣmaʿī] replied: "I do, but look, God's friend did trust his Lord too, and yet he did say[45]: "*[s]how me how Thou wilt give life to the dead,' He said: 'Why, dost thou not believe?' 'Yes', he said, 'but that my heart may be at rest'.*"[46]

[43] See for instance Sprachman 1997: 203.

[44] The renowned Iraqi philologist of the early Abbasid period (2nd/9th c.).

[45] Quran 2:260.

[46] al-Thaʿālibī, *Thimār* I, 70; al-Thaʿālibī, *Iqtibās* I, 153–4; and the same story in a slightly different

> A Bedouin of the Banū ʿUdhra tribe, dining together with [the Umayyad caliph] Muʿāwiya, kept grabbing the morsels of food in front of Muʿāwiya. He would reach here and there, then, catching sight of a particularly greasy bite in front of Muʿāwiya, he took it too. At this [insolence], Muʿāwiya said: "'*[H]ast thou made a hole in it* [viz. in the heap of food] *so as to drown its partakers*'?" And the Bedouin replied: "No, but '*we drive it to a dead land* [i.e. to his own hungry stomach]'."[47]

> Abū l-Ḥasan al-Madāʾinī said: A learned man narrated this: We had a friend from Basra who was a witty and erudite person. Once he promised that he would invite us to his home; however, after that he would just pass by us [in the street]. So whenever we saw him we would say to him: "*When shall this promise come to pass, if you speak truly?*"[48] He would just keep silent, until one day, having prepared [the rich feast] which we wished for, he turned up, and when we had again told him [the usual teasing words], he said: "*Depart to that you cried was lies!*"[49]

After the above stories, which seem to be largely fictional, here is an anecdote that I believe is quite likely to be, as it claims, the record of an actual utterance made in the court of the Seljuk ruler Malikshāh (r. 465/1073–485/1092). The text tells of the embarrassingly lacking elocutionary skills of the vizier al-Mufaḍḍal b. ʿAbd al-Razzāq, who,

> [w]hen he was summoned before the caliph, after having been invested with the office of grand vizier, was [so flustered as to be] unable to utter a word. Upon this, Tāj al-Ruʾasāʾ Nasīb b. al-Mūṣalāyā said to the caliph [with malice]: "Your servant al-Mufaḍḍal b. ʿAbd al-Razzāq serves [you] and says what God said [in the Quran][50]: "*My Lord, dispose me that I may be thankful for Thy blessing.*"[51]

---

wording in al-Thaʿālibī, *Laṭāʾif* 53; al-Ibshīhī, *Mustaṭraf* 111. A humorous motif very similar to this, albeit referring to the story of Moses and not a word-by-word *iqtibās*, is to be found in mediaeval Arabic poetry too: "*La-in aṣbaḥtu murtaḥilan bi-shakhṣī fa-qalbī ʿindakum abadan muqīmu; / Wa-lākinna l-muʿāyina muṭmaʾinnun: li-dhā saʾala l-muʿāyanata l-Kalīmu.*" (An allusion to Quran 7:143.) See Ibn Saʿīd, *Ghāyāt* 119; and in a slightly different version in Ibn Diḥya, *Muṭrib* 92.

[47] al-Tawḥīdī, *Baṣāʾir* I(i), 189; and in a somewhat different version in Ibn al-Jawzī, *Ẓirāf* 50. A far more elaborate version of this anecdote (with a greater number of participants in the repast and with other apposite Quranic citations added) is to be found in English translation in Marzolph 2000: 483. The two quotations in al-Tawḥīdī's version are from Quran 18:71 and Quran 35:9 (and 7:57) respectively. I have slightly altered Arberry's translation of the former verse, which has 'passengers' instead of 'partakers', a word that would make no sense here. The Arabic original uses the noun *ahlahā* ('its people'). The two Quranic phrases cited here evoke the image of a vicious man making a leak in a ship's hull to drown its passengers, and that of God sending a rain-cloud over parched earth, respectively – neither has anything to do with food etiquette.

[48] Quran 67:25. In its original context, this sentence is the unbelievers' sarcastic response to the mention of Hell; see also al-Bayḍāwī, *Tafsīr* II, 512.

[49] Ibn al-Jawzī, *Ẓirāf* 90. The original of the quotation is Quran 77:29, where these words are a description of the Day of Judgement, and more specifically of the doomed who are told to leave for Hell to stay there forever. See al-Bayḍāwī, *Tafsīr* II, 558.

[50] Quran 27:19 and 46:15.

[51] al-Iṣbahānī, *Kharīda* I(i), 94.

This remark was by no means an isolated witticism by an especially quick-witted courtier. The sources strongly suggest that the habit of joking based on the deliberate misinterpretation of Quranic passages was quite common in speech, at least among the educated urban élite. Admittedly, it is conceivable that all these data actually reflect a purely scholarly, written genre that masquerades as the record of original oral utterances – a process not totally improbable in view of the problematic and much-discussed relationship between fiction and historical fact in Arabic literature – yet I do not think it would be realistic to suppose that intellectuals with sufficient skills and wit to invent such jokes in writing would not try to do the same in conversation with friends. This observation is especially true of those intellectuals whom we have sufficient data to describe as having had an easygoing temperament, or even slightly or unabashedly frivolous attitudes – by no means an uncommon breed in the Abbasid and Buyid periods.

Whether one interprets them as genuinely or allegedly oral utterances, remarks based on the misapplication of the Quran's verses are plentiful in the sources. For instance, a witty man is cited as having declared that the Quranic injunction "*when you have had the meal, disperse*" (Quran 33:53) is in fact a warning to tiresome, witless men who bore their interlocutors to death.[52] Another remark, attributed to the famous wit Abū l-ʿAynāʾ (d. 283/896), describes two friends of his teasingly as ne'er-do-well men: "They are like wine and the *maysir* game: *the sin in them is more heinous than the usefulness.*"[53] A rather vulgar joke tells of a person who, having audibly broken wind in public, quotes the Quran (6:96, 36:38, 41:12) without a trace of embarrassment: "*That is the ordaining of the All-mighty, the All-knowing.*"[54] In yet another source (which, not incidentally, seems at times to mimic the witty urban argot of 4th/10th-century Baghdad), the sight of a bowl of fruits prompts someone to give a droll description of the appetising selection, one involving the combination of no less than four passages from the Quran into one appreciative sentence.[55] It

[52] al-Tawḥīdī, *Baṣāʾir* I(ii), 136; al-Thaʿālibī, *Iqtibās* II, 51. In fact the verse in question refers to a not quite unrelated matter, being as it is addressed to the wedding guests of the Prophet Muḥammad who did not display the necessary civility to their host; see al-Bayḍāwī, *Tafsīr* II, 250–1; and Ibn al-Marzubān, *Dhamm* 48–9.

[53] al-Thaʿālibī, *Iqtibās* II, 45; and also (without identifying the author or the objects of the *bon mot*) in al-Ibshīhī, *Mustaṭraf* 261. *Maysir* is an ancient Arabian game played with a set of arrows, which was prohibited by Islam, as were other forms of gambling. The quotation part of the remark comes from Quran 2:219.

[54] al-Tawḥīdī, *Baṣāʾir* I(ii), 85. The *āya* was apparently popular for citation (for serious purposes as well), cf. al-Thaʿālibī, *Iqtibās* I, 62–3.

[55] al-Tawḥīdī [attr.], *Risāla* 307. Further examples of the quick and witty application of textual quotations from the Quran in everyday conversation and friendly jesting: Abū Hiffān, *Akhbār* 124; Ibn Qutayba, *ʿUyūn* I(i), 122; al-Khaṭīb, *Taṭfīl* 33; al-ʿAskarī, *Ṣināʿatayn* 25; al-Thaʿālibī, *Iqtibās* I, 148; II, 18; al-Thaʿālibī, *Yatīma* III, 197, 199–200; al-Thaʿālibī, *Khāṣṣ* 69–70; al-Thaʿālibī, *Laṭāʾif* 67; al-Thaʿālibī, *Thimār* I, 89, 114; II, 834 [here you find a Quranic passage put in a grossly obscene

could not be more obvious that the ability to apply a verse from the Quran to a given situation in an innovative and quick-witted manner, including the intentional twisting of its purport, was a much prized intellectual asset among highly educated mediaeval Muslim intellectuals. How many of them actually had this gift is, however, hard to judge.

Having had a look at the ways prose texts – mainly anecdotes and jokes – and possibly spoken language put *iqtibās* to jumorous uses, we will now turn our attention to the comparable use of such quotations in Arabic poetry, more specifically in *mujūn* poems. In the logic of humorous *iqtibās* there is practically no difference between poerty and prose: in both cases, the purport of the original Quranic verse is intentionally misrepresented in the new context, or (as I will shortly proceed to illustrate with examples) a Quranic verse is put in a highly incongruous, low-brow context to create a funny contrast between the two stylistic registers.

Two examples follow that are based on the misinterpretation of a very famous phrase from the Quran (29:46), which in its original context warns Muslims not to engage in fruitless and unnecessary arguments with the followers of the other monotheistic religions about their respective faiths, and advises that if they do, they should only reply to the tenets of those religions "*with something that is better*" (*bi-l-latī hiya aḥsanu*).[56] This oft-quoted Quranic expression recurs in both of the poems below in correct form and grammar but in a totally and deliberately twisted sense:

context]; al-Tawḥīdī, *Baṣā'ir* I(i), 74, 140, 199; III(vi), 75; al-Tawḥīdī, *Akhlāq* 218, 227; al-Tawḥīdī [attr.], *Risāla* 274, 355 [this again is a gross specimen, placing a Quranic passage into a torrent of vulgar insults]; al-Tanūkhī, *Nishwār* II, 207; VI, 49; VII, 137; al-Bayhaqī, *Maḥāsin* 443, 577, 665; al-Bākharzī, *Dumya* II, 1387; al-Rāghib, *Muḥāḍarāt* III, 478, 495, 530, 532–3; Ibn al-Jawzī, *Ẓirāf* 57, 155, 157, 159, 167; al-Anṭākī, *Tazyīn* 530; al-Ibshīhī, *Mustaṭraf* 204, 264, 268. – In some cases, the misinterpretation of the Quran might well have been an infelicitous yet perfectly *bona fide* mistake originally made by a pious commentator, which would nevertheless end up as an amusing anecdote among less reverent contemporaries. For possible examples of this, see al-Jāḥiẓ, *Ḥayawān* I, 188–9; al-Thaʿālibī, *Thimār* I, 296–7; al-Tawḥīdī, *Baṣā'ir* I(ii), 23–4. For some incredibly absurd, but very amusing, such misinterpretation, also see ibid. I(ii), 231. It must be added that the same motif could be applied to *ḥadīth* texts too; see for instance ibid. III(vi), 114. (The treatment of *ḥadīths* in *mujūn* literature will be discussed at some length in the next section of this chapter.) – The incorporation of Quranic passages in joking texts and their use in humorous contexts were still extremely common and widely regarded as harmless and acceptable in late 19th-century Egypt, as attested in Lane 1895: 280–1. In fact, neither is it absent from today's Arabic dialects; an example would be the almost hackneyed use of the phrase *wa-lā hum yaḥzanūn* ("neither shall they sorrow"; Quran 2:38 and in 12 other verses) as a strange concluding formula at the end of sentences containing multiple negations. See for instance McCarthy, Raffouli 1965: 25, 219. (Attested here in the Baghdadi urban dialect, I have frequently heard it used in casual talk in Tunisia, and as my colleague Saber el Adly informs me, it is widespread in other dialects too. Its Quranic origin, as I have had the opportunity to observe, may not be realised by all Arabic speakers who use it.)

56 See al-Bayḍāwī, *Tafsīr* II, 211. Here I was forced totally to depart from Arberry's English version ("save in the fairer manner") to salvage some of the word-play of the Arabic *iqtibās* in the poems.

> What harm would it do to the gate-keeper of your house, who did not admit me and whom it is no use to ask for permission to enter,
> if he rejected me at your door with civility, or sent me away *with something that is better*?[57]

> We have forgotten the [boy as beautiful as a] gazelle in favour of a girl with a face whose beauty is temptation itself:
> We have stopped our indecent behaviour with him, replacing him *with something that is better.*[58]

Other famous Quranic verses also lent themselves easily to inventive literary uses; one such is the Quranic definition of the responsibility and proper role of the prophets: "it is only for the Messenger to deliver the Message" (*mā ʿalā l-rasūli illā l-balāghu*; Quran 5:99 and with slight differences in wording in a lot of other verses). Like the previous phrase, this one too was built into highly inappropriate contexts in *mujūn* poetry, including, as astonishing or appalling as this may sound, a poem from the Buyid era describing a scene of sexual intercourse (the semantic field of the polysemous noun *balāgh* covering not only 'message' but also 'orgasm', 'ejaculation').[59]

The second type of *mujūn* motifs based on *iqtibās* is closely related to the former, and may be even seen as a variant of it. It consists of putting the lofty quotation in a highly incongruous, low situation, thereby creating a confounding contrast, hence a humorous tension, between the two semantic (and stylistic) levels.

Some expressions of the Quran were, as I have already noted, probably known even to the most uneducated people either owing to their remarkable linguistic oddity or their significance as normative regulations of custom and behaviour. Among such expressions is the Quranic injunction ordering husbands to observe fair behaviour in the case of both divorce and continuation of the marriage, "honourable retention or setting free kindly" (*imsākun bi-maʿrūfin aw tasrīḥun bi-ʾiḥsānin*; Quran 2:229). This Quranic passage, because of its obvious social relevance in matrimonial disputes, was cited very often and in fact seems to have been one of the few Quranic phrases that even illiterate and uneducated women would know by heart. Interestingly, it might have been viewed by dissatisfied wives as a potent argument against slack husbands; it is instructive in this respect that a poem cited

---

57 al-Ibshīhī, *Mustaṭraf* 104.

58 al-Ibshīhī, *Mustaṭraf* 458. The Quranic expression *bi-l-latī hiya aḥsanu* is grammatically feminine.

59 E.g. al-Thaʿālibī, *Tatimma* I, 50; II, 22; al-Thaʿālibī, *Yatīma* II, 354. For further examples of the poetic device in *mujūn* of deliberately misinterpreted *iqtibās*, see Ibn al-Muʿtazz, *Ṭabaqāt* 176; al-Bākharzī, *Dumya* I, 591; II, 731, 1198, 1441; al-Thaʿālibī, *Yatīma* III, 267; IV, 71, 73, 434–5; al-Thaʿālibī, *Tatimma* II, 10, 94, 101; al-Iṣbahānī, *Kharīda* I(i), 44; I(ii), 235; al-Ḥillī, *ʿĀṭil* 105; Wagner 2008: 193. A motif appearing in poetry might well have been used in speech and/or prose too, see for instance al-Bākharzī, *Dumya* II, 854, and v. s. for its use in speech.

in the Perfumed Garden (early 9th/15th c.) depicts the constant nagging of an obnoxious, termagant shrew of a wife by portraying her as "saying day in day out, 'get for me [this and that], you man, start, get a lease, buy, and *observe honourable retention*" (*fī kulli yawmin taqūlu hāti yā rajulu qum wa-ʾktari wa-ʾshtari wa-amsik bi-maʿrūfi*).[60] Similarly, Snouck Hurgronje reports in his late 19th-century description of Meccan society that even the most common, most ignorant women would know this one passage of the Quran by heart, if nothing else.[61] There is little reason to doubt that this particular phrase, of such an obvious societal importance, had been equally well-known in the metropolitan centres of mediaeval Iraq. This is the background one needs to know to appreciate the wit of the following anecdote, a typical one in its highlighting the humorous potential of the incongruity of boorish commoners making attempts to cite the lofty diction of the Quran:

> Abū Hiffān[62] has narrated this: I have seen a stupid man arguing with his wife, whereupon a similarly stupid neighbour of theirs came and told them: "You there, do to this woman as God has commanded [in the Quran]: 'what-d'you-call-it kind of retention or what-d'you-call-it kind of setting free' (*imsākun b-ʾēsh ismuh aw tasrīḥun b-ʾēsh ismuh*)." I had a good laugh at his eloquence.[63]

The scandalously limited knowledge of the Quran – as perceived by mediaeval Muslim intellectuals – among common, illiterate folk is the butt of a considerable number of jokes. Thus, quite a few such jokes show the pattern of portraying ignorant commoners as being familiar with only such Quranic verses as would seem to give support (if properly misinterpreted) to their own unholy predilections or peccadilloes.[64] Another recurrent type of joke is that in which one is supposed to laugh at the grotesquely stupid and ignorant comments of a primitive man on a Quranic passage recited during communal prayer, or in some other respectable context. The

60 al-Nafzāwī, *Rawḍ* 33; and also a slightly different version in Wagner 2008: 142.

61 Snouck Hurgronje 1931: 88.

62 A famous intellectual of the early Abbasid period (d. 255/869), one of the companions of the greatest of *mājin* poets, Abū Nuwās, and author of one of the latter's extant biographies.

63 al-Tawḥīdī, *Baṣāʾir* II(iv), 74. Note the (no doubt quite purposeful and stylistically charged) use of the colloquial form of the interrogative, heightening the contrast between the Quranic quotation and the context. – The same Quranic phrase is incorporated partially (with modifications dictated by the metre and rhyme) in a jesting poem describing the inconvenience caused by thistle ("*Fa-lā yudalliku tadlīkan bi-maʿrifatin wa-lā yusarriḥu tasrīḥan bi-ʾiḥsānī*"); see al-Ibshīhī, Mustaṭraf 259; as well as in a sarcastic verse about empty promises of gratuity ("*Fa-in lam tanwi imsākan bi-maʿrūfin fa-tasrīḥā*"); see al-Bākharzī, *Dumya* II, 1442.

64 A typical example would be the audacious sponger (*ṭufaylī*), a stock figure of mediaeval Arabic entertaining literature, who cites as his favourite Quranic verse the *āya* 18:62 – and inaccurately into the bargain – in which Moses is asking for his lunch. See al-Tanūkhī, *Nishwār* VII, 152; and also cf. al-Thaʿālibī, *Thimār* I, 296; al-Thaʿālibī, *Yatīma* IV, 73, 352; al-Ibshīhī, Mustaṭraf 539. Such jokes, while retaining the same logic, might also use passages from *ḥadīths* instead of the Quran; see for instance al-Thaʿālibī, *Yatīma* II, 378.

protagonist of such texts is often, but not necessarily, a Bedouin, having become by that time one of the archetypes of the 'savage' in Middle Eastern culture, but other kinds of uncouth persons also appear. Whether Bedouins or other ignoramuses, people making inane comments on what they understood to be the purport of a given Quranic verse were apparently a quite popular theme of jokes.[65] A related theme in mediaeval Arabic humour is that in which the protagonist recites the Quran's text making elementary and obvious mistakes, or in a way that completely deprives the text of any meaning. An anecdote recorded in an early 4th/10th-century work is based on the technicality of making stops at designated points in the Quran's text (*waqf*), as it features a less than impeccably learned imam who suspends his recitation in the very middle of a word, and then continues it, after a series of ritual movements and formulae, from the middle of the same word as though this were the most natural procedure in the world.[66]

The contrast to the majestic style of the Quran, as I have observed, is often provided by the banal, unbecoming situation in which it is used, but it can equally well be a materialistic and cynical attitude – no doubt reflecting an existing pattern of speech and behaviour among some libertines. (More about this point later on.) A joke from the Buyid era states that if you hear someone repeating the Quranic verse (28:60) "*and what is with God is better and more enduring*", you can conclude that this person has not been invited to a prestigious banquet.[67] The same contrast of piety and irreverence can be observed in the following anecdote in which a man cites the story of Joseph and Potiphar's wife from the Quran (12:30) and one of his interlocutors remarks, "Now, have we then started to talk about whores?"[68] It is the comic potential of the same contrast that the following two jokes play on. The protagonist of the first is the famously profligate Umayyad caliph al-Walīd b. Yazīd (r. 125–6/743–4). I see no reason to regard this as a historical account, for al-Walīd has forever been proverbial among Muslims for his impiety, which no doubt made him an ideal protagonist of indecent and irreverent jokes:

> When he decided to flee from [the plague epidemic raging in] Damascus, someone said to him: "God says [in the Quran][69]: '*Say: Flight will not profit*

[65] E.g. al-Bayhaqī, *Maḥāsin* 664; al-Ibshīhī, *Mustaṭraf* 262, 531–2; al-Tawḥīdī, *Baṣā'ir* II(iv), 48–50, 108–9.

[66] al-Bayhaqī, *Maḥāsin* 643. For further examples of ridiculous mistakes made in the recitation of the Quran as a source of humour, see ibid. 644. A twist on the themes of contrasting the Quran to dialectal speech and the erroneous citation of the Quran's text by commoners is that based on ignorant people's mistaking some ordinary discourse or a well-known line of poetry for a Quranic passage. See for instance al-Tanūkhī, *Nishwār* III, 133; and the same motif employing a *ḥadīth* in lieu of a Quranic verse in ibid. III, 135.

[67] See this and two similar quips in al-Tawḥīdī, *Baṣā'ir* II(iv), 154.

[68] al-Tawḥīdī, *Baṣā'ir* II(iv), 46.

[69] Quran 33:16.

> *you, if you flee from death or slaying; you will be given enjoyment of days then but little*'." [The caliph] replied: "It's precisely this little that we want."[70]

The second example is quite unequivocally fictitious, featuring as it does one of the stock figures of mediaeval Arabic jokes, Muzabbid (who may originally have been an actual living man in the early Islamic period, but was turned into the legendary buffoon of countless anecdotes):

> A man saw Muzabbid in Edessa wearing a long silken gown, for [Muzabbid] had become quite well-to-do after moving to Edessa. He said to him: "Muzabbid, would you give this gown to me?" He replied, "This is the only one I have." The man said: "But God says [in the Quran][71], '[the righteous are] *preferring others above themselves, even though poverty be their portion.*" Said Muzabbid: "God the Most High is more merciful towards His servants than to send this message to them in Edessa and in December or January; he sent it in the Hijaz [Western Arabia] in June or July."[72]

2.3 Motifs Borrowed from Ḥadīths

Ḥadīths, the characteristic reports about the sayings and deeds of the Prophet Muḥammad, are for all practical purposes almost as important as the Quran as sources of Islamic culture and especially Islamic law, even though they necessarily lack the aura of divine origin that the latter always had. Given their somewhat less forbiddingly holy status, one would expect them to be more freely used in jesting ways, but in fact this does not seem to have been the case. The reason is very simple. It is true that the study of *ḥadīths* was one of the most prominent and extensive fields of religious scholarship among mediaeval Muslims, and *de rigueur* for a decent, comprehensive education for someone aspiring to become an intellectual, yet the level of familiarity with most *ḥadīths* – and one is reminded of the fact that there were tens if not hundreds of thousands of them – was nowhere nearly as profound as the knowledge of the Quran in its entirety. The sheer extent of the discipline precluded the same depth and precision as that displayed towards the Quran's text, and an added factor is that people – even educated people, bar

---

[70] Ibn Saʿīd, *Muqtaṭaf* 186–7. Another source identifies another member of the Umayyad dynasty, Sulaymān b. ʿAbd al-Malik – a less self-evident choice – as the character uttering this cynical *bon mot.* See al-Thaʿālibī, *Laṭāʾif* 15. To appreciate the point of this anecdote fully, it is worth noting that there are a host of Muslim traditions that strongly disapprove of flight in the face of an epidemic, resignation and fortitude being the attitude of choice for a devout Muslim in such a situation. In fact, escaping from an epidemic might even be categorised by some authorities as a *kabīra*, or grave sin. See al-Haytamī, *Zawājir* II, 173–6.

[71] Quran 59:9.

[72] al-Tawḥīdī, *Baṣāʾir* V(ix), 42. Again, there is a different version that places the story in Baghdad and ascribes the remark to, who else, the arch-libertine Abū Nuwās. See Abū Hiffān, *Akhbār* 123–4.

genuine specialists of *ḥadīth* studies – simply did not have the same daily exposure to *ḥadīths* as they did to passages of the Quran. However, the difference is one of degree and not of kind, and it is only reasonable to expect *ḥadīths*, similarly to the Quran, to have become the objects of *mujūn* literature. This is what actually happened.[73]

Inevitably, jokes and poems based on quotations and themes taken from *ḥadīths* have to be regarded as largely scholarly products. Whilst most urban common people did have some superficial knowledge of some Quranic verses, and educated men were supposed to be familiar with the whole text or even to know it by heart, a comparable knowledge of the *ḥadīth* corpus was out of the question for anyone but the most dedicated experts of the discipline. Commoners might not know any *ḥadīths* at all, and ordinary, non-specialist individuals' knowledge thereof was probably quite haphazard. However, this idea should not be pushed too far. In fact, a number of important *ḥadīths* were probably widely known; and the public lectures of some of the most celebrated experts of *ḥadīths* seem to have been frequented by incredible multitudes of men, not just a small circle of specialists, conferring something akin to star status on these experts.[74]

The underlying logic of most of the jesting based on *ḥadīths* is more or less identical to what we have observed about *iqtibās* from the Quran (in fact, the same term might be used in reference to literary quotations from *ḥadīths* too): the source of humour in both cases is either the purposeful, and often shockingly profane, misapplication of a quotation, or its trasfer into a highly inappropriate and incongruous context, and in both cases the resultant subversion of its sublime mood. To illustrate both subtypes, some examples will follow.

The misinterpreation of the purport of *ḥadīth* could not be more obvious in an anecdote about the 'imam of profligacy' (*imām al-bāṭil*), the immensely popular Abbasid-era poet Abū Nuwās (d. ca. 198–200/813–5), the veritable embodiment of *mujūn* in the Arabic tradition. The anecdote is based on the well-known penchant of Abū Nuwās for boys, more specifically for adolescents whose facial hair was only just appearing (called *muʿadhdhar* in Arabic). The *ḥadīth* referred to in the anecdote states that those who reach Paradise will maintain their eternal youth, and expresses this by describing them as remaining forever beardless. Abū Nuwās' comment: "While still in this world, hoard as much as you can of that pleasure which will not be available in Paradise [viz. sex with a *muʿadhdhar*]."[75]

---

[73] Very limited at first, the literary use of *ḥadīths* became more common from the 3rd/9th century on; see Zubaidi 1983: 340–3.

[74] This would be so even if the relevant accounts in al-Samʿānī, *Adab* 17–8, 96 are perhaps exaggerated.

[75] al-Thaʿālibī, *Laṭāʾif* 92. It is interesting to note that this witticism, original though it may look, in fact seems to be just a modification of a widely used vernacular idiom. A common urban locution

The point of the following anecdote – which, by all appearances, recounts an actual *bon mot* by the celebrated vizier of the Buyid era, al-Ṣāḥib Ismāʿīl b. ʿAbbād (326/938–385/995) – relies on the flippant misinterpretation of a famous *ḥadīth*. The narrator, a courtier of al-Ṣāḥib whose name was al-Aqṭaʿ al-Kūfī, would often be among the group of intimate friends who drank and frolicked together with the vizier.

> Once we said to him: "You are fond of perfumes, and keep talking of sex, observing no limits." He replied: "By God, in so doing I am only following the example of our Prophet – may God bless him! – for he declared: *'Of [the pleasures of] this world, I have come to like three [in particular]: perfumes and women...'*." We said: "Why, the *ḥadīth* also mentions [as the third good thing]: '*... and the thing dearest to my heart is prayer*'; and yet you hardly pray at all." He replied: "You fools, should I even pray too, I would also become a prophet, but Muḥammad has affirmed: '*There will be no prophets after me*'."[76]

The third quip, which is recorded in a late source (8th–9th/14th–15th c.), is attributed to an unnamed religious scholar, and it is not difficult to conceive of learned men with a thorough knowledge of *ḥadīths* and a relatively merry temperament engaging in some scholarly joking that they would have regarded as innocuous. (Scholarly attitudes to *mujūn* are one of the topics to be discussed in Chapter Four.) While it is perhaps hopeless to determine who may have invented the joke, I suppose the anecdote must have been widely known in his time for a bigoted scholar such as Ibn Baydakīn al-Turkumānī (a Ḥanafite much influenced by Ḥanbalite thought) to write it down as a horrifying example of some people's frivolity. It involves the deliberately literal (mis)interpretation of a patently figurative *ḥadīth*, thereby creating a grotesque effect:

> A man said to a jurisprudent[, citing a *ḥadīth*]: "*The angels spread their wings [on the ground] for the sake of the man seeking [religious] knowledge.*" To this the scholar jestingly replied: "That's why I've had my wooden clogs studded with nails: to break their wings."[77]

of the Abbasid period characterised a man attracted to beardless boys as "his preference is the dwellers of Paradise" (*sharṭuhu ahl al-janna*); see al-Maydānī, *Amthāl* I, 492.

[76] al-Tawḥīdī, *Akhlāq* 185–6. For further examples of jokes based on the misinterpretation of *ḥadīths*, see al-Tawḥīdī, *Baṣāʾir* III(v), 107 [Juḥā attending a funeral]; III(vi), 78 [the Bedouin and his dog]; Ibn al-Jawzī, *Ẓirāf* 100 [Buhlūl snacking on the street], 116 [a Bedouin on the pilgrimage to Mecca], 143 [Faḍl, his wife and the sacrificial animals]; Yāqūt, *Udabāʾ* V, 2236–7 [a slave-girl's right to her master's penis]; Ibn Saʿīd, *Muqtaṭaf* 178 [the religious scholar buying a new sandal]. For a poem utilising a *ḥadīth*-based motif, see al-Thaʿālibī, *Thimār* I, 82 and al-Thaʿālibī, *Yatīma* IV, 328 [is the ruler God's shadow on the Earth?].

[77] It is very much like the author of this anti-*bidʿa* treatise to add with apparent relish that the cheerful anonymous protagonist was soon afflicted with a terrible calamity. See Ibn Baydakīn, *Lumaʿ* I, 179; and for a somewhat different version of the same anecdote (as recorded in the Buyid period, and minus the sanctimonious concluding comment), see al-Tawḥīdī, *Baṣāʾir* II(iii), 152.

In other cases, as I have indicated above, the cited *ḥadīth* is put in an inappropriate context, which creates a humorous contrast between two very dissimilar registers. The following story is taken from the same source as the previous one, and is obviously a joke – probably a scholarly one. The protagonist, as befits a joke, remains unnamed, but is significantly identified as a Maghrebi man, an archetypal boor in the metropolitan culture of the mediaeval Middle East. The joke makes a reference to the phenomenon of *al-ṭibb al-nabawī*, 'prophetic medicine', that is to say the medical use of the advice contained in a number of *ḥadīths*:

> A Maghrebi man had an inflammation of the eye, and he remembered this *ḥadīth*: "My community can expect a cure from three things: [the recitation of] a Quranic verse, or a spoonful of honey, or the scalpel of a bloodletter." Then the Maghrebi man recited a verse of the Quran, but his eye would not get better. He licked a bit of honey, and still it would not get better. Finally, he had an incision made [near his eye, to let blood], only to get an abscess. At this point, he said: "My beloved, God's messenger, if you know nothing about medicine, why will you meddle in it?"[78]

One finds a relatively limited number of *mujūn* texts containing pseudo-*ḥadīths* instead of genuine quotations. Such texts typically take the form of prose passages showing the characteristically pietistic tone of *ḥadīths* and their pedantic preoccupation with even trivial details, but those trivialities in the context of *mujūn* almost invariably turn out to be of an indecent or outright obscene nature.[79] Such texts are evidently parodistic, which takes us to our next topic.

2.4 Formal Features of Ḥadīths

While *mujūn* texts based on quotations from the *ḥadīths*, as I have argued, show no marked divergence in their logic from those using Quranic quotations (hence, perhaps, the use of the term *iqtibās* by Arabic literary critics for both varieties), there is also another, very special and unique type of *ḥadīth* motifs in *mujūn*. This

[78] Ibn Baydakīn, *Lumaʿ* I, 184–5.

[79] Here is an excerpt (a relatively more publishable, warm-up passage as it were) from the Perfumed Garden, a North African work composed around 813/1410–1 that obviously draws on much earlier material: "It has been transmitted from the Devil – God curse him! – and narrated on his authority that the decent woman will appear riding a [ghastly] bear on the Day of Judgement and sweating profusely, while a voice will cry, 'This is your punishment, oh you who occupied yourself with only one single dick [...]" (and so forth in the same style); see al-Nafzāwī, *Rawḍ* 51. A much earlier source, from the Buyid era, features an old man narrating a pseudo-*ḥadīth* of totally ridiculous purport in what appears to be, significantly, a 'folksy', uneducated accent. See al-Tawḥīdī, *Baṣāʾir* II(iv), 50. Despite the paucity, indeed almost total dearth, of other sources with data illuminating this issue, it might well be the case that such humour was present to some extent in the culture of the lower classes too, unless of course the use of a diction halfway between the vernacular and classical Arabic was simply an attempt to heighten the contrast between the lowly and lofty registers in these texts.

motif is based not on the contents of a *ḥadīth* – neither quoting from or alluding to the text of a particular *ḥadīth* – but on its most recognizable formal characteristic, namely the so-called *isnād* that must precede every trustworthy tradition from the Prophet Muḥammad to give it authority. For students of Arabic, the *isnād* is so familiar a feature that it needs no definition, but for non-specialists, a brief description will be in order. From the formal point of view, the *isnād* ('support') means a chain of authorities that starts with the name of the individual who narrated the account to the *ḥadīth* expert recording it and proceeds backwards in time through a sequence of names, in most cases terminating in the person of a companion of the Prophet, or the Prophet himself: "It was narrated to me by A, who had transmitted it from B, who had transmitted it from C", etc. After an initial period when the veracity of *ḥadīths* was not rigorously examined, an *isnād* – and a repectable one at that – soon came to be regarded a *sine qua non* of an acceptable *ḥadīth*, an absolute prerequisite for even considering the acceptability or otherwise of such a report about the Prophet's sayings and deeds.[80] In fact, *isnāds* might be used extensively in other genres of mediaeval Arabic writing too (e.g. in chronicles), but here we need not concern ourselves with that phenomenon.

Such a striking formal characteristic was bound to be utilised as a conceit in Arabic literature, and it was. This omnipresent feature of a religious discipline was transferred into literary texts with entirely 'secular' subject-matters, where its incongruity must have created an effect of playfulness and wit. Take, for instance, the following verses from an encomium on the Zīrid ruler Tamīm b. al-Muʿizz (454/1062–501/1108) by the celebrated Maghrebi littérateur Ibn Rashīq al-Qayrawānī (390/1000–463/1070–1):

> The most reliable and forceful accounts ever narrated to us concerning generosity are
> The *ḥadīths* narrated by the torrent, which transmitted it from modesty, which had transmitted it from the [inexhaustible] sea, which had transmitted it from the hand of the emir Tamīm.[81]

Almost inevitably, it was not only into such innocuous genres as praise-poems that *isnāds* would be transplanted but into genuine *mujūn* too. In fact, *isnāds* appear

---

[80] On the importance of *isnāds*, see for instance al-Samʿānī, *Adab* 4–7.

[81] Owing to the Western reader's unfamiliarity with the formulae of *ḥadīths* as well as the usual Arabic metaphors for generosity, it is well nigh impossible to convey the elegance and playfulness of the original, which reads: "*Aṣaḥḥu wa-aqwā mā ruwīnā fī l-nadā ʿani l-khabari l-maʾthūri mundhu qadīmi/Aḥādīthu tarwīhā l-suyūlu ʿani l-ḥayā ʿani l-baḥri ʿan kaffī l-amīri Tamīmi.*" See Ibn Diḥya, *Muṭrib* 58, and Ibn Maʿṣūm, *Sulāfa* 50 (citing this and a similar but later piece). For further examples of the use of *isnād* as a literary conceit, see al-Thaʿālibī, *Khāṣṣ* 70; al-Tawḥīdī [attr.], *Risāla* 326; al-Washshāʾ, *Muwashshā* 113; Yāqūt, *Udabāʾ* VI, 2659; al-Ibshīhī, *Mustaṭraf* 277; al-Ṣafadī, *Tawshīḥ* 181; Ibn Maʿṣūm, *Sulāfa* 511.

even in quite provocative and outrageous texts, of which a good example is the following impromptu poem by Muḥammad b. Munādhir (d. 198/813), a famous *mājin* poet of the early Abbasid period. Noticing a beautiful lad in a Baṣra mosque, he propositioned by appealing to a *ḥadīth*, which, needless to point out, had never existed, although the authorities in the *isnād* had been real, existing scholars:

> I have found in the traditions, as part of what the [authorities of] old transmitted to us by way of well-supported *ḥadīths* (*al-musnad*),
> And what al-Aʿmash transmitted from Jābir, ʿĀmir al-Shaʿbī and al-Aswad,
> And what Shuʿba transmitted from ʿĀṣim and what Ḥammād narrated on the authority of Farqad;
> As an admonition to the owners of all cheeks not yet sprouting a black beard:
> They should welcome all who desire intercourse with them. Welcome me, then, for I have no intention of self-restraint.
> [...][82]

The parodistic transplantation of the *isnād* into literary texts can be observed in prose as well as poetry. Perhaps because of the obvious difficulty of adapting a sequence of common names to metre and rhyme, one perhaps encounters it more frequently in prose, where no comparable mastery is needed to fit it into the text. The following anecdotes or jokes, the first of which is one of the best-known pieces of the mediaeval Arabic joke repertoire, exemplify the use of this motif in prose:

> Abū Muḥammad al-Shīrajī, who was one of the witty jurisprudents of Baghdad (*kāna min ẓurafāʾ al-fuqahāʾ bi-Baghdādh*), was travelling on a boat together with a wealthy Christian. When [the latter] brought forth his dinner, he invited [the jurisprudent] to share [the meal], which he did. Having finished eating, [the Christian] had some wine brough to him, which was [as red] as a cock's eye and [as fragrant] as musk. [Abū Muḥammad al-Shīrajī] wanted to come up with some acceptable excuse [to partake of the Christian's wine too], so he asked: "What is this?" [The other] replied: "It is wine bought by my servant from a Jew." Thereupon [the jurisprudent] said: "Why, we experts of *ḥadīth* regard as liars [even such pious authorities as] Sufyān b. ʿUyayna and Yazīd b. Hārūn; are we now supposed to trust a Christian who transmitted [the information] from his servant, who transmitted it from a Jew? By God, the only reason I drink it is because of the weakness of the *isnād*." And he reached for the cup, filled it and drank [the wine].[83]

---

[82] al-Iṣfahānī, *Aghānī* XVIII, 214–5. For a similar but much longer specimen attributed to Abū Nuwās, see Abū Hiffān, *Akhbār* 97–8; and also see Ibn Manẓūr, *Akhbār* 129–30. Abū Nuwās was apparently fond of this motif, judging by the number of poems employing it in Abū Nuwās, *Dīwān* V, 237–43 (and also see Wagner 2008: 86).

[83] al-Thaʿālibī, *Laṭāʾif* 66–7; and in a slightly different wording in al-Thaʿālibī, *Khāṣṣ* 61. In the latter source, the protagonist's name appears as al-Sarjī; and in fact elsewhere the same story displays more of a usual joke format, with an unidentified *ḥadīth* scholar for a protagonist; see for instance al-Ibshīhī, *Mustaṭraf* 527. Another anecdote I have come across cannot but have originated in highly

> Once a *ḥadīth* expert was told by his son: "Father, X has told me that Y had told him that he loathed me." To this his father replied: "Then, my son, you are loathsome by [force of] an *isnād*."[84]

> Once Ashʿab was told: "You have had lots of sessions in the company of [learned] people in pursuit of knowledge; would you care to sit for a while in our company [to share your knowledge]?" So he sat down [with them], and [his interlocutors] asked him: "Transmit your *ḥadīths*." So he started: "I have heard it narrated by ʿIkrima, who said that he had heard it from Ibn ʿAbbās, who said that he had heard it from God's messenger [Muḥammad]: '[There are] two traits that cannot be found together in [anyone worthy of the name of] a believer'..." And here he stopped. They asked him: "What are those two traits?" Said Ashʿab: "One was forgotten by ʿIkrima, the other by me."[85]

The following grotesque pseudo-*ḥadīth* is typical, as the reader will by now recognise, in combining a preposterous directive with an earnest (if in this case not too elaborate) *isnād*. This parodistic text comes from the Buyid period, and appears to me to be a recorded version of a spoken witticism. If so, it would be yet another example of the tendency, already noted, for many spoken quips to become repeated by others and finally migrate to written literature:

> I have heard it from Abū Ṭalḥa al-Ḥadhdhāʾ, who said: "X said, who had transmitted it from Y" – here a long *isnād* followed – "that whoever wakes up on the morning of a Saturday having some amber-coloured *ṭabāhija*[86] at home and having easy access to a seller of fava bean purée (*bāqillānī*), and, despite this, will not start drinking wine – may God never give such a man a happy and wholesome morning!"[87]

The motif of parodistic *isnāds* has apparently survived in later periods too. And as a final example to round off this section, the no less grotesque text that follows is an excerpt from the Perfumed Garden, a relatively late work which nevertheless seems to incorporate a lot of earlier material. Here one observes a mock *isnād* composed of a series of calculatedly comical names – indeed, the last name is a sexually suggestive one – followed by an atrocious communication:

---

educated and literate circles, based as it is on the ever-present possibility of misreading names in an *isnād*. According to this story, for all the pedantry characteristic of *ḥadīth* specialists, one such expert misread the phrase *ʿan Allāh ʿazza wa-jalla* ('from God the Most Powerful and Almighty") as *ʿan Allāh ʿan rajul* ("from God [who transmitted it] from a man"), an egregious and utterly inconceivable mistake for a religious scholar but not entirely impossible spellingwise. See al-ʿAskarī, *Akhbār* 63.

84 al-Thaʿālibī, *Khāṣṣ* 71.

85 Ibn al-Jawzī, *Ẓirāf* 63. (And see Franz Rosenthal's English translation in Rosenthal 1956: 117.) For another joke starring Ashʿab and based on parodying the *ḥadīth* format, see al-Thaʿālibī, *Thimār* I, 262.

86 A meal based on meat, eggs and onions.

87 al-Tanūkhī, *Nishwār* II, 204.

> Abū Bilāl has narrated this, who had transmitted it from Sharīk b. Barīk, who had transmitted it from Salhab b. Malhab, who had transmitted it from Zinṭāḥ b. al-Naṭṭāḥ b. Abī l-Afrāḥ, who had said this concerning the accepted custom: "Kissing and cuddling will not satisfy a lover, unless he can also fuck [...]"[88]

Observing the use of mock *isnāds* in mediaeval Arabic literature, one cannot escape the realisation of the importance of parody in *mujūn* texts.[89] Parody, which will recur as an essential element of many motifs of *mujūn*, is especially important for the next category of motifs to be surveyed, the use of the *termini technici* of the religious disciplines for purely literary purposes. In fact, the highly technical sense of the preposition *ʿan* ('[transmitted] from', as in an *isnād*) may be regarded as one example of the general tendency of the literature of *mujūn* to appropriate the phrases, expressions, and terminology of the 'serious' branches of literature and scholarship and put them to its own parodistic uses. This tendency will be even more pronounced, and hard to avoid noticing, in the following section of this essay.

3. The Stuff of a Sound Education: Religious Disciplines, Theology, and Islamic History

3.1 The Terminology of the Religious Disciplines

Ḥadīths having been the subject of the previous part of this chapter, it will be appropriate to dwell some more on this important product of mediaeval Islamic culture. The reason to do so is that the study of *ḥadīths* among mediaeval Muslims did not stop at collecting and recording a vast number of them, and, correspondingly, neither did the utilisation of *ḥadīths* in *mujūn* literature stop at quoting from them and mimicking their chains of authority. Serious *ḥadīth* scholarship branched off into various subsidiary disciplines, including the all-important study of the reliability of particular *ḥadīth* transmitters (*ʿilm al-rijāl, al-jarḥ wa-l-taʿdīl*). Licentious literature was not slow to incorporate the parodistic use of the specialised vocabulary of this pedantic, meticulous discipline into its repertoire, which resulted in a profusion of puns and all kinds of *double entendre*.[90] All this playful linguistic jugglery, naturally,

[88] This much I consider sufficient here for a sample, but the text goes on and on. See al-Nafzāwī, *Rawḍ* 64. Not incidentally, the most likely original of this prose text is, I believe, a poem by or attributed to Abū Nuwās, the text of which is surprisingly similar to this passage in al-Nafzāwī's book (providing a good example of the movement of *mujūn* motifs across genres and historical periods). See al-Rāghib, *Muḥāḍarāt* III, 515.

[89] That parody is an essential property of *mujūn* is stressed in Meisami 1993: 23–4.

[90] E.g. al-Ibshīhī, *Mustaṭraf* 275, 488. The know-how for inventing such puns seems not to have disappeared in later periods, as attested by a 11th/17th-century example in Ibn Maʿṣūm, *Sulāfa* 58,

does not yield itself to translation into another language, at least not into a Western language that did not borrow its technical terms from Arabic.

However, *ḥadīth* scholarship was not the only branch of the religious sciences to provide linguistic material to utilise or parody in *mujūn* literature. An even more copious source of technical terms on which to base *doubles entendres* was the field of Islamic law, or *fiqh*, as were theology and Muslim philosophy. Obviously, much if not all of this jesting must have been intelligible only to the erudite, as the *termini technici* in question were certainly unknown to an illiterate and uneducated person. Perhaps common people could pick up a limited number of such terms – especially legal terms – in such settings as the court of a *qāḍī*, but it is reasonable to suppose that this particular variety of motifs in *mujūn* literature was largely the preserve of those with sufficient education to appreciate this relatively sophisticated brand of wit. In fact, some intellectuals with a special interest in theology did transfer their knowledge of serious terminology to their lighter poetry too, even if this practice alone does not qualify their products as representative of *mujūn*.[91] Actually, the use of the terminology and ways of argumentation of logic and theology in profane texts – such as love poetry – came to be recognised as a poetic device, and was known as *al-madhhab al-kalāmī* ('theological procedure', 'theological tendency') among mediaeval literary critics and theorists.[92] It must be emphasised, however, that definitely not all – probably only very few – examples of the application of *al-madhhab al-kalāmī* would be classified as *mujūn* by the mediaeval critics. (Here is one area in which the boundaries of *mujūn* appear to be very fluid, and one hesitates to decide just how much frivolity is needed for such a label to be applied with justification.) The playful use of the concepts and terms of religious law in secular poetry (mostly love poems) was another poetic conceit; poems based on this trope were sometimes referred to as *fiqhiyyāt*.[93] Again, the sophisticated wit – at any rate, intended wit – of texts based on the transferring of the terms of jurisprudence into jestful literature is simply impossible to convey in translation.[94]

---

and even one from 20th-century Yemen (which puns with the name of the celebrated *ḥadīth* specialist al-Bukhārī); see Messick 1993: 268 [note 29].

[91] The renowned Muʿtazilī theologian Ibrāhīm al-Naẓẓām (d. ca. 230/845), for instance, is said to have had this habit; see Ibn al-Muʿtazz, *Ṭabaqāt* 129.

[92] Ibn Ḥijja, *Khizāna* II, 453–7; Ibn al-Muʿtazz, *Badīʿ* 147; al-Qazwīnī, *Īḍāḥ* VI, 65–6; al-ʿAskarī, *Ṣināʿatayn* 426–7. For an analysis of *al-madhhab al-kalāmī*, see Bauer 1998: 126–34.

[93] On the term itself, and for several examples composed by Abū l-Fatḥ al-Bustī, a poet of the Buyid period, see al-Thaʿālibī, *Yatīma* IV, 312.

[94] For various examples, see al-Ṣūlī, *Akhbār* 77 [*tawḥīd*, *farḍ*]; al-Tawḥīdī, *Baṣāʾir* I(ii), 98 and al-Ibshīhī, *Mustaṭraf* 531 [*janāba*]; Ibn Rashīq, *Qurāḍa* 88–90 [*ightisāl*]. A poem by the famous Egyptian poet Ibn Nubāta (d. 768/1366), full as it is of puns based on the names of the various Sunni legal schools, is utterly untranslatable but quite worth reading in the original: "*Tafaqqahtu fī ʿishqī lahu mithla mā ghadā khabīran bi-aḥkāmi l-khilāfi yujādilu; / Fa-yā mālikī mā ḍarra law kunta shāfiʿī bi-*

Jesting with the concepts and terms of religious law did not always take the form of puns. A not infrequent type of anecdote portays a pedantic, self-important scholar of jurisprudence who is approached by someone seeking advice on a dilemma, but the question posed is obviously an absurdical one. Obviously to everyone except the scholar himself, and that is the point of such anecdotes: the scholar takes parodistic questions – deliberate nonsense employing the style and terms of *fiqh* – in all seriousness, and tries to figure out an answer to them.[95] (More will be said about joking at the expense of the scholarly class in Chapter Three.) In other instances, while the absurdical use of terminology is retained as the essential element of the story, it is a stupid and ignorant man who poses an asinine question and it is the *faqīh* who, by giving a deliberately nonsensical answer, turns it into a parody.[96] Here is what I consider to be a typical example:

> ʿUthmān al-Ṣaydalānī narrated this: I was present when, on a holiday, Ibrāhīm al-Ḥarbī was called on by a weaver[97], who inquired of him: "Ibrāhīm, what is your counsel regarding a man who has carried out the prayer of the holiday without having first bought some sweetmeats[98]? What's he got to do [in penitence]?" Smiling, Ibrāhīm said: "He has to [distribute] two dirhams' worth of bread as alms." And with [the weaver] gone, he added: "What harm will it do to gladden the poor at the expense of this idiot?"[99]

Interestingly, the motif of consulting a jurisprudent of established piety on a decidedly secular concern and ask for a legal opinion (*fatwā*) from him also occurs in mediaeval Arabic poetry as a witty conceit. In these cases, the motif tends to appear free of

---

waṣlika fa-ʾfʿal bī ka-mā anta fāʿilu; / Fa-innī ḥanīfiyyu l-hawā mutaḥanbilun bi-ʿishqika lā uṣghī wa-in qāla qāʾilu." See al-Ibshīhī, *Mustaṭraf* 446–7.

[95] E.g. al-Jāḥiẓ, *Ḥayawān* I, 366, al-Rāghib, *Muḥāḍarāt* III, 508. (The latter source evidently and explicitly classifies such texts as being *mujūn*, more precisely the even more drastic variety known as *sukhf*: "*al-Mustaftī fī sawʾatihi ʿāliman sukhfan*".) Al-Jāḥiẓ, incidentally, admits his excessive predilection for the absurd nonsense of people debating scholarly topics – notably, theology – that they are totally ignorant of (a kind of unintended parody if you will). See al-Jāḥiẓ, *Ḥayawān* I, 365. – A far more sophisticated manifestation of the deliberately ambiguous use of *fiqh* terminology is the series of inquiries presented in the extraordinary tour-de-force of one of al-Ḥarīrī's (446/1054–516/1122) celebrated *maqāmas*; see al-Ḥarīrī, *Maqāmāt* 332–47.

[96] E.g. Ibn al-Marzubān, *Dhamm* 91; al-Tawḥīdī, *Baṣāʾir* II(iv), 138–9; al-Tawḥīdī, *Imtāʿ* 198; Ibn al-Jawzī, *Ẓirāf* 102–3; al-Rāghib, *Muḥāḍarāt* III, 519; al-Ibshīhī, *Mustaṭraf* 533; van Gelder 1992: 171; and also cf. a story which may or may not have been meant in jest (I rather think it was not) in Ibn al-Jawzī, *Talbīs* 138.

[97] A weaver's trade was a despised one, and weavers often stand in mediaeval Arabic texts as the epitome of stupidity.

[98] The original has the noun *nāṭif*, which was a kind of soft sweetmeat (presumably customary fare on the day of the *ʿīd*), but I have been unable to identify it more precisely. The *Lisān al-ʿarab* gives an eminently circular definition, equating *nāṭif* to *qubbayṭ*, and then defining *qubbayṭ* as the equivalent of *nāṭif*. See Ibn Manẓūr, *Lisān* VI, 209; V, 191.

[99] al-Tawḥīdī, *Baṣāʾir* II(iv), 139.

any palpable malice, being simply a jestful, playful flight of fancy. Typically, one finds it used in love poetry, with the poet's persona citing, in a joking tone, some famous religious scholar's fictitious verdict declaring it licit to yearn for or steal a kiss from one's beloved.[100]

The unswerving concern of *fiqh* experts with deciding which practices are to be regarded as licit (*ḥalāl*) and illicit (*ḥarām*) respectively, as well as establishing a meticulous system of gradations between these clear-cut categories, also proved to be an inspiration and a source of 'raw material' for jesting in the *mujūn* vein. It is perhaps little wonder that the pedantic and often preposterously pernickety discourse of the *fuqahā'* should invite parody. The attempts by jurisprudents at categorising new objects and practices to place them within the framework of this system is the point of an apparently popular joke, which portrays a religious scholar making the verdict, a patent parody of the characteristic *fiqh* style, that "people are of various opinions regarding the [licitness or otherwise of] singing (*samāʿ*), with some of them permitting it and some considering it prohibited; however, I oppose both groups and say that it is obligatory."[101] Another *mujūn* anecdote based on the jurisprudents' system of precise gradations between the extremes of unequivocally permitted and unequivocally forbidden is one that relies on a caricature of the concept of *makrūh*. In its proper legal sense, *makrūh* might be translated as 'disapproved', referring to an act that is not explicitly prohibited but which it is meritorious to avoid. Committing such an act is not punished by God yet avoiding it is rewarded by Him. It is this legal term that the story utilises:

> The nephew of [the governor] Nawfal b. Musāḥiq was brought to justice after he made a girl in the neighbourhood pregnant. [Nawfal] said to him: "Oh you enemy of God, if you insisted on such atrocious misconduct, couldn't you just practice *coitus interruptus*?" [His nephew] replied: " But my brother, I've heard

[100] See several examples of the motif in al-Washshā', *Muwashshā* 107–9; and also Abū Nuwās, *Dīwān* V, 215–6; al-Thaʿālibī, *Tatimma* II, 55; Ibn Saʿīd, *Ghuṣūn* 148; al-Ḥillī, *ʿĀṭil* 117 [where one finds the motif in a vernacular poem]. On the procedure of asking for a *fatwā* in real life, cf. for instance Messick 1993: 136.

[101] al-Thaʿālibī, *Laṭā'if* 81; al-Thaʿālibī, *Khāṣṣ* 63; al-Tawḥīdī, *Baṣā'ir* II(iv), 33. For a joke along the same logic but far more vulgar in meaning ("*mā taqūlu fī l-qabḍ*" etc.), see al-Rāghib, *Muḥāḍarāt* III, 492. For yet another joke on the concept of *ḥalāl*, see al-Tawḥīdī, *Baṣā'ir* I(ii), 134; and for the same as a poetic motif, see Ibn al-Muʿtazz, *Badīʿ* 136; al-Thaʿālibī, *Iʿjāz* 156; Ibn al-Kattānī, *Tashbīhāt* 141. – The concept of 'permitted sorcery' (*al-siḥr al-ḥalāl*; sorcery normally being considered absolutely blameworthy in Islamic law) was a widespread motif in Arabic poetry not classifiable as *mujūn*, and interestingly the phrase, which is used as a metaphor of eloquence and linguistic mastery, seems to originate in a *ḥadīth*. See for instance al-Tawḥīdī [attr.], *Risāla* 200; al-Zawzanī, *Ḥamāsa* II, 83; Ibn Saʿīd, *Muqtaṭaf* 117; al-Ḥillī, *ʿĀṭil* 194; Ibn al-Khaṭīb, *Jaysh* 73. – Not surprisingly, the applications of the *sharīʿa* are a favourite topic of modern Arabic dialectal jokes too; see for instance Ibrahim 1994: 38–40; and on the theme of religious prescriptions in the lyrics of the contemporary North African musical genre *rai*, see Virolle-Souibès 1989: 48.

that onanism is *disapproved* (*makrūh*)." [Nawfal] said: "And haven't you heard that fornication is *prohibited*?"[102]

The following joke also caricatures a concept of jurisprudence, this time that of *qadhf*, 'calumny' (primarily understood to mean a false accusation of adultery against a chaste and virtuous woman, and subject to serious sanctions under Islamic law):

> There was a man of our neighbourhood in Baghdad who had [an adulterous relationship] with the wife of one of his neighbours. One night, having mounted her and fucking her (*ʿalāhā yaḥshūhā*),[103] he says to her: "You woman, do you know people keep saying things about us?" The woman replied: "And what harm will it do to you if they do such a sin [of slander], while you'll be rewarded by God?" Said the man, busy in his doings: "God the Most High will be the judge of all false [calumniators]."[104]

Mediaeval Arabic literature, especially poetry, teems with motifs borrowed from Islamic jurisprudence. In many cases, it is questionable whether the mere presence of such conceits signified *mujūn* for mediaeval Arabic-speaking intellectuals, and I rather think most of the motifs to be discussed in the remainder of this section would not have qualified for such a label. Yet one has to note again that the exact boundaries of *mujūn* were not easily delineable, and personal preferences, tastes and views must have played a great part in a person's understanding of what constitutes licentious or indecent literary material. Outrage was in the eye of the beholder.

A veritable commonplace of Arabic love poetry is the suggestion that the beloved person, by his or her indifference to or outright rejection of the lover's advances, causes the untimely death of the latter, and thus effectively kills him. Pushing this hackneyed expression a step further, many poets sought to appear witty by engaging in rhetorical speculations on the possible legal consequences of such an act of manslaughter. The simple version of this theme would just allude to the proper punishment for homicide (viz. execution), while more sophisticated examples considered the legal significance of the poet's having been a willing slave of the beloved anyway (the sanction for killing a slave being less severe than that for a free person), and indeed might even bring in other circumstances to the full

---

102 al-Tawḥīdī, *Baṣāʾir* I(i), 183; in a slightly different version in al-Ibshīhī, *Mustaṭraf* 167; and in a quite different wording in Ibn al-Muʿtazz, *Ṭabaqāt* 180–1; al-Rāghib, *Muḥāḍarāt* III, 519. Another joke shows a very similar logic in that it features a prostitute who is willing to allow her customer to engage in regular intercourse with her but declines to kiss him because of it taking place during Ramadan, the month of fasting (and, to be sure, of sexual abstinence). See al-Tawḥīdī, *Baṣāʾir* II(iii), 181.

103 The expression is extremely obscene as well as slang.

104 al-Tawḥīdī, *Baṣāʾir* I(ii), 86.

consideration of the 'legal' case.[105] Just like homicide, wine drinking was also subject – in theory if usually not in practice – to a divinely ordained punishment (i.e. one mentioned in the Quran), called *ḥadd* in Arabic. The standard punishment for drinking wine was usually thought to be eighty lashes, which gave rise to the poetic concetto that the poet's persona, drinking together with his beloved, subjects him to the legally applicable number of kisses (*al-ḥadd min al-qubal*) as a sanction for his inebriation.[106] Other areas of religious law that provided material for jesting literary motifs included the regulation of marriage and bridewealth (*mahr*)[107]; the compulsory waiting period to be observed by a woman before remarriage (*ʿidda*) and the Islamic laws of inheritance[108]; and the religiously loaded concept of reprehensible (and in some cases acceptable) innovations (*bidʿa*)[109]. More than one poet used the term *jihād* (holy war) to refer jestingly to committing sodomy with

---

[105] For some examples both in verse and prose, see Ibn al-Muʿtazz, *Ṭabaqāt* 75; al-Thaʿālibī, *Yatīma* I, 90; II, 80; al-Washshāʾ, *Muwashshā* 109–12; al-Iṣbahānī, *Kharīda* I(ii), 56; Ibn Diḥya, *Muṭrib* 50–1. In the last example, an infinitely sophisticated love poem by Yaʿmur al-Khawlānī, one finds as varied categories of Islamic jurisprudence brought into play as homicide, perjury, manumission of slaves, and amends for damages. – A 11th/17th-century anthology offers an example of the continuing use of the motif that we are discussing: "Concerning [the spilling of] my blood you should ask [the lady] with the anklets and the necklace: why did she see it licit deliberately to take my soul? / She has escaped the sanction of execution, as it has been stated that a free person would not be killed in compensation for a slave." See Ibn Maʿṣūm, *Sulāfa* 22. – Similar in logic to this motif is another that applies the legal concept of retaliation for physical injury (*qiṣāṣ*), cited from the Quran, in the context of amorous poetry; see al-Thaʿālibī, *Iqtibās* II, 172–3. – Another popular poetic cliché, that of considering someone who has died of unrequited love to be a martyr (*shahīd*, a word with strong religious overtones in Islam as in Christianity), seems to have been based on a *ḥadīth* attributed to the Prophet Muḥammad. For its uses in poetry, see for instance al-Thaʿālibī, *Yatīma* I, 56 and Abū Firās, *Dīwān* 110; al-Washshāʾ, *Muwashshā* 112–3; al-Zawzanī, *Ḥamāsa* II, 123; al-Ṣafadī, *Tawshīḥ* 71; Ibn al-Khaṭīb, *Jaysh* 118. Incidentally, the theme of martyrdom could be utilised in more outrageous ways too (hence, more unambiguously as the stuff of *mujūn*). A phrase recorded in the Buyid period describes a proficient singer by stating that "getting drunk while/by listening to his voice is [equivalent to] martyrdom"; see al-Tawḥīdī [attr.], *Risāla* 188, and al-Thaʿālibī, *Thimār* I, 269. In a lovely, ironic joke, a man is asked if he has any aspirations to the glory of dying a martyr in the campaign he takes part in. He signals his pious determination in the following words: "Yes, [I swear] by Him whom I beseech to return me safely to you." See al-Tawḥīdī, *Baṣāʾir* IV(vii), 163.

[106] E.g. al-Thaʿālibī, *Laṭāʾif* 106; al-Zawzanī, *Ḥamāsa* II, 100. This jestful application of the concept of *ḥadd* seems to have originated in the spoken language – or at any rate used in speech too. See al-Iṣfahānī, *Aghānī* IV, 280.

[107] See for instance an anecdote about the famous wit of the early Abbasid period al-Jammāz ("*qad ḥaruma l-liwāṭ illā bi-walī wa-shāhidayn*") in al-Rāghib, *Muḥāḍarāt* III, 478; as well as some rather recherché poems from the 11th/17th century presenting the mixing of wine with water as a marriage that demands the surrender of the drinker's sobriety as the adequate brideprice; in Ibn Maʿṣūm, *Sulāfa* 298, 560.

[108] Ibn al-Jawzī, *Ẓirāf* 145; al-Ibshīhī, *Mustaṭraf* 276.

[109] E.g. al-Thaʿālibī, *Yatīma* III, 21; al-Thaʿālibī, *Khāṣṣ* 72; al-Bākharzī, *Dumya* I, 294; II, 764; Ibn al-Jawzī, *Ẓirāf* 86–7; al-Ḥillī, *ʿĀṭil* 183; Ibn Zaydūn, *Dīwān* 413; Ibn al-Khaṭīb, *Jaysh* 77.

non-Muslim boys, and *islām* ('Islam' or 'converting to Islam', but literally 'submission' [to God's will]) to the submissive role of the latter vis-à-vis the Muslim male during intercourse.[110]

As is well known, the tradition of jurisprudence among the Sunnis, who have always constituted the vast majority of Muslims, has been divided into four main legal schools – in addition to a number of less important ones like the *Ẓāhiriyya* – and the various Shiᶜite subgroups also have their own legal traditions. Every legal school (*madhhab*, pl. *madhāhib*) has come to predominate in certain geographical regions, but this has never meant a total absence of the other schools in any region. In particular, urban centres tended to be populated by the followers of more than one *madhhab*, which resulted in a degree of awareness on the part of even ordinary people of the existence of various different legal traditions with often strikingly different regulations for certain domains of social life. What is more important for our present purpose is that those differences were frequently remarkable enough to give fodder for littérateurs searching for witty motifs. It was widely known, for instance, that the *Ḥanafite* school permitted the consumption of date wine and other liquors labelled *nabīdh* (as opposed to grape wine, *khamr*) as long as one did not reach the degree of intoxication, whereas the rest of the legal schools forbade all types of wine-like beverages in any amount whatsoever. Equally well-known was the insistence of the Mālikite school on the permissibility of anal intercourse with one's wife and concubines, in stark contrast to the prohibition thereof by all the other schools. Predictably, such legal differences would end up being the theme of many poems and jokes.[111]

Given the religious diversity of the great cities of the mediaeval Middle East, it was inevitable that some of the notions and practices of the minority religions should also appear in Arabic secular prose and poetry. This is not to deny that most motifs of *mujūn* literature that have to do with religion draw their inspiration from Islam – a reflection of the fact that most poets and writers of Arabic were Muslim and far more familiar with the terminology and traditions of their own religion than with any other – yet the occasional jesting reference to Christianity, Judaism and Zoroastrianism attests to an awareness of some features of the other faiths too. In particular, the Christian identity of many of the boys to whom love poetry was addressed – an unsurprising circumstance, considering the popularity of monasteries and Christian-run taverns as places of drinking parties – would sometimes give rise

110 Wright 1997: 9–10.

111 E.g. al-Thaᶜālibī, *Yatīma* I, 313; II, 9; al-Thaᶜālibī, *Thimār* I, 291–2; al-Tawḥīdī [attr.], *Risāla* 51; al-Zawzanī, *Ḥamāsa* II, 225; al-Rāghib, *Muḥāḍarāt* III, 522; and Wagner 2008: 106–7. On the above-mentioned peculiarities of the Ḥanafite and Mālikite schools of law, see Ibn Hubayra, *Ikhtilāf* II, 145, 292–5; al-Ṭabarī, *Ikhtilāf* II, 124–5.

to a variety of literary witticisms and frivolous motifs about Christian tenets, most notably the Trinity.[112] A less typical reference to Christianity is a *bon mot* attributed to Abū Nuwās (and indeed not unlike him), who identified his Trinity – and by implication the object of his devotion, highly unbecoming for a Muslim – as being composed of the Grape, the Wine and the Raisin.[113]

As has already been noted with regard to various other literary motifs, there seems to have been no rigid boundary between the high register of written literature in classical Arabic and everyday speech. Some motifs seem to have migrated between the two linguistic registers and sociological milieus, and while it is usually hard if not impossible to decide the direction in which a particular motif drifted – whether from writing to speech or vice versa – it remains a valid observation that it is reported from both. In fact, it is striking and potentially significant that the Baghdadian Epistle, a work that appears deliberately to mimic the slang of Baghdad in the Buyid period, offers an unusual wealth of witticisms based on references to theology and religious law. One such passage offers the description of a virtuoso drummer by an enthusiastic member of his audience, who insists: "We must listen to the sound of this drum; we should not make a sentence in absentia; we should not decide [the genuineness of a claimant's] prophecy until we see the evidence: if his proofs are evident, we believe him; if not, we regard him a reprobate...".[114] Whilst I do not wish to pursue this point any further here, it will be worth noting – and here I anticipate some of the findings of Chapter Four – that one complaint against the common people constantly recurring in the writings of ultra-pious scholars is that they enjoyed mocking and parodying the discourse of the learned (the *ʿulamāʾ*) and appreciated the performance of those who were especially good at doing so.

112 E.g. al-Tanūkhī, *Nishwār* IV, 266–75; al-Thaʿālibī, *Yatīma* I, 360. For further examples of poetic motifs derived from religions other than Islam, see al-Thaʿālibī, *Yatīma* II, 259 [motifs from the tenets of various religions]; al-Thaʿālibī, *Tatimma* II, 73–4 [Trinity, and the Dualism of the Manichaeans]; Ibn Diḥya, *Muṭrib* 105 [the Sabbath in Judaism]. The fire cult of Zoroastrians was apparently colourful enough to fascinate Muslim poets and provide them with material for literary motifs; see for instance al-Zawzanī, *Ḥamāsa* II, 113; al-Iṣbahānī, *Kharīda* II(ii), 493; Ibn Saʿīd, *Rāyāt* 171; Ibn al-Kattānī, *Tashbīhāt* 169–70. In a witty saying quoted from Abū Tammām (190/806–232/846), even the names of pre-Islamic goddesses (*al-Lāt* and *al-ʿUzzā*) appear in an ironic sense, but this can arguably be regarded as an example of familiarity with the Quran, which also mentions these false deities (Quran 53:19). See the anecdote in Ibn al-Muʿtazz, *Ṭabaqāt* 134.

113 al-Tawḥīdī, *Baṣāʾir* II(iv), 141. Abū Nuwās seems to have had a thorough familiarity with Christian religious terminology, which he masterfully utilised in his poetry; see Montgomery 1996: 115, 123–4.

114 The original reads: "*fa-dhā ṭabl lā budd min an nasmaʿa ṣawtahu; lā naḥkumu ʿalā ghāʾib; lā naḥkumu bi-l-nubuwwa ḥattā narā l-dalāla in ittaḍaḥa burhānuhu ṣaddaqnā wa-illā fassaqnā* "; see al-Tawḥīdī [attr.], *Risāla* 67. The part about making no judgement in absentia appears in several jokes; see for instance Marzolph 1992: II, 19.

3.2 Motifs Borrowed from the History of Islam

The names and careers of outstanding personalities who had had a formative impact, or a momentous role, in the history of the early Islamic polity were an integral part of the body of knowledge that had crystallised as a sort of general erudition that a Muslim intellectual was expected to possess in the Abbasid era. Such names and data as the most prominent Companions of the Prophet Muḥammad, the Battle of Ṣiffīn, the proverbially debauched and impious figure of al-Walīd b. Yazīd (Umayyad caliph, r. 125–6/743–4), and so on, were probably known even to a man of average education, having simply become a part of the popular mythology of early Islamic times. Supposing that this was indeed so, one will have to consider the strange wording of the following passage, designed to resemble a scolding delivered in a markedly conversational style, to have been perfectly natural for an urban speaker of Abbasid times. The text contains a series of references to the most tragic events of early Islamic history:

> You've tried to oppose the Quran with poems, broken the molars of God's Messenger [Muḥammad], dug up the tomb [of the imam al-Ḥusayn], set up trebuchets against the Kaʿba [sanctuary], [...], beheaded al-Ḥusayn b. ʿAlī, cut off the hand of Jaʿfar b. Abī Ṭālib, eaten the liver of Ḥamza [b. ʿAbd al-Muṭṭalib], torn apart the skin blessed by the hand of God. You worthless man, what makes you laugh (*yā mudbir min ēsh taḍḥak*)?[115]

As far as Classical Arabic, the 'high' literary register of the caliphate, is concerned, there is an ample amount of data showing that poets and writers, fishing for witticisms and literary motifs, would regularly draw upon an established body of historical knowledge about the early Islamic past, such as some episodes of the life of Muḥammad, the civil wars of the first century of the Hegira, the ruthless governorship in Iraq of al-Ḥajjāj b. Yūsuf, and even some events and cultural facts of pre-Islamic Arabia.[116] The bitter controversies and strife of the various sects and theological schools are likewise reflected in the repertoire of motifs in secular literature, both jokes and humorous poetry.[117] A fine example is the following joke, the point of

---

[115] al-Tawḥīdī [attr.], *Risāla* 85–7. The text is referring, respectively, to the appearance in Arabia of false prophets after Muḥammad, the battle of Uḥud, the destruction of Shiʿite shrines by the Abbasid caliph al-Mutawakkil (r. 232/847–247/861), the civil war in the new Islamic state, the battle of Karbalāʾ, the battle of Muʾta, the battle of Badr, and the murdering of the caliph ʿUmar b. al-Khaṭṭāb (r. 13/634–23/644). These are, of course, fairly well known episodes of early Islamic history, but judging from a popular saying recorded in al-Maydānī, *Amthāl* I, 167, even such details of the career of the Prophet Muḥammad as the name of his donkey and his mule must have been widely known among the populace.

[116] E.g. al-Thaʿālibī, *Yatīma* II, 210; III, 49; IV, 239, 324; al-Thaʿālibī, *Thimār* I, 131, 476; al-Thaʿālibī, *Iʿjāz* 116; al-Tawḥīdī, *Akhlāq* 228; al-Zawzanī, *Ḥamāsa* II, 21; al-Bākharzī, *Dumya* I, 389; al-Ibshīhī, *Mustaṭraf* 506[in a dialectal poem from mediaeval Egypt]; al-Ḥillī, *ʿĀṭil* 175; Ibn al-Kattānī, *Tashbīhāt* 50, 277; Ibn Saʿīd, *Muqtaṭaf* 89; Ibn Rashīq, *Qurāḍa* 55–6.

[117] E.g. al-Iṣfahānī, *Aghānī* IV, 276 [the controversy of a Shīʿite and a Murjiʾite]; al-ʿAskarī, *Maṣūn*

which is based on the tragic and relentless tension between Shiᶜites and Sunnis in late Buyid-era Baghdad (and onwards), which cannot fail to call to mind the no less tragic events of recent Iraqi history. As in more modern times, it was apparently already inconceivable in that period for a Shiᶜite to be named Abū Bakr or ᶜĀʾisha, names of early historical figures who were veritable embodiments of evil from a Shiᶜite point of view.

> During the rule of the Buyid dynasty, in the time of the ascendancy of Shiᶜism (*fī ayyām al-Daylam wa-quwwat al-rafḍ*), Abū Bakr b. Qāniᶜ was going somewhere through the Karkh quarter[118], when a woman called him: "My lord, Abū Bakr!" He replied: "At your service, oh ᶜĀʾisha." The woman said: "Why, do you think I'm called ᶜĀʾisha?" Said he: "Now, should they kill me alone?"[119]

This last joke seems like one which may conceivably have been known among illiterate people as well as intellectuals (one of whom, the Ḥanbalite scholar Ibn al-Jawzī [510–97/1126–1200], recorded it in the Seljuk period). And yet, as ever, one cannot but wonder if a real intimacy with the emblematic figures, events and thought currents of early Islamic history was only characteristic of a relatively educated class of people, and whether the illiterate masses knew anything beyond a narrow selection of famous names and catchwords. For instance, whilst it is anybody's guess if ordinary people were aware of any actual historical details of the career of the false prophet Musaylima (killed ca. 10/632) – or the standard, quasi-legendary Muslim version of it anyway – it seems indisputable that the bare name was known to most people, if in no other way than as a proverbial embodiment of falsity and mendacity.[120] There is some textual evidence that appears to strengthen the idea of a very limited and superficial knowledge of early Islamic history and its sectarian strife among commoners; in fact the less than impressive lore of the commoners in this domain was a subject of jokes seemingly popular among the educated class. An example of

158 [a poem by Dīk al-Jinn about the Monday]; al-Thaᶜālibī, *Tatimma* I, 51–2 [an ironic poem by Abū l-Dardāʾ about religious controversies].

118 A predominantly Shīᶜite quarter of Baghdad.

119 Ibn al-Jawzī, *Ẓirāf* 130. The differing name-giving customs of Shiᶜites and Sunnites are also the point of a story – narrated in a deadpan manner as historical fact – about an anonymous Iraqi's visit to Syria where everyone seems to bear names hateful to a Shiᶜite ear. When he comes across the only Syrian whose sons are named after the beloved imams of the Shiᶜites, on closer inquiry it turns out that the man chose those names so as to be able to curse his sons with no feeling of guilt. See Yāqūt, *Udabāʾ* IV, 1854.

120 al-Thaᶜālibī, *Thimār* I, 257–62; al-Thaᶜālibī, *Nathr* 47. Muslims have actually had the habit of adding the epithet al-Kadhdhāb ('the Liar') to Musaylima's name. – Similarly, the historical facts of some of the battles between the followers of ᶜAlī b. Abī Ṭālib and the Umayyads (notably Ṣiffīn and Karbalāʾ) came to be mere metaphors in literary texts – and possibly in popular consciousness too: names symbolising 'direful conflict' and 'ominous event'. See for instance al-Thaᶜālibī, *Yatīma* II, 34; al-Khaṭīb, *Taṭfīl* 28; Ibn Diḥya, *Muṭrib* 35; Ibn al-Khaṭīb, *Jaysh* 86, 96; Ibn Maᶜṣūm, *Sulāfa* 289.

such jokes is the following risqué one recorded in the Buyid period. It is based on the well-known story of Hind bt. ʿUtba, a sworn enemy of the Prophet and an abominable virago in Muslim historical consciousness, biting into the liver of the dead Muslim hero Ḥamza b. ʿAbd al-Muṭṭalib, the Prophet's uncle:

> Abū Sālim the popular preacher (*qāṣṣ*) said: "God's Messenger said that had Hind bt. ʿUtba swallowed the liver of Ḥamza into her stomach when she bit and chewed it, hellfire would have no power over her [so great was the divine blessing in Ḥamza's person]." Said al-Mubarradī: "My Lord, give us some of Ḥamza's liver to eat!"[121]

4. The Religious Obligations

4.1 Prayer

I will not be concerned here with any systematic study of the literary representations of the 'pillars of the faith' in Islam, as that surely lies outside the purview of this essay. The only purpose of this section is to offer a glimpse into the ways four out of the five 'pillars' of a Muslim's religion – namely, prayer, fasting, the obligatory alms tax, and pilgrimage – were treated as topics of light-hearted, secular Arabic literature, and *mujūn* in particular.

Probably the most conspicuous feature of prayer – certainly for someone who is not a practising Muslim – is the call to prayer that precedes it, known as *adhān* in Arabic. Because of the distinctiveness of this melodious and formulaic prelude to prayer, it was practically inevitable that it should claim the attention of poets and

[121] al-Tawḥīdī, *Baṣāʾir* II(iii), 157. For further examples, see al-Tawḥīdī, *Baṣāʾir* I(i), 187 [a joke on sexual intercourse between a Sunni boy and a fanatical Shiʿite extremist]; I(ii), 80 [the relative value of cursing Fāṭima and ʿĀʾisha respectively]; II(iv), 32–3 [clumsy references by various beggars to the personalities of early Islam]; III(vi), 59 [the case of a fanatical Shiʿite father and son with a pro-Umayyad extremist boy]; IV(vii), 52 [an ignoramus knowing absolutely nothing about the Companions of the Prophet]; Ibn al-Jawzī, *Ẓirāf* 130 [a supplication attempting simultaneously to appeal to Shiʿite and Sunni biases]; al-Jurjānī, *Wasāṭa* 365 [a poet who thought that Jesus had been killed by the Christians]; al-Rāghib, *Muḥāḍarāt* III, 481 [another version of the aforementioned joke about the Sunni boy and the Shiʿite extremist]; al-Masʿūdī, *Murūj* II, 29–31 and Ibn Mufliḥ, *Ādāb* II, 172 [several ridiculous examples of the ignorance of the common folk concerning the personalities of early Islam]. – A factor that may have raised the general level of familiarity with early Islamic history – and especially the life of the Prophet and his Companions – is the custom among pilgrims to visit the most important historical sites of Mecca and Medina after having concluded their pilgrimage rites. (One wonders, however, just how widespread this custom was in the Middle Ages; it is reported to have been quite prevalent in the late 19th century. See Snouck Hurgronje 1931: 23.) – Interestingly, modern dialects seem to have preserved plenty of the linguistic imprints of mediaeval sectarian differences and some early historical episodes; for the Egyptian dialect cf. Stewart 1996: 39–40, 45–50, 65; and for a Maghrebi example see Marçais 1954: 128 and 205.

writers of *mujūn* searching for frivolous motifs, all the more so as the formulae of *adhān* were definitely known by heart by virtually every Muslim, if only for its repeated, public recital several times every day. Since the words were so deeply entrenched in the consciousness of Muslims, the humour of modifying it in frivolous ways was, presumably, not lost on anyone. The adaptation of the *adhān* formula for irreverent purposes is a recurrent motif in *mujūn* literature, and is particularly common in wine poems, as attested by the following three short poems, which, despite appearing very similar, in fact originate in different regions and times and represent very different genres:

> If [a devout muezzin] comes forth at dawn, admonishing me and calling, "*On to good deeds*!"
> In my ears, the lute modifies his words thus: "*On to* listening to music and wine-drinking!"[122]

> I did the opposite of what the muezzin was calling me to do –
> He says, "*On to prayer*!", and I say, "*On to* wine-drinking!"[123]

> Fuck any comely boy you meet, and think not of the scandal;
> And take the rebukes of whoever reproaches you as wind that forever blows.
> Hit them [boys] hard with your prick as Khārijite rebels hit with their spears,
> Then dismount and call, as libertines will (*majānatan*), "Oh people, *on to* sex!"[124]

The displeasure of having to get up at dawn to the voice of a muezzin and pray first thing in the morning, when one would prefer to slumber on for some time, was also a much-liked theme in *mujūn*. The nuisance of having to pray when one would wish to be otherwise occupied recurs in poetry as well as in prose.[125]

---

[122] al-Ḥillī, *ʿĀṭil* 191. The end of the first line is, of course, a part of the *adhān* formula, while the end of the second (in the original: *ḥayyā ʿalā qaṣf wa-ʾṣṭibāḥ*) is a frivolous re-formulation of the same. The poem is actually an example of dialectal verse (*zajal*) by the most famous Andalusian master of the genre, Ibn Quzmān (d. 555/1160).

[123] al-Thaʿālibī, *Yatīma* I, 280.

[124] Abū Nuwās, *Dīwān* V, 204. For more sampling of the outrageous ways in which the call to prayer could be adjusted in *mujūn* literature, see al-Thaʿālibī, *Nathr* 85; Ibn al-Jawzī, *Talbīs* 268; Ibn al-Kattānī, *Tashbīhāt* 93. In one particularly interesting text, two brothers, quite independently of each other, happen to refashion the words of the *adhān* so as to convert it into almost identical frivolous invitations to a wine-drinking party, and both versions contain the added funny element of the inclusion of a phrase in Persian. See al-Thaʿālibī, *Yatīma* IV, 72. (I am grateful to Miklós Sárközy for clarifying the translation of the inserted Persian phrases for me.) In a poem by Abū ʿAlī al-Manṭiqī (4th/10th c.), the formula is turned into a call to draw on ('plunder') a man's copious learning; see Yāqūt, *Udabāʾ* V, 2042. – A related but somewhat different motif appears in a poem by Tamīm b. Mufarrij al-Ṭāʾī (early 5th/11th c.), which suggests the muezzin's call as an adequate signal for starting a wine-drinking party; see al-Bākharzī, *Dumya* I, 64. – The idea of reworking the *adhān* formula occurs in other forms too. The judge al-Tanūkhī records an anecdote about a muezzin in Baghdad who customises the *adhān* in a bizarre way to fit his extremist Shiʿite sectarian views; see al-Tanūkhī, *Nishwār* II, 133.

[125] A poem from the Seljuk period states that a night spent with lovemaking would be just perfect "if only [the neighbourhood muezzin] ʿAbbās would keep quiet". See al-Iṣbahānī, *Kharīda* I(i), 188.

Just like the *adhān*, practically no element of the Muslim prayer escaped the ironic attention of the libertine poets and writers of the mediaeval Middle East. Some of those elements, like the characteristic ritual movements of prayer – and especially the prostration, for reasons not too hard to see – easily lent themselves to very frivolous and ruthless caricatures, whilst other aspects of prayer tended to be treated in more good-natured ways. An example of the latter category of motifs is the metaphorical use of the term *qibla*, which literally means the direction of prayer, which for a Muslim is of course the direction of the *Kaʿba* sanctuary in Mecca. Given the powerful image of multitudes of Muslims all over the world who, wherever they happen to live or stay, turn their faces to Mecca at the times of prayer, it was rather inevitable that *qibla* should come to be used figuratively to refer to the focus of someone's attention, love or respect in the broadest possible sense. The motif is as common in poetry as in prose. A typical example – of the kind that one would have to be an extremely narrow-minded individual to disapprove of – is the following sentence describing an extraordinarily useful book: "man regards it as his *qibla* to turn to in prayer, and his fundament to build on" (*ittakhadhahu l-ʿabd qibla yuṣallī ilayhā wa-qāʿida yabnī ʿalayhā*).[126] (Incidentally, one might note the very similar metaphorical use of the name of Mecca in English and other Western languages.) This figurative use of the word *qibla* is usually nothing outrageous, although one does come across the occasional utilisation of the term with sexual overtones, or in the context of bacchic poetry.[127] Other aspects of the prayer appearing in secular poetry, jocular literature and outright *mujūn* include the obligatory ablution before prayer (*wuḍūʾ*), as well as its variety in times of scarcity of water, the substitution of water with sand (*tayammum*).[128]

Similar is the point of a frivolous poem which states that the beloved is sweeter even than sleeping through the designated time of prayer (presumably the ultimate standard of delight); see al-Zawzanī, *Ḥamāsa* II, 105. A joke from the Buyid period features a woman making a similarly ironic comment on the text of the call to prayer; see al-Tawḥīdī, *Baṣāʾir* II(iii), 182. – However, all the aforementioned motifs pale beside what is arguably the most shocking use of the image of the muezzin in *mujūn*. In one of his poems, the prototype of all libertines, the blind, acerbic and infamous Bashshār b. Burd (d. 167–8/784–5) compared his own penis to a muezzin staring at the sky (evidently, to ascertain the proper time for calling to prayer). See al-Iṣfahānī, *Aghānī* III, 198; al-Thaʿālibī, *Iʿjāz* 157. (Incidentally, some sources attribute the execution of Bashshār to one mockery too many of the *adhān*, but I will have more to say about this incident in Chapter Four.)

126 al-Thaʿālibī, *Nathr* 7; and for further examples, see al-Thaʿālibī, *Yatīma* I, 282; II, 216; al-Thaʿālibī, *Tatimma* I, 96; II, 18; al-Tawḥīdī [attr.], *Risāla* 301; al-Iṣbahānī, *Kharīda* II(ii), 657; al-Ibshīhī, *Mustaṭraf* 507; Ibn Diḥya, *Muṭrib* 17.

127 E.g. al-Tawḥīdī [attr.], *Risāla* 212; Abū Nuwās, *Dīwān* V, 163; and Wagner 2008: 41 ["*Kaʿbat al-ladhdhāt*"]. We find it in Persian poetry too; see its use by ʿUbayd-i Zākānī in Sprachman 1997: 204.

128 Abū Firās, *Dīwān* 273; al-Jurjānī, *Wasāṭa* 180; al-Iṣbahānī, *Kharīda* II(ii), 606; Ibn al-Kattānī, *Tashbīhāt* 97; and also Sanni 1998: 129–30. Also in jokes; see al-Tawḥīdī, *Imtāʿ* 198; al-Rāghib, *Muḥāḍarāt* III, 532; and Rosenthal 1956: 67. The metaphorical use of the term *tayammum* (roughly

However, as already noted, of all the elements of prayer it is the prostration (*sujūd*) that provided the most easily exploitable material for *mujūn*. Some jokes and poems simply likened prostration to involuntary collapse, and that is a fairly mild usage as far as the motifs of *mujūn* go:

> A man told his landlord to have the beams of the ceiling repaired, as it kept creaking [forebodingly]. [The landlord] replied: "Fear nothing; it is just praising the Lord (*yusabbiḥ*)". [The lodger] said: "I fear it will be overwhelmed by religious fervour and prostrate itself [before God] (*yasjud*)."[129]

Other uses of the image of *sujūd* were somewhat more scandalous from a Muslim point of view. That one's posterior is above one's head in that moment was commented on in predictable ways in *mujūn* literature, not least in gross allusions to anal intercourse.[130] For instance, this sexual innuendo is evident in the following verse – addressed to a beautiful woman – by the minor poet Rabīʿa b. Thābit al-Raqqī (d. 198/813–4): "When you are praying and prostrating yourself, we say, 'May she remain prostrated for years'."[131] Or, now of a boy (and by a different poet): "Whoever sees him bend his torso (*rakʿa*) during prayer will say, 'Our greatest wish is the prostration following the *rakʿa*'."[132] A poem of six verses by Abū Nuwās, describing two boys having sex in a secluded corner of the mosque, is entirely based on the figurative use of the notion of 'prayer' to refer to sodomy.[133] It might be added that the potential for sexual allusions was also exploited in the case of an important part of the Friday communal prayer, the sermon, with "[going up and] preach on someone's pulpit" serving as a frivolous metaphor for anal intercourse.[134]

---

in the sense of 'the second best thing' or '*faute de mieux*') exists not only in Arabic but in Swahili as well (and perhaps in languages spoken by other Muslim peoples too); see Mkelle 1976: 45.

129 al-Tawḥīdī, *Baṣāʾir* I(ii), 97–8; Ibn al-Jawzī, *Ẓirāf* 141; al-Ibshīhī, *Mustaṭraf* 66; and the same motif appearing in poetry in al-Thaʿālibī, *Yatīma* II, 427; al-Thaʿālibī, *Tatimma* II, 15; Ibn Khafāja, *Dīwān* 70–1. Prostration in prayer could also be a simile for the collapse of a man drunk beyond rescue; see al-Thaʿālibī, *Yatīma* II, 82, 410; Ibn Saʿīd, *Rāyāt* 171; Ibn Saʿīd, *Muqtaṭaf* 119. – Other, fairly innocuous, similes based on the image of prostration can be found in, for example, Ibn al-Kattānī, *Tashbīhāt* 57, 100, 168, 219, 222; Ibn Saʿīd, *Rāyāt* 134. In one anecdote, the movement of prostration during prayer is likened, rather irreverently, to a goat's or ram's butting with the head: "Isn't it enough that I tread the ground, must I ram it too?" See al-Tawḥīdī, *Baṣāʾir* III(vi), 76.

130 al-Thaʿālibī, *Thimār* II, 707–8; Yāqūt, *Udabāʾ* III, 1143; al-Nafzāwī, *Rawḍ* 57. The same image – that of a praying man's buttocks rising above his head – could be fodder for gross folk humour too; see for instance Thesiger 1967: 116. Even though not necessarily related to our topic, it is still interesting to note that grotesque, sexually suggestive parodies of the prayer have been an integral part of the masquerades of many communities in rural Morocco in recent centuries – possibly a very old custom. See Hammoudi 1993: 18, 22.

131 Ibn al-Muʿtazz, *Ṭabaqāt* 72.

132 Ibn Saʿīd, *Rāyāt* 197.

133 Abū Nuwās, *Dīwān* V, 49.

134 E.g. Abū Nuwās, *Dīwān* III, 354; IV, 191; al-Bākharzī, *Dumya* I, 586.

It was not only through sexual innuendoes that the outward, ritual features of prayer would be parodied in literature. Any unconventional manner of praying could be the subject of humorous treatments, especially an unduly hasty or slow pace in performing the prescribed prayers. An evident haste in praying was especially bound to give rise to ironic remarks among friends in everyday life, and it could also be utilised as a motif in invective poetry.[135] Likewise, the distress caused by a too slow performance of communal prayer, especially a sustained prostration – the pace of which is effectively set by the imam leading the ceremony – is a recurring theme in Arabic literature and jokes.[136] In fact, a passage in the monumental *Kitāb al-aghānī* (4th/10th c.) strongly suggests that jestful poems describing scandalously improper ways of performing the prayer might on occasion be simply the reflection of actual acts of vulgar buffoonery at prayer with which certain libertines would amuse themselves and their intimate friends.[137] Nor is it sure that when Abū Nuwās describes himself indecently touching and groping a boy during prayer in a crowded mosque the poem is wholly fictional.[138]

Parodies of the prayer were not always concerned with the outward aspects thereof. One also finds a number of texts that are, for all intents and purposes, caricatures of the usual formulae of prayer and supplication. These parodistic supplications to God are usually put in the mouths of people noted for their ignorance or known libertines. One typical example is the following joke consisting of an entreaty spoken by a popular preacher (*qāṣṣ*), a frequent protagonist in *mujūn* texts: "Lord, bring destruction upon Abū Ḥassān al-Daqqāq, who wishes and does nothing but harm to the Muslims! And his address is the first door in the street on your left."[139] If sufficiently long and elaborate, such mock supplications

---

135 E.g. al-Tanūkhī, *Nishwār* III, 134–5; al-Bayhaqī, *Maḥāsin* 403; Ibn al-Jawzī, *Ẓirāf* 74, 142; Ibn al-Muʿtazz, *Ṭabaqāt* 67 [here the poet, Abū l-Hawl, directs his irony against himself instead of someone else]; al-Thaʿālibī, *Yatīma* III, 38. For further examples of jesting about eccentricities and irregularities in prayer, cf. al-Tawḥīdī, *Baṣāʾir* V(ix), 43 [a drunkard's arguments about observing the prescribed hours of prayer]; Ibn al-Jawzī, *Ẓirāf* 58 [a concluding formula suitable for praying in the company of a bore], 119 [the advantage of travelling as regards prayer]; al-Ibshīhī, *Mustaṭraf* 376 [a joke about prayer with animal protagonists]. The theme is also used in modern spoken Arabic, see for instance Ibrahim 1994: 36–7, 140–1.

136 For instance, this burlesque motif appears in more than one *maqāma*; see al-Hamadhānī, *Maqāmāt* 61–3, 119. Indeed, the motif might have had some real-life basis, if we trust a report by Yāqūt about an imam in mediaeval Damascus who would tease his acquaintances with such antics; see Yāqūt; *Buldān* III, 249–50. The ironic motif of an absurdly long prostration in prayer appears in modern Arabic literature too, notably in a short story by Yūsuf Idrīs; and unnecessarily long prayers were also the topic of some modern Arabic jokes (recorded in the Sudan). See Cachia 1995: 180; Hillelson 1935: 20–1.

137 al-Iṣfahānī, *Aghānī* XIII, 350–1; and cf. ibid. VII, 57.

138 Ibn Manẓūr, *Akhbār* 79.

139 al-Tawḥīdī, *Baṣāʾir* II(iii), 62–3. Another, rather vulgar joke features a devout doctor using the

metamorphose into veritable sermons, and often extremely ribald and obscene ones at that. A mock sermon attributed to a certain ʿUthmān al-Khayyāṭ (an infamous thief and burglar) promotes all sorts of *mujūn*, including sexual deviance, then crowns it all with advice on fashion phrased in religious terms.[140] One cannot help wondering if such parodistic sermons may represent a 'high', literary version of a more unrefined, coarse form of folk humour. Be that as it may, mock sermons – or admonitions to commit all sorts of scandalous acts and misdemeanours, delivered in the style of ordinary sermonising – also appear in poetry, and it seems that even perfectly decent and pious intellectuals would sometimes engage in such jesting in verse to demonstrate their wit.[141] This phenomenon – an observable discrepancy between someone's composing highly immoral literary products and living a quite respectable life at the same time – will be the subject of discussion in a later chapter, as it is a crucial and in many respects illuminative aspect of *mujūn* literature.

4.2 Fasting

Like prayer, fasting in the month of Ramadan was a salient part of a Muslim's duties, and like prayer, it tended to draw the attention of libertines. The reasons that it should be such a popular topic of jocular literature will not be repeated here, beyond stating that the most fundamental and familiar aspects of religious praxis and doctine are apt to serve as ready themes for jokes and poetry.

Of all characteristics of the Ramadan fast, it is with the hardship of going without food and drink and sex throughout the day that *mujūn* was most preoccupied. The difficulty of fasting in Ramadan is a frequent motif in mediaeval Arabic poetry as well as in prose, and as I am going to argue presently, it seems to have been a common topic of jesting in speech too, which is actually likely to have been the source of the motif in written literature. The poetic theme which is often referred to in mediaeval Arabic texts as *hijāʾ Ramaḍān* ('lampooning Ramadan') comes in many varieties, all of which pivot around the difficulty of fasting: it may focus on

medical jargon in his pious supplication to God; see al-Thaʿālibī, *Laṭāʾif* 72. For some further examples, see al-Thaʿālibī, *Laṭāʾif* 92 [the prayer of Abū Nuwās in a vineyard]; al-Tawḥīdī, *Baṣāʾir* II(iii), 75–6 [a supplication by a Kūfan preacher]; II(iv), 218 [a mock prayer about the machinations of Satan].

140 E.g. "... do not wear turbans but face-veils; tall conical caps equal unbelief and leather slippers polytheism" (*wa-daʿū labs al-ʿamāʾim wa-ʿalaykum bi-l-qināʿ, wa-l-qalansuwa kufr wa-l-khuff shirk*). See al-Jāḥiẓ, *Ḥayawān* I, 357–8. A frivolous work from the late mediaeval period also offers an obscene 'sermon' by *al-Ḥājj Bayḍ* ('Sir Balls', more or less); see al-Nafzāwī, *Rawḍ* 50.

141 See for instance a passage on Abū l-Ḥasan al-Rāmhurmuzī and his frivolous poem ("*wa-fīhā tajawwuz kathīr wa-amr bi-khilāf al-jamīl*" etc.) in al-Tanūkhī, *Nishwār* IV, 59. Abū Nuwās composed quite a few such poems; see Abū Nuwās, *Dīwān* V, 199–216.

the extraordinary length of the month of fasting as perceived subjectively (of course, Ramadan is objectively not longer than a regular lunar month), or on the illicit pleasures that have a tendency to diminish during Ramadan even among the most reprobate, or else on the inordinate rejoicing that the arrival of the *ʿīd al-fiṭr* (the holiday marking the end of Ramadan) brings to the poet because it enables him to resume his debauched activities. The exceedingly large number of poems classifiable as *hijāʾ Ramaḍān* – a number that all but justifies treating these poems as a minor genre – is a testimony to the popularity of the motif.[142] Below are three fairly typical specimens of this category:

> Oh you month of fasting, there is no month comparable to you in the eyes of God;
> Even though you have deprived us of the enjoyment of drinking
> And clinking a cup to a cup, and pressing a mouth to a mouth.
> I swear by that person who glorifies you by reciting [the Quran]
> And who spends the whole month with prayers long and short:
> I feel happy about your having passed, even if that means yet more time off my life.[143]

---

[142] The most comprehensive sample of such poems can be found in Ben Cheneb 1922: 62–3, 111–5, 147. For further examples, see for instance al-Thaʿālibī, *Nathr* 156 ["*Ahlan bi-fiṭrin qad anāra hilāluhu, al-āna fa-ʾghdu ʿalā l-mudāmi wa-bakkiri*"]; al-Thaʿālibī, *Thimār* I, 200 ["*Shahru l-ṣiyāmi wa-in ʿaẓẓamtu ḥurmatahu shahrun ṭawīlun baṭīʾu l-sayri wa-l-ḥaraka / Yamshī ruwaydan fa-ammā ḥīna yaṭlubunā fa-lā l-Sulayku yudānīhi wa-lā l-Sulaka*"]; al-Thaʿālibī, *Yatīma* III, 39 ["*Shahrun arāhu yalijju maʿa man yaghtāẓu min ṭūlihi wa-yadradu*" etc.]; IV, 436 ["*Mā tarā l-ṣawma sāra bi-l-aswadayni wa-atānā Shawwālun bi-l-aḥmarayni*"]; al-Thaʿālibī, *Tatimma* I, 45 ["*Bi-laylati fiṭrin qāma fīhā ṭawāʾifu fa-ṣallū wa-qumnā jahratan bi-khilāfihā*"], 83 ["*A-ʾaṣūmu shahran thumma akhruju ghādiyan naḥwa l-muṣallā aqṭaʿu l-amyālā*" etc.]; al-Iṣfahānī, *Aghānī* VII, 219 ["*Hazaztuka li-l-ṣabūḥi wa-qad nahānī amīru l-muʾminīna ʿani l-ṣiyāmī*"]; al-ʿAskarī, *Maṣūn* 159 ["*Ṣubbā ʿalayya l-kaʾsa, inna hilālanā qad ṣabba niʿmatahu ʿalā l-thaqalayni / Lā zāla min bughḍi l-ṣiyāmi mubaghghaḍan yawmu l-khamīsi ilayya wa-l-ithnayni*"]; al-Bākharzī, *Dumya* I, 219 ["*Aqūlu li-shahri l-ṣawmi lammā qaḍaytuhu ʿalayka salāmu ʾllāhi būrikta rāḥilā / Wa-qad kuntu min Saḥbāna afṣaḥa lahjatan fa-ṣayyara ṭabʿī bāqillāʾuka Bāqilā*"]; II, 824 ["*Ḥanānayka ʾstaqalla l-ṣawmu ʿannā wa-ṣāḥa binā l-mudāmu mina l-qilāli*"]; al-Iṣbahānī, *Kharīda* II(i), 375–6 ["*Ṭamʾinū bi-l-mudāmi jaʾsha nufūsin ruwwiʿat li-l-ṣiyāmi fī Ramaḍāni*"]; II(ii), 681–2 ["*Wa-ghadā l-ṣawmu hāziʾan yanshuru l-rawʿata yatlūhu ʿaskaru l-ifṭāri / Wa-maḍā l-nusku wa-l-tarāwīḥu wa-l-tasbīḥu ṭurran muhattaka l-astāri*"]; Yāqūt, *Udabāʾ* IV, 1648 ["*Ramā Ramaḍānu shamlanā bi-l-tafarruqi, fa-yā laytahu ʿannā taqaḍḍā li-naltaqī / La-in sarra ahla l-arḍi ṭurran qudūmuhu fa-inna surūrī bi-ʾnsilākhi lladhī baqī*"]; Ibn al-Khaṭīb, *Jaysh* 29 ["*Wa-lā aʿazza min shahri Shaʿbān...*"]; Ibn Maʿṣūm, *Sulāfa* 460 ["*Qūmū ilā ladhdhātikum yā niyām, wa-nabbihū l-ʿūda wa-ṣifū l-mudām / Hādhā hilālu l-fiṭri qad jānā bi-minjalin yaḥṣudu shahra l-ṣiyām*"]. The same motif appears in a vernacular poem too ("*Ayyā māʿī bī l-waqta ḍāq yā qōm*"); see al-Ḥillī, *ʿĀṭil* 115–8. – The image of the new moon that signals the end of the month of fasting was often used as a metaphor of good tidings; see al-Thaʿālibī, *Thimār* II, 921–2. This usage may have nothing to do with *mujūn*, but could be ascribed simply to the fact that this is one of the two great Islamic festivities, and thus sufficient cause for rejoicing without any undertones of irreverence.

[143] Ibn Saʿīd, *Rāyāt* 265.

> The month of fasting is a blessed month, but [this year] it came in August. Fearing the torment [of Hell], I kept the fast throughout – but this turned out to be just as much torment.[144]

> The month of Ramadan, when it comes in spring, spoils all beauty and pleasure. [Even] a rose cut during the fast is like a beloved person constantly chaperoned.[145]

The *hijāʾ Ramaḍān* 'genre' is one of those manifestations of *mujūn* literature which yield enough data to demonstrate, if not conclusively then with a considerable degree of probability, that *mujūn* had a tendency to draw motifs heavily from spoken culture. To start with, there is a wealth of jokes and anecdotes about fasting; humorous treatments of the duty of the Ramadan fast, including ones that describe inventive attempts to dodge that duty, have been almost commonplace.[146] More specifically and pertinently, the difficulties of observing the fast – more or less along the lines of the *hijāʾ Ramaḍān* corpus – were a recurrent topic of jokes, as was the joy of finally sighting the new moon that signals the end of the holy month.[147] While these jokes have been preserved, naturally enough, in written form, I simply cannot imagine their having been unknown in spoken versions. In an important source from the Buyid period, a frivolous remark made by the famed vizier al-Ṣāḥib b. ʿAbbād (d. 385/995) concerning the wearisomeness of Ramadan is cited as evidence of his depravity and impiety: this remark does not sound like one that would have been made up by al-Tawḥīdī, who recorded it. Concluding an irreverent exchange of mock theological arguments on the Quran, al-Ṣāḥib b. ʿAbbād declares that if Ramadan miraculously ceased to exist, then the only logical consequence would be that "we would not recite the nightly prayers of Ramadan and find rest at last" (*wa-lā nuṣallī l-tarāwīḥ wa-nastarīḥ*).[148]

---

144 al-Thaʿālibī, *Tatimma* I, 66.

145 al-Thaʿālibī, *Yatīma* II, 204.

146 E.g. a joke about a woman postponing fasting for a year in al-Tawḥīdī, *Baṣāʾir* I(i), 167; about irreverent remarks made by the poet Ibn al-Rūmī (221/836–283/896) and the musician Abū Salmān on Ramadan in ibid. III(v), 35; about a woman keeping half a day's worth of fast *per diem* in ibid. III(vi), 236 and al-Ibshīhī, *Mustaṭraf* 538 (and cf. Marzolph 1992: II, 129); two jokes about the idiosyncratic work ethic during Ramadan of two boy prostitutes in al-Rāghib, *Muḥāḍarāt* III, 479; about a Bedouin spending Ramadan travelling around in order to escape the duty of fasting in al-Ibshīhī, *Mustaṭraf* 531 (and the same motif in a vernacular poem from the mediaeval period in al-Ḥillī, *ʿĀṭil* 116).The personification of the name of Ramadan and jesting based on this device were also known in the folklore of 19th-century Mecca; see Snouck Hurgronje 1931: 61, 70. It is not directly relevant here but interesting that it was a custom in Damascus for the officials responsible for waking up the believers before daybreak during Ramadan (*musaḥḥirūn*) to chant funny poems for this purpose. See Kayyāl n. d.: 70.

147 Ibn al-Jawzī, *Ẓirāf* 117; al-Tawḥīdī, *Baṣāʾir* I(ii), 16. Jokes about the difficulty of the Ramadan fast also exist in modern Tunisian folklore; see Chanfrault 1996: 55.

148 al-Tawḥīdī, *Akhlāq* 251–2.

Of course, as always, it could be argued that the movement of the motif was in fact in the opposite direction, resulting in many intellectuals' use in speech of motifs borrowed from written literary products. The following text, however, certainly seems to suggest that in fact we face a case of a spoken witticism making its way into 'high literature':

> Abū Nuwās was asked what was his favourite month, and he replied that it was Shawwāl[, which comes after Ramadan]. When asked whether the reason [for his preference] was that the *ʿīd al-fiṭr* holiday [is in Shawwāl], he answered: "Not at all. It's because [Shawwāl] is the farthest [month] from [the next] Ramadan." Al-Ḥamdūnī then borrowed this [*bon mot*] and composed the following poem: "Shawwāl has done a great service to us, and it is the best placed to do so. / It has brought forth music and feasting and the pleasures of singing-girls. / For me, the loveliest month is that which is farthest from [the next] Ramadan."[149]

Whatever the provenance of *mujūn* motifs and the direction of their movement between the popular and the elite linguistic registers, the fast of Ramadan inspired other poetic motifs as well, not all of which would necessarily be categorised as manifestations of *mujūn*. As ever, the boundaries are blurry. For instance, the widespread use of the verb 'to fast' in the sense of 'to abstain from something', be that thing commendable or not, might be applied in rather indecent contexts as well as innocuous ones. It was, inter alia, often used to refer to stingy hosts, whose guests would be described as keeping a fast by virtue of being entertained by such a host.[150] In the following excerpt, this clichéd usage appears next to the kind of playful, frivolous misinterpretation of a Quranic verse (17:81) that we have seen several examples of, which, taken together, would probably qualify the whole scene as (mild) *mujūn*:

> And then [the scurrilous poet Ibn al-Ḥajjāj] turned to his companions and said: "Are we fasting today (*ṣāyimīn naḥnu l-yawm*)?" At this moment the slave-boy arrived and said: "Please [help yourself to this food.]" [Ibn al-Ḥajjāj] stood up and said: "*The truth has come, and falsehood has vanished away; surely falsehood is ever certain to vanish.*"[151]

---

[149] Ibn Rashīq, *Qurāḍa* 98–9. For a longer and more detailed discussion of the issue of the *hijāʾ Ramaḍān* theme as a loan of written literature from the spoken language, see Szombathy 2005.

[150] E.g. al-Thaʿālibī, *Yatīma* I, 286, 300; II, 157; al-Thaʿālibī, *Tatimma* I, 67–8; al-Tanūkhī, *Nishwār* III, 48; and also cf. al-Thaʿālibī, *Yatīma* III, 273; al-Bākharzi, *Dumya* I, 494; al-Zawzanī, *Ḥamāsa* II, 121; al-Iṣbahānī, *Kharīda* I(ii), 134; Ibn Diḥya, *Muṭrib* 74 ["*afṭarat minhumā ʿaynī wa-sāma famī...*"]; Ibn al-Kattānī, *Tashbīhāt* 255; Ibn Saʿīd, *Muqtaṭaf* 125. The concept of 'fasting' in a sarcastic sense was apparently also used in dialectal poetry; see for instance al-Ibshīhī, *Mustaṭraf* 506.

[151] al-Tawḥīdī [attr.], *Risāla* 292. The Quran verse cited in the text also appears as allusive *iqtibās* in a poem; see al-Washshāʾ, *Muwashshā* 54.

Equally variable in its degree of *mujūn* is another common literary motif, that of likening *Laylat al-Qadr* – a night in Ramadan thought to have extraordinary religious significance – to various profane situations. According to popular belief, the prayers of the believers uttered during this night have far more potency than at any other time of the year, but established Islamic dogma also attributes special importance to this night, as the Quran states in somewhat mysterious language that the Quran was revealed at this time, when angels descend and the grace of God is near (*sūra* 97). Given this background it is easy to see that, depending on the details of a particular frivolous literary comparison with *Laylat al-Qadr*, such a simile might well be seen as truly scandalous *mujūn*. Nevertheless, it came to be a real poetic cliché to liken any memorable and agreeable night – usually a night spent together with one's beloved – to *Laylat al-Qadr*. In a more cautious version of the motif, the night of lovemaking is said to fall just short of equalling *Laylat al-Qadr*, whereas a more daring variety would not even eschew equating the two or even preferring the former to the latter.[152]

4.3 The Alms Tax (Zakāt)

The annual payment of the alms tax, or *zakāt*, is one of the obligations of every adult Muslim man whose possessions reach a certain amount. In theory and more often than not in practice too, this alms tax would be used for charitable and religious purposes such as providing sustenance to the poor, maintaining mosques, and so on. Having observed various examples of the metaphorical uses in literature of the terms for praying and fasting, one will expect the noun *zakāt* to have undergone a similar semantic development, and indeed such was the case. That the possession of any enviable outward or inward characteristic requires the payment of *zakāt* came to be a hackneyed motif in mediaeval Arabic poetry and prose alike; and here again the uses of the motif run the whole gamut from harmless literary commonplace to gross *mujūn*. Poets would elaborate on the notion that someone uncommonly intelligent, powerful or glorious must pay *zakāt* on that desirable quality. Even more common is the poetic conceit – yet another version of the same idea – that the owner of an exceptionally beautiful face must pay the obligatory alms tax on that beauty in the form of kisses or suchlike gratifying gifts, and of course to the benefit of the languishing lover, an appropriate recipient of alms.[153] The motif was also used, and

---

152 For some examples of the motif taken from various eras and geographical regions, see Ibn al-Muʿtazz, *Ṭabaqāt* 86; al-Bākharzī, *Dumya* II, 898, 1179, 1262; Ibn Diḥya, *Muṭrib* 179; Ibn Saʿīd, *Ghuṣūn* 121; Ibn Maʿṣūm, *Sulāfa* 389, 495, 561. For an obscene folk joke about the belief that every man's three wishes expressed during *Laylat al-Qadr* will be granted, see al-Nafzāwī, *Rawḍ* 56–7.

153 See for instance the verses of a Transoxanian poet of the Buyid period, Abū Aḥmad b. Abī Bakr al-Kātib, and the prose version of the same, in al-Thaʿālibī, *Nathr* 34–5; the rhetoric of the vizier

in more than one version, in the spoken language, more particularly in more or less proverb-like phrases.[154] The fact that such a metaphorical use of the term *zakāt* was as common in speech as in poetry is obvious in an anecdote which, while not necessarily the historical record of an actual exchange of words, must have sounded natural enough in its style for the contemporary audience to find it funny. The anecdote is about a slave-girl renowned for her talents of singing, called Zādmihr, whose owner was approached by a friend and asked whether he would let this friend listen to the girl delivering a certain song. The friend added the somewhat tired witticism that this should be regarded as the *zakāt* of the slave-girl's sweet voice ("*ijʿalī hādhā l-ṣawt al-yawm zakāt ghināʾiki*"). When her owner sent a message to the slave-girl telling her to oblige the friend, she wrote on the verso of the message:

> "May God make your eyes hot [with tears]! And supposing this Abū l-Ḥasan [your friend] – may God give him glory! – proposed yet another trifling thing and asked for a ride (*ṭalaba fardan*), saying that I should regard it as the *zakāt* of my cunt, would you also tell me to oblige him?"[155]

4.4 Pilgrimage

We have already seen the metaphorical application of the term *qibla* ('direction of prayer') in the sense of 'focus of attention'. The whole notion of pilgrimage (*ḥajj*) developed into a comparable metaphor for striving to contact someone, sometimes in an amorous sense. The motif could be elaborated further, with such aspects of the pilgrimage as the ritual circumambulation of the Kaʿba (*ṭawāf*) and the kissing of the black stone serving as further elements in a complex metaphorical image, which easily lent itself for use in erotic and love poetry (besides other themes).[156]

Abū Ayyūb al-Mūriyānī in al-Tanūkhī, *Nishwār* VIII, 132; and also see al-Tawhīdī, *Baṣāʾir* V(ix), 65, 168; al-Tawḥīdī, *Muqābasāt* 347; al-Thaʿālibī, *Yatīma* III, 264; al-Thaʿālibī, *Thimār* II, 956; al-Thaʿālibī, *Khāṣṣ* 72; al-Bākharzī, *Dumya* I, 165; Kushājim, *Adab* 44; al-Ibshīhī, *Mustaṭraf* 464.

[154] al-Maydānī, *Amthāl* I, 415.

[155] al-Tawḥīdī [attr.], *Risāla* 230. The same vulgar motif is the point of an obscene joke that defines anal intercourse with a poor (or superannuated) boy prostitute as the '*zakāt* of the prick'; see al-Tawḥīdī, *Baṣāʾir* III(v), 137; al-Rāghib, *Muḥāḍarāt* III, 493.

[156] E.g. al-Thaʿālibī, *Laṭāʾif* 76–7. For further examples, see Abū Nuwās, *Dīwān* V, 34; al-Thaʿālibī, *Thimār* II, 898; al-Thaʿālibī, *Yatīma* I, 308, 373, 398; II, 111, 166; III, 102; IV, 371–2, 398; al-Thaʿālibī, *Tatimma* I, 11, 61, 137, 145; al-Tawḥīdī [attr.], *Risāla* 301; al-Bākharzī, *Dumya* I, 136; al-Iṣbahānī, *Kharīda* I(i), 39; al-Ibshīhī, *Mustaṭraf* 272, 300; Ibn Diḥya, *Muṭrib* 15, 17, 174; Ibn Saʿīd, *Ghuṣūn* 121; Ibn Saʿīd, *Rāyāt* 47; Ibn Saʿīd, *Muqtaṭaf* 94; Ibn al-Kattānī, *Tashbīhāt* 132, 221, 250; Ibn al-Khaṭīb, *Jaysh* 24; al-Ṣafadī, *Tawshīḥ* 107; Ibn Maʿṣūm, *Sulāfa* 62, 552, 566. The motif was also present in vernacular poetry; see al-Ḥillī, *ʿĀṭil* 24 ["*Fa-tarā l-ʿālam yaṭūfū bi-qaṣrak wa-yaqīmū yadak al-ḥajar al-aswad*"]; and it continues to be used in modern folk poetry too; see Jargy 1970: 151 ["*ʿA ṣderek beyt el-Kaʿbe / W-neḥnā l-suwwāḥ ḥejjāje...*"]. – Already in the early Islamic period people seem to have used similar phrases, likening a visit to someone to the pilgrimage. For instance, it could be said about a particularly attractive woman that no pilgrimage would be complete without visiting her. In

The following panegyric, while by no means representing *mujūn* – as I will argue, panegyrics would rarely if ever qualify as *mujūn*, no matter how objectionable their subject-matter, their over-the-top hyperboles, or their style – still illustrates the embellishment of the metaphor of the pilgrimage. The poem, composed by the Moroccan poet Abū l-Rabīʿ b. ʿAbdallāh (fl. late 6th/12th c.), is a complaint addressed to the sultan about the latter's granting access to a recently arrived Syrian delegation but not to his own faithful court poet:

> Oh Kaʿba of generosity, the object of pilgrimage for Syrians, Turks and Daylamī Persians;
> How magnificent it is for those who enjoy your protection and circumambulate this ancient shrine in a pilgrim's garb.
> And how strange that someone from Syria may look at you while an inhabitant of Mecca is denied access.[157]

While these hackneyed metaphors were hardly scandalous to anyone, apart from the occasional slightly offensive erotic overtone, there were other references to the pilgrimage to Mecca that can definitely be described as *mujūn*. One such theme is the jesting description of a libertine's thwarted determination to mend his ways and go on a pilgrimage to Mecca, a plan stopped short at the nearest tavern en route.[158] Such anecdotes would be *mujūn* literature because of their describing *mujūn* behaviour. In addition to this particular theme, quite a number of miscellaneous anecdotes, jokes and poems have been preserved that treat the topic of the pilgrimage and the Meccan sanctuary in a variety of irreverent ways.[159] A case – whether fictive or historical I cannot judge – that seems to have fascinated many intellectuals is the infamous act (or claim) of the proverbial *mājin* Abū Nuwās of exploiting the occasion of the kissing of the black stone in the Kaʿba to kiss an attractive boy doing the ritual. (In another version, he kisses a woman, but in view of Abū Nuwās's known preferences, it seems like an attempt to import a modicum of decency into an indecent account.)[160] Perhaps not coincidentally, the great multitudes of people from all over the Islamic world mingling at Mecca every year tended to give rise not only to strictly chaste and pious concerns, but also to carnal

mediaeval spoken Arabic, there was a colourful expression about the type of person whose company is sought by many although he is somewhat aloof: such a person was "like the Kaʿba", viz. visited by others but not visiting anyone. See al-Maydānī, *Amthāl* II, 204; al-Iṣfahānī, *Aghānī* XVIII, 42; al-Ibshīhī, *Mustaṭraf* 36.

157 Ibn Saʿīd, *Ghuṣūn* 131–2; Ibn Saʿīd, *Rāyāt* 241.

158 al-Iṣfahānī, *Aghānī* XVIII, 110–1.

159 E.g. al-Tawḥīdī, *Baṣāʾir* III(v), 59; III(vi), 197; al-Thaʿālibī, *Yatīma* I, 283; al-Bākharzī, *Dumya* II, 1130; Ibn al-Jawzī, *Ẓirāf* 141.

160 Ibn al-Jawzī, *Talbīs* 390. For the prelude to this famous incident, cf. Abū Hiffān, *Akhbār* 98–9; and also cf. al-Iṣfahānī, *Aghānī* XX, 72. For a later poetic echo of this story, see Ibn Saʿīd, *Rāyāt* 263 ["...*taḥmilu lī qublatan ilā l-ḥajar*"].

ones, not surprisingly in a society normally quite segregated along gender lines. The tradition in Arabic poetry of associating Mecca and the pilgrimage with the beauties arriving there every year goes back, of course, to ʿUmar b. Abī Rabīʿa (d. 93/712 or 103/721) and his brand of love poetry (*ghazal*).[161]

5. Images of Afterlife

5.1 Eschatological Concepts as Literary Motifs

A considerable portion of the Quran is dedicated to vivid images of Paradise and Hell, which have continued to this day to be a formative influence on Muslim folklore and élite culture alike. In fact, the Quran's depictions of the hereafter are so powerful and colourful that it would have been very surprising for Arabic poets and writers not to borrow heavily from that imagery, and borrow they did. That borrowing took place in the context of jocular literature and outright *mujūn* no less than in serious literary products. Taken almost entirely from the Quran (with a small percentage of the material originating in *ḥadīths* and popular eschatological legends), these motifs could arguably be more at home in the section discussing *iqtibās* and the use of Quranic imagery, but the sheer amount of eschatological images in secular literature will perhaps justify treating it within a separate section of this essay.

No more than a cursory look at the wide variety of eschatological imagery in literature will be provided here. To begin with, the very notions of Paradise and Hell – and the terms denoting them – as well as various elements of the imagery of each were used as similes or metaphors for describing pleasant and unpleasant settings and situations respectively.[162] Islamic eschatological elements frequently appearing in secular literature include the two horrific angels thought to interrogate

[161] For some examples from the high Abbasid and Buyid eras, see al-Bākharzī, *Dumya* I, 384.

[162] An admirably elaborate literary utilisation of the Quranic imagery of Paradise can be found in a 12th/17th-century letter cited in Ibn Maʿṣūm, *Sulāfa* 118. A short poem of stunning linguistic brilliance is the following, utterly untranslatable, pun on several nouns: "*Nadīmatī jāriyatun sāqiya wa-nuzhatī sāqiyatun jāriya; / Jāriyatun aʿyunuhā jannatun wa-jannatun aʿyunuhā jāriya.*" See al-Ibshīhī, *Mustaṭraf* 477. For a variety of earlier uses of such motifs (although probably none nearly as luxurious as the text of the letter or as masterful as the previous poem), see Abū Hiffān, *Akhbār* 104–5; Ibn al-Muʿtazz, *Ṭabaqāt* 6; al-Tawḥīdī, *Risāla* 332; al-Thaʿālibī, *Thimār* II, 978; al-Thaʿālibī, *Yatīma* IV, 210; al-Thaʿālibī, *Tatimma* I, 139; al-Bākharzī, *Dumya* I, 114; II, 1251; III, 1492; al-Jurjānī, *Wasāṭa* 303; al-Ibshīhī, *Mustaṭraf* 300; al-Ḥillī, *ʿĀṭil* 31; Ibn al-Kattānī, *Tashbīhāt* 50; Ibn Diḥya, *Muṭrib* 59; Ibn Saʿīd, *Rāyāt* 62, 230; Ibn Saʿīd, *Muqtaṭaf* 107; Ibn al-Khaṭīb, *Jaysh* 13. Of course, motifs of this sort are known in modern Arabic folk poetry too; see for instance Jargy 1970: 54. – Just as 'Hell' could be a metaphor for something very unpleasant, so could be the Quranic phrase *ʿadhābun alīm* ("painful punishment", referring to the torments of hellfire); see for instance al-Thaʿālibī, *Nathr* 147 [where it is used to characterise the conversation of a boring interlocutor].

the deceased in the grave (Munkar and Nakīr); the guardian of Paradise, Riḍwān and his counterpart at Hell's gates, Mālik; as well as the names of various rivers of paradise derived from the Quran's text (*al-Kawthar, Salsabīl, Tasnīm*).[163] Hellish images turned into some of the commonest literary metaphors include the foul, horrific *zaqqūm* fruit and the terrifying sentries called *zabāniya*.[164] The Quranic depictions of the day of the Last Judgement also often appear in the form of literary motifs; by way of a sample, one may single out the images of the trumpet of the last judgement (*al-ṣūr*)[165], the narrow path or bridge that is thought to lead to Paradise (*al-ṣirāṭ*)[166], and the scales on which everyone's good and bad deeds shall be weighed (*al-mīzān*)[167]. In one text, the trumpet that will signal the arrival of the Judgement is evoked as a hyperbolic measurement of a person's deafness; it is suggested that he will fail to notice the event, no matter how hard the trumpet is blown.[168] The tremors of the earth are another apocalyptic image mentioned in the Quran (99:1), and the literary device of *iqtibās* put this well-known Quranic phrase into various contexts, some of them rather *outré*, both in literature proper and in what appears to be the record of spoken jesting.[169]

However, of all the numerous eschatological motifs that poets and writers of Arabic would borrow for secular uses, by far and away the most common one was the comparison of a beautiful girl to a houri (pl. *al-ḥūr al-ʿīn*, the eternal virgins of Paradise awaiting the righteous), and a handsome boy to the 'immortal lads' (*al-wildān al-mukhalladūn*, who will supposedly be the servants of those in Paradise). A veritable cliché in both prose and poetry is the conceit that a person of exceptional beauty is actually a houri or a lad, as the case may be, who has managed to escape from Paradise.[170] The somewhat unclearly defined role of the

---

163 See for instance Ibn Qutayba, *ʿUyūn* I(i), 157; al-Thaʿālibī, *Yatīma* IV, 326; al-Thaʿālibī, *Tatimma* II, 38; al-Thaʿālibī, *Iʿjāz* 204; al-Tawhīdī, *Risāla* 113, 358, 362; al-Iṣbahanī, *Kharīda* II(i), 319–20; al-Ibshīhī, *Mustaṭraf* 105, 277, 306; Ibn Diḥya, *Muṭrib* 3, 170; Ibn al-Kattānī, *Tashbīhāt* 92; Ibn Zaydūn, *Dīwān* 391; Ibn Saʿīd, *Rāyāt* 88; Ibn al-Khaṭīb, *Jaysh* 185; and for an example derived from the spoken argot of mediaeval Baghdad, see Bosworth 1976: I, 160.

164 E.g. al-Tawhīdī, *Risāla* 180, 296, 379; al-Tawḥīdī, *Baṣāʾir* V(ix), 119; al-Thaʿālibī, *Yatīma* III, 270; al-Bākharzī, *Dumya* II, 856.

165 E.g. al-Iṣfahānī, *Aghānī* III, 154, al-Thaʿālibī, *Tatimma* II, 32; Ibn al-Kattānī, *Tashbīhāt* 213, 257.

166 E.g. al-Zawzanī, *Ḥamāsa* II, 116; al-Tawḥīdī [attr.], *Risāla* 332, 378; al-Ibshīhī, *Mustaṭraf* 189; Ibn Diḥya, *Muṭrib* 59; Ibn al-Khaṭīb, *Jaysh* 15.

167 E.g. al-Thaʿālibī, *Yatīma* I, 289–90; al-Thaʿālibī, *Tatimma* I, 27.

168 al-Bākharzī, *Dumya* II, 1068.

169 E.g. Ibn al-Muʿtazz, *Ṭabaqāt* 141 [a scurrilous verse by Abū Saʿd al-Makhzūmī]; al-Iṣfahānī, *Aghānī* III, 154 [outrageous joking of Bashshār b. Burd about this and a number of other Quranic phrases]; al-Thaʿālibī, *Yatīma* III, 272 [a lampoon by al-Ṣāḥib b. ʿAbbād].

170 For mentions of the houris in metaphors and similes, see al-Thaʿālibī, *Yatīma* I, 371; II, 205; al-Tawḥīdī [attr.], *Risāla* 170, 358; al-Iṣbahānī, *Kharīda* I(ii), 77; Ibn Saʿīd, *Rāyāt* 71; Ibn Maʿṣūm, *Sulāfa* 191, 552, 587; al-Ṣafadī, *Tawshīḥ* 159; Ibn al-Khaṭīb, *Jaysh* 161; and also in modern dialectal poetry: Jargy 1970: 219; al-Marzūqī 1967: 110. For the literary image of the paradisiacal lads, see for instance al-Thaʿālibī, *Yatīma* I, 89–90; II, 205; al-Tawhīdī, *Risāla* 362; al-Hamadhānī, *Maqāmāt* 41; al-Iṣbahānī, *Kharīda* I(ii), 77;

paradisiacal lads in the Quran was a standing invitation for innuendoes and quips suggesting an analogous role to that of the houris, as for instance in a jesting remark attributed to Abū Nuwās. Proverbial for his homosexuality as well as his unfettered libertinism, the poet received the pious encouragement from a well-wisher that he should reform his conduct and reap the rewards by entering Paradise and enjoying the bliss of marrying the charming houris. His comment: "Rather the immortal lads."[171] Another notorious homosexual, Yaḥyā b. Aktham (d. 242/857), the chief judge of the caliph al-Ma'mūn (r. 198/813–218/833), is also reported to have made a similar allusion to the potential sexual services of *al-wildān al-mukhalladūn*, and I see no reason to doubt that this witticism may well have been actually uttered by Yaḥyā: "God will honour the believers who reach Paradise by giving them an entourage of young boys as a sign of his satisfaction, for they are worth more than girls. So what should hold us back from striving for this honour and reaching this distinction now?"[172]

5.2 Eschatological Images in Mujūn

The aforementioned remarks of Abū Nuwās and Yaḥyā b. Aktham, both noted libertines, are of the kind that would probably be labelled *mujūn* by any contemporary observer. In the following paragraphs, I will survey a number of such references to Quranic eschatology – and the hereafter in general – as are also likely to have belonged to the same category. That eschatological images should serve as ideal material for *mujūn* is hardly surprising. By their very nature, such images conjure up larger-than-life ideas, yet they are basically just inflated versions of worldly objects and phenomena. This observation is not meant to be disrespectful to religious traditions or frivolous in any way; it is simply a recognition of the obvious fact that for humans to be able to envisage the afterlife, it has to be conveyed in terms somewhat familiar to them, i.e. derived from worldly experiences. However, the tendency of *mujūn* literature – and of pretty much any humour – to exploit the contrast between lofty and lowly would find fertile material on which to flourish by changing the transubstantiated phenomena of Heaven and Hell back into their

Ibn al-Kattānī, *Tashbīhāt* 162; and two pieces by Abū Nuwās in English translation in Wright 1997: 11.

[171] al-Rāghib, *Muḥāḍarāt* III, 474.

[172] al-Thaʿālibī, *Laṭā'if* 62–3; Ibn Saʿīd, *Muqtaṭaf* 208; and in a slightly different wording in al-Thaʿālibī, *Thimār* I, 271. Also cf. al-Jāḥiẓ, *Rasā'il* I(ii), 96; al-Maʿarrī, *Ghufrān* 309. By all appearances, Yaḥyā b. Aktham was noted for his penchant for making scandalous but witty remarks, some of which are recorded in literary and historical sources. One of his famous utterances is a purposeful misapplication of a Quranic verse (34:31) in making a proposition to a servant-boy of the caliph; see al-Iṣfahānī, *Aghānī* XX, 272–3. Whether the paradisiacal boys would perform sexual services in addition to waiting on the believers was a question discussed in the juridical literature too, with most but not all authorities answering in the negative. See El-Rouayheb 2005: 131–6.

original mundane models and thus dragging them into a ludicrously profane context. The creation of such a contrast is the most characteristic manner of handling otherworldly imagery in *mujūn*.

This is one of the areas where there is sufficient evidence to lead one to believe that many *mujūn* motifs actually originated, or at any rate flourished, in everyday speech. Joking in the context of ordinary conversation must have exhibited quite a few instances of the ironic contrast between lofty images and profane contexts, for we find repeated denunciations of precisely such humour in manuals of *fiqh*. (I will not discuss the attitude of jurisprudents to *mujūn* at this point, this being one of the main topics of Chapter Four of this book. What is important for our present purpose is that religious scholars recorded various examples of such irreverent joking.) One Ḥanafite source, dedicated to the condemnation (and presumably the eradication) of reprehensible 'innovations', mentions an outrageous retort that many people were wont to use in answering pious warnings and exhortations: "When you enter Paradise, [remember to] shut the door" (*idhā dakhalta l-janna fa-rudd al-bāb*), presumably to keep sinners out.[173] While these are obviously not scholarly, sophisticated forms of humour, the more learned kind could also rely heavily on the tension between the sublime and the profane, as one can observe in a statement made by Yaḥyā b. Ziyād al-Ḥārithī (2nd/8th c.):

> Date wine (*nabīdh*) has in it one of the qualities of Paradise. God declares [in the Quran], citing [the words of those admitted to Paradise]: "*And they shall say: Praise belongs to God who has put away all sorrow from us*"[174], and date wine also puts away sorrow.[175]

The number of quite irreverent jokes and anecdotes using Islamic eschatological imagery in the mediaeval Arabic literary corpus is considerable. Their topics being extremely variable, the only shared feature in these texts seems to be that they

---

[173] Ibn Baydakīn, *Lumaʿ* I, 182. I am grateful to Khaled El-Rouayheb for discussing with me the likely purport of this phrase. An account in the *Kitāb al-aghānī* about the famous Medinan singer al-Gharīḍ quotes his frivolous joking on the final judgement, which he uttered after hiding behind a rock to have sex with a boy – a very serious offence from a religious viewpoint. See al-Iṣfahānī, *Aghānī* II, 362–3. In another source, frivolous references to the signs of the imminent arrival of the Day of Reckoning ("the proliferation of mosques is a sign of the approach of the Final Judgement...") are ascribed to the Abbasid caliph al-Manṣūr (r. 136/754–158/775), but I find it unlikely that this caliph should have uttered such irreverent words – at least not in public – and would rather take this anecdote for what it seemingly is: an entertaining anecdote with a well-known historical figure added to serve as a protagonist. See al-Tawḥīdī, *Baṣāʾir* I(ii), 18–9.

[174] Quran 35:34.

[175] al-Thaʿālibī, *Laṭāʾif* 86; and also see al-Thaʿālibī, *Iʿjāz* 131; al-Tawhīdī, *Imtāʿ* 196. (In the latter version, the bon mot is attributed to an unnamed *qāṣṣ*.) This text is not unlike a very risqué anecdote that compares the unimpressive performance of a concubine in bed with some attributes of Paradise; see al-Jāḥiẓ, *Rasāʾil* I(ii), 128; al-Tawḥīdī, *Baṣāʾir* II(iv), 156; al-Rāghib, *Muḥāḍarāt* III, 511.

juxtapose, in the manner discussed above, the sublime notion of the hereafter to emphatically banal, prosaic elements of earthly life.[176] Such jokes tend to employ protagonists who came to be standard figures of the mediaeval Arabic joke repertoire (although some of those names did belong to little-known but living men), and thus it is best to regard these texts as fictional, even though some of the punch lines might happen to have originated as actual remarks made by historical personages.

For instance, the scholar Abū ʿAlqama is a stock figure of jokes on grammarians, an important subtype within the *nawādir* corpus. A story shows him heaping exaggerated praise upon the excellence of his mule, whereupon a man advises him to ask God to resurrect the beast next to him on the Day of Judgement, so that he should be able to enjoy a smooth ride into Paradise over the narrow bridge.[177] Another anecdote is based on the trivial use of the expression 'the Resurrection has arrived' (*qāmat al-qiyāma*) to describe a riotous scene, a commotion, uproar and disorder – a usage as widespread in spoken Arabic as it is in written prose and poetry.[178] The gist of the joke is that the protagonist takes the expression at face value, and faults the banal earthly scene for lacking the grandiose attributes of the Quranic description of the resurrection:

> At a time of solar eclipse, coupled with a high wind and a dreadful dust-storm, Muzabbid of Medina heard the people clamour and wail, "The Judgement! The Judgement!" He said: "Damn you; this [would be] a judgement [taken] on an empty stomach! Where is the Beast of the Earth (*Dābbat al-Arḍ*)? Where's the Antichrist? Where's the return of Jesus? Where's the sun rising in the west? I am the witness that this is a meagre resurrection indeed."[179]

---

[176] This contrasting of lofty and banal is not unknown in today's popular Arabic humour either. In an extremely illuminating study of sarcastic quips in popular discourse, a Sudanese anthropologist records a remark that he heard in a village of Northern Sudan to the effect that the tribe's founding ancestor, who stupidly chose a barren stretch of land for his descendants, ought to lie buried under a thick layer of concrete instead of a shrine, so that he should be unable to rise on the day of resurrection. See Ibrahim 1994: 31.

[177] al-ʿAskari, *Ṣināʿatayn* 34–5.

[178] For examples of the use of the phrase in verse, see al-Thaʿālibī, *Yatīma* I, 299; al-Thaʿālibī, *Tatimma* II, 32; al-Bākharzī, *Dumya* I, 101; II, 732; al-Zawzanī, *Ḥamāsa* II, 27; al-Tawḥīdī [attr.], *Risāla* 363; al-Iṣbahānī, *Kharīda* Ii(ii), 615; al-Ibshīhī, *Mustaṭraf* 284. Also in modern dialectal poetry; see for instance Jargy 1970: 104. For some examples in mediaeval Arabic prose, see al-Iṣfahānī, *Aghānī* III, 154; Miskawayh, *Tajārib* I, 112, 206; II, 54, 186; Ibn Maʿṣūm, *Sulāfa* 114.

[179] al-Thaʿālibī, *Laṭāʾif* 87. The same story in a slightly different version can be found in al-Tawḥīdī, *Baṣāʾir* II(iii), 85. *Al-Dajjāl*, usually rendered in English as 'the Antichrist', is a firm part of the Muslim eschatological tradition, and of course appears in frivolous literature too. As this figure was believed to arrive mounted on a donkey, it is rather unsurprising to find an obnoxious person riding a donkey being compared to the Antichrist in a literary text; see al-Tawḥīdī, *Risāla* 131.

The same protagonist appears in another joke, as do similar references to the Muslim conception of the Day of Judgement. In this story, Muzabbid's pregnant wife complains of her craving for roast locusts – perhaps not too costly a delicacy – but the curmudgeonly husband, at the mere notion of such extravagance, starts fulminating: "By God, even if the Antichrist were marching against Medina, and you were in labour to give birth to the Messiah, I wouldn't buy you [locusts] at this price!"[180]

Effeminate men (sing. *mukhannath*) are one of the archetypes in mediaeval Arabic literature of a quick-witted person especially ready with sarcastic repartees. Such a man is the protagonist of a joke that plays with a Quranic image depicting mountains collapsing upon themselves "like plucked wool-tufts" (*ka-l-ʿihn al-manfūsh*; Quran 101:5). It is to this passage that the *mukhannath* in the joke alludes when, exasperated with the trivial inconvenience of a steep ascent to a hill, he says to it: "How glad I'll be the day I see you become *like plucked wool-tufts*."[181] Examples of the grotesque incongruity of combining eschatological concepts and images with prosaic, mundane ones could be multiplied *ad nauseam*: the Angel of Death morosely grumbles about his job when he has to take away an obnoxious bore; the denizens of Hell bewail the damnation of a loathsome, repugnant man because they will have to endure his company; someone offers his condolences to the bereaved but is unable to get right the names of the two interrogating angels even after repeated attempts; and so on.[182] One may wonder if the fascinating prose work of Abū l-ʿAlāʾ al-Maʿarrī (363/973–449/1058), the *Risālat al-ghufrān* (The Epistle of Forgiveness), which displays a somewhat enigmatic ambiguity between seriousness and jestfulness, may not owe much of its effect to a deliberate mixing of banal and sublime elements.[183]

6. Hyperboles in Praise Poetry

It is probably fair to state that praise poems (*madīḥ*), of all of the poetic genres, make the most fertile ground for all sorts of hyperbole, especially shamelessly

[180] al-Tawḥīdī, *Baṣāʾir* II(iv), 205.

[181] al-Tawḥīdī, *Baṣāʾir* I(ii), 98. For a case of *iqtibās* using this Quranic verse in a poem, see al-Bākharzī, *Dumya* II, 840.

[182] al-Thaʿālibī, *Nathr* 147 (and cf. a modern Arabic joke about the tribulations of the dead in Hillelson 1935: 20–1); Ibn al-Muʿtazz, *Ṭabaqāt* 168; al-Tawḥīdī, *Baṣāʾir* IV(vii), 112. In the last reference, instead of the correct Munkar and Nakīr, the first guess is *Yājūj wa-Mājūj* (Gog and Magog), and the second one is *Hārūt wa-Mārūt* (the names of two fallen angels, credited with introducing magic to humanity in Babylon).

[183] On this issue, cf. van Gelder 1992: 177; and for possible examples of such ambiguity, see for instance al-Maʿarrī, *Ghufrān* 248–56 [the comical scene of the tumult and brouhaha of the Day of Judgement], 260–2 [the crossing of the *ṣirāṭ* bridge].

sycophantic exaggerations of magnificence and glory. Magnificence and glory also being one of the natural attributes of God, it stands to reason that panegyrics would easily run the risk of being blasphemous in their too eager praise of a mere mortal. Even so, as praise poetry, however outrageous and blasphemous some of its imagery, would not normally be classified as *mujūn*, the following section of my study will constitute something of a detour from my main topic, even if a necessary one in my opinion. We will not be detained here by the question of why even the most *outré* panegyrics were not usually considered to be *mujūn*, since our present purpose is simply the overview of poetic motifs potentially offensive to religious sensibilities. In Chapter Five of my essay however, this important question will be addressed in some detail.

The genre of *madīḥ*, albeit one of the most conspicuous, extensive and multifarious types of mediaeval Arabic poetry, and despite the fact that it tended to be the most lucrative poetic genre from which to earn a livelihood, was in itself viewed by many devout people as a genre of dubious merits. The pious often felt uneasy with the almost inevitable aggrandisement and sycophancy concomitant with the effusive praise that marked this genre, and tended to view such characteristics in terms of falsity and guile – basically just lying. Given the prevalent perception that temporal rulers were a corrupt breed and their awards to subordinates ill-gotten gains, it is not difficult to comprehend why encomia should be disapproved of by a lot of religious scholars. A particularly strict Ḥanafite source makes this brusque assertion regarding praise to the powers that be: "The Prophet's *sunna* is that no one should be adulated in his presence, or [eulogised/slandered] in excess behind his back."[184] Other authorities were more specific in their condemnation of certain poetic practices, including inadmissible hyperboles, as will be shown at a later point in this book. This, however, never threatened the position of *madīḥ* (or poetry in general) as an omnipresent fact of courtly culture.

Fantastic hyperboles abound in Arabic praise poetry, and some of those hyperboles have the unmistakable air of blasphemy, or near-blasphemy, about them. Some verbal flourishes in panegyrics almost seem designed to flout, or at least disregard, the most elementary doctines of Islam.[185] Eulogy is perhaps similar in this respect to drugs: larger and larger doses are required to produce the desired effect. On the other hand, a poet could obviously get away with phrases and ideas in a praise poem that would surely have caused him difficulties had he incorporated them in works of other poetic genres. For example, a poet claiming to have received divine

---

[184] Ibn Baydakīn, *Lumaʿ* I, 285.

[185] For a sampling, see al-Thaʿālibī, *Yatīma* I, 169–70; II, 420; III, 266; al-Thaʿālibī, *Tatimma* II, 77, 84; al-Bākharzī, *Dumya* I, 435; al-Zawzanī, *Ḥamāsa* II, 187; al-Iṣbahānī, *Kharīda* I(i), 158, 303; I(ii), 294; al-Jurjānī, *Wasāṭa* 229; al-ʿAskarī, *Ṣināʿatayn* 122-3; al-Ḥillī, *ʿĀṭil* 24.

inspiration in composing his poetry – as the prophet Muḥammad did in conveying the Quran – would probably have sounded as if speaking extremely objectionable *mujūn* had he not made the claim in an encomium about a ruler (who after all had the power in practice, although not in theory, to decide what was off limits and what was not).[186] Virtually blasphemous hyperboles in praise poetry are quite varied. One poem compares the respectful kissing of a ruler's hand to the pilgrimage rites at the Kaʿba sanctuary in Mecca, and indeed gives priority to the former over the latter.[187] By the late Buyid period, poets would routinely engage in the verbal excess of calling their royal patrons prophets, a motif which, if taken literally, would imply a clear contradiction of the Islamic tenet of Muḥammad having been the last of the prophets. For instance, one poet calls the celebrated vizier of Seljuk times Niẓām al-Mulk (408/1018–485/1092) a prophet, and his pronouncements a Quran. Another, a court poet of a Fatimid ruler in Egypt, acclaims his patron as a prophet uttering words of divine inspiration.[188] The same cloyingly sycophantic motif – to 20th-century tastes anyway – recurs in the following line addressed to the Abbasid caliph al-Mustaḍīʾ (r. 566/1170–575/1180), who appears to have been pleased by the panegyric as he rewarded the poet with three hundred golden dinars, a luxurious garment, a house and a farm:

> We have asked God to give us an imam to help us live [correctly], but he would give us a prophet [instead].[189]

One of the greatest Arabic poets, Abū l-Ṭayyib al-Mutanabbī (303/915–354/965) – never one to forbear even the most grandiose of hyperboles – went even beyond this when he ascribed what is practically a divine attribute to his patron, whom he characterises as being capable of resurrecting decomposed bones by his benevolence.[190] Al-Mutanabbī was notorious among literary critics for this; his insouciance in regard to pious sensibilities is also evident in the following line which, on the surface, sounds dangerously like questioning the Muslim dogma about God being the sole

---

186 Admittedly, this particular motif comes from a late (11th/17th c.) anthology, where it occurs in a eulogy addressed to the *sharīf* of Mecca: "... *fa-lī fī naẓmi madḥika min Jibrīla ilhāmu.*" See Ibn Maʿṣūm, *Sulāfa* 386; and compare it with a much earlier verse describing the al-Zāhira palace of Andalusia in Ibn al-Kattānī, *Tashbīhāt* 69. The motif of divine inspiration appears not only in praise poetry but in an ironic sense too (which might reflect the influence of spoken language); see al-Thaʿālibī, *Tatimma* I, 85.

187 Ibn Diḥya, *Muṭrib* 15–6; and also see Ibn al-Muʿtazz, *Ṭabaqāt* 97.

188 al-Bākharzī, *Dumya* I, 258, 260; al-Qalqashandī, *Ṣubḥ* III, 497. (And compare it with a poem by Ibn al-Rūmī [221/836–283/896] cited in Gruendler 2003: 87-8; also in Ibn al-Rūmī, *Dīwān* V, 287.)

189 al-Iṣbahānī, *Kharīda* I(i), 330.

190 What is more, the wording is consciously tailored to echo the Quran's text (36:78). See al-Jurjānī, *Wasāṭa* 325.

distributor of livelihood (*rizq*) and the decision-maker about the time of everyone's death:

> It is only your spear's blade that assigns a frightful death, and only your right hand that distributes livelihood.[191]

Even if panegyrics were the real breeding place of excessive hyperboles, other genres of Arabic poetry not usually associated with *mujūn* were not completely devoid of them either. For example, elegiac poetry (*rithāʾ*) might also occasionally employ such exaggerations. A poet of the Buyid era called al-Ḥasan b. Wahb drew perhaps too venturesome a comparison between a great fellow-poet whose death he was lamenting and the Prophet: alluding to the prophet's epithet *khātam al-anbiyāʾ* ('the seal of the prophets'), he called the deceased 'the seal of the poets'.[192] Love poetry (*ghazal*) was also amenable to the use of hyperbolic expressions, in ways analogous to those observed in panegyrics. This similarity is hardly surprising, considering the fact that much of love poetry tended to consist of boundless praise heaped upon the beloved's outward and inward characteristics.[193] Nor is it an unexpected discovery to find a lot of similarly problematic (and potentially offensive) motifs in lampoons too, a genre that, like praise poetry, thrives by exaggeration and hyperbole.[194]

7. Genuine *Mujūn*: A Provisional Summary

This study has repeatedly made the observation that it is not always easy to delineate *mujūn* and distinguish it from less offensive material, there being a very wide margin

191 al-Jurjānī, *Wasāṭa* 249.

192 al-Tanūkhī, *Nishwār* VI, 95.

193 E.g. Abū Hiffān, *Akhbār* 49 ["... *qad aḥalla l-taʿṭīla wa-l-ishrākā*"]; al-Thaʿālibī, *Yatīma* I, 375 ["*mutanaṣṣirun qawiyat ʿalā islāminā bi-l-ḥusni minhu ḥujjatu l-kuffāri*"]; II, 381 ["... *ṣaddaqtu qawla l-ḥulūliyyīna fī l-ṣuwari*"]; III, 423 ["... *āthamu mimman ashrakā*"]; al-Bākharzī, *Dumya* II, 848 ["... *ḥattā ʿiftu islāmī*"]; al-Iṣbahānī, *Kharīda* I(ii), 328 ["*qāla hādhā rabbī wa-lam yatabarrā*"]; Ibn al-Kattānī, *Tashbīhāt* 156 ["... *wa-huwa ʿabdun li-rabbayni*"]. Such exaggerations are also present in modern Arabic folk poetry, at least in Iraq; e.g. al-Khāqānī 1381/1962: I, 35 ["*Lāzim bi-dhichrik mithl al-ʿibāda wird*"]. A common motif in love poetry, which in all probability has always been understood as the conventional hyperbole it was, is the claim that the poet will discard even his religion for his beloved. See for instance Ibn al-Khaṭīb, *Jaysh* 6, 101.

194 A typical example is the following verbal flourish in prose about the great littérateur, poet and politician of the Buyid era, al-Ṣāḥib Ismāʿīl b. ʿAbbād (and a singularly unfair judgement, one may add): "His stupidity belies the wisdom of his Creator; his wealth encourages one to deny the Provider of Sustenance" (*safahuhu yanfī ḥikmat khāliqihi wa-ghināhu yadʿū ilā l-kufr bi-rāziqihi*); see al-Tawḥīdī, *Akhlāq* 106. Similar motifs occur in verse too; see for instance Ibn al-Muʿtazz, *Badīʿ* 163; al-ʿAskarī, *Ṣināʿatayn* 122.

of tolerance for *mujūn* totally dependent on a person's lenience and sensibilities. There is no more accounting for sensitivity or indulgence than there is for tastes. This also implies that one person's *mujūn* could easily be another's light entertainment, and vice versa. As people's insistence on conformity to norms varies, so will their perceptions of norm-breaking too. That said, there certainly were literary motifs and patterns of behaviour that would unambiguously appear as *mujūn* to just about any observer, and it is this category of phenomena that we will briefly turn our attention in this section. As the present chapter has been devoted to motifs potentially offensive from a religious point of view, the manifestations of 'genuine' *mujūn* discussed in the following paragraphs will also represent this category, but it must be added that many motifs flouting norms of common propriety and respectability – the topic of the next chapter – were also obviously regarded as pure, unadulterated, unmistakable *mujūn*. Be that as it may, what follows is a motley collection of motifs and utterances that represent a miscellaneous sample of all the previously surveyed types, and are unified not so much by their subject-matter or their internal logic but by their degree of frivolity and brazenness. Surely, the previous pages also contain a lot of evident and unequivocal *mujūn*, so in that sense there is nothing new here at all, but a condensed sample may still help formulate a better idea of what the term *mujūn* actually means.

A short detour is necessary here. Blasphemy, as I will argue in Chapter Four, is not a Muslim concept in that it does not directly correspond to any one term or category of *fiqh* – in fact the attempt to categorise various statements that appear blasphemous to an outside observer was the subject of an extended and ongoing controversy in traditional Islamic legal theory. Thus the concept of blasphemy corresponds to, if anything, an array of disparate, controversial and much-disputed categories in Muslim thought. These include such concepts as 'derision [of religion]', 'calling God a liar', 'calling God unjust', 'permitting that which is prohibited', 'insulting the Prophet', and so forth. Most of these categories were themselves subject to debate as to what legal consequences they should have, and whether any particular category of *lèse-religion* would qualify as unbelief (*kufr*), or grave sin (*kabīra*), or minor sin (*ṣaghīra*), or iniquity and moral depravity (*fisq*). In short, there was no conceptual framework to deal with either blasphemy or *lèse-religion* as one single category. Without pursuing this point further – which will only be done in Chapter Four – one may simply note that in speaking of manifestations of *mujūn* being 'blasphemous' or 'offensive to religious norms', one is applying a foreign category, albeit a convenient one. The following examples are thus instances of blasphemous (or perhaps even not-so-blasphemous) humour to a modern Western observer, and were certainly instances of *mujūn* for a mediaeval Muslim audience.

1. Comparing mere mortals and their utterances to the Prophet, to the Quran, let alone to God, would never fail to qualify as *mujūn* for mediaeval Muslims, with the probable exception of praise poetry. Such texts are far from exceptional or rare. The following example is a poem composed by the celebrated vizier and intellectual al-Ṣāḥib b. ʿAbbād (326/938–385/995), who describes a boy of stunning beauty with rapturous similes of prophetic mission:

> The brightness of his forehead is like [the light of] true belief, and the blackness of his locks like [dark] error.
> As though God had sent him as a prophet among us, setting his beauty as his strongest argument.[195]

While the Prophet Muḥammad always insisted on his being merely human, the simile is still irreverent, but it is evidently even more outrageous to compare a human being, however jestingly, to God. Yet precisely this is the point of the following poem, although it is an allusion rather than an explicit statement:

> If a cooking pot full of food were boiling in a deep hollow somewhere in Byzantium or the farthest West,
> And you were in China at the moment, you would still get there in time [for dinner], oh you *Knower of Things Hidden* in the pots.[196]

Occasionally one finds not only humans but also inanimate things being given attributes properly belonging to God. Such is the case in a wine poem of Abū Nuwās that mentions 'the most beautiful names' of wine, a Quranic phrase that few Muslims would have failed to recognise as being appropriate only in reference to God.[197] Calling a work notable for its linguistic polish or persuasiveness (or otherwise remarkable) a Quran must also have struck mediaeval Muslims as rather *outré*, yet it is a motif far from uncommon. Abū Ḥayyān al-Tawḥīdī (d. 414/1023), with characteristic vehemence, deplores the morals of the vizier al-Ṣāḥib b. ʿAbbād in one passage with these words: "In debauchery he has an inimitable Quran, in idiocy he has a revealed *āya*" (*lahu fī l-khalāʿa Qurʾān muʿjiz wa-fī l-raqāʿa āya munzala*).[198] Ironically, one of the manifold reasons for which the author faults the vizier is the latter's alleged – and most probably actual – disregard for pious sensibilities.

195 al-Thaʿālibī, *Nathr* 187; al-Thaʿālibī, *Yatīma* III, 253; and cf. Ibn Saʿīd, *Muqtaṭaf* 107 for a poem of similar purport. In another source, the servant who is bringing in the dinner is playfully dubbed a prophet conveying a divine message (*ṣāḥib al-dalāla wa-ḥāmil al-risāla*); see al-Tawḥīdī [attr.], *Risāla* 76.

196 al-Khaṭīb, *Taṭfīl* 26; al-Tawḥīdī [attr.], *Risāla* 64. Of course, Knower of Things Hidden (*ʿālim al-ghayb*) is a common epithet of God, who alone possesses all transcendental knowledge.

197 Zubaidi 1983: 327–8.

198 al-Tawḥīdī, *Akhlāq* 107. For poems that contain similes likening something convincing, beautiful or wonderful to a *sūra* (Quranic chapter) – a more harmless motif by all standards – see al-Thaʿālibī, *Yatīma* I, 229; al-Thaʿālibī, *Tatimma* I, 145; al-Iṣbahānī, *Kharīda* I(i), 37; Ibn Diḥya, *Muṭrib* 111; Ibn al-Khaṭīb, *Jaysh* 108.

2. Misapplying the Quran's verses, twisting its meaning in a deliberate manner, and especially rephrasing the sacred text, were all as popular motifs in genuine *mujūn* as they were outrageous offences to piety. Obviously, the altering of a Quranic verse for frivolous purposes was full-blown *mujūn*, and a very popular sort at that. One of the daughters of the Abbasid caliph al-Mahdī (r. 158/775–169/785) called ʿUlayya is said to have been madly in love with a young servant, whose name was Ṭall ('dew, fine rain'), in the caliphal court. Commanded to refrain, for fear of scandal, from as much as uttering the humble servant's name, she made an indignant yet facetious show of defying the order by obeying it to the absurd degree of suppressing that noun in a Quranic verse (2:265) and reciting a synonym instead.[199] Whilst this incident appears to be a historical one – even if some details may be unreliable – wholly fictitious texts also made use of the device of rephrasing the sacred text. Jokes and anecdotes based on preposterous mistakes made by Quran readers (sing. *qāriʾ*) are a standard type of *mujūn* material. One pertinent example is a joke starring a Quran reciter who misrecites a rather well-known passage (Quran 30:1–3) by mentioning the Turks (*al-turk*) in lieu of the Byzantines (*al-rūm*). When someone in the audience points out the gross mistake – all the more ludicrous as the very title of that chapter of the Quran is *al-Rūm* – he snaps with annoyance: "Both are our enemies, may God destroy them."[200] The implication, of course, is that it is no big deal to alter the divine text, a suggestion so monstrous from a Muslim point of view as to be laughable. It is precisely the enormity of the idea of modifying the Quranic text, whether deliberately or out of ignorance, which makes such jokes sound absurd and therefore funny.[201]

3. As we have seen, placing the sacred texts (both Quran and *ḥadīth*) in an unbecoming or unseemly context, and creating a humorous effect by the resulting discrepancy, was a common device in *mujūn* literature. It is fair to say that all, or most of, such texts would certainly qualify as *mujūn*. Since quite a few such jokes and anecdotes were discussed in the relevant section of this chapter, there is no need to offer another sample here. Let it suffice to say that the sublime character

[199] al-Tanūkhī, *Nishwār* I, 195; al-Ibshīhī, *Mustaṭraf* 50. Incidentally, you find the same *āya* incorporated in a poem in al-Iṣbahānī, *Kharīda* I(ii), 88; as well as in al-Thaʿālibī, *Iqtibās* II, 34.

[200] al-Ibshīhī, *Mustaṭraf* 533. An anecdote about the Kurds is very similar; see it in translation in Marzolph 2000: 486.

[201] For further examples of the motif of deliberate tampering with the text, see al-Tanūkhī, *Nishwār* I, 195 [a lady affecting to be so sensitive as to replace the 'coarse' noun *nafs* with its near-synonym *rūḥ* in reciting Quran 5:116]; al-Tawḥīdī, *Baṣāʾir* V(ix), 10 [Ḥātim al-Aṣamm refashioning the Quran's text to be more suitable to describe his audience]. Such jokes are not unknown in modern Arabic folklore either; see for instance Chanfrault 1996: 55. For examples of the motif of uneducated people misquoting the Quran, see al-Tanūkhī, *Nishwār* II, 244; al-Tawḥīdī, *Baṣāʾir* III(vi), 58; al-Ibshīhī, *Mustaṭraf* 51–2. (However, the protagonist of the last example, Ḥammād al-Rāwiya [d. 155–6/772-3], could hardly be described as uneducated.)

of the Quranic text might be contrasted to such worldly trivialities as the charging of money for the reciting of that text, or the apparent tedium felt by some of the audience in listening to the well-known *āyas*.[202] Regardless of the details, the underlying logic of these jokes is always the same.

4. A significant part of the genuine *mujūn* material we find in the sources displays a markedly cynical, flippant and sarcastic approach to religious obligations, the Quran, or any of the other revered concepts of Islamic culture. In essence, a great many jokes and poems characterisable as *mujūn* are just cynical comments of varying lengths on pious attitudes. A number of such 'comments' follow. The first occurs in a joke that puts a twist on the notion of God's boundless mercy:

> A company of people on a voyage were about to perish in the [tempestuous] sea. They started to invoke God to save them [from destruction]. One of them was asked by his companions why he did not supplicate. He answered: "[God] is [fed up] with me to this point," – and here he pointed to his nose – "so if I as much as utter a word, you'll drown."[203]

The same air of cynicism pervades the following poem by Ibn al-Habbāriyya (d. 509/1115–6), which practically makes fun of the important Muslim concept of *tawba*, or 'repentance':

> Abū Saʿīd asked me, having seen that I had devoutly eschewed drinking [wine] for a year:
> "Which sheikh made you reform your conduct?", and I replied: "Bankruptcy."[204]

Some of what I chose to classify as manifestations of cynicism are really irreverent comparisons or similes, comparing a trivial, worldly image to lofty concepts. In this, they are also analogous to the previous subtype of *mujūn*, where one finds sacred texts – namely the Quran and *ḥadīths* – being brought into incongruous, lowly contexts. The frivolous similes (or quasi-similes) that we are concerned with here show a similar discrepancy between the sublime and the quotidian. Two examples will illustrate this type of *mujūn*. One is a remark attributed to a celebrated

202 E.g. Ibn al-Jawzī, *Ẓirāf* 140; al-Tawḥīdī, *Baṣāʾir* V(ix), 101. For similar examples, see for instance al-Tawḥīdī, *Baṣāʾir* II(iv), 110 [an anecdote about a man attempting to battle his donkey's hunger with reciting the Quran], 115 [a drunk trying to recite the Quran]. – Incidentally, some Sufis might apparently make the occasional overt protest against what was felt to be an inordinately long recitation of the Quran, and the style of such protests, as recorded by Ibn Baydakīn al-Turkumānī, seems to have been quite sarcastic. See Ibn Baydakīn, *Lumaʿ* I, 80. Still more remarkable is the fact that it is not only in frivolous and irreverent contexts that the recitation of the Quran might be considered tedious. No less an authority than Abū Ḥāmid al-Ghazālī (450/1058–505/1111), whose honest piety and serious intent there is no reason to question, acknowledges that studying the Quran is "a burdensome [task] for the soul" (*thaqīl ʿalā l-nafs*). See al-Ghazālī, *Iḥyāʾ* II, 204.

203 al-Tawḥīdī, *Baṣāʾir* III(v), 75–6.

204 al-Iṣbahānī, *Kharīda* I(ii), 92. Possibly an added source of sarcasm is the fact that the term 'bankruptcy' could also be used in a religious sense, to convey a sense of moral emptiness and depravity.

buffoon of a libertine of the high Abbasid period, the clownish Abū l-Ḥārith Jummayn (2nd/8th c.), who had this to say to express his appreciation of *zumāward* (or *bazmāward*, a kind of sandwich made with eggs): "If the *zumāward* were mentioned in the Quran, it would mark a place for prostration [when recited in prayer] (*mawḍiʿ sajda*)."[205] The other is a poem – to be more precise, a piece of vernacular verse from Baghdad recorded in the early 8th/14th century – evoking the concept of God's infinite mercy:

> Enter any public bath, and you'll find my lady's clothes hanging on the wall.
> This woman is like God's mercy: no place is devoid of her [i.e. she is out and about all the time, which a decent lady should not].[206]

5. Descriptions of prohibited activities, especially if coupled with obscenity, would likely qualify as a matter of course for the label of *mujūn*. That literary portrayal of behaviour thought to be *mujūn* would be, by definition, *mujūn* too was noted in Chapter Two. The *par excellence* illustration of this is wine poetry, in particular the kind produced by Abū Nuwās, as well as much of the scurrilous genre of *sukhf*.

6. Literary texts that urged people to engage in forbidden or disapproved activities, usually in a jocular tone, would most certainly be recognised as *mujūn*. Some works almost systematically list every prescription of Islam and make a show of a refusal of obeying them.[207] While such inverted exhortations would often be simple asides within the framework of a larger work – say, in a drinking poem – they occasionally developed into fully-fledged products on their own, which it would not be wrong to call veritable *mujūn* manifestoes. An even more extreme variety of this overt type of *mujūn* can only be characterised as a mock declaration of unbelief. Alternatively, this motif might also take the form of denying the most fundamental, unquestioned tenets of Islam.[208] A handful of quotations will serve to illustrate the degree of studied, explicit offensiveness that such texts can display:

> There is not a trace of piety in my soul; and I am anything but virtuous.
> If someone bargained over my religion, he could take it for a slice of bread.[209]

---

[205] al-Thaʿālibī, *Laṭāʾif* 86. (Incidentally, one source describes *zumāward* as a sort of sweetmeat, but that is unlikely to be accurate; see Ibn Makkī, *Tathqīf* 124.)

[206] al-Ḥillī, *ʿĀṭil* 155.

[207] E.g. al-Iṣfahānī, *Aghānī* VII, 29 [a poem by al-Walīd]. Obviously different are the implications of a similar poem composed by a non-Muslim, even though on the surface of it there seems to be little to distinguish such works from a poem of *mujūn*. See for instance a poem by the Christian poet al-Akhṭal (d. before 92/710) in al-Ibshīhī, *Mustaṭraf* 72.

[208] E.g. al-Tawḥīdī [attr.], *Risāla* 269 [citing a poem by Ibn al-Ḥajjāj]; al-Ḥillī, *ʿĀṭil* 208 [a vernacular *zajal* piece by Mudghalīs].

[209] al-Thaʿālibī, *Yatīma* III, 20.

> When the hour arrives, I will stand before God my Lord as a Jew.[210]
> As regards the firmness of my piety, I have no parallels except an ape,
> Or perhaps [the Umayyad caliph] Yazīd[211]: Yazīd will suffice,
> As he is my true patron, and [you] are my witnesses
> That it is him that I worship. If you do not believe me, just see where I prostrate myself [instead of in the mosque].[212]

> Love is a god worthy of devotion. – Our religion is believing in it only (*dīnunā ilayhi l-tawḥīd*). – Dejection is ever far from us.
> If you look closely, [you find] we are infidels. – We never cease to live in sin,
> – And care nothing about the Lord. – How wonderful these sins are![213]

The last example is part of a strophic poem of the *muwashshaḥ* genre, a rather late development in the history of mediaeval Arabic verse. The following anecdote, which is so widely cited as to leave no doubt of its popularity, shows a comparably audacious explicitness in the (verbal) flouting of religious prohibitions:

> [Abū l-Ṭamaḥān] al-Qaynī was asked what the most negligible peccadillo of his life had been. He answered that it was 'the night of the monastery'. Asked what on earth 'the night of the monastery' was, he replied: "One day I lodged with a nun. I ate some roast pork, drank the wine she had, then stole her clothes and left."[214]

A more explicitly offensive kind of *mujūn* would be hard to envisage. However, as with a good deal of literary libertinism, here again one should be wary of hastily concluding the actual unbelief of the poet from ostensibly defiant statements made in a poem: this could also be a mere affectation, a somewhat extreme form of *Effekthascherei*.[215] Still, offensive it was, and there can be no question of classifying it as *mujūn*.

As already noted, the explicit and provocative flouting of religious norms is a frequent component of wine poetry, a rather natural consequence of the fact that

---

210 That is to say, a non-Muslim.

211 Infamous, indeed proverbial, among mediaeval Muslims for his defiant impiety.

212 al-Tawḥīdī [attr.], *Risāla* 327.

213 Ibn al-Khaṭīb, *Jaysh* 110.

214 al-Bayhaqī, *Maḥāsin* 403. In another version, al-Qaynī broke yet another taboo too by having sex with the nun; see for instance al-Baghdādī, *Khizāna* III, 426; al-Iṣfahānī, *Aghānī* XVIII, 9. (However, as Patricia Crone pointed out to me, al-Bayhaqī's version also makes clear, if implicitly, that the protagonist had sex with the nun: he stole her clothes.) In one version, the protagonist of the story is the far better known poet al-Farazdaq (d. 110/728 or 112/730) rather than al-Qaynī; see al-Thaʿālibī, *Thimār* II, 907.

215 This – admittedly shocking – literary pose should not be confused with genuine-looking, bitter complaints against the perceived injustice of God in meting out undeserved suffering to the poet. Two cases that appear to belong to the latter, more serious category are poems by ʿUbaydallāh b. Aḥmad al-Baladī, an old and almost totally blind poet of Mosul, and the desperately impoverished Abū l-Ḥasan Muḥammad al-Ifrīqī, respectively. See al-Thaʿālibī, *Yatīma* II, 214; IV, 157.

the very genre is based on a refusal to observe one of the universally recognised prohibitions of Islam. Sometimes one finds verses that bring this motif to a truly extreme degree. A classic example of this is the following, notorious line by Abū Nuwās, which was then imitated and paraphrased in various ways by many a later poet: "Oh you who reproach me for the pure, red [wine]: go to Paradise and let me go to Hell".[216]

7. A lot has been said about the next subtype of *mujūn* motifs, the parodistic uses of respectable stylistic features. Mimicking all kinds of venerable and august texts – including ones of religious significance like sermons – is a common device of *mujūn* literature. Since aspects of this topic have been treated at some length in the sections on *ḥadīths* (and more will follow with regard to parodies of the *qaṣīda* openings), as well as elsewhere in passing, I shall not reiterate the observations made there.

[216] Abū Nuwās, *Dīwān* III, 155; and on the circumstances of the composition of this poem, see Abū Hiffān, *Akhbār* 103–4. Another line by Abū Nuwās noted as scandalous by mediaeval critics: "Oh Aḥmad, the man to wish for in times of calamity: come, my lord, let us disobey the Almighty in heaven!" See Abū Nuwās, *Dīwān* III, 57 and al-ʿAskarī, *Ṣināʿatayn* 122. Some further examples of the motif: "Hand me that which will be [counted as] a sin on the Day of Judgement: beautiful as fire, it will land you in fire if you drink it"; see al-Thaʿālibī, *Yatīma* II, 137. "Give me to drink that which is clearly prohibited by the [divine] inspiration of the Quran"; see ibid. III, 66 (and cf. ibid. III, 91). "If he [who reprimands you] says that the religion of Muḥammad prohibits the drinking of wine, convert to Christianity"; see al-Bākharzī, *Dumya* I, 60; and also cf. Ibn al-Kattānī, *Tashbīhāt* 92. For a somewhat less defiant-sounding example, see Ibn al-Khaṭīb, *Jaysh* 160.

3

The Motifs of *Mujūn*: Decency and Propriety

As noted in the preceding chapter, the delineation of the respective spheres of the 'religious' and the 'secular' in mediaeval Muslim society is a largely artificial imposition, a distinction that would have made little sense to an insider in that cultural environment. The all-encompassing scope of the *sharīʿa* meant that a breach of an accepted norm of even ordinary conduct and propriety would likely be viewed in religious terms and disapproved of through appeals to religious principles. Sexuality is one area of human existence which modern, secularised societies typically do not regard as belonging to the domain of religious regulations, but as ongoing controversies concerning abortion and homosexuality show, not everyone agrees even in supposedly secularised countries. Sexual morality and behaviour were definitely viewed by most mediaeval Muslims as fraught with religious consequences and subject to divine regulations. Likewise, politics is supposed to be fully separated from religion in a modern secularised political system, but the separation is evidently never totally complete, nor is it free of vehement controversies. Mediaeval Muslims definitely thought of politics and political leadership as eminently religious affairs – whether or not the piety and justice of a particular ruler were in accordance with religious prescriptions – and we find their political controversies almost invariably employing the phraseology of the religious sciences.

It is therefore for the convenience of the reader, and if truth be told, of this author, that the motifs surveyed below will be discussed under a separate chapter heading. What unifies them is the simple fact that they concern issues of decency, propriety, correct conduct, discretion in social and political relations, and conventions of honour and respectability. Moreover, just as the purview of this chapter is defined somewhat arbitrarily, so will some of its sub-sections appear arbitrary, comprising as they do quite motley material. Let it be stressed, then, that any number of different classifications of the extremely varied repertory of motifs would be equally conceivable and no less valid than the one adopted here; and very few of the types of motifs identified here and in the previous chapter were recognised as a separate category by mediaeval Arab literary experts. (With the notable exception of frivolous *iqtibās* from either the Quran or *ḥadīths*, which were certainly seen, and sometimes discussed, as a category apart.)

One aspect of the following material that may to some extent justify treating it separately is the gradual change that concepts of acceptable behaviour, common propriety, and political authority underwent from the late Umayyad period onwards. This is quite a contrast to the remarkable tenacity and immutability of many religious norms, at least the fundamental ones. One was supposed to pray, fast, show deference to the Quran's text, the Prophet and his companions, and so on: such norms showed little change throughout Muslim history, even if actual conformity to the norms could and did vary. On the other hand, notions (and not just the practice) of what sort of principles a respectable man's daily conduct and interaction with others should comply with, the ways a political leader should treat his subordinates, what composed honourable or sophisticated behaviour, in what ways – if at all – sexuality could be discussed: all these questions were liable to significant changes over time, even if religious scholars might often pretend otherwise. In a sense, then, this chapter is devoted to the breaches of the *furūʿ* ('branches', practical applications) of religious values, while the preceding one discussed those of the *uṣūl* ('roots', general foundations) thereof, even though this distinction is of course meant only half seriously. In any case, changes in dominant norms were always only gradual and incomplete. As will be shown, superannuated norms of behaviour and values did not die a sudden death, and old ideals that had outlived the social and ecological environment that had given rise to them continued to be cherished by many no matter how anachronistic. In particular, some of the ideals of honourable conduct and style closely tied to ancient Bedouin society refused to wither and disappear even in a highly urbanised society – most members of which had never seen a desert or lived in a tent – but influenced the thinking and behaviour of most people and governed the life of a few. Some ancient standards of poetry and oratory also proved to be quite pertinacious. Thus, instead of generalising about the perceptible changes in the norms and attitudes of urbanised Muslim society, it will be more helpful to go into the details and examine the areas most affected by these changes, as well as the role of *mujūn* in that process.

1. Breaches of the Norms of Proper Conduct

1.1 Undignified Presentation of Self

A striking development in the society of the Middle East from late Umayyad times is the growth of a distinctively cosmopolitan culture in the metropolises of the empire, a slow process which entailed not only the absorption of numerous aspects of the various ancient cultures of the region, but also the gradual abandonment of many Arabian (mostly Bedouin) patterns of behaviour. The forsaking of a great part of the tribal cultural heritage was not necessarily deliberate, nor did it characterise the lifestyle and conduct of everyone to the same degree. As will be obvious, some intellectuals – often but not always men of non-Arab descent – would adopt an attitude of mockery and defiance towards the ancient Arabian heritage, while others – perhaps the majority – would simply conform, to varying degrees and without an abrupt change, to new literary fashions without any ill feeling towards older traditions. The gradual change of atmosphere, of course, simultaneously affected a number of domains, not just literature. And gradual it was, for a literary vogue such as *sukhf*(the outrageous combination of obscenity, vulgarity and folly that was born in the early Buyid period) was still unthinkable in the early Abbasid period when poets like Bashshār b. Burd and Abū Nuwās flourished.

The ironic reversal of the established clichés of the literary presentation of the poet's or writer's own persona is one of the areas in which the conscious mockery, indeed subversion, of traditional norms is most evident. Old (pre-Islamic and early Islamic) Arabic poetry had such strong and characteristic clichés of presenting the poet's self, intimately linked to the tribal ethos of Bedouin society, that it was a standing invitation to mockery once the tribal society had undergone profound changes in the process of settlement in towns and cities, urbanisation and growing exposure to other ethicities and civilisations. A poetry that continued to parrot the now empty clichés and sing in the heroic tone of pre-Islamic Bedouin bards while coming from the mouths of individuals who had never set foot in the desert or taken part in a tribal feud must have had an inherently parodistic quality about it in the minds of more perceptive intellectuals. (This is not to deny, of course, the possibility that some of these poems could well be hauntingly beautiful in themselves even if they did not correspond to the social reality lived by the poet.) The ethos of Bedouin society might continue to inform the behaviour of rough tribesmen in the Arabian deserts, but in the social context of the urban centres of Iraq and the adjacent lands the pretense, literary or otherwise, that it was still the most forceful set of norms was an utter anachronism. It was also increasingly ludicrous to many intellectuals, who from the early Abbasid period onwards were less and less willing to take the poetic posture expected of pre-Islamic bards. This posture was composed of several elements, virtually all of which were deliberately subverted and turned into farce by the poets of *mujūn*.

A part of these new, sardonic motifs can be classified loosely under the heading of this section, as 'undignified' ways of presenting the self. In other words, these are manifestations of tart irony directed by the poet towards himself, a sentiment wholly absent from early Arabic poetry. Another large (and motley) cluster of motifs, to be treated separately in the next section, can be described as the introduction of topics theretofore considered unfit for poetry (because either trivial or unbecoming). A third cluster of motifs, again to be treated separately, consists of purposeful, explicit parodies and caricatures of the Bedouin heritage, including its literary aspects.

Before turning our attention to ironic, subversive literary treatments of the mores, norms and poetic conventions inherited from pre-Islamic Bedouin society it will be necessary to take a brief look at what is meant by the 'traditional patterns' of that ancient nomadic culture. Although Chapter One of this book is dedicated to an overview of some tenacious norms, values and principles of mediaeval Muslim society, no account is given there of the norms governing the behaviour of nomads, precisely because that code of conduct had largely ceased to be effective in the urban milieu of the Muslim Middle East. This moral code, which it is needless to emphasise was unwritten, was based on the concept of *murū'a* ('manliness', 'honour'). *Murū'a* was composed of quite a number of aspects, but it is fair to define its underlying value as the cult of manliness, the display of manly behaviour whenever one felt his honour challenged in any way whatsoever. An adult Bedouin man was expected to be ready to protect, by force if necessary, his own interests and his family and dependents, and to retaliate for any perceived slight or wrongdoing to his honour or to his family or tribe. It is little surprising, then, that one of the most highly prized attributes in a man was courage and combativeness. However, as indicated above, a man among Arabian nomads was responsible not only for himself but also for his dependents, including above all his womenfolk and children, his clients and slaves, along with his guests and any outsiders placing themselves under his protection (sing. *jār*). It was his most elementary moral duty to provide for these dependents and defend them, and should any mistreatment befall them, he was supposed to take revenge for the atrocity ruthlessly. Revenge was also his obligation, shared with other adult men of his kinship group, if any member of his lineage (and perhaps even of his larger tribal bloc) was wounded, mistreated or killed. Constant readiness to fight, and engagement in physical violence, formed a natural part of the life of a man among Arabian nomads, so that whoever could not fulfil these obligations was not seen as an honourable, fully valuable male member of a kinship group. An important element within the nomadic honour code of Arabia was the conspicuous display of unreserved hospitality and generosity, which would be expressed by giving food, drink and protection to anyone lodging at one's camp or needing one's support. Extraordinary displays of such altruism, often going to absurd extremes, are the staple of ancient Arabic literature and folklore and have been the admired subject-matter of many a Bedouin story right up to modern times. The ubiquity of the theme of exceptional hospitality is a good indication of the centrality of this norm to Bedouin society. In addition to courage and generosity, a Bedouin man also had to guard his good repute and honour (*sharaf*) by constantly behaving in such a way that his nobility of character and his intellect should not be questioned by anyone. Immaculate behaviour would entail the manifestation of quite a number of praiseworthy characteristics, including perfect composure, sobriety and solemnity, reserve, self-control, temperance and modesty. One ideal that did survive the massive sedentarisation and urbanisation of Arabian Bedouins in regions like Iraq was the expectation that a self-respecting man should not appear 'foolish', frivolous or unduly mirthful, for a man less than fully earnest and determined could not be trusted to look after and defend his dependents at all times. (This norm was described and commented upon in the first chapter.)

The expectations to be met by an honourable Bedouin man with a herd and a family were therefore immensely taxing and the task of cultivating an unblemished reputation arduous, all the more so because of the fact that it was not only one's individual honour but that of his lineage and tribe too that could be at stake. The highly combative and competitive spirit characterising the desert-dwelling, nomadic lifestyle left little room for even a trace of self-deprecation, ironic eccentricity, or waggishness in traditional Bedouin poetry, the revealing of one's weaknesses (or those of one's kin) being no function of this kind of poetry. A Bedouin poet would seek to maximise the heroic, normative aspects of his own poetic persona[1], and even when he portrayed himself as, for all practical purposes, an outcast – as the so-called *ṣuʿlūk* poets did – the image he projected would accentuate heroic characteristics (daring, perseverance, bellicosity, etc.) and steer clear of any clownishness. It is important to note that this observation refers to poetic personae, not actual persons, there being no reason to suppose that no one in Bedouin society ever failed to live up to the exacting ideals depicted in poetry. No one is a hero to his valet, but an ancient Bedouin poet would not mention in poetry the less heroic traits that a valet would have seen. This aspect of Arabic poetry, however, underwent a particularly substantial change in the Abbasid period, in great part owing to the activity of libertine poets and the increasing vogue of *mujūn*.[2] The traditional Bedouin

[1] See for instance Sowayan 1985: 194.

[2] Self-deprecatory wit was already appreciated by some urban intellectuals of the Umayyad era,

diction with its highly conventionalised boasting (*fakhr*), heroic tone and idealised personae certainly continued to flourish – and was even reinvigorated by the likes of al-Mutanabbī – but a different vein of poetry grew alongside it. This new vein, characterised by the conscious abandonment and even ridicule of the anachronistic ideals and conventions of Bedouin poetry, was intimately connected to *mujūn*, even though probably not all manifestations of self-deprecation and waggishness would be recognised as *mujūn* by everyone. Whether classified as *mujūn* or not, farcical self-portrayals were more and more common and part of the 'mainstream' in Arabic poetry from the early Abbasid period on. One finds quite a great variety of comic poetic personae in the works of the 'modern' (*muḥdath*) poets. This tendency culminated in the calculatedly ridiculous, outrageous or offensive personae adopted by many cultivators of *mujūn* and especially *sukhf* poetry, but other, more conventional poets also could and did make forays into this territory either for fun, or to enhance their reputation as men of diverse talents.[3]

A particularly illustrative example of the subversion of ancient norms of poetic self-portrayal is the treatment of the theme of courage by some 'modern' poets. Valour, which was one of the cornerstones of the unwritten code of honour among Arabian nomads, is accordingly also a conspicuous topic within their poetry. However, it is not hard to appreciate that unswerving courage, a crucial quality that would enable a nomad to protect his herds and kin from raiders in the desert, could lose much of its function in the more settled environment of a metropolis, so that the aggressive boldness of a Bedouin man and his readiness to avenge any perceived slights might well appear brash and brutish to an urbanised intellectual. Appear ludicrous it did to quite a few poets, as reflected in a number of *mujūn* works making ruthless fun of the Bedouin conventions of boasting in verse. The subversion of the Arabic poetic tradition of praising bravado was obviously done quite intentionally and carefully, and took the form of boasting of and praising cowardice, an absolute anathema to Bedouin men. The element of calculated parody is quite evident in a

mostly those living in the bigger towns of the Hijaz; see al-Majdhūb 1408/1988: 131.

[3] Of course, not only did genuine libertines not try to idealise their own image but they positively strove to paint it as scandalous as possible; see Ingrams 1933: 8–9. The same tendency, totally alien to ancient Arabian poetry, is manifest in sardonic lampoons directed against the poet's own kin (like siblings, cousins, and even wife and children), giving unflattering details of the latter's failings and shortcomings. See for instance al-Iṣbahānī, *Kharīda* II(ii), 537–9. Such self-deprecating sarcasm which deliberately flouted ancient Bedouin norms of self-presentation could be displayed in speech too, and not only by poets. A pertinent example is a remark made by the great philologist (and one of Abū Nuwās's teachers) Abū ʿUbayda Maʿmar b. al-Muthannā about his own origins in response to a contemptuous Arab aristocrat's question; see Ibn Khallikān, *Wafayāt* V, 240. Abū ʿUbayda's most famous pupil, Abū Nuwās is also said to have "behaved as a typical libertine and fribbled with his [ever-changing] claims [of ancestry] (*wa-kāna Abū Nuwās fī daʿāwīhi yatamājanu wa-yaʿbathu*)". See Ibn Manẓūr, *Akhbār* 42.

story recorded by Ibn al-Muʿtazz. The celebrated aristocratic poet Abū Dulaf al-ʿIjlī (fl. early 3rd/9th c.) composed a work thoroughly conventional in its heroic and boastful tenor, which can be fully conveyed by citing only the opening verse: "Hand me my hauberk; I have missed combat too long!" Hearing of the verses, a considerably more frivolous contemporary called al-Raqāshī felt the need to respond and produced the following poem in the same metre:

> Keep away the hauberk; I have missed the enjoyment of music too long.
> Smash the helmet and the lance, or rather start with the sword;
> Then throw my bow and arrows into the waves of the sea,
> As well as my shield and spear and saddle and bridle;
> And then slaughter my horse – may God afflict my horse with a chronic illness (*ṣidām*)!
> I make no effort to be known as a great fighter;
> It is quite enough that you should see me in the company of fine young men,
> Where we will defeat the wine, should the company wish for a victory.
> Let us leave all the slashes and thrusts directed at the torsos and the heads
> To that miserable wretch who says, 'I have missed combat too long!'[4]

In the previous chapter, it was repeatedly stressed that many motifs of *mujūn* poetry seem to have either originated in ordinary conversational style, or else migrated from written, 'high' literature to everyday speech. Such is the case with the poetic motif of praising cowardice, which also occurred as a widely known urban proverb: "'*He fled, God curse him*' is better than '*He's been killed, God bless him*'."[5] The seepage of such expressions and spoken witticisms into the domain of written literature is not an unreasonable supposition; indeed some anecdotes in *adab* collections appear to be simply records of widely circulating, popular jokes. Although the following joke – a cynical quip on the themes of honourable conduct, conventional civility and cowardice – is presented as a short dialogue taking place between the Prophet's wife and one of his contemporaries, it is obviously an urban joke of the Abbasid period:

> Ibn ʿAtīq made a visit to ʿĀʾisha when the latter was on her deathbed. Entering her room, he asked: "How are you now? May I be the ransom for your life[6]!" She said: "I am about to die, oh my cousin." Said he: "Then may I rather not be the ransom for your life. I thought there was still some room for manoeuvre."[7]

---

4 Ibn al-Muʿtazz, *Ṭabaqāt* 104–5. Also cf. a very similar case in Abū Hiffān, *Akhbār* 58–9; and see a number of comparable poems in Ben Cheneb 1922: 108–10, 141–3; and also see Yāqūt, *Udabāʾ* III, 1045–6. It may not be entirely coincidental that it was only in reference to early (mostly pre-Islamic) Bedouin poets that Arab philologists would use the laudatory noun *faḥl* ('thoroughbred male', 'stallion', and figuratively 'outstanding poet'), for the term is obviously loaded with connotations of virility, vigour, and martial prowess. On the term, see Torrey 1911: 488.

5 al-Maydānī, *Amthāl* II, 109.

6 A phrase of common courtesy in mediaeval Arabic usage.

7 al-Thaʿālibī, *Laṭāʾif* 11–2. The choice of protagonists for frivolous jokes is a subject that needs

The following joke, based on the contrast of down-to-earth common sense and the conventional pose of heroism, is a case in point:

> A libertine (*mājin*) was asked: "Why don't you participate in military campaigns against the infidels?" He answered: "By God, I hate death even [if it finds me] in my own bed; am I supposed to gallop forth to meet it?"[8]

Noteworthy and surely far from accidental is the fact that the protagonist of this anecdote about prudent cowardice is identified as a libertine, which explicitly links this theme to *mujūn*.[9] Like cowardice, avarice – another characteristic deeply abhorrent to Bedouins – also came to be praised, or justified through ironic argumentation, by some intellectuals. Such texts seem to be entirely facetious and not intended as serious discussions; as instances of the playful subversion of ancient Bedouin norms of behaviour and poetry, they can be seen as another manifestation of the attitudes described in this section.[10] Although descent from a powerful tribal group of the Arabian peninsula continued to be a source of immense prestige, urban intellectuals lacking such a pedigree – which is to say the majority of the intellectuals of the Abbasid era – might even dare make a mockery of the prestigious genealogies of the Arab elite.[11]

Traditional Bedouin norms considered gluttony to be every bit as despicable a trait as timidity or niggardliness. Displaying a voracious appetite was understandably seen as a lack of self-restraint and thus an absolute taboo for an honourable man. It is little wonder, then, that the theme of praising certain fine viands and describing one's own craving for them made its début in Arabic literature only in the Abbasid period, and is a markedly 'urbane' motif. As is the case with the praise of cowardice, classifiying this motif as *mujūn* is debatable, but it does fit the overall frivolous mood of libertine literature. Ravenous desire for gourmet food such as various types of sweetmeats is a playful topic elaborated upon by quite a number of poets. For instance, the deliciousness of a cake known in mediaeval Baghdad as *aṣābiʿ Zaynab* ('Zaynab's fingers') is the subject of poems by no less than three different poets in one single anthology.[12] That such facetious motifs might have been borrowed from

to be discussed at some length, which will be done in the next chapter.

[8] al-Bayhaqī, *Maḥāsin* 545.

[9] Another version of the same anecdote replaces the figure of the libertine with a Bedouin, a puzzling choice at first sight but perhaps explicable as a device serving to heighten the humorous tension between the expected and the actual behaviour of the stereotyped Bedouin. See Ibn Qutayba, *ʿUyūn* I(i), 257.

[10] E.g. al-Tawḥīdī, *Baṣāʾir* V(ix), 104; al-Jāḥiẓ, *Bukhalāʾ* 34–43, 59-66, 131–47.

[11] E.g. al-Zubaydī, *Ṭabaqāt* 267–8.

[12] al-Thaʿālibī, *Thimār* I, 490-1; and for similar poems about other kinds of food, see al-Thaʿālibī, *Yatīma* IV, 351; al-Tawḥīdī, *Imtāʿ* 193. A short poem by the Andalusian Ibn Shukhayṣ is dedicated to the portrayal of the poetic persona as a self-conscious glutton, instead of craving for a particular type of food; see Ibn al-Kattānī, *Tashbīhāt* 256. It was not only in poems but in whole monographs that

the spoken, conversational style is indicated by the use of the epithet *Ṣarīʿ al-Fālūdhaj* ('Victim of the Honey-and-Flour Sweetmeat') by a man in Iraq, a parodistic twist on the sobriquet of the well-known poet Muslim b. al-Walīd (d. 208/823), *Ṣarīʿ al-Ghawānī* ('Victim of the Beautiful Damsels').[13]

As shown above, numerous aspects of the traditional Bedouin notion of manliness and honour became targets of the sarcasm and self-mockery of the 'modern' (and often libertine) poets of the mediaeval Middle East. It is perhaps a universal cultural constant that the ultimate disgrace for an adult man – indeed the very negation of virility – is failure in sexual intercourse. It is therefore profoundly telling to find impotency too in the repertoire of themes elaborated by libertine poets in their efforts to make fun of the traditional ideals and norms of self-presentation in Arabic poetry. The theme, which is most closely associated with the names of the poets Abū Ḥukayma (fl. early 3rd/9th c.) and Kushājim (d. ca. 350/961), was versified in manifold ways that usually involve detailed descriptions of the frustrated efforts of the poetic persona during intercourse, as well as his anger at the recalcitrant organ that insists on putting him to shame. It would be an utter misconstruction to conclude that the appearance of such a poetic motif reflects a growing tendency of lyric honesty on the poets' part. As various Arabic sources note, the theme of impotency tended to be a mere frivolous conceit taken up by many a poet with the aim of producing droll and entertaining poetry. Whether any particular poet did suffer from such problems is impossible to tell – and not terribly interesting anyway – because the whole point of the motif was its very outrageousness and its comic negation of the essence of all ancient Bedouin norms. The number and popularity of frivolous verses portraying the author's own sexual inadequacy show, perhaps better than anything else, the vast distance between the traditional Bedouin norm of an idealised self-presentation and the new patterns of urbane Arabic poetry.[14]

1.2 Unworthy Topics

As mentioned in passing above, another strong indication of the increasingly indulgent and frivolous attitudes of the urban intelligentsia of the Muslim Middle East

merry littérateurs might pay tribute to a certain dish. On some book-length exaltations of the popular meat-based *sikbāj*, a specialty of Persian origin, see al-Nadīm, *Fihrist* 162, 164. More recently, the rhymed praise of coffee and hashish has also become a recurrent topic of Arabic poetry; see for instance al-Ḥillī, *Dīwān* 630-1; Ibn Maʿṣūm, *Sulāfa* 56–7, 378–9.

[13] al-Khaṭīb, *Taṭfīl* 38. Of course, the historicity of this information is highly doubtful; it may easily be the product of the author's fancy.

[14] On the relevant works of Abū Ḥukayma and Kushājim, see al-Thaʿālibī, *Thimār* I, 365–8; al-Rāghib, *Muḥāḍarāt* III, 527–8; Yāqūt, *Udabāʾ* III, 1298–9; and for a host of similar poems, also see Ibn al-Muʿtazz, *Ṭabaqāt* 185; al-Bākharzī, *Dumya* II, 1316; al-Iṣbahānī, *Kharīda* I(ii), 69; Ibn Ḥijja, *Khizāna* III, 91; al-Nuwayrī, *Nihāya* I(ii), 101–2; Wagner 2008: 140–1.

from the mid-2nd/8th century onwards is the inclusion of a growing number of trivialities and improprieties, topics previously considered to be beneath contempt for a self-respecting poet, as legitimate themes of literature. The low prestige of any 'unbecoming' and 'unserious' topic has been discussed at some length in the first chapter of this book, as has the fact that such topics were regarded as unfit for literary treatments. The Abbasid era – and the reign of the Buyids in particular – brought fundamental and conspicuous changes in this mentality. The relative prestige of 'serious' and 'unserious' topics certainly did not change in principle, and neither did the notion that a high-ranking man should give priority to 'serious' concerns, but a variety of droll themes were more and more frequently the subject of written literature, no matter how trivial, silly or preposterous. In fact, it seems that the more trivial, silly and preposterous the better, as far as entertainment value was concerned. It is precisely the striking insignificance and folly of some topics that made them ideal subject-matter for facetious literature. In the words of the famous Andalusian poet Ibn Khafāja (d. 533/1139): "Be amusing, play and joke, and leave behind the Bedouin morals."[15]

An indisputably 'unworthy' topic often treated in short poems is the description of the irksome nocturnal activity of tiny parasites like bedbugs, fleas and mosquitoes (*baqq, barāghīth, baʿūḍ*) and the resulting sleeplessness of the poet. Needless to point out, such poems are as far as it gets from old Bedouin concepts of poetry. The transformation of topics fit for small talk into a poetic motif using the elevated diction and metres of classical Arabic poetry speaks volumes about the changing attitudes of the higher, literate classes. The ancient cultural traditions would demand that the poet should sing the hardships of battle against the enemy even if he himself has never participated in one; in view of such expectations the theme of the hardship of fighting bedbugs and suchlike foes was an infinitely ironic gesture as well as a powerful commentary on the vacuity of ancient poetic models. The following verses are fairly typical:

> Valencia has become narrow for me, for sleep has been driven far from my eyes
> By the dance of the fleas to the tune of the mosquitoes' music.[16]

Although there is no hard evidence as to the origins of this theme, it is probably safe to assume that the nuisance caused by small obnoxious bugs had been the stuff of ordinary talk before it became a literary topic – anyone who has ever suffered

---

15 Ibn Khafāja, *Dīwān* 406.

16 Cited in al-Shakʿa 1983: 26. For a host of similar poems, see al-Thaʿālibī, *Yatīma* III, 8–9; al-Thaʿālibī, *Tatimma* II, 106; al-Tawḥīdī [attr.], *Risāla* 308–10; al-Jāḥiẓ, *Ḥayawān* II, 292–4, 298–9; al-Ḥarīrī, *Durra* 276–7; al-Ḥillī, *Dīwān* 639; al-Marzūqī, *Sharḥ* IV, 1843; Yāqūt, *Udabāʾ* I, 150; Yāqūt, *Buldān* I, 466; Ibn Maʿṣūm, *Sulāfa* 528. (The verses quoted in Yāqūt's *Muʿjam al-buldān* are of particular interest in that their author was an aristocrat of extremely high social position, a member of one of the most influential families of Eastern Iran, the Mīkālī lineage. On this family, see Bulliet 1972: 67.)

from the onslaught of such pests and lost sleep as a result is more than likely to comment on it. Whatever the origins of the motif, it was very popular and became something of a poetic convention. Less conventional – but obviously analogous – is the parodistic description of the behaviour of other banes and benefactors of an ordinary house, like mice and cats.[17]

A comparably lowly – and often disgusting – topic is the plaintive description of the effects of certain illnesses (such as catarrh and colic).[18] In a similar vein, a poet called Ibn Abī Karīma composed verses about the foul latrine in his own house and the ordeal of living in its proximity.[19]

Yet another less than traditional poetic theme is the description of the unpleasant and comical aspects of a given town or city. One cannot speak of an established motif here, as the choice of the target settlement seems to have largely depended on the poet's own disagreeable experiences there, but the general topic of comical lampoons against a town can be said to have become a minor convention. Depicting the town of Wāsiṭ in southern Iraq for instance, a poet deemed the pervasive stench of excrement used as manure in the surrounding region as the feature most worthy of memorialising.[20] The famous Transoxanian city of Bukhārā, a prominent centre of Islamic culture throughout the Middle Ages, also earned the derision of a poet of the Buyid era for its suffocating stink and claustrophobic alleyways.[21]

Such was the success of 'unworthy' topics in poetry that some poets even made it their speciality, earning considerable reputation and popularity by virtue of an insignificant, ludicrous but amusing subject they dedicated their efforts to versifying. Such topics came to be regarded more or less as the *de facto* intellectual property of their originator, a highly irregular development in mediaeval Arabic poetry, where the conventionalisation of motifs was almost inevitable. A poet who found a sufficiently funny (because trivial or bizarre) theme would elaborate it in one poem after another. Examples of the phenomenon include al-Ḥamdūnī (3rd/9th c.), whose favourite subject-matter was a piece of threadbare headgear that he received as a gift from a less than magnanimous patron; Abū Dulāma (d. ca. 160/776-7), who kept depicting in minute detail his good-for-nothing mule in his poetry; and Abū Ghilāla al-Makhzūmī, whose speciality, quite akin to Abū Dulāma's, was the description of a comparably useless donkey.[22] Whereas these topics were invented

---

[17] E.g. Yāqūt, *Udabāʾ* IV, 1711.

[18] E.g. al-Thaʿālibī, *Laṭāʾif* 114.

[19] al-Jāḥiẓ, *Ḥayawān* I, 133.

[20] al-Iṣbahānī, *Kharīda* I(i), 182.

[21] al-Thaʿālibī, *Yatīma* IV, 70–1. Also see al-Tawḥīdī [attr.], *Risāla* 309 and 328 [on Baghdad]; Yāqūt, *Buldān* I, 437 [al-Baṣra], 465 [Baghdad]; II, 468 [Damascus]; al-Zawzanī, *Ḥamāsa* II, 127 [al-Kūfa]; Ibn Baṭṭūṭa, *Riḥla* 138 [Naṣībīn]; Ibn Maʿṣūm, *Sulāfa* 202 [al-Mukhā].

[22] al-Kutubī, *Fawāt* I, 173–7; Ibn al-Muʿtazz, *Ṭabaqāt* 176; al-Thaʿālibī, *Thimār* I, 542–5, 550–3;

and monopolised by one single poet, some similarly laughable topics might be taken up by several poets precisely as loftier subjects usually were. An illustration of the tendency is the plethora of poems devoted to the memorable event of a postmaster-general's audibly breaking wind in a reception given by the vizier. 'The fart of Wahb b. Sulaymān' came to be almost proverbial for the sheer number of poems commemorating it.[23] The subject, than which it would be hard to find a sillier one, can be seen as emblematic of the changing role of poetry from the Abbasid era. It is to be observed that the concurrence of several poets in taking up the same trivial subject and composing verses upon it was not always spontaneous; for example, when the celebrated statesman al-Ṣāḥib b. ʿAbbād (d. 385/995) proposed – obviously by way of cultured entertainment – the subject of parodistic elegies (*rithāʾ*) on a dead hack, no less than ten were produced by various poets in his entourage.[24]

The literary fashion of treating grotesque, unworthy topics in classical Arabic verse reached its apogee in the Buyid era. It is during that period that the poets specialising in *sukhf* went from success to success, their practically only stock-in-trade being the audacity to lend all their attention to a style and themes that were shockingly disgraceful to an ordinary, decent man, let alone a traditional Bedouin poet. The term *sukhf* is difficult to render in English with one single word, since it is a combination of obscenity, vulgarity, scatology and all manner of folly and absurdity.[25] As noted above, the unifying element in these varied aspects appears to be the fact that all are phenomena which every self-respecting and honourable adult man would make sure to avoid in speech as well as behaviour. In a sense, *sukhf* is *mujūn* at its very extreme: the purposeful abandonment of all restraints of ordinary decency. It also parallels *mujūn* in the remarkable extent of its success – the favourable reception of Ibn al-Ḥajjāj in the Buyid period was not dissimilar to that of Abū Nuwās several generations earlier, as will be argued at some length in the next chapter. The work of Ibn al-Ḥajjāj can be regarded as the epitome of everything that *sukhf* is about, which is the very negation of all the usual and expected norms for the conduct and speech of a decent person.[26]

II, 860-3; al-Jāḥiẓ, *Rasāʾil* I(ii), 331-2. On the relevant poems of Abū Dulāma, also cf. Ben Cheneb 1922: 82–7, 152–4. Some of these motifs apparently trickled down to the vernacular language in the form of proverbs; see al-Maydānī, *Amthāl* I, 296.

23 al-Thaʿālibī, *Thimār* I, 340–3. A poet even compiled a whole anthology of the numerous poems describing the occurrence; see Yāqūt, *Udabāʾ* I, 284; al-Nadīm, *Fihrist* 163.

24 See Hámori 1999. (An eleventh poem, imitating the original ten, was subsequently composed by an unnamed man living elsewhere; see op.cit. 57 [note 2].)

25 Ibn Manẓūr, *Lisān* III, 259–60; and also see James Montgomery's entry in EI2, s. v. "sukhf ".

26 For a short but representative sample of his output, see for instance al-Tawḥīdī [attr.], *Risāla* 59; and for a full biography (replete with copious citations) see the relevant chapter in al-Thaʿālibī, *Yatīma*.

1.3 Caricatures of the Bedouin Heritage

The gradual and partial shift in attitudes to the old Bedouin poetic tradition manifested itself in a number of other phenomena too. It has to be stressed, as a general observation, that the notion of discarding the early Arabic literary heritage was not entertained by even the most extreme partisans of the 'modern' (*muḥdath*) poetic style; what they did reject was the imperative of slavish obedience to poetic models – including the choice and treatment of motifs and other poetic conventions – that had long become anachronistic.[27] It is this rejection that quite a few works by 'modern' poets of the Abbasid era, both libertines and less adventurous men, give voice to. *Mujūn*, of course, was a suitable domain in which to make fun of certain aspects of the ancient poetic conventions. Foremost among these was the all but obligatory opening motif of the traditional pre-Islamic ode (*qaṣīda*), the object of variegated parodies in the new poetic style.

The introductory section of a *qaṣīda* customarily consists of the motif of nostalgic reminiscences evoked by the poet's stopping at the traces (*aṭlāl*) of the abandoned camping-place of his one-time beloved and her kin. This may rightly be regarded as a Bedouin cultural trait *par excellence* as there are few poetic images more powerfully evocative of the nomadic lifestyle and the desert environment than that of the tribesmen packing up their tents and meagre possessions, leaving the camping-place and driving their herds in search of new pastures elsewhere. Given the highly emblematic nature of this image as well as its having become an immutable cliché, it is little wonder that one finds it being a favourite target of the irony of the 'modern' poets, especially libertines, from the Abbasid period onwards. Parodying the motif of 'weeping over the traces of the camp' came to be so popular a theme among libertine poets that it ended up being a full-blown poetic convention in itself, a development not short of ironic. With the passage of time, *mujūn* had to become more and more crude and vulgar to continue creating the effect of scandalousness (a point on which more will be said in the remaining chapters of this book), and this tendency is certainly reflected in the increasingly merciless and indecorous parodies of the *aṭlāl* motif. A comparison between two examples will illustrate this development. The first is from a poem by Abū Nuwās, arguably the greatest 'modern' poet of the early Abbasid period, and the quintessential libertine[28]:

---

27 It is noteworthy and probably not coincidental that the main outlines of the standard mediaeval Muslim image of the pre-Islamic past (history as well as culture) had just recently been elaborated by philologists. On these efforts, see Drory 1996: 34–5. In other words, no sooner was the Muslim view of ancient Bedouin culture standardised and given a heroic halo than there emerged ironic voices within the urban intelligentsia dissenting from the expected glorification of the Arabian past. One wonders to what extent it was linked to the non-Arabic origins of many intellectuals (and the related *shuʿūbiyya* controversy).

28 Abū Nuwās is likely to have been one of the first poets to use the parodistic *aṭlāl* motif; see

> Say to him who stands weeping at the faded traces [of a camping-place]: What harm would it do if he sat down?
> Leave alone the camping-place and Salmā,[29] and have a drink of ruby red wine from al-Karkh instead!
> [...][30]

The coarsening of the uses of this motif is more than obvious if one compares Abū Nuwās's verses with the following piece from the Buyid era:

> Fuck all the ladies of the tents and all who yearn for the tents [of the camping-place that was]!
> Me, I yearn for a bit of roast veal; I am dying for some roast veal.
> [...][31]

It is not only the opening theme of traditional Bedouin poetry that the 'modern' poets subjected to their irony. The literary heritage of the Abbasid and Buyid periods offers plenty of parodies of various aspects, motifs and genres of ancient Arabic poetry, the tone of which ranges from mild jesting to ruthless sarcasm. One fairly common motif is reminiscent of the frivolous use of *iqtibās* discussed at length in the previous chapter. In a process akin to the purposeful misinterpretation and misapplication of Quranic verses, poets would often take certain well-known phrases, hemistichs or even whole verses from celebrated pre-Islamic odes and incorporate the quoted text into their own frivolous poems on banal topics, which would of course result in a complete distortion of the original meaning of the citation. Being by far the most famous pre-Islamic poem in Arabic, the great ode of Imruʾ al-Qays was a natural hunting-ground for misinterpretable passages. Poets of the Buyid era used verses from it in various poems about, amongst other things, the miserable salary of a state employee, a less than munificent patron, an annoyingly lengthy communal prayer, and a host so mindless as to forget to provide fodder to his guest's riding animal.[32] To give an illustration, here are two lines of verse, the first from a

Ingrams 1933: 11. On the frequent occurrence of the motif in his poetry, see Arazi 1979: 8 [note 1].

[29] A typical female name often appearing in nostalgic Bedouin poetry. Abū Nuwās, of course, was known for preferring boys to women.

[30] Abū Nuwās, *Dīwān* III, 196. For further examples of the parodying, explicit rejection, or mockery of the *aṭlāl* motif from a host of poets, see Ibn al-Muʿtazz, *Ṭabaqāt* 153; al-Thaʿālibī, *Yatīma* I, 376; II, 85; al-Thaʿālibī, *Thimār* I, 552; al-Iṣbahānī, *Kharīda* II(ii), 717–8; Ibn al-Kattānī, *Tashbīhāt* 252; Ibn al-Khaṭīb, *Jaysh* 65. The motif may well have been used in the spoken language too (at least by educated people) by way of joking, as suggested by an ironic remark made by al-Jammāz (fl. 2nd-3rd/8th–9th c.) to an indiscreet singing-girl. See Ibn al-Muʿtazz, *Ṭabaqāt* 177.

[31] al-Tawḥīdī, *Imtāʿ* 193.

[32] al-Thaʿālibī, *Yatīma* IV, 77; al-Tanūkhī, *Nishwār* VII, 252; al-Bākharzī, *Dumya* II, 1258–9; al-Ibshīhī, *Mustaṭraf* 261. For wider sample (including the same works as well), see Ibn Ḥijja, *Khizāna* IV, 129–38. A couplet from the late Buyid or early Seljuk period uses a celebrated line from Imruʾ al-Qays' ode describing his riding horse to give a vivid account of sexual intercourse. See al-Bākharzī, *Dumya* II, 1260. Another couplet extracts a motif from the first line of the same ode in describing

famous early ode by Zuhayr b. Abī Sulmā, and the second a libertine adaptation of it, probably by Abū Nuwās:

> *The disaster, like which there is no other disaster,* is what the Ghaṭafān [tribe] seeks [to do] on the day it loses the way.
>
> *The disaster, like which there is no other disaster,* is having no place to go when a good lay is available.[33]

The point of all these works is naturally the contrast between the lofty diction and atmosphere of the well-known citations and the banality of their new context. While poetry was the most fertile ground for mockery of the masterpieces of early Arabic verse, prose is not devoid of the tendency either. Easily the most ruthless – as well as vulgar – parody of the opening motif of the pre-Islamic ode is an anecdote that features an idiot who, listening to the nostalgic beginning lines of an old *qaṣīda*, is moved to recall sorrowfully a female donkey that he (as well as his brother) used to have regular sexual intercourse with in their youth. Needless to say, the man's words are a blend of jejune obscenity and nostalgic emotions worthy of any traditional ode.[34]

As noted above it was not early Arabic poetry itself – which was admired by practically all educated Arabic speakers including libertines – that the 'modern' poets objected to but the expectation of reducing themselves to being mere imitators of its style and clichés, which was more and more unfit to describe the contemporary reality around them. Neither were they willing to continue glorifying the lifestyle of desert nomads which, as they knew very well, was far inferior to their own urban lives, at least in its relative lack of amenities and pleasures. It bears repeating that most *muḥdath* poets were quite well-versed in the old poetic heritage and capable of imitating it when they needed to, as they did in most of their panegyrics composed in the hope of monetary rewards from their high-ranking patrons. However, an honest comparison of the material conditions of the desert-dwelling Bedouins with those of the sophisticated inhabitants of Baghdad and other urban centres of the Middle East could not but expose the inferiority of the lifestyle of Arabian nomads. Despite the continuing prestige of the Bedouin roots of Arabic culture, this comparison was made, explicitly or implicitly, by a growing number of intellectuals. The material culture of the Arab nomads was increasingly seen as representing an

---

grueling hunger, a topic having nothing to do with the original context. See Ibn al-Muʿtazz, *Badīʿ* 160. In another poem, the same borrowed motif is used to describe stubble on a young man's cheeks; see al-Rāghib, *Muḥāḍarāt* III, 483. Other odes by Imruʾ al-Qays, while not quite as widely known and adored, could also furnish material for parodies; see for instance Ibn Saʿīd, *Rāyāt* 100.

33 Wagner 2008: 31.

34 "*Tadhakkartu ḥimāratan kānat ʿindanā bi-bilādinā bi-baṭn al-wādī kuntu anīkuhā anā wa-akh lī fa-hā anā hāhunā wa-mā adrī mā faʿala ʾllāh bi-akhī wa-lā bi-l-ḥimāra.*" See Ibn Saʿīd, *Muqtaṭaf* 222.

extremely basic stage of development and lacking the most elementary amenities, luxuries and technical achievements taken for granted in mediaeval Muslim cities.[35] In fact, the attitudes of many an intellectual of the Abbasid era traditionally branded a *shuʿūbī* ('anti-Arab'), as well as a considerable part of the whole *shuʿūbiyya* movement, were rooted in this contrast between sophisticated urban living and the pathetic conditions of the nomads, rather than in a conscious anti-Arab stance and an ethnic antagonism. The chauvinism of urban civilisation was expressed by many poets and writers through the denigration of the poor diet and ragged clothes of the nomads and the lack of hygiene amongst them; and this did not necessarily entail a hatred of the Arabs.[36] In this context, it is worth noting that the few extant literary products of the competition between Arab and non-Arab Muslim authors (as in the *shuʿūbiyya* controversy) are often permeated by an unmistakably playful and ironic tone, which makes it very difficult, and very questionable, to define them as wholly serious in purpose.[37]

By the Buyid period, the image of the Bedouin had undergone a profound change in that it would forever be an ambivalent one among Arabs: on the one hand, 'the Bedouin' continued to represent the highest ideals of bravery, manliness and eloquence in speech and poetry, whilst on the other hand, the Bedouin also came to be regarded as the archetypal impoverished boor, the very antithesis of urbanity, elegance and gentility. This latter aspect of the complex image is surely a product of the early Abbasid era and the rise of a cosmopolitan Muslim culture, and some of its earliest expressions are attributable to the early masters of *mujūn*, as shown

---

[35] A particularly emphatic expression of this idea can be observed in a poem by Abū l-Qāsim al-Zaʿfarānī, a minor poet of the Buyid period ("*Lā atbaʿu l-aʿrāba...*" etc.); see al-Thaʿālibī, *Yatīma* III, 345. The words of al-Jāḥiẓ – an author who could hardly be described as hostile to the Arabian cultural heritage – are also expressive of the recognition of the material poverty of Bedouin society: "Do you not see that the Bedouin lives in a tent made of a piece of coarse cloth supported by the bones of dead animals; his dog stays with him in the tent; his clothing consists of a garb made of hides or wool; his medicine is the camels' dung; his perfume is tar and the droppings of gazelles; his wife's only ornaments are shells; for dessert he eats the fruit of the doum palm (*muql*); and the game he hunts is the jerboa. He lives in an arid desert where the only sound to be heard is the hoot of the owls and the howl of the wolves. And yet [the Bedouin] is content with this and proud of it all." Cited in al-Ibshīhī, *Mustaṭraf* 77; and also cf. al-Jāḥiẓ, *Rasāʾil* I(ii), 105; II(iv), 117. The nauseating and pathetic diet of the desert-dwelling Arabs is a recurrent theme in the poetry of the Abbasid era; see Arazi 1979: 48. The rudimentary material culture, uncouth behaviour and lack of refinement of the Bedouins have continued to be despised by many urban dwellers in the Arab world up to the modern period; see for instance Marçais, Guîga 1925: 406 [note 25]; Serjeant 1951: 7; Barth 1983: 5, 59, 70; Yassin 1978: 71 [in this example, a Kuwaiti proverb, the Bedouin is the embodiment of boorishness: "*idha dallēt li-bduwi ʿala bētik wassiʿ il-bāb li-bʿīra*"]. It is noteworthy that the word 'Bedouin' can mean not only 'nomad' in the strict sense but any rural, non-urbanised person; for instance in the modern dialects of Iraq and Western Iran. See Ingham 1976.

[36] For more on this question, see Arazi 1979: 3, 5, 14, 61.

[37] E.g. Ibn García, *Risāla* 247, 250; al-Thaʿālibī, *Laṭāʾif* 20 [the anecdote on Maʿn b. Zāʾida].

above. For an eloquent description of the changing attitudes among the elite vis-à-vis the Bedouins, consider the following account of the reception of the Bedouin poet Abū Nukhayla in the palace of the Abbasid caliph Abū Jaʿfar al-Manṣūr (r. 136/754-158/775):

> Having arrived at the palace of Abū Jaʿfar, Abū Nukhayla asked for permission to enter, which he was denied. The [Persian] people from Khurāsān, who were constantly entering and leaving, were making fun of him – they saw him as a primitive old Bedouin, so they amused themselves by teasing him.[38]

2. Images of Sexuality

2.1 Fornication and Adultery

Depicting sexuality is not in itself an innovation of the masters of *mujūn* in Arabic literature. It is not the topic itself but the way of handling it that was new and specific to *mujūn*. Pre-Islamic poetry was not wholly averse to treating the subject of amorous affairs, and some poets – notably the greatest giant of pre-Islamic poetry, Imruʾ al-Qays – would even go so far as to describe the carnal aspects of love between a man and a woman. Still however, there is a world of difference between such early treatments of sexuality in verse and those composed by the libertines. (Not to mention the fact that Imruʾ al-Qays is highly idiosyncratic among the pre-Islamic poets in his relatively candid and boastful depiction of his sexual escapades.)[39] While even a brief analysis of early Arabic poetry is outside the purview of this study, it is perhaps fair to observe that the idealising tendencies of early Bedouin poetry are generally manifest in its treatment of love affairs too, resulting in a preponderance of a relatively decorous and subdued approach to, and often complete reticence about, the theme of sexuality, at any rate in comparison with the urban poetry of the Abbasid era. The demure attitude of traditional Bedouin poetry to the subject of love reached its apotheosis in the so-called *ʿudhrī* poetry of the early Muslim era (named after the *Banū ʿUdhra* tribe). In this type of love poetry, beside which Victorian attitudes appear positively libidinous, the imperative of decorum and chastity is taken to absurd extremes, and

[38] al-Iṣfahānī, *Aghānī* XX, 423. Contemptuous attitudes towards Bedouins and their poets seem to have already existed among the elite of the Umayyad period, even though they had certainly not been nearly as prevalent as under the Abbasids' reign. Thus did the Umayyad caliph Yazīd b. ʿAbd al-Malik (r. 101/720–105/724) comment on a verse of an early Arab poet: "What does it matter if I don't know what this primitive Bedouin might have meant with this?" See Ibn Qutayba, *Shiʿr* 254.

[39] To put it in a few words, these early Bedouin poets are serious; *mujūn* is not. The invective poetry of the Umayyad period, while comically obscene at times, is different in a similar sense, namely in that it is designed to cause serious offence; *mujūn* is not. (The boundary between *hijāʾ* and *mujūn*, however, is not always possible to delimit so neatly.) More on this issue in the last chapter.

for a lover to die of longing – never mind the mutual attraction – is an inevitability. However, a different streak of love poetry in Arabic had already developed in the Umayyad period, and rather unsurprisingly it was as closely associated with the relatively sophisticated and cosmopolitan environment of Mecca as *ʿudhrī* poetry was with a Bedouin tribe. Light-heartedness, sometimes bordering on cynicism, was a trademark feature of the style of ʿUmar b. Abī Rabīʿa (d. 93/712 or 103/721), the most famous representative of the 'Meccan *ghazal*' (love poem). It was this more frivolous – and more realistic – approach to amorous affairs and poetry that the 'modern', urbane poets of the Abbasid era naturally gravitated towards, adopted, and then went far beyond.[40] Libertines would of course not rest contentedly for long with the playfulness and slight cynicism discernible in some specimens of the love poetry of the Umayyad era, but developed it fully to suit their penchant for flouting ordinary norms of decency. Notably, they introduced the theme of material interests affecting love affairs, a factor surely as present in reality as it was absent from earlier Arabic poetry. Sometimes this theme would involve only hints at the ulterior motives of a beloved girl or boy; at other times the topic of prostitution would be touched upon without inhibitions. Libertine men of letters would quite nonchalantly depict their own experiences with prostitutes, a subject all the more natural for them as a lot of singing and dancing girls and similar female entertainers doubled as prostitutes, which created a close link – in life as well as in literature – between musical or drinking soirées and the trade of sex.[41]

The exchange of money for sex is a topic elaborated upon in quite a number of ways by poets of *mujūn* as well as other libertine intellectuals. (Of course, it is in fact questionable if one is justified to call such texts 'love poetry' in the proper sense, but they do quite consciously exploit and parody the conventions of traditional love poetry.) Consider the following typical product by a notoriously frivolous and jestful Iraqi state official of the Seljuk period called Raḍī al-Dīn Hibatallāh b. al-Ḥasan:

> On my heart are painful wounds from the love I feel for you; and yet I strive
> to hide this love deep in my soul.
> Whether you are angry or satisfied with me, I will only have two advocates in
> my favour – an erect dick and the dirhams.[42]

---

[40] On types of love poetry in the Umayyad period, see Bauer 1998: 38-55.

[41] E.g. al-Iṣfahānī, *Aghānī* XIII, 266; al-Thaʿālibī, *Tatimma* I, 9; al-Rāghib, *Muḥāḍarāt* III, 501–2; al-Ḥillī, *ʿĀṭil* 126–8, 203. In nineteenth-century Egypt, entertainers who sang and danced for largely male audiences (known as *ghawāzī* or *barāmika*) still might earn part of their income as prostitutes. See Lane 1895: 372–6; van Nieuwkerk 1995: 27–8, 31. In fact, even in contemporary Egypt female singers and dancers seem to suffer from the social opprobrium resulting from this traditional association of their trade with prostitution. See van Nieuwkerk 1995: 108, 128–9.

[42] al-Iṣbahānī, *Kharīda* I(i), 179. (The editor chose to suppress one of the key words of the second line, but I am fairly confident that metre and common sense suffice to justify my guess of the missing noun.) For parallels, also cf. al-Iṣfahānī, *Aghānī* XVIII, 178; al-Thaʿālibī, *Yatīma* III, 6; al-Rāghib,

Two examples follow that are similar in tone. The tenor of both poems, even though they are supposed to speak of the poet's beloved, would be perfectly fitting for the discussion of a prostitute. The first piece is by al-Jammāz (fl. 2nd-3rd/8th–9th c.), who expresses his frustration with a eunuch constantly chaperoning the woman he loves:

> I have to share this gazelle with Sinān [the eunuch]: what an odious associate!
> Neither will Sinān have a good fuck nor will he let me have one.[43]

The second poem is an earlier one, composed by Abū Nuwās:

> We have fucked the messenger of [my beloved] ʿInān, a very wise thing to do.
> [We have had] some bread and salt before eating the main course.[44]

Common sense seems to dictate that these poetic themes must have had their origins in ordinary conversation. One indication that they really did may be the following cynical maxim from the Abbasid period: "First your money, and only then your prick (*qaddim khayrak thumma ayrak*)!"[45] The topics of purchasing sex for money and the role of material interests in love affairs must always have been discussed among friends, and therefore it is reasonable to suppose that the only innovation here on the part of the purveyors of *mujūn* was to elevate it all to the level of written poetry. There is some anecdotal evidence about such attitudes being quite common among urban intellectuals. Consider the response of the celebrated 'neo-classical' poet Abū Tammām (190/806–232/846) to the suggestion that his favourite slave-boy was far more eager to please a rich acquaintance than the latter's slave-boy was to please Abū Tammām: "[But of course], since [...] the currency I pay in is words, while he pays my slave in cash."[46] Promiscuous relationships and sexual adventures were apparently quite common among littérateurs, at least those of a libertine bent among them, and were so taken for granted that having sex with the partner of one's friend – usually a female singer or slave-girl of less than puritanical morals – might not even be viewed as cause for the termination of the friendship. Casual attitudes to sexual affairs seem to have been the order of the day among Abbasid-era poets and writers.[47]

Muḥāḍarāt III, 480–1, 485; Ibn al-Rūmī, *Dīwān* II, 14; Abū Nuwās, *Dīwān* V, 304; al-Ḥillī, *ʿĀṭil* 174-5. Money being the key to everything is a theme that appears in 'serious' discourse too, and not necessarily in connection with love affairs. See for instance Ibn ʿĀṣim, *Janna* I, 197.

[43] al-Jāḥiẓ, *Ḥayawān* I, 97.

[44] al-Thaʿālibī, *Thimār* II, 869.

[45] al-Maydānī, *Amthāl* II, 155.

[46] al-Ṣūlī, *Akhbār* 196. The cynicism (or realism?) permeating this story is reminiscent of an anecdote recorded by Ibn al-Muʿtazz in which a young man is asked how sincere the emotions of a man enamoured of him are. He replies that sincere though they may be, but unfortunately not to the extent of actually being expressed in the tangible form of hard cash. See Ibn al-Muʿtazz, *Ṭabaqāt* 192.

[47] For an illustrative case, cf. the story of Muṭīʿ b. Iyās, Ḥammād ʿAjrad and the latter's girlfriend,

Besides outright prostitution and paid sex, the allegedly loose morals of all women and the facility of conquering them are also recurrent topics in *mujūn* works, treated both explicitly and by way of innuendoes and allusions.[48] Another pertinent phenomenon common in *mujūn* is the motif of exhorting the reader to engage in promiscuous sex; this motif often appears in the framework of parodistic, mock 'sermons' that eulogise all manner of debauchery and atrocious norm-breaking.[49]

Given that all *mujūn* seeks to create an effect by the conspicuous breaking of accepted norms, it is to be expected that a universally known and acutely felt proscription of Islamic law, that of *zinā* (fornication, adultery), should feature rather prominently among the topics of this sort of literature. It does in fact constitute an important theme of *mujūn*, treated in a variety of ways, although the overall impression left by a survey of a large number of *mujūn* works is that *liwāṭ* (homosexuality) might be even more prominent a topic of *mujūn* than is *zinā*. If really true, which it might not be, this odd observation may be due to the greater potential of homosexuality for sheer scandalousness and its greater distance from all normative patterns of sexual behaviour.[50] An alternative explanation, and in my view a more probable one, may be that the ubiquity of *liwāṭ* in *mujūn* literature may simply reflect the comparable prominence of homoerotic themes in 'polite' love poetry. However, we will leave this point at that for the time being, and discuss it in the next section of this chapter. Whatever the relative weight of *zinā* as a theme of *mujūn* literature, one does encounter therein quite a few descriptions of illicit sex with women, often combined with breaches of other emphatic taboos like wine-drinking and the failure to pray.[51] The women described as sexual partners are

---

a woman known as Ẓabyat al-Wādī, in al-Iṣfahānī, *Aghānī* XIII, 307–10. Boasting of one's sexual escapades (and drinking binges) appear to have been widely considered a subject fit for informal, friendly conversation; see for instance Ibn Baydakīn, *Lumaʿ* I, 243. However, the degree of indiscretion (bordering on vulgarity) displayed in the case of the caliph al-Walīd (r. 125–6/743–4) with a singer at his court must have been exceptional even in the late Umayyad period. For the story, see al-Iṣfahānī, *Aghānī* VII, 56–7. Of course, there were individuals, even in literary circles, who preferred to be discreet concerning their own extramarital affairs; as can be observed in al-Iṣfahānī, *Aghānī* XIII, 255.

48 E.g. al-Iṣbahānī, *Kharīda* I(i), 182 ["*taḍāyaqī taḍāyaqī, lā budda an tanfarijī* "]; al-Rāghib, *Muḥāḍarāt* III, 502 ["*Idhā hawīta yā ukhayya ghāda*" etc.]; Ibn Maʿṣūm, *Sulāfa* 299 ["*Lam tukhayyib min nawālin rāghiban*" etc.]. The theme also appears in vernacular poetry; see for instance al-Ḥillī, *ʿĀṭil* 83–4 [" *Wa-tbīt lēla māʿū, qālat l-ukhra īh īh* "].

49 E.g. al-Tawḥīdī [attr.], *Risāla* 82–5; al-Bākharzī, *Dumya* I, 445; al-Rāghib, *Muḥāḍarāt* III, 486; al-Ḥillī, *ʿĀṭil* 199.

50 However, see Wright 1997: 9, which argues, and not improbably, the exact opposite of this suggestion.

51 The genre of wine-poems (*khamriyyāt*) furnishes any number of examples. The structure and plot of such poems tends to be similar regardless of whether the object of sexual opportunism is male or female. – In today's Arab world, promiscuous sexuality is an important topic in the lyrics of North African *rāy* (*raï*) music, considered to be a voice of social dissent. See Virolle-Souibès 1989: 48.

usually servant girls, female slaves, singers, and other low-status females, which it is reasonable to attribute to a healthy and prudent reluctance on the part of most libertines to incur the more than predictable wrath of the menfolk of any free woman dragged into the context of *mujūn*. Incidentally, the effort of poets to avoid offending politically influential and wealthy men also manifested itself in their habit of steering clear of the names of any female relatives of their patrons; indeed this custom might also be embraced in prose, as when a prominent secretary kept using synonyms for the feminine form of the adjective 'beautiful' (*jamīla*) because it happened to be the name of the sister of the emir.[52]

As a literary portrayal of fornication, a peculiar poem by a celebrated master of *mujūn*, Ibn al-Ḥajjāj (d. 391/1001), is quite unique. In this work, the poet flatters the Buyid prince Bakhtiyār with the claim that the prince, unlike the prophet Joseph, is so virile that, far from resisting the seductive manoeuvres of Potiphar's wife if faced with such a situation, he would have hastened himself to seduce the woman into adultery without regard for the husband.[53] While the poem is certainly nonpareil in the liberties it takes with all norms of decorum and piety, the cynicism that permeates it is a hallmark of the libertines' approach to amorous affairs.

It is interesting to note the highly unusual presence of female voices in some *mujūn* poems discussing loose morals; for example in a number of short couplets that some libertine women supposedly composed in order to have them written on their own ornamental belts (sing. *tikka*).[54] Besides such short pieces, there are also comparable but longer works that treat the theme of promiscuity.[55] Whether these works were actually composed by women is in my view debatable. Even though the sources do mention, if infrequently, female libertines, it is equally conceivable that male poets would amuse themselves and their friends by inventing such funny pieces – and the accompanying anecdotes – about the lax morals of women. Gert Borg asks this very question in his article on the bawdy material in Ibn Abī Ṭāhir

[52] al-Tanūkhī, *Nishwār* I, 193-4. The same attitudes motivated the insistence of the Buyid ruler ʿAḍud al-Dawla (r. 338/949-372/983) to evade mentioning the name of his own mother while narrating a weird dream had by the latter ("*[...] fa-qāla yā Fulāna wa-sammānī bi-ʾsmī, wa-kadhā kanā l-malik ʿAḍud al-Dawla ʿan al-ism*"). See op. cit. IV, 119; and also cf. al-Maʿarrī, *Ghufrān* 205. For examples of the same phenomenon in verse, see for instance Ibn Zaydūn, *Dīwān* 390; Ibn al-Khaṭīb, *Jaysh* 162. Such tactfulness may well appear exaggerated, even obsessive, to a modern Western observer, but it was perfectly reasonable in a premodern urban society in which malicious gossip could rapidly spread and damage even an innocent person's reputation and there were only limited possibilities of redress. On this problem in 12th/18th-century Aleppo, see Marcus 1986: 176.

[53] al-Thaʿālibī, *Yatīma* III, 45-6. (It is worth noting that the poem was well received by its addressee.) The poem is all the more outrageous for its implicit portrayal of Joseph, who in the Quranic story is a paragon of virtue, chastity and modesty, as a weakling lacking in virility; see El-Outmani 1995: 171-2.

[54] al-Washshāʾ, *Muwashshā* 262; and cf. al-Rāghib, *Muḥāḍarāt* III, 480.

[55] E.g. al-Marzūqī, *Sharḥ* IV, 1840.

Ṭayfūr's *Balāghāt al-nisā'* but, sportingly if unfortunately for us, leaves it unresolved. He notes, however, that the *isnāds* of the stories make it clear that men dominated the transmission (though not necessarily the production) of these texts.[56]

2.2 Homosexuality

Another sexual taboo that appears with remarkable frequency in *mujūn* texts is homosexuality. It was argued in the first chapter of this book that the prevalence of homoerotic flirtations and sex between males should not be taken to mean that mediaeval Islamicate societies ever approved of the phenomenon, just as the common occurrence of extramarital sexual relationships did not lessen the validity of the norm against *zinā*. Let it be repeated here that despite the superficially lenient attitudes towards homoerotic longings and relationships, sodomy (*liwāṭ*) did remain strongly frowned upon and the idea that it constituted a departure from acceptable sexual behaviour was uncontroversial among virtually all mediaeval Muslims, libertines included. That libertines so relished the topic is probably due precisely to the fact that it was a clear-cut case of norm-breaking. Given the ubiquity of homosexual affairs in the greatest cities of the mediaeval Middle East, the difference between an ordinary man pursuing sex with adolescent boys and a libertine doing the same was not the habit itself, but the deliberate lack of discretion on the part of the libertine. Implicit in both the discretion of the ordinary man and the scandal-mongering of the *mājin* was the recognition of the illicit nature of sex between a man and a boy. While the ordinary man who sought sex with a boy would make sure the affair should not become known to anyone except himself and possibly his trusted friends, a libertine would strive to do exactly the opposite, so as to further enhance his notoriety for outrageous conduct and works.[57] It must be added that many a libertine intellectual apparently showed the same indiscretion in conducting his real-life affairs as he did in the depiction of such affairs in poetry. Such intellectuals would make no secret at all of their relationships with adolescents (usually slave-boys), they would speak quite freely of their desire for certain boys, and even proposition boys they fancied in public, sometimes in a half-serious, teasing and ironic manner.[58]

---

56 Borg 2000: 149.

57 It has been observed that the basis for the relative tolerance of homosexuality in traditional Muslim societies, which it would be seriously wrong to misinterpret as a sign of tacit approval or neutrality, was in fact "a widespread and enduring pattern of collective denial in which a condition of the pursuit of homosexual activity [...] is that the behaviour should never be publicly acknowledged". See Schmidtke 1999: 262.

58 For anecdotal evidence, see for instance Abū Hiffān, *Akhbār* 48-9; al-Thaʿālibī, *Yatīma* II, 335;

In this context, it is necessary to make a distinction between the active and passive role in homosexual acts. Mediaeval Muslims, like members of many other societies, viewed the act of penetrating a man as a sin, but a sin that did not lessen the virility of the active partner, while it all but destroyed the honour of whoever played the passive role.[59] From a religious point of view, there was no real difference between the degrees of the abomination of both roles, whereas the traditional code of honour did differentiate, and treated the passive role as infinitely more shameful. This may explain the relative scarcity – although not total absence – of *mujūn* texts in which the author would portray himself as a passive homosexual: posturing as a debauched man having no respect for religious sentiments or common notions of decency is quite another thing to going to the extreme of utter social death by relinquishing one's manly status. (On the other hand, claims of someone else being a passive homosexual are the mainstay of invenctive poetry, a genre that in many respects – in its frequent use of obscenity, its abandonment of ordinary norms of interpersonal contact, and a host of other aspects – shows parallels and a certain affinity to *mujūn*.) The subject of anal sex with boys is commonplace in *mujūn* literature, and some

---

III, 8-9; al-Thaʿālibī, *Laṭāʾif* 93; al-Tawḥīdī, *Baṣāʾir* V(ix), 38; al-Ṣūlī, *Akhbār* 194-5; Ibn al-Muʿtazz, *Ṭabaqāt* 49, 94, 175-6, 186-7; al-Iṣfahānī, *Aghānī* VII, 188; XIII, 351-4; XX, 352-3; al-Bākharzī, *Dumya* I, 172; al-Kutubī, *Fawāt* I, 136-7; al-Rāghib, *Muḥāḍarāt* III, 486; Ibn Saʿīd, *Rāyāt* 71; and for some examples of indecent proposals made in public to boys, see Abū Hiffān, *Akhbār* 32-4; al-Tanūkhī, *Nishwār* VIII, 229-30; al-Thaʿālibī, *Yatīma* IV, 423. It was no secret to practically anyone that the greatest early master of *mujūn*, Abū Nuwās, started his career as the lover of another early libertine, Wāliba b. al-Ḥubāb. See al-Iṣfahānī, *Aghānī* XVIII, 106, 111. The nonchalance of libertine poets about their own homosexual affairs might occasionally be manifested by specialists of dialectal poetry too, as evidenced by the case of a master of the popular *mawwāliyā* genre called ʿĀmir Zurūmī in Ibn Saʿīd, *Muqtaṭaf* 245. In itself, the composition of love poetry addressed to boys does not seem to have been considered shameful, as attested by the obvious pride with which the anthologist Abū l-Ḥasan ʿAlī al-Bākharzī (d. 467/1074-5) cites a selection of such works by his own father; see al-Bākharzī, *Dumya* II, 1254-6.

[59] Tellingly, al-Jāḥiẓ (d. 255/869) refers to inveterate homosexuals who never play the passive role (called *ṣīṣiyya* in the vernacular of his time) as men with an inordinate amount of machismo; see al-Jāḥiẓ, *Ḥayawān* I, 307-8. It is noteworthy that many high-status men of the Buyid period, driven by machismo, would guard their catamites as jealously as they did their wives and concubines, and would react violently to any untoward approach to their slave-boys. For some illustrative cases, see al-Tanūkhī, *Nishwār* V, 135-6; VII, 70; Miskawayh, *Tajārib* II, 199. Also revealing is a story in which a father apparently finds it unobjectionable that his son keeps having sex with other adolescents as long as he always plays the active role; see al-Tawḥīdī, *Baṣāʾir* II(iv), 77. A passage in the *Nishwār al-muḥāḍara* tells of a man known as al-Ḥurr al-ʿĀmilī who would uninhibitedly allude, in front of other people, to his having sex with his slave-boy. See al-Tanūkhī, *Nishwār* II, 227. In contrast, even mere rumours of passive homosexuality could utterly ruin a reputation; see for instance al-Tanūkhī, *Nishwār* III, 173-5. Similar attitudes have continued to be dominant in the Ottoman era and in many places (e. g. Iraq) up to the modern period; see El-Rouayheb 2005: 13-51; al-Wardī 1965: 299, 322-4. Also cf. Schmidtke 1999: 261.

authors would even assume the persona of an irreclaimable homosexual.[60] The theme of homosexuality appears in many forms in *mujūn* poetry; perhaps the most characteristic treatment thereof is the description, in more or less candid terms, of drunken sex with the servant-boy or cupbearer (*sāqī*) as part of a larger wine poem.[61] Less patently offensive is the tone of love poetry addressed to males, even though unequivocal references to the gender of the addressee certainly made such works unseemly and exceptionable in the eyes of many, and albeit common, the genre was undeniably a breach of an important social and religious norm. In any case, the ubiquity of love poetry about boys ensured that it should not be viewed as the exclusive domain of libertines. Obvious signs of a poem being addressed to a boy included the mention of a male personal name (a relatively rare occurrence in love poetry)[62]; explicit references to the beloved being a boy in playful poems describing *ghilmān* (ephebes) of various names, occupations, physiques and origins[63]; and the immensely popular motif of the description of the beloved boy's first growth of facial hair (*ʿidhār*)[64]. It has to be pointed out that the mere use of the grammatical masculine in a love poem should not always be construed as an indication of the addressee's gender, this grammatical form being occasionally used simply because of the requirements of metre and rhyme.[65]

---

[60] For a selection of examples, quite a few of them rather gross, see Ibn al-Muʿtazz, *Ṭabaqāt* 34, 195; al-Jāḥiẓ, *Rasāʾil* I(ii), 136; al-Thaʿālibī, *Yatīma* III, 6, 10, 11, 70; al-Thaʿālibī, *Tatimma* II, 30; al-Tawḥīdī [attr.], *Risāla* 390; al-Tawḥīdī, *Baṣāʾir* I(i), 156; II(iv), 41; III(v), 38; al-Bākharzī, *Dumya* II, 1383; III, 1504; al-Iṣfahānī, *Aghānī* XX, 248-51; al-Iṣbahānī, *Kharīda* II(i), 37; Ibn Saʿīd, *Rāyāt* 124–5; al-Ḥillī, *ʿĀṭil* 124–6, 197; and (an outspoken poem in English translation) in Crone, Moreh 2000: 72–3.

[61] E.g. Abū Nuwās, *Dīwān* III, 346–7, 348–9, 353; IV, 191; V, 34; al-Iṣbahānī, *Kharīda* II(ii), 720. A very outspoken example ("if I wish, [he is] a boon-companion, and if I wish, a riding animal" etc.) can be found in al-Zawzanī, *Ḥamāsa* II, 93.

[62] E.g. Abū Nuwās, *Dīwān* III, 57 [Aḥmad]; V, 114 [Ḥamdān]; Ibn al-Khaṭīb, *Jaysh* 21 [ʿAbd al-Malik]; al-Ḥillī, *Dīwān* 465–71.

[63] al-Thaʿālibī, *Tatimma* II, 85; al-Iṣbahānī, *Kharīda* II(i), 35–8; Ibn Maʿṣūm, *Sulāfa* 226; and also cf. Abū Hiffān, *Akhbār* 32-3.

[64] Bauer 1998: 255–80; Rubiera Mata 1992: 62. For a number of examples, see al-Thaʿālibī, *Nathr* 189–90; al-Thaʿālibī, *Yatīma* I, 89; III, 5, 257-9; al-Thaʿālibī, *Tatimma* I, 138; al-Rāghib, *Muḥāḍarāt* III, 482–4; al-Iṣbahānī, *Kharīda* II(i), 33-5; al-Ḥillī, *Dīwān* 485, 490, 633; al-Ibshīhī, *Mustaṭraf* 275; Ibn Saʿīd, *Ghuṣūn* 22; Ibn Saʿīd, *Rāyāt* 260. The appearance of facial hair on the cheeks of a beloved boy was apparently a topic talked about in playful innuendoes in everyday conversation too; see for instance al-Thaʿālibī, *Laṭāʾif* 34.

[65] A poem expressly mentions that even a beloved person addressed as 'my lord' in verse may actually be a woman, this being a mere formal concession to the demands of the metre. See al-Tanūkhī, *Nishwār* IV, 36. This ambiguity might lead a poet to say explicitly that his (grammatically masculine) addressee is in fact a boy; see al-Bākharzī, *Dumya* II, 1318. Despite the ambiguities, Thomas Bauer's suggestion that the grammatical gender of a poem's addressee in most cases corresponds to that person's biological gender (and should normally be rendered as such in translation) is convincing. See Bauer 1998: 150–62; and cf. El-Rouayheb 2005: 61–6.

In contrast to literary treatments of the active role in sodomy, the passive role – for the reasons mentioned above – was seldom part of a libertine's literary persona, even though it would certainly have given a boost to the outrageousness of a work. However, the scandalous figure of the *mukhannath* (effeminate man; often a male entertainer-cum-prostitute) tends to appear in *mujūn* works as a protagonist of anecdotes spoken of in the third person, rather than as the self-chosen literary persona of the libertine poet or writer.[66] This is not to say that claims of, or allusions to, one's own liking of the passive role in homosexual intercourse were unheard of. Despite the immense disgrace brought about by such predilections, some libertines did go to the extreme of making such outrageous statements, and what is perhaps even more surprising – and very characteristic of *mujūn* – is the fact that these 'admissions' might occasionally be made as an affectation of depravity without any factual basis.[67]

The calculated, overt offensiveness that constituted the trademark of *mujūn* was taken to the extreme in what can be characterised as 'libertine manifestoes', texts resembling pious sermons but with diametrically opposed contents. A prominent

---

[66] More will be said in the next chapter about the *mukhannath* as the hero of risqué anecdotes. On the effeminate men of early Islamic Medina, see Rowson 1991.

[67] Such self-degradation was the speciality of a poet known as Jaḥshawayh (3rd/9th c.), who deliberately spread such rumours about himself, and even made it explicit in many of his verses. The irony is that according to Ibn al-Muʿtazz the poet was in fact not a passive homosexual at all but made this claim solely to boost his reputation of egregious libertinism. See Ibn al-Muʿtazz, *Ṭabaqāt* 184; and also Lagrange 2006: 79–81. A poem attributed to Abū Nuwās mentions his indiscriminate enjoyment of all kinds of sex, including being sodomised; see Wagner 2008: 190. The Andalusian scholar and poet Ibn Yāsmīn al-Ishbīlī (fl. late 6th/12th c.), an erudite black courtier, made no effort to deny or keep secret his own liking for the passive role in sodomy: he would nonchalantly joke about it in conversation and mention it explicitly in his poetry. See Ibn Saʿīd, *Ghuṣūn* 45–6. The Iraqi Abū ʿĪsā b. Bint Abī Nūḥ is claimed to have shown comparable indiscretion about the same habit; see al-Tanūkhī, *Nishwār* II, 228. Even joking about *ubna* (a proclivity for the passive role in anal sex) could be perceived as distasteful. Some intellectuals who certainly did not consistently cultivate a notoriety for passive homosexuality nevertheless succeeded in causing outrage by frivolous innuendos and jesting about the joys of being sodomised. Examples include the reception of a remark by the great littérateur Abū Bakr al-Ṣūlī (d. 335/946); the self-exposing ingenuousness of the poet Abū Muḥammad b. al-Munajjim in his boasting about his beauty as a youth and his relationship with the vizier; and the indignation of the relatives of the libertine poet Muṭīʿ b. Iyās (d. 169/785) because of rumours of his habit of allowing himself to be sodomised (which the poet was not overly eager to deny, observing that no one should reproach him without first-hand experience of the pleasure of the act). See al-Tanūkhī, *Nishwār* II, 229; al-Tawḥīdī, *Akhlāq* 161; al-Iṣfahānī, *Aghānī* XIII, 307 (and also cf. op.cit. XIII, 354 and al-Tawhīdī, *Baṣāʾir* II(iii), 59. For further examples and poems, see al-Rāghib, *Muḥāḍarāt* III, 489–-90; Ibn Manẓūr, *Akhbār* 9. Like libertine poets and writers, some state officials might also display striking disregard for their reputation by admitting a liking for being sodomised. See for instance the bizarre (and surely ironic) argumentation of a certain Ibn Sawwār in favour of the passive role in homosexual acts in al-Tawḥīdī, *Baṣāʾir* II(iii), 98. Also cf. a highly unconventional poem by an unidentified libertine (*mājin*) in op.cit. I(i), 167.

topic in such manifestoes is the exhortation to engage in homosexual acts; indeed this theme would also be developed in separate pieces, which focus solely on the advisability and pleasures of the company of adolescent boys and sodomy. It is necessary to introduce a note of caution here. These texts were clearly designed to be as provocative as possible, and while it is beyond doubt that they may often express a genuine preference for boys it is also conceivable, as with much of *mujūn* literature, that the theme of homosexuality was chosen and elaborated for its shock value, out of simple *Effekthascherei.* However, as the honesty or otherwise of *mujūn* works will be treated in the last chapter of this essay, for the time being the subject will be left aside, and homosexual 'manifestoes' will be taken for what they are on the surface. Such texts occur in prose as well as poetry, and in both cases they tend to emphasise the advantages and the delights of sodomising boys as opposed to heterosexual intercourse in general and licit sex with women in particular.[68] In expanding upon the subject, clever misapplications of Quranic passages – of the kind described in the previous chapter – may be used. Two typical examples follow; one is a poem by the arch-libertine Abū Nuwās (whose honest preference for males is hardly to be doubted), while the second is an excerpt from a jestful epistle titled *al-Wasāṭa bayna l-zunāt wa-l-lāṭa* ('Mediating Between Fornicators and Sodomisers') by Abū l-Faraj ʿAlī b. Hindū, an author and poet of considerable fame in Jurjān in the Buyid period:

> This woman reproaches me for my choice of a boy as beautiful as an antelope;
> And she says I deprive myself of the delights of relationships with fine young girls.
> However, I say to her: "You know nothing; the likes of me will never be duped with nonsense.
> "Am I to choose the sea over firm land, and fish over a gazelle of the desert?

[68] When homosexuality is praised in prose, it is not uncommon to find it within the format of a parodistic verbal duel between two opponents, a long-standing Middle Eastern literary tradition. (On this phenomenon, see Reinink, Vanstiphout [eds.] 1991.) Of course, in such cases the commendation of homosexual sex is put in the mouth of a symbolic 'lover of ephebes' (*ṣāḥib al-ghilmān*), whose odd and funny arguments are then countered by equally smart protestations from a 'lover of girls'. – It is worth observing here that the literary encomia of sex with boys gave rise to analogous works about the superiority of heterosexual relationships (*tafḍīl al-nisāʾ ʿalā l-murd*) – a theme which would have been meaningless had there not been previous works about ephebes to argue against – in which a heterosexual is usually termed *ṣāḥib al-nisāʾ*. See for instance al-Jāḥiẓ, *Rasāʾil* II(iv), 155–66; al-Iṣfahānī, *Aghānī* XIII, 266; al-Rāghib, *Muḥāḍarāt* III, 474; al-Iṣbahānī, *Kharīda* II(ii), 497; and for prose arguments and a small collection of poems defending the preference for women, see al-Washshāʾ, *Muwashshā* 150–3. The terms used in such literary works for men with heterosexual and homosexual preferences respectively seem to have been known in the spoken language too; see for instance al-Tanūkhī, *Nishwār* II, 174 ["*laʿallahum aṣḥāb nisāʾ*"]; Ibn Manẓūr, *Akhbār* 42 ["*kāna akhī ṣāḥib ghilmān*"]. One finds in literary texts another, remarkable usage which playfully refers to sexual preferences as a sort of quasi-sectarian conviction: a bisexual might be described as someone who 'believes in women as well as boys' (*yaqūlu bi-l-niswān wa-l-ghilmān*), a heterosexual as 'one of those who believe in the clitoris' (*mimman yaqūlu bi-l-baẓr*). See al-Thaʿālibī, *Laṭāʾif* 57–8; al-Thaʿālibī, *Yatīma* III, 46.

"Leave me alone; reproach me not; for I will continue to do, to the day of my death, that which you disapprove of.
"This is what God's Scripture [the Quran] advises us to do: to give preference to the boys over the girls."[69]

[...] The superiority of men over women is indisputable, since even God accords them preferential treatment in [dividing up] a legacy. What a huge difference there is between a boy – who offers you company in travels and at home, is an adornment of our entourage when you ride out, massages your shoulders if you wish so, listens to every wish you may have when you have a party, is a boon-companion if the two of you are alone, [acts like] a ferocious lion in the saddle of his horse and [like] a delicate gazelle under the blanket – and a woman, who causes the hairs in your beard to turn white with her sighs and those on your head too with the expenses she occasions; who destroys all pleasures, wears out your body, shortens your life, showers you with offspring and diminishes your wealth [... etc.].[70]

Like a host of other motifs in *mujūn* literature, the laudation of homosexual relationships also seems to be rooted in everyday speech. Here as elsewhere, written literature – both poetry and prose – appears not to have been averse to borrowing

[69] Abū Nuwās, *Dīwān* V, 14. For further examples, see Abū Nuwās, *Dīwān* V, 92–103; al-Jāḥiẓ, *Rasāʾil* I(ii), 111–3; Abū Hiffān, *Akhbār* 27, 31; Ibn Manẓūr, *Akhbār* 75, 91–3, 136; al-Jāḥiẓ, *Ḥayawān* I, 98; al-Thaʿālibī, *Yatīma* I, 373, 374; al-Thaʿālibī, *Thimār* II, 885; al-Rāghib, *Muḥāḍarāt* III, 474–5 [incl. a prose version of the last verse of Abū Nuwās's poem]; al-Iṣbahānī, *Kharīda* II(ii), 488; Ibn Maʿṣūm, *Sulāfa* 492. Needless to point out, the final verse in Abū Nuwās's poem deliberately and grossly misrepresents the purport of the Quranic passage referred to (4:11), which speaks of the preferential treatment of boys in the context of inheritance, ruling that a son should be given twice the share of a daughter when dividing up the legacy. The use of the verb *awṣā* ('advise' or 'rule') in the verse certainly suggests that the reference is to this *āya*, but there are additional possibilities of allusion too: to sarcastic Quranic verses deploring the belief that God has daughters among pagan Arabs who for their part prefer to have sons (e.g. 37:153, 43:16; the occurrence of the noun *iṣṭifāʾ* ['choice'] in the first verse of the poem reinforces this hint); to the Quranic statement (4:34) that God has 'preferred' men over women by making them responsible for the maintenance of their womenfolk (note the use of the word *tafḍīl* ['preference'] in the last verse); etc. – The use of 'sea' as a metaphor for women and heterosexual intercourse, and 'land' as a metaphor for men and homosexual acts, which occurs in works by other poets too, seems to have been invented by Abū Nuwās. It is probably based on the the fact that the usual mode of travelling by land was to ride on the back (*ẓahr*) of a creature, while a voyage by sea would involve entering the 'belly' (*baṭn*) of a ship. In a sexual context, *ẓahr* would refer to the rear part of the human body, and *baṭn* to the front part. I thank G. J. van Gelder for clarifying this trope for me.

[70] Cited in al-Thaʿālibī, *Tatimma* I, 143–4. Cf. an excerpt from Abū l-ʿAnbas al-Ṣaymarī's (d. 275/888-9; author of various obscene works (*v.i.*) including a *Kitāb tafḍīl al-satihīn ʿalā l-ḥariḥīn wa-l-lāṭa ʿalā l-jammāshīn* ('Book of the Superiority of Arse-Lovers to Cunt-Lovers and Sodomisers to Womanisers [lit. Flirts]') in Abū Nuwās, *Dīwān* V, 156–7. For further examples, see al-Jāḥiẓ, *Ḥayawān* I, 357–8; al-Tawḥīdī, *Baṣāʾir* V(ix), 79; and of course the celebrated epistle of al-Jāḥiẓ on the advantages of loving boys and women respectively (*Mufākharat al-jawārī wa-l-ghilmān*) in al-Jāḥiẓ, *Rasāʾil* I(ii), 91–137.

phrases and ideas from oral culture and incorporating them into the higher register of elite literature in Classical Arabic. A number of witticisms that one finds in *adab* works and poetry have their origins as spoken *bons mots*, which are sometimes attributed to concrete individuals.[71] Whether or not the attribution of such utterances is correct in any given case, it seems reasonable to suppose that they did circulate in oral form before being recorded in writing.

3. Stylistic Features: Punning, Double Entendre, Obscenity, and Parody

Although *mujūn* works do favour and often display certain linguistic and stylistic characteristics, it would be misleading to regard the latter as the distinguishing mark of *mujūn*. In style as in content, the boundaries of *mujūn* are not sharply defined. However, whenever the thematic conventions surveyed in the foregoing chapters of this book appear in combination with the stylistic features to be treated here, it is more than likely that the work bearing these characteristics can be classified as *mujūn* even if it is not expressly described as such in any mediaeval source. As a rule of thumb it is probably fair to state that obscenity tends to be a hallmark of libertinism in poetry – except in *hijāʾ* (invective poetry), which is often exceedingly obscene without usually being perceived as *mujūn* – and that punning and other clever and funny linguistic devices occur with sufficient frequency in *mujūn* literature to justify devoting some attention to them. A literary analysis of *mujūn* not being an ambition of this essay, neither phenomena will be discussed in depth in what follows; and the subject of word-play and punning in particular, which are far from being an exclusive property of *mujūn*, will only be examined very briefly. On the other hand, the close association of vulgarity, scurrility and obscenity with *mujūn* makes it indispensable to accord them serious consideration, all the more so as such language ran counter to ordinary norms of linguistic propriety. As an element clearly enhancing the norm-breaking potential of a *mujūn* work, the obscenity observable in a lot of such works is directly relevant to the main concern of this study.

---

[71] One example is the frivolous claim that a boy makes a better partner than a woman does because "he is suitable for the bed as well as the battle" (*yaṣluḥu li-l-firāsh wa-l-hirāsh*). This quip is ascribed to a military officer of the Abbasid period, although other versions attribute it to the chief *qāḍī* Yaḥyā b. Aktham. (The reason for the latter variant may well be the notoriety of the *qāḍī* as a pederast.) See al-Thaʿālibī, *Laṭāʾif* 28; al-Thaʿālibī, *Thimār* I, 271; al-Thaʿālibī, *Khāṣṣ* 51. Another relevant example is the cynical saying that as a sexual partner a boy is superior to a woman in that "he neither mentruates nor lays eggs" (*lā yaḥīḍu wa-lā yabīḍu*). The originator of the quip is identified as a *qāḍī ʿĀfiya;* at any rate, the phrase would make its appearance in written poetry in due course. See al-Rāghib, Muḥāḍarāt III, 475; al-Jāḥiẓ, Rasāʾil I(ii), 104.

3.1 Paronomasia and Word-Play

With the increasing refinement of Middle Eastern urban society and culture, it was inevitable that a corresponding sophistication should manifest itself in the literary language too. The educated class – to which most of the purveyors of *mujūn* belonged, if only by virtue of their using the written language in their works – laid more and more emphasis on the necessity of proving one's linguistic virtuosity in literary products, and with the explosion of highly erudite works of poetry and prose from the early Abbasid era onwards, a successful literary career required more and more aptitude for and skill in playful linguistic devices. The Buyid and Seljuk periods saw the proliferation *ad nauseam* of all kinds of puns, *double entendre* and word-play in the 'high', written literature, which, together with the tendency of motifs rapidly to become conventionalised, lent an increasingly *recherché* quality to many a literary product. This development can be observed in *mujūn* literature too. Two linguistic devices in particular seem to have been remarkably in vogue in works of *mujūn*, to wit, ironic *doubles entendres* based on technical terms of various branches of serious scholarship, and the utilisation of vernacular (and often vulgar) words and expressions in written literary works.

Puns in most cases are difficult if not impossible to render in any language other than the original, a quite unfortunate fact in view of their popularity in mediaeval Arabic literature. It can be observed as a general rule that most learned puns are based on a *double entendre* involving a word's primary, banal meaning and another, specialised sense of the same word in one of the disciplines of Muslim scholarship, typically Arabic grammar, Islamic theology or jurisprudence. Many of the terms of classical Arabic grammar obviously lend themselves to being utilised in sexual innuendoes. Thus *naṣb* as a grammatical term means the accusative, while its literal meaning is 'hoisting', 'raising', and figuratively 'erection'; *fiʿl* means 'verb', but its literal meaning being 'deed', 'action', it is often used elliptically in reference to the sexual act; likewise, *fāʿil* (grammatical subject, lit. 'the doer') may have the sense of 'fornicator', 'adulterer', 'sodomiser' and *mafʿūl* (grammatical object, lit. 'that to whom/which an act is done') may mean 'a man sodomised by another', 'a passive homosexual'. Taking another example, this time from religious terminology, *ākhira* ('afterworld') also means 'the back part' of something, and applied to a human body it may refer to the buttocks; no commentary is needed to guess the sort of punning this polysemy occasioned in many frivolous poems. Given the propensity of *mujūn* for the theme of sexuality, it is hardly surprising to find a copious amount of such puns in the relevant sources, in verse and prose alike. The use of *termini technici* naturally signals that these jestful texts, unlike many other aspects of *mujūn*, cannot be regarded as having originated in popular culture but must have been invented by intellectuals familiar with the curriculum of a standard Islamic education.[72] It is important to add, however, that the élite origin of such texts does not preclude a preceding spoken version. Consider the following account:

> [...] It was narrated by Ibrāhīm b. al-Mudabbir: al-Faḍl al-Yazīdī, al-Buḥturī and Abū l-ʿAynāʾ met in my house, and al-Faḍl sat down to give a lecture to our young people (*ʿalā baʿḍ fityāninā*) on grammar. Abū l-ʿAynāʾ said: "This is about me and [your] mother (*hādhā bābī wa-bāb al-wālida*) [viz. about the concepts of 'the active' and 'the passive'], may God preserve her!" Al-Faḍl got angry and left. Al-Buḥturī went from Baghdad to Sāmarrā and sent to me a poem [...] in which he lampooned al-Faḍl, saying: "*The greater part of his [knowledge] is hesitation about who of his parents is the active and who is the passive [partner]* (jullu mā ʿindahu l-taraddud fī l-fāʿili min wālidayhi wa-l-mafʿūli*)*." (Ibrāhīm continues the story:) So I gave orders to write a reply to his letter and send him a hundred dinars. [Presently] Abū l-ʿAynāʾ visited me and I showed him the poem, and he said: "Give me half of the hundred [dinars] because, by God, he lampooned him with my own [spoken] words!" He took fifty [dinars], and I sent fifty to al-Buḥturī, informing him of what had happened. He wrote to me: "By God, he told the truth; I based my verses on his idea."[73]

The growing sophistication of the society of the great Middle Eastern cities is also indicated by the appearance and popularity of other learned forms and intricate devices of literary expression, the most striking example being the well-known, charming *maqāma* genre. Of course, literary works might indulge in a great deal of word-play and related amusements without being necessarily perceived as closely

---

[72] E.g. al-Thaʿālibī, *Yatīma* III, 272 [*istiṭāʿa, jabr*]; IV, 312 [*lāzim lā yataʿaddā*]; al-Thaʿālibī, *Tatimma* I, 42 [*rafʿ, naṣb, khafḍ*]; al-Thaʿālibī, *Khāṣṣ* 68 [*rafʿ, naṣb, ṣifa, ḥadhf*]; al-Thaʿālibī, *Laṭāʾif* 115 [*ḥāl, naṣb, khafḍ*]; al-Tawḥīdī, *Baṣāʾir* III(v), 131 [*naṣb*]; III(vi), 67–8 [*hamz, jarr*]; al-Tawḥīdī, *Akhlāq* 159 [*fāʿil, mafʿūl*]; al-Tawḥīdī, *Imtāʿ* 197 [*hamz*]; al-Iṣbahānī, *Kharīda* II(i), 45 [*khafḍ, ḥarf ḍaʿīf, iḍāfa*]; II(ii), 517-8 [*ṭawīl, ziḥāf, muʿtall, taṣrīf, dakhīl, zāʾid, ḥadhf*]; al-Rāghib, *Muḥāḍarāt* III, 478 [*fiʿl, naṣb, fāʿil, mafʿūl, ḥarf jāʾa li-maʿnā, iḍāfa*], 491 [*ṭawīl, madīd, basīṭ, wāfir, kāmil, fāʿil, mafʿūl*]; al-Ḥillī, *Dīwān* 636 [*ḥarf jāʾa li-maʿnā*]; al-Ḥarīrī, *Durra* 142 [*wāw al-ʿaṭf*]; Ibn Maʿṣūm, *Sulāfa* 258 [*ism fiʿl, ʿāmil, ḍamīr*], 299 [*mafʿūl, ḥāl, fiʿl, tamyīz*], 409 [*iʿrāb, ḍamm, jamʿ, ḥaraka, sākin, ʿāmil*], 552-3 [a whole poem based on a plethora of puns]; Abū Nuwās, *Dīwān* V, 135–6 [*ḥaraka, sākin*]; Abū Nuwās, *Dīwān* V, 26-7 and Ibn Manẓūr, *Akhbār* 83–4 [*ākhira*]; al-Ṣafadī, *Tawshīḥ* 117 [*mālikī, iʿtizāl*]. This literary device was known in mediaeval Arabic poetics as *tawriya* or *īhām*, although some authors preferred the term *tawjīh*. See al-Qazwīnī, *Īḍāḥ* VI, 38; al-Ḥillī, *Sharḥ* 122–3, 135–6; and Sperl 1989: 107–8. Although punning with the technical terms of a branch of scholarship obviously required at least a modicum of erudition, the phenomenon was even known in dialectal poetry; see for instance the text of a late mediaeval *mawwāl* containing puns on the terms *rafʿ, naṣb, jarr,* and *ḥarf jāʾa li-maʿnā* in al-Khāqānī 1381/1962: I, 22. This type of erudite punning has not been forgotten in the modern Arab world either. A pertinent example is a lovely – but, alas, totally untranslatable – *bon mot* of an Iraqi politician of the 1930s Yāsīn al-Hāshimī cited in al-Qishṭaynī 1992: 111. Double entendre is a much-used device in Arabic proverbs as well as modern Algerian *rāy* (*raï*) music, in which the sexual connotations of certain words are often exploited. See Virolle-Souibès 1989: 49; and Westermarck 1930: 22.

[73] Yāqūt, *Udabāʾ* V, 2178–9.

connected with *mujūn*, but the element of playfulness does create an indirect (and in some cases direct) link. Other amusing literary forms include versified riddles, poems incorporating the date of their own composition by the numerical value of the letters of the last hemistich (such poems being often inscribed on edifices to commemorate the construction thereof), verses obeying certain rules self-imposed by the poet (such as the stipulation of using only dotted or undotted letters, or of using a certain letter in every single word of a poem, etc.). The habit of quoting a part or the whole of a verse from a previous poem (*taḍmīn*) in the context of a new composition – often, especially in *mujūn* works, in an ironic sense – is yet another indication of the intellectuals' increasing appetite for complex, advanced literary devices.[74]

Interest in the common folk's vernacular and even the urban argot of the underclass was growing too. In addition to the occasional *mujūn* work composed entirely in a combination of classical Arabic grammar with the beggars' and urban vagabonds' vocabulary, we find many instances of poems in classical Arabic being peppered with some odd vernacular words, and the recording of the amusing malapropisms and grotesque linguistic mistakes of uneducated or semi-educated people.[75] The trend of vernacular linguistic elements seeping into 'high' literature – mostly to create a humorous effect – is closely related to another novel phenomenon, that of macaronic verses, lines of Arabic poetry containing phrases or even whole hemistichs (frequently obscene in content) in a foreign language, usually Persian.[76] Persian having been widely spoken and understood in the big Iraqi cities, including Baghdad, it is justified to view this as a variant of the incorporation of the urban vernacular or slang into classical Arabic works.

A word of caution is in order here. It would be a mistake to see in this interest a reflection of a growing sympathy with the lower orders of society; in fact the only thing it is likely to reflect is a curiosity for the bizarre and odd not unlike the

[74] On versified riddles, see Ibn Ḥijja, *Khizāna* IV, 166–202; al-Iṣbahānī, *Kharīda* II(ii), 502–3; al-Ḥillī, *Sharḥ* 212–3; Abū Nuwās, *Dīwān* V, 281–6. On chronograms, see Ibn Maʿṣūm, *Sulāfa* 57, 64, 288, 569–70. For examples of the stipulation of extra rules for the outward appearance of a poem (or even a prose piece), see al-Ḥarīrī, *Maqāmāt* 495–500; Yāqūt, *Udabāʾ* V, 1952–4; al-Jurjānī, *Wasāṭa* 51 [*taṣḥīf*]; al-Iṣbahānī, *Kharīda* II(i), 299; II(ii), 616–24, 661–2; Ibn Maʿṣūm, *Sulāfa* 204–6, 454–5; and for comparable works from modern Arabia, see Sowayan 1985: 171–2. On the device of *taḍmīn* (also, if more rarely, known as *īdāʿ*), see for instance Ibn Ḥijja, *Khizāna* IV, 106–61; al-Qazwīnī, *Īḍāḥ* VI, 143; al-Jurjānī, *Ishārāt* 318–9; Ibn Rashīq, *Qurāḍa* 81–2; al-Thaʿālibī, *Thimār* I, 82–3, 552–3; II, 861–3; al-Bākharzī, *Dumya* I, 294 ["... *nāma ʿan laylī wa-lam anami* "]; Ibn al-Muʿtazz, *Badīʿ* 159; and also Jones 1991: 64, 71-3. As a general observation, it may be argued that intertextuality (in a host of forms) came to be a key aspect of mediaeval Arabic poetry. See Sperl 1989: 167–75.

[75] See for instance the quotations of the texts of Ibn Sakrān and Abū l-Ḥasan al-Qummī in al-Tanūkhī, *Nishwār* VII, 186–9, 230.

[76] E.g. al-Tawḥīdī [attr.], *Risāla* 288; al-Bākharzī, *Dumya* I, 542–3, 550–2.

curiosity of a helminthologist for the objects of his studies. A highly learned littérateur might find the language of the masses amusing and deplorably primitive and deficient at one and the same time – or indeed he might find it amusing precisely because, in his eyes, it was deplorably primitive. And just as the vulgar phrases and ways of commoners might be cited and described in written literature (especially *mujūn*) to add spice to it, so did it become possible – and fairly common – for gross obscenities to appear in 'high' literary products. By no means should it be misconstrued as the elevation of such language to the dignity of a respectable form of expression.

3.2 Vulgarity and Obscenity

As noted above, obscenity[77] is an aspect of *mujūn* literature that merits special consideration. First, it is quite common in such literary products; and secondly, it is a clear-cut case of the breach of an important norm of ordinary speech and writing. As Thomas Bauer warns, the exact contours of the notion of obscenity vary from culture to culture and from one historical period to another,[78] but a detailed analysis of the issue is beyond the scope of this essay. At any rate, it seems to be generally true that among mediaeval Arabic-speaking Muslims, a self-respecting and respectable adult man was supposed to refrain from using obscene language, part of the more general expectation of displaying reserve, coolness and self-restraint (*ḥilm*) in all situations. This quality had already been one of the most highly prized and admired personal traits in the pre-Islamic period, which it continued to be among Muslim Arabs throughout the Middle Ages. Aloofness, composure and a cool disdain of even the most outrageous provocations were thought to be signs of real nobility of character, as was the deliberate avoidance of foul language and swearing, no matter how offensive the challenge. Conversely, the use of gratuitous swearwords, insults and gross expressions was a mark of lowly breeding. Accordingly, it was regarded as particularly unbecoming for a high-status person. Learning of a couplet containing obscene words that his son had composed, the vizier Abū l-Faḍl Ibn al-ʿAmīd (d. 360/970) exploded in anger: "Someone like my son write obscenity and immorality like this (*a-mithl waladī yaktubu mithl hādhā l-fuḥsh wa-l-fujūr*)?"[79] The disapproval of offensive and vulgar language and the ideal of composure and self-control are also well illustrated in the following story, in which there is not a trace of ambiguity about who the villain is. The passage presents the climax of a

---

[77] Roughly equivalent to the Arabic terms *badhāʾa* and *fuḥsh*; see Ibn Manẓūr, *Lisān* I, 179; V, 96. On the relationship of obscenity and humour, see Douglas 1968: 371–2.

[78] Bauer 1998: 8.

[79] Yāqūt, *Udabāʾ* IV, 1891–2.

conflict between the notoriously vulgar vizier of the caliph al-Muqtadir (r. 295/908–320/932), Ḥāmid b. al-ʿAbbās, and another courtier called ʿAlī b. ʿĪsā:

> [...] And then [Ḥāmid] began to curse him in an obscene manner, yet all that ʿAlī b. ʿĪsā kept repeating was this: "Peace, peace." This was an allusion to the Quranic verse "*[The servants of the All-merciful are those (...)] who, when the ignorant address them, say 'Peace'.*"[80] One day, incensed at this [display of self-restraint], Ḥāmid concluded a torrent of vulgarities with the words: "How much more are you going to repeat this 'Peace', which can go fuck your sister Asmāʾ!" Thereupon ʿAlī b. ʿĪsā stood up, saying: "This is the end of everything [between us]." He would never speak to him again.[81]

So much for ideals. Lest it should be misunderstood to mean that the majority of mediaeval Arabs avoided obscenities, let me reiterate the point stressed in the first chapter that a norm may not be statistically predominant in actual behaviour, a general acceptance of it as an ideal being sufficient to maintain it as a norm. (In other words, a norm may dominate conduct in either a descriptive or a prescriptive sense.) In the absence of overwhelming evidence, there is simply no way to determine the extent to which obscenities formed a part of the ordinary speech style of mediaeval Middle Eastern Muslims but such evidence as we do have does not seem to suggest a widespread reluctance to use indecent language. It seems probable that indecencies were, while frowned upon, by no means uncommon. Some of these usages are even reported in the sources, although it is fair to assume that among mediaeval Arabs as in other cultures writing was a medium less amenable to the toleration of gross language than speech is. Ḥāmid b. al-ʿAbbās is not the only high dignitary of the Buyid period who would insouciantly utter vulgarities and obscene abuses; the same habit was noted (not implausibly, even if by an admittedly hostile source) about the great statesman-cum-littérateur al-Ṣāḥib b. ʿAbbād (326/938–385/995), whose "manners were bad, and his tongue obscene (*sāʾa adabuhu wa-*

---

80 Quran 25:63.

81 al-Tanūkhī, *Nishwār* VIII, 88. The grossly obscene style of the vizier scandalised almost everyone in the court; see Miskawayh, *Tajārib* I, 62–3. – One finds quite a few modern examples too of the norm against the use of indecent language. A pertinent one comes from an anthropological description of the poetic competitions called *bāla* in the Yemeni highlands. At these contests it is customary to interrupt the exchange of verses when one of the participants uses an offensive phrase, because on the one hand it is discreditable behaviour, and on the other hand verbal aggression may immediately spill over into actual fighting. See Caton 1990: 119–21. Among the Swahili today (an entirely Islamised society), obscene language is an absolute taboo ("*katika utamaduni wa Kiswahili inakatazwa kutumia lugha chafu*"), to the extent that even remarks meant to be insulting must be phrased in the form of allusions (sing. *kijembe*); see Sheikh 1994: 11; and Hirsch 1998: 232. The Touareg also very strongly disapprove of abusive and indecent language; see Casajus 1987: 102–3. Whilst Islamic religious texts certainly regard obscenity and offensive expressions in a very negative light, the toleration of such phenomena – as will be obvious from the following pages – has not been uniform through the centuries of the history of Islamicate societies.

badhuʾa lisānuhu)".[82] At roughly the same time, a Christian intellectual who served the Buyid state as a secretary was widely known by the obscene sobriquet *Baẓr Umm al-Dunyā* ('The Clitoris of the World's Mother') because he kept using this gross expression in conversation.[83] It seems, then, that the norms against vulgarity did not always and necessarily inform speech behaviour even in the highest echelon of society, the use of outspoken language being a long-standing tradition in Arabic culture.[84]

In the coming chapter, it will be stressed that the boundaries of acceptable behaviour were to a large extent determined by the circumstances being perceived as 'private' or 'public' respectively, these two types of social situation calling for quite different norms of conduct, especially among the political and intellectual élite. Anticipating that discussion let it be stated here that it was not in all situations that scurrility and obscenity had to be avoided but rather in settings considered to be 'public', although some people would certainly carry their avoidance of indecent speech over into their private life too. However, if analogies with modern Arab societies can be allowed, it appears likely that most intellectuals who took pains to behave and speak respectably in public would not necessarily be averse to scurrilous humour in exclusive situations, when only trustworthy friends or close relatives were present.[85] Apart from analogies of doubtful validity, explicit accounts from mediaeval sources also support the postulate that the use of obscenities and vulgarities was rampant among intellectuals, particularly those identified as libertines, in strictly private situations (viz. in the exclusive company of friends). In such settings, the use of strong, scurrilous language seems to have been regarded

---

[82] al-Tawḥīdī, *Akhlāq* 143.

[83] al-Tanūkhī, *Nishwār* III, 115. Furthermore, there is some anecdotal evidence (including poems) that even men of the highest rank and prestige in the early Islamic era might occasionally use vulgar words. For some examples, see al-Thaʿālibī, *Laṭāʾif* 11; and for a (perhaps fictitious) account of an incredibly obscene teasing taking place between the caliph al-Ma'mūn (r. 198/813–218/833) and one of his concubines, see al-Suyūṭī, *Mustaẓraf* 69.

[84] On this, see for instance Sadan 1983: 20–4; Khayati 1989: 139.

[85] See for instance Abu-Lughod 1999: 17, 156; and E. W. Lane's observations on the secrecy surrounding wine-drinking and friendly drinking parties in Egypt in Lane 1895: 153. Even the presence of certain close relatives may necessitate discretion about displaying disreputable forms of conduct, including the use of swearwords and obscenities. In Morocco for instance, it is inconceivable for a son, whether a minor or a grown-up man, to utter an obscenity or allude to sexuality in the presence of his father, and a man may even leave a café when his father enters it since it is by definition a locale of coarse and indecent talk. See Rosen 1984: 36. The fact that the relationship of a researcher and an informant is not classified as 'private' or 'intimate' puts all but insurmountable hurdles in the way of research on sexuality in Middle Eastern societies. A good indication of the constraints on acceptable topics for public discourse in many Arabic-speaking countres is the observation of an Omani sociologist (who naturally wished to remain anonymous) to a prominent Western anthropologist that no ethnological monograph containing a discussion of sexual practices would have any chance of being translated into Arabic and published there. See Eickelman 1989: 190.

as a source of fun rather than a cause for indignation and shame.[86] Libertine intellectuals would take remarkable liberties with their friends, including the use of abusive terms and vulgar phrases as a source of fun. Indeed, a reliable source claims, on the authority of the well-informed al-Jāḥiẓ (d. 255/869), that some of the best-known poets and writers of the early Abbasid period, forming a circle of habitual drinking pals, often amused themselves by composing biting lampoons about one another ("*wa-yahjū baʿḍuhum baʿḍan hazlan wa-ʿamdan*"; "*hijāʾ [...] ʿalā sabīl al-ʿabath* ").[87] The obscenity of some poems appears to reflect the ordinary speech style of everyday chat in private situations.[88] The following excerpt illustrates the fact that educated people might have no qualms to use or endorse vulgarities in circumstances defined as private:

> Bashshār [b. Burd] asked the transmitter of his works (*rāwiya*) to recite some verse by Ḥammād [ʿAjrad] to him. The latter recited: "You call Burd your father, while it was someone else; but let's grant it was Burd, may I fuck your mother: whoever is Burd?" At this point, Bashshār asked: "Is there anyone nearby who might overhear what I'm going to say?" [The transmitter] replied: "No." Said Bashshār: "The son of a bitch is good at what he does (*aḥsana ibn al-zāniya*)."[89]

A more sophisticated way of being vulgar was by allusion, avoiding explicit obscenities yet making the meaning clear to anyone with a minimal knowledge of conversational Arabic. The story is narrated by Abū ʿAlī al-Ḥasan al-Īdhajī, a *qāḍī* known for his libertine ways:

> As a young man I went to al-Baṣra to acquire learning, erudition and good manners. My company was sought by [the poet] Abū ʿAbdallāh al-Mufarrijī, who came to be my only [close friend there]. One day, when the weather had turned terribly cold, he wrote [the following verses] to me: "Oh you excellent man, for you are an excellent man even when hardly anyone is worthy of the description: / How nice is the condition of someone who, come winter, possesses cups, cash, comestibles, and clothes!" Then he added on the piece of paper: "And there is yet [another thing with an initial] *c* that I could mention if I did not wish to keep your expenses low." [...] I sent him everything he had asked for.[90]

---

86 E.g. al-Iṣfahānī, *Aghānī* VII, 188; XIII, 307-10; Ibn al-Muʿtazz, *Ṭabaqāt* 50 [a story about Ibn Munādhir and al-Ḥajjāj al-Ṣawwāf]. However, not everyone was glad to tolerate jesting abuses. As few people wished to see what had started as a joke turn into serious friction, it was important to consider the interlocutor's temper before any rude joke. See for instance al-Tanūkhī, *Nishwār* III, 155.

87 al-Iṣfahānī, *Aghānī* XVIII, 107, 201.

88 E.g. al-Bākharzī, *Dumya* II, 828–9.

89 al-Ṣūlī, *Akhbār* 181.

90 al-Tanūkhī, *Nishwār* III, 287. The list in the Arabic original contains items with an initial *kāf* (namely *kaʾs*, *kīs*, *kisra*, *kisā* and the unstated *kuss*). Literal translation has been sacrificed for the sake of alliteration, as *kīs* really means 'purse' or 'sack', and *kisra* 'a piece of bread'. This allusion to things with initial *kāf* letters occurs in the text of a well-known *maqāma* too, as well as in Iraqi dialectal

The evidence for the prevalence or otherwise of obscenity in the speech of the lower orders of urban society is extremely limited and mostly indirect; an added problem is that what little data we have at our disposal may or may not be wholly fictitious.[91] That vulgarity was well received, perhaps even favoured, by a considerable number of common people is suggested by the following observation in an anthology about a poet known as Abū l-Yanbaghī: "His invective poems against Rajā᾽ b. al-Ḍaḥḥāk are considered particularly witty despite their foolish [i.e. calculatedly obscene] expressions (*ʿalā sukhf lafẓihi*). But such [language] is used on purpose so that even the common masses and the children should take up and transmit it."[92]

Whatever the *de facto* prevalence of obscenity and indecency in élite and popular culture, *mujūn* literature utilised them with no inhibitions, and its later offshoot known as *sukhf* (lit. 'folly', gross indecency and scatology) all but gorged on such language, making it practically its most recognisable stylistic feature. Obviously, some topics were especially amenable to the application of gross and outspoken language. Sexual congress is certainly one of those topics, and they are a common theme in *mujūn* literature, as are detailed descriptions – sometimes almost anatomically precise, sometimes grotesque – of the male and female sexual organs, erection, penetration, and ejaculation and semen.[93] Weird or shameful forms of sexuality, like masturbation, the use of a dildo, bestiality and other perversions, also occur with considerable frequency in frivolous literature, usually serving as a source of

poetry. See al-Ḥarīrī, *Maqāmāt* 251–2 ["*talaqqaytu l-shitā᾽ bi-kāfātihi* "]; al-Khāqānī 1381/1962: I, 24. The Arabic letters *lām* and *mīm* were also used in sexual innuendoes (in reference to the penis and anus respectively) – not because the letters occur in the Arabic equivalents but because their shape in the Arabic script may be suggestive of the organs in question – Freud would be delighted to hear of it. For an example of such innuendo in verse, see Yāqūt, *Udabā᾽* IV, 1874.

[91] A passage in the Baghdadian Epistle of Abū Ḥayyān al-Tawḥīdī, which seems to attempt to evoke the vernacular style of the inhabitants of the city, narrates the rather gross mumblings of a chess player; another passage recounts the rant of a drunk in a comparable manner; see al-Tawḥīdī [attr.], *Risāla* 282, 354. For an anecdote based on an obscene exchange of words between a libertine and a woman that takes place in the setting of a street, see al-Tawḥīdī, *Baṣā᾽ir* I(ii), 43; for two comparably obscene conversations, see al-Ibshīhī, *Mustaṭraf* 62, 262; and see some similar examples in al-Rāghib, *Muḥāḍarāt* III, 529. Contemporary Arabic culture also yields examples of thoroughgoing obscenity in various 'popular' contexts like the carnivalesque *Bilmawn* festival of Moroccan folklore, and dialectal poetry (e.g. "*Dabbūs inglīzī yō yō; / Yeghres b-ṭīzī yō yō*" etc.); see Hammoudi 1993: 20, 74–5, 82–3; and Jargy 1970: 145–7.

[92] Ibn al-Muʿtazz, *Ṭabaqāt* 55.

[93] E.g. al-Iṣfahānī, *Aghānī* II, 401; XIII, 339; XVIII, 201-2; al-Thaʿālibī, *Yatīma* I, 349-55; III, 9–13, 70; al-Thaʿālibī, *Tatimma* I, 70; al-Tawḥīdī [attr.], *Risāla* 76–7, 212, 305, 367–9; al-Tawḥīdī, *Baṣā᾽ir* III(vi), 57; al-Tawḥīdī, *Imtāʿ* 194-5; al-Bākharzī, *Dumya* I, 200–1, 616–7; II, 947–8; al-Iṣbahānī, *Kharīda* I(ii), 98, 132; al-Rāghib, *Muḥāḍarāt* III, 505–32; al-Nuwayrī, *Nihāya* I(ii), 99–101; al-Marzūqī, *Sharḥ* IV, 1847–51; Abū Nuwās, *Dīwān* V, 29, 37–8, 345–6; Ibn Saʿīd, *Muqtaṭaf* 222–4; al-Jāḥiẓ, *Ḥayawān* I, 356; Ibn al-Muʿtazz, *Badīʿ* 117; al-Suyūṭī, *Mustaẓraf* 26; al-Nafzāwī, *Rawḍ* 2, 22–3, 30–3. Tales might also contain descriptions of the sexual act; cf. Rescher 1919: 84.

amusement and fun.[94] Sexuality must surely have been a favourite topic of conversation among friends,[95] and it is perhaps not unreasonable to suppose that *mujūn* borrowed many jokes and motifs from the spoken language, drawing them into the orbit of 'high' literature through the medium of writing and Classical Arabic. (The reader is referred back to the aforementioned examples of libertines amusing themselves with lampoons and obscenities directed at one another.) In this context, it is noteworthy that Classical Arabic, whilst being a literary tongue, does have a plethora of words for the human reproductive organs – ranging from euphemisms to humorous terms to obscenities – which must have facilitated the literary treatment of such topics.[96] Besides sexuality (indeed often in combination with it) scatological humour and allusions to the biological, bodily functions were likewise common motifs in *mujūn* literature, and came to constitute the primary subject matter of many poets. It was especially so in the case of a later version of *mujūn* known as *sukhf* (lit. 'folly'), which tends to luxuriate in disgusting, naturalistic images of bodily emissions both fluid and gaseous, and the most bizarre aspects of the human body's metabolism.[97] As could be expected, the genre of *hijāʾ*, or invective poetry, was as fertile a soil for obscenities as all manner of *mujūn*, which can probably be regarded as the strongest link between the two distinct but not unrelated phenomena.[98]

---

94 E.g. al-Rāghib, *Muḥāḍarāt* III, 498–500, 530-1; Yāqūt, *Udabāʾ* III, 1145, 1403; al-Jāḥiẓ, *Ḥayawān* I, 204–5; Ibn Manẓūr, *Akhbār* 94–5; al-Thaʿālibī, *Yatīma* IV, 449; al-Thaʿālibī, *Tatimma* II, 30; Ibn Saʿīd, *Muqtaṭaf* 219–20; Ibn al-Muʿtazz, *Badīʿ* 161; al-ʿAskarī, *Ṣināʿatayn* 383–4. Abū l-ʿAnbas al-Ṣaymarī (d. 275/888–9), a judge of the town of al-Ṣaymara in Iraq and a noted auhor on assorted libertine topics, wrote full-length works dedicated to such subjects as lesbianism and male prostitution (*Kitāb al-saḥḥāqāt wa-l-baghghāʾīn*), masturbation (*Kitāb al-khaḍkhaḍa fī jald ʿUmayra*), and 'the superiority of the anus over the mouth' (*Kitāb faḍl al-surm ʿalā l-fam*). See Yāqūt, *Udabāʾ* VI, 2422.

95 See for instance an account of the conversation of the caliph Hārūn al-Rashīd and his vizier about the sexual excellence of concubines and slave-girls in al-Thaʿālibī, *Laṭāʾif* 75–6; the discussion of the meaning of the vernacular word *zurnūq* by an anonymous woman in al-Tawḥīdī, *Baṣāʾir* I(ii), 169; and an anecdote recounted by the poet al-Ḥamdūnī (3rd/9th c.) about an uncomfortable encounter in the crowded bazaar in Ibn al-Muʿtazz, *Ṭabaqāt* 176. Whereas none of these accounts can be assumed to be factual (nor, for that matter, pure fiction), the portrayal therein of casual discussions of sex certainly does not sound unrealistic.

96 The early 9th/15th-century frivolous work known as The Perfumed Garden lists no less than 37 synonyms for 'penis' and 40 for 'vagina'; see al-Nafzāwī, *Rawḍ* 24, 27–8. Persian apparently also possesses the vocabulary for very obscene discussions of sex and other staples of *mujūn*; see for instance a sample of the relevant works of the great al-Saʿdī (d. 691/1292) in Sprachman 1995: 33–43.

97 For an unsavoury sample, see for instance al-Tawḥīdī [attr.], *Risāla* 52, 59, 211–7, 384–7; al-Tawḥīdī, *Baṣāʾir* II(iv), 221; al-Thaʿālibī, *Yatīma* I, 316–9, 349-55; al-Thaʿālibī, *Tatimma* 140; al-Ḥarīrī, *Durra* 373–6; al-Rāghib, *Muḥāḍarāt* III, 535–46; Ibn Saʿīd, *Muqtaṭaf* 221; al-Ibshīhī, *Mustaṭraf* 261. Such scurrility can safely be presumed to have been present in oral culture too (see for instance al-Tawhīdī, *Baṣāʾir* I(i), 129); and it also occurs in the Arabian Nights; see Rescher 1919: 85. On scatological humour, cf. Douglas 1968: 364.

98 E.g. al-Tawḥīdī, *Akhlāq* 63-4 [a prose version of *hijāʾ*]; al-Bākharzī, *Dumya* II, 1384–6; al-

3.3 Stylistic Parodies

Some of these subversive texts we have already encountered in the preceding part of the book, such as 'mock sermons' and frivolous texts cast as *ḥadīths* in the previous chapter, as well as parodies of Bedouin poetical conventions (e.g. the traditional opening motif of the *qaṣīda*) and love poetry in this chapter. Here I will confine myself to some examples of the parodying of the form and content of certain branches of serious scholarship. Such parodies, naturally, presuppose the existence of the disciplines in question, and a sufficiently recognisable and intricate scholarly style and vocabulary. They also require an audience that is, first, sufficiently erudite to appreciate the general point and the nuances of the parodies – that is to say, they must be familiar with the technical vocabulary of the parodied disciplines – and second, sufficiently broad-minded and detached to relish the humour without feeling offended. Most libertines writing in Arabic meet both conditions, but there is no reason to suppose that the parodies discussed below were the exclusive preserve of the specialists of *mujūn*. Here again the boundaries of *mujūn* are not sharply defined.

Various branches of traditional Muslim scholarship, with their highly specialised vocabulary and peculiar scholarly style, provided an easy target for mockery by frivolous-minded intellectuals. A favourite object of such parodies was the figure of the *naḥwī*, or grammarian, the ultimate embodiment of the ludicrous remoteness of many scholars from real-life concerns and their ivory tower existence. The discipline of Arabic grammar certainly lent itself to parodistic uses, given the prevailing situation of diglossia, which made the use of pure Classical Arabic in mundane contexts instantly grotesque. Even though the vastly greater prestige of Classical Arabic vis-à-vis the dialects was never seriously questioned by anyone, and continues to be generally accepted, using the literary language for quotidian purposes was and is entirely inappropriate.[99] No easier target, then, than the experts of this discipline if one was to parody the insularity of the scholars' world and concerns. Consider the message of the following joke:

> [The grammarian Abū ʿAlqama] said to a slave-girl he was in love with: "Oh maiden, methought thou hadst tenderness towards me, and lo! thou hadst but antipathy. How is it that pine though I may for thee, thou abhorst me (*yā kharīda qad kuntu ikhāluki ʿarūban fa-idhā anti nawāri; mā lī amiquki wa-tashnaʾīnanī*)?" Said the girl: "You idiot, I've never seen a man love someone and then go insult her."[100]

Iṣbahānī, *Kharīda* II(ii), 539, 543–4, 759. Vulgarity had been the stylistic hallmark of the *hijāʾ* genre from a very early time; see Pellat 1963: 356.

[99] Cf. Foley 1997: 337.

[100] al-ʿAskarī, *Ṣināʿatayn* 35 (and for a German translation, see Weipert 2009: 120–1). For further examples, see op.cit. 33–5; Ibn al-Jawzī, *Ẓirāf* 125–7; Ibn al-Jawzī, *Taqwīm* 93–4; al-Naḥḥās, *Ṣināʿa* 240-1; Yāqūt, *Udabāʾ* IV, 1637–40; al-Tawḥīdī, *Imtāʿ* 194; al-Tawḥīdī, *Baṣāʾir* I(i), 155 [the story of

In other texts – more precisely, poems by noted libertines of the Buyid period – the great authorities of Arabic linguistics are referred to in abusive and often obscene terms; the point of singling out these prestigious scholars for insults appears to be the same as above, viz. the pretentious and affected linguistic usage associated with them.[101]

Whether anecdotes that show grammarians using the literary language in everyday situations have any factual basis is, for our present purposes, neither here nor there. What is important is the existence of a large number of texts that parody the style of Arabic linguistics, grammar and philology by placing the high-prestige linguistic register of Classical Arabic in inappropriate, mundane contexts and thereby making fun of the pretensions of many scholars. That said, there might well have been instances of certain presumptuous scholars showing off their erudition by such incongruent linguistic habits, but it is hard to determine definitively.[102] One indication of this possibility is a passage in the above-cited work by the philologist Abū Hilāl al-Ḥasan al-ʿAskarī (fl. late 4th/10th c.) that states, "a common man, when you address him in the language of the élite, will mock and make fun of you (*al-ʿāmmī idhā kallamtahu bi-kalām al-ʿilya sakhira minka wa-zarā bika*)".[103] Another clue is a passage about the grammarian Abū l-ʿAbbās Thaʿlab (d. 291/904), cited on the authority of one of his pupils. This account clearly shows that it was thought to be worthy of recording that this celebrated grammarian used colloquial forms *in his speech*.[104]

Ibn Sayyāba in Egypt]; al-Ibshīhī, *Mustaṭraf* 535; al-Ḥarīrī, *Durra* 579; al-Zajjājī, *Amālī* 14–5; and al-Qishṭaynī 1992: 39. Also see Weipert 2009: 70–146 and Marzolph 1992: II, 2, 8, 50, 152 for jokes on grammarians in German translation. A peculiar anecdote features an insane man answering, in the learned style of the grammarians, a 'grammatical problem' as absurd as it is obscene; see al-Tawḥīdī, *Baṣāʾir* I(ii), 15. Not incidentally, the clash of pompousness and excessive respectability with the trivial and the quotidian is a universal theme of humour; see Douglas 1968: 363.

101 E.g. al-Thaʿālibī, *Yatīma* II, 352; III, 31–2; al-Thaʿālibī, *Thimār* II, 919; al-Tawḥīdī [attr.], *Risāla* 187.

102 A fairly sure case is Abū Bakr Ibn al-Jawālīqī (fl. early 4th/10th c.), who is said to have insisted on using classical case endings in speech and kept talking about syntactical questions, a habit that made him loathsome (*baghīḍ*) to many contemporaries; see Yāqūt, *Udabāʾ* VI, 2468. To denote the ostentatious use of Classical Arabic words (and possibly grammatical forms) in situations where the dialect would have been the natural choice the verb *taqaʿʿara* was applied. This verb must have been widely known, for in al-Andalus it even gave rise to a dialectal (from the point of view of grammarians, 'incorrect') form, *taqaʿwara*. See al-Zubaydī, *Laḥn* 264. Another verb, *tashaddaqa*, was also often used as a synonym of *taqaʿʿara*; see for instance al-Ghazālī, *Iḥyāʾ* II, 149–50. Ironically, the effort of some scholars to avoid using vernacular ('incorrect') forms often led to errors of hypercorrection; see Ibn Makkī, *Tathqīf* 295–301. For an attentive overview of these Arabic terms and concepts, see Weipert 2009: 25–55.

103 al-ʿAskarī, *Ṣināʿatayn* 38.

104 Yāqūt, *Udabāʾ* II, 541. Elsewhere in this work, the same habit – doing without case endings in speech, as in the dialects – is called 'the tradition of the most distinguished savants (*sunnat jillat al-ʿulamāʾ*)'; op.cit. V, 2254.

It is perhaps not erroneous to detect in texts mocking the grammarians signs of the antipathy of the less solemn kind of Muslim intellectuals – libertines included – towards a certain type of their educated colleagues.[105] (It is worth bearing in mind that these are texts that could only be produced and appreciated by erudite intellectuals well versed in Classical Arabic grammar and vocabulary.) The clash of differing mentalities among scholars is unmistakable in the arguments put forward in quite a few perfectly serious works that explicitly deplore various supposed shortcomings of certain scholarly groups such as philologists, religious scholars, theologians, and of course grammarians. The objections include accusations of greed, hauteur, arrogance, envy, ignorance, and so forth.[106] That the ostentation of learning through anachronistic linguistic usages and by other means felt both ridiculous and obnoxious to quite a number of scholars despite – or because of? – their own unassailable erudition seems certain. And the artificiality of Classical Arabic was an all too obvious symbol of that ostentation, hence the symbolic value of 'the grammarian' as the embodiment of scholarly pretentiousness and mannerisms. Besides, grammar in itself was a dry and boring discipline for an *adīb* (a highly cultured, urbane intellectual); consider the following warning by the philologist Khalaf al-Aḥmar (d.

---

[105] I am referring to the type exemplified by the grammarian Aḥmad al-Qaysī al-Qurṭubī al-Aʿraj (d. 345/956–7), whom the *Muʿjam al-udabāʾ* portrays as a man who never relaxed his forbidding mien so that no-one dared joke in his presence ("*kāna waqūran muhīban lā yuqdimu aḥad ʿalayhi wa-lā ʿindahu bi-l-hazl*"). See Yāqūt, *Udabāʾ* II, 484. – Failure rigorously to observe the rules of Classical Arabic usage did not necessarily disqualify an intellectual as a witty and refined person; see for instance al-Anbārī, *Aḍdād* 239. Al-Jāḥiẓ, for one, opined that the humorous utterances of commoners lose their entertaining quality if they are transformed to the medium of Classical Arabic, which should not be done even in writing. See al-Jāḥiẓ, *Bukhalāʾ* 73. Even among religious scholars, there was some palpable annoyance with the pretentious and incongruous speech style of some linguists, which was called 'odious affectation' (*al-takalluf al-mamqūt*) and duly condemned, even in the form of a number of (obviously fabricated) *ḥadīths*. See al-Ghazālī, *Iḥyāʾ* II, 149–50; Ibn Makkī, *Tathqīf* 62; and cf. Ibn al-Jawzī, *Talbīs* 126. Affecting a classical style in speech might also in some instances be linked with false claims of Arab genealogy, a particularly ridiculous combination, as in the case of the secretary ʿAlī b. al-Haytham Jawanqā (fl. early 3rd/9th c.); see Yāqūt, *Udabāʾ* V, 2006.

[106] E.g. al-Ghazālī, *Iḥyāʾ* I, 83, 87, 94–5; II, 182; Ibn al-Jawzī, *Talbīs* 115, 118. Sufis too were occasionally criticised for similar reasons; see for instance Ibn Maʿṣūm, *Sulāfa* 98. Also instructive is the following passage by the literary expert Abū Bakr al-Ṣūlī (d. 335/946): "[...] they [...] claim to know everything, never uttering 'I do not know' about anything. [...] And there is the kind [of scholar] whose only goal is to peruse some [ancient] poems and memorise the rare motifs therein, or learn a couple of grammatical problems, or look into a book on linguistics, and then to attend [scholarly] gatherings, not with the aim of further edification or learning, but to [wait till] the lecturer happens to make a mistake or fails to remember something, and then to take up the word and carry the day. [Such people] believe that by virtue of their having memorised a verse or a motif that the lecturer has not, they have instantly surpassed the latter in learning, while the lecturer may well know a thousand other data or even more..." See al-Ṣūlī, *Akhbār* 9–11. The ignorance and greed of certain religious scholars is still a common subject of popular jokes in Yemen (as no doubt in other Arabic-speaking countries too); see Lambert 1997: 39.

ca. 180/796): "You cling to linguistics too much, and neglect all other things. Seldom does anyone rise to excellence that devotes himself to it exclusively, and therefore do study poetry and all manner of stories too."[107] The idea that 'serious' branches of scholarship – as opposed to jocular literature and poetry in general – are boring is a recurrent motif in *mujūn*; indeed the religious disciplines and linguistics are often explicitly portrayed as the very antithesis of gaiety, entertainment and *joie de vivre*.[108]

The language of Sufism (*taṣawwuf*) was as distinctive and recognisable as that of Arabic linguistics, and the same is true of the style of Islamic theology (*kalām*). Some examples follow that show the ease with which both discourses lent themselves to parody. A parody of the style of Islamic mysticism appears in an anecdote recorded in the Buyid era that shows a group of dervishes in Iran sitting in a circle over a bowl of sweetmeats. When one of the mystics shows too obvious rapacity by reaching over to the far side of the bowl to get the best morsels, the sheikh al-Būshanjī points out to him the unseemliness of that conduct and the fact that eating somewhat less swiftly he will still reach the best part of the meal. To this rebuke, the offending Sufi replies in the quintessential pietistic style of mystics: "Oh sheikh, my hopes do not reach far enough to allow my soul to aspire to reach there." Hearing the unctuous words, the more sanctimonious members of the group start crying, while those capable of perceiving the irony burst out laughing.[109] While this, as befits an anecdote, is a fairly short (but dense) parody of the Sufi parlance, the following story contains a more sustained caricature that is also complete nonsense:

> It was narrated by Aḥmad b. Muḥammad al-Madā'inī: While in Baghdad, I stopped in the al-Madīna central mosque beside a group of Sufis who were busy discussing ecstatic occurrences and afflations and questions resembling delusions that I could not understand (*yataḥāwarūna ʿalā l-khaṭarāt wa-l-hawājis wa-masāʾil tushbihu l-wasāwis lam afhamhā*). I fancied the idea of having some *mujūn*-like fun at their expense (*amjunu bihim*), so I said [to their master]: "Oh honourable sheikh, [I have] a question." He said: "Go ahead." Said I: "Tell me, if you were a Sheikh in your Meaning, appendant to the Essence of your Soul, and a silvery-white sabre tore to shreds the crown of your head in the Way of Knowledge while you were under [the power of] Volition – would then your Attributes be

[107] al-ʿAskarī, *Maṣūn* 122. What I translated as 'all manner of stories' can be anecdotes, historical accounts, *ḥadīths* and other relatively short pieces of edifying or entertaining information as well, all these senses being covered by the Arabic term *akhbār*.

[108] E.g. al-Thaʿālibī, *Tatimma* I, 51–2; al-Bākharzī, *Dumya* II, 787 ["*Mā anā wa-l-nusku wa-l-taqarrī wa-inna Zaydan wa-inna ʿAmrā*" etc.]; al-Ḥillī, *ʿĀṭil* 32 and 201 ["*Lawlā l-sharāb wāsh kān baqī, narjaʿ faqī*"; "*Ṭalab al-ʿulūm ʿandī shaqā*"], 203 ["*Anā barī min shughli fīh ʿadhāb*" etc.]; Ibn Maʿṣūm, *Sulāfa* 299 ["*Ayyuhā l-qawmu lladhī fī l-madrasa*" etc.].

[109] al-Tawḥīdī, *Baṣāʾir* II(iii), 114–5.

harmed despite your holding on to the rope of Capacity, oh Hero (*akhbirnī idhā kunta shaykhan fī maʿnāka ḥalsan fī dhāt nafsika fa-aṣāba yāfūkhaka taqṭīʿ bi-ʿaḍb khazarī ʿalā sabīl al-ʿilm wa-kunta taḥta l-irāda hal yaḍurru awsāfaka shayʾ maʿa taʿalluqika bi-ḥabl al-qudra yā baṭṭāl*)?" Those around him took this for a [bona fide] question, and began to discuss the correct answer. The sheikh, however, was instantly aware of the situation; and being afraid that he would turn [his disciples] loose on me, I decamped.[110]

As for scholastic theology (*kalām*), its highly artificial technical terms – often borrowed from translations of Greek philosophy – and its abstract concepts made it a prime target of frivolous mockery. The great prose writer al-Jāḥiẓ (d. 255/869), whose penchant for irony is more than evident in a lot of his writings, makes the point that nonsense cast in the style of *kalām* cannot fail to entertain: "There are two things that I find extremely witty amusement (*wa-anā astaẓrifu amrayn istiẓrāfan shadīdan*): listening to the stories of the Bedouins, and to a debate on theological questions between two men who know nothing about such things. This is so uniquely funny that it will make even a bereaved mother and an infuriated man laugh."[111] Note the abundance of turgid abstract nouns in the following anecdote:

Abū Ḥātim al-Sijistānī says that there was a man, a scholastic theology enthusiast, who frequented Ḥusayn al-Najjār's company. He was a bore with a pompous style (*kāna thaqīlan mutashādiqan*), so that [Ḥusayn] would not know what to say to him for a while, until he realised that he would prepare a reply in the same vein as the question had been, thus stopping and silencing him. So one day, when [that man] asked him, "What do you say – may God bring you happiness – on the terminal point of the annihilation of delusions at the prime of closeness to the reaching of the final goals (*fī ḥadd talāshī l-tawahhumāt fī ʿunfuwān al-qurb min dark al-maṭālib*)?", Ḥusayn replied: "This is part of [the issue of] the existence of the closeness of conditionality in the manner of aspectuality, by which mutual negation and affinity take place with neither encounter nor separation (*hādhā min wujūd qurb al-kayfūfiyya ʿalā ṭarīq al-ḥaythūthiyya wa-bi-mithlihi yaqaʿ al-tanāfī wa-l-mujānasa ʿalā ghayr talāqin wa-lā ʾftirāq*).' Then the man said: "This will require some consideration and deduction." And he replied: "Just think it over, for we have found rest at last."[112]

[110] al-Tanūkhī, *Nishwār* I, 99. The adjective *khazarī* might mean 'Khazarian', while *baṭṭāl* seems to be deliberately ambiguous: in Classical Arabic it would rather have the meaning 'idle', but the disciples apparently took no offence at the term being addressed to their master, which suggests that they understood it in its more vernacular sense of 'hero', 'courageous man'. – On Daniel Beaumont's quite convincing suggestion that various passages of al-Jāḥiẓ's *Kitāb al-bukhalāʾ* be best read as parodies of various types of educated discourse (those of Sufis, *ḥadīth* scholars, philosophers, etc.), see Hoyland 2006: 35–6.

[111] al-Jāḥiẓ, *Ḥayawān* I, 365.

[112] al-Tawḥīdī, *Baṣāʾir* I(ii), 183–4.

4

The Reception of *Mujūn*

Having attempted, first to determine the patterns of behaviour that tended to be perceived by mediaeval Arabic speakers as *mujūn*, and then to paint a tableau of the numerous motifs and themes that, taken together, constituted the literary version of libertinism, it is now possible to turn our attention to the social environment in which *mujūn* flourished (or as the case might be, languished). In fact, it is at this point that our research into the implications of *mujūn* for the understanding of mediaeval Muslim society begins in earnest, the previous two chapters having simply served to illustrate in a cumulative way the complex concept of *mujūn*.

The overview of *mujūn* offered in the previous chapters, coupled with the sheer amount of literary material of a libertine bent, may suggest total and unlimited tolerance, indeed indulgence, when it came to *mujūn*. After all, the bare fact that such an astonishing number of *mujūn* works – poetry as well as prose – have been recorded in writing in the first place and then handed down to subsequent generations, and ultimately to us, is very revealing as to the acceptance of this literature (and, by necessity, the attitudes underlying it). No less astonishing is the existence of many texts that strike even the jaded 21th-century reader as outrageous and were nevertheless deemed fit to be included in entirely 'respectable' literary anthologies that enjoyed great prestige among mediaeval Arabic intellectuals. That such texts were thought to be worthy of recording and preserving is a remarkable fact in itself, and definitely seems to be an indication of a permissive atmosphere in the society at large. It is, however, just one side of the coin, and one would do well to pause before rushing to the conclusion that everyone really was at liberty to indulge in *mujūn* to his heart's content. While the abundance of *mujūn* material may well leave such an impression, it is a quite erroneous one which we seek to nuance, and thereby correct, in this chapter.

Given that *mujūn* is routinely understood (at least implicitly) as the manifestation of a sort of deviance by modern scholars both Western and Muslim, it is quite imperative to analyse societal reactions to the phenomenon, this being the only way to determine whether, and precisely in what sense – and, to be sure, by whom –

mujūn was perceived as deviant. It has been proposed that in researching deviance in any form, the reactions of people to what they perceive as deviant must be regarded an extremely important aspect of the study, since those reactions tend not only to illustrate but also virtually define the society's dominant notions about what is acceptable and what is not.[1]

Although, as will be obvious from the remainder of this study, I do not find the label 'deviance' adequate for characterising the phenomenon of *mujūn* in mediaeval Middle Eastern society, and indeed regard it as positively misleading, an analysis of the responses of society to libertinism is for various reasons still indispensable to the understanding of the phenomenon. One such reason is that the study of a normatively ambiguous phenomenon speaks volumes about the general norms and values of a society, as well as about the internal disagreements within the society and the resulting tensions. If studied over an extended period of time, observing societal reactions to such challenging phenomena can also yield some insights into gradual shifts in the culture. In short, where norms are broken there is a prime opportunity better to observe those norms: the reactions that breaches of norms provoke (or fail to provoke) highlight the nature of the norms themselves and the underlying values as few other situations do. However, there are other lessons that can also be learned from a closer look at the reception of *mujūn* in the various social subgroups. A better understanding of the methods of control over literary and other forms of expression is one potentially momentous result of this line of inquiry, especially in view of the fact that such control can be exerted in myriad unofficial, informal and *ad hoc* ways as well as through brutal, overt repression. The constraints and limits to which the expression of one's opinions and predilections is subject in every human society are highly peculiar to each culture (and often vary from one historical period to the next); also they are not necessarily predictable and mechanical in all cases, leaving a lot of room for negotiation and differing interpretations. What a 'chartered libertine' is allowed to say and write is often not the same as what the next man may; too many factors can influence the limits of expression to allow for a clear-cut picture. Studying those factors is an important concern of this chapter. The various possible ways of sanctioning unacceptable manifestations of *mujūn* (either as behaviour or as literature) will also be discussed. However, as we will observe, *mujūn* occasioned as much kudos and material rewards as reproach and sanctions, and this aspect of the phenomenon is equally important and revealing. Scandalous behaviour and literary products – whether affected or genuine – can actually be a very profitable enterprise, as many modern artists are in a position to verify. Now *mujūn* certainly seems to have been a lucrative literary pursuit at least for the top names in the business. Sporadic though

[1] For more on this issue, cf. Denzin 1970: 120.

the data may be, but some textual evidence does suggest that a reputation for mastery of *mujūn* could earn a person more than notoriety, and the pecuniary aspects of libertine careers have an obvious relevance to a realistic assessment of the *mujūn* phenomenon.

The expression 'societal reactions' is of course quite unhelpfully vague, and it glosses over the evident fact that every society is composed of many different constituent subgroups, the values and norms of which tend to show considerable differences on most issues. The absence of uniform views and attitudes shared by all members of a society naturally necessitates a more nuanced analysis that takes into consideration the potentially huge differences between the attitudes and norms of any two subgroups of a society. While this is a fairly obvious desideratum, the problems do not end here. A requisite initial step is to identify those subgroups within the larger community that can be assumed to have had more or less uniform cultural norms – a gigantic undertaking in itself well beyond the scope of this study. At the very least however, one can attempt a division of the society into constituent parts which, while not precluding internal disagreements among members over any number of norms, can still meaningfully be seen and handled as units of a sort and which further seem to have been perceived as discrete social units by their members too. Certainly no such division will be ideal or unassailable. However, the one that will be adopted here has the practical merit of making the formidable task of analyzing a wide array of attitudes and norms more feasible, and the theoretical merit of not being totally alien to the mediaeval Muslim conception of the composition of society.

For even a roughly workable division, some crucial factors must be taken into account. The minimal criteria for a viable demarcation of the subgroups of society must include, first and foremost, literacy and learning as well as political power or the lack thereof. Further factors to be reckoned with are the nature of a group's erudition (whether leaning to the religious or to the secular, although no strict separation existed), their relationship to the court, their status and prestige in religious and political terms, as well as their wealth. Occupation, ethnic origins, and language must also be important considerations; and of obvious significance is the issue of urban or rural residence.

This latter factor can be disposed of rather quickly here. For a virtually complete lack of data, there is no way to study reactions to *mujūn* among rural folk. Even if peasants and other village folk were aware of the existence of *mujūn* beyond vague stereotypes of urban profligacy and extravagance, which we have no reason to suppose they were, there would be no way of knowing and much less proving it. This problem, for this reason, must needs be off our compass, but in fact the likelihood that *mujūn* (at least as literature) was much of a concern to simple and illiterate villagers in any way is infinitesimal. Bedouins are spoken of more often in the sources than the sedentary agriculturalists, but reliable data about their views on such a specific issue as *mujūn* are again practically nonexistent. All that one can safely say is that the stereotypical image of Bedouins has always tended to be one of honour-bound people, and clearly *mujūn* would not have sat very well with such a deeply conservative tribal code. Even if there is no hard evidence – no evidence at all really – that *mujūn* was an essentially urban phenomenon, it is perhaps not wildly adventurous to assume that it must have been.

On the other hand, the regional differences in attitudes to *mujūn* are a factor to consider. As will be argued in this chapter, there were perceptible variations to which a given community allowed any display of libertinism, and the popularity of *mujūn* seems to have varied from place to place. Here again, data is not always forthcoming – to put it mildly – but the tantalisingly sporadic evidence does point to existing regional differences, as well as an awareness (indeed, stereotyping) of such differences. Of particular importance are the differing attitudes of the Muslim West and East respectively, which will be the subject of a brief discussion.

Turning back to the problem of dividing the society into meaningful, workable subgroups suitable to serve as units of analysis, one that is readily available – and native to the culture – but extremely vague and crude is the distinction between the *ʿāmma* and the *khāṣṣa*, 'the commoners' and 'the élite' respectively. These important terms of mediaeval Muslim thought have already been touched upon in the first chapter of this book, and I will not repeat those observations here. Other native terms that may prove helpful for the contemporary researcher include *ʿulamāʾ* (roughly equivalent to 'religious scholars', 'those learned in the religious disciplines') and *kuttāb* ('secretaries'), a term corresponding to all sorts of literate state officials, generally with a somewhat more secular kind of learning and of varying influence and wealth. However, mapping mediaeval Muslim society in fully native terms seems to be neither possible nor quite desirable. Thus, while a tripartite division into the political élite, the religious élite and a massive, undifferentiated category of 'commoners' would represent a scheme not unrelated to native notions, it would still be too crude for our purposes because it would overlook very important internal differences in the social status, political influence and wealth of the members of each subgroup.[2] Instead another tripartite division will be adopted here. It consists of, firstly, the rulers, their courtiers and other associates: the courtly milieu that incorporated the highest echelon of the *kuttāb*

[2] These considerations owe a lot to the generous advice that I received from Patricia Crone, as does the scheme that I have come to adopt. However, certainly none of the possible errors that my assertions will be found to contain can be traced to that advice, which focused on clarifying a number of indisputable guidelines for the analysis.

as well as some outstanding *ʿulamāʾ*, in addition to the rulers, their families, and their entourage. Secondly, we will treat as a separate group the 'petty' intellectuals, those living outside the orbit of the court. This category, which basically represents the less influential section (at least politically) of the literate class, comprises such elements as the bulk of the ordinary *ʿulamāʾ*, the petty *kuttāb*, the scribes (*warrāqūn*) and other literate 'day-labourers'. Surely quite a number of the poets and writers producing *mujūn* belonged to this category; but perhaps as many were part of the previous group, the courtly milieu. (Also, upward mobility in this sense was quite a possibility for talented individuals among the small intelligentsia, and especially for successful poets.) The third great category to be distinguished will be the illiterate masses, which might actually include quite affluent elements like some uneducated merchants, and which does largely correspond to a widespread understanding of the term *ʿāmma*. As must be evident, the two main criteria for this scheme are literacy and connections to the ruler's court, while consideration of material possessions and the exact nature of a person's educational background is given only secondary importance, ethnic origins even less. However, in surveying the courtiers' group, internal distinctions will be recognised and taken account of, and the same can be said of the second category.

In his book on sexuality in Islamicate societies, Abdelwahab Bouhdiba makes the sweeping statement that "[e]ach social category had its *mujūn*", adding that the phenomenon spread beyond the courts and the moneyed classes. In a similar spirit, Julie Scott Meisami asserts that the "popularity of *mujūn* poetry [...] permeated all classes".[3] That may well be the case, but the claim is far from self-evident and needs careful and detailed substantiation before it can be accepted.

1. The Reception of *Mujūn*

1.1 The Attitudes of the ʿĀmma

Evidence – more often than not anecdotal evidence – for the reception of *mujūn* is more readily available for some groups than for others, not surprisingly given the scholarly and élitist bias of much of mediaeval Arabic writing. In particular it will be far easier to study the attitudes of religious scholars and courtiers than those of the urban masses. The lamentable lack of hard data means that there are few conclusions one can draw beyond impressionistic observations and tentative speculations. However, in a way this also reflects the scant regard the purveyors of *mujūn* themselves – in common with most of the literate élite – had for the *ʿāmma*.

[3] Bouhdiba 2004: 130, 131; Meisami 1993: 16.

In fact the judgements of the ordinary, illiterate masses had relatively little impact on the livelihood and status of a libertine intellectual, at least in comparison with the views of the élite: the commoners must simply have had very limited possibilities to vent their dissatisfaction, or else express their applause, as the case might be. It is hard to imagine how a common man could have given voice to their disapproval of *mujūn* beyond trying to complain, indirectly rather than directly, to the powers that be or actually forming a mob to lynch the audacious wretch; and it is equally inconceivable that they would have been able to show their appreciation, if that is what they felt, by giving significant material rewards to the poet or writer. With their livelihood being largely independent of the common people's responsiveness, the libertines had no pressing reason to be preoccupied with this issue. Moreover, the culturally pervasive low esteem for the *ʿāmma* would actively discourage a more serious consideration of the tastes of the *plebs*, let alone catering to those tastes. The *ʿāmma* were clearly no part of the group of moral entrepreneurs – the elements of the population most instrumental in setting the standards of decency and propriety – in mediaeval Muslim society.

Another very significant factor is the undeniable fact that quite much of *mujūn* poetry and prose must simply have been beyond the comprehension of illiterate commoners, partly because of its language being classical written Arabic, and partly because of the presumable lack of the necessary erudition to grasp the point of a lot of *mujūn* humour. For example, if you do not recognise a phrase for the Quranic quotation it is, there is precious little reason to feel offended by it and regard its use as improper. Admittedly this observation is valid only for a certain type of *mujūn*, and the more accessible sorts like scurrility, obscenity or scatology would pose little obstacle for popular comprehension. Nonetheless, the limited knowledge possessed by a typical urban commoner would certainly prevent a real understanding of many a *mujūn* motif, hence also lessen the danger of a public outcry over frivolity and libertinism. A passage in an important source from the Buyid era suggests an awareness among witty littérateurs of the need to address different audiences according to their respective levels of erudition. It tells of a young man with a jocular temperament who invented deliberately convoluted and nonsensical arguments about why date-wine (*nabīdh*) should be regarded as permitted – a subject of heated controversy among the Islamic legal schools. One argument, which obviously mocks the theological style, was the assertion that God had not created anything without a purpose; and given that the existence of the violet cannot have any other purpose than for people to inhale its sweet smell while drinking date-wine (flowers being a customary accompaniment to drinking at the time), therefore date-wine must be licit to drink. What is relevant to our discussion here is the comment that follows this account: "He would present these words as a serious argument to those whom he considered to be weak [in intellect] and as jesting to knowledgeable men" (*wa-kāna yukhriju hādhā l-qawl mukhraj al-jidd li-man yastaḍʿifuhu wa-mukhraj al-hazl maʿa ahl al-ʿilm*).[4]

Even if some *mujūn* was in all probability incomprehensible to uneducated people either owing to its language or its relatively intricate cultural references, a lot of *mujūn* was not. As I have noted above scatological humour and vulgarity, for instance, need no erudition on the part of the recipient. Some of the jesting with religious motifs was also accessible to the *ʿāmma* – indeed transmitted (or even produced) by members of the common populace. One can state this with a fair degree of certainty because evidence is forthcoming from the most unlikely quarters: the most pious type of Islamic religious literature. In treatises dedicated to the condemnation of reprehensible innovations (sing. *bidʿa*), as well as in some collections of *fatwā*s (legal opinions or decisions of leading religious scholars) and other *fiqh* manuals, there is an abundance of denunciations of the wicked speech habits and deplorable locutions of the common folk, and such complaints tend to come replete with specific examples. (Ironically much of those 'deplorable' expressions would not have come down to us were it not for the preservation thereof in these tomes.) Most of the phrases cited by such sources are clear examples of *mujūn*.[5] They offer a rare and fortunate insight into the urban popular humour of the mediaeval Middle East, and buttress the supposition that frivolity was by no means an exclusive feature of high-status and learned circles. The pious sources do not really address the question of the ubiquity or otherwise of such expressions in the speech of the *ʿāmma*, but the number of examples adduced does suggest that it was not an uncommon or sporadic phenomenon. The corpus of objectionable utterances among the common folk shows a remarkable variety of types and motifs. Some passages are jokes not unlike the kind encountered in collections of *mujūn* anecdotes. There are for instance jokes about *ḥadīths* and about the prophet Muḥammad. Some jokes feature well-known heretics making breathtakingly indecent or blasphemous remarks.[6] A great many examples are simple phrases. Among these, one finds several frivolous and irreverent oath formulae; for instance the assertion that the speaker will not do something, or insists on doing something, even if the archangel Gabriel or the prophet Muḥammad himself appeared in person to ask him to change his mind. Some examples are ironic remarks on certain Quranic passages – and here it is worth restating that some bits of the Quran were very widely known

[4] al-Tanūkhī, *Nishwār* III, 141–2.

[5] Of course, *mujūn* of the spoken variety, but that is only to be expected, and is at any rate irrelevant here. The religious scholars' assessments of the phenomenon and their general attitude to *mujūn* will not be discussed here but in a separate section later in this chapter.

[6] The choice of protagonists for jokes is an important question which will be addressed later in this chapter.

and quoted, even if the whole text was not – whilst other phrases are similar to the purposeful misapplications of Quranic quotations discussed at great length as part of the survey of the motifs of literary *mujūn*. And finally, a considerable part of this corpus of popular *mujūn* utterances culled from religious works is composed of what can be described as disrespectful replies to 'commanding right and forbidding wrong' (*al-amr bi-l-maʿrūf wa-l-nahy ʿan al-munkar*, essentially pious reprimands delivered to perceived wrongdoers).[7]

This finding is also supported by another kind of related – and again not quite explicit – data. A highly indirect hint of the popularity of *mujūn* amongst the illiterate class, which I do not wish to push too far, is the fact that some texts that seem to mimic to some extent the uneducated speech style of the urban masses do contain a lot of material resembling *mujūn*.[8] An urban proverb from the Abbasid period, which must reflect existent (but not necessarily dominant) attitudes among the commoners, is a clear testimony to the popularity of jokes and funny anecdotes: "Tell anecdotes, even about your own mother (*qul al-nādira wa-law ʿalā l-wālida*)".[9]

There are sporadic references which are more or less outspoken regarding the fame and popularity of some libertine poets, notably Abū Nuwās, among the *ʿāmma*.[10]

---

[7] For a wide array of such material, see for instance Ibn Baydakīn, *Lumaʿ* I, 181–5. A particularly blasphemous phrase, mentioned by Ibn Baydakīn al-Turkumānī (8th–9th/14th–15th c.), looks rather innocuous on the surface: "[That's all right, but] Sheikh ʿAdī is quite another thing." The necessary background information, however, puts it in another perspective: A heretic sect especially popular among the Kurds treated the 6th/12th-century Sufi sheikh ʿAdī al-Hakkārī virtually as a god – the greatest anathema to Islamic monotheism – and while recognising the prophethood of Muḥammad, they were wont to add that Sheikh ʿAdī was a quite different (i.e. superior) category. This clear blasphemy was used by many Muslims in an ironic way, roughly (as it appears) in the sense of 'a different kettle of fish'.

[8] See for instance al-Tawḥīdī [attr.], *Risāla* 322 ["*ēsh taʿmal bi-dārī ... dār taʾassasat ʿalā ghayr al-taqwā bi-ḥamd Allāh...*" etc.].

[9] al-Maydānī, *Amthāl* II, 155.

[10] E.g. Ibn al-Muʿtazz, *Ṭabaqāt* 91 ["*wa-aḥabbahu l-khāṣṣa wa-l-ʿāmma*"]; Abū Hiffān, *Akhbār* 51 ["*wa-man lā yaʿrifuhu? innī la-aḥsabu ḥimārī hādhā yaʿrifuhu, wa-hal yakhfā l-qamar?*"]. By the time of Ibn al-Muʿtazz (247/861–296/908), the common people already routinely attributed any poem with characteristically *mujūn*-like contents to Abū Nuwās, a measure of his fame (or notoriety), if not necessarily of his popularity. However, Muhalhil al-ʿAbdī, better known as Ibn al-Muzarraʿ (fl. early 4th/10th c.), adds that many in the lower classes were enthusiasts for Abū Nuwās. See Ibn al-Muʿtazz, *Ṭabaqāt* 34; Ibn al-Muzarraʿ, *Sariqāt* 31–2. Although the sources do seem to support the idea of Abū Nuwās having been a widely recognised and much-loved poet even among the commoners, as does his later career as a quasi-legendary personality in Arabic and Muslim folklore, James E. Montgomery still cautions (and I believe rightly) that we cannot simply conclude that the greater part of the poetic *oeuvre* of Abū Nuwās was actually widely known among the people. On this question, see Montgomery 1996: 116–7 and 118 (note 13). On the figure of Abū Nuwās in the folklore of the Arabs of the Middle East as well as the Swahili of East Africa, see Ingrams 1933: 19–47, 48–85; Knappert 1970: 128 (note 1); Knappert 1978: 6, 112–22, 209–10. (Interestingly, another great Arabic poet, al-Mutanabbī, also appears in the role of a quick-witted trickster in Swahili folklore, although far less frequently than

An ironic verse attributed to Abū Nuwās, supposedly delivered by him as a repartee to the pious exhortations of a fellow-poet, seems implicitly to suggest an awareness of his own popularity among the populace: "Can you imagine me marring my glory among the people through piety (*A-turānī mufsidan bi-l-nuski ʿinda l-qawmi jāhī*)?"[11] Certainly, Abū Nuwās is such a giant of Arabic literature – and was already perceived to be so in his own lifetime (he died around 198–200/813–5) – that he is hardly representative of the libertine intellectuals in general. However, assertions about his massive popularity do suggest the absence of a dominant atmosphere of intolerance for *mujūn*, an impression somewhat reinforced by the fact that particular *mujūn* works by other poets are also occasionally described in the sources as having been as popular among the commoners as among the higher classes. Some of the *mujūn* works of various poets that happened to have a fairly accessible form and content are reported to have been picked up by the commoners as well and transmitted among them as poems or songs.[12]

Whilst tolerant – and possibly even indulgent – attitudes are certainly part of the tableau of the commoners' approach to *mujūn*, by all appearances they are not the whole picture. To begin with, urban mobs were notoriously excitable in certain historical circumstances, and with some prodding, their wrath could easily turn against anyone suspected or accused of heretical tendencies in the broadest sense. The common people having been unqualified to weigh sophisticated arguments for and against pious indictments of persons deemed blasphemous or irreligious in any sense, it is reasonable to suppose that given the right amount of incitement, mere libertines could easily become the target of the mob's mayhem. The Ḥanbalite-led, aggressive and destructive outbursts of popular anger against the Shiʿites, as well as against individuals disliked for any reason by the Ḥanbalite preachers are a powerful indication of the limits of popular religious and cultural tolerance. While the main objects of the violence of the Ḥanbalites and the impoverished masses of the Sunni quarters tended to be the Shiʿites, just about anyone identified as not sufficiently pious by the fanatics could become targets.[13] Here the infinitely disgraceful incident of al-Ṭabarī's (d. 310/923) funeral comes to mind. This outstanding scholar, one of the greatest historians and exegetes of the mediaeval

Abū Nuwās; see Knappert 1978: 125–7.) More will be said about the reception of the works of Abū Nuwās towards the end of this chapter.

[11] al-Iṣfahānī, *Aghānī* IV, 106; Abū Nuwās, *Dīwān* V, 235.

[12] E.g. al-Iṣfahānī, *Aghānī* II, 405 ["*ḥattā in kāna l-mukārī* ..." etc.]; III, 142 ["*ʿahdī bi-l-Baṣra wa-laysa fīhā ghazil*..." etc.]; XIII, 309 ["*fa-lam tabqa bi-l-Kūfa saqqāʾ wa-lā ṭaḥḥān*..." etc.].

[13] On the influence of the Ḥanbalites in Baghdad, see Mottahedeh 1980: 25; Cahen 1958–9: II, 48–9. For a description of the riots and rampages of the plebeians of Baghdad, see for instance al-Iṣbahānī, *Kharīda* II(i), 325–6. Also cf. Yāqūt, *Udabāʾ* V, 2325 on the case of the Quran expert Ibn Shannabūdh (esp. on the contribution of the *ʿāmma* to his tribulations).

Islamic world, was branded a heretic and sacrilegious man by some Ḥanbalite foes, who roused the mobs violently to obstruct the burial of al-Ṭabarī so that the scholar's body could only be laid to rest stealthily at night, and within the protection of the walls of his own house.[14] In general, the urban masses appear to have often been quite susceptible to the manipulations of all manner of street preachers, miracle-mongers and demagogues.[15] Although a systematic study of the history of such agitations falls outside the purview of this book, it must be noted that the anger of the masses is of course easier to incite and manipulate in times of economic hardship and widespread poverty, and despite the cultural efflorescence of the Buyid period, it was an era characterised by economic stagnation if not decay, increasing corruption, a disappearing sense of solidarity and social responsibility, along with alarming levels of urban poverty.[16] The highly specific historical and economic circumstances of the Buyid era do not allow extrapolating from the levels of popular intolerance, sectarian strife and mob activity observed in this period.[17] One conclusion that can be drawn, however, is that *given the right set of circumstances*, the lower classes could display quite as ruthless intolerance towards perceived 'wrongdoers' and 'heretics' as any learned zealot or fanatical ruler.

In fact the ruler and the political élite could occasionally be far more indifferent or accommodating to libertine behaviour or 'heretical' views – that is to say non-normative opinions or conduct – than were certain elements within the lower classes.[18] One of the most repulsive historical characters of the Buyid period, a certain Ḥanbalite zealot called al-Barbahārī (d. 329/941) was intrumental in inciting several rounds of bloody anti-Shiʿite disturbances in Baghdad, veritable pogroms by the urban mobs of the capital. He also succeeded in turning the popular custom of employing professional female mourners into a virtually lethal risk, by encouraging his fanatical followers to lynch the perpetrators of such a godless iniquity. Tellingly, it was not the common folk but the caliph al-Rāḍī (r. 322/934–329/940) and his courtiers who finally felt disgusted with the activity of this Savonarola-like preacher, and decided to ban his incendiary sermonising.[19]

---

[14] Miskawayh, *Tajārib* I, 84.

[15] See for instance al-Tanūkhī, *Nishwār* II, 126–8.

[16] Kraemer 1986: 51–2.

[17] It may serve as a cautionary note, for instance, that in Damascus under the Mamlūk régime (7th/13th to early 10th/16th c.), the intermittent purificatory zeal of the authorities seem to have often failed to meet with the approval of the common populace; see Pouzet 1991: 370.

[18] For example, in 284/897 an enraged mob marched to a prison in Baghdad to demand that the caliph al-Muʿtaḍid (r. 279/892–289/902) and his vizier take measures against godless conduct and execute a servant who was said to have uttered disrespectful words about the prophet Muḥammad. See al-Alūsī 1987: 186. Also cf. the case of the Muʿtazilites with the governor of Baṣra in al-Tanūkhi, *Nishwār* II, 208.

[19] al-Tanūkhī, *Nishwār* II, 233; Miskawayh, *Tajārib* I, 322–3; and also Cook 2000: 116–8; and Kraemer 1986: 60–3.

Even sans political incitement, 'impious' intellectuals, especially if not of a very agreeable personality, could be ostracised by many, or all, neighbours and acquaintances. Ostracism is a very extreme reaction, but milder forms of pressure could also be applied. Notably, there are occasional references in the sources to libertines being lectured and reproached by family members or friends with the intention to convince them to abandon their sinful lifestyle; the idea that such admonishments alone would lead anyone to reform his ways does not appear overly realistic.[20]

Good-natured warnings and reprimands by friends or kin were just one possible expression of popular disapproval. That the activity of some *mājin* poets might arouse the disapproval of their neighbours is evident, for instance from the case of the irascible Bashshār b. Burd (d. 167–8/784–5).[21] A similar conclusion may be drawn from a passage in the *Ṭabaqāt al-shuʿarāʾ* which tells of the daily vexations at the hands of the common people of al-Kūfa of three famous littérateurs of the early Abbasid period, saying that "all of them had a reputation for being ungodly heretics, and whenever people saw any of them, they would shout 'kill the heretic!' (*wa-kānū jamīʿan yurmawna bi-l-zandaqa wa-idhā raʾā l-nās wāḥidan minhum qālū zindīq uqtulūhu*)".[22] Of course the text only says 'the people' (*al-nās*) without specifying status or class, but it is hardly conceivable that this vivid scene of the bullying of 'deviant' intellectuals could refer to any type of agents other than a sort of uneducated urban canaille. An important poet of the early Abbasid period, Ibn Munādhir (d. 198/813), was ostracised and almost literally chased away from Baṣra by members of his own lineage, having drawn the ire of the local community by his increasingly libertine lifestyle and his ever more vicious, vulgar tongue:

> Ibn Munādhir used to be the imam of the mosque in [the quarter of] his lineage. [However,] once he had begun overtly to live the life of a dissolute libertine (*aẓhara mā aẓharahu min al-khalāʿa wa-l-mujūn*), they grew fed up with his leading them during times of prayer and their following his lead obediently. So

---

[20] For instance, the relatives of the infamous libertine poet Muṭīʿ b. Iyās (d. 169/785) made attempts to persuade him to terminate his affair with a singing-girl and refrain from immortalising it in poems. They employed a friend of the poet as intermediary, presumably because of deeming it unlikely that the poet would listen to *their* advice. See al-Iṣfahānī, *Aghānī* XIII, 312. Abū Nuwās was apparently often on the receiving end of (futile) admonishments from both friends and kin over his notorious drinking and homosexual affairs. See Abū Hiffān, *Akhbār* 50–7. It is worth noting that reproaches by family members might often be motivated by considerations having nothing to do with honestly felt outrage over sinfulness: the scandalous reputation of an individual would certainly reflect negatively on his whole kinship group and possibly besmirch their honour too. On this important point (with supporting evidence from a much later period, 12th/18th-century Aleppo), see Marcus 1986: 177.

[21] See the passage recounting the comment of a neighbour of Bashshār at hearing the joking of the latter with various religious motifs and concepts, in al-Iṣfahānī, *Aghānī* III, 153–4.

[22] Ibn al-Muʿtazz, *Ṭabaqāt* 24.

> they composed a poem outlining this and exposing his shame, and they left the piece of paper [containing the verses] in the prayer-niche (*miḥrāb*) of the mosque. After the prayer, [Ibn Munādhir] read the paper, then he turned it and wrote on its back [the following verse]: "I have learned of some verses written by those whose honour I will destroy. / Whoever has transmitted these verses: let him fuck the mother of the poet, and let the poet fuck that of the scribe!" That done, he threw the piece of paper before them and thereby ceased to be their imam.[23]

Sensing the general resentment surrounding him, the poet – probably wisely – chose to flee his hometown and settle as far away as Arabia.[24] In his case as in that of Bashshār b. Burd cited above, invective poetry trampling on the honour of various members of the community – rather than *mujūn* – seems to have been the main factor in turning public opinion against the libertine poets. It is a very important distinction in our discussion of the phenomenon of *mujūn* and reactions to it, and it will be emphasised and elaborated upon later in this chapter.

1.2 The Courtly Milieu

A thorny problem that deeply affects any discussion of the higher classes' attitudes to non-normative cultural practices and products is the potential divergence of theory and practice. It is quite conceivable that a large number of authors should say one thing in their writings and do another in their actual life; and therein lies the problem of drawing any confident conclusions from the corpus of data at our disposal. Given that the lower classes did not produce durable (i.e. written) records of their experiences, this problem is far less acute in discussing the attitudes of the common people to *mujūn* (but the absence of this difficulty is more than made up for by the lamentable scarcity of data). With the courtly people and the literate people outside the courts, however, the dilemma of the idealised portrayal of the state of affairs comes to the fore. Whenever an author indicates his disapproval of some manifestation of *mujūn*, or describes some respectable person disapproving of it, the suspicion of lip service being paid to dominant norms is inevitable and must be addressed. (Often indeed, the only honest way for the researcher to deal with this is to leave the question unresolved.) Although it may intuitively seem to be less likely, the opposite distortion cannot be ruled out *a priori* either: someone might well produce *mujūn* out of deference to a literary or cultural fashion or a desire for fat earnings, yet

---

[23] al-Iṣfahānī, *Aghānī* XVIII, 177.

[24] Ibn Munādhir had been having a love affair with the son of a local religious dignitary. It was more or less public knowledge locally, and indeed he made references to it in a lot of poems, but did so in a relatively chaste – romantic rather than erotic – style. However, the sudden death of the young man clearly dealt a blow to his sense of dignity and propriety too, as he started to churn out one lampoon after another about the inhabitants of his quarter. It was this change that proved to be his undoing. See al-Iṣfahānī, *Aghānī* XVIII, 174.

condemning it in his heart of hearts and never for a moment departing from an exemplary, respectable Muslim lifestyle. Unlikely as this tendency may sound, serious thought has to be given to this possibility as well, as will be argued in the next chapter. The problem of prescriptive writings obscuring the actual attitudes of a group as manifested in its day-to-day interactions is particularly overwhelming in the case of the *ʿulamāʾ* class, in which individual behaviour and degree of leniency appear to have varied widely, while their writings do not by far betray the same degree of diversity (despite a multitude of controversies regarding types of reprehensible conduct). Considering the influence of the theoretical viewpoints and prescriptions of the religious scholars, it is imperative to lend as much attention to their theories (handed down to us in the form of manuals of religious law, *fatwā* collections, manuals for judges or market inspectors, etc.) as to their practice (as recorded in chronicles, biographies, anecdotes, etc.). A comparison of the two sets of data must offer interesting insights into patterns of conformity and non-conformity to, and enforcement of, dominant norms.

Unlike success or failure with the masses, the appreciation or condemnation of a poet's work on the part of the ruler along with the courtly people could make the difference between a decent standard of living and poverty. With the opinions of the courtiers being a question of primary monetary importance for aspiring poets and writers, and with the political leaders having the means to punish perceived deviance from norms, the purveyors of *mujūn* certainly had to be alert to the reception of their works in courtly circles. This is in no way contradicted by the fact that some poets did earn their living from sources other than the munificence of the rulers, governors and powerful courtiers: in the main, a poet needed a high-ranking and affluent patron to support and perhaps protect him.[25] Even for littérateurs whose primary audience was outside the court, it was probably advisable to be aware of the attitudes and policies of the authorities, as attested by the episode of the persecution of many intellectuals branded 'heretics' in the early Abbasid period (which will be discussed below). These observations are meant to suggest that a general antipathy to *mujūn* among the rulers and their entourage simply cannot be envisaged, as this would have effectively put an end to this literary vogue in no time at all.

[25] A notable exception is an Iraqi poet of the Buyid era called Ibn Tammār al-Wāsiṭī, who "composed [his poetry] to provide entertainment, not to make a living (*wa-innamā kāna yaqūluhu taṭarruban lā takassuban*)". See al-Thaʿālibī, *Yatīma* II, 370. On the question of the livelihood of poets, also see Kilpatrick 1997: 117. It is noteworthy that some works of *mujūn* were obviously commissioned by high-ranking members of the court élite. Even as late as the early 9th/15th century – and in the relatively conservative atmosphere of North Africa – a *mujūn*-type treatise on sexuality like the Perfumed Garden was written on the order of, and financed by, the Tunisian vizier Muḥammad ʿAwāna al-Zawāwī, whose attention had been caught by a previous work of the same author on sexuality, titled *Tanwīr al-wiqāʿ fī asrār al-jimāʿ*. See al-Nafzāwī, *Rawḍ* 2–3.

The first barrier to understanding and appreciating *mujūn* – and 'high' literature in general – could have been a limited erudition in Classical Arabic as well as the finer points of Muslim culture (such as Quranic quotations, or the terminology of the religious disciplines, or the details of Islamic history, etc.), all absolute requirements for comprehending much of *mujūn*. While this certainly was a problem for the masses, and could be a problem for some members of the higher classes too, quite a few rulers, viziers, courtiers, and political and military leaders of the mediaeval Middle East were remarkably well educated. Some of the Abbasid caliphs, for instance, had a thorough grounding in the religious and secular scholarship of the period – usually by virtue of childhood studies under a renowned scholar – and there is anecdotal evidence showing some caliphs being quite appreciative of wit, eloquence and erudition in their courtiers. For example, the caliph al-Mustanjid (r. 555/1160–566/1170) had the habit of conversing with his chief treasurer in a weird private lingo based on the misspelling of the letters of the Arabic alphabet (*taṣḥīf*), an exercise that obviously required a ready wit and great erudition.[26]

There is no shortage of data demonstrating that many members of the courtly milieu, often including the rulers themselves, had a strong penchant for various types of jokes, witty remarks and manifestations of *mujūn* – usually, but not necessarily, enjoying such entertainment in private. The ability to amuse the ruler or a vizier – whether by sophisticated jokes and poems or by more down-to-earth buffoonery[27], as the case might be – was an immensely valuable asset for a poet or intellectual who had been given entry to the court and wished to make a living from his talents. For instance, a famous vizier of the Buyid era, al-Muhallabī (d. 352/963) had a court poet in his entourage whose main stock-in-trade was his adroitness in imitating various stereotypical accents and manners, a skill much appreciated by the vizier.[28] Much of that intellectual amusement can obviously be described as *mujūn*, and some of it was quite outrageous too. The overall impression is of an atmosphere in which the appreciation of *mujūn* did not automatically preclude respectability.[29] Like al-Muhallabī in the Buyid era, the celebrated vizier and maecenas Niẓām al-Mulk (d. 485/1092) was one of the most prominent statesmen in his own era (the Seljuk period), but he apparently had no problem with patronising Abū Yaʿlā Muḥammad b. al-Habbāriyya, a poet of Baghdad whose work is described

[26] al-Iṣbahānī, *Kharīda* I(i), 187. Not incidentally, jesting based on *taṣḥīf* seems to have been a well-liked source of humour – one that, by definition, could only be appreciated by literate people. See for instance al-Thaʿālibī, *Khāṣṣ* 53.

[27] A celebrated court poet of the early Abbasids called Abū Dulāma is a representative of the clownish 'court jester' category of libertines. See for instance Ben Cheneb 1922: 29–30, 45, 47, 63.

[28] al-Thaʿālibī, *Yatīma* II, 377.

[29] See for instance the identification of the narrator of a quite indecent joke in al-Tawḥīdī, *Baṣāʾir* I(i), 167 ["*samiʿtu shaykhan nabīlan...*"].

thus in an anthology: "the majority of his poems consists of lampoons, jesting and obscene silliness (*sukhf*); he was cast in the same mould as Ibn al-Ḥajjāj[30], as were their styles, except that he even surpassed the latter in his shamelessness and libertinism (*fī l-khalāʿa wa-l-mujūn*)."[31] The ready audience that quite number of notorious people found for their *mujūn* at the court indicates the degree of the acceptance of this phenomenon within the ruling class. The best-known examples of such success include the careers of Yaḥyā b. Aktham (an insouciant *mājin* who also happened to be the chief judge at the court of the caliph al-Maʾmūn [r. 198/813–218/833] and was a close friend of the caliph), the littérateur al-Jammāz (fl. 2nd–3rd/8th–9th c.), the unparalleled master of scurrility Ibn al-Ḥajjāj (d. 391/1001) at the Buyid court, and, for that matter, the iconic libertine Abū Nuwās too.[32] And consider the following summary of the career of the secretary and poet Aḥmad al-Battī, who pursued religious studies first but later switched to writing libertine poetry and telling indecent anecdotes, the better to flourish at the Buyid court:

> He was a secretary at the caliphal bureau. [...] Later on his morals came to be dominated by jesting (*hazl*), and he turned his back on seriousness, devoting himself to playfulness. His appearance and talk, and the anecdotes he told, all prompted [people] to frequent his company and wish to pass time with him. He attended the gatherings of [the Buyid ruler] Bahāʾ al-Dawla [r. 379/989–403/1012] as one of his boon-companions, and achieved unsurpassable success with him. Amongst the men of high rank, no one felt perfectly glad and cheerful unless [al-Battī] was present; they passed him from hand to hand and never left him alone. He was a boon-companion of the viziers until he ended up being a drinking companion of Fakhr al-Mulk, who grew extremely pleased with him and showered him with favours.[33]

Of course, the almost universal custom among rulers and their courtiers of engaging in regular wine-drinking sessions must have greatly enhanced their receptiveness to *mujūn* – both risqué anecdotes and licentious poetry. Indeed, in my opinion the highly private sphere of wine-drinking parties is likely to have been the most amenable setting for the circulation of *mujūn* texts and utterances, at least among the élite. The accumulated weight of the data, scattered though they may be over the pages of miscellaneous sources, does allow the stating of one thing: caliphs, sultans and their courtiers were not necessarily averse to *mujūn*, and could even be

---

30 *V.i.*

31 al-Iṣbahānī, *Kharīda* I(ii), 70–1.

32 From Persian literature, one may add the name of ʿUbayd-i Zākānī (8th/14th c.), scion of a family of distinguished jurists and religious scholars, and celebrated court poet in Shiraz. See Sprachman 1995: 44.

33 Yāqūt, *Udabāʾ* I, 374.

a very appreciative audience for it.[34] The growing penchant amongst the highest élite for frivolous topics was noted by some intellectuals of the Buyid era, either in a matter-of-fact manner or in an indignant tone as the case might be. Even intellectuals who clearly had no aversion to *mujūn* might feign the decency of calling it a sign of the decadence of their times.[35] Significantly even rulers with a reputation for piety and religious zeal might loosen their rigid norms of conduct amongst friends and have some spontaneous fun of the *mujūn* type. For example, the last thing the Ghaznavid ruler Maḥmūd b. Sabuktakīn (r. 388/998–421/1030) was noted for is frivolity and lax religious standards – he carefully cultivated his well-earned reputation of a devoted Muslim warrior of the faith – and yet the following account paints a very different picture. (Whether it is true or not is hard to decide, but it does appear more like the recounting of a concrete scene than a literary cliché.)

> The conqueror emir Abū l-Qāsim Maḥmūd b. Sabuktakīn – may God rest him in peace! – once narrated the following [religious tradition] to his boon-companions: "King Solomon, the son of David, would [have the energy to] visit each one of his forty wives within the course of one single night." To this, Abū Naṣr [b. Mishkān] replied: "Not a big deal, with the wind obeying him and running at his command."[36] The emir could not but guffaw at this talk, which delighted him.[37]

What is more, one observes that some politically powerful men of the court not only enjoyed listening to the frivolity of other, lesser individuals, but also produced

[34] E.g. al-Iṣfahānī, *Aghānī* VII, 193; XVIII, 105–6; XX, 354; al-Thaʿālibī, *Yatīma* III, 30; al-Thaʿālibī, *Tatimma* I, 14–5; al-Bayhaqī, *Maḥāsin* 517–8; al-Tawḥīdī, *Baṣāʾir* II(iv), 190–1 ["*raʾā Yaḥyā b. Aktham...*" etc.]; III(vi), 143 ["*anshidnī ashʿar mā taʿrif fī l-mujūn...*" etc.]; Ibn al-Muʿtazz, *Ṭabaqāt* 177 [Jaʿfar b. al-Qāsim al-Hāshimī and al-Jammāz]; al-Kutubī, *Fawāt* I, 60 [Abū Jalank's vulgar remark]; Ibn al-Kattānī, *Tashbīhāt* 284; Ibn Saʿīd, *Muqtaṭaf* 208, 221; Ibn Diḥya, *Muṭrib* 57–8. In the court of the caliph Hārūn al-Rashīd (r. 170/786–193/809) lived a man called Ibn Abī Maryam al-Madanī whose services to the caliph consisted of purveying jokes and anecdotes of the *mujūn* type; see al-Ṭabarī, *Tārīkh* V, 1750–1. One of the Buyid rulers would even allow a court poet widely celebrated for his foul mouth to felicitate him with a shockingly frivolous and indecent – but entertaining – poem on the occasion of the greatest Muslim holiday, in front of the whole court. See al-Thaʿālibī, *Yatīma* III, 67. (This instance of the enjoyment of *mujūn* by high-status people in a public setting is highly unusual. This important aspect of our subject will be discussed at more length later in this chapter, as well as in the next one.)

[35] E.g. al-Thaʿālibī, *Nathr* 84. It is reported about a famous vizier of the Buyid period, Abū l-Faḍl b. al-ʿAmīd (d. 360/970), that his criterion for assessing the excellence and intelligence of a person was whether that person favours Baghdad (presumably as the epitome of sophisticated metropolitan culture) and the works of the celebrated prose writer al-Jāḥiẓ (d. 255/869). Any mention of erudition in the religious sciences is conspicuously absent. See al-Thaʿālibī, *Thimār* II, 740. – Mores and tastes had certainly changed since the Umayyad era, when jesting with the Quran's text – a staple of *mujūn* literature and popular humour from the Abbasid period – was apparently sufficient grounds for a governor to execute a man (as it happened, an effeminate male, an embodiment of indecency even sans the frivolous joking). See al-Iṣfahānī, *Aghānī* IV, 220–1.

[36] An allusion to a well-known story in Quran 21:81 and 34:12.

[37] al-Thaʿālibī, *Laṭāʾif* 51.

such jokes, remarks or poems themselves. There could hardly be more convincing proof of the fact that political power and a frivolous attitude were by no means mutually exclusive properties. The most celebrated example of a personality who, for all his high standing in the court and great political power, would engage in producing *mujūn* himself is the vizier al-Ṣāḥib Ismāʿīl b. ʿAbbād (326/938–385/995). It is evident that his portrayal (and also that of another vizier, Abū l-Faḍl b. al-ʿAmīd) as presented by the embittered al-Tawḥīdī in his *Akhlāq al-wazīrayn* is a tendentious caricature aimed at denigrating the celebrated personality at any cost, and accusations of a penchant for indecency and libertinism fit all too well into that effort. However, many of the anecdotes about the vizier's love of *mujūn* bear all the hallmarks of genuine (if gossipy) information gathered from courtly insiders; and the vizier's liking for *mujūn* seems also to be supported by other evidence, including his own literary output. Be that as it may, manifestations of *mujūn* have been recorded in the sources about more than one vizier and political leader.[38]

However, this is only one side of the coin. To maintain the image of a pious political leader – and in principle (if not necessarily in practice) piety was an absolute prerequisite for a position of political leadership – an individual did have to distance himself from overt *mujūn*, by paying at least lip service to dominant norms and making an outward show of discouraging frivolity. This is what it mostly entailed: lip service to norms. While it is undeniable that quite a few rulers and politically powerful individuals seem to have had an accommodating attitude to *mujūn*, a too close association of their name with it would have been out of the question. (Suffice it here to refer to the fates of the Umayyad al-Walīd b. Yazīd and the Abbasid al-Amīn [r. 193/809–198/813].[39]) The occasional show of frowning upon frivolity and libertinism probably sufficed to preserve a ruler's Islamic credentials, and posture they did as pious leaders if the need arose. Nor is there a reason to doubt that sometimes they might honestly frown upon what they perceived as too extreme libertinism, even if they enjoyed the milder variety. (This point will be discussed more fully in the last chapter.) Whether arising from genuine dismay or an

---

[38] E.g. al-Tawḥīdī, *Akhlāq* 214 [al-Ṣāḥib b. ʿAbbād], 452 [Ibn al-ʿAmīd]; al-Thaʿālibī, *Laṭāʾif* 40 [al-Faḍl b. Marwān]; Miskawayh, *Tajārib* I, 371 [Abū ʿAbdallāh al-Barīdī]; al-Tanūkhī, *Nishwār* II, 70–1 [Ibn Muqla]. It would seem reasonable to regard the infamous Umayyad caliph al-Walīd b. Yazīd (r. 125–6/743–4) as an early example. However, this determined tippler and libertine can hardly be called typical, and in any case his scandalous conduct, once he came to occupy the highest religious post in the Muslim empire, was not tolerated much longer. Although for all his impulsivity he appears to have taken care to restrict his debauchery to the private sphere, it did not take long before it was public knowledge anyway, and eventually it cost the caliph his life. See al-Iṣfahānī, *Aghānī* VII, 6, 24, 59–60, 96; and on the proverbial dissoluteness of al-Walīd, also cf. al-Suyūṭī, *Tuḥfa* 99.

[39] This is not to suggest that notoriety for lax religious observance and for frivolity was the only factor in the downfall of either ruler, but it certainly was an excellent pretext, readily exploited by foes, in both cases.

opportunistic attempt at pious posturing, shows of symbolic disapproval were a substitute for, rather than a form of, punishment and they seem to have entailed no long-range consequences. This tendency may have already governed the behaviour of some political leaders living in urban centres in the considerably stricter atmosphere of the Umayyad period, when *mujūn* had not begun in earnest. For example this is the impression that one gets from the following excerpt about the celebrated but notoriously effeminate and shameless singer al-Dalāl, which is not as implausible an account as it may look at a superficial glance:

> Praying in the mosque of Mecca, al-Dalāl heard the imam recite, "*And why should I not serve Him who originated me, and unto whom you shall be returned?*"[40] Said al-Dalāl: "By God, I don't know." At this, most of those present began to laugh, interrupting their prayer. The governor, when he had completed his prayer, ordered [al-Dalāl] to come to him and said to him, "Won't you then ever give up this shamelessness and silliness (*hādhā l-mujūn wa-l-safah*)?" And [al-Dalāl] replied, "I thought that you worshipped God, and when I heard what you asked, I thought you might have doubts about the Lord, so I gave a boost [to your faith]." [The governor] said, "Me, having doubts about the Lord, and you giving me a boost? Go away from here, may God curse you; and do not let it happen again, because – I swear by God – I will punish you severely."[41]

In a later period, when *mujūn* had already become a widely accepted part of the cultural landscape of many Middle Eastern cities, the renowned poet Abū Tammām (190/806–232/846) used an impudent poem, containing some frivolous jesting with the Quran's text, to express his exasperation with his patron over the latter's failure to invite him into his presence and reward him for his poetic efforts. The aristocratic patron unsurprisingly felt rather annoyed with the insolence, yet he could not help laughing at the verses and was content to upbraid the poet with no more than the following message: "Tell Abū Tammām to avoid producing a similar poem again, because the Quran is too sublime for its text to be incorporated into such verses."[42] The show of disapproval is as important an aspect here as the ultimate lack of serious consequences. A ruler could not afford to be perceived as someone giving encouragement to conspicuous breaches of norms, so much so that even if he personally happened to have no objection to libertinism, it was advisable for him

[40] Quran 36:22.

[41] al-Iṣfahānī, *Aghānī* IV, 278. Joking during prayer – indeed interrupting prayer with any triviality – was regarded by religious scholars as not permissible; see for instance al-Ṭabarsī, *Makārim* 234.

[42] al-Ṣūlī, *Akhbār* 211; and also see Sanni 1998: 138–9 and van Gelder 2002–3: 6 for accounts in English of this incident. Another story that has a comparable ending is one about the caliph al-Ma'mūn and his chief judge Yaḥyā b. Aktham (see al-Iṣfahānī, *Aghānī* XX, 272–3), but the fact that other versions depict a very different situation and a very different reaction on the caliph's part makes the authenticity of this story highly suspect.

to pretend to have to some extent.[43] It seems indisputable that the arch-libertine Abū Nuwās was imprisoned several times by caliphs who, equally indisputably, were admirers of his poetry or at least did not really mind its libertine tone. The most absurd, hence the most revealing, case must be the incarceration of this poet by the caliph al-Amīn (r. 193/809–198/813), a ruler of not inconsiderable notoriety for his love of boys and drinking sprees, and – not incidentally – the occasional boon-companion of Abū Nuwās. The charge: drinking wine. According to the chronicle of al-Ṭabarī, the immediate motive of this truly hypocritical act was the disturbing news that the caliph's image as a pious ruler was beginning to be eroded by widespread rumours of his associating with the disreputable libertine.[44] Likewise, it appears to be out of concern for the caliph's reputation that the bohemian poet Wāliba b. al-Ḥubāb was never invited to the caliphal court of al-Mahdī (r. 158/775–169/785) to serve as boon-companion.[45] Similarly, courtiers who did not keep a

---

[43] One example of a ruler having to go to great lengths to affect pious disapproval of non-normative conduct while avoiding actual punishment of the 'offender' is the case of the caliph al-Manṣūr (r. 136/754–158/775) with the poet Ibn Harma. It is alleged that the caliph devised an ingenious way of allowing the poet to continue his habitual drinking without interference from the police and yet not contradicting the prescriptions of the *sharīʿa*: he had it announced that if anyone reports on the drinking binges of Ibn Harma or brings him in a state of intoxication to the police, the poet will get the eighty lashes prescribed by the *sharīʿa* (as no one has the right to forgo the sanctions of the holy law), but the accuser will get one hundred as discretionary punishment by caliphal order. According to the story, the drunken Ibn Harma would subsequently meet police patrols with the confident, cheerful bawl: "Who'll buy a hundred for eighty?" See Ibn Qutayba, *Shiʿr* 388; al-Iṣfahānī, *Aghānī* IV, 368; and also cf. ibid. XX, 425 [the case of Abū Nukhayla with the head of the police in al-Kūfa]. (The story about Ibn Harma sounds so well-rounded as to appear a bit apocryphal; however, its basic premise must have been familiar to its audience – namely, that even a caliph may not openly support reprehensible conduct, much less abrogate legal punishments, whatever his personal level of tolerance. And that is precisely the point of my argument above.)

[44] al-Ṭabarī, *Tārīkh* V, 1821–2. This explanation of the caliph's behaviour is reinforced by another account, which claims that the new caliph, al-Maʾmūn (al-Amīn's brother and rival) would initially be at pains to cultivate the image of a pious ruler, totally refraining from listening to singers for twenty months. He continued to exercise discretion for another four years, with his musical soirées taking place in strict privacy, but finally resumed his normal participation in drinking parties and concerts like most other Muslim rulers. See Yāqūt, *Udabāʾ* II, 601. In another version, charges of immorality and licentiousness are also added, and yet another account identifies some verses offensive to the honour of the Caliph's lineage as the real reason, with wine-drinking and blasphemies providing only an opportune pretext. Elsewhere the real offense is said to have been a wine poem containing sarcastic criticism of al-Amīn as a ruler. See Ibn Manẓūr, *Akhbār* 82–3, 127–8, 191. Incidentally, it is also reported by some sources that on one occasion al-Amīn almost ordered the beheading of Abū Nuwās because of the latter's hints of his amorous feelings for the young (and famously attractive) caliph. Of course, speaking of a ruler as the object of another man's lust is about as offensive and insufferable as talk or poetry can ever get. See al-Thaʿālibī, *Thimār* I, 314–5.

[45] Wāliba, who happens to have been the master of Abū Nuwās, and apparently his first lover too, produced works much appreciated by the caliph, but his oeuvre gained such notoriety as to make it advisable for the ruler not to associate with him. Sources, however, single out one particular couplet

sufficiently solemn public façade risked giving their rivals and adversaries – which everyone had in the intensely competitive atmosphere of a ruler's court – a good pretext to attack and perhaps undo them.[46]

The above observations already anticipate an important distinction to be made here, that between the private and public spheres. A factor of paramount significance, this distinction merits more than a fleeting mention. Whereas there was no serious obstacle to a caliph or a lesser ruler indulging himself if he liked entertainment of the *mujūn* type, such entertainment had to be kept in the private domain. This means not the immediate family but the circle of the most intimate, trusted friends. Trust in the discretion of one's closest friends was particularly essential for drinking parties – both because of the theoretical impropriety of drinking wine and for keeping whatever happened in a state of inebriation secret – but it was, understandably enough, a universal requirement for any kind of intimate friendly gathering or soirée (*majlis al-uns*). Boon-companions (sing. *nadīm*) being inevitably privy to a lot of information potentially damaging to a ruler's image, it is no wonder this position was considered to be one signifying a great deal of intimacy and trust, and was viewed as strictly separate from more formal positions.[47] Given the right choice of tried and trustworthy friends, a ruler might be as merry and frivolous among friends as he wished and still cultivate an immaculately respectable, even solemn image of himself for the public.[48] This distinction between the private and public spheres

by this poet as the immediate reason for excluding him from the court milieu: «Between us only, I say to the servant-boy: ‹Draw your head closer to mine; / Come closer and lie down before me – I am a man who will have sex with his companions›.» The caliph remarked that he had no need to be known as the boon-companion of the author of these verses. See Ibn al-Muʿtazz, *Ṭabaqāt* 34; al-Ṭabarī, *Tārīkh* V, 1685; al-Tawḥīdī, *Baṣāʾir* I(i), 156. Another source from the high Abbasid era also suggests the advisability to keep a safe distance from notorious libertines; see Abū Hiffān, *Akhbār* 23 ["*hādhā ʿayyār shārib shawwāẓ yunādim al-sifla wa-l-sūqa wa-yantāb al-ḥānāt wa-yarkab al-fawāḥish yarā dhālika ghunman wa-inna fī munādamatihi tashniʿa ʿalā amīr al-muʾminīn*"]. Occasionally even a member of the caliphal lineage who was too indiscreet to make a scandal might be punished so as to dissociate the ruling dynasty from any conspicuous shameful behaviour. This is what happened to Abū ʿAlī b. al-Rashīd, a half-brother of al-Maʾmūn, after a wild and all-too-public carousal at a Christian monastery. See Kilpatrick 2003: 29–30.

46 The malicious stories about the vizier Ismāʿīl b. ʿAbbād recorded by al-Tawḥīdī are instructive in this respect. (Many of these are concerned with the vizier's penchant for obscenity and *mujūn*.) See al-Tawḥīdī, *Akhlāq* 144–51, 175, 178–9, 214.

47 Precisely with an eye to keeping the public and private spheres separate, it was commonly deemed to be inadvisable to include the biggest office-holders in the state machinery like the viziers in the group of the ruler's boon-companions. Incidentally, the early Abbasid caliphs also maintained the old Persian custom of hiding from their companions behind a curtain during drinking parties, a symbolic enhancement of privacy that was discontinued under their later successors. See Chejne 1965: 329–31.

48 For some illustrative cases, see for instance the account about the caliph al-Maʾmūn and the *mājin* youngsters in al-Bayhaqī, *Maḥāsin* 617; the case of the same caliph with a *qāḍī* of Damascus producing questionable poetry in al-Ṭabarī, *Tārīkh* V, 1875–6; and the story of the drinking sessions

seems to have been the context in which *mujūn* could flourish in aristocratic circles. It is also the context that helps reconcile the ostensibly incongruous evidence of the most dignified, august and upright caliphs and rulers (the ilk of Maḥmūd the Ghaznavid for instance) enjoying and even sponsoring and commissioning various manifestations of *mujūn*. This separation between the public and the private was by no means perceived as dishonesty – not by everyone anyway – but as behaving in a manner appropriate for each setting.[49] The expectation of solemnity and respectability in public situations was a fundamental one for a ruler (especially a caliph) for religious as well as social reasons, but this did not presuppose a total eschewal of entertainment and frolicking in a private setting, as long as strict discretion about it was observed. (Fortunately for the contemporary researcher, discretion in a huge royal or caliphal court could apparently never be airtight, hence the data at our disposal to demonstrate the reception of *mujūn* in the highest echelon of society.) A particularly striking example of the disconnect between the private and the public personae of rulers is the case of the Abbasid al-Qāhir (r. 320/932–322/934), a caliph who issued a harsh order banning singing, wine and other alcoholic drinks and ordering the expulsion of singers from Baghdad, and who at the same time was virtually an alcoholic and an avid aficionado of music and singing concerts in the privacy of his palace quarters.[50]

The separation of the private and public spheres was not as simple and straightforward as one might imagine, and the ambiguity of this norm – or rather of its concrete application – could easily give rise to many a distressing and embarrassing situation. Keeping one's privacy and secrets might not always be easy in the court milieu; and people might have quite differing interpretations of a certain situation being private or otherwise. Such ambiguities are eminently borne out in the following account of a funny incident involving some courtiers of the caliph al-Wāthiq (r. 227/842–232/847):

> Al-Ḥasan b. Wahb served as secretary to Muḥammad b. ʿAbd al-Malik al-Zayyāt, the vizier of al-Wāthiq. Ibn al-Zayyāt, when he was informed of what was going on between al-Ḥasan b. Wahb and [the renowned poet] Abū Tammām on account of their respective slave-boys[51], told some of his sons – who happened to work

of the Umayyad caliph al-Walīd (perhaps an account of dubious historical authenticity) in al-Iṣfahānī, *Aghānī* VII, 96. On the distinct norms for informal conduct befitting a private setting (*ṭarḥ al-takalluf*), see Sadan 1983: 40. While there certainly were individuals who would never relax even in the most informal of situations, preferring to keep their solemnity whatever the circumstances, such behaviour seems to have been eccentric enough to serve as the subject of somewhat bewildered anecdotes. See for instance al-Tanūkhī, *Nishwār* I, 47.

[49] This point will be revisited in the last chapter.

[50] Miskawayh, *Tajārib* I, 269.

[51] Each was in love with a slave-boy owned by the other, and they made no effort to hide the fact from each other.

> under al-Ḥasan b. Wahb – to let him know what these two men were up to and what was [actually] happening. Now, the slave-boy of Abū Tammām wanted to have phlebotomy performed on him, and he wrote to [his lover] al-Ḥasan to ask him to send him a bit of date-wine. [Al-Ḥasan] responded by sending him a hundred jugs of it, as well as a hundred dinars, a festive garb, incense, and a small note [containing this verse]: "I wish I knew, o you most beautiful in my eyes, do you seek a cure for my absence through bloodletting? / [...]" The note was placed under the prayer-mat of the boy. [The vizier] Muḥammad b. ʿAbd al-Malik, when hearing of the missive, hastily sent for al-Ḥasan to distract him while someone takes the message and brings it to him. Having read it, [the vizier] wrote a reply in the name of Abū Tammām: "I wish I knew what this 'I wish I knew' means: Are you being serious, or are you kidding? / [...]" Then he ordered that the note should be put back to where it had been taken from. When al-Ḥasan read it, he said: "In God's hands we are! By God, we have been put to shame in the eyes of the vizier." He sent a message to Abū Tammām telling him about what had happened, and enclosed the small note too. At this, they went to Muḥammad b. ʿAbd al-Malik and told him, "These two [boys] have merely served as an excuse for us to exchange poetic messages with each other." Replied the vizier: "And who's accused you of anything else?" His [sarcastic] remark only added to their embarrassment.[52]

Ambivalent situations – ones that the concerned parties could and did interpret differently as either private or non-private – were probably not uncommon. Accordingly, the dilemma of whether to exercise caution and stick to the norms of formality, or relax one's conduct and let frivolity prevail, was forever a potential difficulty to be dealt with in the court milieu. This problem presented itself for instance to a vizier of the Abbasid caliph al-Muʿtaḍid (r. 279/892–289/902) when the latter casually mentioned the information that he was aware of the drinking and frolicking that the vizier had engaged in the previous night. Realising that his supposedly 'private' party had obviously been under close scrutiny the vizier panicked, only to be told by the caliph: "What is there to be nervous about? What's the matter? If I'd known that I would cause you such [consternation], I wouldn't have said a word to distress your soul..."[53] Whereas it is fairly obvious that misinterpreting a situation could be fraught with peril for a subordinate interacting with someone of a higher rank, caution might also be necessary on the ruler's part.

[52] al-Ṣūlī, *Akhbār* 196–9. It is quite obvious that the vizier finds the whole incident very amusing, as is the fact that he is supposed to disapprove of such a shameless behaviour in his capacity as a high dignitary of the state. The tension in the story seems to be rooted in the ambiguity of the vizier's rapport with his subordinates: certainly not camaraderie, but not exactly a sheer exercise of power either.

[53] al-Tanūkhī, *Nishwār* III, 277. To decide to whom to admit drinking wine and to whom to keep silent about it was apparently an important issue requiring a lot of tact and prudence in the courts of the rulers. See for instance al-Thaʿālibī, *Thimār* I, 114.

At the very least, he might also face serious embarrassment if his perception of a 'private' and relaxed setting turned out to be interpreted otherwise by his interlocutor, as happened between the Buyid sultan of al-Rayy, Fakhr al-Dawla (r. 366/977–387/997), and his celebrated vizier al-Ṣāḥib b. ʿAbbād. Given that the latter was widely known for his strong inclination for frivolity, ribaldry and lechery – in short, all kinds of assorted *mujūn* – it was not unreasonable for the monarch to expect an encouraging response for his attempt at jesting, but al-Ṣāḥib b. ʿAbbād simply refused to take his cue. The source quotes the vizier's own words describing the incident:

> Whenever I asked for permission to enter into the presence of Fakhr al-Dawla while he was being entertained among friends, the session would immediately become a formal one (*intaqala ilā majlis al-ḥishma*) before he would give me permission to enter. I do not recall him ever relaxing his solemnity in my presence and joking with me except once, when he said to me during the course of a conversation: "I've heard that you think the right school of theology is the *Muʿtazila*, and the right form of fucking is to fuck men." At this, I showed my displeasure with his jocosity (*inbisāṭ*). Saying, "We have enough serious concerns to preoccupy us from joking", I stood up as if in indignation. He would apologise several times in writing before I began to frequent his company again. He would never again attempt to jest or banter with me.[54]

In view of the considerable ambivalence of the notion of a 'private setting' and the resulting need for circumspection, it is hardly surprising that some libertines were somewhat unenthusiastic about constant attendance at the court, a potential source of trouble even with the most benevolent and indulgent of rulers. Paradoxically, a distinction that would ordinarily provide a great deal of freedom in some situations might also add an extra element of discomfiture. With even the dominant party in a social interaction, such as a ruler, being unable to assess the nature of every situation with total certainty, the possibility of a *faux pas* was much more pronounced for the lower-status party. A ruler might also have his caprices or be subject to a sullen or irritable mood, especially when drunk, which increased the potential danger to his interlocutors and boon-companions even further. Weighed against this factor, the ostensibly odd fact that some intellectuals preferred to keep

---

[54] al-Thaʿālibī, *Yatīma* III, 199; Yāqūt, *Udabāʾ* II, 707 (and for a French translation of the story, see Lagrange 2006: 69). It is worth setting this account against another passage in the same source, which cites a letter written by al-Ṣāḥib b. ʿAbbād to a friend, teasing the latter and inquiring about the intimate details of a sexual escapade. See al-Thaʿālibī, *Yatīma* III, 248. For an account of a comparable misunderstanding of a situation in roughly the same period; see Yāqūt, *Udabāʾ* IV, 1586. (This incident also elicited indignant words of rebuke – "When did you hear me joke or play the libertine, so that you should [dare to] joke and play the libertine with me [*wa-matā raʾaytanī amzaḥu fa-tamzaḥa maʿī aw amjunu fa-tamjuna bī*]?" – and it was also settled more or less amicably.)

their distance from the caliphs appears less puzzling. Although the court remained the most remunerative venue for plying their craft, some genuinely frivolous poets seem to have tried as best they could to avoid 'private' entertainment with the ruler, however enviable that opportunity may have seemed to other, less favoured courtiers. (On the other hand, there is no reason to suppose that they did not strive as much as everyone else to market their panegyrics and 'serious' poetry at the court and get their material rewards.) Two of the most outstanding poets and libertines of the early Abbasid period, Abū Dulāma (d. ca. 160/776–7) and Abū Nuwās (fl. late 2nd/8th c.) are described alike as disinclined to spend their leisure time with the reigning caliph:

> [The caliph] Abū l-ʿAbbās al-Saffāḥ was fond of Abū Dulāma and would spend all his time in his company, for [the latter] was erudite and a great poet ready with a lot of entertaining jokes and stories about all kinds of people. Abū Dulāma was a debauched libertine (*mājin*) who kept fleeing from [the caliph], preferring to frequent the taverns in which he would drink wine with his friends. He hated the company of the caliphs, as that is a tiresome nuisance calling for constant caution, while Abū Dulāma loved relaxed conversation, something that he had little opportunity for in the sessions with the caliph. Therefore he would flee from him, and Abū l-ʿAbbās would reproach him, saying: "Damn it, I see that you are indisposed to us and our gatherings, nay actively avoiding us. If only I knew why!" [Abū Dulāma] replied: "Oh Commander of the Faithful, the best, noblest, most virtuous and excellent activity is to be with you or wait for permission to enter into your presence and serve you. However, we wish that you should not be bored by us, and therefore we hold back somewhat, so that we can continue to be in your favour." Abū l-ʿAbbās said: "Never have we been bored by you; and it is not the way you claim, but you have become habituated to frequenting taverns in the company of all kinds of scum, rabble and libertines." Then he placed him under surveillance and obligated him to spend all his time in his company and say all the [prescribed] prayers together with him. Aggrieved over this, Abū Dulāma mentioned it in a poem: "Don't you know that the caliph has confined me to his mosque and palace – what business have I in the palace? / Diligently I say the dawn prayer with him, and the afternoon prayer – woe unto me for both! / He detains me from a company I would enjoy, where I could imbibe music as well as wine. / By God, I have no liking for his prayers; piety and a virtuous, decent life are not for me. / What harm would it do him, if he lives a godly life, if all the sins of the world were upon me?" When Abū l-ʿAbbās heard these verses, he said: "By God, this man will never mend his ways. Let him [go and be] with his friends."[55]

> [Abū Nuwās] kept fleeing from the caliphs and rulers, sparing no efforts [to avoid their company]. He would say: "It is only the greatest men who utterly

[55] Ibn al-Muʿtazz, *Ṭabaqāt* 20–1.

> devote themselves to it (*al-fuḥūl al-munqaṭiʿūn*) that have the patience [for the task], those who never relax their conduct and only utter a word when permitted to do so. By God, I feel as though I were burning in fire whenever I enter into the [rulers'] presence, until I can go away to my friends and my drinking companions. That is because when I am with [the ruler], it is not me who decides my own business."[56]

As has been noted in a previous chapter of this study, the frivolity and irreverence of libertines might also manifest itself in political and personal topics as well, and while the genre of lampoons (*hijāʾ*) was not usually considered to be representative of *mujūn*, the delineation of the two categories is in fact not so simple. Given that there appears to have been some overlapping between *hijāʾ* and political poetry on the one hand, and the concept of *mujūn* on the other, the reactions of the political elite to the latter must have been affected to some extent by the political and invective poetry produced by the same poets. (Bashshār b. Burd is a conspicuous case of a libertine who was also a prolific purveyor of *hijāʾ*, and one has to take into account both aspects when assessing contemporary responses to his oeuvre.) In other words, there is the ever-present possibility, especially when it comes to punishments for poetic works, that a ruler who felt personally insulted by the political loyalties or the biting sarcasm of a poet would choose to disguise his motives as pious indignation over *mujūn*. As this problem will shortly be discussed as part of the wider issue of the variety of sanctions for *mujūn*, it need not detain us here, but I will anticipate my argument somewhat by pointing out that the powers that be tended to have much more patience for frivolity and *mujūn* than for political criticism or perceived slights to their own honour.[57] (Heterodox, heretic and sectarian tendencies were also viewed much more harshly than the casual irrevence of a libertine.) In practical terms, this means that a libertine who happened to have great currency at the court as a poet and wit would be very wise to refrain from meddling in politics and court intrigues, and composing *hijāʾ* about politically powerful individuals or their kin. Albeit rulers and their courtiers in the metropolitan centres of Muslim culture tended to be amenable to the menifestations of *mujūn*, even within the courts there were caveats

---

[56] Ibn al-Muʿtazz, *Ṭabaqāt* 91.

[57] See for instance al-Tawḥīdī, *Baṣāʾir* I(ii), 74. Although an analysis of the mechanisms of criticising the authorities constitutes an undertaking far beyond the scope and ambition of this essay, the above observations should not be taken to imply that rulers were always and completely impervious to any sort of political criticism. The question seems to have been rather one of style and vocabulary: the language of piety and appeals to religious sentiments – which allowed the ruler to project the image of a honourable and devout man yielding to God rather than to human rivals or contenders – naturally had better chances of success than an abusive and/or challenging tone. Listening to criticism phrased as religious discourse would probably mean an increase, instead of a loss, of honour for the ruler. See for instance al-Shayzarī, *Nihāya* 7–8; Ibn Riḍwān, *Shuhub* 111; and also cf. Bulliet 1972: 61.

to be aware of. The ambivalence of the court elite's attitudes to *mujūn* could bring nasty surprises to an unwary libertine.

1.3 The 'Lower Literate Class'

Before proceeding to survey the attitudes of two very influential groups of mediaeval Muslim society, the 'secretaries' (*kuttāb*) and the religious experts (*ʿulamāʾ*), it is important to clarify a point. The treatment of these two groups in this section is not meant to imply that *all kuttāb* and *ʿulamāʾ* can be relegated to the category – somewhat clumsily defined to begin with – of the 'lower literate class', that is the category of literate professionals having no direct relationship to the court. In fact some of the *kuttāb* were very much a part of the court milieu, as were some religious scholars. If the vizier al-Ṣāḥib b. ʿAbbād is a good example of the former group, the *qāḍī* Yaḥyā b. Aktham is representative of the latter. Moreover, many scholars' and secretaries' careers took them into the court at times and out of it at other times, so social mobility (upward and downward) was quite a possibility in this sense. (In fact even people from the deepest pits of the common populace, such as slaves, could and not infrequently did end up in the court as military and political leaders.) Nevertheless, for the sake of convenience it seems to be a better choice to discuss both the *ʿulamāʾ* and the *kuttāb* in this section – where the bulk of their numbers probably belonged – but with due emphasis on the fact that some members of both categories were indisputably part and parcel of the royal or caliphal courts.

The two most important subgroups of the lower intelligentsia, the *kuttāb* (the literate elements with a more 'secular' outlook) and the *ʿulamāʾ* (the scholarly class focusing on religion, especially the Quran, the *ḥadīth* and the *sharīʿa*), were characterised by markedly dissimilar patterns of behaviour, values and norms. This corresponded to, indeed resulted from, a differing educational background, although of course secretaries were expected to be conversant to some degree with the religious disciplines too (certainly with the Quran's text and some *ḥadīth* scholarship). Conversely, quite a few religious scholars had some measure of familiarity with such things as ancient and even recent Arabic poetry.

1.3.1 THE RELIGIOUS SAVANTS

Certainly in principle and sometimes in practice too, the opinion of the *ʿulamāʾ* mattered. It was thought to matter in every issue, including ones that a modern observer may not recognise as having any religious significance. However, the extent to which an individual religious scholar, and even the *ʿulamāʾ* as a group, could convert his or their theoretical influence into actual, practical control varied widely. This is due to several reasons, analysing which would far surpass the scope of this book, but some of them are worth mentioning here. First, as is well known, the customs of any given region often proved too deeply entrenched for the interpretations of Islamic law of the *ʿulamāʾ* to displace them. Secondly, political leadership tended to be largely divorced in practice, if never in theory, from religious leadership, and in some circumstances the latter would even be in opposition to the state. Thirdly, disagreements within the group of *ʿulamāʾ* were so pronounced (on virtually every question beyond the most basic tenets of Islam) as to render any operation as a unified pressure group utterly impossible. Fourthly, the *ʿulamāʾ* were a very heterogeneous group, with some members of it being quite wealthy and practically in symbiosis with the courtly elite, others serving as the petty local intelligentsia of a provincial town or a quarter within a metropolis, and yet others consciously maintaining a pietistic attitude far removed from the give-and-take of political struggles.[58] However, lip service to the opinions of *ʿulamāʾ* was a widespread norm even in situations where their actual influence was minimal. A consequence of this for our study is that those opinions, as far as they touch upon the issue of *mujūn*, will have to be studied at some length before we try to examine how much of that corpus of theoretical views was put into practice.[59]

As will be obvious, there was little consensus among the *ʿulamāʾ* in their assessment of various aspects of *mujūn*. To the extent that books of Islamic law deal with literary topics and motifs, a number of curious features characterising their approach stand out. First of all, in no *fiqh* work do we find a separate section or subsection on literature as such; remarks on various aspects of literary production are as a rule scattered over different sections of the book. The reason I believe is simple enough. Manuals of *fiqh* show a similar arrangement of chapters to that found in *ḥadīth* collections, and few *ḥadīths* treat the subject of literature.[60] The Quran itself has little to say on literature, apart from the famous verses (26:224–7) warning against the fraudulence of poets who do not believe, which are duly cited in some *fiqh* manuals when the occasion arises. Not quite sympathetic to poetry in its original context, the Quranic passage was nevertheless commonly utilised later to defend it against its detractors by pointing out its fictitious nature: poets cannot be mechanically assumed to behave in the way they depict in their works, since "they say that which

58 In fact, the very definition of a 'religious elite' in reference to a Muslim society is far from unproblematic; see Cachia 1995: 176–7.

59 On the social prestige of the *ʿulamāʾ* as a group (bearing in mind that the prestige of a group does not necessarily presuppose the popularity of its individual members), see for instance Stambouli, Zghal 1976: 11–2. The observations of the authors refer to the urban society of North Africa, but they seem to be roughly valid for other regions of the Arabic-speaking world as well.

60 A widely accepted *ḥadīth* compares poetry to pus filling the poet's stomach, but this stark condemnation was tempered, indeed all but explained away, in inventive ways by commentators. See for instance Ibn Mufliḥ, *Furūʿ* III, 638; al-Naḥḥās, *Ṣināʿa* 29.

they do not". In any case, the Quran and the Traditions between them offered very little in the way of pegs on which to hang juridical rulings about literary works. Even such aspects of literature as have an obvious religious dimension – like quotations from the Quran in literary works (*v. i.*) – had no fixed place of their own within manuals of Islamic jurisprudence; scholars who did have something to say on the subject had to choose the section in which to do so in a rather haphazard manner.[61] Secondly, one of the most striking aspects of the jurists' treatment of literature is the ubiquitous failure (and sometimes explicit refusal) to distinguish various types of utterances: literary texts from ordinary speech, speech from writing, poetry from prose, and – in many but not all cases – utterances that are serious from those that are not. For many *fuqahāʾ*, these were all simply *statements* from a legal point of view, no matter what their purpose, genre or mode of delivery. Statements could then be classified as commendable, neutral, or harmful; and when harmful, a statement that someone made might constitute immorality (*fisq*) or unbelief (*kufr*), as the case might be.[62] In such sections of large *fiqh* works, as well as in the few shorter treatises devoted entirely to this issue, the author typically proceeds by amassing concrete examples – rather than identifying abstract principles – and trying to decide in each case whether it signals unbelief, or immorality, or else is innocuous.[63] (The meticulous preoccupation with precise phrases is hardly unique to this issue; *fuqahāʾ* also accumulated myriad examples of acceptable and unacceptable formulae for such things as legally binding oaths, divorce, guaranteeing, the postponed manumission of slaves [*tadbīr*], and so on.[64]) Apart from short sections in larger *fiqh* works, there exist separate treatises dealing with the problem of classifying utterances and specifying those that are to be considered clear expressions of *kufr*. (Ḥanafite and Shāfiʿite scholars seem to have lent particular attention to the issue.[65]) For instance, a collection of *fatwā*s by the Ḥanafī authority Abū l-Layth Naṣr al-Samarqandī (d. 375/985–6) includes a chapter titled *Faṣl fī-mā yūjibu l-kufr wa-fī-mā lā yūjibu* ("Chapter on What Must Be Regarded as Unbelief and What Is Not

[61] al-ʿAskar 1425 (A.H.): 10–1.

[62] In most Muslim communities, declaring someone an unbeliever was thought to be the exclusive preserve of the *ʿulamāʾ*; see Kruse 1984: 426–7.

[63] A typical example is the subject of some oath formulae ("I'll have nothing to do with Islam if ...", "I'll be a Jew if ...", etc.) somewhat reminiscent of the literary frivolities of libertines, which were rather controversial: some *fuqahāʾ* considered them to constitute *kufr*, others did not; not to speak of the fundamental question of whether such phrases are to be considered binding oaths. See for instance Ibn Juzayy, *Qawānīn* 163–4; al-Samarqandī, *Fatāwā* 239, 241; al-Walwālijī, *Fatāwī* II, 231–2; al-Haytamī, *Zawājir* II, 184–5; al-Ṭūsī, *Nihāya* II, 569; Ibn Miftāḥ, *Muntazaʿ* IX, 21–3.

[64] E.g. al-Marwazī, *Ikhtilāf* 487–92; al-Ṭabarī, *Ikhtilāf* I, 1–3; II, 51–3; Ibn Miftāḥ, *Muntazaʿ* IX, 7–69.

[65] In the words of the Shāfiʿite author al-Haytamī, "those who took an interest in this topic were mostly the Ḥanafites and then our fellow[-Shāfiʿite]s". See al-Haytamī, *Iʿlām* 347.

So"). Another scholar of the same legal school, Abū l-Fatḥ al-Walwālijī (d. 540/1145–6) also treated the question in a separate section under the title *Kitāb fī l-alfāẓ allatī tajrī ʿalā l-lisān fa-yukaffaru bihā wa-mā lā yukaffaru bihā* ("Book on Statements That Slip from the Tongue and Lead to the Charge of Unbelief and What Does Not Lead to It"). Later on, a number of Ḥanafite jurisprudents wrote separate, book-length treatises on the subject, compiling and relying on the legals opinions of earlier authorities. An example of the genre is the *Risāla fī l-alfāẓ al-mukaffirāt* ("Epistle on Words that Make One an Unbeliever") of Muḥammad b. Ismāʿīl b. Muḥammad, known as Badr al-Rashīd (d. 768/1366–7). A notable Shāfiʿite scholar who devoted a separate work to the subject is the Meccan Abū l-ʿAbbās Aḥmad al-Haytamī (d. 974/1567), author of *al-Iʿlām bi-qawāṭiʿ al-Islām* ("Information on What Puts an End to Being a Muslim").[66] It is remarkable that in its not infrequent failure to take into account the purpose and tone of an utterance, such jurists' approach shows a marked contrast to the thinking of other Muslim intellectuals, as will be shown below. In any case, much of this literature can be safely assumed to have remained mere theory that never really informed legal and ordinary practice.

The above-mentioned lack of distinction between serious and facetious utterances (*jidd* and *hazl* respectively) was far from universal but neither quite uncommon among experts of Islamic law. A key term in pietistic discourse that signals the absence of distinction between seriousness and humour is *kadhib*, 'lying, fabrication, untruth' (and the synonym *buhtān*)[67]; and through this prism practically all kinds of frivolous text – which is to say all *mujūn* – could be viewed as pure falsehood. But that was not the worst possible assessment of libertine texts. Frivolous literary motifs – and jesting in general – would sometimes be subsumed under the sinister heading of *istihzāʾ*, 'derision' (sinister because forms of the term are used in the Quran [e.g. 4:140, 6:10, 30:10, 43:7, and a lot of other verses] in a very negative sense, to refer to the hostile attitudes of unbelievers to Islam and God's messengers, and it is thus practically tantamount to a charge of *kufr*, or unbelief). By using this term, some *fuqahāʾ* could present jesting remarks as the expression of something more serious and more profoundly wicked than mere frivolity, indeed an attack on Islam itself. The Ḥanbalite author Ibn Mufliḥ al-Maqdisī (d. 763/1362) asserts that words suggesting unbelief, even if obviously uttered in jest (*wa-law hāzilan*), are to be regarded as full apostasy, and elsewhere he adds: "[...] whoever makes a mocking show of unbelief is an unbeliever (*al-mustahziʾ bi-l-kufr yakfuru*)".[68] Another term

---

[66] al-Samarqandī, *Fatāwā* 286–8; al-Walwālijī, *Fatāwī* V, 417–22; Badr, *Risāla*; al-Haytamī, *Iʿlām*.

[67] As mediaeval Muslim literary critics used the term, *kadhib* might virtually correspond to the modern Western concept of 'fiction'; see Hoyland 2006: 17.

[68] Ibn Mufliḥ, *Furūʿ* III, 413, 416. (The principle *al-mustahziʾ bi-l-kufr yakfuru* is also cited from the *Furūʿ* in al-Haytamī, *Iʿlām* 390.) It is perhaps not without significance that one finds the term *mustahziʾ* paired up with the Arabic for 'libertine' ("*ʿādat al-mujjān wa-l-mustahziʾīn*") in a rather

frequently used so as to put frivolous humour on a par with serious affronts to religion and thereby highlight its heinousness is *istikhfāf [bi-l-Qur'ān* etc.] ('showing disrespect [to the Quran etc.]'). Another pliable concept that in its proper sense was applicable to a 'serious' crime but could be expanded by some legal experts to include certain frivolous literary motifs is the portrayal of God as unjust or tyrannical in what He decrees (*taẓlīm Allām* or *tajwīr Allāh*). This concept was initially used in reference to theological views that held God to be the originator of all human deeds, good or bad.[69] That the same term should be utilised to characterise – and advise action against – playful remarks or literary motifs is yet another example of the perhaps wilful failure of some jurists to distinguish jest from earnest. The attitude manifests itself in other ways too. For instance the celebrated Mālikite author al-Qāḍī ʿIyāḍ al-Yaḥṣubī (496/1103–544/1146) classifies irreverent jesting about the Prophet Muḥammad ("*ʿabath fī jihatihi l-ʿazīza bi-sukhf min al-kalām*") as equal to serious insults to his person, nor does he regard the offender's rash or frivolous personality as acceptable excuses. Indeed, if such jesting is a habit rather than an isolated incident, al-Yaḥṣubī regards it as a proof of unbelief (*kufr*).[70]

As noted above, some authorities would also expressly refuse to make any distinction between literary and ordinary statements, assessing both according to the same criteria. This is hardly surprising given the lack of a mediaeval Arabic term corresponding to the modern concept of 'literature'. Native terms did, however, include 'poetry' (and, for that matter, 'prose'), which was an all-important element of Arabic culture yet was viewed with suspicion by some bigots. It is at least partly with the aim of defending poetry from such attacks that the majority of jurists treated it as any other form of discourse. One of the greatest Muslim jurisprudents ever, al-Shāfiʿī (d. 204/820) is a notable representative of this tendency and a model for other scholars. As he puts it,

> Poetry is [a kind of] speech: whatever is good [in poetry] is like good speech, and whatever is bad in it is like bad speech (*al-shiʿr kalām, ḥasanuhu ka-ḥasan al-kalām wa-qabīḥuhu ka-qabīḥ al-kalām*), except that it is a durable and widely known [type of] speech, which is its extra feature vis-à-vis [ordinary] speech. Thus, if a poet is not known for denigrating and hurting the Muslims and doing so repeatedly, nor for lying a lot in praise-poetry, his testimony should not be rejected.[71]

---

harsh 6th/12th-century Mālikite work on dealing with disrespect to the Prophet's memory. See ʿIyāḍ, *Shifāʾ* 343–4.

[69] See al-Bustī, *Baḥth* 6, 12. For the application of the concept to mere frivolous phrases or casual, sarcastic remarks, see for instance al-Haytamī, *Iʿlām* 363, 371, 378; ʿIyāḍ, *Shifāʾ* 373.

[70] ʿIyāḍ, *Shifāʾ* 345, 353–4, 386–7.

[71] al-Shāfiʿī, *Umm* VII, 513. (The refusal to accept someone's legal testimony signified his status

The tendency to make a commonsense distinction between serious statements and mere frivolity varies dramatically from jurist to jurist, and does not appear to correspond to any consistent, identifiable pattern of difference between one school of jurisprudence and another. A good illustration is a commentary to a treatise on blasphemous statements written by the Ḥanafite author known as Badr al-Rashīd (d. 768/1366–7). A large proportion of the contents of this commentary – the work of another Ḥanafī jurist, Nūr al-Dīn ʿAlī b. Sulṭān Muḥammad al-Qāriʾ al-Harawī (d. 1014/1605) – consists of all-too-obvious efforts to allow for exceptions from the monotonous string of harsh verdicts of *kufr* (unbelief) that dominate the original treatise. The basis for the exceptions is mostly the analysis of the real intention of the speaker or author making the outrageous utterance, that is to say a conscious distinction between jest and earnest. Al-Qāriʾ al-Harawī seems to be as charitable in his evident endeavour to help offenders come up with acceptable excuses to ward off imputations of unbelief as Badr al-Rashīd is offhanded in distributing the potentially fatal label of 'unbelief', yet both belong to the same legal school.

Like al-Harawī, quite a few mediaeval Muslim jurists did take into consideration the declared or inferred intention (*niyya*) of the person making a statement (as well as other circumstances), thereby extending a principle commonly observed in assessing a host of other legal issues (e.g. oaths).[72] This principle, when applied to *mujūn*, virtually amounted to making a distinction between the seriously offensive and the merely frivolous. Thus, the Muʿtazilite authors Abū Hāshim al-Jubbāʾī (d. 321/933) and al-Qāḍī ʿAbd al-Jabbār al-Hamadhānī (d. 415/1025) seem to have recognised that an offensive act done by way of irony and frivolity (*ʿalā wajh al-sukhriyya wa-l-majāna*) should not be regarded as a proof of unbelief (*kufr*) even if initial impressions would suggest so. Most Zaydite authorities, like the Imam Abū Ṭālib al-Nāṭiq (d. 424/1032), apparently dismissed this distinction.[73] The majority of Sunnite scholars, however, were not so rigid. As the Ḥanafite jurist al-Walwālijī (d. 540/1145–6) quite benevolently puts it, "the words of Muslims should be interpreted in the best and nicest possible way (*yuḥmalu kalām al-muslimīn ʿalā aḥsanihi wa-ajmalihi*)".[74] Like him, a lot of Sunnite jurists would probably have

as an immoral man [*fāsiq*], of which more anon.) A later Shāfiʿite scholar quotes al-Shāfiʿī's dictum in a slightly different wording (*al-shiʿr kalām, ḥasanuhu ḥasan wa-qabīḥuhu qabīḥ*) and says that it is a *ḥadīth mursal*; see al-Haytamī, *Zawājir* II, 215. – The Ḥanbalite Ibn Mufliḥ al-Maqdisī (d. 763/1362) echoes al-Shāfiʿī's principle in the opening words of a short passage on the legal aspects of poetry: "Poetry is like [ordinary] speech (*wa-l-shiʿr ka-l-kalām*)". See Ibn Mufliḥ, *Furūʿ* III, 638.

72 E.g. Ibn al-Ṣalāḥ, *Fatāwā* II, 664; al-Haytamī, *Iʿlām* 361 ["*law qāla lā akhāfu l-qiyāma...*" etc.]; al-Samarqandī, *Fatāwā* 210; al-Walwālijī, *Fatāwī* II, 352 ["*anā lā uḥibbu l-qarʿ...*" etc.] (and cf. V, 418).

73 Ibn Miftāḥ, *Muntazaʿ* X, 510–2.

74 al-Walwālijī, *Fatāwī* V, 417. However, this author seems to be somewhat undecided about the issue, because elsewhere he declares that, despite the difference of opinion among the *ʿulamāʾ*, a man

agreed with the following opinion stressing the necessity of investigating the intention of a person who made an ostensibly outrageous statement:

> If [a religious scholar] is asked to give a *fatwā* concerning a man who uttered something that turns him into an unbeliever – like saying that "prayer is mere play" or "the pilgrimage is an absurdity", or similar things – then [the scholar] should not hastily pronounce that this man's blood can be freely spilt (*ḥalāl al-dam*) or that he must be killed. Instead, he should say [in his legal advice]: "If this has been proved by trustworthy testimony or his own confession (*idhā thabata ʿalayhi dhālik bi-l-bayyina aw al-iqrār*), the ruler must ask him to repent, and if he does, his repentance will be accepted. If he insists and does not repent, he should be killed and such-and-such actions should be taken against him." And he should stress the heinousness of that man's deed. Now, if the words uttered by [the offender] allow various interpretations some of which do not make him an unbeliever, then [the mufti] should not issue a reply; he is free to say [instead]: "Ask him what he meant by saying what he did. If he meant such-and-such, then my reply is such-and-such; and if he meant such-and-such, then the [right] decision is such-and-such..."[75]

And here is a similar opinion from a Ḥanafite author:

> If in the case [being investigated] there are several possible interpretations leading to a charge of unbelief (*wujūh tūjibu l-takfīr*) and one single interpretation that will prevent this charge, then the mufti must incline to that which prevents a charge of unbelief, supposing the best he can about a fellow-Muslim.[76]

The standard sources of *fiqh* provided jurisprudents with a number of categories and terms to facilitate dealing with literary offences against cultural and religious norms. To begin with, certain behaviours associated with libertines were clear cases of transgression, with the *sharīʿa* specifying the appropriate (if not always uncontroversial) punishment as well. Examples include drinking, illicit sex (*zinā* and *liwāṭ*), and to some extent music and dancing too. This sort of legal case presented few difficulties, apart from the question of how to prove that someone did in fact engage in an illicit activity, which is not unique to cases of libertine offenders, and the problem of whether a literary text may be taken for an admission of guilt, which is.

In other cases, jurists would utilise well-known and fairly obvious legal categories, such as *qadhf* (calumny, slander); insults to God, the angels, the prophet Muḥammad or earlier prophets (*sabb Allāh / al-malāʾika / al-rasūl / al-anbiyāʾ*); or *zandaqa* (heresy),

who utters words indicating unbelief without being a genuine unbeliever (*aṭlaqa kalimat al-kufr illā annahu lā yaʿtaqidu*) is probably to be regarded as an unbeliever 'because he has made light of his religion' (*istakhaffa bi-dīnihi*). See op.cit. V, 422.

[75] Ibn al-Ṣalāḥ, *Fatāwā* I, 77.

[76] al-Qāriʾ, *Sharḥ* 230.

and then – disregarding all difference between jesting and serious statements – treat certain literary motifs as being tantamount to such an offence.[77] This procedure had the undeniable advantage of making it easier to specify the proper punishment, and the disadvantage of often requiring tortuous arguments to present a literary passage as a positive, affirmative statement of offensive opinions. A relevant example is the legal treatment of charges of illegitimate descent or illicit sex by innuendo (*kināya* and *taʿrīḍ*) instead of explicit allegation – a mainstay of *hijāʾ* poetry and not unknown in *mujūn* either. Here some jurists took pains to show that saying or writing such a thing amounted to a case of calumny (*qadhf*; technically a false accusation of fornication or adultery) and should be punished accordingly, while other jurists disagreed with this view. (Even addressing a man contemptuously as 'you son of a tailor' could be interpreted by some as an instance of *qadhf* if the man's father had not actually been a tailor. In the same way, calling an Arab a Berber or Persian might qualify as prosecutable calumny.) Subtleties of the issue gave rise to further disagreements.[78]

In yet other cases, the absence of directly applicable categories in the *sharīʿa* led scholars to have recourse to terms of rather obscure meaning encountered in the main sources of the *sharīʿa* – especially in the Quran – and equate such terms with certain types of statements or behaviours typical of libertines. Foremost on the list of these elastic terms must be *fisq* ('immorality'). While the legal consequences of someone being a *fāsiq* (an immoral person) were roughly clear, much more controversial was the issue of precisely what turns a man into a *fāsiq*. Be that as it may, there was little doubt among Muslim jurisprudents that a libertine (*mājin*) was to be regarded as *fāsiq*, with all the legal consequences thereof. Among the things mentioned in legal sources as constituting *fisq* are quite a few that also happen to be commonly associated with the behaviour and speech of libertines. Examples include the neglect of prayer, drinking wine, and so on.[79] Some activities might be

77 On the legal concept of *sabb Allāh* etc., and that of *zandaqa* (all these being manifestations of unbelief, *kufr*), as well as on the recommended legal action against these offences, see for instance al-Haytamī, *Iʿlām* 381 sqq; ʿIyād, *Shifāʾ* 345–75, 388–9; al-Wansharīsī, *Miʿyār* II, 327 sqq; Ibn Juzayy, *Qawānīn* 370–1; Ibn Mufliḥ, *Furūʿ* III, 417; Ibn al-Ṣalāḥ, *Fatāwā* II, 465–6; al-Ṭūsī, *Nihāya* II, 751; Ibn Ḥazm, *Muḥallā* XII, 431–9; and also Fierro 2001: 463–6. For some jurisprudents, the concept of 'insulting the Prophet' was apparently elastic enough to be applicable to cases of jestful *mujūn*. A pertinent example is the case of a North African poet who, being told that the Prophet had been seen in a dream condemning one of his poems, playfully remarked: "Poor Muḥammad, taking all the trouble [of travelling] from Medina to here." See al-Wansharīsī, *Miʿyār* II, 364–5.

78 E.g. Ibn Juzayy, *Qawānīn* 362; al-Wansharīsī, *Miʿyār* II, 422–3; Ibn Mufliḥ, *Furūʿ* III, 371–4; al-Shāfiʿī, *Umm* VIII, 359–62; al-Māwardī, *Aḥkām* 348–50; Ibn al-Ṣalāḥ, *Fatāwā* II, 470; al-Nawawī, *Fatāwī* 128, 129; al-Samarqandī, *Fatāwā* 260–1; al-Walwālijī, *Fatāwī* II, 248–9, 253; Ibn Ḥazm, *Muḥallā* XII, 219 sqq; al-Ṭūsī, *Nihāya* II, 743–4, 749–50; Ibn Miftāḥ, *Muntazaʿ* X, 99–101, 108–11; Ibn Hubayra, *Ikhtilāf* II, 194–5, 197.

79 Some authorities went further and classified more controversial activities – such as gossiping (*ghība*), playing chess or backgammon, listening to music – as grounds for exclusion from legal

less clear-cut cases of *fisq*, but still cause for legal disadvantages. Some authors, like the Ḥanafite Abū Bakr Aḥmad al-Khaṣṣāf (d. 261/874), even explicitly state that behaviour which can be categorised as *mujūn* and *sukhf* (licentiousness, frivolity and vulgarity), whether or not constituting *fisq*, disqualifies the perpetrator from testifying in a legal case (*v. i.*). For instance, using abusive terms about people is according to this author a form of *mujūn*, as are such activities as the frequenting of the shameless drinking parties of dissolute men (*majālis al-majāna ʿalā l-shurb wa-l-fujūr*), singing, playing musical instruments, and other types of dishonourable conduct. All of these misdeeds are treated similarly to *fisq*.[80]

In theory, *fisq* would entail a number of negative legal consequences. (Whether these were in fact applied in practice is a different question, and will be treated below.) First and foremost, according to the practically universal consensus of the religious scholars, the legal testimony of a *fāsiq* was to be rejected; the only circumstance in which it would be heard and accepted was after the *fāsiq* had repented and sufficient time had passed to ascertain the honesty of his contrition. But even this exception was subject to controversy among the *ʿulamāʾ*, with some

testimony (that is to say, manifestations of *fisq*). Indeed, any activity that potentially marred one's reputation (*yusqiṭ al-murūʾa*) sufficed. In a brief but very telling passage, the Ḥanbalite authority Ibn ʿAqīl (d. 513/1119) not only states that unblemished respectability (*murūʾa*) is a prerequisite of being accepted as a witness in court, but goes on to list people who tell droll stories (*yaḥkī l-ḥikāyāt al-muḍḥika*) among those whose testimony cannot be allowed. Another eminent Ḥanbalite scholar, Ibn Mufliḥ al-Maqdisī (d. 763/1362), held similar views, and in one of his books – partly drawing on earlier authorities – gives a detailed list of attributes incompatible with *murūʾa* and therefore with testifying in legal cases. For this study, the most important items on the list are the following: talking about sex with one's womenfolk or addressing them in a bawdy manner (*khiṭāb fāḥish*) in the presence of other people, narrating drolleries (*ḥākī l-muḍḥikāt*), loud or rowdy laughter (*tashadduquhu bi-ḍaḥik wa-qahqaha*), habitual playing (*dawām al-laʿib*). And the list goes on and on. – Authors belonging to other legal schools might also emphasise dignified conduct as a necessary attribute of an acceptable witness; the Ḥanafite commentator al-Jaṣṣāṣ (d. 370/980) even specifies that a man of advanced age who talks silly and droll things in public places ("*waqafa ʿalā l-nās fī l-aswāq wa-takallama bi-l-sukhf wa-l-hazl*") cannot be allowed to testify in court, although he adds that this behaviour in itself is not prohibited and does not constitute *fisq*. Al-Shāfiʿī (d. 204/820) holds that a man whose habit is to drink alcoholic beverages other than grape-wine (*anbidha*) in the company of indiscreet good-for-nothings (*ahl al-safah al-ẓāhir*) cannot be allowed to testify, not because of his drinking *per se* but because of his disregard for respectability and his overtly unbecoming conduct (*bi-ṭarḥihi l-murūʾa wa-iẓhārihi l-safah*). A very similar view is expressed by the Transoxanian Ḥanafite authority Abū l-Fatḥ al-Walwālijī (d. 540/1145–6). On these and other aspects of the issue (including the legal grounds of *fisq* and some of its attributes), see for instance Ibn Juzayy, *Qawānīn* 313; Ibn ʿAqīl, *Tadhkira* 359–60; Ibn Mufliḥ, *Furūʿ* III, 637; al-Samarqandī, *Fatāwā* 393–4; 396; al-Khaṣṣāf, *Adab* 45, 51–2; 305, 311; al-Shāfiʿī, *Umm* VII, 512, 514–5, 518; al-Walwālijī, *Fatāwī* IV, 42–4; al-Nawawī, *Fatāwī* 137; al-Haytamī, *Iʿlām* 355; Ibn Miftāḥ, *Muntazaʿ* IX, 416–7; X, 158; al-Bustī, *Baḥth* 3–4, 93; Hamdan, Schmidtke 2008: 113–5; Kruse 1984: 432; and also Fofana 1425 (A.H.): I, 30–3. For a helpful analysis of the Muslim legal concept of *fisq*, cf. Mezziane 2008: 281 [note 14], 291–2.

[80] al-Khaṣṣāf, *Adab* 303–6.

legal schools allowing and some rejecting the possibility, in addition to contested procedural minutiae.[81] It is in a Twelver Shiʿite legal source of the 5th/11th century – an influential work by Abū Jaʿfar Muḥammad al-Ṭūsī (d. 460/1067) – that I have found the most explicit verdict concerning the position of a libertine in a courtroom: "The testimony of a libertine or a foul-mouthed man must not be accepted (*wa-lā tuqbalu shahādat mājin wa-lā faḥḥāsh*)".[82] Secondly, persons known for their *fisq* were theoretically disallowed from occupying certain prestigious posts such as those of mufti, judge, imam, muezzin, or manager of a pious endowment[83] – not that they were likely to apply in the first place. Thirdly, some jurists would give judges the power to place what they called a *safīh* under tutelage (*ḥajr*), a status properly belonging to minors only. While the exact definition of a *safīh* (a vague term meaning all of 'foolish, silly, vulgar, impertinent, prodigal, careless, irresponsible') was open to debate, some authorities (most notably al-Shāfiʿī) apparently considered reckless and shameful behaviour – commonly associated with *mujūn* as well as *fisq* – to be the hallmarks of a *safīh* person. This stance, however, was hotly disputed by the majority of *ʿulamāʾ* (most notably by Abū Ḥanīfa) who were adamant that adult men should be given the right to control and manage their own property whatever their moral and religious shortcomings.[84] Furthermore, some jurists urged that decent men should avoid being friends with a *fāsiq* – let alone taking part in his sinful conversations and parties or otherwise socialise with him – although they usually did not object to ordinary, polite social interaction with him.[85]

---

[81] E.g. Ibn Hubayra, *Ikhtilāf* II, 414–5; al-Marwazī, *Ikhtilāf* 555; Ibn Mufliḥ, *Ādāb* I, 66, 73–4; Ibn ʿAqīl, *Tadhkira* 361; al-Walwālijī, *Fatāwī* IV, 52; al-Khaṣṣāf, *Adab* 118; al-Ghazālī, *Fatāwā* 264; al-Ṭūsī, *Nihāya* I, 329–9; Ibn Miftāḥ, *Muntazaʿ* IX, 399–400; and especially Fofana 1425 (A.H.): II, 735–950. A related problem was whether it was legally acceptable for someone to repent from a particular type of sin instead of all sinful activities. Muʿtazilites, for instance, considered the notion an absurdity. See Ibn Mufliḥ, *Ādāb* I, 62–3.

[82] al-Ṭūsī, *Nihāya* I, 328.

[83] E.g. Ibn al-Ṣalāḥ, *Fatāwā* I, 21, 44; al-Khaṣṣāf, *Adab* 117; Ibn ʿAqīl, *Tadhkira* 45–6; al-Nawawī, *Fatāwī* 95; al-Wansharīsī, *Miʿyār* I, 131–2; and especially Fofana 1425 (A.H.): I, 110–38, 223–6, 515–9; II, 105–45.

[84] On this issue cf. Fofana 1425 (A.H.): I, 561–71; and Ibn Hubayra, *Ikhtilāf* I, 426–7; Ibn Juzayy, *Qawānīn* 325–7; Ibn ʿAqīl, *Tadhkira* 140–1; al-Shāfiʿī, *Umm* IV, 459–60; Ibn al-Ṣalāḥ, *Fatāwā* II, 721; al-Samarqandī, *Fatāwā* 419; al-Khaṣṣāf, *Adab* 271–2, 282; Ibn Miftāḥ, *Muntazaʿ* IX, 580.

[85] al-Haytamī, *Zawājir* I, 110; II, 197; Ibn Miftāḥ, *Muntazaʿ* X, 543–7; Ibn Baraka, *Jāmiʿ* I, 181–2; al-Samarqandī, *Fatāwā* 286. Some authorities even regarded eating the flesh of animals slaughtered by a *fāsiq* to be disapproved (*makrūh*); see Ibn Juzayy, *Qawānīn* 186. The Mālikite author al-Lakhmī (d. 468/1075–6) even allows the possibility that a man of disreputable behaviour – specifically, one who drinks and frequents the company of similar people – may in certain circumstances be forced to divorce his wife. See Ḥalūlū, *Masāʾil* 317. The Twelver Shiʿite jurist Abū Jaʿfar al-Ṭūsī (d. 460/1067) thinks that it is undesirable for a father to allow her daughter to marry an indiscreet *fāsiq*, but he opines that once the marriage takes place it is to be considered valid. See al-Ṭūsī, *Nihāya* II, 470; and also cf. Fofana 1425 (A.H.): I, 335–8. In addition, Muʿtazilite authors discussed the

After these observations concerning the general approach of jurists in formulating their views on literary texts, we can now turn our attention to the actual literary phenomena they had anything to say on. Among the literary themes and devices that many jurisprudents touch upon in their works are hyperboles (especially in praise-poetry), various motifs of malicious invective poetry (*hijāʾ*) – especially sexual innuendoes – and of course a number of *mujūn* motifs.

It has already been noted in the first chapter, in discussing some of the dominant norms of mediaeval Muslim society, that a negative view of any kind of 'unserious', 'childish', 'unworthy' discourse and conduct is a recurrent attitude in Middle Eastern culture. While it definitely cannot be ascribed to Islam – defenders of humour and jesting would phrase their arguments in Islamic terms, as did opponents – this mentality was undeniably characteristic of a certain type of religious scholar. (Ironically, the attitude belittling jesting and all unworthy subjects has much more to do with ancient Bedouin conceptions of manliness and honourable conduct than with any specifically Islamic precept.) The pious avoidance of 'wasting time' on 'valueless subjects' (i.e. anything not directly relevant to religion) probably remained an ideal rather than an actual pattern of behaviour in most cases – after all, it is not so easy to resist humour and merriness when everyone else is having a good time. A handful of *ʿulamāʾ*, however, did manage to maintain a dour attitude against all odds, and some of them would even make attempts to force others to abandon all kinds of *mujūn*, irony or humour. Whether such attempts were successful is a different question, and it seems that most often they were not. In fact, it might be precisely the failure effectively to censor and control behaviour and speech that makes the tone of some religious scholars so belligerently self-righteous. Not surprisingly, scholars embracing the often austere Ḥanbalite school of law tended to display particular harshness and inflexibility in their views on *mujūn*. A good example is the famous Ḥanbalite jurisprudent Ibn Taymiyya (d. 728/1328); a scholar notorious for his stringency, and as a consequence a rather marginal figure in his own time.[86] However, similar inflexibility characterises the views of the Ḥanafite author Ibn Baydakīn al-Turkumānī too. The unequivocal condemnation of all frivolous or humorous uses of Quranic phrases and citations expressed by this savant seems to be a fairly standard Ḥanbalite approach to the phenomenon. (Not incidentally, the excerpt also hints at the ubiquity of such joking in popular culture, being as it is too specific and detailed to stem from the author's own imagination.) Note, in particular, the verdict of this scholar that such uses of the Quran's text tend to constitute unbelief:

---

question of whether one should thank a *fāsiq* for some favour rendered; see Hamdan, Schmidtke 2008: 57–8.

[86] See for instance Shoshan 1993: 68–9; Calder 2000: 78.

> Reprehensible innovations in the domain of speech (*al-bidaʿ al-qawliyya*) include jesting with the words of the Quran. This makes the perpetrator either an unbeliever or blameworthy. An example of the kind that constitutes unbelief is when a man stands on an elevated place, with the people gathered beneath him, and starts to imitate preachers and those delivering the sermon [at the Friday prayer]. He cites the words of the Prophet[87], then, in a dragging voice and swaying his head, he says [in typical Quranic style]: "Oh you people (*ayyuhā l-nās*)..." And those around him are in paroxysms of laughter. This renders all of them unbelievers.[88]

This author was not alone in regarding the public delivery of mock sermons amidst a laughing audience as constituting unbelief. However, the harsh conclusion of al-Turkumānī quoted here is far from representing the consensus of religious experts on the issue; indeed, many *ʿulamāʾ* expressly rejected it.[89]

The sanctioning of linguistic usages on the basis of stern and unrealistic ideals of piety was an ambition of quite a few religious scholars, but the possibility of actually enforcing such speech controls was of course infinitesimal. Religious ideals of acceptable speech – artistic or otherwise – generally included the avoidance of lying, calumny, gossip, gratuitous oath formulas, sarcasm, allusions, mockery, vulgarity, obscenity, and the recounting of debauched or improper behaviour. That list, as will be obvious to the reader, pretty much approximates a full inventory of the motifs of *mujūn*. Lying in particular was broadly defined – as noted earlier in this chapter – so that a lot of common poetic motifs would fall in this category: poetic hyperboles, innuendoes in invective poetry, and any fictitious (hence factually 'untrue') statement. One finds an outline of such attitudes in the ethical work of the Shāfiʿite scholar al-Ghazālī (450/1058–505/1111), as well as that of the Ḥanbalite

87 I am not sure that this translation of the word is correct. The Arabic text has *yatlū kalām al-ḥabīb* (lit. 'he cites the speech of the beloved'), and my tentative translation is based on the fact that a common epithet of the Prophet Muḥammad among Muslims has been 'God's beloved'. That it could be a reference to citing love poetry (and scandalously prefacing it to a mock religious sermon) is a possibility, but to me it does not appear very likely. The context does not really support it, and in Arabic love poetry the beloved tends to be described rather than made to speak, although some poets (e.g. Abū Nuwās) did occasionally use the motif of quoting the words of the beloved.

88 Ibn Baydakīn, *Lumaʿ* I, 178–9.

89 Cf. al-Haytamī, *Iʿlām* 362. For more on mock sermons (*waʿẓ ʿalā sabīl al-istihzāʾ*), see op.cit. 372–3; and Badr, *Risāla* 30; al-Qāriʾ, *Sharḥ* 159–60. Elsewhere in al-Haytamī's work, an unspecified Ḥanafite scholar (or scholars: *baʿḍ al-Ḥanafiyya*) is quoted who considered even those who listen to and laugh at blasphemous talk to have become unbelievers; see al-Haytamī, *Iʿlām* 397. (There is no chronological difficulty that would exclude the possibility that al-Haytamī is referring to Ibn Baydakīn al-Turkumānī here.) That passive participation in blasphemous joking (i.e. listening to and enjoying it) is as grave a sin as actively engaging in it is a view shared by various Ḥanafite authorities, such as al-Ṭāhir b. Aḥmad al-Bukhārī (d. 542/1147–8, author of *Khulāṣat al-fatāwī*) and Aḥmad b. Muḥammad b. Abī Bakr al-Ḥanafī (d. 522/1128, author of *Majmaʿ al-fatāwī*); see Badr, *Risāla* 19; al-Qāriʾ, *Sharḥ* 117–8.

Ibn Mufliḥ al-Maqdisī (d. 763/1362).[90] Like al-Ghazālī, other *ʿulamāʾ* of various legal schools would also allow some room for 'innocuous' humour (very narrowly defined) and make efforts to specify impermissible forms of joking (very broadly defined).[91]

Some scholars of religion displayed an uncompromisingly harsh attitude to poetry in general as a condemnable pastime that, at best, distracts from more important, pious concerns.[92] Others were more discriminating in this respect. Mention has already been made of al-Shāfiʿī's opinion – shared by many other authorities – that poetry is just like any other type of discourse as regards its evaluation: whatever is acceptable in prose or ordinary talk is so in poetry too. As reprehensible forms of poetic expression, he singles out invective verse (*hijāʾ*), excessive hyperboles ('lying') in panegyrics, love poems about women other than the poet's wife (but only if the object of the poem is named in it). He also adds that prose texts that may be damaging to someone's reputation are to be disapproved (*yukrahu*). Joking (*mizāḥ*) he apparently finds innocuous in itself, except when it involves malicious insinuations about another man's descent, hurtful remarks, or bawdiness (*fāḥisha*).[93] A later Shāfiʿite author, Abū l-ʿAbbās Aḥmad al-Haytamī (d. 974/1567), states that describing sinful behaviour (e.g. drinking or fornication) in a frivolous way with the aim of making fun is prohibited (*al-taḥadduth bi-l-maʿṣiya tafakkuhan [...] ḥarām*).[94] In another work, he strongly condemns frivolous treatments of the themes of Islamic religious duties, especially prayer and the Ramadan fast.[95] (As we showed in Chapter Two, both were favourite motifs of *mujūn* literature.) This scholar, who devotes considerable attention to the issue of literature, also strongly objects to certain types of love poetry: first, any love poem addressed to a boy, be he mentioned by name or remain unnamed (although some Shāfiʿite authorities, like al-Adhruʿī [d. 783/1381], allowed amorous poetry about an unnamed boy); secondly, love

90 al-Ghazālī, *Iḥyāʾ* II, 143–4, 150–7, 159–65; Ibn Mufliḥ, *Ādāb* I, 14–21. Also see al-Sakhāwī, *Iʿlān* 88 [Shāfiʿite]; al-Haytamī, *Zawājir* I, 118; II, 22 [Shāfiʿite]. On the significance of such passages, see Ibrahim 1994: 67–8.

91 According to a Ḥanafī authority, joking with women unrelated to oneself and with handsome youths is prohibited, and doing so with 'innovators' (*mubtadiʿ*), unjust men, despots, and reprobates is to be disapproved of. There are no limits, however, to joking with old women. On the other hand, utterly forbidden is to use joking as an excuse for saying anything even remotely questionable, especially about the *ʿulamāʾ*. See Ibn Baydakīn, *Lumaʿ* I, 160, 178–80; and also see Ibn Qutayba, *ʿUyūn* I(i), 44; Ibn Mufliḥ, *Ādāb* III, 172–3.

92 See for instance Ibn Baydakīn, *Lumaʿ* I, 92. In contrast, a manual for *muḥtasib*s even advises the teaching of poetry to schoolchildren provided it is not of the silly and indecent variety ("*mā yustaḥsanu fī [...] al-ashʿār dūna sakhīfihā wa-mustardhalihā* "), viz. not *mujūn* and *hijāʾ*. See Ibn Bassām, *Nihāya* 161.

93 al-Shāfiʿī, *Umm* VII, 513–4.

94 al-Haytamī, *Zawājir* II, 127.

95 al-Haytamī, *Iʿlām* 371–2; and also cf. Badr, *Risāla* 46; al-Qāriʾ, *Sharḥ* 214–5.

poems about a woman who is not the poet's wife or slave-girl if she is mentioned by name; thirdly, love poems about an unnamed woman if it contains obscene language or the mention of private parts.[96] Hurtful invective poetry against a fellow-Muslim is generally condemned by Shāfiʿites – even if there remained some minor disagreements as regards certain aspects of the issue – and so are excessive ('mendacious') or outright blasphemous hyperboles in praise-poetry.[97] Ḥanafites seem to have differed little from the Shāfiʿites in their attitudes to literary frivolities. For a Ḥanafite jurist of Transoxania, Abū l-Fatḥ al-Walwālijī (d. 540/1145–6), it is what appears to be *mujūn*-like poetry that is particularly problematic: "Reading the verses of Arabs, if they contain mentions of immorality and wine, is disapproved because it means the mentioning of abominations (*qirāʾat ashʿār al-ʿarab idhā kāna fīhi dhikr al-fisq wa-l-khamr makrūh li-annahu dhikr al-fawāḥish*)."[98] The Ḥanbalite scholar Ibn Mufliḥ al-Maqdisī (d. 763/1362), whose pietistic dislike of many aspects of poetry has just been noted above, specifies invective poetry, exaggerated panegyrics, appreciative descriptions of wine, and delicate love poetry addressed to boys or to a particular woman who is not the poet's wife or concubine. On the other hand, he finds no fault with love poems about one's own wife or slave-girl; and the literature of the pre-Islamic period he calls useful.[99] This latter topic is also mentioned by Abū l-ʿAbbās al-Wansharīsī (d. 914/1508), whose collection of North African and Andalusian *fatwā*s offers glimpses into Mālikite views on certain aspects of Arabic literature with a relevance to *mujūn*. He says that Mālikite scholars generally saw no problem with studying the great pre-Islamic odes, even in study-groups congregating in mosques, but were wary of the 'untrue' and indecent contents ("*mā fīhā min al-kadhib wa-l-fuḥsh*") of the *maqāmas*, some scholars banishing the teaching thereof from the mosque precincts.[100] Elsewhere in the same work a *fatwā* of Ibn Rushayd al-Fihrī al-Sabtī (657/1259–721/1321) is cited concerning the permissibility or otherwise of graphic descriptions of the bodily charms of the

96 al-Haytamī, *Zawājir* II, 211–2. For more on the legal issue of the permissibility of addressing love poems to the above-mentioned categories of persons, see El-Rouayheb 2005: 141–5.

97 al-Haytamī, *Zawājir* II, 212–6; al-Haytamī, *Iʿlām* 384.

98 al-Walwālijī, *Fatāwī* II, 320. Poetry in itself he does not consider to be discreditable, and, somewhat surprisingly, he even states that it is licit to sing bawdy poetry (as long as it is not one's own composition). Elsewhere he also states that expressing the wish that there were no compulsory fasting in Ramadan – which we showed in Chapter Two was a frequent theme of *mujūn* poetry – does not constitute unbelief. See op.cit. IV, 145, 146; V, 419. (And cf. Badr, *Risāla* 45 and al-Qāriʾ, *Sharḥ* 211–2 on the wish not to have to fast.)

99 Ibn Mufliḥ, *Furūʿ* III, 638.

100 al-Wansharīsī, *Miʿyār* I, 24; XI, 13. (The *maqāmas* of al-Ḥarīrī [d. 516/1122] formed part of the usual curriculum of traditional Muslim institutions of higher learning.) Some jurists also strongly condemned folk epics like those about ʿAntar, Dhū l-Himma (*vulgo* 'Dilhimma') and al-Baṭṭāl, labelling them 'lying' (*kadhib*); see op.cit. XI, 172.

beloved. He observes the lack of consensus among scholars, and then quotes approvingly an earlier (Ḥanbalite) view to the effect that this poetic theme is not prohibited. However, he proceeds to specify that this verdict is only valid under certain conditions, namely, if the poem is about one's own wife or concubine, or about an unnamed woman, whereas a love poem about a male is only permissible as a poetic exercise or when the use of the masculine is merely a grammatical or metrical necessity. Even then the practice is disapproved, or *makrūh*.[101] Another important Mālikite scholar, al-Qāḍī ʿIyāḍ al-Yaḥṣubī (496/1103–544/1146), also has something to say on the subject of literature in his *Kitāb al-shifāʾ*, but the specificity of the book's topic – namely, how to deal with insults to the Prophet's memory – inevitably limits the scope of this discussion. This author very strongly condemns all careless literary treatments of any of the prophets, especially similes and metaphors likening any person to the prophets or angels in any sense, and does not exclude jesting (*qaṣd al-hazl*) from this general condemnation. He apparently dislikes even such ubiquitous, hackneyed phrases as the saying that someone has shown the patience of Job (*ṣabr Ayyūb*) – as common in Arabic poetry as in speech. In common with other jurists just discussed, hyperboles in praise-poetry are particularly odious in his eyes. For most of these motifs, he advocates imprisonment and painful corporal punishment as appropriate chastisement for the poet.[102] Finally, to cite an opinion outside the Sunnite schools of law. The eminent Shiʿite author Abū Jaʿfar al-Ṭūsī (d. 460/1067) declares that earning money with lampoons (*hijāʾ*) against decent Muslim men is prohibited (*ḥarām*) – rather than just disapproved – while composing panegyrics about such men, even for money, is unobjectionable as long as no 'lying' is involved ("*bi-l-ṣidq min al-aqwāl*").[103]

One aspect of *mujūn* literature – indeed, of literature in general – that drew the particular attention of some jurists is the use of Quranic quotations (*iqtibās*). Some religious scholars issued detailed legal opinions (*fatwā*) dedicated to the subject, while others discussed it in passing within the framework of a larger manual of Muslim law.[104] (Many, perhaps most, *ʿulamāʾ* remained silent on this issue.) Muslim

---

[101] al-Wansharīsī, *Miʿyār* XI, 48.

[102] ʿIyāḍ, *Shifāʾ* 357–9. He singles out for special condemnation some very common motifs of Arabic poetry – such as playful metaphorical references to Riḍwān and Mālik, the guardians of Paradise and Hell respectively – as well as a number of poets like al-Mutanabbī, Abū Nuwās, Ibn Hāniʾ al-Andalusī, and Abū l-ʿAlāʾ al-Maʿarrī.

[103] al-Ṭūsī, *Nihāya* I, 367, 369; II, 751.

[104] For a list of authors (including *ʿulamāʾ* as well as littérateurs) who wrote full treatises on the subject of *iqtibās* and its permissibility or otherwise, cf. al-ʿAskar 1425 (A.H.): 6–8. The *fatwā* given by the famous Egyptian Shāfiʿite scholar Jalāl al-Dīn al-Suyūṭī (d. 911/1505) under the title *Raqʿ al-libās wa-kashf al-iltibās fī ḍarb al-mathal min al-Qurʾān wa-l-iqtibās* to clarify the subject is especially interesting, as it summarises the findings and opinions of earlier authorities. See its text in al-Suyūṭī, *Ḥāwī* I, 248–72.

jurists would lend attention to such aspects of the issue as whether the Quranic wording is slightly altered, and whether the Quranic phrase is transplanted into prose or verse, and into a serious or facetious text. Predictably, verbatim *iqtibās* was less problematic than one with a slight alteration of words, prose by and large less problematic than verse; and serious contexts most certainly less problematic than facetious ones.[105] For instance, al-Suyūṭī (d. 911/1505) states that the total consensus of his fellow-Shāfiᶜites is that *iqtibās* in prose is permissible (*jāʾiz*). As for verse, he observes that despite the ubiquity of the practice in Arabic poetry old and new, Muslim jurists failed to come up with explicit guidelines about it, and proceeds to deduce from their silence on this matter that *iqtibās* in poetry must be as permissible (*jāʾiz*) as it is in prose, or else they would have declared it prohibited. He adds that the fact that many earlier Muslim scholars of good repute have themselves used *iqtibās* in their own poetry is further proof of the permissibility thereof. However, other scholars – al-Bāqillānī (d. 403/1013), al-Nawawī (d. 676/1277) and Bahāʾ al-Dīn al-Subkī (d. 773/1371–2) for instance – would permit Quranic quotations in prose but regarded it as reprehensible (*makrūh*) in verse, probably because the text of the Quran itself insists that it is not poetry. According to al-Suyūṭī, such disapproval does not mean that *iqtibās* in poetry is prohibited.[106] These observations all pertain to serious uses of Quranic quotations only, not to *mujūn* and frivolities ("*wa-maḥall dhālika kullihi fī ghayr al-hazl wa-l-khalāᶜa wa-l-mujūn*"). Regarding jestful *iqtibās*, al-Suyūṭī states – on the authority of al-Nawawī among others – that Quranic quotations in humorous contexts are to be disapproved (*yukrahu*).[107] Corresponding closely to al-Suyūṭī's opinion, the general attitude of Muslim jurists seems to have been that *iqtibās* is problematic only if the context into which the Quranic citation is inserted is a frivolous one, and the purport of the quoted verse is thereby altered in an unseemly way. That is to say, *iqtibās* in *mujūn* texts is by definition problematic. Indeed Muslim jurists almost unanimously disapprove of it, if with varying vehemence. Whether the practice must be censured and punished was somewhat unclear, as was the appropriate punishment applicable in such cases. For instance, the Ḥanbalite scholar Ibn ᶜAqīl (d. 513/1119) simply says that using Quranic quotations in an improper context is not allowed (*lā yajūzu*).[108] In an interesting passage by the Shāfiᶜite jurist Abū l-ᶜAbbās al-Haytamī (d. 974/1567) we find more specific instructions on what to make of frivolous *iqtibās*. Al-Haytamī first cites what he apparently considers a particularly hideous example of outrageous *iqtibās* by 'some rash and frivolous men' (*baᶜḍ al-mujāzifīn al-mutahawwirīn*), which

105 Cf. al-ᶜAskar 1425 (A.H.): 28–33, 59, 64–5.
106 al-Suyūṭī, *Ḥāwī* I, 248, 265–6, 271.
107 al-Suyūṭī, *Ḥāwī* I, 251, 266.
108 Ibn Mufliḥ, *Ādāb* II, 226. On the subject, see al-ᶜAskar 1425 (A.H.): 59–60, 73, 79.

is based on the deliberate misapplication of Quranic phrases, in this case the much-discussed mysterious letters appearing at the beginning of certain chapters of the Quran. Then follows his verdict: "This is monstrous frivolity, and yet the general statement that it constitutes unbelief is unlikely [to be correct], except in [the case of a poet] who says that that is indeed the meaning of those letters [in their Quranic context] (*wa-hādhā tahawwur fāḥish wa-maʿa dhālika iṭlāq al-kufr fīhi baʿīd illā fī-man qāla inna hādhā maʿnā tilka l-ḥurūf*)".[109] The Ḥanafite scholar Ibn Ḥijja al-Ḥamawī (d. 837/1434) classifies *iqtibās* into the three categories of acceptable (*maqbūl*), permissible (*mubāḥ*) and unacceptable (*mardūd*), and relegates all facetious uses of Quranic quotations (*taḍmīn āya karīma fī maʿnā hazl*) to the third category.[110]

In addition to *iqtibās* in the context of *mujūn* literature, a lot of scholars from the earliest times also deplored the gratuitous use of Quranic phrases in speech in mundane, banal contexts, a widespread custom by all appearances. Indeed, some ʿulamāʾ even classified many utterances of this kind (if used in a sarcastic or frivolous sense) as indicating unbelief (*kufr*).[111] Besides jesting with Quranic phrases, another type of *iqtibās* practically all scholars agree on condemning is the use of Quranic phrases pertinent to God in reference to humans.[112] (As must be obvious from the material presented in Chapter Two, these virtually unanimous views of jurists seem to have had little influence on the production of *mujūn* literature.)

The *ʿulamāʾ* were a group whose job it was explicitly to formulate norms, mostly defined in religious terms, and they naturally had an interest in enforcing conformity to those norms once they were established. Thus one would intuitively expect this group to have been the most severe in their condemnation of *mujūn* and the least flexible in granting a margin of tolerance. The most likely candidate for a group having a serious conflict with libertinism and libertines is, it seems, the *ʿulamāʾ*. While this intuition cannot be said to be entirely wrong, the religious scholars, like any other constituent part of the society, were not a monolithic bloc. We have already remarked on the variety of opinions within the *ʿulamāʾ* class, but internal differences

[109] The point of the poem is very hard to do justice to in a language other than Arabic, but it can be summarised as follows. The poet treats the letter combinations *a-l-m* and *a-l-m-ṣ* (Quran 2:1 and 7:1) as though they were the Arabic words 'pain' (*alam*) and 'sucking [the saliva of the beloved]' (*al-maṣṣ*), respectively, which they are not. He then asks his beloved to cure the former with allowing him to do the latter. See the discussion in al-Haytamī, *Iʿlām* 368.

[110] Which he immediately illustrates with an outrageous couplet setting two Quranic verses in an obscene context. See Ibn Ḥijja, *Khizāna* IV, 357. It is questionable if, in expressing this opinion, the author is wearing his jurist's hat – for he was also a noted littérateur and this work is a work of *adab* – but al-Suyūṭī obviously regarded this passage by Ibn Ḥijja as a valid legal opinion because he cites it (in a slightly different wording) in his *fatwā* on the subject of *iqtibās*; see al-Suyūṭī, *Ḥāwī* I, 266.

[111] al-ʿAskar 1425 (A.H.): 89–90. See some examples (replete with condemnation) in Badr, *Risāla* 23–5; al-Qārī', *Sharḥ* 133–4, 136, 138–9; al-Haytamī, *Iʿlām* 369; and al-Suyūṭī, *Ḥāwī* I, 249.

[112] al-ʿAskar 1425 (A.H.): 65, 74–5, 78.

apparently went well beyond that dimension.[113] One ought not to forget that not everyone is incorruptible, and unless we posit that a clerical vocation in itself ennobles human character, material interests can be thought to be a factor in the views, and certainly the behaviour, of religious scholars. On the most basic level – which is quite important and relevant to our purpose in this study – the group of *ʿulamāʾ* was composed of individuals with a wide range of personalities. Some of them extremely intolerant, others remarkably lenient, their characters definitely had an impact on their practice, and quite possibly on their theory too. (It would be hard to fail to detect the hallmarks of the personality of an Ibn Taymiyya or an al-Suyūṭī in their respective legal opinions.)

Despite the evident and predictable failure to make most people conform to their rigorous ideals of language use, even the most tolerant scholars formulated their prescriptions, and the more intolerant among them – often but not exclusively Ḥanbalites – would not cease to rail against the depravity of their contemporaries. Thus one strict Ḥanafite authority displays especial dissatisfaction with the use of jocular religious references in the funny rhymed ditties that sellers in the market used to advertise their products.[114] However, such quixotic attempts at actually policing speech habits (beyond pious admonitions) seem to have been very few.

Later in this section, we will come across markedly secular arguments, made by mediaeval Arabic literary critics, for the permissibility of vulgar and scurrilous motifs in literature. However, it must also be noted that the defence of joking and humour – although not of *mujūn* in general – could be phrased in religious terms no less than could the opposite view. To wit, it was pointed out that a number of *ḥadīths* unequivocally show the Prophet Muḥammad engaging in light-hearted joking, and if he did, then it must surely be allowable to later generations of Muslims too. At least some of the relevant *ḥadīths* were widely recognised as reliable.[115]

---

[113] On this question, see for instance Mottahedeh 1980: 137.

[114] E.g. "[Buy] beans, and God bless the prophet (*al-fūl wa-l-ṣalāt ʿalā l-rasūl*)", "Lentils from Hebron, and peace upon Abraham (*ʿadas al-Khalīl wa-ʿalā l-Khalīl al-salām*)". According to the author, people using such formulas ought to be disciplined; see Ibn Baydakīn, *Lumaʿ* I, 232. Such usages were apparently disapproved of because they were seen as vain and frivolous uses of sacred names and concepts in the highly mundane context of business transactions; see for instance al-Samarqandī, *Fatāwā* 295; al-Walwālijī, *Fatāwī* II, 331. – The tendency to hold up totally and patently impracticable standards of decorous speech might take some savants to the point of declaring the diminutive form of the nouns 'mosque' or 'Quran manuscript' inadmissible. Others insisted, on theological grounds, on having to avoid all references to God not explicitly Quranic in origin (like the expression 'God's palms' instead of the correct 'God's hands'). On such attitudes, see al-Jāḥiẓ, *Ḥayawān* I, 184; al-Thaʿālibī, *Tatimma* II, 83; al-Ghazālī, *Iḥyāʾ* II, 202–4; al-Ḥarīrī, *Durra* 635; Yāqūt, *Buldān* I, 456; Ibn al-Muʿtazz, *Badīʿ* 105–6.

[115] al-Ṭabarsī, *Makārim* 14, 21; al-Ibshīhī, *Mustaṭraf* 528–9; Ibn Mufliḥ, *Ādāb* II, 178–9; al-Thaʿālibī, *Iqtibās* I, 77; and cf. Sadan 1983: 68; al-Qishṭaynī 1992: 31; Marzolph 2000: 482. In addition to *ḥadīths* presenting examples of the Prophet's jesting, there are about 50 traditions that show him

Mujūn could be manifested in conduct as well as in language. The case of patterns of behaviour associated with libertines differs to some extent from *mujūn* as literature and speech. A number of behaviours classifiable as *mujūn*, notably drinking wine, fornication and sodomy, were explicitly condemned and prosecutable in Islamic law. Other forms of conduct, while technically not illicit (indeed possibly customary), could still be liable to discretionary punishment, at least in theory. For instance, appearing nude before others in the public baths (*ḥammām*) was a common practice, yet experts of religious law were fairly unanimous in their verdict that it should not be permitted.[116]

The influence of a religious scholar over his contemporaries in many cases seems to have been in inverse proportion to his inflexibility and rigour. Although this – as we have seen in the case of the control of Ḥanbalī preachers like al-Barbahārī over the Sunni mobs of Baghdad – is certainly not true of all historical situations, extremely intolerant *ʿulamāʾ* would often be seen in a very negative light by a lot of people. This is hardly surprising given the haughty, either condescending or hostile, attitudes of some religious experts towards everyone who did not belong to their class. It is easy to imagine that conspicuous, disdainful displays of superiority by virtue of an education in the religious disciplines would certainly not endear a savant to either the commoners or the 'secular' intelligentsia.[117] In fact, under ordinary circumstances a particularly intolerant religious scholar would have precious few means to enforce his own strict views, which may have to do with the notable acridity of their tone in discussing the lowly morals of their contemporaries. The

in the act of laughing. On these texts, see Ammann 1993: 40–5, 47–69, 144–53. Shiʿites could additionally invoke examples of jesting by ʿAlī b. Abī Ṭālib; see Walther 2002: 514.

116 Disapproval of widespread but reprehensible customs like nudity in the baths would usually be kept within the written universe of jurisprudence, but some zealous scholars might take steps to suppress such habits. See for instance Ibn Baydakīn, *Lumaʿ* I, 197; Ibn Baṭṭūṭa, *Riḥla* 29; and cf. al-Shayzarī, *Nihāya* 88; Ibn al-Jawzī, *Talbīs* 399–400; Marcus 1986: 168–9. Also cf. Shoshan 1993: 68. In the modern period too, one occasionally observes the situation of a ubiquitous custom being strongly condemned by some elements of the community, who at the same time make no serious efforts to eradicate the custom. See for instance Hammoudi 1993: 3, 65, 88–9. Compromise with prevalent customs was in fact such a strong practical imperative as to be a formative factor in the development of Islamic law, in which consideration of the actual situation was allowed in certain circumstances. On this issue in more detail, see Hallaq 1986: 427–50.

117 For a glimpse of the haughty attitudes of some *ʿulamāʾ*, see al-Yaḥṣubī, *Ilmāʿ* 28, 41. – An anthropologist who did his fieldwork in Yemen makes the interesting point that the ivory-tower attitudes and the airs of superiority displayed by some members of the *ʿulamāʾ* class may be a psychological result of the insular ambience of their education. On this topic, see Messick 1993: 83–4. It must also be kept in mind that while in theory the ranks of the *ʿulamāʾ* class were open to every sufficiently assiduous aspirant, in practice the religious elite would often form a closely-knit, exclusive community composed of a limited number of lineages, a group which offered scant possibility of entry for an outsider. (Of course, this is a general statement the validity of which varies from one historical situation to another.) See Bulliet 1972: 56–7.

recommendation of a Ḥanafite author of the 8th–9th/14th–15th century that one ought to refuse to greet or answer to the greeting of sinful and dissolute people speaks volumes about the range of possibilities open to such scholars.[118] (Obviously, this observation is general and certainly not equally applicable to all historical situations.) In mediaeval Iraq, the Arabic adjective often used specifically in reference to strict, holier-than-thou religious scholars who had not even a modicum of tolerance for human foibles and peccadilloes was *baghīḍ*. This word, whose literal meaning is 'odious' or 'repugnant', was closely associated with excessive religious zeal and a general killjoy attitude.[119] In a collection of entertaining texts from the Buyid era, there is an anecdote which portrays a religious savant citing a Quranic verse to reprove a woman passing by and to recommend the use of a face-veil to her. The woman replies: "You odious man, are you shaming me with the Quran (*yā baghīḍ tuḥashshimunī bi-l-Qur'ān*)?"[120]

This anecdote is a good example of an annoyed, resentful response to pious admonishment. Albeit calling someone else's attention to the sinfulness of an activity in which he or she is engaging is not only commendable but indispensable in Muslim thinking (this being one interpretation of the famous concept of *al-amr bi-l-maʿrūf wa-l-nahy ʿan al-munkar*, 'commanding right and forbidding wrong'), this did not stop many people from feeling irritated and saying so in so many words.[121] Such

118 Ibn Baydakīn, *Lumaʿ* I, 284. Jonathan Berkey made the important observation that the 'innovations' (sing. *bidʿa*) so vehemently denounced by religious experts have in common the significant trait that all "lay beyond the control of the established religious and scholarly authorities". See Berkey 1995: 58 (and the idea elaborated at more length in pp. 58–60). On the often quite limited influence of *ʿulamā'* in Iraq in the Saljūq period, also see Ibn al-Jawzī, *Quṣṣāṣ* 170, 319; Ibn al-Jawzī, *Talbīs* 388–9. Already in the Buyid era, Baghdad had seen the proliferation of not only frivolity and profligacy in speech and conduct but the more alarming phenomenon of serious crime too. For example, even though it was common knowledge that a hardcore criminal living in the Bāb al-Ṭāq quarter made his living from organised gambling, drinking and prostitution – with his prostitutes occasionally offering their sexual services in plain view of the public in the open courtyard of his house – he was practically beyond the reach of law for a long time as he made sure to bribe an important military leader on a regular, monthly basis. (As so often happens in business, the costs of bribery were also borne by the general population since he gathered it by extortion, robbery and blackmail.) See al-Tanūkhī, *Nishwār* I, 349–50; and cf. Miskawayh, *Tajārib* II, 51.

119 E.g. al-Iṣfahānī, *Aghānī* I, 390; VII, 192; al-Tanūkhī, *Nishwār* I, 90; Ibn al-Muʿtazz, *Ṭabaqāt* 177; Yāqūt, *Udabā'* I, 9; IV, 1478, 1843.

120 al-Thaʿālibī, *Laṭā'if* 74–5.

121 Apart from the types of retorts we are discussing here, dismissal of pious meddling is a recurrent motif in *mujūn* poetry too (yet another example of the possible origins of some *mujūn* motifs in spoken language). The rejection of the warnings of an *ʿādhil* or *ʿādhila* (a male or female 'reproacher') is a stock motif in mediaeval Arabic poetry. In addition to this motif one finds more sophisticated literary responses as well. Note, for instance, the reflection of the scholarly discussions going on concerning the legal concept of *fisq* in one of the most famous poems of Abū Nuwās. The verses in question ("*Fa-qul li-man yaddaʿī fī l-ʿilmi falsafatan...*" etc.) – part of a bacchic poem (see Abū Nuwās, *Dīwān* III, 2–4) – are meant to taunt the Muʿtazilite scholar Ibrāhīm al-Naẓẓām (d. 231/845) for the theory

responses, which are a powerful indication of the limits of the popular appeal and influence of piety, are quoted aplenty in some sources, and show both remarkable variety and wit. Notably, a part of the extant corpus of such repartees makes use of phrases borrowed from the Quran or *ḥadīth* and applied ironically, a link (or at least parallel) to *mujūn* literature. The following two phrases illustrate the attitude manifested in such replies: "You kill me with this great religiosity of yours; every sheep will be hanged by its own leg [to be flayed]." And "look after your own souls", which is in fact a verbatim quotation from Quran 5:105.[122]

Whilst it is incontestable that the ideal of strict piety never ceased to inform the outlook of a great many mediaeval Muslims, whatever their social status, and in this sense it was one of the most fundamental social norms, this did not necessarily translate into an automatic approval of ultra-strict religious views. There is a plethora of evidence to suggest that, for all the prestige of Islamic piety, bigotry was widely perceived to be an undesirable extreme, and moderation (in religious fervour as in other domains of culture) was preferred. For example, a poem from the Buyid era expresses the noteworthy sentiment that the golden mean in religion and morals is best, and portrays the libertine and the devout believers as two unsavoury extremes.[123]

---

of the 'intermediate status' (*al-manzila bayna l-manzilatayn*) of a person who commits grave sins (viz. the *fāsiq*): the idea that such people will be regarded in the afterworld as neither proper Muslims nor fully unbelievers. Here is a libertine commenting on religious scholars commenting on libertinism.

[122] Ibn Baydakīn, *Lumaʿ* I, 182–3; Ibn Makkī, *Tathqīf* 369. The first expression is, of course, a figurative way of saying that everyone will have to answer for his or her own sins only. As for the Quranic phrase, it is certainly intended ironically when used as a repartee to a pious admonition. However, it must be noted that the original verse in the Quran does have a similar purport, pointing out that each and every human is answerable for his or her own deeds. In this sense, there is no misapplication of the Quran's text here. For the interpretation of the *āya*, see al-Bayḍāwī, *Tafsīr* I, 286. However, some *ʿulamāʾ* sought to give the verse a different interpretation precisely because of its potential use to ward off pious meddling; see Cook 2000: 30–1. For other examples of similar retorts, see Ibn al-Jawzī, *Talbīs* 391; al-Haytamī, *Iʿlām* 371–2; Badr, *Risāla* 32; al-Qāriʾ, *Sharḥ* 165; and Cook 2000: 498–9. In one source, a rich merchant brusquely rejects pious advice on correcting his way of praying, calling it officious interference (*fuḍūl*); see al-Tanūkhī, *Nishwār* III, 134–5. The Ḥanafite scholar al-Walwālijī mentions the case of a man who labelled people 'commanding right and forbidding wrong' riffraff (*ghawghāʾ*), and adds that saying such a thing looks perilously close to unbelief ("*khīfa ʿalayhi l-kufr*"); see al-Walwālijī, *Fatāwī* V, 419–20; and also Badr, *Risāla* 49; al-Qāriʾ, *Sharḥ* 225. An incorrigible libertine like the poet Abū l-Hindī, an alcoholic and a recidivous debauchee (early 2nd/8th c.), would not even hesitate to retort to the quite sensible reproaches of the local governor in an abusive yet witty manner. There is no reason, however, to believe that such extreme audacity was ever common. See the story in al-Iṣfahānī, *Aghānī* XX, 348. Sarcastic retorts to religious admonitions occur in today's spoken Arabic too. An example is given in Piamenta 1979: 47, who says that to the pious phrase "have patience, God is with those who are patient" (*uṣbor, inna ʾllāha maʿa l-ṣābirīn*), a flippant answer is "provided they do have patience" (*iza ṣabaru*).

[123] al-Thaʿālibī, *Nathr* 21–3 (and also see Gruendler 2005a: 64). The verse in question, in which the poet boasts of his own agreeable character, reads "*Wa-lastu bi-l-nāsiki l-mushammiri thawbayhi wa-lā l-mājini l-qabīḥi l-waqāḥi*", and its gist is also given in a prose version: "*wa-lastu bi-l-nāsik*

The ease with which many specialists of theology (*kalām*) were wont to label their opponents unbelievers – a verdict that in theory would have sinister consequences for the person branded, although this was seldom the case in practice – provoked negative feelings and a strong dislike of the theologians among some intellectuals on both secular and religious grounds.[124]

Markedly negative perceptions of intolerance and uncompromising zeal were obviously held by a lot of people and extended to many fields of social interaction. Some examples will illustrate the ubiquity of such views, which might manifest themselves either implicitly or explicitly, as the case might be. We find, for instance, that the so-called *muḥtasib* (the supervisor of the markets and of public morals) was advised to refrain from displaying intolerance and rigidity; and it is remarked that some caliphs were quite averse to a strict, sermonising style.[125] In high society, a man who refused to join others in drinking and carousing could be viewed simply as a spoilsport. Regarded as callous and impolite, such behaviour would elicit a negative response; and religiously motivated teetotallers would sometimes be prodded, at times all but coerced, to stop spoiling the fun but join it instead.[126] An *adab* collection admiringly recounts an act of one of Hārūn al-Rashīd's uncles, ʿAbd al-Malik b. Ṣāliḥ, as an illustration of nobility of character (*makārim al-akhlāq*): widely known for his devout religiosity, this man was nevertheless loath to derange a wine-drinking party of two friends he had inadvertently happened upon, preferring to drink some wine for the first and last time in his life and then, after a while, take his leave discreetly.[127] The following account is directly relevant to the issue of

---

al-bārid wa-lā l-fātik al-mārid wa-lā bi-l-mutaʿaffif al-mutaqashshif wa-lā bi-l-khalīʿ al-mutakashshif" etc. On this topic, also cf. van Gelder 1992: 91–2. – The ideal of respectability, when taken to the extreme, has a tendency to provoke negative responses in other cultures as well; see Ball 1970: 340.

124 For some negative appraisals of the theologians as a group, see for instance al-Jāḥiẓ, *Ḥayawān* I, 97; al-Tawḥīdī, *Baṣāʾir* II(iii), 17, al-Ghazālī, *Iḥyāʾ* I, 59–60; al-Wansharīsī, *Miʿyār* II, 456–7. It seems that the experts of *ḥadīth* had their detractors too; see for instance al-Yaḥṣubī, *Ilmāʿ* 39 ["*Qul li-man yunkiru l-ḥadītha...*" etc.]; Ibn al-Marzubān, *Dhamm* 84 ["*inna hāʾulāʾ thuqalāʾ*"]; and cf. al-Thaʿālibī, *Yatīma* III, 422 ["*Hādhā zamānun laysa yuḥẓā bihi ḥaddathanā l-Aʿmashu ʿan Nāfiʿi*"].

125 al-Shayzarī, *Nihāya* 9; Ibn Bassām, *Nihāya* 13–4. In mediaeval Cairo, most *muḥtasib*s seem to have been immensely unpopular, perhaps owing to their corrupt practices. See Shoshan 1993: 63.

126 E.g. al-Iṣfahānī, *Aghānī* VII, 71. Reluctance to join others in a wine-drinking party could occasion rather rude practical jokes; see for instance ibid. XIII, 341–2; and also see the reaction of the drinking pals of Manṣūr al-Namarī to his professed unwillingness to drink in ibid. XIII, 172. An interesting (but certainly very distant) parallel is the curious fact that in modern Yemen, the prevailing custom at the afternoon *qāt*-chewing parties dictates that the first half-hour or hour should only be spent discussing facetious topics, and whoever tries to initiate serious conversation in this phase is considered a tedious man and gets his due share of teasing. See Lambert 1997: 36, 38.

127 al-Ibshīhī, *Mustaṭraf* 427–8. Conversely, some religious authorities held that not only drinking but even sitting in the company of people drinking wine was forbidden; see al-Ṭabarsī, *Makārim* 426. Of course, in practice drinking wine was commonplace and mostly regarded leniently, and its ubiquity made it all but natural that someone stumbling upon a company of friends in the midst of a drinking

negative perceptions of rigidity among the *ʿulamāʾ*, and the preference of tolerance and moderation:

> [...] Also illustrative of the amicability (*waṭāʾa*) of [certain] stringent *qāḍīs* towards those seeking their counsel (*li-l-mustaftīn*) and their tolerance in situations necessitating it is an anecdote about Ḥāmid b. ʿAbbās. Once he asked ʿAlī b. ʿĪsā in the bureau of the vizierate (*dīwān al-wizāra*) what was the remedy of a hangover, from which he was suffering. He would not, however, talk to him [about such a matter], saying only: "What have I to do with such a question?" In embarrassment, Ḥāmid turned to the chief *qāḍī* Abū ʿUmar, and asked him [the same question]. The *qāḍī* cleared his throat and said: "God says, *'Whatever the Messenger gives you, take; whatever he forbids you, give over.'*[128] Now, the Prophet – peace be upon him – said, 'In every craft, seek the counsel of him who is an expert of it.' Well, the person with the most expertise in this craft [viz. that of wine-drinking] in the pre-Islamic period was al-Aʿshā, who says [in one of his poems]: 'One cup [of wine] I drank for the pleasure of it, another to cure myself of the first.' Then in the Islamic period came Abū Nuwās, who says: 'Leave off reproaching me, for reproach is but encouragement; but do cure me with that which caused the illness'." With a face now cheerful, Ḥāmid told ʿAlī b. ʿĪsā: "Now, what harm would it have done to you, you humourless man (*yā bārid*), if you'd answered in the manner the *qāḍī* has? In order to give an answer, he quoted, first God, and then the Prophet, clarifying his legal opinion, driving home his point, and evading any [personal] responsibility (*bayyana l-futyā wa-addā l-maʿnā wa-tafaṣṣā min al-ʿuhda*)." At [hearing] these words, ʿAlī b. ʿĪsā felt even more embarrassed before Ḥāmid than the latter had before him when he initiated this whole issue.[129]

We have already noted the frequent use of the adjective *baghīḍ* ('odious') to characterise persons with overly pietistic attitudes. The nomenclature of unpleasant personal attributes in classical Arabic also includes some other terms which express a dislike of stringency. One such adjective that occurs in the sources very often is *thaqīl*. This word, whose literal meaning is 'heavy', or more faithfully to the original 'burdensome', was meant to describe a tedious, boring individual whose presence in a company is a veritable ordeal for his interlocutors. The stereotyped personification of this quality came to be one of the stock figures of jocular Arabic literature.

party should join them. An anecdote quotes the ironic words of a poet of Abbasid-era Baghdad to this effect: "Ibn Shabāba once joined a company where wine-drinking was going on. A friend who was with him said: 'Woe unto us if it's wine that they are drinking!' Said Ibn Shabāba: 'Woe unto us if it isn't wine that they are drinking'." See Ibn al-Muʿtazz, *Badīʿ* 136–7. For a more serious (and disapproving) discussion of the phenomenon, see Ibn al-Jawzī, *Talbīs* 399. Also cf. Rescher 1919: 13.

128 Quran 59:7.

129 al-Ḥarīrī, *Durra* 444–5. Another, shorter, version of the same story can be found in al-Thaʿālibī, *Laṭāʾif* 64; al-Thaʿālibī, *Khāṣṣ* 61–2. In another source one sees an unnamed imām showing similar indulgence to other people's peccadillos by being complicit in a witty scheme of seducing someone. See al-Iṣfahānī, *Aghānī* XVIII, 161.

Besides *baghīḍ* and *thaqīl*, a third related term, commonly used to describe a person lacking any sense of humour, was *bārid* (lit. 'cold'), the use of which we have already come across in the excerpt quoted just above.

It may perhaps reflect, at least partly, the impact of such negative perceptions of 'excessive' rigidity and intolerance that a number of *ʿulamāʾ* apparently saw no problem in adopting a more easygoing attitude. A good example of that – if it is reliable – is the aforementioned report about the chief *qāḍī* Abū ʿUmar, and it is by no means exceptional in that the attitudes it depicts recur in many another account on the conduct of religious scholars. Some celebrated savants whose dedication to Islamic norms and general propriety cannot be seriously doubted would not have serious qualms about cracking jokes themselves or sanctioning other's jesting by listening to it and showing no disapproval thereof.[130] The pious Muḥammad b. Sīrīn (d. 110/729), for instance, was apparently not averse to the enjoyment of poetry – even poetry having a *mujūn* content.[131] The Quran expert Ibn Mujāhid (d. 324/936) is said to have been "given to jesting and of an amiable disposition (*kathīr al-mudāʿaba ṭayyib al-khuluq*)", for all his well-known excellence in religious studies,

---

[130] E.g. Ibn al-Jawzī, *Ẓirāf* 25–7, 36–52 [quite a few examples]; Abū Hiffān, *Akhbār* 97–8 [Shuʿba]; al-Tawḥīdī, *Baṣāʾir* II(iv), 139 [Ibrāhīm al-Ḥarbī]; al-Ibshīhī, *Mustaṭraf* 50 [Ibn al-Munkadir]; al-Thaʿālibī, *Laṭāʾif* 12 [al-Ḥasan al-Baṣrī]. For later examples of respected religious scholars cultivating 'light' poetic genres like *ghazal*, see Bauer 1996. It is noteworthy that in Baghdad even some Ḥanbalite scholars – normally the group least likely to be associated with leniency towards any manifestation of frivolity – were characterised as 'refined' or 'sophisticated' (a term usually closely connected with *mujūn*, as will be argued in the next chapter). See Ghazi 1959: 67. Of course, the anecdotal nature of much of this evidence and its provenance from entertaining collections may cast serious doubt on the reliability of any one example. However, taken together these data do seem to imply that educated people saw no contradiction between someone's being a religious scholar and his enjoyment of frivolous humour. – Regarding the story about al-Ḥasan al-Baṣrī, it must be added that whether or not he really appreciated some forms of joking, this scholar was nevertheless the object of intense antipathy on the part of the libertine poet Bashshār b. Burd, another celebrity of the same town. See al-Iṣfahānī, *Aghānī* III, 163. If one trusts the testimony of al-Washshāʾ, a number of religious scholars apparently did not object to their names being cited in light-hearted love poems as 'authorities' for jocose arguments designed to soften the beloved's heart; see al-Washshāʾ, *Muwashshā* 107–8.

[131] al-Ibshīhī, *Mustaṭraf* 529; Ibn Rashīq, *ʿUmda* 21. Another account portrays Ibn Sīrīn as possessing a good deal of dry humour himself. Asked about his opinion of the claims of religious mystics who professed to be seized by an irresistible ecstasy at hearing the sublime text of the Quran and to lose their consciousness, he commented: "We should return to [discussing] this question when they have taken seats on top of a high wall, and then the Quran has been recited to them from beginning to end; if they still lose their consciousness in that condition, it is indeed the way they claim." See al-Ibshīhī, *Mustaṭraf* 112. The Ḥanbalī jurist Ibn Mufliḥ also confirms that Ibn Sīrīn (as well as al-Shaʿbī, another respected scholar) was anything but averse to jokes; see Ibn Mufliḥ, *Ādāb* II, 179–80; and for a jestful mock *fatwā* by al-Shaʿbī, see Ibn al-Marzubān, *Dhamm* 63. A story portrays al-Shaʿbī as having a strong dislike to socialising with tedious *ḥadīth* experts and preferring jestful companions; see Yāqūt, *Udabāʾ* IV, 1478. On Ibn Sīrīn and other pious scholars not averse to jesting (including the imam Jaʿfar al-Ṣādiq), see Ammann 1993: 84–8.

and a similar characterisation is given of the Basran scholar Zakariyyā al-Sājī (d. 307/919–20).[132]

In the case of some *ʿulamāʾ*, the dismissal of all *mujūn* and related poetic phenomena was clearly a mere theoretical stance that they had no intention of applying, or enforcing, in real life. Such is demonstrably the case with the Ḥanbalite scholar Ibn al-Jawzī (d. 597/1201); it is instructive to juxtapose his deprecatory comments on various motifs of *mujūn* literature in his *Talbīs Iblīs*[133] to practically the whole of his collection of amusing *mujūn* anecdotes titled *Akhbār al-ẓirāf wa-l-mutamājinīn*. Also, quite a few widely admired religious authorities, some of them with a well-earned reputation for honest piety, are the subjects of passages showing them enjoying facetiae of various sorts.

In particular, some of the *oeuvre* of Abū Nuwās had its share of admirers among the *ʿulamāʾ*. As a literary anthology notes, the poems of Abu Nuwās were quite popular and circulated widely among the members of the religious elite ("*wa-mā zāla l-ʿulamāʾ wa-l-ashrāf yarwūna shiʿrahu wa-yatafakkahūna bihi wa-yufaḍḍilūnahu ʿalā ashʿār al-qudamāʾ* ").[134] This assessment is admittedly somewhat vague and general, but more concrete evidence is also available, like a passage about the impeccably devout Sufyān b. ʿUyayna (107/725–196/811), who is claimed to have been fond of the love poetry (if not other genres) of Abū Nuwās, a genre usually considered to be beneath the dignity of a religious scholar and unbecoming for a respectable man with a high social standing. The great anthologist al-Thaʿālibī (d. 429/1038) comments at some length on this apparent discrepancy:

> ʿUmar b. Shabba tells us that Sufyān b. ʿUyayna, for all his asceticism and piety, was a great admirer of the poetry of Abū Nuwās. One day he said to someone from al-Baṣra: «How original this [poet] of yours from al-Baṣra is. By God, he is so marvellous, inventive and witty when he says [in a poem]: ‹I caught sight of a gazelle at a funeral lamenting among her companions. / She is crying: shedding pearls [from eyes resembling] narcissi, and beating roses [i.e. her rosy cheeks] with [hennaed fingers as red as] jujube berries.›» Now, if Sufyān for all his godliness liked it so much, what to say of others?[135]

The inescapable conclusion seems to be that the degree of one's appreciation or otherwise of frivolity and humour did not primarily depend on one's métier but one's personality. Whatever the recommendations of the manuals of religious law,

---

132 Yāqūt, *Udabāʾ* II, 521; III, 1326.

133 Ibn al-Jawzī, *Talbīs* 128–9.

134 al-Baghdādī, *Khizāna* I, 168; and the passage is also cited in Abū Nuwās, *Dīwān* I, 9. For an example of a libertine poet in a later period enjoying a great deal of popularity within the class of religious savants, see Ibn Maʿṣūm, *Sulāfa* 414 [Sharaf al-Dīn Yaḥyā al-Aṣīlī].

135 al-Thaʿālibī, *Laṭāʾif* 98. (And cf. Ibn Manẓūr, *Akhbār* 164–5.) I owe the correct interpretation of the imagery in the two verses to G. J. van Gelder.

a uniform attitude to humour and frivolity simply did not exist in the actual behaviour of *ʿulamāʾ*. One cannot but agree with the assessment of Roy Mottahedeh that "the piously minded and the ulema were not identical categories".[136] This helps understand such ostensibly implausible (even self-contradictory) labels as 'the witty among the jurisprudents of Baghdad' (*ẓurafāʾ al-fuqahāʾ bi-Baghdādh*), 'the libertines among the experts of *ḥadīth*' (*mujjān aṣḥāb al-ḥadīth*), 'the reprobates among the experts of *ḥadīth*' (*khulaʿāʾ aṣḥāb al-ḥadīth*), and so on.[137] A religious dignitary of the Buyid period known as Abū ʿIṣma is described in a source with the epithet *mājin*, and the citation of the man's obscene comments about his responsibilities as an official preacher in ʿUkbarā (Iraq) certainly gives substance to that description.[138]

As in the case of Abū ʿUmar and the notorious Yaḥyā b. Aktham, judges were often perceived, even stereotyped, as being more lenient and perhaps more susceptible to *mujūn* than other categories of religious savants. A number of anecdotes will illustrate the manner in which tolerance, and in some cases even indulgence, on the part of *qāḍīs* would be viewed almost as a matter of course. The first text describes an incident that is supposed to have taken place in the late Umayyad period:

> Al-Awqaṣ al-Makhzūmī was appointed *qāḍī* in Mecca. People had never before seen a man as virtuous and noble-minded as him. One night, sleeping in a wing of his house, [he was startled by] a drunken man passing there, who was singing: "Turn towards us, oh lady in the fine camel-saddle!..." Looking at him out of his window, [the *qāḍī*] told him: "Man, you have had forbidden drink, then you wake up those who are sleeping, and you sing incorrectly [into the bargain]. Listen how I do it." He then taught him the correct [tune], and let him go.[139]

[136] Mottahedeh 1980: 149.

[137] al-Thaʿālibī, *Laṭāʾif* 66; Ibn al-Jawzī, *Ẓirāf* 123; al-Tawḥīdī, *Baṣāʾir* II(iii), 152.

[138] al-Tanūkhī, *Nishwār* I, 122, 124. On the other hand, an account of the vulgar tomfoolery of a 4th/10th-century religious savant of Baghdad called Abū Naṣr al-Binṣ, presented in his own words, is so outrageous that it verges on implausibility. See ibid. I, 97. – A curious passage in the *Kitāb al-aghānī* (al-Iṣfahānī, *Aghānī* I, 389) seems to imply that the religious elite of Iraq had the reputation of being more rigid and intolerant than that of the Hijaz (Western Arabia). I have no idea what to make of this suggestion, which seems to be at odds with the general stereotype of the cultural atmosphere of Iraq (*v.i.*).

[139] al-Iṣfahānī, *Aghānī* II, 361. (And cf. a story on the remarkably tolerant behaviour of Abū Ḥanīfa in al-Ibshīhī, *Mustaṭraf* 421.) While Abū Ḥanīfa's legal opinions do bear witness to his uncommonly lenient personality, I find it hard to give credence to the story about the incident involving al-Awqaṣ al-Makhzūmī and the drunk. However, its historicity is largely irrelevant, as what I am concerned with here is the popular perception of the attitudes of *qāḍīs*, and the anecdote *is* presented as factual by Abū l-Faraj al-Iṣfahānī. – A *qāḍī* of al-Baṣra called Muḥammad b. Ḥafṣ al-Tamīmī was also remembered as having displayed remarkable leniency regarding an affair involving the arch-libertine Abū Nuwās; see al-Iṣfahānī, Aghānī XX, 76-7; and cf. Abū Hiffān, *Akhbār* 113–4. – On the attutudes of *qāḍīs* and the literature produced by members of this group, see Bauer 1996: 277, note 6.

The next passage, a fairly well-known account about the *qāḍī* al-Tanūkhī, is much more plausible despite the odd and *outré* revelry depicted in it, as it comes from a near-contemporary, appears to be based on widely circulating gossip, and is very specific (in identifying names among others things):

> It is said that [the *qāḍī* al-Tanūkhī] was one of those judges who were the boon-companions of the vizier al-Muhallabī and gathered in his chamber two nights every week to cast aside all reservations, and giving free rein to romp and profligacy (*ʿalā ʾṭṭirāḥ al-ḥishma wa-l-tabassuṭ fī l-qaṣf wa-l-khalāʿa*). Among them were Ibn Qurayʿa, Ibn Maʿrūf, al-Tanūkhī, and a number of others – all of them men with long, gray beards, just like the vizier al-Muhallabī. When they began to feel good, all in high spirits, and they enjoyed the music that carried them all away, they would abandon piety for wine and plunge into reckless and rash conduct. Each would grab a golden cup full of wine from Quṭrabbul or ʿUkbarā, weighing a thousand *mithqāl* or more, and then he would dip his beard in it, and soak it until it was all saturated with wine. Then they would set to sprinkling one another with [the wine in their beards], dancing unrestrained. [...] Progressing from drink to drink, they kept yelling this word: "*Harr, harr*!" [...] And then the next morning they would resume their usual magisteriality and godliness, their dignity worthy of a *qāḍī* and reservation worthy of a great sheikh.[140]

Whereas the exact way in which these judges chose to amuse themselves is strikingly bizarre, the fact that *qāḍīs* could behave in a less than dignified manner when in a private setting is not quite so extraordinary.[141] However, as often in the preceding paragraphs, it is to be emphasised that personal disposition was a decisive factor, and certainly not all *qāḍīs* were drawn to drolleries and indecency. For an instructive counter-example from the same era – the times of the Buyid dynasty – one may cite the case of Abū Khāzim, a *qāḍī* renowned for his honest piety and scrupulosity. Persistent gossip held that a certain piece of love poetry had actually been composed by this devout man, incredible though it might sound. To establish the veracity or otherwise of the implausible claim, the vizier sent a trusted retainer of his to inquire of the *qāḍī* himself, an extremely delicate task. In the words of the envoy himself,

> Early one morning I went to see him and sat there until he was left alone save for one man wearing the garb of a judge and an ornate headgear. Then I said [to Abū Khāzim]: "There is something I'd like to talk to you about *tête-à-tête*." He said that I could go ahead, since he had no secrets to hide before that man. I told him the whole story and asked him about the verse and the occasion [which prompted its composition]. Smiling, he said: "This is an affair of my youth; I

[140] al-Thaʿālibī, *Yatīma* II, 335–6.

[141] For another example from roughly the same period, see al-Tanūkhī, *Nishwār* III, 287–8 ["*wa-takhālaʿa wa-tahattaka bi-mā lā yajūz li-l-quḍāt*"].

addressed the poem to the mother of this" – and he pointed to the man, who thus turned out to be his son – "who quite enthralled my soul. She was a slave-girl of mine; and yet my heart was no less a slave of hers. However, I've given up doing such things for years, and haven't composed a poem for a long time, and I ask God's forgiveness for what happened in the past." The young man had become sullen and was sweating heavily with embarrassment. I returned to the vizier al-Qāsim and told him everything. Laughing at the youth's embarrassment, he said: "Were there a man completely untouched by love, it would have to be Abū Khāzim with his extreme puritanism (*maʿa bughḍihi*)."[142] Later on, we would keep recounting the case a lot.[143]

1.3.2 THE SECRETARIAL CLASS

Like that of the religious scholars, the category of 'secretaries' (*kuttāb*) was a very heterogeneous one too, encompassing individuals doing a variety of jobs requiring literacy and some level of education. At best, a 'secretary' was an embodiment of the highest ideal of the genteel and polished man (*adīb*) with a wide-ranging interest and erudition, and such people were the mainstay of the courtly culture too. At the lowest level, a 'secretary' was just a scribbler in some obscure bureau, a man with next to no influence and with a less than impressive erudition barely enough to enable him to avoid manual work. What unified this 'class' seems to be their literacy, their state jobs and their not being religious specialists.[144]

Clearly, a lot of the poets and writers who produced *mujūn* belonged to this category. Of course, this fact alone is highly indicative of the great measure of acceptance that libertinism and its literary expressions enjoyed within this group; and furthermore one can observe that if there was one social group readily identified with the attitudes and products of *mujūn*, it must be the 'secretaries'. In this group of people, one finds at least four prerequisites that are arguably of paramount importance for the appreciation of frivolous literature: literacy, a degree of familiarity with the religious and secular cultural heritage, some leisure time, and a lack of religious zealotry (although not, in most cases, of religious faith). There is ample anecdotal evidence showing that many of the manifestations of the frivolous spirit of *mujūn* reviewed in the previous chapters were relished by state functionaries of

[142] *V.s.* on the idiomatic use of the adjective *baghīḍ* in the sense of 'overly, unpleasantly pious'.

[143] al-Tanūkhī, *Nishwār* I, 89–90. Not all judges had such qualms about love poetry. The same source tells us about two respectable *qāḍīs* of Baghdad in the late third/ninth century, Abū Bakr al-Ẓāhirī and Ibn Surayj, that they had a heated debate concerning who of the two had composed better love poetry in his juvenile years. See ibid. VIII, 187.

[144] The group of the *kuttāb* and that of the religious scholars represented two very separate, and sometimes even opposed, cultural milieus in the first three centuries of Islamic history. This opposition, however, seems to have gradually faded to a noticeable extent by the forth century of the Hegira. See Mottahedeh 1980: 143.

various levels.[145] It is a telling detail concerning the dominant stereotypes of the *kuttāb* in the high Abbasid period that some people considered resigning from a job in a state bureau (*dīwān*) to be a form of contrition and personal moral reform.[146] Even more pertinent to our subject is the observation that some 'secular'-minded intellectuals showed a palpable hostility to the more intolerant representatives of the *ʿulamāʾ* group, and had no reservations about voicing their animosity in the most mordant manner possible.[147]

A special weight is conferred upon the views of the literary critics, not because of their wider influence or power, which was next to nonexistent, but because they were specialists of the topics we are dealing with. Perhaps some poets would even listen to such voices.

Given the close association of *mujūn*, 'light poetry', and more broadly a 'secular' outlook, with the *kuttāb*, it would be understandable to presume that there was no opposition to *mujūn* literature in these circles. Understandable, but wrong. Not everyone among the literary experts approved of frivolous poetry, and there was a way of thinking – a minority opinion by all appearances, but noted by several mediaeval Arabic writers – that displayed a marked prejudice against either 'unworthy' genres and poetic subjects (especially love poetry) or 'modern' (*muḥdath*) poetry as a whole. This attitude would typically contrast these 'unbecoming' genres or the 'decadent' contemporary period to the grand poetic diction and solemn, heroic content of pre-Islamic and early Islamic Bedouin odes.[148] Of course, in a comparison

[145] For instance, a state official of early 3th/9th-century Iraq called Abū Muḥammad al-Ḥizāmī saw no problem with amassing funny and creative arguments to support his own parsimony, a despicable characteristic in the traditional Arabian honour code; see al-Jāḥiẓ, *Bukhalāʾ* 101. A highly erudite functionary in the administration in al-Rayy (Northern Iran) under the last Buyids or early Seljuks would often amuse his colleagues with extremely indecent and obscene poems, a pastime they seem to have had no objections to. See al-Bākharzī, *Dumya* II, 828–9. The teacher of the caliph al-Mustanjid's sons, ʿAbdallāh al-Khashshāb (d. 567/1172) was forever joking and loved all sorts of less than respectable pastimes and entertainments; see Yāqūt, *Udabāʾ* IV, 1495. Homosexuality was notoriously rampant among the *kuttāb*, indeed it was closely associated with this group; see for instance al-Jāḥiẓ, *Rasāʾil* I(ii), 112. A certain Raḍī al-Dīn Hibatallāh b. al-Ḥasan, a state official of the Seljuk period wrote self-deprecating poems making use of the less than flattering epithet that others had branded him with ('Rat'). See al-Iṣbahānī, *Kharīda* I(i), 179.

[146] al-Jāḥiẓ, *Ḥayawān* I, 96; and also cf. Kraemer 1986: 11. (However, this notion might also have to do with the widespread perception of most of the state revenues as ill-gotten plunder, for many taxes were not levied in accordance with the *sharīʿa*.)

[147] When a jurisprudent of al-Kūfa slighted the poetry of ʿUmar b. Abī Rabīʿa, considering it to be too indecent, the famous littérateur-cum-philologist Ḥammād al-Rāwiya publicly remarked that he was quite willing to impregnate the savant's mother, so that she might hopefully give birth to a more talented poet; see al-Iṣfahānī, *Aghānī* I, 85. Also see al-Tawḥīdī, *Baṣāʾir* III(vi), 91 [Yaḥyā b. Ziyād's poem on the pious].

[148] For some citations and discussions of such opinions, see al-Jāḥiẓ, *Ḥayawān* I, 228; al-Tawḥīdī, *Akhlāq* 7–8; al-Jurjānī, *Wasāṭa* 20, 53; and for a general discussion of the phenomenon, see von

by such standards *mujūn* (by definition 'modern' and 'of no consequence') could not fare too well. However, the negative opinions were all the more pronounced perhaps owing to their representing a minority position. For all the critical voices, there was no denying the immense popularity of the new, 'modern', urban poetry, not exactly baffling in view of the far greater accessibility of the new poems' style and vocabulary. Although classical Bedouin poetry did have continuing prestige among the erudite, the fact remained that "the verse of [the modern poets] reflects the contemporary era better, and people cite it more often in their gatherings, in their books, by way of proverbial expressions, and for various purposes (*wa-shiʿruhum ashbah bi-l-zamān wa-l-nās lahu akthar istiʿmālan fī majālisihim wa-kutubihim wa-tamaththulihim wa-maṭālibihim*)."[149] This excerpt suggests the important point that in some cases there might be an element of sour grapes in vehement dismissals of 'modern' poetry. Whether in spite of or because of the popularity of the modern poetic style, among literary specialists and in genteel society the debate raged on and on. The celebrated littérateur Abū Bakr al-Ṣūlī (d. 335/947) offers a somewhat sarcastic but not unrealistic summary of the controversy, which like all matters of taste was essentially irresolvable:

> The scholars [who depreciate modern poetry], when asked to give commentaries on the verses of Bashshār, Abū Nuwās, Muslim [b. al-Walīd], Abū Tammām and other [modern poets], will never say 'I do not know it' but belittle it instead. [...] What else is a man supposed to do who will insist on everyone having to seek his instruction in learning the poetry of the ancients, only to turn out to know nothing when he is asked about the poems [of the modern poets]. What other refuge could he find but belittling that which he is ignorant of...[150]

Literary experts had their own (sometimes quite idiosyncratic) opinions not only on the respective merits of old and new poetry, but on some specific features of the newer genres too. Frivolous quotations from the Quran are one such topic. We have already examined the opinions of some *ʿulamāʾ* about *iqtibās*, including the jocular kind, but the more 'secular' discourse also had things to say about the phenomenon. As with most matters discussed in this chapter, there seems to have been no unanimity

---

Grunebaum 1944: 249–50; Bonebakker 1967: 193, 198–9. Beatrice Gruendler very convincingly shows that the ostensibly academic 'ancients versus moderns' controversy had a crucial social dimension, namely the emergence of a new élite, hence a new type of literary patron and a new audience, under the Abbasids. See Gruendler 2005a: 74, 80. Interestingly, the attitude of belittling contemporary poetry can still be observed among some scholars in the Ottoman period; see for instance Ibn Maʿṣūm, *Sulāfa* 7. On continuing negative views of poetry (especially love poetry) on a popular level, see Abu-Lughod 1990: 35; Abu-Lughod 1999: 250–1.

149 al-Ṣūlī, *Akhbār* 17; and also cf. al-Qazwīnī, *Īḍāḥ* V, 198.

150 al-Ṣūlī, *Akhbār* 14–5. For an anecdote that appears strongly to buttress this assessment, see ibid. 175–6. Also see al-Jurjānī, *Wasāṭa* 54–5.

of opinion; what is remarkable is the absence of a truly truculent tone even among those opposed to jocular *iqtibās*.[151] The chapter on objectionable forms of *iqtibās* in al-Thaʿālibī's sizeable book on this literary device is remarkable for its shortness only, and says little about the motifs of *mujūn*, apart from some technicalities and a few words condemning the application to humans of Quranic phrases describing God. One cannot but note the lack of any vehemence in the author's tone.[152] Al-Suyūṭī (d. 911/1505) makes the general observation that the experts of rhetoric and literature tend not only to allow *iqtibās* but also consider it a marvellous rhetorical device.[153]

Obscenity – a common accompanying feature of *mujūn* literature – is another topic that occasioned controversies among literary critics. Their views apparently ranged from extreme prudery to appreciation; and the words of the highly influential al-Jāḥiẓ (d. 255/869) are typical of the latter attitude:

> There are people who, when they hear the words 'cunt', 'dick', or 'fuck', recoil, feign disgust and assume a mien of deep piety. Most of those whom you see doing so boast only this much of modesty, excellence, nobility and piety – this affectation. However, all that a sanctimonious hypocrite manages to prove [thereby] is his vileness and ingrained baseness.[154]

Some literary critics also voiced their opinion on the treatment of the subject of love in 'modern' poetry. The cynicism of *mujūn* poetry towards love affairs was abhorred by quite a few urban littérateurs who favoured the *ʿudhrī* conception of ethereal love instead. Even at the height of the popularity of *mujūn*, not everone was happy to cultivate cynical and admittedly 'immoral' literature. Despite the florescence of libertine poetry, the chaste style of *ʿudhrī* love poetry, a long-standing

---

[151] For an in-depth discussion of the opinions of mediaeval Arab literary critics on humorous *iqtibās*, see van Gelder 2002–3, esp. 3–4, 7, 9–10, 13; and also see al-Ḥillī, *Sharḥ* 326–7. (Instead of *iqtibās*, quite a few literary experts preferred the term *taḍmīn*; see al-ʿAskar 1425 [A.H.]: 18. When the Quranic quotation was woven into a prose text, other synonyms might also be used to refer to the practice, namely *ḍarb mathal*, *tamaththul* and *istishhād*; see al-Suyūṭī, *Ḥāwī* I, 248.)

[152] al-Thaʿālibī, *Iqtibās* II, 57–8. For an overview of the sections of this book, and the topics treated in each, cf. Gilliot 2000: 496–8.

[153] al-Suyūṭī, *Ḥāwī* I, 272.

[154] al-Jāḥiẓ, *Ḥayawān* I, 376; and in a slightly different wording in al-Jāḥiẓ, *Rasāʾil* I(ii), 92. (After this verdict, al-Jāḥiẓ proceeds to buttress his argument with citations containing rather indelicate words from some authorities of impeccable reputation in early Islam.) If an anecdote about a remark made by al-Jāḥiẓ in a public bath can be accepted as a historical account – which in my view is improbable – then it leaves no doubt that the great prose writer was as little concerned with prudish considerations in his daily conduct as in his literary *oeuvre*. See al-Thaʿālibī, *Laṭāʾif* 54. The shunning of supposedly 'indelicate' vocabulary items was seen as a ludicrous affectation by several other influential literary experts too; see for instance Ibn Qutayba, *ʿUyūn* I(i), 44–6; al-Thaʿālibī, *Thimār* I, 365–6 ["*dhikr al-aʿḍāʾ lā yuʾaththimu...*" etc.]; and also cf. al-Rāghib, *Muḥāḍarāt* III, 504; and Lagrange 2006: 76–7.

convention of Arabic verse, continued to have its promoters and its grateful audience. These poets, who might with some irony be called a kind of literary *arrière-garde*, were as fully urban as any libertine and definitely as alien to Bedouin culture, yet were drawn to the idealised images of chastity, modesty and virtue to be found in early Bedouin poetry, a strong contrast to the actual lifestyle of Middle Eastern metropolises.[155]

That there should be within the *kuttāb* class – as elsewhere in society – individuals disgusted by the new fashion of wit, frivolity and *mujūn* is only to be expected and seems indubitable. At any rate, some writers thought it necessary to defend the trends, and argue against what they regarded as narrow-minded and fretful attitudes to humour and frivolity. Abū Ḥayyān al-Tawḥīdī (d. 414/1023) was one of the literary specialists sympathetic to *mujūn* and its various manifestations:

> I warn you not to turn away with repulsion from these things said in jest and intended to sound silly (*al-maḍrūba bi-l-hazl al-jāriya ʿalā l-sukhf*), for if you avoid them altogether, your intellect will weaken and your nature will grow dull. Nothing sharpens the mind like observing the affairs of the world and learning the good and the bad, the obvious and the hidden therein. [...] If you do not give your soul a taste of the joy of jesting, it will be afflicted with the melancholy of seriousness...[156]

A view that appears to have been quite widely – but not universally – shared among mediaeval Arabic literary experts is the need to distinguish between assessments of an author's actual lifestyle and his literary legacy. In other words, even the relatively pious-minded among them would reject to regard a 'sinful' life as casting a shadow over the man's *oeuvre*. We find quite a few authorities voicing this opinion, and it persisted into more recent times as well, as attested by the exceedingly positive review in an anthology of a certain Meccan poet's talents and output immediately after an account of his chronic alcoholism and promiscuity.[157] Such an approach

[155] For a principled defence of the superiority of platonic love poetry over frivolous works, see al-Washshāʾ, *Muwashshā* 113–5. For some examples, see al-Zawzanī, *Ḥamāsa* II, 81–2; al-Iṣfahānī, *Aghānī* XX, 230; al-Thaʿālibī, *Tatimma* I, 3; al-Bākharzī, *Dumya* I, 152; Ibn Zaydūn, *Dīwān* 30; al-Washshāʾ, *Muwashshā* 69; al-Iṣbahānī, *Kharīda* II(i), 290; Ibn Saʿīd, *Rāyāt* 185. Also cf. al-Thaʿālibī, *Tatimma* I, 108, where the themes of platonic love and chastity appear in a homosexual context, which makes this work all but unique.

[156] al-Tawḥīdī, *Baṣāʾir* I(i), 55; and also see ibid. II(iv), 43–4. An earlier genius of mediaeval Arabic prose, Abū ʿUthmān ʿAmr b. Baḥr al-Jāḥiẓ (ca. 160/776–255/868–9), was equally convinced of the merits of humour and joking, and – judging from his immense popularity among other things – a very substantial part of his educated urban contemporaries shared his predilection. On this issue, see Pellat 1963: 359–60. The idea that seriousness unrelieved by doses of humour leads to ennui was widely held and stated by mediaeval Muslim authors; see Sprachman 1995: xxii–xxiii.

[157] Ibn Maʿṣūm, *Sulāfa* 213. The same indulgence in turning a blind eye to personal defects was

was commonplace in the mediaeval period, and some literary experts, as exemplified by the three excerpts that follow, even explicitly stated it. The texts also implicitly demonstrate – by their polemical tone – that the approach had its detractors:

> If [the poet's unsound] religiosity were to deface [his] poetry and and mistaken beliefs justified the disesteem of a poet, then the very name of Abū Nuwās should be effaced from all collections of poetry and should not be mentioned when the generations [of poets] are enumerated. And it is all the more true of [the poets of] the pre-Islamic period. [...] However, these are two completely separate matters: religion has nothing to do with poetry.[158]

> It is also part of [the negative aspects of al-Mutanabbī's poetry] that he overtly mentions therein his tenuous faith and shaky piety. However, religiosity is not a measure of a poet's [worth]; incorrect religious convictions cannot be grounds for rating a poet low.[159]

> There are people who accuse [Abū Tammām] of unbelief, indeed treat it as a fact and use it as a reason to depreciate his poetry and brand the very best of his poems repugnant. I do not think, however, that unbelief will decrease the value of any poetry, nor that faith will increase it. [...] And they might feel inclined to curse other poets who[, unlike Abū Tammām,] were indisputably unbelievers and whom the caliphs executed on the basis of both confessions and evidence. Yet it does not diminish the value of their poetry in the least, nor does it make it of lesser quality: it is only they [the poets] themselves who became less because of this, and it is only themselves that their unbelief harmed. Likewise, those four people who every expert acknowledges have been the most talented poets ever – namely Imru' al-Qays, al-Nābigha al-Dhubyānī, Zuhayr and al-Aʿshā – did not harm their poetry at all with their unbelief; they harmed themselves.[160]

Such opinions, which are discussed in the above passages in earnest, could also be expressed in a sarcastic tone, more or less suggesting that too pious versifiers tend to produce mediocre poetry and therefore piety is not a desirable quality in a poet.[161]

A corollary to the principle of poetry being outside the purview of religious ethics is the treatment of serious and jesting texts (*jidd* and *hazl* respectively) as two separate fields, with dissimilar criteria of judging them. Obviously, the jesting register (*hazl*) would allow for infinitely more tolerance than texts with a serious

---

apparently not accorded to the scholarly class (even specialists of more 'secular' disciplines); see Kopf 1956: 38–9.

[158] al-Jurjānī, *Wasāṭa* 66.

[159] al-Thaʿālibī, *Yatīma* I, 168.

[160] al-Ṣūlī, *Akhbār* 172–4. Also cf. Ibn Saʿīd, *Ghuṣūn* 7–8. Such views are succinctly summarised by G. J. H. van Gelder: "Poetry and the criticism of poetry lie outside the domain of ethics, in the view of [...] the majority of Arab critics." See van Gelder 1992: 188.

[161] See for instance Ibn Qutayba, *Shiʿr* 139; al-Thaʿālibī, *Thimār* I, 358.

purport.[162] This resulted in the slightly schizophrenic practice on the part of some anthologists of happily enjoying the *mujūn* of libertine poets while heaping curses on the religiously skeptical poetry of Abū l-ʿAlāʾ al-Maʿarrī (363/973–449/1058), presumed to be serious in intent.[163] Another pertinent example is the heated denunciations of countless motifs of the poetry of Abū l-Ṭayyib al-Mutanabbī (303/915–354/965) and others cultivating obviously 'serious' genres (especially panegyrics), a striking contrast to the treatment accorded to most *mujūn* works even if it is likely that personal rancour and *jalousie de métier* often played a part in the case of reactions to al-Mutanabbī.[164] We will take up the pivotal issue of the differentiation of seriousness and jesting again in the next chapter.

This differentiation was dominant but not absolute. Some anthologists and literary experts expressed ambivalent feelings towards the drollery of *mujūn*, simultaneously acclaiming it for the wit thereof and criticising it for its perceived immorality. Of course, one can only speculate as to the honesty of such sentiments either way – not only righteousness but also a 'sophisticated' taste for humour might well be feigned. Consider this critical appraisal of some verses from the Seljuk era:

> [The following satirical poem was composed by Abū Tammām al-Dabbās] about Kathīr b. Samālīq al-Wakīl preparing for going on the pilgrimage to Mecca: "My Lord, your sanctuary is one that people are obligated to visit. / And therefore Kathīr has now departed towards you; but you have to block his way / Before he, with all his crooked arguments, dispossesses you of this sanctuary." This motif he had borrowed from another poet's work: "O Lord of Creation other than whom there is no one we can depend upon! / My brother, whom you know best, has departed as a pilgrim towards you out of hypocrisy. / Beware, do not let him enter Mecca, for he will grab it away from you." Now, such [talk] may well please one as an entertaining conceit, yet for someone to address God with such words is a sign of fickle faith and piety. We beseech God to make us persevere in correct faith![165]

---

[162] E.g. al-Thaʿālibī, *Yatīma* III, 30 ["*wa-lawlā anna jidd al-adab jidd...*" etc.]. The distinction was commonly recognised by rulers too. For instance, unlike jestful libertines, people who would utter disrespectful remarks about the Prophet or his relatives or companions in earnest (e.g. out of sectarian conviction) could expect very harsh chastisement. See for instance al-Tanūkhī, *Nishwār* VI, 64–5. – It is regrettable that in many cases the modern Western reader is quite unable to decide with certainty whether its mediaeval author intended a text to be serious or jestful or both. See van Gelder 1992: 88.

[163] E.g. al-Bākharzī, *Dumya* I, 157–8; Ibn Maʿṣūm, *Sulāfa* 386–7. On the nature of al-Maʿarrī's poetry, cf. Sperl 1989: 99.

[164] E.g. al-Qazwīnī, *Īḍāḥ* VI, 63–4; Ibn al-Muʿtazz, *Ṭabaqāt* 82; al-Thaʿālibī, *Yatīma* I, 146, 161 ["*wa-kathīr min al-ʿahr aḥsan min hādhā l-ʿafāf*"], 167–70; II, 214; IV, 418; al-Thaʿālibī, *Tatimma* II, 113; al-ʿAskarī, *Ṣināʿatayn* 122–3, 384; al-Jurjānī, *Ishārāt* 321–2; al-Qalqashandī, *Ṣubḥ* III, 497. (One finds plenty of vehement derogations like "he would deserve a slap in the face for this poem", and so on.)

[165] al-Iṣbahānī, *Kharīda* I(ii), 331–2.

This text also illustrates the usual extent of drawing religious considerations and judgements into the discussion of literature on the part of literary specialists like anthologists and critics. Apart from the occasional token expressions of pious disapproval – in Frédéric Lagrange's apt phrasing, some "*affectation de quelques froncements de sourcils*"[166] – there tends to be little criticism of *mujūn* from a religious point of view, and almost no sustained and systematic arraignment of it. The very fact of the inclusion of 'offending' works, often in full, in literary anthologies is pregnant with implications and all but belies the disapproving comments that may accompany the cited work. In some cases, even that much criticism is absent. And in other cases, all the commentary is highly, even enthusiastically, positive.[167] An interesting example of the efforts of some literary specialists to eat their cake and have it is the strikingly mild criticism appended to a sample of verses clearly expressing unbelief (*kufriyyāt*) by Abū Nuwās. The author, who is elsewhere in his treatise quite outspoken about his admiration for the great libertine poet and states his intention to compose a separate work in his praise, indicates disapproval in phrases like "I do not know why he had to say that, given he did not really believe it (*lā adrī li-mādhā qālahā wa-lā yaʿtaqiduhā*)" and "I see no excuse for his having uttered such things, given his belief in the divine law of Islam and its requirements (*lā aʿrifu lahu fī l-bawḥ bihā ʿudhran maʿa mā kāna ʿalayhi min iʿtiqād sharīʿat al-islām bi-sharāʾiṭihā*)".[168]

166 Lagrange 2006: 55.

167 The poet-cum-anthologist Ibn al-Muʿtazz gives a wholly positive assessment ("*wa-mimmā yustaḥsanu min shiʿrihi qawluhu fī l-mujūn...*") of a poem describing a sexual intercourse; see Ibn al-Muʿtazz, *Ṭabaqāt* 127–8. The author of *Yatīmat al-dahr* had no qualms either about this subject. The only comment we find on a shockingly, unspeakably obscene and naturalistic poem describing anal intercourse is this: "[The poet] is in total control of his subject-matter in this verse, which is devoid of any artificiality; nothing comparable has so far been composed in this topic." In the same anthology, a real literary success by the standards of the period, al-Thaʿālibī shows himself very favourably disposed to the obscene poetry of Ibn al-Ḥajjāj too (who was extremely successful anyway). He dwells long upon the unique talents of the poet and all he says by way of criticism is the banal phrase "I ask for God's pardon and forgiveness". See al-Thaʿālibī, *Yatīma* I, 349–55; III, 30, 99. The anthologist ʿAlī b. al-Ḥasan al-Bākharzī (d. 467/1074–5) volunteers no explicit assessment of the quite witty *mujūn* poetry of his own father, but its inclusion in the selection from the father's *oeuvre* can surely be taken as a sign of tacit approval, nay pride. See al-Bākharzī, *Dumya* II, 1260. In the anthology *Kharīdat al-qaṣr*, a poem mocking a muezzin and his profession elicits only this commentary: "[it is] popular" and "wonderful"; see al-Iṣbahānī, *Kharīda* I(i), 188. The Andalusian anthologist Ibn Diḥya al-Balansī (6th–7th/12th–13th c.) offers this criticism about the use of the motif of a patron's hand being even more deserving of a grateful kiss than the black stone in the Kaʿba in Mecca: "It is an instance of exaggerations and embellishments by the poets", but "what a difference there is between the hand [of a human] and the Black Stone in this world and the next!" See Ibn Diḥya, *Muṭrib* 15–6; and cf. al-Ḥillī, *ʿĀṭil* 208. Also see van Gelder 1988: 78–95, a whole chapter devoted entirely to the stark contrast between anthologists' declarations of disapproval of hurtful *hijāʾ* poetry and the striking amount of hurtful *hijāʾ* the same authors' anthologies tend to contain.

168 Ibn al-Muzarraʿ, *Sariqāt* 144–6.

2. Sanctions and Rewards

The foregoing sections of this chapter have shown that the existence of a remarkable amount of extant *mujūn* material, both as a body of fictitious literature and as a supposedly truthful description of a pattern of behaviour, does not by any means testify to a unanimous acceptance of such a phenomenon in any of the classes and subgroups of society. Even at the height of its popularity, *mujūn* was irredeemably controversial. And where there is virtuous disapproval, there must be attempts to suppress the objectionable. We have seen the wide variety of views among the ultimate moral entrepreneurs of mediaeval Muslim society – the class of *ʿulamāʾ* – regarding libertinism, and their almost unanimous tendency to frown upon the phenomenon while disagreeing as to the desirable legal consequences. We have likewise noted the fact that such theoretical stances did not necessarily – or even commonly – inform actual praxis, even among these religious experts themselves. The remarkable discrepancy between patterns of conduct in private and public respectively has also been commented upon in discussing the attitudes of the courtly elite. However, it would be too hasty simply to conclude that libertines were condemned in theory and given a blank check in practice. Not only hasty but incorrect as well, because libertines did expose themselves to the danger of punishment for their behaviour and literary output, and such penalisation was often, indeed usually, justified with the need to put a stop to indecency or irreverence. In other words, *mujūn* was widely regarded as liable to (less than precisely specified) legal penalties, and that principle was in some cases put into practice. Even though it is probably true that the purveyors of *mujūn* faced no ill consequences in the majority of cases, they certainly did not enjoy total immunity. It is to the issue of the actual ways of sanctioning and curtailing *mujūn* that we turn our attention in the following sections, before having a brief look into the profitability of *mujūn* literature, that is to say the material rewards that would counterpoise and justify the usually slender risks involved in this literary pursuit. As will be obvious from the following paragraphs, I use the concept of 'sanctions' in a very broad sense which includes quite informal, even casual ways of expressing disapproval as well as tangible legal measures taken by the powers that be. This spacious use of the term is deliberate. First, it must be realised that in no society today are sanctions and punishments applied completely systematically and consistently, and the element of haphazardness is all the more pronounced in the case of premodern societies, which lacked the resources of the machinery of a modern state to control its citizens. This in itself introduced a certain amount of fluidity into the enforcement of conformity to norms, and the researcher can only hope, at best, to identify certain tendencies in punishing offenders instead of clear-cut rules. This is especially relevant to a situation in which the legal framework for dealing with a phenomenon is subject to controversy and offers no clear guidelines, as was the case with the legal consequences of *mujūn*. More important still is the fact that the sanctions that a society applies to breaches of norms are more often than not informal and unofficial, and legal action is usually just a last resort that does not affect the majority of cases.[169] Therefore, in the discussion below, any way in which a libertine considered to be breaking a norm was urged to move closer to compliance with that norm qualifies as a way of sanctioning, no matter how benign and peaceful the rectifying efforts. For our present purposes, the important point is whether, how often, and in what ways a *mājin* would be encouraged to conform to norms and thus, by definition, renounce some of his *mujūn*. As we will see, such pressure might range from token disapproval to legal restrictions to the relatively rare instances of the death penalty. It will also be shown that the pressure to conform, although typically not particularly violent, was strong enough for many littérateurs to choose to refrain from certain (or all) forms of *mujūn* of their own accord and thus stay on the safe side.

2.1 Repression and Control: Premodern Forms of 'Censorship'

Various informal ways of expressing disapproval and attempts at censorship (including virtual ostracism by the community and pious exhortations) have been discussed above in the sections dealing with the reception of *mujūn* in the various echelons of the society. The reader can refer back to those passages to see instances of informal societal pressure on libertines to conform. The focus in this section will be on more formal ways of exercising control over literary production and pressuring libertines to conform their behaviour and works to established norms.[170]

Mediaeval Arabic literature offers relatively few examples of active, drastic official censorship such as the public burning of books or the banning of concrete works, at least as far as belles-lettres – as opposed to theological treatises and similar 'serious' works – are concerned.[171] However, rulers might occasionally decide to prohibit certain

[169] On this important point, see Clinard 1965: 18–20, 149; and also cf. Denzin 1970: 122–25; Ball 1970: 359–60.

[170] I am aware of the element of anachronism in using the term 'censorship', so it is to be understood in the very loose, non-technical sense of any attempt, official or otherwise, to restrict the production or circulation of certain literary works. On this point, and for a more thorough treatment of the subject-matter of this section, see Szombathy 2007.

[171] A pertinent case is the killing of the famous mystic of Baghdad, Manṣūr al-Ḥallāj (244/857–309/922). After his execution, the authorities reportedly summoned all the scribes and copyists of Baghdad, who had to take an oath never to circulate or sell the works of the 'heretic' Sufi. See Miskawayh, *Tajārib* I, 82; and for a comparable example, see ibid. I, 285. The Zaydite authority Abū l-Ḥasan Ibn Miftāḥ (d. 877/1472) advises that 'the books of unbelief' (*dafātir al-kufr*) – which he

poets (usually temporarily) to compose works in some genres deemed provocative or offensive. The genres singled out for such proscription would typically be lampoons, love poetry, and bacchic poetry. There is some reason to suppose that such cases almost always involved previous complaints against the offending poet, that is to say such a ban would result from a prior scandal rather than an overall desire on the part of the ruler to suppress objectionable poetry in general. A case in point is the injunction to stop producing love poetry directed to the famous blind libertine Bashshār b. Burd (d. 167–8/784–5). His outspoken and catchy love poems addressed to various women being in vogue among the population of Baṣra, it was feared – and denounced by many – that these works had a pernicious influence over the morals and chastity of the young people of both sexes in Baṣra. It was in response to such complaints that the caliph prohibited Bashshār from composing amorous verse.[172] (As we will argue, lampoons were the genre most likely to be affected by such attempts at casual 'censorship'.) But the sanctioning of literary production by decree of a sovereign could work both ways, as a ruler could equally well order the composition of 'indecent' or 'immoral' works by a court poet extremely reluctant to oblige.[173]

The occasional effort to suppress literary works mainly affected those having a political content or containing exorbitant invective. (As the boundaries of *mujūn* and *hijāʾ* could be fluid at times, *mujūn* might be susceptible to censorship in this way.) Thus the literary heritage of an infamously malevolent abusive poet of Seljuk-era Baghdad, Jamāl al-Mulk al-ʿAbsī, is largely lost due to the caliph's order, issued immediately after the poet's death, to confiscate and destroy the whole *oeuvre* of the deceased.[174] While this *post mortem* act of censorship can hardly be described

defines as the writings of heretics (*zanādiqa*) and partisans of an anthropomorphic conception of God's attributes (*mushabbiha*) – should be burned. See Ibn Miftāḥ, *Muntazaʿ* X, 532–3; and see Fierro 2001: 472 on cases of burning certain books in the Muslim West. Religious tendencies and views officially considered to be errant, as well as customs seen as reprehensible, could also be subject to banning at times. See for instance Shoshan 1993: 13, 49–51; and cf. Ibn al-Ṣalāḥ, *Fatāwā* I, 232 [on the necessity of banning unusual Quran readings]. The Abbasid caliphs would sometimes even take steps to repress certain Christian heresies – totally indifferent from a Muslim point of view – when petitioned to do so by the religious leaders of the Christian community. See Cooperson 2001: 376–82.

[172] al-Iṣfahānī, *Aghānī* III, 176–9. Another version attributes the caliph's decision to his own excessively jealous character instead of pressure from others; see ibid. III, 238. However, both versions clearly agree on the role of ulterior motives, and neither explanation suggests any preoccupation on the ruler's part with the admissibility of such poetry in general.

[173] Such is the case of Abū l-ʿAtāhiya, who is claimed to have spent over a year in prison for his firm refusal to purvey love poetry as commanded by the caliph Hārūn al-Rashīd (r. 170/786–193/809). Having repented his past sins, the poet was determined to write only decorous and upright poetry thenceforth, but the caliph apparently would not hear of such tenacity. See al-Iṣfahānī, *Aghānī* IV, 33–4, 68–9.

[174] al-Iṣbahānī, *Kharīda* I(ii), 52–4. Some of his poems, however, escaped destruction at the hands of the caliph's agents; for a sample, see ibid. I(ii), 66–8.

as drastic, for a poet to get entangled in political controversies could be an invitation to violent attempts to suppress his poetry and a source of real peril; an example is the almost unanimous reticence of court poets after the assassination of the short-lived caliph Ibn al-Muʿtazz (296/908), apprehensions of the murderers' vengeance being enough of a disincentive to the production of any dirges as would have been customary.[175] (The issue of killing people for certain literary products will presently be taken on below.)

Apart from a ruler, there were few people in a position to decide the suppression of a literary work. To be sure, an anthologist could deliberately exclude certain works from his compilation. Criteria for omission were, needless to say, highly idiosyncratic, even whimsical perhaps – after all, it is a matter of taste and mood to determine what is over the top. In some anthologies one finds the occasional remark that a given poem, or some verses of it, were found to be too indecent, irreverent or obscene for inclusion, but such indications seem to be quite infrequent. More often than not, the language of anthologists commenting on their own decision to bowdlerise is somewhat opaque, and the sheer amount of truly outrageous material in the same compilations must leave the reader wondering what particular aspect of the censored work caused the anthologist to draw the line where he did and why. Wherever any reason is given, we typically find political or sectarian considerations playing a role; in other cases the phrasing is totally impenetrable and allows no inference to be made.[176] It is all the more regrettable as a sufficiently extensive corpus of comments by anthologists on their own criteria of bowdlerisation and deletion would certainly speak volumes about prevalent notions of the limits of freedom in literary expression. More helpful are those cases when an anthologist does not actually delete a certain work or parts of it, but in a perfunctory nod to dominant norms records his disapproval after a full citation of the objectionable passages.[177]

[175] One poet was, however, bold enough to compose an explicit elegy, while another – betraying more circumspection – disguised his commemorative poem on the ill-fated caliph as a parodistic dirge on a tomcat. See al-Thaʿālibī, *Thimār* I, 320–1. This collective dread to touch the subject of the murdering of Ibn al-Muʿtazz appears to be atypical. When for instance the caliph Hārūn al-Rashīd (r. 170/786–193/809) turned against the family of his vizier, the Barmakids, in 187/803, and had the vizier executed, quite a number of poets subsequently composed sympathetic elegies on the disgraced family. See al-Ṭabarī, *Tārīkh* V, 1731–2.

[176] Explicit attacks against the powers that be (especially the caliphate) as well as extremist sectarian (typically Shiʿite) views might not always pass the test of the anthologist's sensitivity. In other cases, laconic sentences like «there is [in this poem] such content as I protect my book from» offer no clue to the nature of the omitted material. See for instance al-Iṣbahānī, *Kharīda* I(ii), 84; II(i), 208; al-Thaʿālibī, *Tatimma* I, 70. Particularly vulgar and offensive lampoons were sometimes left out of anthologies; it is not unreasonable to suppose that in such decisions a desire to avoid offending the targeted person (or his descendants) would be an important factor. For a late mediaeval example, see Ibn Maʿṣūm, *Sulāfa* 244–8 [on Ibrāhīm b. Yūsuf al-Muhtār and his works].

[177] E.g. al-Iṣbahānī, *Kharīda* I(ii), 328, where we read: "You see what [the poet] has committed

While *mujūn* poetry and prose rarely faced the prospect of being banned, legal consequences for producing such works were not unheard of. As ever, a wide discrepancy between theory and practice is a distinct possibility, and here we will focus on what we can know of the real-life application – or lack thereof – of the legal principles and prescriptions discussed earlier in this chapter. As discussed at length above, one of the negative implications of being a libertine that the legal sources most consistently insist on is the loss of the status of a trustworthy witness (*ʿadāla*) in legal proceedings. This meant that a person infamous for his impropriety and licentiousness (whether in behaviour, speech or writing) would not be allowed to testify in a disputed case (*baṭulat shahādatuhu*), as he was considered to be too nonchalant about the responsibility it entailed, hence of dubious veracity. It must be emphasised, however, that behaving or speaking like a libertine was only one of many characteristics and activities that could result in being deprived of the status of *ʿadāla*. The process of verifying the credentials of an individual as a trustworthy witness (*taʿdīl*) was supposed to be a careful and meticulous one, and a lot of factors could contribute to the verdict that someone was not to be trusted. Some jurisprudents would advise rejection of a witness who provided musical intruction to his female slaves or entertained his guests with the singing of slave-girls, others were adamant in disallowing the testimony of anyone ever seen naked in a public bath.[178] *Mujūn* was clearly treated pretty much like any other manifestation of improper behaviour or speech unbecoming for a serious man.

This for one is a legal precept that appears to have been followed by and large, although certainly not in every case. As the very notion of *mujūn* is a complex one – the label, as has been shown in the previous chapters, in fact described a wide variety of behaviours and literary motifs unified by the irreverent and frivolous attitudes manifested by them – it is hardly surprising that a host of phenomena associated with libertines might lead to exclusion from the status of reliable witness. Notoriety for habitual drinking – especially if indiscreet – was obviously one of such behaviours.[179] An observable lack of respectability and solemnity, a trait closely associated with libertines, was likewise a potential cause for disqualification from the status of *ʿadl*, a trustworthy witness.[180] It bears emphasis that the rejection of a

for the sake of this exaggeration; we ask God's forgiveness for such talk."

[178] Ibn Baydakīn, *Lumaʿ* I, 173–4; Ibn al-Ṣalāḥ, *Fatāwā* II, 498; al-Tawḥīdī, *Baṣāʾir* III(vi), 118.

[179] See for instance the information on al-Sarī b. ʿAbd al-Raḥmān and his drinking pals in al-Iṣfahānī, *Aghānī* XX, 215. Also cf. Ibn Maʿṣūm, *Sulāfa* 417.

[180] Some legal experts advised rejection of the testimony of a man with a jestful character. It appears that judges did apply such strictures, at least occasonally: a *qāḍī* in Baghdad immediately withdrew the status of trustworthy witness from a man who had expressed his satisfaction at acquiring the coveted status with a merry dance; and another *qāḍī* turned away a witness sporting a laughable and frivolous nickname. Too evident hypocrisy might also lead to disqualification: the judge Abū ʿUmar al-Azdī refused to accept the testimony of a man who made a show of disgust at sniffing the

man's legal testimony did not usually entail other negative consequences, nor did it necessarily reflect any personal animosity or disdain on the part of the judge. Indeed, the *qāḍī* might easily be on friendly and even bantering terms with the person whose testimony he refused to accept.[181]

That said, deciding a person's status for purposes of legal testimony depended to a great extent on an individual and highly subjective set of criteria, including quite whimsical ones, which may explain the fact that some men widely known for their mirthful temperament and their partiality for joking and banter could still pass muster as reliable witnesses, and indeed even achieve appointment to positions requiring high moral integrity.[182]

Imprisonment of a poet for *mujūn* works seems to have been rather unusual, and execution for the same offence even more so. Although in many – perhaps most – cases the passing references available in the sources hardly allow us to decide with absolute certainty whether *mujūn* was truly the cause of such a violent reaction or only an opportune excuse, the point is moot, for in either case *mujūn* provided an opportunity to the authorities to imprison or jail a poet, and therefore could be a source of danger. As the sources are often totally reticent or else speak in elusive terms about the nature of the wrongdoing that led to the incarceration of a poet or writer, the reader is left speculating.[183] However, the sporadic and highly unsystematic

bouquet of wine. As Abū ʿUmar quite sensibly observed, that wine is illicit does not mean that it is also disgusting, and therefore the man must be either a hypocrite or an oaf. See al-Khaṭīb, *Kifāya* 139; al-Tawḥīdī, *Baṣāʾir* I(i), 89; al-ʿAskarī, *Ṣināʿatayn* 158; al-Tanūkhī, *Nishwār* II, 171. Also see Ibn Qutayba, *ʿUyūn* I(i), 136–9; Messick 1993: 161–2.

181 E.g. al-Tanūkhī, *Nishwār* I, 307. On the other hand, the acceptance or rejection of a man's testimony was a delicate business, and some individuals would come to bear great animus towards the judge who had disqualified them. See for instance Ibn ʿĀṣim, *Janna* I, 174; and also Messick 1993: 180. (Still, it is reasonable to suppose that libertines who deliberately flouted established norms would be the least likely to react with acrimony to such a sanction.)

182 See for instance an illuminating characterisation of a certain Abu l-Fatḥ Hibatallāh al-Wāsiṭī: "He was among the most esteemed witnesses and the witty men of Wāsiṭ. Fond of stories and anecdotes, his joking and chat were engrossing..." See al-Iṣbahānī, *Kharīda* II(i), 403. Also see ibid. II(ii), 489 ["*kāna min ẓurafāʾ Wāsiṭ wa-aʿyānihā*"]. If one trusts a report in the *Kitāb al-aghānī* concerning the poet Muṭīʿ b. Iyās, even disreputable libertines might be appointed to high official posts (although chronological problems make this account rather improbable); see al-Iṣfahānī, *Aghānī* XIII, 344 ["*wa-wallā l-Mahdī Muṭīʿ b. Iyās ʿalā ṣadaqat al-Baṣra*"]; and Vajda 1938: 212. Some singers, however, were accepted as trustworthy witnesses despite the widespread religious opposition to their métier; see Kilpatrick 1997: 97. – It is worth noting that some authorities opined that disqualifying someone as a witness was justified only in rare cases of truly momentous moral objections; see Ibn Qutayba, *ʿUyūn* I(i), 133. On the institution of legally acceptable witness; also see Cahen 1958–9: I, 232.

183 For instance, the successful and rich Iraqi poet al-Muʾayyad al-Alūsī spent a decade in prison under the caliph al-Muqtafī (r. 530/1136–555/1160), during which he lost his eyesight, and was only set free under the next caliph. However, the sources available to me identify the cause in a hopelessly opaque wording: "he staggered by [decree of] Fate", "things that are not proper were told about him and his companions", etc. See Yāqūt, *Udabāʾ* VI, 2737–8; al-Iṣbahānī, *Kharīda* I(ii), 172–3. One case

application of such drastic measures does suggest that *mujūn* must have been a handy excuse rather than the real offence in the majority of cases. It remains to be seen what the genuine cause in every case might have been. Whenever it can be guessed with a degree of probability, it seems that personal rancour or political considerations – not too surprisingly – played a part. A display of disrespect towards the powers that be could sometimes lead to imprisonment, if not worse. Of course, disrespect could be manifested in a lot of ways. For example, writing lampoons against rulers and members of the courtly elite was risky business, indeed probably the most frequent cause of violent reactions on the part of the offended parties.[184] Because of the intense rivalry within the political elite, even a poet's refraining from composing satirical poetry altogether did not totally shield him from the possibility of furious retributions. Permitting no sign of disloyalty, rulers might strongly resent their court poets' composing panegyrics praising other patrons.[185] However, even complete loyalty to one patron would not necessarily ensure immunity for a poet: patrons, as all humans, die, and in the atmosphere of heavy intrigue characterising mediaeval courts, they could also fall from grace. If a former patron's foe rose to prominence, a poet – and indeed any member of the entourage – might get into trouble. Ironically, too much loyalty to one patron would in such a case be just as dangerous as too little of the same could be, as a rival would seek to eliminate (or remove from the court) not only his political and/or personal opponent but also anyone too closely associated with that opponent. A case in point is the fate of a renowned poet and close associate of the vizier Ibn Hubayra (d. 560/1165), who was imprisoned on charges of offending a high-ranking man, and subsequently died in prison.[186] Similarly, Bashshār b. Burd immediately revised one of his particularly abusive lampoons when his patron died, being well aware that leaving the verses

of a man being punished for what definitely appears to be jesting of the *mujūn* type took place in North Africa (Tunis) and is therefore unrepresentative of tendencies further east (*v.i.*). This account tells of a student of religion (*rajul min ṣinf al-ṭalaba*) who entertained others with frivolous jokes ("*ʿalā wajh al-taḍāḥuk wa-l-istihzāʾ wa-ʿadam al-ihtibāl fī-mā yulqīhi min al-kalām al-muḍḥik mimmā fīhi sakhāfāt wa-qabīḥ al-manṭiq...*") involving irreverence towards God and the Prophet, which was reported to the chief judge of the town. There being no trustworthy man among the many available witnesses, he got the relatively mild sentence of a one-year prison term (plus eighty lashes on being released). See al-Wansharīsī, *Miʿyār* II, 374.

[184] For a detailed discussion of the possible consequences of lampooning a politically powerful individual, see Szombathy 2009: 92–105.

[185] The officially declared cause of a stint Abū Nuwās spent in the Abbasid caliph's prison was his audacity in employing a flippant poetic motif offensive to Islamic sensibilities – a usual enough phenomenon, as we have seen, in both his oeuvre and *mujūn* in general – but it seems almost certain that the real reason was the fact that the poem in question was addressed to a patron other than the caliph himself (the governor of Egypt). See Ibn Qutayba, *Shiʿr* 419.

[186] al-Iṣbahānī, *Kharīda* II(i), 302. Nor does it seem to be an atypical incident; see for instance Ibn al-Muʿtazz, *Ṭabaqāt* 56; and also Kilpatrick 1997: 114–5.

(and especially the names appearing therein) intact could cost him his life. In the event, the revision seems to have saved him from the wrath of the poem's target.[187]

As noted, imprisonment itself was not a prescribed and uncontroversial penalty for insults to the honour of political leaders, and therefore any uniformity in the length of such a prison term was out of the question. In the absence of a fixed penalty, once a court poet was imprisoned, he might well remain in jail practically indefinitely, unless someone interceded successfully on his behalf.[188]

Languishing in jail is bad enough, but worse could also befall a poet or writer. The capital punishment for a literary product was not unheard of in the mediaeval Middle East, but again patterns are rather hard to pin down. In legal theory, a few motifs of *mujūn* literature – especially anything classifiable either as 'insulting the Prophet' or as unequivocal 'apostasy' – would be subject to prosecution and could lead to the execution of the offender. (The reader is referred back to the discussion of the views of jurisprudents on various facets of *mujūn*.) However, the considerable distance between theory and practice makes the task of the researcher very complicated. Some accounts of the application of the death penalty are suspiciously lacking in specific data, and in my view reflect wishful thinking rather than historical fact.[189] In some few cases, jesting remarks of the *mujūn* type did demonstrably lead to capital punishment, although such incidents tend to have taken place in very specific circumstances, and political considerations seem to have played an important part.[190]

It bears repetition that the officially stated reasons for executing – or otherwise punishing – an offender might well mask ulterior motives, and could thus often be simple pretexts. Nevertheless the use of such pretexts to get rid of enemies or annoying people does mean that producing *mujūn* texts could become dangerous under certain circumstances and in certain historical periods. Yet even in such cases the establishment of an acceptable legal basis for the execution might pose problems and take quite some time. The process would typically involve considerable efforts, and on occasion even repeated unsuccessful attempts, by a ruler to recruit some prestigious savants willing to be accomplices to what was basically an abuse of religious law.[191] Accusations of blasphemy and frivolity could also be used as

[187] al-Iṣfahānī, *Aghānī* III, 149–50, 211; al-ʿAskarī, *Maṣūn* 162–4.

[188] E.g. al-Iṣfahānī, *Aghānī* IV, 70; al-Ṭabarī, *Tārīkh* V, 1820–1.

[189] A legal source mentions an unnamed imam who ordered that 'an Iraqi man' (who is not named) be decapitated for a frivolous remark on a Quranic passage, a decision endorsed by 'the caliph' (again, anonymous); see Ibn Baydakīn, *Lumaʿ* I, 181–2. For another case with somewhat more concrete details, see Badr, *Risāla* 33; al-Qāriʾ, *Sharḥ* 167.

[190] For an analysis of two such cases in Muslim al-Andalus, see Fierro 1990: 104–9.

[191] An illustrative example is an account of the machinations of the Abbasid caliph al-Muʿtaḍid (r. 279/892–289/902) with the aim of having his vizier Ismāʿīl b. Bulbul executed. Lacking any legal grounds for such a course of action, he sought to convince one of the religious notables at the court

opportunistic weapons in courtly intrigues, although such ruses did not necessarily succeed. Under the relatively zealous Almohad rulers, in the relatively conservative cultural atmosphere of North Africa, a poet called Abū Ḥafṣ ʿUmar al-Sulamī (early 7th/13th c.) was the target of such charges, but still he escaped unscathed.[192]

One particular period of Muslim history, however, did feature an episode of widespread accusations of ill-defined 'heresy' or 'godlessness' (*zandaqa*) – sometimes with sinister consequences for the accused – and libertines, frivolous poets and other secular-minded individuals were an especial target of the persecution.[193] Practically all manifestations of *mujūn*, both literary and behavioural, would provide an obvious excuse for indictment. The persecution of 'heretics' was systematised and intensified during the reign of the caliph al-Mahdī (r. 158/775–169/785), with a special official (the *ṣāḥib al-zanādiqa*) appointed to prosecute any intellectual suspected of the crime. The career of many a famous poet and man of letters suffered from such harrassment, and indeed some even lost their lives. Not surprisingly, some people

to pronounce a reasonably plausible charge against the vizier, only to be rejected by the conscientious scholar. Another high religious savant had no moral qualms, however, and delivered the required death sentence. See al-Tanūkhī, *Nishwār* III, 97–8. A comparable case which took place in 8th/14th-century Syria (in the coastal town of al-Lādhiqiyya) also involved a religious scholar who was willing to oblige the governor by carefully designing a case (based on charges of blasphemy) against a local poet. This case is all the more pertinent to our subject-matter as the real reason of the execution of the poet was his having lampooned the governor and other notabilities – a fact evident even to a passing visitor to the town. See Ibn Baṭṭūṭa, *Riḥla* 48. Also cf. Ibn al-Muʿtazz, *Ṭabaqāt* 76–7 [on the possible reasons of the death of al-ʿAkawwak]; Yāqūt, *Udabāʾ* III, 1108 [on religious charges being a mere pretext in the execution of al-Ṭughrāʾī]. As Maribel Fierro convincingly shows, the occasional charges of 'heresy' in the history of Muslim al-Andalus can almost always be taken to have been politically motivated ("una excusa para acabar con un adversario político"); see Fierro 1994: 207; and cf. the charges and the real motives involved in the pertinent case of Ibn al-Khaṭīb (d. 776/1375) in Calero Secall 2001: 434–47. The need for such legal duplicity resulted from the fact that Muslim political theory very clearly circumscribed those felonies and misdemeanours that the authorities were entitled to punish. For a concise discussion of these, see Redissi 1998: 136–8.

192 Ibn Saʿīd, *Ghuṣūn* 92.

193 I am deliberately avoiding the use of the term 'Manicheanism', the usual translation of *zandaqa*. The reason is that this word, like many another denoting unacceptable political or sectarian leanings, came to be used as a general pejorative term, a sort of undifferentiated, all-out abuse. It is especially misleading to understand it in its original meaning when applied to an accused intellectual of the early Abbasid era; it is indispensable to examine each case separately to see what the label of *zandaqa* might have entailed. On this issue, see Vajda 1938: 173, 221; al-Alūsī 1987: 57, 201–2; and for a comprehensive analysis, see ʿAṭwān n.d. Most of the libertine poets and writers accused of *zandaqa* were simply too indifferent, and perhaps even ironic, about theological and religious disputes to become followers of any strict sectarian view, whether a heresy or not. Nonetheless, quite a few littérateurs were killed or lost their possessions in this brief period of persecution. See for instance Ibn al-Muʿtazz, *Ṭabaqāt* 34–5 [Ṣāliḥ b. ʿAbd al-Quddūs], 36 [Ibrāhīm b. Sayāba]; al-Baghdādī, *Khizāna* I, 542 [Ḥammād ʿAjrad]. On the background of several interesting cases, see Vajda 1938: 183–4, 198–9, 218–20. It is noteworthy that at least some modern Arabic dialects seem to have preserved the use of *zindīq* as a term of general abuse. For its use in Morocco, see Westermarck 1930: 86.

would be all too willing to denounce their personal enemies or professional rivals as 'heretics' to the authorities.[194] Consider the following highly insightful advice, reportedly given to Abū Nuwās by a well-wishing friend after the libertine poet recited a characteristically skeptical and blasphemous verse to him: "Man, you do have enemies on the lookout for your missteps so as to utilise them to find a way to accuse you and smudge your reputation before the ruler! Fear God, in your own best interest, and stop all this unrestraint and *mujūn*. [...] And if these verses of yours haven't yet become known, forget and hide them well."[195] What is remarkable from the point of view of this study is the way fairly ordinary *mujūn* motifs would sometimes be identified as sufficient grounds for branding someone a 'heretic'. The harrassment of the celebrated poet Abū l-ʿAtāhiya (d. 210/825 or 211/826), best known for his ascetic poetry yet the author of much love poetry in his youth, is a case in point. It is on the pretext of some playful, mildly frivolous references to Paradise in a poem that a personal foe brought charges of heresy against Abū l-ʿAtāhiya ("*shannaʿa ʿalayhi Manṣūr b. ʿAmmār bi-l-zandaqa wa-qāla yatahāwanu bi-l-janna wa-yabtadhilu dhikrahā fī shiʿrihi bi-mithl hādhā l-tahāwun*").[196] This despite the fact that such poetic conceits were not only common but veritable clichés, as we have shown in Chapter Two of this study. However, the logic of process was apparently rather haphazard, as other cases show that sometimes *mujūn* was explicitly distinguished from genuine 'heresy', or *zandaqa*, and treated much more leniently.[197]

Apart from the relatively brief intermezzo of the official persecution of *zandaqa* under the early Abbasids, the political authorities do not appear to have concerned themselves with the content of belles-lettres in any systematic way. As noted repeatedly above, this does not mean an official endorsement of *mujūn*, or even an overt toleration thereof, only a discreet indifference to its existence (often combined with a personal penchant for it in contexts of privacy). On the other hand, the genre of invective poetry, or *hijāʾ*, was quite another kettle of fish. Lampoons obviously

---

194 See for instance the case of the notorious libertine Muṭīʿ b. Iyās with his neighbour in al-Iṣfahānī, *Aghānī* XIII, 319–20; and the conflict of Ḥumayd b. Saʿīd and Aḥmad b. Abī Du'ād; ibid. XVIII, 159.

195 Abū Nuwās was not one to hide his outrageous poetry. Predictably, he was denounced to the caliph, who imprisoned him for the verses. It is noteworthy that a certain al-Rabīʿ b. Yūnus, a courtier who insisted on the need to punish the poet for his grave *lèse-religion*, had been previously offended by a sarcastic remark of Abū Nuwās, which goes a long way toward explaining his attentiveness to the poet's *faux pas*. See the case in Abū Hiffān, *Akhbār* 45–7.

196 al-Iṣfahānī, *Aghānī* IV, 55; and Ibn Qutayba, *Shiʿr* 409, 411–2. The consequences of those charges against Abū l-ʿAtāhiya are not perfectly clear, but it seems that the man also tried to incite the mob against the poet with some success ("*[...] wa-awqaʿa lahu hādhā ʿalā alsinat al-ʿāmma fa-laqiya minhum balāʾan*").

197 E.g. Abū Hiffān, *Akhbār* 122–3 ["*wa-huwa yushbihu annahu rajul mājin laysa bi-zindīq...*" etc.].

had the potential to incite the wrath of a ruler (or a lesser but still powerful individual, as the case might be), and revenge would often, although not always, take very violent forms. Much more than *lèse-religion*, *lèse-majesté* could easily lead to the assassination of the offending poet, and as we have seen, even cases of execution ostensibly based on offences against the sanctity of religion can be more meaningfully understood as thinly disguised acts of revenge for personal slights or political challenges. The whole issue of *hijāʾ* is tied to the preoccupation with honour among high-status males, and therefore it is little surprise to observe that within the circles of 'bohemian' men of letters, libertines and people of low status, lampoons were often regarded as just a kind of jesting with no consequences.[198] The mirthful casualness about lampoons of persons with no honour to guard contrasts starkly with the obsession of people of high prestige with defending themselves against the opprobrium of putting up with malicious satire.[199] It did not even matter if the satire was clearly untrue, trite and flimsy; in fact the more vernacular and accessible the style, the more damaging the piece could end up being, given the potentially wider circulation of a work comprehensible to everyone.[200] Needless to say, a poem could be infuriating without its belonging to the genre of satirical poetry *sensu stricto*: for instance, love poems addressed to a female relative of a ruler and scathing political criticism could provoke as violent reactions as any *hijāʾ*.[201] There is no shortage of reports about the killing of poets for a piece of *hijāʾ*; what complicates the picture is the fact that Islamic law in no way allows this practice, which meant that revenge would often have to be carried out surreptitiously and yet deliver a clear message to all potential offenders. Besides the killing of the offender, other drastic reactions to *hijāʾ* were also possible, on condition that they sufficiently highlighted and restituted the full honour of the offended party.[202] Thus there are reports about

---

198 See for instance al-Ibshīhī, *Mustaṭraf* 256. The frivolous poet al-Jammāz is described in a source as someone totally immune to *hijāʾ* – while very dangerous as a composer of damaging lampoons – because of his utter nonchalance about being satirised and his lack of any honour to protect ("*lā ʿirḍ lahu*"). See al-Iṣfahānī, *Aghānī* XIII, 260–1. The libertine poet Muṭīʿ b. Iyās almost instinctively vented his anger at the unfaithfulness of his girl-friend in impromptu *hijāʾ* verses; al-Iṣfahānī, *Aghānī* XIII, 339.

199 For some illustrative cases, see al-Bayhaqī, *Maḥāsin* 287; al-Ṣūlī, *Akhbār* 178; al-Iṣfahānī, *Aghānī* VII, 232–3; XX, 180–2, 188; Ibn Diḥya, *Muṭrib* 169 and Rubiera Mata 1992: 89–93 [on the career of Ibn ʿAmmār].

200 al-Jurjānī, *Wasāṭa* 35; and cf. Ibn al-Muʿtazz, *Ṭabaqāt* 92, 125.

201 E.g. al-Ḥillī, *ʿĀṭil* 14–5; García Gómez 1940: 35. A unique case of offensive love poetry with potentially lethal consequences is the story of Abū Nuwās composing some amorous verses about the beauty of the young caliph al-Amīn (r. 193/809–198/813). Although the caliph was very appreciative of Abū Nuwās's talents, there can be no doubt that he would not have hesitated to execute the poet to protect his own honour if he had learnt of the unspeakable impudence. See Abū Hiffān, *Akhbār* 101–2.

202 This question is treated more fully in Szombathy 2009: 95 sqq.

invective poetry leading to various poets' being threatened with a severe beating, or actually flogged, or sodomised by way of shaming, or having to go into exile from the whole territory of the Iberian peninsula.[203] It bears repeating that none of these sanctions – with the possible exception of a public flogging ordered by a famous *qāḍī* offended by a lampoon, which might have been justified as *taʿzīr* or *taʾdīb* (discretionary punishment) – had any secure basis in Islamic law, being instead demonstrations of an ability to defend one's honour regardless of legal principles. The self-imposed exile of some poets out of a fear of the wrath of a high-ranking individual insulted by their *hijāʾ* is indicative of the very real possibility of the most extreme measure against an offending poet, that of washing off the insult with the offender's blood. This eventuality was actually not at all uncommon. Poets who habitually lampooned people with considerable political power all but courted death, as shown by the cases of quite a few poets who lost their lives in exactly such circumstances. An early example is the famous Bashshār b. Burd (d. 167–8/784–5), although some accounts of his liquidation on the orders of the reigning caliph mention blasphemous jokes made by Bashshār in public – no doubt an instance of the usual custom of using charges of *lèse-religion* as a pretext to kill someone for satires or political criticism.[204] Similar pretexts were cited by those offended by the Andalusian poet Abū Jaʿfar al-Battī, but it seems incontrovertible that his disgraceful death was caused by one lampoon too many that he had composed.[205] Another south Iraqi poet with a notoriety for his obsession with the genre of *hijāʾ*, a certain Murajjā b. Battāh al-Baṭāʾiḥī, also met his death at the hands of murderers sent by an offended local ruler.[206]

[203] al-Iṣfahānī, *Aghānī* IV, 242–3; al-Ibshīhī, *Mustaṭraf* 110; al-Iṣfahānī, *Aghānī* IV, 25–6; Ibn Diḥya, *Muṭrib* 147–8. For other cases of flogging or beating for *hijāʾ*, see Ibn al-Muʿtazz, *Ṭabaqāt* 140, 151; al-Bākharzī, *Dumya* I, 370–2. For an account of a poet, to wit Ḥammād ʿAjrad (d. 161/777–8), being forced to flee because of a lampoon he had composed, see Ibn al-Muʿtazz, *Ṭabaqāt* 23. Other poets of the Abbasid period who had to flee for their lives because of a piece of *hijāʾ* against a powerful political leader include Diʿbil al-Khuzāʿī and Ibn al-Dawraqī; see al-Iṣfahānī, *Aghānī* XX, 131–2; Ibn Qutayba, *Shiʿr* 441; Ibn al-Muʿtazz, *Ṭabaqāt* 159. It is remarkable that even the great Abū l-Ṭayyib al-Mutanabbī (303/915–354/965) would only dare to compose lampoons against the ruler of Egypt, Kāfūr al-Ikhshīdī, from a safe distance after his departure from Egypt. This was apparently rather embarrassing for devotees of al-Mutanabbī's gallant poetry, which may explain the attempts (started by the poet himself) to reinterpret all his panegyrics on Kāfūr as satires in disguise. For a liberal serving of such attempts (not too convincing, to put it charitably), see Ḥusāmzāda, *Risāla*.

[204] al-Iṣfahānī, *Aghānī* III, 240–5; al-Ṭabarī, *Tārīkh* V, 1684; Ibn al-Muʿtazz, *Ṭabaqāt* 2–3, Ibn Qutayba, *Shiʿr* 392. (One version of the story claims that the aristocrats of Basra, previous targets of Bashshār's *hijāʾ* to a man, expressed their gratitude for the poet's execution with lavish gifts.)

[205] It is explicitly stated by the anthologist that al-Battī made a lot of enemies with his numerous satirical poems, who would accuse the poet of heresy, atheism, and neglecting the Quran in favour of focusing on Avicenna's works. See Ibn Diḥya, *Muṭrib* 124.

[206] al-Iṣbahānī, *Kharīda* II(ii), 532–3, 546; and for a sample of his invective, see ibid. II(ii), 537–9.

An important conclusion that can be drawn from the above survey of the remarkably desultory patterns of punishments for literary products is that *mujūn* was treated with far more indulgence than invective poetry and works having a political content.[207] Even when certain motifs classifiable as *mujūn* did occasion penalties – sometimes very serious ones – ulterior motives can be easily detected in most cases. In other words, whilst producing *mujūn* could undeniably turn out to be dangerous for the author, it hardly ever was so in isolation: for frivolity actually to be punished, it needed to be combined with other types of offensive activities or works.

2.2 Subtle Ways of 'Self-Censorship'

As noted above, the potential threat of formal or informal sanctions persuaded some poets and writers to tone down their own *mujūn* – or other types of objectionable literature – or else abandon certain genres altogether. This tendency, which, allowing for a certain degree of anachronism, may be described as self-censorship, was arguably as common as, if not more common than, the actual penalisation of *mujūn*.

In Chapter Two, the issue of the ubiquity of quasi-blasphemous hyperboles in panegyrics has already been discussed, as has the impression that *madīḥ* seems to have been more amenable to the toleration of such exaggerations than most other genres of mediaeval Arabic literature. Some motifs, nevertheless, were perceived as problematic even in the context of praise poetry, an awareness that is rather obvious from recurrent qualms voiced by anthologists and literary critics, and which is also likely to be indirectly responsible for some poetic devices observable in panegyrics that clearly served to blunt the edge of potential blasphemy. I do not think that the variety of cautious qualifying clauses appearing in quite a few praise poems were only introduced to get rhyme and metre right. Such qualificatory expressions positively seem designed to dispel sanctimonious objections to the poem's verbal exorbitance. A number of examples from various works will illustrate the point, with the restrictive clause marked in italics in each verse:

> I swear that, *were it licit* to prostrate oneself to a benefactor, I would bend my waist and prostrate in front of you.[208]

---

[207] The riskiness of writing *hijā'* is in no way contradicted by the existence of a number of rulers who were noted for their extraordinary tolerance of such provocations. The very remarkability of such lenience shows that it was the exception rather than the rule. Rulers whose forbearance of at least some forms of provocation is commented on in the sources include the Abbasid caliphs al-Manṣūr (r. 136/754–158/775) and al-Wāthiq (r. 227/842–232/847), as well as the Sāmānid sovereign Naṣr b. Aḥmad (r. 301/914–331/943). See al-Bayhaqī, *Maḥāsin* 422; al-Iṣfahānī, *Aghānī* XX, 306–7; al-Thaʿālibī, *Yatīma* IV, 69–70; and also cf. al-Ibshīhī, *Mustaṭraf* 127–8, 199–200; Ibn Riḍwān, *Shuhub* 101–10.

[208] al-Ibshīhī, *Mustaṭraf* 248. This cautious clause appears in love poems too; see for instance al-Thaʿālibī, *Yatīma* I, 107 ["*law jāza l-sujūdu lahu sajadnā...*"]; III, 414 ["*law jāza an yaʿbuda ʾmruʾun ...*"].

> His being mentioned is *as though* the verses [of the Quran] were mentioned among the people.[209]
>
> *Were there* two gods reigning over the creatures, then Fakhr al-Dawla would be the second one.[210]
>
> *Could there be* any prophet after Muḥammad, we would consider you a prophet for your generosity.[211]

The same cautious wording also tempers the florid style of many prose texts lauding various types of performances by comparing them to the Quran, a potentially blasphemous utterance. A remark supposedly made in the Umayyad period but in fact appearing in a much later (4th/10th–century) work praises the voice of a singer with the following, carefully and prudently worded hyperbole: " *Were there* a Quran in the domain of singing, it would be like this."[212] A passage in rhymed prose in a much later source (11th/17th c.) displays comparable circumspection in its description of an admirably written epistle: "it deserves to be described – *were it not* for religiosity – as being the Quran itself" (*al-ḥarī an yuqāl fīhi lawlā l-diyāna annahu l-Kitāb al-Mubīn*).[213] These conditional clauses are by no means coincidental or purely conventional, even if they recur in several works; the effort of mincing one's words to stay on the safe side is quite palpable in them.

Mediaeval literary critics would regularly call attention to the impropriety of excessive hyperboles and the inherent danger of falling into blasphemy on account thereof. The author of a major comprehesive work of Arabic literary theory makes this point in a quite unequivocal manner when he states that too daring hyperboles "are not considered to be agreeable, except when they come combined with something that make them more acceptable, like the word 'perhaps' to express a degree of probability, or the phrase 'were it not for' [to convey the sense of] impossibility, or 'almost' [to express] relativity, and other such forms of approximation (*taqrīb*)."[214]

---

209 Ibn al-Khaṭīb, *Jaysh* 60. The original sounds much less cumbersome: "*Ka-annamā dhikruhu āyātu dhikrin fī l-anāmi.*"

210 al-Thaʿālibī, *Yatīma* III, 267. This motif recurs in other poets' works too; see for instance ibid. III, 307–8.

211 al-Iṣbahānī, *Kharīda* I(ii), 47.

212 al-Iṣfahānī, *Aghānī* I, 304. Also see al-ʿAskarī, *Maṣūn* 210 [*lawlā anna ʾllāh ʿazza wa-jalla khatama...*" etc.].

213 Ibn Maʿṣūm, *Sulāfa* 103. The phrase *al-kitāb al-mubīn*, strictly speaking, simply means 'clear book', but of course it is an epithet of the Quran – used in the sacred book itself – and that is indisputably the sense meant here. In the same anthology, another epistle puns on the noun *bayt* ('verse line', and 'house', by extension 'the sanctuary in Mecca') and purposefully misapplies the Quran's text in the process, but limits the offence by saying "Were it not that it could be said I went beyond all bounds, I might write that..." etc. See ibid. 214.

214 Ibn Ḥijja, *Khizāna* III, 142.

There were other ways too of mollifying the bite of a *mujūn* text. One particularly widespread device that obviously served to distance the narrator of a joke or (more rarely) the composer of a poem from the godlessness inherent in the text was the introduction of a fictitious protagonist. The choice of a protagonist for texts of the *mujūn* type can be quite revealing, although some figures seem to have begged to be utilised in this way. A wide range of stereotypical personalities appear in frivolous jokes. However, regardless of the actual choice of a protagonist, the message the author (or anthologist) sends is basically the same: "I did not say it, he did".[215]

In the case of a blasphemous utterance, one particularly obvious possibility to distance oneself from it was to attribute it in the narrative to some stereotypical representative of impiety. A person known to have been a heretic would be an ideal choice. And indeed, we find the person of the Muʿtazilite theologian-become-freethinker Ibn al-Rāwandī (d. 298/911) serving such a purpose. This man, who was famous, or infamous, for his radical and extreme views in matters of divinity, was transmogrified in popular culture (and literature) into a caricature whose sole function was to give voice to ideas and punchlines felt to be too risky perhaps. An anti-*bidʿa* treatise from 8th–9th/14th–15th-century Syria complains of the tendency of people to ascribe all manner of blasphemous jokes to Ibn al-Rāwandī and then feel free to spread them ("... *yatajarrad al-ʿabd bi-mazḥihi ʿalā ʾllāh taʿālā wa-yuḍīfuhu ilā ʾbn al-Rāwandī* ").[216] The role played by Ibn al-Rāwandī might also be given to an unnamed 'false prophet' (*mutanabbiʾ*), an infinitely ignominious character given the unanimous Islamic insistence on Muḥammad having been the last prophet.[217]

Ignorant, vulgar commoners constitute another preferred category of protagonists in *mujūn* texts. An undifferentiated 'commoner' – which for mediaeval Arab intellectuals implied an ignoramus – may sometimes appear as the hero of a *mujūn* anecdote. In such a case, small linguistic devices (like the retaining of a vernacular noun or interrogative) might be added to enhance the air of ignorance and

---

215 At least some religious scholars were apparently alert to this trick, and we find them condemning even the telling of 'the drolleries of libertines' (*maḍāḥik al-mujjān*), 'the anecdotes of silly people (*nawādir al-sukhafāʾ*)' and 'engaging in "it was said" and "he said so" (*al-khawḍ fī qīl wa-qāl*)'. See ʿIyāḍ, *Shifāʾ* 360–1; al-Wansharīsī, *Miʿyār* II, 359–60; al-Haytamī, *Iʿlām* 385.

216 Ibn Baydakīn, *Lumaʿ* I, 184. Besides criticising, the author also preserves a number of Ibn al-Rāwandī anecdotes that, but for his pious indignation, would in all probability have been lost. In one joke, Ibn al-Rāwandī leaves a pot in the open, which is then broken by a sudden hailstorm. Bringing a metal mortar outside, he addresses the Lord: "Now break this if you are so clever." Another joke, based as it is on a pun, is unfortunately untranslatable (it makes fun of the folk pronunciation of the phrase *astaghfir Allāh*, 'I ask God's forgiveness'), but it is every bit as blasphemous as the previous one. – You find a comparably outrageous joke from modern Tunisia in Chanfrault 1996: 56. On the historical Ibn al-Rāwandī, cf. al-Nadīm, *Fihrist* 216–7.

217 Professing to be a prophet being effectively tantamount to ceasing to be a Muslim, a person making such a claim is an ideal candidate for saying all sorts of blasphemous things. See a number of such jokes in Ibn al-Jawzī, *Ẓirāf* 107–8, 133; Ibn Saʿīd, *Muqtaṭaf* 178.

uncouthness. For instance, one has little doubt that the suggestion that the Quran has not only good passages but also bad ones ("*w-ēsh fī hādhā, hādhā huwa l-Qur'ān fīh jayyid wa-radī...*" etc.) would have been rather intolerable even as a joke had it not been put into the mouth of an ignorant commoner; the gist of the joke is thus ostensibly shifted from the scandalous *lèse-religion* to the risible nescience and denseness of the commoner.[218]

In such a case, as we have observed, nothing else is specified – it is just an ordinary, common man, an *ʿāmmī* – but in many cases one finds stereotyped figures playing the role of the naïve, stupid, uncouth hero. For instance, it might be a *Daylamī*, an inhabitant of the highlands of Northern Iran, a barely civilised barbarian with but a veneer of Islamic identity. (Not surprisingly, this stereotype seems to have originated in the early Buyid era [mid-4th/10th c.], when a new dynasty came to power even in Baghdad with the support of rough Daylamī mercenaries.) Says a Daylamī highlander in an anecdote from the Buyid period, attempting an oath: "[I swear] by God, other than whom there is no god, I mean divorce and the manumission of all my slaves (*wa-'llāhi 'lladhī lā ilāha illā huwa aʿnī bihi l-ṭalāq wa-l-ʿitāq*)".[219]

The ultimate ignoramus, however, is a character other than those mentioned so far. It is the Bedouin. In fact, while highly stereotyped, 'the Bedouin' of Arabic literature is a figure of ambiguous properties – simultaneously idolised and despised. On the one hand, his stereotypical courage and toughness would make him a kind of 'noble savage' in the eyes of the urban dwellers of the mediaeval Middle East; and on the other hand, his lack of sophistication and his rudimentary grasp of the essentials of Islamic dogma and praxis made him a target of ridicule.[220] It is the latter aspect of the image of the Bedouin that was amply exploited in *mujūn* literature to shift the blame away from the actual narrator of jokes. Consider the following joke, which is typical:

> A Bedouin was asked: "Do you know how to supplicate to your Lord?" He said he did, whereupon they told him: "Go ahead, supplicate." So he said: "My God,

---

[218] al-Tawḥīdī, *Baṣā'ir* II(iv), 43–4. Ignorant schoolboys were another perfect choice for the same function, as shown by an anecdote based on absurd and blasphemous misreadings of Quranic passages. See al-Ṣūlī, *Adab* 124.

[219] al-Tanūkhī, *Nishwār* VII, 168–9. While it was customary to swear by God, it was an equally common oath formula to say that if one was unable to accomplish the specified condition, one would divorce his wife and set all his slaves free. Of course, the point of the anecdote is that the Daylamī, rustic brute as he is, regards the two formulas as synonymous or commutable. – Incidentally, such stories of the primitiveness of tribesmen might well have some basis of actual observation. I wonder if the appallingly stupid (and distinctly un-Islamic) boasting of a *Zenāta* Berber tribesman reported in al-ʿUmarī, *Masālik* III(iv), 72 may be a historical report, but it is not at all inconceivable that it is.

[220] On the Bedouin as a *Witzfigur* in Arabic literature, see Binay 2006: 171–85.

> you've given us Islam, though we hadn't asked for it; so please don't deny us Paradise, which we do ask for!"[221]

Another anecdote shows a Bedouin listening to a lute concert and being so carried away by the (for him) unfamiliar experience of an instrument and tunes that he ends up enthusing in what for all practical purposes amounts to a caricature of the Muslim creed. The story is presented by the Bedouin himself in the first person singular:

> I sat in front [of the musician] and asked him: "My mother and father [be the ransom] for you; what's this creature (*dābba*) that is unknown to the Bedouins and which must have been created just recently?" He said that it was a lute (*barbaṭ*). I asked him: "My mother and father [be the ransom] for you; and what's this thread at the bottom?" He said it was the [string called] *zīr*. I asked: "And the next one?" He said it was the *mathnā*. I asked: "And the third one?" He said it was the *mathlath*. I asked: "And the one at the top?" He said: "It's the *bamm*." And I said: "I believe, first in God, secondly in you, thirdly in the lute, and fourthly in the *bamm* string!"[222]

The list of possible protagonists for *mujūn* does not end here. We find, for instance, that the role could be played by simpletons (sing. *mughaffal*) and outright 'fools'; as well as by the effeminates (sing. *mukhannath*) so feared for their biting tongues and sarcasm. Given the utter disregard of the *mukhannath* for even the most elementary norms of male comportment, it is hardly surprising that they would be serve as ideal protagonists for indecent and/or irreligious texts, especially ones involving quick and witty repartees.[223] Often the same function – that of a protagonist who can say things an ordinary man would not – is accorded to named individuals, who might be either wholly fictitious figures like the omnipresent Juḥā of Arabic jokes, or else (perhaps) living persons so much transmogrified as to have become for all practical purposes fictitious (Ashʿab, Muzabbid, Buhlūl, etc.).[224] Jokes presenting obscene talk by a woman often feature a Medinese woman called Ḥubbā who may or may not have lived but for practical purposes can be regarded as the stereotyped figure of the lecherous woman.[225] Juḥā has indisputably been, and still is, the most popular choice among these fictitious or quasi-fictitious persons. (He is, by the way, an obvious analogue to the Nasreddin Hoca of Turkish jokes.) While

---

221 Ibn Simāk, *Zaharāt* 149.

222 al-Iṣfahānī, *Aghānī* XVIII, 201.

223 The *mukhannath* is often portrayed flinging back a witty and biting retort. As a source puts it, "women are capable of fearful repartees, and the *mukhannath* is feared because he resembles a woman [in this respect]." See al-Tawḥīdī, *Baṣāʾir* I(i), 167; I(ii), 43; II(iii), 60, 62; II(iv), 78; IV(vii), 93; al-Tanūkhī, *Nishwār* II, 224–6.

224 Cf. Marzolph 1992: I, 238. On the literary image of Ashʿab, and the possible historical background thereof, see Rosenthal 1956, esp. pp. 17–9, 23.

225 Borg 2000: 152–3, 158, 160.

Juḥā is an all-purpose protagonist of jokes, and thus plays many narrative functions, not infrequently he serves to give voice to near-blasphemous observations, precisely like the rest of the joke protagonists mentioned in this section. Consider this example:

> Once Juḥā was told: "Beseech your Lord to save you from the terrors of the Day of Judgement!" And he said: "Who in this world will live long enough to see the Day of Judgement?"[226]

The tendency to employ fictitious persons notwithstanding, a simpleton appearing in a *mujūn*-type joke might also bear the name of an actual historical personality, just as was the case with literary 'heretics'. A prime example is a certain Ibn al-Jaṣṣāṣ (d. 315/927–8), originally a wealthy jeweller and financier in Baghdad and a close associate of the Abbasid caliph al-Muʿtaḍid (r. 279/892–289/902). As the *qāḍī* al-Tanūkhī informs his readers, the reason this man ended up playing the role in jokes of a half-wit uttering inadmissible, irreligious – indeed sometimes quite blasphemous – nonsense is that all the malicious intigues at the court persuaded him to pretend to be more naïve than he actually was, and apparently the carefully cultivated image came to have a momentum of its own. Be that as it may, as time passed the image of Ibn al-Jaṣṣāṣ had less and less to do with historical facts, simply becoming a convenient distancing device for narrators of *mujūn* anecdotes ("*aṭradat ʿalayhi l-ʿāmma wa-ashbāh al-ʿāmma min al-khāṣṣa hādhihi l-nawādir wa-hādhihi l-shubah*").[227]

Thus several devices were available to a writer, a poet or an anthologist who wished to allay the scandalousness of the *mujūn* content of his work. This, however, was not thought to be sufficient in many cases. When it came to more outrageous literary products – including but not limited to *mujūn* – more radical forms of self-censorship also existed which might lead to the destruction of certain works. Whilst sources usually fail to identify motives behind such decisions, which are hard to judge anyway, and whilst it is reasonable to suppose that fear might sometimes play a role, in quite a few cases the decisions appear to have been piety-driven. Such is especially likely to have been the motivation in cases when a poet decided to destroy his literary output only in his old age, with its concomitant increase of religious ardour and dread of hellfire. Of course, a resolution to do away with all of one's past writings would run into serious difficulties after those works had already started to circulate widely. Feasible or not, such attempts were made by some repentant poets, like Saʿīd b. Wahb of Basra (2nd/8th c.), who gave up composing poetry when growing old, and whenever he could lay his hands on a poem of his, he made

226 al-Tawḥīdī, *Baṣāʾir* I(ii), 141.

227 al-Tanūkhī, *Nishwār* I, 29–30; and al-Thaʿālibī, *Thimār* II, 661; al-Kutubī, *Fawāt* I, 374–6; al-Tawḥīdī, *Baṣāʾir* II(iv), 105–6 [in the last two sources one finds several jokes about this personality].

sure to destroy it (*fa-kāna idhā wajada shay'an min shiʿrihi kharaqahu wa-aḥraqahu*).[228] This may represent a very extreme turnabout, as there were also poets who strove to suppress only their more 'improper' literary products, such as lampoons (*hijā'*), bacchic poetry, hyperbolic praises, love poems, and generally anything that was even remotely related to *mujūn*.[229] An interesting – and some may say slightly schizophrenic – type of attrition for frivolous poetry is reported from al-Andalus, although it may well have been known elsewhere too. Whereas it did not involve the actual destruction of 'improper' works, the poet did seek to expiate the sinfulness of producing *mujūn* poetry, in the event by composing a pious poem for each frivolous one he wrote, so as to counterbalance bad with good. Such poems were called *mukaffirāt* ('expiatory [verses]').[230] Repentance might thus take many forms, and it is to be noted that it might not always even be sincere. With an irony that can be described as quintessential *mujūn*, a libertine called Abū l-Fatḥ b. Qirān (fl. mid-6th/12th c.) made a mockery of the remorse of some of his colleagues, making a great show of his deep contrition (*tawba*), only to turn back to his sinful ways in haste and depict the unnerving experience in a vintage *mujūn* piece.[231]

2.3 The Success and Profitability of Mujūn

Someone steeped in the Western literary clichés of the last two centuries will find it all too natural to think of the destiny of 'libertines' and 'bohemians' along the lines of, say, *Les fleurs du Mal*: at best, independent souls whose refusal to compromise with the hypocrisies and insincerities of society condemns them to a

---

[228] al-Iṣfahānī, *Aghānī* XX, 351. Cf. a passage about Khalaf al-Aḥmar in al-Ibshīhī, *Mustaṭraf* 69; and also see Kilpatrick 1997: 109.

[229] The famous poet known under the sobriquet *Ḥayṣ-Bayṣ* (d. 574/1179) extirpated every lampoon from the volume of his collected poems ("*lam ara shay'an min ahājīhi fa-innahu nazzaha dīwānahu minhā*"), and had a tantrum whenever he heard anyone reciting such a work of his composition; see al-Iṣbahāni, *Kharīda* I(i), 349–50. See also the case of the poet Abū Ghassān Damādh ("*fa-lammā asanna ankara mā hajā bihi l-nās*") in Yāqūt, *Udabā'* III, 1307. A repentant poet might alternatively ask anthologists to refrain from selecting certain genres of his *oeuvre* for inclusion in a poetic anthology. See for instance al-Thaʿālibī, *Yatīma* IV, 433. Some references to changes driven by contrition can be positively puzzling, as the mention in one source of a 'sophisticated', 'polished' and 'agreeable' moral turnaround by a poet, which is further described as unlike the 'devotion of non-Arabs' ("*wa-lam yansuk nuskan aʿjamiyyan bal ẓarufa ẓarfan adabiyyan wa-salaka maslakan min al-birr marḍiyyan*"). See Ibn Diḥya, *Muṭrib* 149.

[230] al-Ḥillī, *ʿĀṭil* 10–11. Another name for this kind of poetry was *mumaḥḥiṣāt* ('purificatory [verses]'), a term applied by the celebrated man of letters Ibn ʿAbd Rabbihi (d. 328/940), who in his old days had the habit of atoning for every frivolous poem he had produced in his youth (like love poetry or wine poems) with a 'serious' piece full of devout exhortations. See Ibn Diḥya, *Muṭrib* 154; Yāqūt, *Udabā'* I, 465, 467. This practice was adopted not only by poets but also by some philologists engaged in the study of 'unserious' (that is to say, literary) topics. See Kopf 1956: 34–35.

[231] al-Iṣbahānī, *Kharīda* I(ii), 342–43.

life of poverty and rejection, and at worst avant-garde rebels utterly wrecked by their own self-destructive, insuppressible talents and the hostility of the philistines. Quite apart from the question of whether this romantic image corresponds to the reality in Western literary history, it is certainly very far from an accurate description of the lives of libertine poets and writers in the mediaeval Middle East. The effort to assess the profitability of producing libertine literature might appear somewhat cynical, but only if we accept the aforementioned stereotypes – which are rooted in relatively recent developments in Western culture – and such a line of research is in fact an indispensable part of an analysis of the relationship of *mujūn* to prevalent norms.

That said, the length of this section is severely limited by the scarcity of data on the monetary aspects of *mujūn* literature and the earnings of those who produced it. Also, some types of evidence must be approached with suspicion, like the clichéd accounts of the lavish gifts rulers handed out for literary products or entertaining remarks delivered in their presence. This is not to say that such things did not take place; otherwise it would be hard to conceive how the cliché might have arisen in the first place. However, judging the historicity of any individual case, and especially its concrete details, is all too often mere guesswork.

That there was considerable demand for works of *mujūn* in high-status circles seems incontestable. That the authors of such works were often remunerated for their efforts is also certain. Handouts of money for witty sayings (examples of which will be treated at more length in the next chapter) were not uncommon, and of course, as already noted, the sources teem with instances of monetary rewards for reciting poetry both serious and facetious, in both public and private settings. Although the main source of income for a court poet would certainly be praise poetry addressed to a patron (or several patrons), other types of works that met the liking of a ruler, including bacchic poems or other genres containing *mujūn*, could also elicit quite tangible rewards. By the Buyid period, there were poets who decided to turn to treating frivolous topics and *mujūn* expressly to ensure a better livelihood and earn more, given the huge demand for such literary products.[232] Even before that period, the clownish literary figure known as Abū l-ʿIbar (d. 250–5/864–9) had given up a career as a serious poet, enticed by hopes of living better that made him take up facetious and silly topics (*al-hazl wa-l-ḥamāqāt*) instead. By all accounts, he was not disappointed in his calculations: he is said to have found instant success and gathered a fortune greater than any 'serious' poet of his age.[233] This demand is also highlighted, if indirectly, by a passage in the literary anthology *Nathr al-durr*

[232] E.g. al-Thaʿālibī, *Yatīma* I, 314, 326; al-Thaʿālibī, *Tatimma* I, 14–5.

[233] Yāqūt, *Udabā'* V, 2298. For more on Abū l-ʿIbar (d. 250–5/864–9), and on the penchant of the caliph al-Mutawakkil (r. 232/847–247/861) for frivolities, see Gruendler 2005b: 106.

by Abū Manṣūr al-Ābī (d. 426/1030), in which this author explains that he decided to spread frivolous and facetious material all over his compilation, alternating it with serious subjects, in order to ensure that readers actually peruse the whole book. Had he collected all unserious material in one separate chapter, he says, readers would have gone for that one part of the work and neglected all the rest.[234] Some works containing *mujūn*, or wholly consisting of such material, were actually commissioned by a ruler or a rich literary patron, examples including the Perfumed Garden of al-Nafzāwī (fl. early 9th/15th c.), *al-Imtāʿ wa-l-muʾānasa* by al-Tawḥīdī (d. 411/1023) and possibly even the *Akhlāq al-wazīrayn* by the same author. Even *mujūn* works that were not produced on assignment from a wealthy person could end up fetching high prices, although after the death of the author it would be the copyists and editors who benefited from the profitability of the writings. For instance, a source mentions that a copy of the collected poems (*dīwān*) of the great libertine poet Abū Nuwās would sell for the hefty sum of several golden dinars, albeit the exact price would depend on the particular redaction, out of many in circulation, of the work.[235]

It is instructive to have a look at the financial aspects of the literary career of one of the most famous and successful (and, significantly, most outrageous) exponents of *mujūn*, the court poet Ibn al-Ḥajjāj (d. 391/1001). Copies of the collected poems of this specialist in obscenity and scatology (*sukhf*) fetched quite exorbitant prices – as much as between fifty and seventy golden dinars – and their market was forever bustling.[236] It is noteworthy that the extraordinary obscenity of most of the literary output of Ibn al-Ḥajjāj did not stop al-Sharīf al-Raḍī (359/970–406/1016) – a man of impeccable reputation, a theologian and for a time the marshal (*naqīb*) of the Prophet's lineage in Baghdad – from producing a redaction of his own of the poet's works, which he admired.[237] The resounding success of

[234] Quoted in English translation in van Gelder 1992: 170.

[235] Abū Bakr al-Ṣūlī (d. 335/947) claimed to have produced the most sought-after and expensive version by far; see al-Ṣūlī, *Akhbār* 55–6; and also Gruendler 2005b: 104. The number of people undertaking to collect and edit Abu Nuwās's *dīwān* shortly after his death is yet another good indication of the success of the poet. See al-Nadīm, *Fihrist* 182. Several respected literary critics heaped flowery praise upon the talents and works of Abū Nuwās; see for instance Ibn Manẓūr, *Akhbār* 1–2, 45–7. As Ewald Wagner has shown, Abū Nuwās is by far the most frequently cited poet in most literary collections of the 3rd/9th to 5th/11th centuries; see Bauer 1998: 74–7. The poetry of Abū Nuwās did not take long to become known and popular among Arabic speakers of al-Andalus too, where they had a lasting influence on the local 'modern', urbane poetic style. See Rubiera Mata 1992: 66; Jones 1991: 61; Schippers 2001: 120.

[236] al-Thaʿālibī, *Yatīma* III, 30–1, 34.

[237] Kraemer 1986: 16. He also paid his respect to the poet in an elegy. Moreover, Ibn al-Ḥajjāj, a Shiʿite, was also honoured by being buried next to the shrine of the Imam Mūsā al-Kāẓim in Baghdad. See Yāqūt, *Udabāʾ* III, 1047–8. Another noted scholar who edited a selection of the poetry of Ibn al-Ḥajjāj (with the title *Durrat al-tāj min shiʿr Ibn al-Ḥajjāj*) was the successful mathematician,

Ibn al-Ḥajjāj and his ilk was expressed in a popular saying circulating in Baghdad concerning the two most frivolous poets of the period: "An era that has given us Ibn Sukkara and Ibn al-Ḥajjāj is a generous era indeed."[238] It is hardly controversial to contend that the image is not one of a marginal, tragic genius battling the philistinism of an uncomprehending society. And the success of Ibn al-Ḥajjāj proved lasting, judging by two types of circumstantial evidence. One of these is the existence of many epigones who modelled their own poetry after the highly regarded brand of *mujūn* and *sukhf* characterising Ibn al-Ḥajjāj's poetry.[239] Another, indirect but quite cogent, indication of the poet's success is the insistence of several manuals for the overseers of markets and public morals (sing. *muḥtasib*) on the necessity of teachers making sure minors should not get access to and memorise any of the works of Ibn al-Ḥajjāj and those of another successful libertine of Baghdad, an epigone of the former known as *Ṣarīʿ al-Dilāʾ* (d. 412/1021–2).[240] Surely had these works not enjoyed wide popularity, efforts to limit their circulation would have made no sense.

A conclusion that can be drawn from the regrettably patchy evidence is that there was a sufficient number of affluent and financially libertines who owed their fortune to precisely their *mujūn* products to rule out a direct link between poverty and *mujūn*. When a poet or a man of letters known for his *mujūn* was marginalised and destitute, the cause must be sought elsewhere. Although one cannot state that *mujūn* ensured material success for its author, in many cases it did, and therefore it was marketable merchandise. However, individual talents in marketing it varied.

---

astronomer and physician al-Usṭurlābī (d. 534/1139–40). It bears witness to the continuing popularity of this *oeuvre* more than a century later. See Yāqūt, *Udabāʾ* VI, 2770.

238 al-Thaʿālibī, *Yatīma* III, 3.

239 E.g. al-Thaʿālibī, *Yatīma* I, 310 [*'wa-huwa bi-l-Shām ka-ʾbn al-Ḥajjāj bi-l-ʿIrāq*"]; al-Thaʿālibī, *Tatimma* I, 14 ["*wa-tashabbaha bi-ʾbn al-Ḥajjāj*"]; al-Bākharzī, *Dumya* I, 550 ["*lahu ashʿār sakhīfa nasaja fīhā ʿalā minwāl Ibn al-Ḥajjāj*"]; al-Iṣbahānī, *Kharīda* II(i), 375 ["*... wa-dhakara annahu ʿamilahā ʿalā uslūb Ibn al-Ḥajjāj*"].

240 In the words of a manual written in the 6th/12th century, "the elementary school teacher ought to prevent children from memorising or looking into any of the poems of Ibn al-Ḥajjāj and beat them if they do, and likewise the collected poems of Ṣarīʿ al-Dilāʾ, which have nothing worthwhile in them" (*wa-yanbaghī li-l-muʾaddib an yamnaʿ al-ṣibyān min ḥifẓ shayʾ min shiʿr Ibn al-Ḥajjāj wa-l-naẓar fīhi wa-yaḍribahum ʿalā dhālik wa-kadhālik dīwān Ṣarīʿ al-Dilā fa-innahu lā khayr fīhi*). See al-Shayzarī, *Nihāya* 104–5; and the same passage cited verbatim in Ibn Bassām, *Nihāya* 162, a work probably composed in Egypt in the early 9th/15th century. The manual of al-Shayzarī also advises the banning of books giving voice to extremist Shiʿite views, and recommends that schoolchildren should be required to memorise pious poetry instead. The desideratum of restricting access to the poetry of Ibn al-Ḥajjāj and Ṣarīʿ al-Dilāʾ appears in various other *ḥisba* manuals too; see Bosworth 1976: I, 65.

3. Regional Differences in the Reception of *Mujūn*

The vast majority of the data that have been utilised in the foregoing discussion of responses to *mujūn* behaviour and literature predominantly comes from a particular region and a special kind of social setting within the Middle East, namely the metropolitan centres of Iraq and some of the adjacent lands. In a sense, this is hardly surprising. It may simply reflect the cultural weight of these urban centres, and the gravitation of a great number of aspiring intellectuals (of both the *ʿulamāʾ* and *kuttāb* type) towards these centres throughout the centuries. The preponderance of these cities and this region can certainly be observed in other domains of mediaeval Arabic writing too, and therefore the same tendency with regard to *mujūn* is almost predictable. However, this may well be only part of the explanation of the regional imbalance when it comes to works of *mujūn*. The following section attempts to suggest some further factors at work, although the scarcity of hard evidence makes these findings more like a conjecture than an induction.

Although Islam has certainly served as a factor of cultural unity, it would be unreasonable to suppose that norms were uniform at any given historical moment over as vast a geographical area as the Middle East and North Africa.[241] Even when a norm was the same, the degree of conformity felt to be absolutely necessary might differ from one community to another. In the hypothetical case of the same literary work being presented to various communities, the ostentatious and calculated flouting of norms upon which *mujūn* was based would certainly not provoke identical, or even broadly similar, reactions in an isolated oasis of the Arabian Peninsula, an agricultural village along the Nile in Egypt, among nomads in Syria, the ancient towns of Iran or Transoxania, or such cosmopolitan cities as Baghdad, Cairo or Cordoba. Leaving aside the villages and other rural communities where literacy was extremely restricted if not nonexistent and which are rarely mentioned in the available sources anyway, the cities and towns of the various regions also appear to have accommodated manifestations of frivolity in general and *mujūn* literature in particular to different degrees. Differences in lifestyle, predominant modes of livelihood, local cultural traditions, the varying influence of the legal schools (sing. *madhhab*) and religious sects, the homogeneity or otherwise of the local population, can all be reasonably expected to have played a role in forming typical reactions to norm-breaking. In view of the above discussions of the attitudes of the different subgroups of society, local configurations of social stratification, and the possible overrepresentation of some social group or class, could be a decisive factor too. (For instance, a town with a robust tradition of religious scholarship might easily be unusually intolerant of perceived non-compliance with norms.) Whereas these

[241] Not to speak of changes in norms over time, on which cf. Sherif 1936: 15, 43, 85–7, 198–9.

general considerations can be accepted more or less intuitively, some textual evidence can help add concrete substance to them. As in many other cases, most of the data are anecdotal in character, but taken together they do seem to suggest some general tendencies.

A conspicuous regional difference that was observed and commented on by mediaeval Arabic authors is the contrasting attitudes in the Western and Eastern parts respectively of the mediaeval Muslim world. Notably, the cultural ambience in the Maghreb was perceived as leaning more towards austerity and conservatism than elsewhere in the Arabic-speaking world. To start with, the stereotype of the greater religious rigour of the Muslim West compared to the East has been a persistent one in the consciousness of Arab scholars.[242] The general conservatism seems to have expressed itself in literary matters as well; as an 8th/14th-century author from the region observed, the littérateurs of the Maghreb tended to stick to pre-Islamic and early Islamic Arabic poetry as an ideal and dismiss the 'modern' poetic fashions of the East, presumably including *mujūn* ("*[...] kuttāb al-Maghrib yuḥāfiẓūna fī shiʿrihim wa-kitābatihim ʿalā ṭarīqat al-ʿarab wa-yadhummūna mā ʿadāhā min ṭuruq al-muwalladīn...*").[243] Also, insofar as the vogue of frivolity and *mujūn* did drift over to the Muslim West – as it did to some extent in al-Andalus – it was widely perceived by Eastern littérateurs as distinctly inferior to its Iraqi models, which generated considerable resentment on the part of many a Maghrebi intellectual visiting the East.[244] However, the protests of such intellectuals notwithstanding, it does seem to be the case that the output of 'modern' poetry (including *mujūn*) in the Western Islamic lands simply could not be compared to its counterpart in the East. It is an indication of the differing attitudes that manuscript volumes of the somewhat frivolous vernacular poems (sing. *zajal*) of the Andalusī poet Ibn Quzmān (d. 555/1160) were in more demand and sold better in Baghdad than in any of the cities of the Maghreb, although the dialect spoken in Baghdad was obviously farther from that of the Iberian peninsula.[245] Another interesting detail that may be pertinent here is the relative scarcity of citations of Abū Nuwās in the anthology *al-Ḥamāsa al-Maghribiyya* by Aḥmad al-Jurāwī (d. 609/1212) as compared to similar works produced in the Muslim East. As Thomas Bauer notes, not only is Abū Nuwās

[242] On this point, see Berkey 1995: 42; and also see Kraemer 1986: 59. For a first-hand discussion of this view, see for instance Ibn Jubayr, *Riḥla* 55–6.

[243] al-Shāṭibī, *Ifādāt* 158.

[244] See for instance Ibn Diḥya, *Muṭrib* 145 and 148–9 about perceptions of the respective merits of the poetry of Abū Nuwās and his Andalusī epigones. On the widespread image of the cultural inferiority of the Maghreb, see al-ʿUmarī, *Masālik* IV(v), 2–3, 7–8. Ironically, such stereotypes were replicated within the Muslim West; notably, the inhabitants of al-Andalus regarded themselves as culturally superior to those of North Africa. See García Gómez 1981: 7.

[245] Ibn Saʿīd, *Muqtaṭaf* 263.

underrepresented in this anthology, the selection also leans towards his 'decent' works, resulting in "ein geradezu groteskes Abū Nuwās-Bild".[246] There is also some explicit textual evidence testifying for the widespread perception that Eastern intellectuals showed more openness to frivolity and humour in comparison with their colleagues in the West. Two excerpts follow in which the stereotyping of Maghrebis as dull, insipid and austere is quite manifest. In the first text, the famous Andalusī anthologist and writer Ibn Saʿīd (d. 685/1286) describes his impressions of an Egyptian scholar named al-Asʿad b. Muqrib:

> When in Alexandria, I frequented his sessions. He was knowledgeable in various branches of scholarship, but he had gained particular fame in the study of *ḥadīth* and jurisprudence; and he was also [known as] a witty man. One day, when I was with him, a boy of captivating beauty entered, and I was unable to avoid staring at him. [Al-Asʿad] asked me whether there were [boys] of such beauty in the Maghreb, which filled me with embarrassment. He said: "Relax, leave off this Maghrebi character of yours! When we are in intimate company, we can be childish/sensual (*idhā khalawnā ṣabawnā*)." Then I asked him: "And who is this [boy] than whom I have never seen someone more beautiful?" He answered that it was his son. I asked him what [the boy's] occupation was, and he said: "His business is with pricks [ḥamām, lit. 'pigeons']." Then another boy, younger and even more beautiful than the first, entered. I said: "And not a sign We showed them...", and [al-Asʿad] snapped: "Complete the *āya*!"[247] This let me know that it was the brother of the previous [boy]. I asked [al-Asʿad]: "And what is the occupation of this one?" He said: "Balls [*bayḍ*, lit. 'eggs']." I felt I'd die of embarrassment, but he said: "Haven't I told you to leave off this Maghrebi character of yours? This country hasn't had any influence on you yet. And all the while I'm supposed to be a specialist of religious matters, and you an unrestrained littérateur."[248]

The next passage features another visitor to Egypt from the Muslim West, a certain Ibn Mundhir al-Baṭalyawsī, who tried to persuade the vizier Najm al-Dīn b. Mujāwir to grant him some favour. With growing annoyance, the vizier is striving to fend off the persistent petitioner with as much civility as possible:

> Trying to evade him, [the vizier] said: "My good man, you have to know that he who asks for an impossible thing only exhausts himself as well as the ear of his addressee." [Ibn Mundhir] then asked: "Vizier, do you promise that you

---

246 However, it may be an important factor that the anthology was compiled in the Almohad period. See Bauer 1998: 76–7.

247 Quran 43:48. A typical example of frivolous *iqtibās* in conversation as a manifestation of quick wit, the exchange is an allusion to the Quranic verse saying "*And not a sign We showed them, but it was greater than its sister sign* [viz. the previous one]."

248 Ibn Saʿīd, *Muqtaṭaf* 219. I thank G. J. van Gelder for pointing out to me the likely meaning of the word *ḥamām* in this passage.

> won't look for excuses if I ask you for something quite feasible?" [The vizier] replied that he would not look for excuses in a matter he was capable of accomplishing. [Ibn Mundhir] said: "Then I don't ask more than that you should go back to teach children in the school where you used to work! In this way you'll be able to relax after all the petitions of the people, and the people can also relax after this crappy vizier who is of no use yet occupies the position, blocking the way of those who'd be happy to do what people petition them for and wouldn't spare their efforts to deserve the praise of the people!" At this point, the vizier began to laugh as he had never been seen doing, and said: "Why, are you such a man then! You do have a sense of humour and aren't one of those uncouth Maghrebis. You deserve my support; and if God wills, I might be able to do more for you than what is in my power alone." And he took him to [the ruler] al-ʿAzīz, to whom he recounted the exchange of words between them. [The sultan] found the story amusing, and made [Ibn Mundhir] one of his closest circle of courtiers...[249]

Thus it seems to be justified to say that the Eastern part of the mediaeval Middle East had the reputation of offering a somewhat more amenable environment to levity, frivolity and also probably *mujūn*, and there is some amount of evidence, albeit relatively meagre, to suggest that that stereotype did correspond to real differences in culture. However, regional differences existed within the Eastern lands too. It is rather trivial to observe that the focal point of all new cultural trends before the Mongol invasion (656/1258) was Baghdad, the capital of the Abbasid caliphate. The ultimate model of urbane culture was Baghdad, to which all sorts of intellectuals gravitated from the Middle East and North Africa. The attraction and cultural influence of Baghdad was felt even as far as the Iberian peninsula, let alone in such less distant urban centres as Aleppo in Syria or Shiraz in Iran. In al-Andalus, the nucleus of Eastern influence was, unsurprisingly, Cordoba.[250] Baghdad, and in a broader sense Iraq, offered the highest standard of urbane sophistication in mediaeval Muslim eyes. That this region (and this city) was the epitome of human civilisation beside which any other place can only qualify as 'rural' and backward came to be a largely undisputed idea, despite the occasional dissenting noise made by scholars from other regions.[251]

---

249 Ibn Saʿīd, *Ghuṣūn* 20–1. The stereotyped image of the tedious, boring (*thaqīl*) Maghrebi man recurs in other sources too; see for instance al-Muqaddasī, *Taqāsīm* 216.

250 In Cordoba, cultural patterns borrowed from Baghdad included the fashions dictated by the tastes of the renowned musician Ziryāb (fl. early 3rd/9th c.), an immigrant from the east. The impact of Eastern cultural models was for some time so strong that the term *bagdadización* has been used to describe the phenomenon. Cordoba would in turn serve as a point of transmission from which Baghdadi influences spread to lesser urban centres in al-Andalus, especially Seville. See Rubiera Mata 1992: 16–7, 22, 56; Blachère 1930: 16, 35; Ghazi 1959: 48–50, 65–6.

251 See for instance al-Tanūkhī, *Nishwār* V, 171 ["*man lam yarahā lam yara l-dunyā*"], 173 ["*idhā kharajta min al-ʿIrāq fa-l-dunyā kulluhā rustāq*"]; al-Thaʿālibī, *Thimār* II, 739 and Yāqūt, *Buldān* I,

Beyond the trivial fact of the empire's greatest metropolis being reputed as the centre of civilisation and high culture, another stereotype that is more relevant to our purpose also developed. It is the image of Baghdad (and generally Iraq) as the home of the quality expressed in Arabic by the term *ẓarf* (wit and refinement). The close association of the concept of *ẓarf* with *mujūn* will be discussed in the next chapter, and it will suffice here to refer to the existence of such a connotation. The stereotype of Iraqi (or Baghdadi) sophistication and wit is articulated in a somewhat recherché style in the following passage by al-Thaʿālibī (d. 429/1038) describing the art of a poet originally from Baghdad: "His poems are [typical] of a witty, polished littérateur which have imbibed the waters of the Tigris and been nourished by the zephyrs of Iraq."[252]

A key ingredient of the image of Baghdad as a sophisticated place was precisely the licentiousness and levity that characterised the cultural atmosphere of the city in the popular consciousness. Such perceptions are evident in quite a few texts, although, as so often is the case, the available evidence is largely anecdotal. Consider the following excerpt from a *mujūn* work that compares the bohemian air of Baghdad to the perceived conservatism of Isfahan (hardly the most repressive of towns itself):

> [Here in Isfahan] I see no witty, well-groomed boon-companions reciting poetry, recounting stories and literary matters to one another. Instead, I see a gathering of wretched, miserable, primitive and lowly men [...] who keep debating about schools of jurisprudence and religions...[253]

There is no shortage of passages expressive of a similar stereotyping of Baghdad – minus the favourable appraisal – as a den of frivolity. More to the point, there are instances of an explicit association of Baghdad with *mujūn*, of which some examples follow. The work already quoted above states that "the stories concerning

461 ["*Baghdād ḥāḍirat al-dunyā wa-mā ʿadāhā bādiya*"]. Also cf. Ibn Ḥawqal, *Ṣūra* 210; al-Munajjim, *Ākām* 33. Some authors would strive to find scientific explanations for the perceived cultural superiority of Baghdad and Iraq; see al-ʿAẓma 1991: 61–9. Part of the cultural weight of Baghdad was simply a function of numbers, with the city's population reaching as much as half a million in its golden age; see Kraemer 1986: 26, 47. In the Umayyad period (41/661–132/750), before the foundation of Baghdad, the Hijaz (Western Arabia, incorporating the towns of Mecca and Medina) was stereotyped as the centre *par excellence* of urbane, frivolous culture. See al-Majdhūb 1408/1988: 17; and cf. Enderwitz 1989: 135.

[252] al-Thaʿālibī, *Tatimma* I, 63. Also see ibid. II, 36 ["*ẓarf al-ʿIrāq*"]; al-Bayhaqī, *Maḥāsin* 166 ["*uṭlub lī rajulan ʿāqilan min ahl al-ʿIrāq ẓarīfan*"]; al-Muqaddasī, *Taqāsīm* 130 ["*wa-hum ahl al-ẓarf*"]; al-Nuwayrī, *Nihāya* I(i), 345 ["*baghdādiyyūn fī ẓarfihim wa-naẓāfatihim wa-riqqat akhlāqihim*"]; and also cf. the relevant passages in the editor's introduction in Ibn al-Marzubān, *Dhamm* 8–9. In Ibn al-Jawzī, *Ẓirāf* 62–3 one finds an anecdote intended to illustrate that in Baghdad even the water-carriers behave like refined gentlemen elsewhere. In a poem from the late Buyid era, the phrase "Iraqi heart" is used to describe a gentle, sensitive soul; see al-Bākharzī, *Dumya* I, 427.

[253] al-Tawḥīdī [attr.], *Risāla* 176.

the libertinism of [the people of Baghdad] (*akhbār mujūnihim*) are too numerous to count, and too well known to need mentioning".[254] An account about the famous Ibn al-Mubārak (d. 181/797), a man remembered for his great piety, claims that he decided to reject a prospective disciple of good credentials and unobjectionable morals simply because of the latter's having originated from Baghdad, and it was not before lengthy endeavours to persuade him that the scholar finally changed his mind.[255] The idea that the real home of *mujūn* is Iraq, and more particularly Baghdad, is articulated even in an Arabic poem from al-Andalus.[256] Another anecdote from the Buyid period, while it does not explicitly use the term *mujūn*, is certainly also based on the popular image of Baghdad appearing in the preceding examples; in fact, the very point of the joke relies on that image:

> One of the Prophet's descendants smuggled a whore into his house. When he was about to [touch] her, she said: "Give me the money." The man replied: "Come off it, damn it, I'm a kinsman of the Prophet!" Said the woman: "Enough of it! Go to the whores of Qumm! The whores of Baghdad won't buy this!"[257]

The extent of the acceptance of *mujūn* has certainly been variable from one historical period to another as well. Any systematic study of this important aspect is beyond

---

[254] al-Tawḥīdī [attr.], *Risāla* 241.

[255] According to the story, after the student had given the correct answers to several test questions, Ibn al-Mubārak asked him where he was from, and the mere mention of Baghdad made him snap: "Go away!" To the repeated protests and entreaties of the flabbergasted student, he recited some verses about the frivolous atmosphere of Baghdad by way of justification. See al-Yaḥṣubī, *Ilmāʿ* 238–9. As in many other texts, it is not so much the strict historical veracity of this account as the stereotypes expressed in it that are important. However, it is noteworthy that Ibn al-Mubārak was especially adamant about the necessity of avoiding all (by definition corrupting) contact with rulers, and therefore the story – assuming that its true – may well reflect a dislike for anyone coming from the recently founded centre of worldly power. On Ibn al-Mubārak's uncompromising views about contact with the political leaders, see Cook 2000: 53. The perceivedly 'worldly' and 'godless' attitudes of the inhabitants of Baghdad were also commented on by some visitors from elsewhere; see for instance Ibn Jubayr, *Riḥla* 194–5; Yāqūt, *Buldān* I, 464, 466.

[256] Ibn Saʿīd, *Rāyāt* 158.

[257] al-Tawḥīdī, *Baṣāʾir* II(iii), 87. Qumm, which is today one of the most important scholarly centres of Twelver Shiʿism, was already known as a centre of serious scholarship among the Shiʿites, who of course have always had a particular reverence for the Prophet's descendants. See Yāqūt, *Buldān* IV, 398; al-Samʿānī, *Ansāb* IV, 542–4. The point of the joke is not, however, the difference between Shiʿite and Sunni attitudes, since the population of Baghdad also incorporated a large percentage of Shiʿites. (The Prophet's descendants enjoyed unparalleled privileges in many parts of the Middle East, including Southern Iraq; cf. al-Wardī 1965: 246–7.) – For some more anecdotal data on the reputation of Baghdadi women as somewhat loose in morals but quick-witted (*mutamājināt Baghdād*), also see al-Tawḥīdī [attr.], *Risāla* 227–9, 232 ["*wa-l-jāriya baghdādiyya, lā taʿrifu illā l-dunyā wa-l-dīnār*"]; and an anecdote about a woman of Baghdad in Ibn Saʿīd, *Muqtaṭaf* 178. There is also an indecent but very funny joke (already cited above) about a boy prostitute from Ḥimṣ prospering in the licentious milieu of Baghdad in al-Rāghib, *Muḥāḍarāt* III, 479.

the scope of this book, but some general observations will be in order. First, it bears emphasis that the amount and intensity of *mujūn* material in the extant sources is only partly reliable as a measure of the place of libertinism in the culture of a given historical period, since it is quite conceivable that such material, considered as it typically was to be 'unserious' and of no consequence, would flourish and be accepted liberally yet circulate only in oral form, as the stuff of entertaining conversation. I went to some length to show that in fact at least some of the *mujūn* that one finds in the sources is but a written version of jokes, witticisms and remarks that had circulated in spoken form before.[258] Thus, even in the absence of copious amounts of *mujūn* texts in the written literary corpus of a certain era, one can never quite rule out the possibility that such material was simply deemed to be unworthy of recording but flourished in speech. (Such a possibility is especially obvious to someone who has ever taken part in conversations at friendly gatherings of highly educated intellectuals in otherwise repressive Middle Eastern countries where official censorship routinely suppresses the publication of 'indecent' and 'irreverent' texts.) In a way, the notion of different margins of tolerance for spoken and written discourse respectively is perhaps applicable to every society. Charles Pellat notes that the literary corpus of entertaining anecdotes, which was treated as an integral part of the written 'high' culture by mediaeval Arabic-speaking intellectuals, has in later times gradually moved towards the domain of folklore and oral literature.[259] If this has indeed been so, which appears likely, then *mujūn* has not so much dwindled as returned to its origins. Far from shrivelling from lack of an audience, it reverted to a more spontaneous context, that of merry conversation among friends, where it continued to be present even in the heyday of written *mujūn* literature. It is noteworthy in this context that today's spoken Arabic shows a joke repertoire and patterns of wit that are often quite reminiscent of the inventory of humorous and frivolous motifs analyzed in the survey of *mujūn* literature offered in the previous two chapters.[260]

Another factor that has to be reckoned with in any consideration of libertinism is the issue of changing patterns of urbanisation over the centuries. Because *mujūn* is likely to have been a largely urban phenomenon, the degree of urbanity and the geographical distribution of metropolitan centres in any given period must have influenced the acceptance of this phenomenon to a great degree. For example, a heavy influx of Bedouins or other rural folk into a theretofore highly urbanised area could easily shift attitudes closer to the norms of these newcomers. (And such

---

258 But cf. Marzolph 2000: 487.

259 Pellat 1963: 359. Some genres – notably popular joke collections, partly in colloquial Arabic – have continued to flourish in print too; see Marzolph 1992: I, 82–3, 85–6.

260 See for instance al-Qishṭaynī 1992: 153.

influxes, of course, did happen several times over the course of Middle Eastern history; suffice it to point to the waves of Arabian tribal immigration to Mesopotamia, or the invasion of the agricultural lands of the Maghreb by the *Banū Hilāl* and *Banū Sulaym* in the mid-5th/11th century). Obviously these changes of population did have an impact on the cultural patterns of the affected regions, including the tolerance or otherwise of non-normative discourse. One extremely important event is the occupation of Baghdad by the Mongols in 656/1258, which effectively terminated the pre-eminent position of that city within Arabic culture. A concomitant development was the rise to eminence of other great cities (which is not to say that those cities had not long played an important role as regional cultural centres before). The image of Egypt, or more properly Cairo, as a milieu particularly amenable to mirth and frivolity whose inhabitants have a great affinity to humour might be traced back to such changes.[261]

Whatever the reasons, the general impression is that attitudes (at least elite attitudes) in the Arab world in the last two centuries have become much less tolerant of cultural phenomena that overtly flout dominant norms (in matters of both religion and propriety). *Mujūn* is inevitably one of first casualties of such a shift towards conservatism and stridency. The process was an incremental one – no one suddenly outlawed *mujūn* literature in Muslim history – and seems to have started roughly in the Seljuk period.[262] However, it gained real momentum only in the early 14th/20th century, when the bowdlerising of editions of mediaeval Arabic texts as well as censorship of contemporary 'indecent' content became commonplace. Enter editorial diatribes against the moral vices of earlier generations of poets and writers, exit whole sections of works deemed to be 'corrupting'. Notable victims of the expurgation of 'improper' literary material include the Arabian Nights, the *Maqāmāt* of al-Hamadhānī, and the *Dīwān* of Abū Nuwās, with widely used obscene words and explicit descriptions of sexuality (especially homosexuality) usually having pride of place in the removed content.[263] These practices are not uniformly followed

[261] This is a mere surmise on my part, unsupported by any hard evidence. Edward Lane noticed this image in the 13th/19th century (Lane 1895: 207–8), but similar stereotypes were already recorded in the early 6th/12th century; see for instance al-Idrīsī, *Nuzha* III, 324 ["*wa-fī ahlihā rafāha wa-ẓarf shāmil wa-ḥalāwa*"]; al-Andalusī, *Risāla* 24 ["*wa-ammā akhlāquhum fa-l-ghālib ʿalayhā ittibāʿ al-shahawāt wa-l-inhimāk fī l-ladhdhāt wa-l-ishtighāl bi-l-turrahāt...*"]. Also see al-Qishṭaynī 1992: 110. Baghdad also lost its leading position in 'serious' scholarly pursuits to Cairo, and to a lesser extent to Damascus; see for instance al-Sakhāwī, *Iʿlān* 300. It is interesting to note that a contemporary scholar reports that wit – even the more risqué brand – is much appreciated as an important virtue by the intellectuals of Wādī Ḥaḍramawt in Yemen. See Serjeant 1951: 7. Of course, centuries of emigration and overseas trade have created in the towns of Ḥaḍramawt a remarkably cosmopolitan society and culture.

[262] Kraemer 1986: 30.

[263] See for instance El-Rouayheb 2005: 158, 160; Sprachman 1997: 192; and also the countless

even today, even if they are sufficiently prevalent to be a serious nuisance. An unintended yet emblematic display of the changing attitudes towards *mujūn* can be found in Muḥammad Bahja al-Atharī's edition of parts of the anthology *Kharīdat al-qaṣr* by ʿImād al-Dīn al-Iṣbahānī. Many of the poets whose works appear in the selection practically luxuriate in vulgarity, irreverence and other manifestations of *mujūn*, not surprisingly for the men of literature of the Seljuk era. The anthologist does make some disapproving noises at some points in his work, and he also claims to have omitted some texts that he considered too gross for inclusion in the collection. However, these are token gestures at most, in contrast to the practice of the editor, who (while producing a technically good edition of the text) adds his own comments in footnotes, a succession of embarrassingly moralistic remarks and even sustained tirades castigating the long-dead poets for their failures in the decency department.[264]

As we have argued, an interplay of several factors must have contributed to such a cultural change, with the growing influence of religious reform movements in recent times being an obvious component of the new atmosphere. Ironically, Victorian prudery might have had as powerful an influence as any home-grown factor; when Muslim peoples were most directly exposed to Western influence British (and French) culture was nowhere as permissive and tolerant of 'indecency' as it is today.[265] A special type of indirect outside influence may also have been (and still be) at play. It stands to reason that the margin of tolerance for behaviours and speech patters not conforming to accepted norms will be considerably smaller in situations when the very cultural integrity or even the survival of a community is threatened. In other words, threats from outsiders – whether real or putative – tend to diminish the toleration of internal dissent and non-conformity. A community feeling under

omissions in the edition I used of Abū Hiffān, *Akhbār*. A recent example is Hindāwī's new edition of the *Balāghāt al-nisāʾ* of Ibn Abī Ṭāhir Ṭayfūr, with the whole section on *mujūn* (consisting of obscene talk ascribed to women) missing from the volume with no acknowledgement of the mutilation. See Ibn Abī Ṭāhir, *Balāghāt*, and for the missing part in English translation see Borg 2000: 150–9. On the treatment – or indeed, in most cases, omission – of *mujūn* by editors in modern Iran of mediaeval Persian literary oeuvres, see Sprachman 1995: xxix, xxxi, xxxiv.

[264] Given that the editor refrained from actually bowdlerising the text, one cannot but wonder to what an extent honesty (as opposed to outside pressure) motivated these comments. See al-Iṣbahānī, *Kharīda* I(i), 44, 330; I(ii), 47, 80, 84, 98, 294; II(ii), 546, 759. Also cf. Bouhdiba 2004: 128.

[265] It is instructive to read E.W. Lane's comments on what he considered to be the inadmissibly licentious speech and poetry of the Egyptian natives. Palpably squeamish, the author awards special attention to the scandalous fact that an Arabic poem mentions God's name in the concluding part, after descriptions of wine-drinking and a sexual escapade, and that Egyptians see nothing wrong in such a text. See Lane 1895: 279–80; and cf. Marzolph 1992: I, 44, 131; El-Rouayheb 2005: 156–60. Here I would like to thank Khalid Kishtainy for the important insight that earlier European influence may well have been an important factor in shaping modern Arab attitudes to humour (email communication). – Modern Muslim thought sometimes bears the impact of Western influences in quite unexpected ways; see for instance Mahdi 2000: 62–3; van Gelder 1988: 137.

siege will permit far less fooling around with its values than one confident of its position. And indeed, it can be shown that periods of outside threats in the Muslim world were often accompanied by increasingly strict attitudes to norm-breaking. One salient example is the treatment of joking based on Islamic concepts in al-Andalus. When local Christians developed the nasty habit of publicly denigrating Islam and the Prophet Muḥammad, Muslims grew far less tolerant of jocular treatments of Islam by Muslims as well; and the same hardening of attitudes emerged during the wars of the *Reconquista*.[266] That a similar sense of beleaguerment prevails in much of today's Arab (and Muslim) world would be hard to deny.

When all is said and done, this book cannot, and will not, venture to give any satisfactory explanation to the progressively less lenient and less permissive cultural atmosphere of the last two centuries. It is almost certain that no one single factor can be identified as *the* cause; a combination of factors is much more likely to explain the phenomenon.

[266] I am indebted to Maribel Fierro for this idea, as well as the supporting evidence. For further details on the topic, see Fierro 1990: 109, 117; Fierro 1994: 210–4. – As a rule, the existence of an unmistakable 'other' tends to fortify the self-identification of a community and heighten awareness of its distinguishing features (including, presumably, its norms). On this point, see al-ʿAsrī 2001: 6–7. (I am grateful to Professor al-ʿAsrī for making a copy of this study available to me.)

5

Mujūn, Values and Norms

Kam min fatā taḥsabuhu nāsikan yastaqbilu l-layla bi-amrin ʿajīb
Alqā ʿalayhi l-laylu astārahu fa-bāta fī lahwin wa-ʿayshin khaṣīb
Wa-ladhdhatu l-aḥmaqi makshūfatun yasʿā bihā kullu ʿaduwwin murīb.

Many a young man you consider devout will spend the night in curious affairs.
Once the night has cast its shroud on him he spends it with amusements and delights.
It is a stupid man whose pleasures are unconcealed so that every suspicious adversary could carry news of them around.

(The vizier Yaḥyā b. Khālid al-Barmakī, offering advice to his indiscreet son)[1]

An overview of the reception of *mujūn* in the metropolitan culture of the mediaeval Middle East – especially in that of Baghdad and a number of cities with a similar cultural atmosphere – has revealed the ubiquity of a relatively tolerant attitude towards humour, frivolity and even libertinism among the educated classes and the political leaders. While never unambiguously endorsed, the exponents of *mujūn* nevertheless benefited from a remarkable degree of acceptance and might even derive considerable popularity and material success from their output. Indeed, some noted libertines are to this day counted among the greatest Arabic poets and writers. That works of *mujūn* often sold extremely well is beyond doubt; that some libertines formed part of the closest circle of a ruler's confidants and courtiers is obvious; that the production and circulation of literary works containing *mujūn* would normally encounter few if any negative sanctions is more than probable. For these and other reasons *mujūn* seems to have only the most tenuous of connections with mere deviance and norm-breaking. To treat *mujūn*, this Muslim intellectual variety of libertinism, purely as an aberration in the conduct of some individuals is to misrepresent it totally; nor is it tenable to regard mediaeval Muslim libertines as a group of social outcasts or pariahs languishing on the margins of society and tolerated only because of their humility or inconspicuity. In a sense, the producers of literary *mujūn* were very much a part of the cultural mainstream of their time.

[1] Yāqūt, *Udabāʾ* VI, 2812.

That said, it is no less obvious that virtually all of the literary material perceived as *mujūn* goes counter to accepted, ordinary norms of speech and behaviour in mediaeval Muslim society in some way or another. In fact, the very essence of *mujūn* appears to be a conscious breach or questioning of those norms, or more appropriately, a frivolous disregard thereof. And often the more outrageous the trespass of ordinary norms, the more favourable the reception of the work. This spells out the fundamental contradiction: authors of literary works clearly forming part of the cultural mainstream sought to make fun of the values and norms of that mainstream, and often proved extremely successful and drew a good income from such products. Members of the cultural élite seem to have amused themselves with ridiculing the values of the cultural élite to which they firmly belonged. Why did they do so? Is it best understood as a subversive discourse, a challenge to norms felt to be outdated or tedious, or simply as a form of entertainment, or as something else altogether? Is there anything that links *mujūn* to deviance in the usual sense of the term? Does it make any sense after all to speak of *mujūn* in terms of norms and values? A host of similar questions surround any attempt at analysing the social background of *mujūn* literature; and these are some of the questions to which the remainder of this study is devoted.

1. *Mujūn* vis-à-vis Dominant Values

1.1 Heterogeneity and Cultural Variety of Middle Eastern Societies

One of the factors to be taken into consideration when analysing the degree of conformity to norms in a complex society – like the mediaeval Middle East – is the existence of many subgroups, each with a different set of norms and values besides the shared cultural heritage. The multiplicity of conflicting viewpoints, traditions, and norms can be bewildering even when studying a relatively small-scale community, a point more and more cultural anthropologists seem to have realised in recent decades, and one that is as relevant to a study of the mediaeval Middle East as to the anthropology of contemporary societies. To quote the cautionary words of Lila Abu-Lughod:

> One type of phenomenon that resists analysis in terms either of a theory of culture or a theory of ideology is the coexistence of contradictory discourses, especially when one seems to subvert the other. I found this not in a place like colonial Morocco but within a relatively homogenous group where the contradictory discourses were linked to different groups defined by gender or age and even characterized the same individual speaking in different contexts.[2]

[2] Abu-Lughod 1989: 274.

The many participants of daily social interactions (literally as many as there are individual members of that society) will typically speak in a multitude of voices. Even within such a distinctive social subgroup as the religious experts (*ʿulamāʾ*) – or perhaps *especially* within such a group – one finds a continuous debate and struggle of opposed, and sometimes downright irreconcilable, ideas and norms; and there was hardly less controversy and conflict in other sectors of society and other domains of culture even though sources are less readily available to show it now. There has never been a unified Islamic viewpoint. Nor, importantly, is the cultural variety reducible to a simple dichotomy of high and popular culture.[3] The essentialistic assumption that the countless local ('folk') varieties of Islam and cultures stressing their allegiance to Islam are so many modifications – or indeed distortions – of some original, genuine form of Islam ('real Islam' as it were) is absolute nonsense. Yet for a patent nonsense that few scholars would now explicitly endorse, it has been a remarkably influential idea in an implicit way, since quite a few anthropologists and Islamicists have largely concurred with a considerable part of the Muslim religious élite in assuming the existence an immutable, ahistorical core Islamic culture and its primacy over local varieties. Indeed some researchers, again concurring with a lot of Muslim scholars, would take pains to define what constitutes this core.[4] Even apart from the absurd notion of the reclamation of an uncorrupted original Islam, overemphasising the unifying factors in various Islamicate societies, above all the regulations of the *sharīʿa*, is in itself a serious mistake. On the one hand, there never was consensus on any element of the *sharīʿa* beyond the most basic tenets of Islam, and on the other hand, at no moment of premodern history did the *sharīʿa* fully organise the life of any Muslim society. As Talal Asad observes,

> [...] the notion of a totalitarian Islam rests on a mistaken view of the social effectivity of ideologies. A moment's reflection will show that it is not the literal scope of the shariʿa which matters here but the degree to which it informs and regulates social practices, and it is clear that there has never been any Muslim society in which the religious law of Islam has governed more than a fragment of social life. If one contrasts this fact with the highly regulated character of social life in modern states, one may immediately see the reason why. The administrative and legal regulations of such secular states are far more pervasive and effective in controlling the details of people's lives than anything to be found in Islamic history.[5]

---

[3] Berkey 1995: 39–40. Also cf. Ibrahim 1994: 5–6. Not incidentally, it seems to be a universal tendency that whereas within every human society one finds ongoing controversies on what is morally acceptable and what is not, most members of those same societies will assume that such categories are clear, well-defined and universally valid. See Douglas 1970: 15, 19–20.

[4] On this issue, see el-Zein 1977: 227; Eickelman 1989: 203, 258, 260.

[5] Asad 1986: 13.

That said, it is equally important to avoid turning the heterogeneity of the Islamic world into an absolute rule and abandon all quest of regularities and similarities. Odd as that may sound, this extreme stance has also had its advocates. Accurately observing the baffling variety of opinions among Muslim élites and the equally striking multiplicity of lifestyles, social relations, customs and beliefs among and within Muslim communities, some scholars concluded that it was spurious and conceptually unhelpful to uphold what they regarded as the fiction of the unity of Islamic culture and preferred to use the very term Islam in the plural ('islams').[6] Partly owing to the influential ideas of Edward Said regarding Orientalism and partly because of theoretical currents within anthropology, there is a palpable reluctance among some anthropologists to make general observations, however innocuous and justified, about the culture of the Middle East or the Muslim world, viewing all generalisations as inherently hostile, a form of cultural aggression as it were.[7] This is unwarranted. It is unwarranted for a number of reasons: first, it would be hard to deny the existence of a few obvious factors of unity within the Islamic world (not least the subjective feeling of unity expressed in the concept of *umma*) even though factors of diversity may predominate; second, identifying patterns and structures is a legitimate goal of social science; and third, the status of an outsider (a Western scholar studying a contemporary Muslim community or any scholar, Western or Muslim, studying mediaeval Muslim communities) does necessitate some degree of generalisation if one is to gain a better understanding of the society under scrutiny.

To begin with the issue of the unifying features of Islamicate societies. An approach suggested by the anthropologist Talal Asad I find extremely insightful and constructive; the gist of his proposition is that Islamic culture, like other cultures, can be understood as essentially a distinct tradition, or better, as a form of discourse. Its being a discourse means that all the controversies and conflicts going on within it form an integral part of it. What is relatively uniform in the world of Islam is not the solutions and the answers that Muslim groups or individuals may find to the problems they face but the conceptual framework in which they seek solutions and answers.[8] Muslims have no common opinions, but they do have a common cultural

---

[6] el-Zein 1977: 242; Eickelman 1989: 262.

[7] On this tendency, see Lindholm 1995: 809–10.

[8] Asad 1986: 11, 14, 16; and also cf. Calder 2000: 69–70, 75–6. Brinkley Messick arrives at a conclusion similar to Asad's when he contends that the *sharīʿa* is not so much a unified 'Islamic law' as a 'general societal discourse'. See Messick 1993: 253. The existence of a general 'Islamic discourse' must also mean that studying a given Muslim community in isolation – as a discrete cultural entity and without considering the wider cultural and historical background – is quite infelicitous. Religious, cultural and economic links with the wider world of Islamic civilisation are a crucial aspect of the study of any Muslim community. See Salzman 1978: 540.

vocabulary – a common discourse – to discuss their differences of opinion. As all long-standing traditions, the discourse of Islamicate societies must needs leave ample room for debate, dissent, change and innovation, but the possibilities, modes and patterns of controversy and change were largely established, more or less definitively, during the first centuries of the development of this tradition.[9] (For instance, the norm that you may innovate but should under no circumstances call it 'innovation', *bidʿa*.)

As noted above, it is also important to reject the crude notion of generalisations as *ipso facto* distorting. Jumping from the observation of the undeniably huge variety of voices within Islamicate societies to the conclusion that no regular patterns at all can be identified in that variety is a *non sequitur*. As a matter of fact, the many voices of a society will usually fall in a number of recognisable types of general discourse, with recognisable patterns of subgroup-specific judgements and opinions.[10] While it is true that various social subgroups and even individuals embraced different values and priorities, this fact should not lead the researcher to the abandonment of all attempts at finding recognisable patterns of culture and behaviour, structures of social relationships and normative systems. No two individuals are identical, but most people do succumb to norms of conduct that are to a large extent (albeit not entirely) predictable and observe social rules and cultural guidelines that they share with countless other persons. Finding general patterns in people's lives may not be easy and straightforward, but it is nonetheless a legitimate aspiration of anthropological and historical research.[11]

With that caveat in mind, we may now return to the problem of the heterogeneity of the society of mediaeval Muslim cities, and what it entails for the purposes of an analysis of *mujūn*. At least four levels of diversity must be reckoned with: first, the differences between one particular Muslim community and another (such as between Baghdad and a rural community in the *sawād*; between Baghad and, say, Isfahan; or even between a Shiʿite and a Sunni quarter of Baghdad); second, between the norms and customs of one social subgroup and another (e.g. the ʿulamāʾ and the

[9] el-Zein 1977: 229–30.

[10] Cf. Sherif 1936: 27–8, 139.

[11] The danger that the commendable quest for the recognition of the heterogeneity and individual differences in foreign societies may turn anthropological analysis into amorphous, inconsequential storytelling is pointed out by Charles Lindholm in the context of the review of an otherwise quite interesting and original anthropological monograph. As he observes, laudable though it is to portray the diversity of Middle Eastern peoples and call attention to the myriad voices to be heard there as elsewhere, yet the statement that Arabs are individuals like everyone else is a somewhat meagre and self-evident one for a conclusion: "We are left wondering [...] whether we can say anything about the Middle East except that it is full of complicated individuals with varied life histories who live in very different historical and cultural contexts." See Lindholm 1995: 812–3, for more on the problem pp. 809–13, and for examples of a better approach, pp. 813–8. Also cf. Salzman 1978: 555–6.

kuttāb; or the *ʿulamāʾ* and the petty traders; allowing for overlaps); third, differences of opinion and debates within one particular social subgroup (e.g. various theological views or divergence of legal opinions among the *ʿulamāʾ* of the same city); and of course individual dissimilarities resulting from difference of personality and experiences. Much has already been said about the different attitudes to *mujūn* in the various regions of the mediaeval Arab world (especially in the Maghreb and the eastern lands respectively), and we will not be detained with this level of diversity here. Of the factors contributing to the variability of Islamicate culture, it is the differences on the level of the subgroup and the individual – in other words, diversity of opinion, belief and practice within the same community – that will be the object of inquiry in the following pages. The varied responses to *mujūn* in all social classes, as well as the varied nature of the material labelled *mujūn* itself suggest that the heterogeneity of mediaeval Muslim society and culture may offer a clue to understanding this strange literary phenomenon.

Reading *mujūn* texts, one is often struck by the distinctly 'folksy' character of a considerable part of this material, especially in the case of *nawādir* (anecdotes, or better said, jokes). Furthermore, it has repeatedly been noted in the preceding chapters that quite a few *mujūn* motifs (in poetry and prose alike) were demonstrably borrowed from humorous phrases and quips heard in ordinary conversation. This justifies, indeed begs, the question whether and to what an extent the appearance and growing popularity of *mujūn* may have had to do with the impact of popular culture upon élite culture. Differences in norms and culture between one social subgroup and another – namely the *khāṣṣa* and the *ʿāmma* of a given locality – might be found to have been a crucial factor in the emergence of *mujūn*. To put it in simpler terms: can *mujūn* be seen as an aspect of the culture of the lower classes that came to be adopted by many within the élite and adapted to higher literary forms? How much, if any, of *mujūn* literature really reflects 'lower' tastes and values appropriated by the literate classes for their own ends (mainly for entertainment)?

Of course, the very notion of 'popular' is of dubious merit and is to be treated with due caution. In addition to the problem of defining the term, there never seems to have been a watertight separation between 'popular' and 'élite' culture – be the two categories defined as they may – in Middle Eastern history (nor indeed in other complex societies).[12] Although a serious analysis of the issue would go far beyond the scope of the present essay, it is still important to note that the concept of 'popular culture', when used in a mediaeval Middle Eastern context, can refer to at least two sharply different phenomena, which I will conveniently call 'old folklore' and 'new

---

12 On the progressive abandonment of this crude paradigm in Middle Eastern studies, see Berkey 1995: 38–9. (Although this essay cannot address the question, note that the neat separation of the oral and the written is not unproblematic either; see Foley 1997: 425.)

folklore' respectively, although the difference between them is not primarily chronological. The main difference is rather the strikingly dissimilar attitude to each of urban Muslim intellectuals. By 'old folklore' is meant the pre-Islamic and early Islamic Bedouin culture (by definition wholly oral), which Muslim élite culture regarded as its fountainhead of information, ideals and partly of ethical and behavioural norms too, and which for that reason enjoyed exceedingly high prestige among urban intellectuals. The contrast with 'new folklore' could not be more evident, the latter term covering the oral culture of the urban and rural lower classes, including the urban poor, the peasants of the villages as well as all Bedouin tribesmen from about the 4th/10th century onwards. This type of 'contemporary' folklore had very low prestige; indeed it was the object of derision and almost no urban intellectuals were interested in it (and then only for such curiosity value as it might have). We can quickly pass over 'old folklore': it was the object of serious study and the source of 'serious' linguistic, historical, ethnographic and philological data, and as such had little if anything to do with *mujūn* literature. It did not offer the cultivators of *mujūn* much in the way of borrowable material, and when it did the borrowed motifs would invariably be put to parodistic uses, as in the case of the poetic motif of the 'deserted camping-grounds' (*aṭlāl*) and some aspects of the ancient Bedouin ethos (*v. s.* in Chapter Three). 'New folklore', on the other hand, is quite another kettle of fish. One particular type of 'new folklore', the living oral culture of the *urban lower classes*, did perceptibly influence the style and contents of written *mujūn* literature. Albeit virtually every libertine poet and writer known to us was literate and relatively well educated, and some were quite erudite and wealthy too, the impact of the *ʿāmma* on the literature they produced can be shown here and there. It is slightly ironic that not all members of the lower classes – as shown in the previous chapter – were necessarily glad to see their élite play with frivolous literary motifs, no matter if those motifs had partly been borrowed from popular culture.

That a number of motifs that appear in libertine poetry originated as orally transmitted jokes or quips is undoubtable.[13] Some illustration of this has been provided in the preceding chapters, but for additional evidence, here is a passage from the *Dīwān* of Abū Nuwās:

> Abū Nuwās says [in one of his poems]: "When the fox of disaffection (*ṣudūd*) appeared before us, I sent the hound of intimacy (*wiṣāl*) to chase it. / It brought him in chained up, with the tail over the head." Now, Abū Nuwās was once in a park when he caught sight of a group of lowly people (*jamāʿa min al-sifal*),

[13] Besides the cases mentioned in passing in the second and third chapters, also see Beaumont 1993: 159 for what appears to be another possible example. On this kind of osmosis, also cf. Sadan 1998: 4–5, 22.

one of whom was talking to the rest telling a story about the person he loved, saying: "He tries to evade me like a fox, and I run in his wake like a hunting dog, right at his tail." So Abū Nuwās composed these two verses in imitation of this [man's words].[14]

Indeed, even popular idioms might pass for *mujūn* and be occasionally taken up by élite intellectuals.[15] Nor is there, in my opinion, compelling reason to doubt that in many if not most cases it was an oral joke that metamorphosed into a written motif and not vice versa – with the exception of motifs that are clearly based on aspects of scholarly culture that might still be understood by uneducated people (e.g. the parody of the *isnād* format). The fact of cultural borrowage from the lower classes is indisputable in one particular aspect of *mujūn* texts: the not infrequent use of colloquialisms and even elements of genuine, unalloyed urban argot in both prose and poetry.[16] That some libertine poets sought to enhance the effect of their works by deliberately merging dialectal items into the written Arabic text is shown by sporadic but quite explicit evidence. Such, for instance, is the clear implication of the following characterisation of the Iraqi poet Abū l-Ḥasan Muḥammad al-Buṣrawī (d. 443/1051): "Still alive, he plays the libertine in his poetry by [using] the language and the tales of the Baghdadians (*wa-huwa baʿd min al-aḥyāʾ yatamājanu bi-lughat al-Baghdādiyyīn wa-khurāfātihim bi-shiʿr*)..."[17] The celebrated Ibn al-Ḥajjāj (d. 391/1001) claimed to have learned the necessary vocabulary for his startlingly vulgar poetry by making written notes of the obscene insults he had overheard as a youth on summer nights from a tavern next to his family's house.[18] Of some relevance here is the increasing popularity among highly educated intellectuals of such dialectal verse forms as the Andalusian (and later also Eastern) *zajal*, the Iraqi *mawwāliyā*

---

[14] Abū Nuwās, *Dīwān* V, 286.

[15] E.g. Yāqūt, *Udabāʾ* VI, 2772. Here, a respectable courtier of the caliph al-Muqtafī (r. 530/1136–555/1160) utilises for his own purposes a phrase identifiable as *mujūn* and common in the dialect of the Baghdad folk (*mathal yatamājanu bihi ahl Baghdād*).

[16] For the impact of the vernacular, see for example al-Tawḥīdī [attr.], *Risāla* 280; al-Tawḥīdī, *Baṣāʾir* I(i), 111 ["*tūbatnāʾ* "]; II(iv), 87 ["*shiqq istik ṣayrafī* "]; V(ix), 55–7 [various phrases and proverbs]; al-Thaʿālibī, *Thimār* 667 [*bāzī Juḥā*]; al-Iṣbahānī, *Kharīda* I(ii), 314–5 ["... *qāma bihi l-Burhānu li-l-nāsi* "]; II(i), 216–8 [*shubbāra*]; Ibn Maʿṣūm, *Sulāfa* 50 [*awḥashanā unsukum*], 89 ["*nawrazūnā mimmā tanawraztumā minhu*..."], 110 ["*zāda ... al-māʾ ʿalā l-daqīq*"]. Also cf. van Gelder 1992: 185; Shoshan 1991: 101–4. On a well-known case of the impact of slang on *mujūn* literature, see al-Thaʿālibī, *Yatīma* III, 353; and the whole of the two volumes of Bosworth 1976. – It must be noted, however, that libertine poets writing in Classical Arabic could also occasionally have an influence on vernacular poetry. A recent example is the case a humorous poem in the Iraqi dialect by Ḥusayn Qassām al-Najafī, which he meant to be a reply to a similar verse in Classical Arabic composed by Īliyā Abū Māḍī. See al-Khāqānī 1381/1962: 9.

[17] al-Bākharzī, *Dumya* I, 347.

[18] Van Gelder 1988: 82.

and other genres, and the Yemeni type of the *muwashshaḥ*.[19] Some of these kinds of dialectal poetry – notably the *zajals* of Ibn Quzmān (d. 555/1160) – lent themselves to *mujūn*-like content. Indeed, the unpretentious and spontaneous medium of the dialects was obviously more adequate for conveying certain (as a rule, trivial and/or humorous) messages. In spite of the practically undisputed prestige of Classical Arabic, even intellectuals – most intellectuals anyway – would find the use of this elevated linguistic medium in distinctly quotidian contexts both incongruous and ludicrous.[20] According to Abū Bakr al-Ṣūlī (d. 335/946), it is said that solecisms [against the rules of Classical Arabic] (*laḥn*) are more unseemly in writing than they are in speech. Most scholars will themselves speak incorrectly[21], lest they should be thought of as irksome and pompous (*akthar al-ʿulamāʾ yalḥanu fī kalāmihi li-allā yunsaba ilā l-thiqal wa-l-bughḍ*). However, in writing and in reciting poetry this would be unseemly and unacceptable.[22]

The observation of the incongruity of an elegant Classical Arabic in treating trivia is especially pertinent to some of the material classifiable as *mujūn*. Jokes, particularly indecent jokes, are an obvious example. Consider the following commentary, coming right after the punchline of a joke, by the renowned man of letters Abū Ḥayyān al-Tawḥīdī (d. 414/1023):

> These are the exact words (*lafẓ*) of this ignoramus [the protagonist of the joke]; the joke would have been ruined by correct [usage, viz. of Classical Arabic] (*wa-l-ṣawāb fīhi yukhillu bi-l-nādira*). There is no harm in solecisms and mistakes if one quotes a silly or worthless man (*wa-lā yunkaru l-laḥn wa-l-khaṭaʾ idhā kānat al-ḥikāya ʿan safīh aw nāqiṣ*).[23]

---

[19] About these and other comparable forms, see for instance al-Ḥillī, *ʿĀṭil* 7, 12–3, 71–5, 136; Ibn Saʿīd, *Muqtaṭaf* 239, 263; Ibn Maʿṣūm, *Sulāfa* 243–4; al-Khāqānī 1381/1962: 16. Of course, by no means did the growing (but still limited) appetite for dialectal verse imply a decrease in the appreciation of Classical Arabic poetry, whose prestige and superiority were never in jeopardy. The Muslim intelligentsia would relish dialectal works as a complement to, not a substitute for, verse in the written language. See, for instance, al-Bayhaqī, *Maḥāsin* 478.

[20] E.g. al-Thaʿālibī, *Tatimma* I, 30. (This fact was noted and commented on in Chapter Three in the context of discussing parodies, in particular jokes on grammarians. Also cf. Szombathy 2004: 95–7.)

[21] That is to say not conforming to the rules of Classical Arabic (which does not mean that they would commit errors in terms of using the vernacular).

[22] al-Ṣūlī, *Adab* 130.

[23] al-Tawḥīdī, *Baṣāʾir* I(i), 111. For a similar opinion concerning proverbs circulating among the common people, see op.cit. V(ix), 58. G. J. H. van Gelder pointed out to me that more than a century and a half earlier al-Jāḥiẓ had already held the opinion, which he repeatedly expressed in his works, that the vernacular is a more suitable medium than grammatically correct Classical Arabic for narrating jokes and frivolous trifles (see for instance al-Jāḥiẓ, *Ḥayawān* I, 375). The literary theoretician Ḥāzim al-Qarṭājannī (d. 864/1285) also considered the use of colloquialisms to be apposite to jestful texts; see Meisami 1993: 14.

The appearance – in a very limited measure – of urban slang in 'high' literature corresponded with a similarly moderate but perceptible increase in curiosity about the lowest class (indeed the underclass) of city dwellers, like beggars, thieves, vagabonds, mountebanks. This interest, which can be dated to the Buyid period, did not peter out altogether in the succeeding centuries.[24] A rare instance of explicit acknowledgement of debt to popular culture can be found in the biography of ʿAbdallāh b. Aḥmad al-Khashshāb (d. 567/1171–2) of Baghdad, who, although a specialist of Classical Arabic grammar and a real bookworm, made a point of using purely dialectal language in speech, and was fond of socialising with commoners and frequenting venues of such low-prestige entertainment as the performances of popular storytellers and jugglers (*arbāb al-ḥikāya wa-l-shaʿbadha*) on the banks of the Tigris river. He also had lively interest in the commoners' speech, and a sympathy for this class of people most uncharacteristic of men of his social standing. When reproached by educated friends for stooping so low, he would defend his habit thus: "From time to time [one hears] from them anecdotes than which nothing is better or finer (*innahu yanduru minhum nawādir lā yakūnu aḥsan minhā wa-lā alṭaf*)."[25]

The links of *mujūn* with the culture of the lower classes went beyond borrowings of style, vocabulary and themes. Whilst it was argued in the previous chapter that at least some elements among the common people could be quite unsympathetic to what they perceived as the immorality and impiety of certain intellectuals, and would occasionally give violent expression to their dissatisfaction, it remains true that most littérateurs, libertines included, must have had daily or near-daily contact with various people of lower social status. Even those who achieved success in a ruler's court and came to be part of that milieu were more often than not of modest origins, and must typically have maintained contact with their kin. Then there were those, not few in number, who had to complement their undependable earnings from poetry or prose writing with more regular income from some ordinary craft, which definitely ensured continuing familiarity with the commoners' ways.[26] Mention was

[24] Cf. Bosworth 1976: I, 30, 96, 105. For some illustrative examples, see al-Tanūkhī, *Nishwār* II, 358; al-Tawḥīdī, *Akhlāq* 365.

[25] Yāqūt, *Udabāʾ* IV, 1497–8.

[26] A relevant case is the career of the poet ʿAbd al-Sayyid b. Jakar (early 6th/12th c.), who initially sold confectionery in Wāsiṭ (Southern Iraq) but became a success with the governor of the city as a poet and narrator of anecdotes. According to some sources, however, he would later on make a living as a shoemaker in Baghdad. See al-Iṣbahānī, *Kharīda* II(i), 359–60. Some successful poets undoubtedly pursued quite ordinary métiers for a living. Al-Waʾwāʾ al-Dimashqī worked in his youth as an auctioneer at the fruit market of Damascus, and gained his poetic skills as an autodidact while pursuing his trade. The libertine poet al-Nāshiʾ (d. 365/975) made and repaired brass objects to earn his livelihood. The sobriquet of a poet of Northern Iraq known as al-Khabbāz al-Baladī ('the baker from Balad') tells all about his métier. Incidentally, this poet, despite his mastery of Classical Arabic verse, seems to have remained illiterate all his life. The same can be said about another baker-cum-poet, the celebrated

made in the last chapter of more than one libertine poet's express preference for low-class venues of entertainment (especially the cheap drinking dens of Baghdad and the surrounding settlements) and for the company of an assortment of less than illustrious folk, the primary reason being that in a lowly tavern, unlike in a ruler's court, there was no need to conform to excessive etiquette. It is worth adding here that it was not unusual for witty littérateurs, poets, singers, and their admirers to choose the shop or workshop of a known libertine as the venue of their regular soirées or informal gatherings.[27]

It is not a totally misguided quest, then, to search for interfaces, or points of overlapping, between libertinism and the culture of the urban masses. Low-class urban folklore did have a demonstrable, if limited, impact upon *mujūn*. However, that folklore represents but one of many influences that converged to produce libertine literature and lifestyles, and most of those influences originated with the cultural and political élite. To put it in the simplest possible terms, *mujūn* belonged to the élite as much as, and probably far more than, it did to the lower classes.[28]

---

al-Khubzaruzzī ('the maker of rice-bread'; d. 327/938–9). One of the libertines of Basra and a known homosexual, he would recite his own poetry as well as amusing anecdotes while working in a baker's workshop, with people congregating nearby to listen to his talk, including a lot of young boys who hoped he would mention them in amorous poetry and thereby make them famous. Even the successful court poet Ibn Lankak did not deem it beneath his dignity to attend this bizarre 'literary salon'. Yet another informative sobriquet is that of al-Sarī al-Raffāʾ, a famous poet from Mosul, who earned his living by darning worn clothes. See al-Thaʿālibī, *Yatīma* I, 272; II, 208–9, 365; Yāqūt, *Udabāʾ* IV, 1785–6; VI, 2745; al-Bākharzī, *Dumya* I, 510–1; and also see al-Iṣbahānī, *Kharīda* I(ii), 323 [Ghazāl]; and several examples in al-Alūsī 1987: 73–7. Also see Gruendler 2005b: 88 on the poverty of Abū Hiffān (d. 255/869), an accomplished littérateur and poet, and an associate of Abū Nuwās.

[27] During the reign of al-Muʿtaṣim (218/833–227/842), a shop where beer was sold is said to have been a place much frequented by young boys of dubious morals and poets and singers desirous of meeting them ("... *wa-huwa yakhruju wa-yajlisu ʿinda Fulān al-fuqqāʿī wa-dukkānuhu maʾlaf li-l-ghilmān al-murd wa-l-mughannīn*" etc.); see al-Iṣfahānī, *Aghānī* XX, 302. A poet of the Seljuk period called Abū l-Maʿālī al-Shurūṭī owned a shop in Baghdad which served as, for all practical purposes, a literary salon ("... *adhkuruhu fī awān ayyām al-ṣibā wa-dukkānuhu fī Bāb al-Nūbī majmaʿ al-ẓurafāʾ wa-l-udabāʾ wa-huwa yaʿmalu l-shiʿr wa-yulaqqinuhu ṣunnāʿ al-ghināʾ...*"). In the same period the bookshop and copyist's workshop of a certain Saʿd al-Ḥaẓīrī appears to have played roughly the same role in the lives of another circle of intellectuals ("*sūq al-adab qāʾima bi-makānihi fī sūq al-kutub ... wa-lam yazal majmaʿ al-faḍl dukkānuhu*"). See al-Iṣbahānī, *Kharīda* I(ii), 308; II(i), 31–3. It is in the 3rd/9th century that bookshops began to play the role of important venues of literature and culture in the bigger cities, especially in Baghdad; see Toorawa 2005: 302. This is not to say that high-class venues never hosted the gatherings of men of letters: a famous example of a distinctly aristocratic literary salon is that of the royal princess al-Wallāda in Córdova (late 5th/11th c.); see for instance Ibn Diḥya, *Muṭrib* 8; and on some precursors thereof in the Hijaz under the Umayyads, cf. al-Majdhūb 1408/1988: 20. On the institution of *majlis* ('session', intellectual gathering or 'salon', a sort of *tertulia*) in Arabic culture, see Depaule 1997.

[28] It follows that the assertion of Sylvette Larzul (Larzul 1996: 38) that outrageous or daring views could only be presented in quasi-'popular' literature – for instance, in the Arabian Nights – is, to put it mildly, wide of the mark.

What the *ʿāmma* did contribute to the florescence of *mujūn* was mostly in the form of such curious usages, phrases, customs and peculiarities as the educated élite happened to find diverting and cared to lend selective and condescending attention to. Also this attention was never systematic, and involved no trace of esteem or recognition of debt. The prestige of the common people and their culture remained as low as ever.

Despite the interesting evidence reviewed above for links between *mujūn* and the lower classes there is no reason to interpret libertinism simply as a reflection of lower tastes and norms in 'high' literature. An equal or greater number of data could be adduced to show links to the cultural élite; thus differences in norms between one social subgoup or class and another – even if they may have played a minor role – cannot provide a full answer. It rather appears that the differing responses to *mujūn* had more to do with a lower level of diversity, with controversies within subgroups and with variation in individual attitudes.

1.2 Alternative Values

By definition, norms are supposed to be shared by the majority of the members of a community. However, this statement does not mean that every member of a society is expected to conform to all norms to the same extent. For a norm to be valid, it is even possible that it should be complied with by a minority only, provided they are influential enough to set the tone for the rest of the society. In short, the various social subgroups tend to face differing expectations as to conformity to dominant norms. The political élite in particular, as well as the religious élite, were expected to display a far higher degree of conformity, if only in the form of outward shows of normative behaviour or rhetorical support. This observation, which is not specific to mediaeval Muslim society, is true with some reservations; notably, it is behaviour in the public space that required a high degree of compliance with norms of piety, decency, and respectability, while the private domain was less regulated even for the highest echelons of society. (Furthermore, public conformity had little direct correlation with honest commitment and heartfelt morality – more about this important point below.) Nevertheless, it is generally valid that members of the élite, because of their conspicuous position, were supposed to behave and talk in conformity with cultural ideals and the concrete norms expressing those ideals. In the case of mediaeval Muslim societies, these expectations would typically include self-control, tact, courtesy, and the avoidance of all kinds of scandal and notoriety. It is somewhat ironic that higher status and social prestige would (and will) result in not less but more behavioural constraints and compulsions, but the tendency is in fact easily explicable, the likely reason being that it is precisely the highest-status members of a society that symbolise honour and, practically, the sum of the values of the community. In a sense, they embody the values of their community, and therefore their behaviour must represent the norms that give observable structure to those values in everyday life. This principle, which anthropologists like Pierre Bourdieu and Lila Abu-Lughod have observed in Muslim communities of the contemporary Middle East and North Africa[29], seems to be equally valid for the mediaeval period.[30] What is more, the heavy pressure on high-status members of a society – whose position makes them paragons of normative conduct – to guard their behaviour and conform to ideals at least in public, can be shown to recur across various cultures; indeed it appears to be a well-nigh universal tendency.[31]

Norms were thus different for each social subgroup. In fact, even within the same social rank and the same kinship unit, norms of proper behaviour and speech would differ on the basis of biological age: old men were expected to behave quite unlike the young. More specifically, mature people were supposed to eschew all manifestations of 'silliness' and frivolity, traits regarded as far more tolerable – indeed all but inevitable – in youths. It was widely considered, as it often is today, to be natural that young men should sow their wild oats, whereas an old man engaging in identical activities would surely make a scandal.[32] In judging discreditable behaviour, the perpetrator's advanced age was certainly a serious aggravating circumstance. Consider the obvious implication of a passage in the *Kitāb al-badīʿ* of Ibn al-Muʿtazz (d. 296/908), which tells of a well-educated man (*rajul min ahl al-adab*) who, upon reaching the age of forty, made the abrupt decision to give up

[29] See for instance Abu-Lughod 1999: 97. A concrete example is the differing ways contumelious language would be received and judged in the Yemeni highlands depending on the social status of the person delivering it, with women, children and people of low status being treated with remarkable leniency and tribesmen of full honour being liable to serious censure and possibly painful consequences as well. See Caton 1990: 55; vom Bruck 1996: 152–3. Given the different expectations corresponding to the different social subgroups, it is far from surprising to note that the greatest negative attention tends to be aroused by behaviour inappropriate for the actor's social status; see Messick 1993: 179. On the impact of social status upon the individual's habitus and conduct, see for instance Foley 1997: 260, 308.

[30] See for instance Lagrange 2006: 63.

[31] Goode 1960: 255. As a possible corollary to the idea that norms may be defined either in a descriptive (statistical) or a prescriptive sense (see Chapter One), it has been suggested that the statistical predominance of norms may show a connection with social class, with the lower classes tending to accept the prescriptive aspect of a norm but failing to conform in practice, and dominant groups showing a greater degree of actual conformity. See Testé 2003: 21.

[32] For some poetic reflections of this attitude, see for instance Ibn al-Muʿtazz, *Ṭabaqāt* 29–30; al-Zawzanī, Ḥamāsa II, 46; al-Thaʿālibī, *Tatimma* II, 39; and for a detailed summary of the issue, see A. Arazi's entry in EI2, s. v. "al-shayb wa ʾl-shabāb", esp. p. 385. (Abdullahi Ali Ibrahim mentions an interesting case showing the permanence of such a view in contemporary Sudan. When Sudanese president Jaʿfar al-Nimayrī introduced *sharīʿa* law in 1983, many in the country commented that while it is only to be expected that an aging man should at some point make up his mind to abandon carousal and womanising, it is unreasonable that he should turn his decision into law. See Ibrahim 1994: 37.)

drinking and making merry. When asked by his friends about his motives, he pleaded that at his age such pastimes would be shameful ("... *wa-anā astaḥī min sinnī*").[33] The same principle is put succintly by the ever-eloquent al-Jāḥiẓ (d. 255/869):

> The men of seriousness are not the same as those of jesting. And a thing may well be pleasing when done by a youth and repulsive when done by an old man (*wa-qad yaḥsunu al-shay' bi-l-shabāb wa-yaqbuḥu mithluhu min al-shuyūkh*).[34]

It should be clear by this point that norms are very flexible guidelines whose applicability for a given person will usually depend on a host of factors like social status, family background, and biological age. And the issue is complicated further by the existence of what can be termed *alternative values*, the main subject of this section of the present chapter. Let me remind the reader that the values endorsed by the *ʿulamāʾ*, the religious élite – although not without ongoing controversies – may not have actually informed the totality of the customs and cultural practices of society, yet most people of all social classes would, by and large, accept those values as part of their identity and refuse to question them explicitly.[35] The consensus regarding the most elementary values was thus fairly pervasive (in principle if not always in practice). This had important consequences for *mujūn*. There can be no questioning that people of integrity, honour and social prestige regarded the behaviour of libertines with disapprobation and considered their literary products immoral.[36] It is safe to say that the moral disapproval of libertinism was widespread among mediaeval Muslims at least on a rhetorical level. And yet, ironic as it is, this disapproval did not necessarily entail a lack of appreciation, *because values of morality were not the only basis on which to judge works of art.* According to other, alternative criteria – on an altogether distinct scale of equally valid values – a libertine might pass the test of excellence, and indeed might appear superior to the most devout and respectable patrician. This point must be emphasised repeatedly, as it is one of the most central observations of the present essay: because of the simultaneous existence of alternative value scales within the same cultural

---

33 Ibn al-Muʿtazz, *Badīʿ* 94.

34 al-Jāḥiẓ, *Ḥayawān* I, 111.

35 Stambouli, Zghal 1976: 14; el-Zein 1977: 245. That subgroups within a complex society will borrow elements or even a substantial part of the value system of each other is not unusual, but the most typical direction of such borrowings is from a subgroup of higher status to another of a lower status. (The opposite process may also take place but is relatively rare.) See Wolf 1966: 20.

36 Nor is there reason to doubt the honesty of a lot of educated Muslims in forming such judgements, but it is obviously impossible to ascertain the matter. Their honesty is in fact immaterial to an analysis of *public* attitudes to libertinism, although it does affect the issue of *privately* held and voiced attitudes. The sincerity of the professed views of Muslim intellectuals concerning libertinism, as well as the relationship of a libertine literary persona to the actual author's conduct, will be discussed shortly.

collectivity, it is possible and in fact very common that a person's behaviour (or lifestyle) should be judged improper and dishonourable according to a certain set of norms, and yet admired for its distinction according to another set of norms.[37] *The dominance of a certain value system does not preclude the validity of other, alternative – and perhaps conflicting – values.*

There being various scales on which to judge the performance of social actors and alternative sets of criteria by which to assess the cultural output of intellectuals, it was quite possible for a mediaeval Muslim to fall short of the established norms in one respect, yet perfectly conform to a different set of norms. Of course, the choice and management of various value scales by individuals is more often than not an instinctive practice rather than a conscious one. The effort to maximise one's social standing is never uncomplicated, value systems being rarely made explicit in any society, and therefore intuition probably plays a greater role than positive knowledge. However, if asked, most people will usually betray an awareness of alternative value systems through the use of such expressions as 'So-and-So is really stupid, but he is a first-rate athlete'. As will be presently shown, judgements along these lines directly affected assessments of libertinism (and other ambiguous cultural phenomena) among mediaeval Muslims.

Because of the crucial significance of this point for my conclusions, I will dwell on it at some length, and quote a selection of texts I find particularly illustrative. The first of these, unlike the rest, does not relate to *mujūn* in a direct fashion, but it does show the rare instance of a purposeful manipulation of alternative values to gain prestige (or rather rescue some prestige). The remark in question, which can be found in the *Kitāb al-bukhalāʾ* of al-Jāḥiẓ (d. 255/869), is part of a passage in which the author states his decision not to identify the niggardly protagonists of his funny anecdotes, many of them personal acquaintances still alive at the time of writing who would probably be embarrassed by the exposure. After this general principle, al-Jāḥiẓ proceeds to say:

---

[37] Besides the case of *mujūn*, discussed at length here, other interesting examples of the simultaneous impact of alternative value systems can be cited from Middle Eastern social history. Lila Abu-Lughod, for instance, describes the attitudes of the *Awlād ʿAlī* Bedouin of Egypt, who view the oral genre of love poetry with marked ambivalence reminiscent (*mutatis mutandis*) of the mediaeval Muslim intellectuals' views of libertine poetry. In another study she also shows that even though modesty and submissiveness are among the most highly valued qualities a Bedouin woman can have, headstrong, refractory women are not necessarily viewed with disapproval (because they embody another important, if conflicting, element of the Bedouin value system, pride and autonomy). See Abu-Lughod 1990: 35–6; Abu-Lughod 1999: 110. Alternative value scales are likewise reflected in judgements of the genre of *saḥir* (lit. 'sorcery'; succinct, witty and often sarcastic remarks) among the *Rubāṭāb* of Northern Sudan; see Ibrahim 1994: 3. In modern Iraq, people would equally admire violent daredevils (*ashqiyāʾ*) – for their bravery and physical strength – and the pious (*akhyār*) – for their devotion and good works; see al-Wardī 1965: 295.

> In some cases, however, I will name my friends [featured in the book], if they are the sort of people who frequently joke about it [i.e. their own pitiful avarice] and whom we have seen make witty remarks about it (*mimman yumāziḥu bi-hādhā kathīran wa-ra'aynāhu yataẓarrafu bihi*), and *who ensure, precisely by this wittiness (*ẓarf*), that [their avarice] should not disgrace them* [emphasis added].[38]

Many other passages are directly relevant to an analysis of the alternative values inherent in *mujūn*. The following text cites a conversation between two illustrious, highly respected aristocrats of the early Umayyad period, who disagree on whether they would degrade themselves by taking refuge from a torrent of rain in the house of a notorious effeminate (*mukhannath*). Note that whereas the two interlocutors virtually embody the quintessence of all the ordinary values of a Muslim man of their time, the effeminate man, known as Ṭuways, can be said to represent the exact opposite, the very negation of normative conduct. On the other hand, *mukhannath* men were famous – indeed stereotyped – for their witty and entertaining conversation as well as their singing skills:

> [ʿAbdallāh b. Jaʿfar said:] "Shouldn't we enter the house of Ṭuways? It's nearby, so we can find refuge there, and he'll tell us stories and make us laugh." [...] To this ʿAbd al-Raḥmān b. Ḥassān b. Thābit replied: "[...] What do you want of this Ṭuways? May God's wrath fall upon this effeminate man whose very acquaintance is a disgrace!" ʿAbdallāh said: "Don't say such a thing. He's a witty and entertaining man we can have a pleasant time with (*fa-innahu malīḥ khafīf lanā fīhi uns*)..."[39]

It is evident that neither interlocutor disputes the immorality of the singer's character, but one of them introduces a different criterion of judging him – in other words, an alternative value scale – which does show him in a better light and makes his company more desirable. It is in like manner that a mediaeval Muslim intellectual could argue that *mujūn* was not altogether negative, devoid of any value:

---

38 al-Jāḥiẓ, *Bukhalā'* 99.

39 al-Iṣfahānī, *Aghānī* III, 33. (The remarkably tolerant ʿAbdallāh was in fact a close relative of the Prophet; see his genealogy in Ibn Ḥazm, *Jamhara* 68.) On Ṭuways, see Rowson 1991: 677–81. For a summary of the stereotyped merits of the *mukhannath* (told in the form of comical bragging), see al-Rāghib, *Muḥāḍarāt* III, 496; and for a surprisingly similar stereotyping (including both positive and negative aspects) of boy prostitutes in contemporary coastal Kenya (a predominantly Muslim but not Arabic-speaking region), see Shepherd 1978a: 134. A much later but comparable case illustrating the coexistence of alternative value scales is an assessment given by the chronicler al-Dhahabī (d. 748/1348 or 753/1352–3). A pious and virtuous Muslim by all accounts, he could not but express admiration for the wit, sophistication and other qualities of a certain ʿAlam al-Dīn Aḥmad, son of a Mamlūk vizier, while he deplored his infamous profligacy and libertinism. See Pouzet 1991: 364. – Thomas Bauer speaks of "mindestens zwei verschiedene in der Gesellschaft wirksame Idealbilder", which he chooses to call 'religious' and 'secular' respectively (see Bauer 1996: 284); these are very close to the alternative value scales I am discussing here.

> I have heard from several people that there is such *mujūn* as one can find entertainment in. The [primary] meaning of *mujūn* is 'the twisting of the true [sense of] words to turn it into something else (*ṣarf al-lafẓ ʿan ḥaqīqatihi ilā maʿnā ākhar*)', [an ability] which signals intelligence.[40]

The gist of this theoretical stance was apparently applied in practice as well. One could hardly find a better exemplar of libertinism both in literature and in everyday behaviour than Abū Nuwās, whose remarkable popularity as a poet was commented on in the last chapter. The following two excerpts show how people would rationalise their penchant for the notorious libertine's poems – and indeed for his person – by citing alternative values. The first text recounts a discussion that took place between the narrator (the great philologist al-Aṣmaʿī [2nd/9th c.]) and the grand vizier:

> [...] And then he [the vizier] said: "By God, if people did not report so much [depravity] about him [viz. Abū Nuwās], I would not part with him for a moment; but when I reflect on what he is like, I will conclude that he is a shameless, profligate, carousing libertine (*mājin*). And therefore I will rather do without his advantages because of his shortcomings." To this I replied: "May God support you, vizier! However, [Abū Nuwās] is a very polished man. I have met him at countless gatherings, where all sorts of littérateurs and scholars convened, yet he was as *au courant* in every topic as any, and indeed appeared superior to them. And as for poetry, you know how he excels in it..."[41]

The second text comes from a disciple of al-Aṣmaʿī – and, not incidentally, a close acquaintance of Abū Nuwās – called ʿAbdallāh b. Aḥmad al-Mihzamī but better known as Abū Hiffān (d. 255/869):

> [The Abbasid caliph] Muḥammad al-Amīn was excessively fond of Abū Nuwās; he insisted on [Abū Nuwās's] presence whenever he felt like drinking wine. On one occasion, he sent for him, but [Abū Nuwās] was nowhere to be found. Al-Amīn continued drinking for days on end, dispatching his men to search for [the poet] and comb every tavern and all the places where he was likely to be found, but all efforts failed. Thereupon [the caliph] became really furious. Now, one of [the caliph's] boon-companions was envious of the [favoured] position that Abū Nuwās enjoyed with al-Amīn. This man now found the opportunity to speak [in order to revile and harm the poet]. He disparaged and maligned the latter, saying: "O Commander of the Faithful, that man is an idler and a foul-mouthed drunkard who keeps drinking wine with the riffraff and the commoners (*al-sifla wa-l-sūqa*), frequenting the taverns and engaging in debauchery, and he considers it all to be time well spent (*yarā dhālika ghunman*). To be his boon-companion is degrading for the Commander of the Faithful." When the man insisted in his

[40] Ibn al-Jawzī, *Ẓirāf* 27.
[41] Ibn al-Muʿtazz, *Ṭabaqāt* 99.

diatribe, Muḥammad [al-Amīn] told him: "Enough of this talk! By God, it is exactly such a man that a caliph should choose as his boon-companion, given his erudition, wit, knowledge and excellent qualities (*fī adabihi wa-ẓarfihi wa-ʿilmihi wa-kamāl khiṣālihi*). The only reason I feel angry with him is that I resent having to make do without [his company]."[42]

Awareness of alternative value scales directly affected assessments of literary works in the mediaeval Muslim world. In fact, some sources offer all but explicit elaborations of the notion that literary works should be judged according to criteria quite different from those appropriate for other domains of life, especially everyday affairs. The argument is that religion and literature are two separate provinces, and criteria for judging matters in each are very dissimilar. It is both interesting and highly significant to find this idea developed in a facetious epistle consisting of a fictitious argument between a man preferring girls and another preferring boys, a text clearly representative of *mujūn* literature. When the aficionado of heterosexual affairs resorts to religion-based, moral arguments to support his preference, his opponent responds:

You cite the Quran, the ḥadīths (*al-āthār*) and the [opinions of] jurisprudents – well, we too have read whatever you have read, and listened to whatever you have listened to. If you choose to consider the gratifications and pleasures of this world, then our opinion is right. [...] If your point of view is that of self-denial and abstention from pleasures, then it is better to relinquish all pleasures – women and everything else. If you are to be fair, please submit arguments like our ones [viz. about the carnal pleasures of heterosexual affairs]. However, your quoting the Quran and bringing up well-chosen ḥadīths means the end [of all possibility of a jestful debate].[43]

A curious account about a famous jester of the Umayyad period mentions that a typical *mujūn* joke – namely, one based on the deliberate misinterpretation of the purport of a Quranic verse – earned the quipster a hundred painful lashes on the one hand and an award of a hundred dinars on the other.[44] Why the simultaneous punishment and prize, one might ask. In fact, by recognising the impact of alternative value scales one can make perfect sense of the story: the remark was felt to be intolerable because of its religious overtones, hence the discipline, but it was at the same time charming because of its wittiness, hence the bonus.

It is time now, having reviewed a selection of illustrative cases, to attempt to identify the value content of *mujūn*. The question to be asked, which is absolutely central to this essay, is the following: in order to gain social recognition and acclaim,

42 Abū Hiffān, *Akhbār* 23.

43 al-Jāḥiẓ, *Rasāʾil* I(ii), 116–7 (and the same idea is put forward again on p. 119).

44 Cited in Rosenthal 1956: 114 (note 3), 115.

what alternative to behaving honourably could there be for a mediaeval Muslim intellectual? Or, put in the briefest possible manner: what value was felt to be there in *mujūn*? To answer the query, it will be worthwhile to go over the above excerpts and examples again, and identify the 'redeeming qualities' (or, in the more abstract terminology applied here, alternative values) that are mentioned therein. (Of particular relevance are those texts that contain express references to *mujūn* rather than to some of its familiar aspects.) Doing so, one finds a number of virtues picked for praise, including such properties as good companionship and a flair for entertaining talk, intelligence, erudition, poetical excellence, and above all a sense of humour and wit, this last quality being repeatedly mentioned in the sources. The Arabic terms employed to describe these values include adjectives like *malīḥ* and *khafīf* (roughly 'entertaining, light-hearted'), the nouns *uns* ('sociability, affability, friendly atmosphere') and *adab* ('culture' as well as 'good manners'), and most frequently an adjectival or nominal form of the root ẓ-r-f (*ẓarīf* and *ẓarf* respectively). The recurrent use of the last term is supremely significant and in my view offers the best clue to the value content of *mujūn*. It will be noted that in the final analysis practically all the positive qualities of a libertine identified above can be covered by the term *ẓarf*, an important and loaded concept of Arabic the meaning of which will be examined in detail in the next section of this chapter. An actual libertine could and would be admired if he conformed to the cultural ideal of a 'typical' libertine – amusing, witty, clever, frivolous, and irreverent. To express it all with a single term, a libertine could earn respect with his *ẓarf*.

1.3 The Value of Mujūn: Wit and Refinement (Ẓarf)

If *ẓarf* really is the underlying quality that gave positive value to libertinism and prevented a purely condemnatory judgement thereof, which I believe it is, it will be necessary to understand what this concept consisted of, and what its relationship with *mujūn* was. These two questions will consitute the subject of the following pages.

An absolutely fundamental concept in the culture of mediaeval Muslim cities, *ẓarf* is as characteristic of that cultural setting and almost as hard to render in English by a single term as *mujūn* itself. (Moreover, as has been observed and will be argued in more detail, the two concepts are in fact closely related.) Even at first sight, the Arabic noun *ẓarf* seems to have very broad semantics. Depending on the context, it may be the equivalent of such English terms as 'sophistication' and 'refinement', 'wit' and 'humour', and 'elegance', 'finery'.[45] This is the term usually employed

[45] Ibn al-Jawzī, *Ẓirāf* 29–31; Ibn Manẓūr, *Lisān* IV, 221–2. It appears that in the vernacular speech of Iraq in the Seljuk period the word was used exclusively in the sense of 'elegance'; see Ibn al-Jawzī, *Taqwīm* 154.

by mediaeval Arab writers to refer to the qualities of an urbane, educated man whose companionship is forever pleasant and whose conversation never fails to entertain. It is commonplace to find, for instance, well-liked authors, cultured *charmeurs* and fine musicians being characterised in the sources with the adjective *ẓarīf*. On closer inspection, it is obvious that at the core of the term *ẓarf* is urban sophistication: it is the very opposite of what rural dwellers, peasants, louts, oafs, and barbarians represent.[46] (In a sense, it is also the opposite of Bedouin manners and culture, understood as a materially primitive and savage culture, although the image of Bedouins among educated urban Muslims was far from unambiguous.) As the summation of all urbane values, *ẓarf* is also a strongly positive concept, even if it was not applicable to *every* educated and respected person, as we will show shortly. In this book, I have either translated *ẓarf* with one of its possible English equivalents or used the original Arabic word, and will continue to do so, but it is to be noted that the sense most relevant to our present discussion is that of 'wit', 'humour'.

One of the pillars of *ẓarf* is keen perception, ready wit and quick ripostes. The term was often used to describe people who instantly recognised what was expected of them and could immediately respond to challenges in an appropriate and intelligent way.[47] A sense of humour and a cheerful disposition were apparently also indispensable ingredients of the quality of *ẓarf*.[48] Of the aforementioned endowments of the mediaeval Muslim wit, it is the aptitude for quick repartee that was particularly highly prized by the educated élite, who had no appreciation for *esprit d'escalier* but relished quick repartees no matter how cynical, pert or insolent. A prompt reply to a challenge, or even to a neutral remark, was one of the most direct ways of displaying one's wit. Indeed, some anthologists appreciated this ability so much that they would reserve a separate section in their literary collections to the most memorable ready ripostes under the heading *al-ajwiba al-muskita* ('Replies That Reduce the Opponent to Silence'). A very significant fact is that, as one observes in the sources, this talent was often recognised in people who would otherwise command little or no respect – a notable example is the category of homosexual prostitutes and effeminates (sing. *mukhannath*), who were collectively noted for their skills in quick and witty repartee, as were many women.[49] The fact that a

---

46 In the opinion of Mhammed Ferid Ghazi the best approximation in French to the original meaning of the Arabic plural form *ẓurafāʾ* is 'raffinés'; see Ghazi 1959: 39.

47 See for example al-Tanūkhī, *Nishwār* IV, 37, 226–7 (and also cf. V, 206–7); Yāqūt, *Udabāʾ* VI, 2602. Also see al-Ibshīhī, *Mustaṭraf* 50 ["*mā aẓraf hādhā l-wāw...*"].

48 E.g. Abū Hiffān, *Akhbār* 17 ["*Atatabbaʿu l-ẓurafāʾa...*" etc.].

49 Such talents in inferior categories of people were not only admired but feared too, which made respectable individuals reluctant to provoke a *mukhannath* and thereby unleash his devastating comments. On quick repartees (and/or on the competence of effeminates in this regard), see for instance

certain reply was rude, offensive or abusive was no obstacle to its being enjoyed, nor to its being recorded in writing; what mattered was the perception of its being funny – its quality of *ẓarf.* In fact, even persons on a friendly footing could occasionally not resist the temptation of making malicious and often obscene remarks about one another regardless of the potential consequence of seriously offending a friend. Hence the occasional recording in mediaeval Arabic sources of cases of mock squabbles between friends, which may sometimes appear quite offensive at first sight because of the vulgar style employed by the participants, the sole purpose of such exchanges of words being the display of one's quick wits and verbal skills. Intellectuals would apparently engage in such duels in prose as well as verse, in writing as well as speech.[50] These verbal contests had very deep roots in Arabic culture: duels based on the impromptu show of each side's deftness and verbal skills are an age-old Arabic tradition, which is still practised in various Arabic-speaking communities and widely regarded as a truthful gauge of a man's cleverness and intelligence.[51] For that reason, whoever desired to be known as a witty man could hardly dispense with the making of malicious yet original remarks. Consider the following anecdote about a famous wit of the high Abbasid period:

> Once al-Suddī told al-Jammāz: "Last night a son was born to me, who is [as beautiful] as a golden coin with a florid inscription." Said al-Jammāz: "Take the

---

al-Thaᶜālibī, *Iqtibās* II, 37–48; al-Ibshīhī, *Mustaṭraf* 65; al-Thaᶜālibī, *Tatimma* I, 73 ["... *annahu aẓraf al-nās ... wa-aḥḍaruhum jawāban*"]; al-Tawḥīdī, *Baṣā'ir* I(ii), 43; II(iii), 162; IV(vii), 17; al-Tawḥīdī [attr.], *Risāla* 186 ["*rajulan ẓarīfan ... in khūshina ᶜaqarat bawādiruhu*"]; al-Iṣfahānī, *Aghānī* IV, 9; and on the appreciation of quick repartee (*al-radd al-sarīᶜ*) in an Arabic-speaking community of the contemporary Sudan, see Ibrahim 1994: 114. For the most detailed treatment of the subject (replete with bibliography), see Sadan 1983: 81–3; and for further examples, see Ibn Abī Ṭāhir, *Balāghāt* 261–6; al-Ṣūlī, *Akhbār* 72, 264; al-Iṣfahānī, *Aghānī* II, 28; XIII, 328; al-ᶜAskarī, *Maṣūn* 113–4; al-Ḥarīrī, *Durra* 418; al-Thaᶜālibī, *Thimār* I, 95; al-Tanūkhī, *Nishwār* II, 224–6, 278; Ibn Saᶜīd, *Ghuṣūn* 69-70; Ibn Simāk, *Zaharāt* 70–1. An Egyptian author who lived in Iraq for some time in the early 4th/10th century notes the fondness of intellectuals of the secretarial class for 'fine responses' (*ḥusn al-jawāb*), although the example he cites is decent in tone. See al-Naḥḥās, *Ṣināᶜa* 240–1.

[50] E.g. al-Iṣfahānī, *Aghānī* XIII, 125–6, 354–5; XX, 247–8; al-Baghdādī, *Khizāna* III, 458; Ibn al-Muᶜtazz, *Ṭabaqāt* 24, 197; al-Thaᶜālibī, *Yatīma* IV, 78; al-Thaᶜālibī, *Tatimma* I, 110–1; al-Bayhaqī, *Maḥāsin* 668–9; al-Iṣbahānī, *Kharīda* I(i), 94; al-Rāghib, *Muḥāḍarāt* III, 473–4. In an important passage, some versified abuses directed against a person to whom their author felt no hostility at all – abuses whose sole purpose was to entertain – are referred to as behaviour characteristic of a *mājin* ("*a-turā Abā Saᶜd yatamājanu ᶜalayya...*"); see al-Iṣfahānī, *Aghānī* XX, 183.

[51] Such verbal duels (usually in verse) go by various names in the dialects of the modern Arab world: *galṭi* or *mrādd* in Central Arabia, *musājala* in the Northern Sudan, *bāla* in the Yemeni highlands. See Sowayan 1985: 142–3; Al-Shahi 1986: 69; Caton 1990: 96–7, 114–8; and cf. Ibrahim 1994: 72. Within the Islamicate world, it is not only among Arabic speakers that one finds similar duel-like forms of demonstrating verbal and poetic skills; for instance, the Swahili of East Africa also have a comparable tradition (*mashairi ya kujibizana*); see Sheikh 1994: 10.

case to court."[52] The anecdote was recounted to Abū l-ʿAynāʾ, who commented thus: "I'd give up everything I've ever said if I could claim this [remark as my own]."[53]

As is obvious from this text and the preceding observations, *ẓarf*, while admired by most intellectuals, was quite a different thing than the constituents of ordinary respectability, which mainly stemmed from careful conformity to established norms. Not so *ẓarf*. Indeed, the latter quality appears to have been very closely associated with *mujūn*, of all things. *Ẓarf*, this peculiar combination of wit, refinement and elegance, was apparently widely stereotyped as being concomitant with libertinism and frivolity. This widespread attribution of wit and sophistication to libertines is attested by countless literary and historical texts from the mediaeval period. Despite a lone but important dissenting voice – that of the author of the *Muwashshā*, a late 3rd/9th- or early 4th/10th-century monograph on refinement – the evidence for the correlation of *mujūn* with *ẓarf* is compelling. Some examples will give substance to this assertion, which is pivotal to this essay's argument.[54]

Firstly – to start with the most indirect type of evidence – it is remarkable that the period that saw the phenomenal rise of the fashion of *ẓarf* (an enthusiasm that verged on veneration among some sectors of the cultural élite), that is to say roughly

[52] It is not a literal translation of the original, which could only be given at the expense of brevity and appositeness. The Arabic reads *lāʿin ummahu*, the approximate meaning of which is "take the mother of the newborn to court and make a public allegation of adultery that will require her to swear that you are indeed the son's biological father".

[53] al-Tawḥīdī, *Baṣāʾir* I(ii), 46. It is reported elsewhere that al-Jammāz had already distinguished himself by his witty repartees when still a little boy; al-Thaʿālibī, *Iʿjāz* 132. As for Abū l-ʿAynāʾ (d. 283/896), he was not at a loss for quick and sarcastic replies either, as evidenced by a wealth of such witticisms attributed to him; see for instance al-Tawḥīdī, *Baṣāʾir* IV(vii), 47; Yāqūt, *Udabāʾ* VI, 2605–10; and the wording of two descriptions of his character in al-Nadīm, *Fihrist* 138 ["*ḥāḍir al-jawāb sarīʿ al-ijāba*"] and Yāqūt, *Udabāʾ* VI, 2602 ["*min ẓurafāʾ al-ʿālam, āya fī ... surʿat al-jawāb*"].

[54] For a more thorough treatment of why al-Washshāʾ's book cannot be taken seriously as a mirror of the relevant views of the majority of Muslim intellectuals in his time, see Szombathy 2006. My basic contention in that article, which I see no reason to modify here, is that al-Washshāʾ (d. 325/937) presents his own highly anachronistic mind-set, especially his strong dislike of frivolity and 'sinful' or 'untoward' conduct, as the consensus of his educated contemporaries, which it demonstably was not. *Pace* M. F. Ghazi (who draws most of his data from al-Washshāʾ), the *Muwashshā* is anything but a reliable, undistorted reflection of the views and lifestyle of a large group of intellectuals in the Abbasid era (see Ghazi 1959: 51–2), although it may be a useful source in a limited way, insofar as the material aspects of *ẓarf* (food, clothing) are concerned. – To mention only the most glaring absurdities of the assertions made in the *Muwashshā*. Al-Washshāʾ states that a *ẓarīf* man will in all circumstances refrain from joking (!), embrace a chaste and decorous lifestyle and speech style, eschew all oscene vocabulary and love affairs not purely platonic, and abhore sexual adventures and homosexuality. (It is a fine giveaway, however, when one finds al-Washshāʾ complaining of the callosity of his contemporaries and their failure to live up to these ideals of *ẓarf*.) See al-Washshāʾ, *Muwashshā* 21–3, 66–73, 113–7, 150–3, 194–5, 219–26.

the two centuries subsequent to the reign of Hārūn al-Rashīd (170/786–193/809),[55] should happen to correspond to the golden age of *mujūn* literature. This may have to do with the ascendance of the 'secretarial class' (the *kuttāb*) and the formative impact of their tastes and preferences in this period, in contrast to later ages when the *ʿulamāʾ* (the religious élite) came to the fore and mores and cultural trends within the élite changed accordingly.[56] And – despite all examples of surprisingly liberal religious savants reviewed in the last chapter – it is obvious that poets of the Abbasid period were far more closely associated with the kind of erudition the *kuttāb* tended to boast than with scholarly achievements.[57]

Secondly, one observes the adjectives 'witty, refined' (*ẓarīf*) and 'libertine' (*mājin*, or closely related terms like *khalīʿ*, *sakhīf*) routinely juxtaposed in descriptions of mediaeval Muslim intellectuals, which alone precludes the possibility of an outright opposition between the two concepts (as the author of the *Muwashshā* would have us believe). Clearly, a person could easily be a libertine *and* a famous wit, as lots of mediaeval Muslim intellectuals had a reputation for both qualities. Abū Nuwās for instance was remembered for what a source calls his "witty talk of a licentious and wanton sort (*kalām ẓarīf fī l-mujūn wa-l-khalāʿa*)".[58] And here is a characterisation given by Abū Manṣūr al-Thaʿālibī (350/961–429/1038) about two outstanding poets of the Buyid era who also happened to be siblings: "Both of them were among the wittiest, most libertine, and most entertaining of men (*wa-humā min aẓraf al-nās wa-amjanihim wa-amlaḥihim*)."[59] The same author, in another of his many books, treats the qualities of *mujūn* and *ẓarf* as belonging essentially to the same category of people, to which he contrasts that of "ascetics and wise men", that is to say men with serious and respectable concerns.[60] One may add that the opposite combination – that of the qualities of devoutness and wit – is, while not inexistent, definitely

---

55 See Ghazi 1959: 46–7.

56 Kraemer 1986: 209, 286.

57 Kilpatrick 1997: 107.

58 Ibn Manẓūr, *Akhbār* 186.

59 al-Thaʿālibī, *Tatimma* I, 69. For further examples, see for instance al-Tawḥīdī, *Baṣāʾir* I(i), 27 ["*ẓurafāʾ mujjān*"]; Yāqūt, *Udabāʾ* I, 201 ["*kāna min al-ẓurafāʾ al-khulaʿāʾ*"], 373 ["*ẓarīf al-mazḥ wa-l-mujūn*"]; VI, 2852 ["*kāna shāʿiran mujīdan ẓarīfan mājinan*"]; al-Suyūṭī, *Mustaẓraf* 26 ["*mashhūra bi-l-ẓarf wa-l-mujūn*"]; al-Tawḥīdī [attr.], *Risāla* 46–7 ["*kāna ʿayyāran wa-ẓarīfan wa-sakhīfan*"]; al-Ṭabarī, *Tārīkh* V, 1874 ["*kāna shāʿiran ẓarīfan khabīthan munkaran*"]; Ibn Manẓūr, *Akhbār* 122 ["*amjan ghulām wa-aẓrafuhu*"]; al-Khāqānī 1381/1962: 21 ["*kāna maṭbūʿan ẓarīfan khalīʿan*"; citing the words of Ibn Kathīr's *Bidāya*]. In the Ottoman period we still find the two concepts being comfortably placed together to characterise the same individual, in the case a littérateur from Lebanon: "all redolent of *ẓarf* [...], he had an intimate knowledge of the jokes of *mujūn*, with which he would embellish his conversation..." See Ibn Maʿṣūm, *Sulāfa* 355. On the connection between *ẓarf* and *mujūn*, also see Ghazi 1959: 41.

60 "*[...] wa-lā l-mujjān wa-l-ẓurafāʾ bi-aḥraṣ ʿalayhi min al-zuhhād wa-l-ḥukamāʾ*"; see al-Thaʿālibī, *Iqtibās* I, 38.

very rarely mentioned in the sources.[61] Going beyond explicit mentions of wit and libertinism in the same man's character, one also observes that some of the most notorious libertines of mediaeval Arabic literature – even proverbial representatives of *mujūn* – are regularly described in written sources as *ẓarīf*, 'refined' and 'witty'. The list of relevant names is long, and includes the Umayyad caliph al-Walīd b. Yazīd, Wāliba b. al-Ḥubāb, Bashshār b. Burd, al-Ḥusayn b. al-Ḍaḥḥāk, Ibn al-Ḥajjāj, and of course the greatest *mājin* of all, Abū Nuwās.[62] Besides, some of the typical themes of literary libertinism were, on occasion, explicitly characterised as possessing the property of *ẓarf*. Homosexuality is an example: in a poem composed in the Buyid era, it is presented as being not only compatible with *ẓarf* but even an indispensable component thereof – although it would be rash to regard this calculatedly scandalous assertion as literally true.[63]

Frequent though the juxtaposition of wit and libertinism is in biographical portrayals, it might still be largely accidental and need not in itself reflect a close connection between the two attributes. Yet copious evidence of various kinds does make such a connection more than likely. Firstly, spoken remarks obviously classifiable as *mujūn* are as a matter of course labelled witty or sophisticated, using some form of the root ẓ-r-f.[64] The same is true of written literary works. For example, the author of a 7th/13th-century anthology, in commenting on a poem that treats an Islamic religious precept in an irreverent and frivolous way, states that he has never heard a wittier piece of poetry (*mā samiʿtu aẓraf minhu*).[65] In another work, a cynical couplet on the merits of money is the object of similar praise.[66] Secondly, and even more significantly, there are strong indications that in fact *ẓarf* would often be explicitly contrasted to a pious and decorous personality as, for all practical purposes, mutually exclusive characteristics, or at the very least two qualities unlikely to be found in the same person. Consider the following assessment of the virtues of the great writer Abū ʿUthmān al-Jāḥiẓ (d. 255/869) by one of his contemporaries: "I

[61] An example ("*wa-kāna nāsikan ...ẓarīfan*") can be found in al-Zajjājī, *Amālī* 59.

[62] al-Iṣfahānī, *Aghānī* XVIII, 105; VII, 6, 169, 173; Ibn al-Muʿtazz, *Ṭabaqāt* 2, 87, 91; Yāqūt, *Udabāʾ* III, 1394; Abū Hiffān, *Akhbār* 22; Abū Nuwās, *Dīwān* I, 14, 19. A remark attributed to an Ibrāhīm b. al-ʿAbbās al-Ṭawīl specifies the knowledge of Abū Nuwās's poems as one of the signs of a man's *ẓarf*, see Ibn Manẓūr, *Akhbār* 47. It is remarkable that an important anthology should call the blind Syrian poet, Abū l-ʿAlāʾ al-Maʿarrī (d. 449/1058) *ẓarīf*, see al-Thaʿālibī, *Tatimma* I, 9. Certainly not a libertine, al-Maʿarrī was often accused of being a heretic and a godless fellow because of his well-known agnosticism.

[63] al-Thaʿālibī, *Yatīma* I, 374.

[64] See a remark attributed to a certain Fazāra concerning the theological controversies on the Quran in al-Tawḥīdī, *Baṣāʾir* II(iv), 41; and Ibn ʿĀʾisha's appreciative comment on the frivolous and insolent jesting of his son in al-ʿAskarī, *Maṣūn* 199–200.

[65] Ibn Saʿīd, *Ghuṣūn* 25.

[66] Ibn ʿĀṣim, *Janna* I, 197.

trust his wit, but do not trust his religiosity (*anā athiqu bi-ẓarfihi wa-lā athiqu bi-dīnihi*)."[67] (It is wholly irrelevant here whether this verdict was warranted.) Also, people known for their excellent wit would often be accused of heretical thought. This is Abū l-Faraj al-Iṣfahānī's description of the infamous libertine poet Muṭīʿ b. Iyās (d. 169/785): "He was a witty and profligate man, pleasant as a companion and full of amusing anecdotes, a libertine who was accused of heresy (*kāna ẓarīfan khalīʿan ḥulw al-ʿishra malīḥ al-nādira mājinan muttahaman fī dīnihi bi-l-zandaqa*)."[68] Moreover, the close connection of *ẓarf* and irreverence was taken so far that in time the association of the former with the concept of heresy (*zandaqa*) came to be a commonplace notion, often compressed into a quasi-proverbial expression. This conceptual link is likely to have originated in the events of the early Abbasid period, more precisely the reign of al-Mahdī (158/775–169/785), when quite a few libertine poets and other intellectuals were charged with heresy and exposed to serious persecution from the authorities.[69] It was thus demonstrated as starkly and drastically as possible that if there were any correlation between *ẓarf* and piety it was negative rather than positive; and the lesson did sink in, as all the references in written sources to the supposed wit and sophistication of the *zindīq* (heretic) attest. The following account about an Iraqi poet of the early Abbasid period called al-Khārakī is an eloquent expression of this idea:

> Al-Khārakī, whose given name was Muḥammad b. Ziyād, pretended to be a heretic in order to appear witty (*kāna ... yuẓhiru l-zandaqa taẓārufan*). That is why Ibn Munādhir says of him [in one of his poems]: "Oh Abū Jaʿfar b. Ziyād, you exhibit a religion other than you truly harbour inside you. / You are a heretic outwardly, in your words, and inwardly a decent Muslim believer. / You are no heretic; you only wish to be known for your wit (*aradta an tūsama bi-ẓarfī*)."[70]

Orthodox piety and its behavioural signs might, then, be perceived as the very antithesis of *ẓarf*, and heresy as a frequent accessory of the latter. It shows very well the degree to which the concept of *ẓarf* was divorced in the mediaeval Muslim consciousness from social prestige and normative conduct; but more evidence can be adduced to support that conclusion. Given the admiration that *ẓarf* tended to elicit among Muslim intellectuals, it is somewhat counterintuitive to find that this coveted and adorable quality was by no means the exclusive preserve of the élite

---

[67] Yāqūt, *Udabāʾ* V, 2104.

[68] al-Iṣfahānī, *Aghānī* XIII, 303. For comparable characterisations of the poets Yaḥyā b. Ziyād and Ibn al-Khayyāṭ, see op.cit. XVIII, 187; XX, 5.

[69] al-Thaʿālibī, *Thimār* I, 298. For more evidence of the close connection of *ẓarf* with *zandaqa*, see Abū Nuwās, *Dīwān* I, 189; al-Tawḥīdī, *Baṣāʾir* II(iv), 162; al-Jurjānī, *Wasāṭa* 64.

[70] al-Iṣfahānī, *Aghānī* XVIII, 187. Also cf. al-Thaʿālibī, *Thimār* I, 299; and Vajda 1938: 214; Enderwitz 1989: 136.

(*khāṣṣa*) in the broadest possible sense of the term. Apparently, one need not even be literate to be *ẓarīf.* There are texts in which the most despicable, uneducated, low-class persons earn the label with a *bon mot.*[71]

There is more to consider. Not only was *ẓarf* considered to be perfectly compatible with an utter lack of all usual norms of piety, decency and respectability, but also it might even be treated as a quality expressly undesirable for a man of honour and social standing. It could even be considered unflattering, nay downright insulting, to a honourable man of high rank and prestige if he be characterised as *ẓarīf.* The sense of offence may have to do with the lower value generally ascribed to jocular themes (*hazl*) vis-à-vis 'serious' concerns (*jidd*) in mediaeval Islamicate culture, as has been discussed in the first chapter of this book. If the cultural ideal is that a respectable man ought to be occupied in conducting momentous and solemn affairs, it is logical that 'witty' is not the most fitting adjective to describe the cultural ideal. Consider this passage about an ugly *faux pas* committed by the poet Abū l-Bakr al-Khawārizmī (4th/10th c.):

> One of his ugly blunders is the following couple of verses in a [praise] poem addressed to al-Ṣāḥib [b. ʿAbbād]: "He is held in awe, as though people are sinners before him, for which they must suffer humiliation. / He is also *ẓarīf,* as though every single act he does were a bride being exhibited before the wedding guests." But [the quality of] *ẓarf* must not be attributed to great, respectable men, as it is a descriptive term suitable for mere boys, singing-girls and youngsters. Yet [the poet], not content with his blunder in [using] this word, went on to compare [his patron's] deeds to brides being exhibited before the guests. Now, had he wished to praise an effeminate man (*mukhannath*), he could not have gone further! But perfect is he whose mistakes can be counted...[72]

One finds similar reasoning in the dictionary *Lisān al-ʿarab,* whose author states that the word *ẓarf* "is only used to describe fine young men and fine girls, but not old or high-ranking men (*yūṣafu bihi l-fityān al-azwāl wa-l-fatayāt al-zawlāt wa-lā yūṣafu bihi l-shaykh wa-lā l-sayyid*)."[73] An interesting passage in Ibn Rashīq al-

---

[71] E.g. a lawless tramp and beggar, a thief, a Jewish tavern-keeper; see al-Iṣfahānī, *Aghānī* IV, 21; Ibn Manẓūr, *Lisān* IV, 222. In a passage in the huge *adab* collection *al-Baṣāʾir wa-l-dhakhāʾir* (4th/10th c.) an Iranian boy prostitute is called 'witty' on the basis of an extremely cynical remark he makes concerning his trade. See al-Tawḥīdī, *Baṣāʾir* III(vi), 82. Another anecdote presents an uncouth Bedouin behaving in a markedly undignified manner, who is nevertheless called *ẓarīf* because of two insolent verses he cites on his own parasitic character. See Ibn al-Marzubān, *Dhamm* 83–4. Al-Thaʿālibī calls *ẓarīf* a character in an anecdote who quotes the Quran in a distorted sense to describe his own shameless parasitism; see al-Thaʿālibī, *Iqtibās* I, 173.

[72] al-Thaʿālibī, *Yatīma* IV, 222.

[73] Ibn Manẓūr, *Lisān* IV, 221. The adjective *zawl* is (among other things) more or less a synonym of *ẓarīf* (see op.cit. III, 216) which I chose to translate here simply with 'fine' because of the many possible meanings of the latter.

Qayrawānī's *Kitāb al-ʿumda* (mid-5th/11th c.) suggests that the art of panegyrics – arguably the most illustrious and honourable (and most 'serious') of all the genres of Arabic poetry – was seen as inappropriate for a 'refined' poet, for it is claimed that al-ʿAbbās b. al-Aḥnaf (d. 192/808, a famous master of amorous poetry) would not write panegyrics 'out of sheer sophistication' (*fa-innahu mimman anifa ʿan al-madḥ taẓarrufan*).[74] *Ẓarf* and august respectability, it seems, were mutually exclusive domains. A mediaeval Muslim intellectual had the option of becoming known either for his dignified, honourable conduct and good repute, or else for his cheerful and witty character.[75] The two choices, while necessitating quite different strategies and lifestyles, could equally bring fame and high esteem.

Yet *ẓarf* was unquestionably a positive quality. The term is practically always applied to express acclaim, never in a pejorative sense. That people who possessed it were admired for it cannot be doubted. The limits of its applicability neither devalued *ẓarf* nor turned it into an ambiguous quality, only set the framework and the bounds of its validity. How to make sense then of the curious fact that an unequivocally and explicitly positive trait would often be considered inappropriate for, and undesirable in, precisely the most prestigious members of a society? This question, I believe, takes us nearer to an understanding of the responses to *mujūn* among mediaeval Muslim intellectuals. We have argued earlier that *ẓarf* was very intimately linked to libertinism and frivolity; indeed, this close association justifies the contention that it is precisely the quality of *ẓarf* that rescued *mujūn* from being viewed with pure disapproval and conferred upon it a perceptible cultural value. Be libertinism ever so discreditable, it did possess the value of *ẓarf* in the eyes of most Muslim intellectuals of the Middle Ages. To put it another way, *the value inherent in* mujūn *can be identified as wit and urbane sophistication.* Thus *ẓarf* (wittiness, refinement) – a recognised cultural value of mediaeval Muslim society – is the very reason *mujūn* was not considered to be entirely devoid of value and would not be unconditionally condemned and sanctioned. The status of wit among the higher classes of mediaeval Muslim society can be understood as an alternative value – an alternative to ordinary patterns of respectability and thus, in a sense, as normative as the latter even if distinct from it.

That humour and wit were values cherished by a significant part of the political and intellectual elite cannot be doubted in the light of substantial textual evidence. The appreciation of wit is particularly evident in stories – some obviously fictitious, some probably historical even if stylistically polished – wherein an intellectual is

[74] Ibn Rashīq, *ʿUmda* 70.

[75] The distinction was not absolute, for almost all 'witty' poets produced 'serious' works as well, and in many *adab* works serious and frivolous material alternates. However, the overall reputation of any one poet or writer would typically gravitate towards either of the two poles.

saved from the ire of the ruler by a droll remark, which turns the latter's irritation into amused laughter. An apposite and succinct utterance, especially if funny as well, was often seen – as it should – as a sign of bright intellect, which was one of the most highly esteemed, indisputable values in the literate and courtly sectors of urban Muslim society. To be sure, the individual characteristics of a political leader – to start with the most obvious factor, his sense of humour and his disposition to gaiety – must have played a decisive role in responses to witty remarks, but prevalent norms must have had an impact on even the dourest of rulers. And the norm that wittiness is a value to be appreciated by a refined person was a relatively prevalent one, at least within the elite. Whether any individual ruler or vizier really enjoyed, or just feigned enjoyment of, a *bon mot* made by a courtier or a littérateur is therefore a moot point, for what is important for our study is the obvious fact that such an appreciation of wit was expected from a sophisticated, high-status man. There is considerable evidence to suggest that a well-designed, eloquent remark could even save a man about to be executed, let alone one sentenced to lesser punishments.[76] What is more, even unmistakably flippant and pert pleasantries (both in prose and verse) were liable to be received in good humour provided they betrayed smartness, *esprit* and wit (qualities summed up by the Arabic term *ẓarf*, already discussed above). The ability to offer quick repartees (*ajwiba muskita*, lit. 'replies that reduce the opponent to silence') was particularly savoured by educated people, rulers and the ruled alike.[77]

In fact, some court poets had it as their primary responsibility to deliver such witty and amusing talk on a regular basis, even if it involved a normally intolerable degree of audacity. The licence of *ridendo dicere verum* granted to these witty individuals makes them not unlike a sort of glorified court jesters.[78] Most libertines, however, did not make a whole career out of impudent antics at the court but only occasionally engaged in such behaviour, presumably when the temper of the ruler

---

[76] E.g. al-Iṣfahānī, *Aghānī* III, 261–2; al-Ibshīhī, *Mustaṭraf* 202; al-Anṭākī, *Tazyīn* 531; Ibn Simāk, *Zaharāt* 83–4. Interestingly, anthropological studies of modern Arab societies also yield comparable examples; for one such from Yemen, see Caton 1990: 41.

[77] See for instance al-Ṭabarī, *Tārīkh* V, 1645; Ibn al-Muʿtazz, *Ṭabaqāt* 2–3, 197; Ibn Qutayba, *Shiʿr* 367; al-Tanūkhī, *Nishwār* VII, 252; al-Tawḥīdī, *Baṣāʾir* I(ii), 199; al-Thaʿālibī, *Tatimma* I, 22; Yāqūt, *Buldān* IV, 398; al-Iṣbahānī, *Kharīda* I(i), 94; al-Ibshīhī, *Mustaṭraf* 536–7; Ibn Simāk, *Zaharāt* 73–4. For more on *ajwiba muskita*, *v.i.*

[78] A celebrated example of this type of courtly intellectual is a famous poet of the early Abbasids, Abū Dulāma (d. ca. 160/776–7) – a man of black slave ancestry and a notorious libertine – who owed his immense wealth to his considerable wit and his trademark unbridled impudence. See Ibn al-Jawzī, *Ẓirāf* 121; Ibn al-Muʿtazz, *Ṭabaqāt* 17–8, 53; al-Ṭabarī, *Tārīkh* V, 1658; Ibn Qutayba, *Shiʿr* 400; al-Ibshīhī, *Mustaṭraf* 319; and Ben Cheneb 1922: 102–3. (The authoritative overview of the poet's career and *oeuvre* remains Ben Cheneb's book.) On a comparable, somewhat clownish court poet called Abū l-ʿIbar, see El-Outmani 1995: 166–9. For more on court jesters in the mediaeval Middle East, see Pellat 1963: 357.

appeared to be amenable to flippant jokes. If the jest happened to meet the liking of the ruler, its author could expect considerable and tangible rewards, usually in the form of a sum of money. Such was the outcome, for instance, of a remarkably bold-faced prank displayed by a poet of the early fourth/tenth century called al-Hamdānī, which certainly seems like a gamble on his part: he interrupted a public recital of a panegyric praising his patron with a breathtakingly flippant, extemporised verse corresponding in rhyme and metre, though not in content and style, to the panegyric. A gamble as it was, it turned out to be successful, as his audacious wit was appreciated by the patron, who expressed his approval with a generous gift.[79]

Although the risks involved in such antics meant that similar gestures of flippancy tended to be made only spontaneously, on the spur of the moment, they may have been premeditated in some rare cases. The propensity of certain rulers to reward humorous if impudent jokes, news of which must have spread quickly at the first sign of it, might have emboldened some people to prepare audacious jokes beforehand and perform them in front of the ruler, but the only evidence I have for this appears fictitious, and therefore much should not be made of it:

> It is said that a man came to the presence of [Hārūn] al-Rashīd, and said: "O Commander of the faithful, I have composed a lampoon against the Shīʿites [who oppose Abbasid rule]." [The caliph] said: "Let me hear it." The man recited: "Sun and rancour and olive tree and injustice from their receiving tyranny from the two sheikhs." The caliph said: "Now, do explain it." Said the man: "O Commander of the Faithful, you are [served] by hundreds of thousands, and yet you fail to understand it; do you expect poor me alone to understand it?" The caliph laughed at this and gave him a reward.[80]

Even supposing the historicity of this anecdote, it remains undeniable that in most cases of deliberately impudent jokes appealing to the ruler's sense of humour the act was done on the spur of the moment. Rewards could then take any number of forms, but they usually involved an amount of money given to the author of the jest, and/or the forgoing of some punishment. The latter case can be exemplified with what took place between the vizier of the Abbasid al-Muqtadir (r. 295/908–320/932) and a certain Abū l-Jahm b. Sayf:

---

79 Yāqūt, *Buldān* III, 359; al-Tanūkhī, *Nishwār* VII, 108. Remarkably, this prank is not unparalleled in the sources, even if such irreverence to elementary norms of courtly behaviour and decency cannot have been too common. A public recital of a praise poem by the outstanding but notoriously conceited poet al-Buḥturī (d. 284/897) was cut short by a certain Abū l-ʿAbbās (or Abū l-ʿAnbas) al-Ṣaymarī barging in with a couple of immensely obscene and insulting verses. The addressee of the panegyric, the Abbasid caliph al-Mutawakkil (r. 232/847–247/861), could not hold back a fit of laughter, and liberally rewarded the joke. See Ibn Rashīq, *ʿUmda* 176–7.

80 al-Bayhaqī, *Maḥāsin* 486; al-Naḥḥās, *Ṣināʿa* 244–5.

> The vizier of al-Muqtadir, Abū l-Fatḥ b. Furāt dismissed [Abū l-Jahm] from his post and ordered that he should be subjected to a slapping [in his presence]. However, [Abū l-Jahm] would not moan even once but started to count the slaps on his fingers instead. Astonished at his conduct, the vizier asked him what he was doing, and he answered: "May God increase your glory! I am counting so that I should be able to reciprocate with an equal number of slaps later on when I come to be the vizier. I should not be unjust either to you by giving you more [than your due] or to myself by giving you less." Thereupon the vizier began to laugh, unable to contain his laughter – for these were turbulent times – and then he said: "Go home, may God not protect you!" And he waived the money that he had demanded of him before.[81]

As for cases of monetary rewards for audacious but witty remarks, some of these have already been mentioned above, and there are more in the sources. For example, when a son of the celebrated poet Abū Tammām (190/806–232/846) – a considerably less talented man than his father had been – recited a mediocre piece of praise poetry glorifying the emir of Khurāsān at his time the latter, unsatisfied with the encomium, ordered one of his court poets to improvise a satirical poem in response, which would serve as the only reward for the poetaster. Abū Tammām's son then observed that exchanging a product for the same product with a slight increase is defined as usury (*ribā*) – which Islamic law absolutely forbids – and the exchange could only be transformed into a licit one by adding a different merchadise to the reward. The impertinence of the poet paid off, as the emir could not help laughing, and rewarded the poet with three thousand dirhams. Significantly, he stated that it was not the man's poetic talents, which were nonexistent, but his wit that justified the gift ("*in lam yakun maʿahu shiʿr abīhi fa-maʿahu ẓarf abīhi*").[82]

It is noteworthy that rulers might reward a good but ruthless joke or verse line even if the laughter was at the expense some high functionary present at the occasion.[83] (But then the reward would obviously have to be weighed against the perils of having made an influential enemy.) The ability of quick and witty repartee could trump many other qualities when success at the court was concerned, although it is anyone's guess how lasting such success would be. An illustrative case is a story about the favourable reception of an irreverent *bon mot* by the famous libertine

[81] Ibn Saʿīd, *Muqtaṭaf* 204. (This was an instance of the all but customary *muṣādara*, the confiscation of part or all of the property of a dismissed state official (on the opportunistic but not necessarily unfounded rationale that he must have amassed his wealth by bribery and the raiding of the state coffers).)

[82] al-Ṣūlī, *Akhbār* 261–2.

[83] A poet of the Seljuk period called Abū Tammām al-Dabbās received a sum of money from the vizier for an insult disguised as a riddle in verse directed against one of the high religious dignitaries in attendance. See al-Iṣbahānī, *Kharīda* I(ii), 330. Also cf. Ibn al-Muʿtazz, *Ṭabaqāt* 25–6; al-Thaʿālibī, *Thimār* I, 80–1.

Bashshār b. Burd (d. 167–8/784–5), and yet no less significant is the fact that it was on orders of the same caliph that Bashshār would later be executed:

> Bashshār was once sitting in the palace of the caliph al-Mahdī in the company of others, waiting to be admitted. A member of the retinue of al-Mahdī said to those present: "What do you think about [the meaning of] the following passage of the Quran: '*Thy God revealed unto the bees, saying: 'Take unto yourselves, of the mountains, houses, and of the trees'...*"[84] Bashshār replied that 'bees' means what everyone commonly understands by this term. [The attendant] said: "No it doesn't, Abū Muʿādh, in fact 'bees' is [a reference to] the Hāshimite lineage[85], and the [next] verse – '*Then comes forth out of their [the bees'] bellies a drink of diverse hues wherein is healing for men*' – is a reference to the great knowledge [of the Hāshimites]." Thereupon Bashshār told him: "May God ensure that all your food, drink and cure should consist of that which comes out of the bellies of the Hāshimites, if you must speak such nonsense." Angered, the man heaped abuse on Bashshār. Being told of the incident, al-Mahdī summoned the two of them and asked them how this really had been. Bashshār narrated it, whereupon the caliph began to laugh so much that he had to hold his sides, and then said to his retainer: "That's true; may God ensure that all your food and drink should consist of that which comes out of the bellies of the Hāshimites, since you're such a witless idiot."[86]

As noted above, impudent witticisms were basically a gamble, a bet on the ruler's disposition to appreciate irony and daring humour, and like all bets, it could prove to be a losing one. Unless someone was totally confident in gauging the limits of a ruler's good humour, as well as his temper at that moment, the risk of angering him always loomed over an exchange of less than respectful and decorous words. And an irked ruler might decide to vent his irritation in quite nasty ways, the least of which was to dismiss the offender from his post.[87] A sovereign who saw it fit to reward what he regarded as a manifestation of sophisticated wit could be equally inclined to punish what he deemed dull-witted ineptitude. Consider the following story for example:

> It has been narrated by al-Ḥusayn b. Samaydaʿ al-Anṭākī: There was a governor in our town Antioch, who had been appointed by the emir of Aleppo, and this governor had a stupid scribe. Once, when two ships of the Muslim fleet battling the Byzantines, of the kind called *shalandī*, were wrecked, the scribe wrote the following [letter] on behalf of his lord to the emir in Aleppo: "In the name of

[84] Quran 16:68. The Quranic verse cited a few lines on is 16:69.

[85] Of which the Abbasids formed a subgroup. More shameless sycophancy it would be hard to devise.

[86] al-Iṣfahānī, *Aghānī* III, 151–2.

[87] E.g. al-Tawḥīdī, *Baṣāʾir* I(i), 87; al-Iṣbahānī, *Kharīda* II(ii), 515.

> God the Beneficent and Merciful. I inform the emir – may God increase his glory – that two *shalandīs* (i.e. warships) have been wrecked (i.e. they submerged) because of the fury of the sea (i.e. the force of the waves), and everyone on board perished (i.e. died)." The reply sent by the ruler of Aleppo was this: "Your letter has got here (i.e. arrived), and we have understood (i.e. comprehended) it. And you teach your scribe good manners (i.e. slap him well), and seek another (i.e. dismiss him), for he is an idiot (i.e. a cretin). Peace upon you (i.e. the letter ends here)."[88]

While this account appears to bear the marks of either utter fictionality or considerable editing and styling, the following one, in my opinion, must be factual, self-deprecatory as it is throughout. The narrator is a poet of considerable reputation in the Buyid period, who recounts a maladroit witticism he made and the negative reaction of the ruler to it:

> It has been narrated by the poet al-Salāmī: I entered [the palace of the ruler] ʿAḍud al-Dawla, and recited a panegyric on him, which he rewarded with a gift of plenty of clothes and money. There was a cup in front of him, and when he noticed how eagerly I was eyeing it, he threw it to me, saying: "There, [take it]." At this, I said: "*Everything good that is with us is from him.*" To which he replied: "From your father." Utterly perplexed, I had no idea what he might mean by that. Then I went to see one of my teachers to tell him the story, whereupon he said: "You've made a colossal mistake, because this quotation is from [a poem by] Abū Nuwās, in which he describes a dog: "*I am speaking of a [hunting] dog, who exerts himself for his owners, / Their fortune being dependent on his own fortune; / And everything good that is with us is from him.*" Then, clad in an ample robe, I went back to the presence of the ruler, shaking vehemently. He asked me what the matter was, and I answered that I had a fever. He asked me if I knew the cause of my fever, and I said: "I've looked into the poetry of Abū Nuwās, which gave me a fever." Said he: "Fear not, this fever will do no harm to you." I threw myself at his feet, and then left.[89]

It is obvious that humour was a prized talent that could also bring tangible benefits, but it is equally obvious that much of its effect would depend on the particular social setting and the participants. As *ẓarf*, a basically positive quality, could be regarded undesirable in certain categories of men and in certain kinds of situations,

---

[88] al-Tanūkhī, *Nishwār* VII, 178. Of course, providing glosses on difficult words immediately after they occurred was a common custom in mediaeval Arabic writing, but on the one hand there are no really difficult words in either letter, and on the other hand a letter to one's superiors was hardly the place in which one was expected to give explanations, linguistic or otherwise, for the benefit of the uncomprehending. (In fact, a book of professional advice for secretaries explicitly states that even vocalising the text of a letter addressed to one's superior was seen as very bad form, suggesting as it did that the sender harboured doubts about the addressee's linguistic abilities. See al-Ṣūlī, *Adab* 57.)

[89] Ibn al-Jawzī, *Ẓirāf* 84–5.

so would responses to *mujūn* also vary according to the particular circumstances of its production and dissemination and its producers and audience.

1.4 Situational Values

Alternative value scales were not the only factor that affected the reception of libertine behaviour and literary works. Another level of fluidity and ambiguity was also at play when it came to the actual impact of norms and values in everyday life. Different situations might call forth different norms of behaviour and speech, even in the case of the same individual. It has been widely observed by sociologists that the nature of a situation and the circumstances of a social interaction determine to a very large extent the norms of acceptable behaviour.[90] Human behaviour is thus never reducible to a limited number of fixed, absolute and unalterable rules independent of the concrete situation and social context, nor can any theoretical model presupposing such fixed rules be adequate to describe the daily working of any society. As Jack D. Douglas puts it,

> the most basic principle of any analysis of social meanings and actions [is] the principle of the contextual determination of meaning: the concrete meaning of anything (rule, statement, and so forth) is adequately given to members [of a community] only when its concrete or situated context is provided.[91]

The fluidity of norms informing day-to-day behaviour has been observed, and described at length, by anthropologist Lawrence Rosen during his fieldwork in Sefrou, Morocco. He found that the expectations and norms that governed people's conduct in their interactions, far from being fixed and rigid, were in fact – in his words – "open" and "malleable" and could only be grasped to the limited extent that they appeared in and shaped concrete situations.[92]

Accepting the dominant norms is not tantamount to a blind, mechanical application in daily life of a set of practical rules. An overall uniformity and consistency of values might – just might – be hypothesised to exist in an extremely primitive and homogeneous, small-scale community; however, this could certainly never have been the case in a highly complex social setting such as mediaeval Baghdad.[93] The society of a mediaeval Middle Eastern city, even one much smaller than the capital of the Abbasid caliphate, was an infinitely diverse one. As argued above, differences

---

[90] See for instance Herzfeld 1980: 343; Dubois 4, 7.

[91] Douglas 1970: 9. (The author discusses what he calls 'meanings of morality' but his observation is equally relevant to the issue of norms regarding libertinism.)

[92] Rosen 1984: 1–2. (And cf. Mottahedeh 1980: 4.)

[93] On this important difference between small-scale and complex societies, see Benedict 1966: 27; Clinard 1965: 11–3.

in the respective values of social subgroups contributed to the diversity, but so did the fact that even the same person could embrace different norms and patterns of behaviour according to the particular circumstances he found himself in. The single most important factor governing this variation was the distinction between public and private settings.

It was stressed in the last chapter that there was considerable pressure on high-ranking men, especially political leaders and religious dignitaries, to conform to moral and behavioural norms at least outwardly, even if their conduct in the private sphere might diverge astonishingly from their public shows of devoutness and respectability. Most written sources, for example, apparently take it for granted that almost all rulers, caliphs included, will take part in wine-drinking parties and even get drunk – and there is little reason to doubt that the rulers' ordinary subjects would suspect as much – but this was a pastime that had to be kept strictly behind closed doors. Likewise, I have shown that many rulers, high functionaries and even respected religious scholars did entertain themselves by listening to or composing *mujūn* works, yet in order to avoid becoming notorious for such predilections they would be wise to confine that sort of entertainment to gatherings of trusted friends. The potential damage to a man's reputation, should disgraceful information leak, was apparently great, witness anecdotal accounts about the most private sexual perversions of certain aristocrats; one cannot but wonder about the way such sordid details would reach the wider public – and eventually land on the pages of a book – from a circle of supposedly trustworthy confidants.[94]

The Arabic noun *satr* – literally 'covering, concealment, screen', but here used in the specific sense of the concealment of shortcomings and sins – eloquently expresses the principle behind this dichotomy of norms: namely, the recognition that every human being has failings and peccadilloes, yet precisely because they are universal it is shameful for a particular person to earn a notoriety for them. A respectable man therefore must make sure his weaknesses are kept secret – or at any rate known only to a few discreet and benevolent confidants. In this remarkably sensible conception of human nature, a decent, honourable, 'covered' (*mastūr*) man is not one who is devoid of imperfections and conforms to ideals to the minutest detail – for such a person does not exist – but one who does his best not to exhibit his failings and his deviations from the ideals. To behave properly is obligatory in certain situations; yet one can relax one's conduct in trusted company, in private settings.[95]

---

[94] E.g. al-Tawḥīdī, *Baṣāʾir* I(i), 96–7; and a large part of al-Tawḥīdī, *Akhlāq* (which typically relies on information received from the viziers' close associates and courtiers). It is little wonder that the divulging of what had happened in a ruler's private gathering would be considered inexcusable treachery and punished brutally; it is probably for that reason that the caliph al-Muʿtaḍid (r. 279/892–289/902) ordered the execution of one of his boon-companions. See Chejne 1965: 334.

[95] On this dichotomy in Iranian society today, see Eickelman 1989: 235–7.

It would be rash to dismiss the tendency to split social behaviour into private and public as a typically Middle Eastern form of all but institutionalised dishonesty or dissimulation. If anything, the separation of the norms of public and private behaviour was an explicit recognition of a duality that, as a matter of fact, exists in all societies including the modern West. A relevant and very important distinction that probably few human communities fail to make is that between formal and informal situations with a corresponding difference between patterns of conduct and speech expected in each. It is usually in highly formal settings – especially those involving evaluation and moral judgement – that normative patterns of behaviour are 'activated'.[96] On a more general level, norms of behaviour tend to differ from any specific type of situation to another; indeed manners considered appropriate in one situation can be totally unlike expected conduct in a different kind of social interaction. To mention just a few obvious examples, both the topics and the speech style of a conversation will differ considerably depending on the presence or absence of women among the participants; members of a group will often modify their talk if outsiders are present; and in many communities joking is taboo in the presence of people of higher status.[97] Nearly universal, situational norms are a way of giving flexibility to social interaction while maintaining the general normative framework of the society; they have nothing to do with hypocrisy, which mediaeval Muslims regarded in very negative terms (and which they referred to with an unrelated term, *nifāq*). Even if norms informing appropriate behaviour varied according to the various types of situations, they were widely known and therefore felt to be equally valid. It may be said that a norm would rarely be absolute but in most cases situational, and if one keeps that caveat in mind, the false question of hypocrisy in normative behaviour disappears. Aware as they are that 'proper' conduct depends on the specific situation, people can strongly and honestly identify with a normative system and still behave in starkly divergent ways in some types of social setting.[98] This approach is at odds with an all too common conception of norms – "the primitive hedonistic theory, so characteristic of Western notions about sin, which views human action as arising from a choice between individual desire and

[96] On the concepts of formality and informality, see Irvine 1979: 774–80. On the concept of the 'activation' of norms, see Dubois, Beauvois 2003: 241. In an essay on certain forms of public speech in contemporary Algeria, Hadj Miliani observes that public discourse tends to be subject to special constraints because of its function of presenting widely accepted values and codes of behaviour to audiences already familiar with them. See Miliani 1997: 119.

[97] E.g. Rosen 1984: 35; Abu-Lughod 1990: 35; Abu-Lughod 1999: 31, 152–6, 186–7, 227; Eickelman 1989: 90, 233–4. – A mediaeval Arabic manual for boon-companions of rulers advises that one should first ascertain the ruler's readiness for jests before venturing any funny talk ("*fa-ammā l-ʿabath wa-l-mizāḥ fa-lahu min al-munādim mawqiʿ laṭīf wa-maḥall khaṣīṣ idhā tabayyana l-nadīm minhu nashāṭan li-dhālik*"); see Kushājim, *Adab* 14.

[98] On this issue, see Abu-Lughod 1990: 32–3; Abu-Lughod 1999: 236–8.

the norms which oppose such desires"[99] – but seems to offer a better understanding of mediaeval Muslim attitudes to various forms of norm-breaking, including *mujūn.*

As an individual might choose among several alternative value scales in any given situation, so could others judge his choice varyingly, according to their own understanding of the situation. The important point is that alternative values and norms resulted not only from different social subgroups having different preferences but also – even more crucially – from practically everyone complying with one set of norms in a given social setting and with another in a different setting. Resulting from the availability of various *alternative value scales*, norms were also *situational*, that is to say their applicability would, to a large extent, depend on the situation. And, as noted above, there was nothing necessarily hypocritical about such flexibility. Obviously, the same man who would whole-heartedly enjoy and appreciate the mischievous wit of his friends' frivolous conversation during a nightly drinking-party might with equal enthusiasm identify with pious norms when, say, listening during Ramadan to a poignant sermon about the suffering of fellow-Muslims from Byzantine raids in the borderlands of the caliphate. In the former case, his responses would likely be judged according to the criterion of *ẓarf* (wit, sophistication); in the latter, the criterion would be piety and Muslim solidarity. As an adage-like remark attributed to the Quran expert Ibn Mujāhid (d. 324/936) – not necessarily apocryphal given this savant's reputation for cheerfulness – puts it, "Playing the sage in a garden [viz. a pleasant, informal setting] is as [bad as] playing the libertine in a mosque (*al-ta'āqul fī l-bustān ka-l-takhāluʿ fī l-masjid*)".[100] There is no question that the variety of social situations a person finds himself in allows him earnestly to espouse disparate values. True that one man may give priority to one set of values and norms, and another to a different one, but extreme cases must have been relatively rare. Apart from the truly, uncompromisingly bigoted on the one hand and the irredeemably dissolute and godless on the other, most people would perhaps derive pleasure and pride from religiosity as well as from other values.

In brief, the same person may, and typically will, embrace various – even contradictory – values and norms. If one accepts this idea, the popularity of libertine poetry and indecent talk among high-ranking, respectable men will appear far less of a sociological puzzle. The situational nature of norms helps explain the conspicuous difference in mediaeval Muslim reactions to *mujūn* and to forms of behaviour considered really deviant.

The pervasive distinction of the private and public domains extended to a lot of situations and made some social settings and some forms of expression more amenable to *mujūn* than others. Thus *mujūn* was probably more acceptable in speech

[99] Goode 1960: 251.

[100] Yāqūt, *Udabāʾ* II, 523.

than in writing, and friendly gatherings would be more natural and safe venues for libertine fun than public assemblies. In general, the more informal a setting, the more room for engaging in libertine talk and behaviour. The grammarian known as al-Wajīh (d. 612/1215) would lavishly sprinkle his serious lectures with all manner of entertaining stories and poems (*al-akhbār wa-l-ḥikāyāt wa-inshād al-ashʿār*), a habit that greatly irritated many in his audience.[101] While the source does not specify the reason, I have no doubt that, given the demonstrable popularity of such light genres in Baghdad, it must be the unsuitability of the material for a respectable scholarly gathering that the students found vexing. The way *mujūn* works circulated is also likely to have affected the degree of their acceptance. It is notable just how much of the *mujūn*-type material in the sources suggests a casual context rather than grand literary enterprise, a lot of *mujūn* prose being comprised of either jokes or funny remarks recorded in writing, a lot of *mujūn* poetry, of versified messages between friends, teasing and gibes, and extemporised occasional poetry of various sorts. With the growing vogue of literary libertinism – especially from the Buyid period – such ephemeral products would increasingly find their way into respectable anthologies and gain the dignity of 'literature'. Exchanges of poems or pleasantries between friends on slips of paper (*riqāʿ*) might be kept by one party or both and later, if found to be sophisticated enough, end up recorded by some acquaintance.[102] However, it is reasonable to suppose that it is only a fraction of the *mujūn* spoken (and done) at soirées and parties that was ever recorded – orality was bound to remain a more fitting medium for *mujūn* than writing.

Just like some social situations, some poetical genres (*aghrāḍ*) were more accommodating to *mujūn*, and this again may have had to do with the perceived 'informality' or otherwise of the genre in question. Thus praise poetry would as a rule never be considered *mujūn*, even though some of the hyperboles used in panegyrics were no less outrageous from a religious point of view than any hardcore *mujūn*. Lampoons (*hijāʾ*) were a rather ambiguous case, and might occasionally be labelled *mujūn* because of their calculatedly offensive motifs and imagery, yet most often they were treated as *sui generis* and separate, in intent if not in content, from libertine poetry.[103] The crucial factor here, in my view, is whether a work was meant

101 Yāqūt, *Udabāʾ* V, 2263.

102 See the case of Aḥmad al-Ṣaffārī's friendly correspondence in Yāqūt, *Udabāʾ* I, 405.

103 Cf. Rowson 1998: 546–7. There exist sporadic references to the contents of some *hijāʾ* poems being *mujūn*, as in the following passage: "[...] a lot of lampoons, which we have preferred to omit because of the silliness and *mujūn* therein (*ahājin kathīra aʿraḍnā ʿan dhikrihā li-mā fīhā min al-sukhf wa-l-mujūn*)". See Yāqūt, *Udabāʾ* III, 1198. Amorous poetry (*ghazal*), romantic and idealised as its tone tends to be, is a domain rather distant from *mujūn*, although the kind of love poetry cultivated by ʿUmar b. Abī Rabīʿa (23/643–93/711) displays a playfulness, even slight cynicism, that is remotely reminiscent of the attitudes of some later libertine works. Of course, the carnal descriptions of flirting and intercourse in the bacchic poems of the likes of Abū Nuwās, Bashshār b. Burd and other libertines

in seriousness (*jidd*) or jesting (*hazl*). *Mujūn* was by definition unserious, humorous[104], not to be taken in earnest, and that made it an eminently 'informal' phenomenon. It is the underlying reason why *madīḥ* (praise-poetry), no matter how abundantly blasphemous its hyperboles, would not qualify as *mujūn*[105] – nor would early Bedouin poetry of any type, even the most vivid descriptions of sexual affairs by a poet like Imru' al-Qays. The distinction between jest and earnest can also account for the difficulty of drawing a definite boundary between love poetry and *mujūn*. In fact, poems appearing to belong to the genre of *ghazal* (amorous poetry) may turn out to be *mujūn*, provided they approach the subject in a frivolous or ironic tone.[106]

2. The Sociology of *Mujūn*

2.1 Was Mujūn Really Subversive?

After the first superficial impressions of a conservative social milieu, many Western visitors to Middle Eastern cities discover an extraordinary level of tolerance for officially prohibited activities – drinking, extramarital and homosexual liaisons, and so on – provided such things are pursued strictly in discretion. Activities that would create a scandal if done overtly can go on largely undisturbed if secrecy is observed. One would suppose that the inhabitants of mediaeval Muslim cities were not much different in this regard. Secrecy was and still is the key to this toleration of 'improper' conduct; there is no question that respect for privacy in such cases did and does not signal permission, let alone approval. As I argued above, the fact that dominant norms and cultural ideals are not always perfectly applied in practice, indeed are sometimes totally ignored, does not lead to the conclusion that such norms and ideals have no validity for the majority.[107] The effort to keep a 'forbidden' activity

are quite another matter. Wine poetry (*khamriyyāt*) was, not surprisingly, a fertile ground for *mujūn*; indeed it constitutes one of the genres most intimately associated with libertinism, albeit not every wine poem is necessarily a specimen of *mujūn*. In prose literature, anecdotes (*nawādir*) are probably the most natural locus of *mujūn*, but it must be remarked that the *maqāma* genre often contains a lot of *mujūn* material too.

104 Indeed, according to Paul Sprachman the word mediaeval Persian authors most frequently used to refer to *mujūn*-type literary texts is *hazl*. See Sprachman 1995: xxii.

105 The formal poetry of Ibn al-Ḥajjāj (d. 391/1001) addressed to his Buyid patrons often does contain a mixture of *mujūn* and *madīḥ*. It is so unusual in mediaeval Arabic poetry as to appear a speciality of this master of *sukhf* ('folly', obscene and scatological poetry). See an example (a congratulatory poem on the occasion of the *ʿĪd al-Aḍḥā* holiday which doubles as a wine poem) in al-Thaʿālibī, *Yatīma* III, 67.

106 See for instance Bauer 1998: 480–1.

107 See for instance Marcus 1986: 178.

secret is a strong indication that the transgressor is aware of the error and sinfulness of his ways; it may even be argued that the secrecy reinforces the validity of the norms, sending the message that it would be shameful to be seen doing such things.

Whereas this kind of tolerance for discreet misconduct, which is hardly unique to mediaeval Muslim civilisation, has been an important influence, it is largely irrelevant for an analysis of responses to libertinism. It is for a very simple reason that the fashion of *mujūn* certainly could not rely on the tacit toleration of clandestine breaches of norms: *mujūn* was never discreet. Note that libertines deliberately sought to be scandalous, outrageous talk and deeds being the distinguishing mark of *mujūn* and its very *raison d'être*. In spite of the unequivocal Islamic prohibition thereof, lots of people would regularly drink wine, yet someone who valued his good reputation would be discreet about it – but libertines did not follow this unspoken rule of thumb. Extramarital sex and homosexuality were far from uncommon, yet it was advisable for a respectable man not to brag about such affairs – libertines were again an exception with their careless abandon. Presumably not every male fit the cultural ideal of fearlessness and gallant feats in campaigns, but it is unlikely that many would publicly own up to their own lack of valour – except libertines, who would make jestful remarks and verses about it. Examples could be multiplied to show how impossible it would be to attribute the popularity of *mujūn* and those who cultivated it to the tacit toleration of discreet misconduct.

In the last chapter, much was written about the legal category of *fisq* (immorality) and the legal consequences of the label. It was noted that while the term is somewhat opaque, a typical libertine would certainly be classified as a *fāsiq* (immoral person) in the legal sense. Indeed, a libertine was not only the quintessential *fāsiq* but also an indiscreet, overt *fāsiq*, which was a category apart: overt immorality (*al-mujāhara bi-l-fisq*) was judged differently (and more severely) from discreet misconduct, and certain forms of protection or indulgence granted to a discreet *fāsiq* were not available to the self-advertising libertine. The distinction was formulated explicitly in the principle – buttressed by ḥadīths – that a discreet *fāsiq* should not be gossiped about and thus exposed and put to shame, unlike an indescreet one, who should. This principle seems to have been accepted across many but not all schools of law.[108]

[108] Ibn Juzayy, *Qawānīn* 433; al-Samarqandī, *Fatāwā* 291, 393–4; al-Khaṣṣāf, *Adab* 310–1; Ibn Miftāḥ, *Muntazaʿ* X, 537–8; al-Haytamī, *Zawājir* II, 16, 18, 214–5; Ibn al-Ṣalāḥ, *Fatāwā* II, 497–8; Ibn Baraka, *Jāmiʿ* I, 358–9. (Note that the last source, an Ibāḍite work of jurisprudence, makes no distinction between a discreet and an indescreet *fāsiq*.) – In a *fatwā* of his, the Shāfiʿite Abū Ḥāmid al-Ghazālī (d. 505/1111) also advises that the testimony of an immoral man who is indiscreet about it (*idhā kāna l-fāsiq mutaẓāhiran bi-l-fisq*) cannot be allowed even after he makes an outward show of repentance. See al-Ghazālī, *Fatāwā* 264. According to the Ḥanafite scholar Abū Yūsuf (d. 182/798), an indiscreet *fāsiq* may not marry a decent woman, while a discreet one whose outward *murūʾa* (respectability) is intact may; see Fofana 1425 (A. H.): I, 336. On some legal consequences of indiscreetness (*mujāhara* or *taẓāhur*) in sinful behaviour, also cf. al-Māwardī, *Aḥkām* 376–7. For an

Yet indiscreet though *mujūn* was by definition, it was anything but subversive. As shown in the preceding pages, what *mujūn* represented for the contemporary audience is not the denial of or opposition to a single valid system of values, but the occasional, temporary application – in a certain type of social setting – of another, alternative set of values (centred on refinement and wit). To put it in more concrete terms: there would be no denying that libertinism was dishonourable (because indecent and irreverent), yet at the same time it would be appreciated because it was charming and witty. The appreciation of its entertainment value did not have to entail a denial of its immorality. In this way, there could be ample room for valuing the wit of *mujūn* without abandoning or subverting any of the dominant norms.

It is important to note that a huge distance separates ostentatious norm-breaking from the denial and subversion of the norms. Libertines never went over that distance. As we have argued, a libertine would routinely poke fun at ordinary norms, but he would not question their validity, let alone proposing new norms to replace the old ones. In this sense, he was halfway between the discreet transgressor and the subverter of norms. Political dissidents or sectarian agitators – and in the mediaeval Islamic world the two categories often merged – had precious little in common with even the most inveterate libertines. (And, as will be shortly shown, this difference was commonly acknowledged by mediaeval Muslims.) A libertine would ostentatiously disregard – or, in many cases, pretend to disregard as a literary pose – compliance with norms that he treated as valid for other people, but he would never pursue a project of changing or improving them. For instance, the poetical praises of the virtues of wine and drinking wine – the genre of *khamriyyāt* – were never understood as a positive stance, a serious proposal to invalidate the Islamic interdiction of liquor.[109] Naughty rather than subversive, the theme was obviously not interpreted by the audience as a challenge to established norms. This view of *mujūn* works is manifest in an Andalusian account about the practice of detaining at the ruler's court the sons of some recalcitrant lineage heads. It was advised that these boys should not be exposed to ancient, heroic Bedouin poetry as part of the school curriculum but they should be taught love poetry, the wine poems of Abū Nuwās 'and similar drolleries' (*wa-shibhahā min al-ahzāl*) so as to help turn them into harmless and unambitious men.[110]

It is utterly misleading to understand libertinism as subversive, a voice of social or cultural dissent as it were; *mujūn* was not a project of changing norms or values

enlightening discussion of the differences between modern Western and traditional Muslim concepts of privacy, see Cook 2000: 480–2, 593–4.

[109] Arazi 1979: 14.

[110] Ibn Simāk, *Zaharāt* 122–3.

but merely a form of entertainment. From a societal point of view, *mujūn* was harmless – more than anything, it was empty, inconsequential chatter.[111] *The fact that libertinism posed no danger to the maintenance of moral and religious norms is probably one of the chief reasons it rarely triggered off violent reactions and sanctions, unlike truly subversive cultural tendencies and forms of political and social dissent, which usually did.* Transgressing norms is always far more tolerable than questioning them.[112]

There is a particularly good indication of the narrow limits of the libertines' challenge to prevalent norms. I am referring to two telltale facts: first, for all their scandalous merry-making, these poets and writers never ceased to stress that their acts were *sinful*; and second, one of their constant themes is the possibility of eventual repentance (*tawba*) and God's forgiveness to the sinner. The emphasis on *tawba* is a literary convention, but it may be more than that. As shown in the last chapter, gestures of penitence were not unheard of among libertines. And Islamic thought generally insists on the possibility of repentance (and divine forgiveness) right until the moment of an individual's death; indeed a sinner who believes in God and finally humbles himself before Him can be in a better position than an arrogant sciolist. Here is the notable opinion of Abū Ḥāmid al-Ghazālī (d. 505/1111), a man of integrity, honest piety and exceptional scholarly credentials, on God's forgiving of sins:

> [Even] the most sinful commoners (*al-ʿawāmm al-ʿuṣāt*) are in a more hopeful condition (*asʿad ḥālan*) than men ignorant of the ways of religion who [nevertheless] believe that they are learned. That is because the sinful commoner acknowledges his shortcomings and [may] ask for God's forgiveness and repent, while that ignorant man who considers himself learned [...] will neither repent nor ask for God's forgiveness but continue as ever right until his death.[113]

Thus, fully acknowledging the sinfulness of their own behaviour, libertines were perceived as being much less of a threat to the moral order than they would have been had they disputed it. This distinction is not merely an interpretation put forward by the researcher living in the modern age; in fact it was pointed out, in so many words, by several mediaeval Muslim religious scholars. Consider, for instance, a quite explicit explanation by the Iraqi Shāfiʿite scholar Ibn al-Ṣalāḥ al-Shahrazūrī (fl. early 7th/13th c.) about why an immoral lifestyle (*fisq*) is to be judged less

[111] In this regard, cf. the instructive observations of Lambert 1997: 47–8.

[112] See for instance Goode 1960: 257. The words of Joel L. Kraemer regarding responses to heresy are also pertinent to our topic: "Orthodox religions and other ideologically closed systems tend to wink at infringement of the rules provided that lip-service is paid to the guiding ideology [...]." See Kraemer 1986: 13. For more on this issue, cf. Calder 2000: 67; and Lagrange 2006: 62.

[113] al-Ghazālī, *Iḥyāʾ* I, 111.

severely than incorrect religious beliefs: "Immorality may [merely] consist of sinful practices while the religious beliefs [of the sinner] are sound (*wa-l-fisq qad yakūnu fasādan fī l-ʿamal maʿa salāmat al-ʿaqīda*)."[114] The experts of *fiqh* – of all established legal schools – took pains to distinguish between what constitutes unbelief (*kufr*) on the one hand and sin ('disobedience', *maʿṣiya*) on the other, and made fine distinctions when they searched a transgressor's motives in, for instance, failing to pray, or drinking wine. The considering of forbidden things as licit (*istiḥlāl*) was an offence far more serious than any immoralities libertines were notorious for. Mere neglect of prayer, they would insist, was to be distinguished from the questioning of the duty of prayer, with the latter being tantamount to apostasy, whereas the former would be counted as a mere misdemeanour. Likewise, drinking wine or eating pork was simply an immoral act, while considering it permissible was a sign of unbelief (and potentially punishable by death).[115] And it is exactly the same distinction that a story about Abū Nuwās cites him as pointing out in order to defend himself from charges of unbelief. The libertine poet observes that he cannot be an infidel, given his acknowledgement of his sin ("*aqrartu bi-l-dhanb*"): at most, he can be blamed for his postponement of repenting (*taʾkhīr al-tawba*).[116] Coming from (or put in the mouth of) the arch-libertine of Arabic literature, it is a powerful testimony to the cogency of the distinction I have been describing; and it is immaterial for my argument whether the story is factually true; what matters is the existence of such a conceptual framework. As noted above, breaches of norms will usually be viewed with more lenience than explicit opposition to them. Even recurring misconduct cannot be equated with a conscious challenge to the normative system.

In some respects, responses to *mujūn* show similarities with the indulgence with which the moral entrepreneurs[117] of a society tend to treat the excesses of carnivals.

---

[114] Ibn al-Ṣalāḥ, *Fatāwā* I, 219.

[115] E.g. Ibn ʿAqīl, *Tadhkira* 73; al-Khaṣṣāf, *Adab* 305; Badr, *Risāla* 46–7; al-Shāfiʿī, *Umm* II, 563–5; al-Haytamī, *Iʿlām* 353; al-Ṭūsī, *Nihāya* II, 734; Ibn Baraka, *Jāmiʿ* I, 463–4; al-Shahrastānī, *Milal* I, 144; Ibn Miftāḥ, *Muntazaʿ* X 114–5; Hamdan, Schmidtke 2008: 91. Ḥanafite jurists would make the same distinction in the case of someone having sex with a menstruating woman, a forbidden act; see for instance al-Samarqandī, *Fatāwā* 276; Badr, *Risāla* 47. The only exception is some extremist (and marginal) elements among the Khārijites (notably the *Ṣufriyya*) who refused to differentiate certain grave sins – especially the neglect of prayer – from *kufr*, and regarded those who failed to pray for whatever reason as unbelievers in every respect. The *Azāriqa* subgroup was even harsher, considering as they did *all* sinners to be unbelievers in the full sense of the word. See al-Shahrastānī, *Milal* I, 122, 137.

[116] Ibn Manẓūr, *Akhbār* 103–4.

[117] I have borrowed this term from an article by Donald W. Ball, who defines this category as those members of a society who "go about the business of manufacturing the definitions of deviant or reprehensible conduct and thereby respectable and otherwise selves, identities and characters". See Ball 1970: 357.

Not incidentally, carnival-like festivals were customary in quite a few Muslim communities, mediaeval and modern, urban and rural. An example is the *Nawrūz* festival (of Persian origin) in mediaeval Egypt, during which the celebrants would openly consume wine and various kinds of beer and engage in teasing with erotic overtones – for instance drenching one another's clothes to make them cling to the body and reveal its shape – while prostitutes and transvestites would dance in the streets and high dignitaries had literally to ransom themselves with money if they wished to pass unharmed through the throngs of wild revellers.[118]

Such carnivals are similar to *mujūn* literature in that neither means a permanent subversion of the prevailing moral order and normative framework, and in both cases a number of people get an implicit license, in very special circumstances, to engage in activities that would normally be frowned upon and possibly punished too. Like *mujūn*, carnivals are allowed to take place precisely because it is obvious to everyone that ordinary norms of behaviour and morality continue to be as binding as ever: far from losing their force, they are just playfully suspended for a well-defined period.[119] Likewise, the existence of a handful of chartered libertines did not represent a serious challenge to the established moral order; the implicit licence granted to these people depended on the clear understanding that such people are few and, even more importantly, a departure from otherwise well-defined and valid norms. The parallels between *mujūn* and carnivals has led at least one literary expert to borrow Bakhtin's concept of 'carnivalised literature' to characterise the sort of mediaeval Arabic literary products usually labelled *mujūn*.[120]

It is the strength, rather than the weakness, of dominant norms that phenomena like libertinism and carnivals signify, for had the norms been felt to be unstable and disputable, the moral entrepreneurs of the society would certainly have reacted with rage against the least challenge. This, as has been noted towards the end of the previous chapter, may offer part of the explanation as to why Muslims in certain periods of threat from the outside – as in the contemporary Middle East or during the *Reconquista* in al-Andalus – appear to have become more sensitive to all perceived affronts to their culture, including mere frivolity.

A final word about *mujūn* having little to do with the subversion of norms. Scholars trying to analyse the effect of humour have sometimes argued that jokes are basically vigorous challenges to the existing social order and its control over

---

118 Shoshan 1993: 42–4.

119 Shoshan 1993: 47–8; Hammoudi 1993: 92. Abdellah Hammoudi notes that participants of the *Bilmawn* carnival among the Berbers of the High Atlas are themselves quite aware of the impropriety of some features of this festival, and therefore ask God's forgiveness for these, and are reluctant to discuss the carnival with outsiders. See Hammoudi 1993: 59, 65.

120 El-Outmani 1995: 166. (To the best of my knowledge, this terminological proposal, however apt, has not been adopted by specialists of Arabic literature.)

the individual. While this view is not self-evidently wrong, it has also been noted that the 'subversive' effect of a joke is always and strictly momentary, and since a joke cannot be but ephemeral and never offers a real alternative to the existing distribution of power and the normative system, it is totally harmless. Someone who jokes does not aspire to disturb, much less change, the social order; he or she is merely a "privileged person who can say certain things in a certain way which confers immunity", and the jokes are "in a sense the comments of the social group upon itself".[121] In a foregoing part of this chapter I mentioned the apparently frequent tendency for rulers to restrain themselves and pardon an offender in acknowledgement of a sufficiently funny remark or verse. Part of the reason for such lenience is that comicality neutralises a potentially subversive act and makes it innocuous: what is not serious is not threatening.[122] Joking is no violence. Just as jokes poking fun at a certain ethnicity as a rule express mild teasing rather than stark hostility, the mediaeval Arabic joke repertoire about religious themes reflects anything but opposition to religion.[123] Indeed, the purpose of joking can often be so far from challenging the established order that in many societies 'joking relationships' become institutionalised and, conforming to fixed conventions of theme and style, may serve as a way of relieving social tensions.[124] While humour was never conventionalised to this extent amongst mediaeval Arabs, neither can it be described as a subversive social factor.

2.2 The Conventionalisation of Scandal: Libertinism as a Social Role

The human types that appear in the traditional Arabic poetry of the early Middle Ages are largely predictable, falling as they do into a limited number of categories. No less predictable are the 'plots', as it were, of these mediaeval poems. The genre of a poem to a great extent determines the protagonists and the ways in which they will be portrayed as behaving and speaking. The lionised objects of traditional

121 Douglas 1968: 364–5, 372.

122 For example, questioning the tenet that Muḥammad had been the last of the prophets was normally perceived as an extremely savage assault at the very fundaments of Islamic religion and culture. However, there are stories about the arrest of certain pretenders to a prophet's status which conclude with the release of the offender following a comical answer to the interrogations. The logic is that such men are too ridiculous to be punished seriously. See an example in al-Tabarī, *Tārīkh* V, 1682. (Of course, with a ludicrous 'false prophet' being a favourite type of protagonist in *mujūn* jokes, the historicity of any such account is, to say the least, unlikely.)

123 On ethnic jokes, see Davies 1987: 42; on jokes on religion, see Rosenthal 1956: 28.

124 This kind of relationship, which has been termed 'category-routinized joking', is especially common in, but not restricted to, traditional tribal societies in Africa and elsewhere. On the phenomenon, see Hamdelman, Kapferer 1972: 485, 497–8, 507; Radcliffe-Brown 1940: 195–6, 208–10; Freedman 1977: 154–6, 158–9.

panegyrics have little individuality – as opposed to a set of stock attributes expressed in similes and metaphors – and one heroic Bedouin bard differs little in his general features from another. Similarly, poets writing *ghazal* (amorous verse) would follow predictable patterns when portraying the pangs of love, their suffering, the beauty of their beloved, the jealousy of censorious relatives and neighbours, etc. (Let it be stressed that these remarks on the conventional personae in this poetry are not meant as a judgement of poetic value, there being lots of other criteria of aesthetic evaluation – this essay has no room, nor intention, to treat this much-discussed subject.) There was little variation in the voices to be encountered in, say, love poetry, or those in heroic verse, and a host of other genres. Convention is the pillar of the thematic aspects of old Arabic poetry.[125] Given the remarkably conventional patterns of the available repertoire of poetic personae and roles, the appearance of an entirely new type of role – to wit, that of the *mājin* – in this fixed catalogue is pregnant with particular significance and is worth the keen attention of a sociologist and cultural anthropologist because of what it has the ability to reveal about momentous changes in the society. For it must have been important changes in the socio-cultural landscape that gave rise to the novel possibility of a poet assuming the persona of the shameless, frivolous, scandalous and debauched libertine – almost the exact antithesis of the heroic model of a traditional Arabic bard.

Ironically, the literary figure of the libertine went the way of all other roles (and motifs) of mediaeval Arabic poetry: it ended up being a regular poetic convention. It is richly ironic that *mujūn* – a literary phenomenon that began as a conscious, innovative breach of established norms – should gradually become conventional, indeed as fully conventional as any of the earlier poetic clichés and poses it sought to mock, yet this is what happened to *mujūn* relatively soon. It developed its own topoi and conventional motifs – reviewed at length in Chapters Two and Three of this book – just as 'serious' literature had. Just how conventional a lot of the motifs of *mujūn* literature eventually came to be is, hopefully, obvious from the footnotes to those two chapters.[126]

The conventionalisation of *mujūn*, of course, must have been a gradual process. With the growing familiarity of literary libertinism, its acceptance also grew. At first, around the beginning of the Abbasid period, it is only a handful of poets who dared experiment with outrageous motifs, but seeing their considerable success among urban intellectuals (and, no less importantly, their impunity), others would

---

[125] See for instance García Gómez 1940: 42. On the typical 'dramatis personae' of mediaeval Arabic panegyrics, see Gruendler 2003: 39. On the role of convention in mediaeval Arabic poetry, also see von Grunebaum 1944: 234–5; Hamori 1969: 5.

[126] A particularly good example is the parody by 'modern' (*muḥdath*) poets of the opening motif of ancient Arabic odes, which ended up being every bit as conventional as the original motif. See Hamori 1969: 10.

follow suit. According to an account, a poet of the early Abbasid period called al-Khārakī was the first in Basra to have the courage to treat in his poetry themes that would soon become staples of *mujūn* poetry: wine-drinking parties, visits to taverns, sex with adolescent boys. Thereby he would start an enduring vogue, for his example inspired a lot of poets active in the city – including Abū Nuwās – to use such frivolous motifs in their poetry quite openly, a novelty as local poets had formerly been treating such themes, if at all, only in secret.[127] Likewise, it is said that the libertine poet al-Nāshiʾ (d. 365/975) was something of a pioneer of a certain type of *mujūn* in the Bāb al-Ṭāq quarter of Baghdad who found quite a number of epigones ("*wa-lahu fī l-mujūn wa-l-walaʿ ṭabaqa ʿāliya wa-ʿanhu akhadha mujjān Bāb al-Ṭāq kulluhum hādhihi l-ṭarīqa*").[128] It was thus only gradually that the conventions of *mujūn* literature crystallised and thereby, to borrow a phrase from Mary Douglas, "the permitted range of attack" was explored and found to be quite wide.[129] When *mujūn* had become a recognisable literary tradition and in most respects conventional, its themes and motifs – as well as the behaviour associated with it – became, accordingly, quite predictable. In this sense, *mujūn* was transformed from being an informal, tentative kind of norm-breaking in acts and speech to being a remarkably formalised literary and social phenomenon, if we understand formality as "an increased structuring and predictability of discourse".[130] *Mujūn* ended up being like love poetry among contemporary Egyptian Bedouins in so far as in neither case does the poet give spontaneous and free expression to his innermost feelings but follows established conventions of both form and content. The general awareness that supposedly improper and objectionable verses are part of a tradition that defines their style and themes does confer a measure of protection and esteem upon the poets.[131]

The fact that, with the exception of the very first libertine poets' innovative works, much *mujūn* was conventional in themes, imagery and style must alert us to the potentially great distance between the literary persona of a supposedly 'libertine' poet or writer and his actual lifestyle. Just as a master of grand, heroic verse like al-Mutanabbī need not have been a valiant man in real-life encounters, so is it quite possible that the loud libertinism of a libertine poet was a mere pose. Once

---

[127] Ibn al-Muʿtazz, *Ṭabaqāt* 145 (and also cf. the additional passages taken from the book of al-Mubārak b. Aḥmad in the section of editorial notes, p. 38).

[128] Yāqūt, *Udabāʾ* IV, 1785. Al-Nāshiʾ's speciality in *mujūn* seems to have been the unabashed blending of outrageous and often obscene comments into serious theological debates.

[129] Douglas 1968: 372.

[130] Irvine 1979: 774. (Of course, as Irvine observes on p. 784, all poetry is in a sense a discourse with an increased level of structuring.)

[131] On such factors influencing the status of love poetry among Bedouins, see Abu-Lughod 1999: 238–40.

conventions of how a *ẓarīf* (witty, urbane, refined) intellectual should behave, talk and write had been accepted, a would-be libertine had to take those conventions into consideration, given that the most important embodiment of *ẓarf* came to be the libertine intellectual. But the reverse is equally true: whoever wished to gain recognition as a witty man had better conform to the stereotyped style of a *mājin* (libertine). This conventionalisation of *mujūn* is what makes it extremely hard to judge the 'sincerity' or otherwise of a lot of *mujūn* literature. Apart from a few obvious cases, it is difficult to tell the difference between the literary outpourings of a man's genuine libertinism and the wholly conventional poses of another. Consider the following verdict on Abū l-Ḥasan al-Ṣā'igh al-Rāmhurmuzī (d. 312/924–5), author of what appears to be a poem with typical *mujūn* content: "It is full of excess and urging [to do] things that are sinful. He composed it by way of posing as a reprobate and jester, while [in his heart] he was virtuous and a true believer (*wa-fīhi tajawwuz kathīr wa-amr bi-khilāf al-jamīl; qālahā ʿalā ṭarīq al-takhāluʿ wa-l-taṭāyub wa-kāna ṣāliḥan muʿtaqidan li-l-ḥaqq*)."[132] Or consider the following argument offered by a Shāfiʿite jurist in favour of permitting the composition of amorous verses about an unnamed boy: "Typically the poet will only say it so as to make his poem more delicate and to show off his mastery, not because he is genuinely in love (*wa-l-ghālib anna l-shāʿir innamā yaqūluhu tarqīqan li-shiʿrihi wa-iẓhāran li-ṣunʿihi lā annahu ʿāshiq ḥaqīqatan*)."[133] The famous scholar Abū l-Rayḥān al-Bīrūnī (d. after 442/1050) is said to have been "a nice companion, licentious in his words, chaste in his deeds (*ṭayyib al-ʿishra khalīʿan fī alfāẓihi ʿafīfan fī afʿālihi*)".[134] These are not isolated cases; one finds even the libertine extraordinaire Abū Nuwās being the object of a similar judgement (whether or not warranted is irrelevant for our present purpose): "He does believe in resurrection, but *mujūn* leads him to say [irreligious] things that he does not really believe (*innahu la-yu'minu bi-l-baʿth wa-yaḥmiluhu l-mujūn ʿalā dhikr mā lā yaʿtaqiduhu*)."[135] (I remind the reader of the

[132] al-Tanūkhī, *Nishwār* IV, 59. This opinion all but echoes another (written so as to explain a scandalous gesture by an earlier poet): "He did this merely by way of *mujūn*, but he was not irreligious (*innamā faʿala dhālika mujūnan wa-lam yakun radī' al-dīn*)." See Ibn al-Muʿtazz, *Ṭabaqāt* 40. (Also see Ibn al-Muʿtazz, *Ṭabaqāt* 146.)

[133] al-Haytamī, *Zawājir* II, 211.

[134] Yāqūt, *Udabā'* V, 2334.

[135] al-Bayhaqī, *Maḥāsin* 268. In another, rather dissimilar version of the same story, the poet himself is cited as making a comparable claim: "By God, nothing but Islam is my religion, but *mujūn* will occasionally carry me away so that I say monstrous things (*lā, wallāhi, lā adīnu ghayr al-islām wa-lākin rubbamā nazā bī al-mujūn ḥattā atanāwala l-ʿaẓā'im*)." See Abū Hiffān, *Akhbār* 38 (and cf. op.cit. 49 on the religiosity of Abū Nuwās); and a different wording of what is practically the same assertion in Ibn Manẓūr, *Akhbār* 198. Another specialist in the oeuvre of Abū Nuwās, Ibn al-Muzarraʿ (fl. early 4th/10th c.), also insists on Abū Nuwās having been a true believer despite all the frivolities and blasphemies he stuffed his verses with, and so does Ḥamza al-Iṣbahānī (on the authority of some members of the Nawbakht family). See Ibn al-Muzarraʿ, *Sariqāt* 144, 146; Abū Nuwās, *Dīwān* V,

observation made in the previous chapter that at least some mediaeval Muslim jurisprudents made a distinction between serious affronts to basic Islamic norms, which they regarded as proofs of unbelief (*kufr*), and mere *mujūn*, which they did not.) Clearly mediaeval Muslims considered it quite possible that *mujūn* might be a mere convention witty intellectuals were expected to try their hands at, rather than the spontaneous spurt of a shameless soul. Moreover, it will be noted that even the most incorrigible reprobates among the libertine poets and writers would sometimes have their episodes of (perhaps genuine) repentance; and perplexingly, some of them would occasionally go as far as to produce works denying any involvement in illicit or immoral activities.[136] Conversely, it would be mistaken to assume that morally upright persons, for all their pious advice to others, would never engage in a bit of discreet or not-so-discreet revelry.[137] Words, whether frivolous or pious, cannot always be taken at face value.

Thus, one cannot state with absolute certainty the 'sincerity' of the self-portrayal of even the most infamous, proverbial libertines, and perhaps surprisingly, there might be reason to question many aspects of the much vaunted depravity of poets and writers quite emblematic of *mujūn*. Abū Nuwās – arguably the best-known libertine that Arabic poetry has ever produced – is a case in point. It has been suggested (*v. s.*) that his actual religious convictions were in fact very dissimilar to the scandalous statements to be found in many of his poems. It has also been suggested that, for all his notoriety in this respect, he was not in fact a homosexual at all, only cultivating this poetic theme to enhance his reputation as a libertine. I am not advocating the idea that these suggestions are to be accepted as true; indeed my impression is that Abū Nuwās must have had a frivolous attitude to practically all serious matters, including religious orthodoxy, and to me the evidence for Abū Nuwās's homosexuality appears to be compelling and the counter-evidence meagre.[138]

335–6. All this despite the striking and well-known disregard of this poet for ordinary religious sensibilities, an attitude summed up by the littérateur al-Ṣūlī thus: "I have never seen anyone as extravagant with [talk that betrays] unbelief, as steady in making it public, and as persistent in being frivolous about the Quran as Abū Nuwās... (*mā ra'aytu aḥadan ashadd badhkhan bi-l-kufr min Abī Nuwās wa-lā akthar iẓhāran lahu minhu wa-lā adwam taʿabbuthan bi-l-Qur'ān*)". See al-Thaʿālibī, *Iqtibās* II, 202.

[136] The most ludicrous claim may easily be one in a poem disavowing all kinds of immorality ("*wa-lastu bi-fāsiqin...*" etc.) that was composed Ḥusayn b. al-Ḍaḥḥāk, one the most notorious libertines of the early Abbasid period. See al-Iṣfahānī, *Aghānī* VII, 241.

[137] E.g. Abū Hiffān, *Akhbār* 56–7.

[138] The indiscreet homosexuality of who was undeniably one of the greatest poets of all time in the Arabic language has been a continuing embarrassment for a lot of intellectuals in later generations. (It is even more of an embarrassment today, if all the brutal bowdlerising going on in contemporary editions of the poet's *oeuvre* is anything to go by.) I believe this uneasiness explains the palpable enthusiasm of many authorities (especially in the modern period) about the story of the poet's supposed infatuation with the slave-girl Janān, a minor episode in his life at best, a sarcastic joke at worst. A

However, the point is that one should never take for granted that a libertine's literary self-portrayal is a true mirror of his lifestyle and convictions. Apparently, the possibility that *mujūn* may be a mere literary posture, an affectation bearing little resemblance to the author's real self, was recognised and reckoned with by mediaeval Muslim literary experts, as has been illustrated above. The obvious practical consequence for the modern researcher is that each individual case is to be judged on its own merits – supposing one finds this line of research an interesting and fruitful one – and hardly any judgements can be made that will not be open to differing interpretations and controversy.

One observation that all the foregoing evidence allows us to make is that mediaeval Muslims had definite expectations of how a libertine – or for that matter, a religious dignitary, a political leader, a patriarch, and so on – should typically behave and express himself. As has been argued, this does not mean that any given individual was expected always and unfailingly to conform to the same expectations regardless of the situation – quite the contrary – but 'the libertine' was nevertheless a recognisable type of person with a recognisable set of behavioural and communicational attributes. A *mājin* intellectual tended to display so predictable characteristics and conduct that it strikes the modern reader as a sort of ritualised role-playing. Indeed for a relatively fixed and recognisable social type such as this, many sociologists have been using the technical term *social role*, and I believe it is not too far-fetched to apply this term to the version of 'the libertine' known in mediaeval Muslim urban society. Before laying out some of the reasons why I find this term both applicable to *mujūn* and helpful in explaining it, a precise definition is in order, which I borrow from William J. Goode. A social role is

source makes the claim that the real Janān, who was a slave-woman in Sāmarrā, made a decidedly unprepossessing sight to look at, and Abū Nuwās, uninterested as he was in women (*lam yakun yuʿtaddu bi-l-nisāʾ wa-lā yuʿrafu bi-ʿishqihinna*), wrote love poems to her out of mischievous humour (*wa-lam takun fī mawḍiʿ ʿishq wa-lā kāna madhhab Abī Nuwās al-nisāʾ wa-lākinnahu ʿabath kharaja minhu*). Even those authorities who view the poems about Janān as an expression of genuine feeling for her tend to agree that Abū Nuwās never entertained amorous sentiments for another woman (e.g. "*lam yaṣduq fī ḥubbihi imraʾa ghayrahā*"). I find it more probable that love poems addressed to Janān were the poet's way of showing his mastery of the genre of *al-ghazal bi-l-muʾannath*, love poetry addressed to a woman. Incidentally, Abū Nuwās is claimed to have married a woman towards the end of his life, but turned even this occasion into a full-blown scandal by escaping from the wedding with a group of boys. In any case, Abū Nuwās became the ultimate emblem of homosexuality in the Arabic-speaking world. See al-Iṣfahānī, *Aghānī* XX, 71, 74, 77–8; Abū Hiffān, *Akhbār* 27, 28, 106; Ibn Manẓūr, *Akhbār* 163; and cf. Ingrams 1933: 28. The significance of a minor poet like Naṣr b. Aḥmad al-Khubzaruzzī (d. 327/938–9) was apparently not sufficient to occasion such controversies, and therefore his homosexuality has not been disputed or glossed over. See al-Thaʿālibī, *Yatīma* II, 366; Yāqūt, *Udabāʾ* VI, 2745. However, when all is said and done I cannot but agree with J. S. Meisami that the issue of the 'sincerity' of a poetic persona in this regard is ultimately irrelevant; see Meisami 1993: 17–8.

> a set of mutual (but not necessarily harmonious) expectations of behavior between two or more actors, with reference to a particular type of situation. These expectations are backed by normatively based sanctions applied by ego, alter, and others. Thus, both ego and alter know, or believe they know, what the other will, in fact, do in the situation. The expectations are both cognitive and normative.[139]

Here we have to make a distinction between the related but different concepts of social role and status. There does not appear to be a sharp difference between them, but it is still possible to treat them as separate concepts. 'Status' tends to be understood by sociologists as an ideal, a position far more institutionalised than a 'role' is; while 'role' is typically treated in terms of real behaviour (as opposed to ideals), especially in the course of social interactions between two (or more) people. In a real-life interaction, a person may fulfil or fail to fulfil the expectations attendant on his perceived role – and assessments of whether and how he does fulfil them in a concrete situation can differ dramatically – and this introduces a great deal of fluidity into the actual performance of a role.[140] As a society becomes more and more complex – for instance by way of the process of urbanisation and the growing division of labour – the tendency is that the number of possible social roles will increase, giving individuals a greater range of choice in assuming their own role in social interactions.[141] Putting terminological questions aside, I prefer to make use of the concept of *social role*, rather than status, as a useful tool for the purposes of this analysis.

In essence, I contend that the role of a libertine (*mājin*) intellectual in mediaeval Islamic urban culture came to be so well-established and its attendant discourse and behavioural traits so conventionalised and predictable that it is possible and meaningful to understand the *mājin* as a *social role* in the usual sociological sense of the term. In treating *mujūn* in terms of a social role, it is necessary to emphasise that a role is by no means a mere theoretical construct of sociologists but an entity even ordinary people in the society are fully aware of. As the anthropologist S. F. Nadel pointed out, speakers of a language tend to give a name to every social role, and this labelling clearly indicates their recognition of the existence of those distinct

---

139 Goode 1960: 249. Also cf. Banton 1969: 28; and Sherif 1936: 52–3.

140 Goode 1960: 247–9. Because to some extent a 'role' does involve an idealised, abstract set of expectations, T. H. Newcomb proposed that the actual performance of a role in daily life should be called 'role behaviour'; see Banton 1969: 26–7. (I will not adopt this further distinction in this study.) – Outside of sociological research, one occasionally finds social roles being referred to in quite inappropriate terms. In an interesting article on the boon-companions (*nudamā'*) of caliphs and other rulers – a social role if ever there was one – such people are talked of as a 'class' ("[they] constituted a class by themselves"), although it is hard to believe the author would mean 'class' in its sociological sense. See Chejne 1965: 327.

141 Benedict 1966: 25–6.

roles as 'ready-made' models of behaviour.[142] This is obviously the case with 'the libertine' in mediaeval Islamicate society.

There are further reasons that allow *mujūn* to be interpreted as a distinct and recognised social role. Firstly, one such reason is that roles are by definition neither exclusive nor perpetual: the same person may play quite a number of different roles as he or she grows older, and even at the same age but in different situations.[143] This feature of a social role is clearly applicable to libertine careers in view of the evidence presented in this book. Secondly, the discourse and behaviour associated with a certain role tend to follow highly conventional patterns, which *mujūn* obviously did. And thirdly, roles are not a petrified, rigid set of prefabricated rules that the incumbent will follow in a mechanical, robotic fashion; social actors display different degrees of loyalty to their roles and different skills in performing role expectations. A half-hearted and clumsy football player is still perceived as playing the role of 'football player' as long as he is tottering on the field. Likewise, the ranks of *mājin* intellectuals ranged from the few notorious chartered libertines – such as Abū Nuwās, Abū Dulāma or Ibn al-Ḥajjāj – to what may half-jokingly be called 'recreational' libertines (people who only occasionally amused themselves with *mujūn* in private settings) to those who only rarely wrote and never did *mujūn*. As hinted at above, any person's performance of a role in a given situation is open to differing assessments (his own, and those of other participants in the situation as well as onlookers). Previous expectations may differ to a considerable extent; some people are more fastidious than others in judging their own or others' actions; and in addition to all these factors, two participants in a social interaction may have totally different understandings of the nature of the situation.[144] Thus, instead of slavish conformity to clear-cut rules, the enacting of a social role is best understood as *an effort or attempt* to conform, one always fraught with potential ambiguity, misapprehension and conflict. In this context, I remind the reader of the many cases (reviewed in the previous chapter) of people's misjudging the privateness or publicness of a situation and the resulting conflicts.

It is possible to categorise roles according to varying criteria (although to me all such criteria seem ultimately related). Thus, roles may be either vague and negotiable

[142] Banton 1969: 28.

[143] Banton 1969: 127, 131, 139; and cf. El-Rouayheb 2005: 11–2.

[144] Goode 1960: 249; Banton 1969: 150. The anthropologist Lawrence Rosen offers some discerning insights into social relations in a Moroccan town, the general principles of which seem to be by and large applicable to the milieu that sustained mediaeval Muslim libertines. Interpersonal relationships in Sefrou generate certain expectations as to the proper behaviour each participant should display; however, every participant may understand the situation and their own role in it differently, and even when the general character of the situation is roughly clear, "different individuals may draw on the repertoire of relational possibilities differently". See Rosen 1984: 163–4.

or rigid and conventionalised (e.g. the role of 'friend' is obviously of the former category, and that of 'patient' more like the latter); they may involve either a lot of or just a little prescribed behaviour; and they also differ in the extent to which they inform the whole life of a person. This last criterion allows us to distinguish roles that are 'highly pervasive' – those seen as "central definitional aspects of a person's identity" – from those that are not.[145] Whether the role of 'libertine' among mediaeval Muslims was a pervasive one is a difficult question, and the answer must vary from case to case.

It has been proposed – not unreasonably – that the more pervasive a role is the more conventionalised the discourse associated with it tends to be. So much so that some highly pervasive roles may actually be all but defined by their particular style or form of discourse that everyone who aspires to the role is expected to become proficient in.[146] There is no doubt that libertines did develop their conventionalised form of discourse (or significant speech style[147]) – the kind of talk and/or literature mediaeval Muslims labelled *mujūn* – which is the subject of this book. In this sense, the role of *mājin* was a highly pervasive one. However, commitment to the libertine lifestyle varied from person to person, and it would be difficult to claim that a high dignitary who would play the *mājin* during drinking parties among good friends but return to a respectable job and family life at all other times qualifies for a 'highly pervasive' identity as a libertine. Thus the role of 'libertine' was pervasive in some cases and definitely not pervasive in others. It is perhaps rather common that very conspicuous roles with a peculiar style of speech and behaviour which evoke mixed reactions from the society should attract people to differing degrees, with some incumbents fully identifying with the role and others wavering on the periphery. The hard core of *mujūn* was composed of men like Abū Nuwās who had no qualms about being identified as shameless libertines; and that is certainly a pervasive role. On the other hand, it seems that many intellectuals would make literary or real-life forays, so to speak, into *mujūn* by way of entertainment but stop short of letting the label of 'libertine' stick to them.[148] For these men, being a *mājin* was most definitely an occasional role at most. And then there was a presumably far more numerous category which comprised the passive audience of *mujūn*: urban dwellers

---

145 Foley 1997: 311. For a slightly different but related classification of roles into *basic* (all but inescapable), *general* (highly pervasive) and *independent* (informal and casual) ones, see Banton 1969: 39–40.

146 Foley 1997: 359.

147 A technical term used by Dell Hymes and defined by him thus: "The criterion of a *significant speech style* is that it can be recognized, and used, outside its defining context, that is, by persons or in places other than those with which its typical meaning is associated, or contrasted with relation to the persons and places with one or more other styles." See Hymes 1974: 440.

148 Cf. Crone, Moreh 2000: 174–5.

– in a large proportion intellectuals but also traders, musicians, singers, commoners, all classes of youngsters – who liked the works of libertines and enjoyed their conversation. Such people might still be referred to as *mujjān* (pl. of *mājin*) insofar as they participated in a less than respectable event and listened to indecorous talk, but only in this single context. The label of *mājin* therefore signifies quite miscellaneous a category. As mentioned above, it certainly included people who led a decidedly nonconformist life, with perhaps many if not most of them quitting as they got older. The following passage, while it is not about libertines as such, still sheds some light on what the ingredients of a nonconformist lifestyle may have been:

> [...] It is said that a number of young men (*fityān*) came together as a group of equals, everyone among them being well-to-do, a fugitive from his kin, and content [to live] with his friends. One of them recounted: "We rented a house in a lane off a busy and populous street of Baghdad. We didn't see it as extravagant at all (*lā nastakthiru*) that one single person among us, provided he had the means, should cover all our expenses, nor that one of us, provided he had nothing, should be forever paid for by the rest. So, when we had the money, we ate the best food, wore the finest clothes, and invited male and female entertainers [to the house] (*daʿawnā l-mulhīn wa-l-mulhiyāt*), staying [at such occasions] on the ground floor. When there was no music to listen to, we'd sit in a room [on the upper floor] (*ghurfa*) to have fun looking at the passersby. Date-wine we'd never do without, whether we had money or not, even if we had to sell some of our clothes..."[149]

[149] al-Bayhaqī, *Maḥāsin* 261. The use of the noun *fityān* ('young men') at the beginning of the excerpt appears to be a reference to the well-known phenomenon of *futuwwa*, urban groups of young men with a range of functions, but often serving as a sort of urban militias. However, it is fairly obvious that here it is not the militarised variety of a *futuwwa* community that one reads about but a coterie of friends who for some reason – shameful conduct perhaps? – had had to leave their families and whose main aim was to be merry and have fun. The similarities with libertines are clear. (I have no evidence that libertines would typically have been ostracised by their kin – although in some cases they were, they would mostly face only reprimands. Entertainment and frequent drinking was, however, a typical feature of the *mājin* lifestyle.) On the possible connexions between the early phase of *futuwwa* and *ẓarf*, cf. Enderwitz 1989: 125, 127–9. A rather enigmatic text from the 6th/12th century also shows vague links to hardcore libertines and their spirit, but I find it altogether hard to interpret it with any certainty. The subject-matter of this text is certainly not libertinism but a type of transgressor called *ibāḥatī* ('permissive'), which seems to refer to a sort of heresy. (It is not clear to me if the label was the self-identification of the group or a contemptuous epithet invented by outsiders.) An added factor of ambiguity is the fact that whereas the greater part of the text seems to describe a kind of antinomian heresy with a set of explicit tenets (even though sarcasm may conceivably be at play), the cited verse and the accompanying explanation almost certainly originates in the domain of *mujūn*, being as it is a frivolous, cynical poetical conceit rather than a positive religious principle. And now to the text: "[*Ibāḥatī*] is an adjective referring to a group (*ṭāʾifa*) of accursed infidels, for the reference is to the permitting of things prohibited by the *sharīʿa*. They say: 'Do whatever you would, and you will commit no sin.' Their abominable belief (*iʿtiqāduhum al-khabīth*) holds that the world belonged to Adam, who

Having argued that it is possible to analyse libertinism in terms of a social role, it is here, towards the end of my essay, that I find it opportune to say a few words about whether the sociological concept of 'deviance' is applicable to *mujūn* so as to gain a better understanding of the latter. In fact by having deliberately avoided the use of the term 'deviance' so far in this book, I have already committed myself to a negative answer and given an indication thereof. While quite a few roles in any society can obviously be classified as 'deviant', I do not believe that the role of libertine would qualify without stretching the concept too far. Surely much depends on how one will define 'deviance'[150], yet whatever the definition, *mujūn* seems to be a very special case having so little resemblance to unequivocally deviant social roles – such as those of 'alcoholic' or 'tramp' or 'beggar' – that applying the same term to categorise it would be positively misleading. The mere fact that a libertine did prohibited or undignified things – drinking wine, squandering money on diversion, or having illicit sex – does not necessarily make his role a deviant one; the most prestigious elements in the society also did such things from time to time. Deviant acts are ubiquitous, deviant roles are not. Occasional deviant behaviour,

---

then left it as a heritage to his descendants, so who decided what is permitted and what is prohibited? Who could ever permit this and prohibit that, [given that] everything belongs to the descendants of Adam? Sheep and pig, as well as their flesh, are equal in their eyes. By way of proof, they will cite the following Quran verse [7:32], which they interpret according to their nefarious views: '*Say: Who has forbidden the ornament of God which He brought forth for His servants, and the good things of His providing?*' [They opine that] it is equally licit to sleep with one's mother and wife, and '*they say: There is nothing but our present life; we die, and we live, and nothing but Time destroys us.*' [Quran 45:24]. Nay, some of them would even recite the following verse: '*Gamble, sodomise, drink openly, and always cite the words of some imam [to justify your conduct] (qāmir wa-luṭ wa-ʾshrab jahāran wa-ʾḥtajij fī kulli masʾalatin bi-qawli imāmi)!*' This verse is [an ironic] repartee at [the expense of] the imams of the Muslims, alluding to the fact that al-Shāfiʿī considers chess permissible, as does Mālik anal intercourse with women and Abū Ḥanīfa the drinking of date-wine – may God have mercy on all [three] of them!..." See al-Samʿānī, *Ansāb* I, 69.

[150] Deviance is sometimes defined simply as the lack of conformity to norms (or to a given norm). However, such a simplistic dichotomy seems to be quite problematic. Other sociologists give deviance the meaning of an act subject to penalisation. Yet another possible definition is that advanced by J. M. Marques and R. G. Serôdio, for whom "a deviant act is one which endangers the value attributed to the ingroup". See Testé 2003: 17–8, 20. Some specialists, like N. K. Denzin, seem to give 'deviance' a meaning so broad as to include any type of behaviour that just about anyone views with disapproval – for instance, a married couple having a quarrel. In this conception, deviance is not a definable category (not even a vague one), but a continuum that extends all the way to peevishness and the tedious repetition of a familiar story. Denzin also states that deviance may be admired and envied by some outsiders, citing the Hell's Angels and similar groups as an example. (While that is true, it is questionable if 'people who matter' – the political and cultural élite – were ever quite so appreciative of such gangs.) See Denzin 1970: 132–3, 138. Of course, in this broadest of senses *mujūn* – and just about anything else – *is* deviance, and all people deviant. However, I prefer to use the term in a more restricted sense which excludes both occasional imperfections that every person is prone to and activities that a substantial part of the élite values highly.

which practically everyone engages in at times, is to be distinguished from fixed social roles recognised to be deviant. The latter have characteristic attributes and are associated with recognisable patterns of behaviour, and expectations are as clear as in the case of more respectable roles. Low prestige seems to be an important aspect of deviant roles.[151] It is this factor that makes it particularly problematic to treat libertinism as a deviant social role: it has been argued above that a great deal of the ambiguous reception and status of *mujūn* resulted from its distinct value content. *Mujūn* was both objectionable and delectable, and its prestige, accordingly, somewhat ambivalent because of its widely recognised positive quality, *ẓarf*.

The important thing here is that libertines were not only *tolerated* but further *admired* for their wit. This is what really sets it apart from deviance. Toleration would not in itself suffice: some fully deviant activities are also found to be tolerated in all societies, and sanctions are often lenient as well as variable; indeed informal ways of sanctioning are as often as not preferred to legal ones, and there tends to be a (shifting, unpredictable and situational) 'margin of tolerance' that allows a certain degree of deviance to go unpunished.[152]

All things considered, mediaeval Muslim perceptions of *mujūn* can hardly be described with the term 'deviance', even though there is no denying the general disapproval of what was seen as the immorality and impropriety of libertines. (As shown above, even libertines themselves quite accepted this characterisation of their activity.) However, deviance proper does not fare highly on any normative value scale, neither does it elicit the praise of the highest echelons of society, which *mujūn* routinely did. Unlike the unmitigated negative image of a deviant role, libertinism did have saving graces, and important ones too, hence its ambiguous reception within all levels of the society, including the cultural and political élite.

Mujūn meant the flouting of all ordinary norms of speech and behaviour, and for that it was viewed with disapproval. That it developed its conventions and ended up being a distinct social role accorded it toleration. That it involved a quality highly valued by the higher classes of mediaeval Muslim society – namely, sophistication and wit (*ẓarf*) – gave it a certain lustre and prestige. When they had become incumbents of a recognised social role through the conventionalisation of their antics, libertines came to be a familiar phenomenon to most urban dwellers, and a familiar phenomenon, be it ever so unseemly, is relatively easy to live with and relate to – it is unthreatening. This familiarity, coupled with the considerable value

---

[151] *Prestige*, which is a property of the social role, is not to be confused with *esteem*, which results from and varies with a person's good or bad performance in enacting the role. Esteem thus serves as basis for judging individuals, prestige as the measure of comparing roles. See Banton 1969: 37.

[152] Denzin 1970: 122–5; Testé 2003: 22, 24; Clinard 1965: 19–20; and also cf. Goode 1960: 255–6.

attached to the most salient attribute of a *mājin* – his sophistication and wit – could not but confer upon him a measure of social acceptance, even esteem of a sort. The reception of *mujūn* shows that norm-breaking may itself have its norms, and disrepute – if acquired in the proper manner – may prove quite profitable.

Afterword: On Defining *Mujūn*

In the first chapter of this book, attempts at defining *mujūn* were briefly discussed, and the difficulty of offering a neat and totally satisfactory definition stressed. Having had a look into some of the typical motifs of literary *mujūn*, surveyed the reactions of the various social classes to the phenomenon, and proposed possible explanations of the remarkable tolerance of *mujūn* among mediaeval Muslims, this essay might well be expected to offer a definition of its own. After all, *mujūn* being the main subject of the book, it is not unreasonable to presume that it ought at least to be defined – if no sooner, at least at the end of a long study. However, the complexity of the picture that has unfolded before our eyes quite possibly makes the task not easier but more difficult than at the outset.

We have noted that the different social classes had different norms of conduct to observe, and within one social class norms of acceptable behaviour differed in accordance with the nature of the situation. Furthermore, even in the same situation the various social actors might well have differing understandings of it. Obviously, personality played an additional role of considerable importance. This fluidity and ambiguity of applicable norms could not have failed to affect perceptions of what was to be considered a transgression of norms. One person might judge a given type of behaviour or a certain line of poetry quite transgressive while another could regard it, if perhaps slightly light-hearted, yet well within the bounds of propriety. This ambiguity is reflected in the great heterogeneity of the material labelled *mujūn* in mediaeval Arabic sources, which after all are our only guide as to what was, or could potentially be, perceived as constituting *mujūn*. The inescapable conclusion is that *mujūn* was an extraordinarily vague term whose application depended on a lot of variables. Indeed, this continues to be the case. More than one person who took the time to read the first draft of the manuscript of this book reacted to this or that motif mentioned in the second and third chapters of the book by pointing out that the motif in question actually did not sound outrageous at all to them. How anyone could object to such harmless pieces of drollery and label them 'libertinism' is a question that was formulated in various ways by these readers. It is a valid question but ultimately an unresolvable one, as all questions concerning value judgements are. At the end of the day, *mujūn* was and is in the eye of the beholder.

I have stressed in the first chapter that *mujūn* is definitely not a separate literary genre comparable to, say, love poetry (*ghazal*) or panegyrics (*madīḥ*) or invective verse (*hijāʾ*) despite the sporadic existence of separate sections in poetic *dīwān*s sporting the heading *mujūniyyāt*. The use of that title is deceptive for various reasons, the most important one in my opinion being that pieces lumped together in the special '*mujūn* section' of a book may, and often expressly do, belong to other definable genres including those just mentioned. In the *mujūn* section of the collected poems of Abū Nuwās one finds lampoons, love poetry, bacchic poems and a lot of other content that can easily be identified as belonging to some known genre of Arabic poetry. With so much overlap between *mujūn* and well-defined genres, it is in my view meaningless to speak of it as a separate genre – it is an altogether different category. Furthermore, there is usually no mistaking a panegyric or an elegy, which – to put it mildly – cannot be said of *mujūn*. *Mujūn* shows a tendency to prey on (quote or allude to) texts representing 'serious' genres and 'respectable', normative tradition, and turn them to parodistic uses. The parodistic tendencies of *mujūn* literature prompted J. S. Meisami to call *mujūn* "a counter-genre which inverts the conventions" of the traditional, serious genres of Arabic poetry.[1] This strongly suggests that *mujūn* is something very special, not just an ordinary genre, one among many that could be treated analogously to the rest.

Because of the lack of agreement as to where the exact boundaries of *mujūn* lay, it is inadvisable to try to work out our own guidelines of qualifying or disqualifying, including or excluding, anything as *mujūn*. Instead, I propose that in handling such a fuzzy notion as *mujūn* it is best to rely on the instincts and conceptions of authors chronologically closer to the phenomenon. As hinted above, our best help, or indeed our sole help, in identifying any type of material as *mujūn* is the application of that label to it in some primary source. The epithet is used in two typical ways. In some works (especially some *adab* collections and the *dīwāns* of certain poets), *mujūn* is treated in a separate chapter carrying this heading. In other instances, *mujūn* of various types is scattered over other types of content and where it occurs it may or may not be explicitly identified as such; here we should be concerned only with those cases where it is. Both kinds of reference to *mujūn* are equally helpful. Given that mediaeval Arabic dictionaries offer so opaque definitions and apparently assume the term to be self-evident, without these explicit references there would be practically nothing to rely on. This is all we have, full stop. In other words, what I would advocate is to take the label *mujūn* seriously wherever it appears in Arabic works of belles-lettres, no matter how incongruous some of the material so classified might be with our current notions of 'libertinism' or 'licentiousness'. Surely this approach – which is more or less what I tried to follow in the preceding chapters – will result

[1] Meisami 1993: 19.

in some degree of overreaching: whatever any author anywhere ever perceived (or by oversight misplaced in his anthology) as *mujūn* will be admitted as such. One result and sign of this problem is the inevitable question, noted and commented on above: "How could anyone ever object to such a harmless piece of drollery and label it libertinism?" But the fact is that at least someone, somewhere, once did.

Even a cursory look into the sections on *mujūn* in anthologies and other collections shows that the material is strikingly heterogeneous. I will rely here on three such texts to form an idea of what the concept entailed. Each widely known and acclaimed and popular, all three works contain material explicitly identified as *mujūn* in the chapter heading and treated as such apart from other types of material; and some of them repeatedly and emphatically use that label within the chapters' text too in reference to certain motifs. The three texts are the following: the twelfth section (*bāb*) of Ḥamza al-Iṣbahānī's recension of the *Dīwān* of Abū Nuwās (first half of the 4th/10th c.), the eighteenth night in al-Tawḥīdī's *Kitāb al-imtāʿ wa-l-muʾānasa* (late 4th/10th c.), and the sixteenth thematic category (*ḥadd*) in al-Rāghib al-Iṣbahānī's *Muḥāḍarāt al-udabāʾ* (late 5th/11th c.).

This selection of *mujūn* texts contains poetry as well as prose, and obvious candidates for the status of *mujūn* as well as less self-evident ones. Composed exclusively of texts explicitly stated to represent *mujūn*, the sample must surely help define the concept. So what do we find in these sections? It is fair to say that between them they contain most of the selection of themes and motifs presented in Chapters Two and Three of this book.

To start with the *Dīwān* of Abū Nuwās, we find a remarkably heterogeneous collection of material presented as *mujūn*. Some of the themes – for instance, obscene language and images, vivid, explicit descriptions of sex as well as caustic innuendoes – are obviously classifiable as *mujūn*, and few would have failed to recognise them as such. All this being close to the modern Western understanding of the 'bawdy' and needing little familiarity with specifically Islamicate cultural concepts, this type of material is also what is most commonly identified as *mujūn* in the secondary literature. Sex is evidently a subject closely associated with *mujūn* – it is easy to be indecent about. Thus the praise of affairs with boys and arguments for preferring them to women is not difficult to recognise as *mujūn*; verses on preferring women to boys (there is one single poem of that kind attributed, rightly or wrongly, to Abū Nuwās) are not so obvious a case, but their presence in the section on *mujūn* is comprehensible if one recalls the fact that the whole topic of women versus boys was meant as something of a burlesque. Love poetry (*ghazal*) in itself was a respectable genre, even if pious scholars had their reservations. It may therefore come as something of a surprise that the chapter on *mujūn* contains a lot of poems belonging to this genre, a reminder of the fact that *mujūn* cut across boundaries of genres. Thus one encounters examples of love poetry addressed to various categories of persons: street boys and aggressive urchins armed with daggers, boys working in the state bureaus or studying in the Quranic school, boys met in the mosque, Christian and Zoroastrian boys. Making references to the religious terminology and imagery of those non-Muslim communities, this last-mentioned class of poems takes us to the other large category of *mujūn*: texts playing with religious texts and concepts instead of norms of common propriety. To be sure, this category is also amply represented in the *mujūn* section of the *Dīwān*. We find a lot of humorous *iqtibās* (some of it in fairly harmless contexts but nevertheless classified as *mujūn*); many uses of parodistic *isnād*; the lampooning of Ramadan and complaints about the difficulty of fasting (*hijāʾ Ramaḍān*); mock advice poetry – in some cases outright 'anti-sermons' – urging people to have no restraint in seeking illicit pleasure; expressions of the poet's insistence on following his own sinful ways and his rejection of the pious reproachers' advice; verses making light of the threat of Hell and containing frivolous appeals to God's mercy and His forgiveness of all sins.

Some motifs are not easily recognisable to a contemporary Westerner as 'libertinism', and it seems to be their parodistic intent that justified their being classified as such. Parody is heavily represented in the corpus of Abū Nuwās's *mujūn*. Such motifs include parodies of the *aṭlāl* motif of ancient Arabic odes; imitations of the speech of madmen or maniacs; humorous uses of proverb-like expressions, Persian phrases, riddles and puns; seemingly ordinary poems in a traditional Bedouin style so exaggerated that, according to Ḥamza al-Iṣbahānī, it must be meant as mockery (*sukhrī*); the use of tropes that appear to be so over-the-top, unconventional and bizarre as to be funny (and probably sarcastic). Poems speaking of the poet's lack of heroism and his preference of entertainment to brave exploits can also be understood as a parody of the characteristic tone of early Arabic tribal poetry.

The section on *mujūn* ends with miscellaneous material consisting of prose anecdotes featuring Abū Nuwās, some of them hardly offensive at all, just examples of quick repartee that silences the opponent (a proof of a man's *ẓarf*, as we will recall); as well as his jestful correspondence with friends, which again contains nothing patently offensive or obscene – perhaps the style was so exaggeratedly courteous and compliment-laden that it appeared to be parodistic.

The *Kitāb al-imtāʿ wa-l-muʾānasa* offers a similarly variegated material, most of it in prose. Since much of it represents the same types of themes and motifs that have just been listed with regard to the *Dīwān* of Abū Nuwās, I am giving only a very brief inventory here. One finds, for instance, lots of humorous *iqtibās*; the theme of *hijāʾ Ramaḍān*; a mock *fatwā* by al-Shaʿbī to a stupid petitioner; a prose invective (*hijāʾ*) with some religious imagery that can hardly be characterised as very offensive; metaphors with very slight references to religious concepts (and no vulgarity involved); descriptions of sex with boys and praise of sodomising them; descriptions of the promiscuity of today's women (and men) and of the lack of romantic sentiments among them; expressions of unheroic attitudes in talk and poetry; descriptions of one's own gluttony and praises of certain foods; obscenities and scatological humour; a joke featuring Juḥā (with no obscenity or blasphemous motifs in it). Linguistic humour – most of it showing no trace of vulgarity at all – is amply represented in the selection: instances of double entendre based on grammatical terms; parody of the affected 'classical' speech style (*taqaʿʿur*) of grammarians; examples of quick repartee designed to silence the opponent; examples of apposite phrases in Classical Arabic and in the vernacular; many apposite, witty phrases used by commoners and by *mukhannath* men; an inventive (and somewhat folksy) torrent of abuse with some religious references but no real vulgarity; the boasts of a vagabond remarkable for their slight vulgarity and creative similes; imitations of the clumsy style of common people. On the whole, here again it is remarkable how much of this collection of material is not patently offensive to a modern Western observer.

The chapter on *mujūn* and *sukhf* in the *Muḥāḍarāt al-udabāʾ* is composed of material that appears considerably less varied than the selections just reviewed. It is divided into four main thematic subsections, devoted respectively to depictions of illicit sex (sodomy, boy prostitutes, passive homosexuality, effeminacy, forms of non-consensual sex, prostitution and pimps, fornication), descriptions of the sexual organs and intercourse, lesbianism, and scatology (to be more precise, the theme of farting). As can be seen, this material seems to be restricted basically to two topics: sex and embarrassing bodily functions. At first sight, nothing that I discussed in Chapter Two appears in this selection. However, within the chapter we do find examples of varied types of *mujūn* already discussed, including motifs having to do with religion. Examples include lots of humorous *iqtibās*, the use of mock *isnād*, parodistic *fatwās*, apposite and/or frivolous remarks, quick ripostes, references to Islamic eschatological concepts in mundane contexts, playful metaphorical references to the religious obligations (e. g. the *zakāt* and the pilgrimage), jesting arguments in favour of preferring males and females respectively as sexual partners, descriptions of one's own sexual impotence, instances of double entendre based on theological and grammatical terms, praise of the facial hair (*ʿidhār*) of adolescent boys, invective poems with or without explicit vulgarities, parodies of well-known pre-Islamic verses, jokes, and so on.

In the light of this combined material of the three collections, our modern perceptions of 'offensiveness' are clearly no guidance, indeed hardly any help at all, in trying to define *mujūn*. The overall impression is that sections on *mujūn* served as a container into which to deposit anything which was found lacking in decency or seriousness, or felt to be parodistic or low-brow or otherwise departing from the usual norms of polite literature. It is obvious from the above survey of the material that the concept of 'offensiveness' – especially as interpreted by a modern observer – is simply irrelevant. Exactly what is 'offensive' about an apposite saying applied ironically at the right moment, or about a parodistic twist on an old Arabic poetic motif? Surely, if someone is quick to take offence, he might find both 'offensive', but that is beside the point when we try to define *mujūn.* Indeed, the issue of 'offensiveness' invites more questions that it answers. In precisely what ways are these motifs 'offensive', and more crucially, to whom? And then, how 'offensive' could they be to an anthologist who, after all, did select them as being worthy of inclusion in his collection?

Despite the heterogeneous nature of the *mujūn* material, some unifying factors can be identified. One constant seems to be that *mujūn* is always tongue-in-cheek – it is almost by definition in the jesting mode (*hazl*). However, the contours of the jesting mode are themselves ambiguous – and what is more, sometimes the ambiguity is purposeful – and therefore this guideline is not an absolute one. Moreover, not everything uttered or recorded in jest was meant and perceived as *mujūn.* Still, it is safe to assume that *mujūn,* however coarse or rude on occasion, is closely associated with playfulness and humour. Secondly, *mujūn* is always associated with transgressing ordinary norms, even though, as noted above, norms are neither agreed upon nor clearly defined. (And recall that the transgression in a piece of *mujūn* text may be as harmless as the mocking of an old literary convention.) With the increasing conventionalisation and acceptance of *mujūn,* transgressing norms was also more and more a notional concept. Thirdly, shamelessness ('not caring'), or an affectation of it anyway, is another necessary element of *mujūn* in most cases, although this again will often be found to have been highly relative. It is easy not to care about consequences when they are likely to be in the form of amused laughter at worst and monetary rewards at best. Indiscretion was expected of libertines, and they delivered.

Traditional Muslim culture has quite a number of concepts that have no direct parallels in Western culture and thus pose a problem of translation. *Mujūn* is one of them. To define it is better accomplished through listing and sampling than through concise abstractions. I, for one, certainly find this approach preferable to trying to reduce this colourful literary and social phenomenon to a brief sentence. However, if a definition must be given, mine would be approximately as follows. *Mujūn* is any text or behaviour which is meant or perceived to constitute a breach of ordinary norms of writing or conduct, and which is meant or perceived to be jesting rather than serious. The words 'meant or perceived' are crucial for this definition, as they allow ample room for the indefiniteness of the concept and for the sometimes conflicting perceptions of whether a particular motif or behaviour is really *mujūn* (or something still more innocuous, or indeed something more serious). This ambiguity, as I hope to have sufficiently stressed, is an intrinsic part of *mujūn* and a factor in its attractiveness, and it also determined the remarkable variety of reactions to the phenomenon. Every person's norms will differ, if ever so slightly, from the next man's. Consequently, every person's *mujūn* will differ from the next man's. For a student of mediaeval Muslim culture, it is probably best to accept as *mujūn* anything that is referred to as such in the sources, no matter how inoffensive to our modern sensitivities.

Sources

In Arabic names, the definite article (*al-*) will not affect alphabetical order, according to the scholarly convention. However, in cases when an Arab author transcribes his own name in the orthography of a Western language, the spelling will be left intact and, for purposes of alphabetical order, the definite article will be regarded as part of the name. (Obviously, such cases can only occur among secondary, modern sources.) Thus, with a sacrifice of strict consistency, al-Marzūqī will appear under the letter *M*, while El-Outmani will be found under *E*.

References to secondary sources follow the system usual in the social sciences (i.e. surname of author plus year of publication), while primary sources, for better recognisability, are referred to by name of author plus first significant word in the title.

Abbreviations

AA	*American Anthropologist*
BSOAS	*Bulletin of the School of Oriental and African Studies*
EI2	The Encyclopaedia of Islam, 2nd edition (Leiden: E. J. Brill, 1960–2002)
IJMES	*International Journal of Middle East Studies*
JAL	*Journal of Arabic Literature*
JAOS	*Journal of the American Oriental Society*
JRAI	*Journal of Royal Anthropological Institute*
MIDEO	*Mélanges de l'Institut Dominicain d'Etudes Orientales du Caire*
RMMM	*Revue du Monde Musulman et de la Méditerranée*
QSA	*Quaderni di Studi Arabi*
SI	*Studia Islamica*
ZDMG	*Zeitschrift der Deutschen Morgenländischen Gesellschaft*

Primary Sources

Abū Firās, *Dīwān* = *Dīwān Abī Firās al-Ḥamdānī.* Ed. Yūsuf Shukrī Farḥāt. Beirut: Dār al-Jīl, 1413/1993.

Abū Hiffān, *Akhbār* = Abū Hiffān ʿAbdallāh b. Aḥmad b. Ḥarb al-Mihzamī, *Akhbār Abī Nuwās.* Ed. ʿAbd al-Sattār Aḥmad Farrāj. Cairo: Maktabat Miṣr, n.d.

Abū Nuwās, *Dīwān* = *Dīwān Abī Nuwās al-Ḥasan b. Hāniʾ al-Ḥakamī (Der Dīwān des Abū Nuwās).* Eds. Ewald Wagner, Gregor Schoeler. Wiesbaden: Franz Steiner Verlag [5th vol. Berlin: Klaus Schwarz Verlag], 1958–2003. [5 vols.]

al-Anbārī, *Aḍdād* = Muḥammad b. al-Qāsim al-Anbārī, *Kitāb al-aḍdād.* Ed. Muḥammad Abū l-Faḍl Ibrāhīm. Sidon, Beirut: al-Maktaba al-ʿAṣriyya, 1407/1987.

al-Andalusī, *Risāla* = Abū l-Ṣalt Umayya b. ʿAbdallāh al-Andalusī, "al-Risāla al-miṣriyya". In ʿAbd al-Salām Muḥammad Hārūn (ed.), *Nawādir al-makhṭūṭāt.* Cairo: Maktabat Muṣṭafā al-Bābī al-Ḥalabī wa-Awlādihi, 1392/1972: I, 6–56.

al-Anṭākī, *Tazyīn* = Dāwūd b. ʿUmar al-Anṭākī, *Tazyīn al-aswāq fī akhbār al-ʿushshāq.* Beirut: Dār al-Hilāl, n.d.

al-ʿAskarī, *Akhbār* = Abū Aḥmad al-Ḥasan b. ʿAbdallāh al-ʿAskarī, *Akhbār al-muṣaḥḥifīn.* Ed. Ṣubḥī al-Badrī al-Sāmarrāʾī. Beirut: Maktabat al-Nahḍa al-ʿArabiyya, 1406/1986.

al-ʿAskarī, *Maṣūn* = Abū Aḥmad al-Ḥasan b. ʿAbdallāh al-ʿAskarī, *al-Maṣūn fī l-adab.* Ed. ʿAbd al-Salām Muḥammad Hārūn. Kuwait: Maṭbaʿat Ḥukūmat al-Kuwayt, 1960.

al-ʿAskarī, *Ṣināʿatayn* = Abū Hilāl al-Ḥasan b. ʿAbdallāh al-ʿAskarī, *Kitāb al-ṣināʿatayn al-kitāba wa-l-shiʿr.* Eds. ʿAlī Muḥammad al-Bajāwī, Muḥammad Abū l-Faḍl Ibrāhīm. Cairo: ʿĪsā al-Bābī al-Ḥalabī wa-Shurakāʾuhu, n.d. [1971?].

Badr, *Risāla* = Muḥammad b. Ismāʿīl b. Muḥammad [Badr] al-Rashīd, *Tahdhīb Risālat al-Badr al-Rashīd fī l-alfāẓ al-mukaffirāt.* Beirut: Muʾassasat Nādir, 1411/1991.

al-Baghdādī, *Khizāna* = ʿAbd al-Qādir b. ʿUmar al-Baghdādī, *Khizānat al-adab wa-lubb lubāb lisān al-ʿarab.* Beirut: Dār Ṣādir, n.d. [4 vols.]. [Reprint of the Būlāq edition.]

al-Bākharzī, *Dumya* = ʿAlī b. al-Ḥasan b. ʿAlī al-Bākharzī, *Dumyat al-qaṣr fī ʿuṣrat ahl al-ʿaṣr.* Ed. Muḥammad Altūnjī. Beirut: Dār al-Jīl, 1414/1993 [3 vols.].

al-Bayḍāwī, *Tafsīr* = Naṣīr al-Dīn Abū Saʿīd ʿAbdallāh b. ʿUmar al-Bayḍāwī, *Anwār al-tanzīl wa-asrār al-taʾwīl.* Beirut: Dār al-Kutub al-ʿIlmiyya, 1408/1988 [2 vols.].

al-Bayhaqī, *Maḥāsin* = Ibrāhīm b. Muḥammad al-Bayhaqī, *al-Maḥāsin wa-l-masāwiʾ.* Ed. Muḥammad Sawīd. Beirut: Dār Iḥyāʾ al-ʿUlūm, 1408/1988.

al-Bustī, *Baḥth* = Abū l-Qāsim Ismāʿīl b. Aḥmad al-Bustī, *Kitāb al-baḥth ʿan adillat al-takfīr wa-l-tafsīq.* Eds. Wilferd Madelung, Sabine Schmidtke. Tehran: Iran University Press, 2003.

al-Ghazālī, *Fatāwā* = Abū Ḥāmid Muḥammad b. Muḥammad al-Ghazālī, *al-Fatāwā.* Ed. ʿAlī Muṣṭafā al-Ṭassa. Damascus, Beirut: Dār al-Yamāma li-l-Ṭibāʿa wa-l-Nashr wa-l-Tawzīʿ, 1425/2004.

al-Ghazālī, *Iḥyāʾ* = Abū Ḥāmid Muḥammad b. Muḥammad al-Ghazālī, *Iḥyāʾ ʿulūm al-dīn.* Cairo: Dār Miṣr li-l-Ṭibāʿa, 1998 [5 vols.].

Ḥalūlū, *Masāʾil* = Abū l-ʿAbbās Aḥmad b. ʿAbd al-Raḥmān al-Zulayṭinī al-maʿrūf bi-Ḥalūlū, *al-Masāʾil al-mukhtaṣara min kitāb al-Barzalī.* Ed. Aḥmad Muḥammad al-Khalīfī. Beirut: Dār al-Madār al-Islāmī, 2002.

al-Hamadhānī, *Maqāmāt* = *Maqāmāt Badīʿ al-Zamān Abū l-Faḍl Aḥmad b. al-Ḥusayn al-Hamadhānī.* Ed. Muḥammad Muḥyī l-Dīn ʿAbd al-Ḥamīd. Beirut: Dār al-Kutub al-ʿIlmiyya, n.d.

al-Ḥarīrī, *Durra* = Abū Muḥammad al-Qāsim b. ʿAlī al-Ḥarīrī, *Durrat al-ghawwāṣ.* Ed. ʿAbd al-Ḥafīẓ Faraghlī ʿAlī al-Qarnī. Beirut, Cairo: Dār al-Jīl, Maktabat al-Turāth al-Islāmī, 1417/1996.

al-Ḥarīrī, *Maqāmāt* = Abū Muḥammad al-Qāsim b. ʿAlī al-Ḥarīrī, *al-Maqāmāt al-adabiyya.* Beirut: Dār al-Kutub al-ʿIlmiyya, 1413/1992.

al-Haytamī, *Iʿlām* = Abū l-ʿAbbās Aḥmad b. Muḥammad b. ʿAlī b. Ḥajar al-Haytamī, *al-Iʿlām bi-qawāṭiʿ al-islām.* (In vol. 2 of al-Haythamī, *Zawājir.*)

al-Haytamī, *Zawājir* = Abū l-ʿAbbās Aḥmad b. Muḥammad b. ʿAlī b. Ḥajar al-Haytamī, *al-Zawājir ʿan iqtirāf al-kabāʾir*. Beirut: Dār al-Maʿrifa li-l-Ṭibāʿa wa-l-Nashr, n.d. 2 vols.

al-Ḥillī, *ʿĀṭil* = Ṣafī al-Dīn Abū l-Faḍl ʿAbd al-ʿAzīz b. Sarāyā al-Ḥillī, *al-Kitāb al-ʿĀṭil al-ḥālī wa-l-murakhkhaṣ al-ghālī*. Ed. Wilhelm Hoenerbach. Wiesbaden: Franz Steiner Verlag, 1956.

al-Ḥillī, *Dīwān* = *Dīwān Ṣafī al-Dīn al-Ḥillī*. Beirut: Dār Ṣādir, 1410/1990.

al-Ḥillī, *Sharḥ* = Ṣafī al-Dīn Abū l-Faḍl ʿAbd al-ʿAzīz b. Sarāyā al-Ḥillī, *Sharḥ al-Kāfiya al-badīʿiyya fī ʿulūm al-balāgha wa-maḥāsin al-badīʿ*. Ed. Nasīb Nashāwī. Beirut: Dār Ṣādir, 1412/1992.

Ḥusāmzāde, *Risāla* = ʿAbd al-Raḥmān b. Ḥusām al-Dīn al-Rūmī, *Risāla fī qalb Kāfūriyyāt al-Mutanabbī min al-madīḥ ilā l-hijāʾ*. Ed. Muḥammad Yūsuf Najm. Beirut: Dār Ṣādir, 1413/1993.

Ibn Abī Ṭāhir, *Balāghāt* = Abū l-Faḍl Aḥmad b. Abī Ṭāhir Ṭayfūr, *Balāghāt al-nisāʾ*. Ed. ʿAbd al-Ḥamīd Hindāwī. Cairo: Dār al-Faḍīla, 1998.

Ibn ʿAqīl, *Tadhkira* = Abū l-Wafāʾ ʿAlī b. ʿAqīl b. Muḥammad b. ʿAqīl al-Baghdādī, *al-Tadhkira fī l-fiqh ʿalā madhhab al-imām Aḥmad b. Muḥammad b. Ḥanbal*. Ed. Nāṣir b. Suʿūd b. ʿAbdallāh al-Salāma. Riyadh: Dār Ishbīliyā li-l-Nashr wa-l-Tawzīʿ, 1422/2001.

Ibn ʿĀṣim, *Janna* = Abū Yaḥyā Muḥammad b. ʿĀṣim al-Gharnāṭī, *Jannat al-riḍā fī l-taslīm li-mā qaddara Allāh wa-qaḍā*. Ed. Ṣalāḥ Jarrār. Amman: Dār al-Bashīr, 1410/1989 [3 vols.].

Ibn Baraka, *Jāmiʿ* = Abū Muḥammad ʿAbdallāh b. Muḥammad b. Baraka al-Bahlawī al-ʿUmānī, *Kitāb al-jāmiʿ*. Ed. ʿĪsā Yaḥyā al-Bārūnī. [Muscat]: Wizārat al-Turāth al-Qawmī wa-l-Thaqāfa, 1391-3/1971-3. 2 vols.

Ibn Bassām, *Nihāya* = Muḥammad b. Aḥmad b. Bassām al-Muḥtasib, *Nihāyat al-rutba fī ṭalab al-ḥisba*. Ed. Ḥusām al-Dīn al-Sāmarrāʾī. Baghdad: Maṭbaʿat al-Maʿārif, 1968.

Ibn Baṭṭūṭa, *Riḥla* = *Riḥlat Ibn Baṭṭūṭa*. Beirut: Dār Ṣādir, 2001.

Ibn Baydakīn, *Lumaʿ* = Idrīs b. Baydakīn b. ʿAbdallāh al-Turkumānī, *Kitāb al-lumaʿ fī l-ḥawādith wa-l-bidaʿ*. Ed. Ṣubḥī Labīb. Cairo: Deutsches Archäologisches Institut Kairo, 1406/1986 [2 vols.].

Ibn Diḥya, *Muṭrib* = Abū l-Khaṭṭāb ʿUmar b. Ḥasan b. Diḥya al-Balansī al-Dānī, *al-Muṭrib min ashʿār ahl al-Maghrib*. Eds. Ibrāhīm al-Abyārī, Ḥāmid ʿAbd al-Majīd, Aḥmad Aḥmad Badawī. Cairo: no publisher indicated, 1993 [1st ed. Cairo: al-Maṭbaʿa al-Amīriyya, 1954].

Ibn García, *Risāla* = "Risālat Abī ʿĀmir b. Gharsiyya fī l-shuʿūbiyya.» In ʿAbd al-Salām Muḥammad Hārūn (ed.), *Nawādir al-makhṭūṭāt*. Cairo: Maktabat Muṣṭafā al-Bābī al-Ḥalabī wa-Awlādihi, 1392/1972: I, 246–54.

Ibn Ḥawqal, *Ṣūra* = Abū l-Qāsim b. Ḥawqal al-Naṣībī, *Kitāb ṣūrat al-arḍ*. Beirut: Dār Maktabat al-Ḥayāt, 1979.

Ibn Ḥazm, *Jamhara* = Abū Muḥammad ʿAlī b. Aḥmad b. Saʿīd b. Ḥazm al-Andalusī, *Jamharat ansāb al-ʿarab*. Ed. Muḥammad ʿAlī Bayḍūn et al. Beirut: Dār al-Kutub al-ʿIlmiyya, 1418/1998.

Ibn Ḥazm, *Muḥallā* = Abū Muḥammad ʿAlī b. Aḥmad b. Saʿīd b. Ḥazm al-Andalusī, *al-Muḥallā bi-l-āthār*. Ed. ʿAbd al-Ghaffār Sulaymān al-Bundārī. Beirut: Dār al-Fikr, n.d. 12 vols.

Ibn Hubayra, *Ikhtilāf* = Abū l-Muẓaffar Yaḥyā b. Muḥammad b. Hubayra al-Shaybānī, *Ikhtilāf al-aʾimma al-ʿulamāʾ*. Ed. Yūsuf Aḥmad. Beirut: Dār al-Kutub al-ʿIlmiyya, 1423/2002. 2 vols.

Ibn Ḥijja, *Khizāna* = Abū Bakr b. ʿAlī b. ʿAbdallāh b. Ḥijja al-Ḥamawī, *Khizānat al-adab wa-ghāyat al-arab*. Ed. Kawkab Diyāb. Beirut: Dār Ṣādir, 1421/2001 [5 vols.].

Ibn al-Jawzī, *Quṣṣāṣ* = Abū l-Faraj ʿAbd al-Raḥmān b. ʿAlī b. al-Jawzī al-Baghdādī, *Kitāb al-quṣṣāṣ wa-l-mudhakkirīn*. Ed. Muḥammad b. Luṭfī al-Ṣabbāgh. Beirut: al-Maktab al-Islāmī, 1403/1983.

Ibn al-Jawzī, *Talbīs* = Abū l-Faraj ʿAbd al-Raḥmān b. ʿAlī b. al-Jawzī al-Baghdādī, *Talbīs Iblīs*. Ed. Muḥammad Munīr al-Dimashqī. Cairo: Maṭbaʿat al-Nahḍa, 1928.

Ibn al-Jawzī, *Taqwīm* = Abū l-Faraj ʿAbd al-Raḥmān b. ʿAlī b. al-Jawzī al-Baghdādī, *Taqwīm al-lisān*. Ed. ʿAbd al-ʿAzīz Maṭar. Cairo: Dār al-Maʿrifa, 1966.

Ibn al-Jawzī, *Ẓirāf* = Abū l-Faraj ʿAbd al-Raḥmān b. ʿAlī b. al-Jawzī al-Baghdādī, *Akhbār al-ẓirāf wa-l-mutamājinīn*. Ed. ʿIrfān Muḥammad Ḥammūr. Beirut: Dār al-Shūrā, 1983.

Ibn Jubayr, *Riḥla* = *Riḥlat Ibn Jubayr*. Beirut: Dār Ṣādir, n. d.

Ibn Juzayy, *Qawānīn* = Abū l-Qāsim Muḥammad b. Aḥmad b. Juzayy al-Kalbī al-Gharnāṭī, *al-Qawānīn al-fiqhiyya*. Tripoli, Tunis: al-Dār al-ʿArabiyya li-l-Kitāb, 1982.

Ibn al-Kattānī, *Tashbīhāt* = Abū ʿAbdallāh Muḥammad b. al-Kattānī, *Kitāb al-tashbīhāt min ashʿār ahl al-Andalus*. Ed. Iḥsān ʿAbbās. Beirut: Dār al-Thaqāfa, n.d.

Ibn Khafāja, *Dīwān* = *Dīwān Ibn Khafāja*. Ed. Yūsuf Shukrī Farḥāt. Beirut: Dār al-Jīl, n. d.

Ibn Khallikān, *Wafayāt* = Abū l-ʿAbbās Shams al-Dīn Aḥmad b. Khallikān, *Wafayāt al-aʿyān wa-anbāʾ abnāʾ al-zamān*. Beirut: Dār Ṣādir, 1397/1977 [8 vols.].

Ibn al-Khaṭīb, *Jaysh* = Lisān al-Dīn Muḥammad b. ʿAbdallāh b. al-Khaṭīb, *Jaysh al-tawshīḥ*. Eds. Muḥammad Māḍūr, Hilāl Nājī. Tunis: Maṭbaʿat al-Manār, 1967.

Ibn Makkī, *Tathqīf* = Abū Ḥafṣ ʿUmar b. Khalaf b. Makkī al-Ṣiqillī, *Tathqīf al-lisān wa-talqīḥ al-janān*. Ed. ʿAbd al-ʿAzīz Maṭar. Cairo: Dār al-Maʿārif, 1981.

Ibn Manẓūr, *Akhbār* = Abū l-Faḍl Jamāl al-Dīn Muḥammad b. Mukarram b. Manẓūr al-Ifrīqī, *Akhbār Abī Nuwās*. Ed. Muḥammad ʿAbd al-Rasūl Ibrāhīm. Cairo: Dār al-Bustānī li-l-Nashr wa-l-Tawzīʿ, 2000.

Ibn Manẓūr, *Lisān* = Abū l-Faḍl Jamāl al-Dīn Muḥammad b. Mukarram b. Manẓūr al-Ifrīqī, *Lisān al-ʿarab*. Beirut: Dār Ṣādir, 1997 [7 vols.].

Ibn al-Marzubān, *Dhamm* = Abū Bakr Muḥammad b. Khalaf b. al-Marzubān, *Dhamm al-thuqalāʾ*. Ed. Muḥammad Ḥusayn al-Aʿrajī. Cologne: Al-Kamel Verlag, 1999.

Ibn Maʿṣūm, *Sulāfa* = ʿAlī Ṣadr al-Dīn b. Aḥmad b. Maʿṣūm al-Madanī, *Sulāfat al-ʿaṣr fī maḥāsin al-shuʿarāʾ bi-kull miṣr*. Doha: Maṭābiʿ ʿAlī b. ʿAlī, 1382 A. H.

Ibn Miftāḥ, *Muntazaʿ* = Abū l-Ḥasan ʿAbdallāh Ibn Miftāḥ, *al-Muntazaʿ al-mukhtār min al-ghayth al-midrār al-maʿrūf bi-Sharḥ al-Azhār*. Ṣaʿda: Maktabat al-Turāth al-Islāmī, 1424/2003. 10 vols.

Ibn Mufliḥ, *Ādāb* = Shams al-Din Abū ʿAbdallāh Muḥammad b. Mufliḥ al-Maqdisī, *al-Ādāb al-sharʿiyya wa-l-minaḥ al-marʿiyya*. Eds. ʿĀmir al-Jazzār, Anwar al-Bāz. Al-Manṣūra: Dār al-Wafāʾ, 1419/1999. 3 vols.

Ibn Mufliḥ, *Furūʿ* = Shams al-Din Abū ʿAbdallāh Muḥammad b. Mufliḥ al-Maqdisī, *Kitāb al-furūʿ fī fiqh al-imām Aḥmad b. Ḥanbal*. Ed. ʿAbd al-Razzāq al-Mahdī. Beirut: Dār al-Kitāb al-ʿArabī, 1422/2002. 3 vols.

Ibn al-Muʿtazz, *Badīʿ* = Abū l-ʿAbbās ʿAbdallāh b. al-Muʿtazz, *Kitāb al-badīʿ*. Ed. Muḥammad ʿAbd al-Munʿim Khafājī. Beirut: Dār al-Jīl, 1410/1990.

Ibn al-Muʿtazz, *Ṭabaqāt* = Abū l-ʿAbbās ʿAbdallāh b. al-Muʿtazz, *Ṭabaqāt al-shuʿarāʾ al-muḥdathīn*. Facsimile edition, ed. ʿAbbās Iqbāl. London: Cambridge University Press, Luzac and Co., 1939.

Ibn al-Muzarraʿ, *Sariqāt* = Muhalhil b. Yamūt b. al-Muzarraʿ al-ʿAbdī, *Sariqāt Abī Nuwās*. Ed. Muḥammad Muṣṭafā Haddāra. Cairo: Dār al-Fikr al-ʿArabī, n. d. [1957?].

Ibn Qutayba, *Shiʿr* = Abū Muḥammad ʿAbdallāh b. Muslim b. Qutayba al-Dīnawarī, *al-Shiʿr wal-shuʿarāʾ*. Ed. Mufīd Qumayḥa. Beirut: Dār al-Kutub al-ʿIlmiyya, 1401/1981.

Ibn Qutayba, *ʿUyūn* = Abū Muḥammad ʿAbdallāh b. Muslim b. Qutayba al-Dīnawarī, *ʿUyūn al-akhbār*. Ed. Mufīd Muḥammad Qumayḥa. Beirut: Dār al-Kutub al-ʿIlmiyya, 1418/1998 [2 vols., 4 parts].

Ibn Rashīq, *Qurāḍa* = Abū ʿAlī al-Ḥasan b. Rashīq al-Qayrawānī, *Qurāḍat al-dhahab fī naqd ashʿār al-ʿarab*. Ed. al-Shādhilī Bū-Yaḥyā. Tunis: al-Sharika al-Tūnisiyya lil-Tawzīʿ, 1972.

Ibn Rashīq, *ʿUmda* = Abū ʿAlī al-Ḥasan b. Rashīq l-Qayrawānī, *Kitāb al-ʿUmda fī naqd al-shiʿr wa-tamḥīṣihi*. Ed. ʿAfīf Nāyif Ḥāṭūm. Beirut: Dār Ṣādir, 1424/2003.

Ibn Riḍwān, *Shuhub* = Abū l-Qāsim b. Riḍwān al-Mālaqī, *al-Shuhub al-lāmiʿa fī l-siyāsa al-nāfiʿa*. Ed. ʿAlī Sāmī al-Nashshār. Casablanca: Dār al-Thaqāfa, 1404/1984.

Ibn al-Rūmī, *Dīwān* = *Dīwān Ibn al-Rūmī*. Ed. ʿAbd al-Amīr ʿAlī Muhannā. Beirut: Dār wa-Maktabat al-Hilāl, 1998. 6 vols.

Ibn Saʿīd, *Ghuṣūn* = Abū l-Ḥasan ʿAlī b. Mūsā b. Saʿīd al-Andalusī, *al-Ghuṣūn al-yāniʿa fī maḥāsin shuʿarāʾ al-miʾa al-sābiʿa*. Ed. Ibrāhīm al-Abyārī. Cairo: Dār al-Maʿārif, n.d. [3rd ed.].

Ibn Saʿīd, *Muqtaṭaf* = Abū l-Ḥasan ʿAlī b. Mūsā b. Saʿīd al-Andalusī, *al-Muqtaṭaf min azāhir al-ṭuraf*. Ed. Sayyid Ḥanafī Ḥasanayn. Cairo: al-Hayʾa al-Miṣriyya al-ʿĀmma li-l-Kitāb, 1984.

Ibn Saʿīd, *Rāyāt* = Abū l-Ḥasan ʿAlī b. Mūsā b. Saʿīd al-Andalusī, *Rāyāt al-mubarrazīn wa-ghāyāt al-mumayyazīn*. Ed. Muḥammad Riḍwān al-Dāya. Damascus: Dār Ṭilās li-l-Dirāsāt wa-l-Tarjama wa-l-Nashr, 1987.

Ibn al-Ṣalāḥ, *Fatāwā* = Taqī al-Dīn Abū ʿAmr ʿUthmān b. ʿAbd al-Raḥmān Ibn al-Ṣalāḥ al-Shahrazūrī, *Fatāwā wa-masāʾil Ibn al-Ṣalāḥ fī l-tafsīr wa-l-ḥadīth wa-l-uṣūl wa-l-fiqh*. Ed. ʿAbd al-Muʿṭī Amīn Qalʿajī. Beirut: Dār al-Maʿrifa, 1406/1986. 2 vols.

Ibn Simāk, *Zaharāt* = Abū l-Qāsim Muḥammad b. Muḥammad b. Simāk al-Mālaqī al-ʿĀmilī, *al-Zaharāt al-manthūra fī nukat al-akhbār al-maʾthūra*. Ed. Maḥmūd ʿAlī Makkī. Madrid: al-Maʿhad al-Miṣrī li-l-Dirāsāt al-Islāmiyya fī Madrīd, 1404/1984.

Ibn Zaydūn, *Dīwān* = *Dīwān Ibn Zaydūn*. Ed. Ḥannā al-Fākhūrī. Beirut: Dār al-Jīl, 1410/1990.

al-Ibshīhī, *Mustaṭraf* = Shihāb al-Dīn Muḥammad b. Aḥmad al-Ibshīhī, *al-Mustaṭraf min kull fann mustaẓraf*. Ed. Mufīd Muḥammad Qumayḥa. Beirut: Dār al-Kutub al-ʿIlmiyya, 1413/1993.

al-Idrīsī, *Nuzha* = Abū ʿAbdallāh Muḥammad al-Idrīsī, *Nuzhat al-mushtāq fī ʾkhtirāq al-āfāq*. Eds. E. Cerulli et al. Naples: Instituto Orientale di Napoli, 1970–80 [8 vols.].

al-Iṣbahānī, *Kharīda* = al-Kātib al-Iṣbahānī ʿImād al-Dīn Muḥammad b. Muḥammad al-Qurashī, *Kharīdat al-qaṣr wa-jarīdat al-ʿaṣr*. Ed. Muḥammad Bahja al-Atharī. I: *[al-Qism al-ʿIrāqī]*. Baghdad: Maṭbaʿat al-Majmaʿ al-ʿIlmī al-ʿIrāqī, 1375–84/1955–64 [2 vols.]. II: *[al-Juzʾ al-Rābiʿ]*. Baghdad: Dār al-Ḥurriyya li-l-Ṭibāʿa, Maṭbaʿat al-Ḥukūma; 1393/1973 [2 vols.].

al-Iṣfahānī, *Aghānī* = Abū l-Faraj ʿAlī b. al-Ḥusayn al-Iṣfahānī, *Kitāb al-aghānī*. Eds. Yūsuf ʿAlī Ṭawīl, ʿAbd al-Amīr ʿAlī Muhannā, Samīr Jābir. Beirut: Dār al-Fikr, 1415/1995 [2nd ed.] [25 vols.].

ʿIyāḍ, *Shifāʾ* = al-Qāḍī Abū l-Faḍl ʿIyāḍ b. Mūsā al-Yaḥṣubī, *Kitāb al-shifāʾ bi-taʿrīf ḥuqūq al-Muṣṭafā*. Ed. Nawāf al-Jarrāḥ. Beirut: Dār Ṣādir, 1427/2006.

al-Jāḥiẓ, *Bukhalāʾ* = Abū ʿUthmān ʿAmr b. Baḥr al-Jāḥiẓ, *Kitāb al-bukhalāʾ*. Ed. Muḥammad Altūnjī. Beirut: Dār al-Jīl, 1414/1993.

al-Jāḥiẓ, *Ḥayawān* = Abū ʿUthmān ʿAmr b. Baḥr al-Jāḥiẓ, *Kitāb al-ḥayawān*. Ed. Yaḥyā al-Shāmī. Beirut: Dār al-Hilāl, 1986 [2 vols.].

al-Jāḥiẓ, *Rasāʾil* = *Rasāʾil al-Jāḥiẓ*. Ed. Muḥammad ʿAbd al-Salām Hārūn. Cairo: Maktabat al-Khānjī, 1399/1979 [2 vols., 4 parts].

al-Jurjānī, *Ishārāt* = Muḥammad b. ʿAlī b. Muḥammad al-Jurjānī, *al-Ishārāt wa-l-tanbīhāt fī ʿilm al-balāgha*. Ed. ʿAbd al-Qādir Ḥusayn. Cairo: Dār Nahḍat Miṣr li-l-Ṭibāʿa wa-l-Nashr, n.d.

al-Jurjānī, *Wasāṭa* = Abū l-Ḥasan ʿAlī b. ʿAbd al-ʿAzīz al-Qāḍī al-Jurjānī, *al-Wasāṭa bayna l-Mutanabbī wa-khuṣūmihi*. Ed. Aḥmad ʿĀrif al-Zayn. Sousse, Tunis: Dār al-Maʿārif li-l-Ṭibāʿa wa-l-Nashr, 1992.

al-Khaṣṣāf, *Adab* = Abū Bakr Aḥmad b. ʿAmr al-Shaybānī al-Khaṣṣāf, *Kitāb adab al-qāḍī bi-sharḥ al-Jaṣṣāṣ*. Ed. Farḥāt Ziyāda. Cairo: American University in Cairo Press, 1978.

al-Khaṭīb, *Kifāya* = Abū Bakr Aḥmad b. ʿAlī al-Khaṭīb al-Baghdādī, *al-Kifāya fī ʿilm al-riwāya*. Ed. Aḥmad ʿUmar Hāshim. Beirut: Dār al-Kitāb al-ʿArabī, 1406/1986 [2nd ed.].

al-Khaṭīb, *Taṭfīl* = Abū Bakr Aḥmad b. ʿAlī al-Khaṭīb al-Baghdādī, *al-Taṭfīl wa-ḥikāyāt al-ṭufayliyyīn wa-akhbāruhum wa-nawādir kalāmihim wa-ashʿārihim*. Damascus: Maṭbaʿat al-Tawfīq, 1346 A. H.

Kushājim, *Adab* = Abū l-Fatḥ Maḥmūd b. [sic] Kushājim, *Kitāb adab al-nudamāʾ wa-laṭāʾif al-ẓurafāʾ*. Alexandria: Maṭbaʿat Jurjī Gharzūzī, 1329 AH.

al-Kutubī, *Fawāt* = Muḥammad b. Shākir al-Kutubī, *Fawāt al-wafayāt wa-l-dhayl ʿalayhā*. Ed. Iḥsān ʿAbbās. Beirut: Dār Ṣādir, 1973–4 [5 vols.].

al-Maʿarrī, *Ghufrān* = Abū l-ʿAlāʾ al-Maʿarrī, *Risālat al-ghufrān*. Ed. ʿĀʾisha ʿAbd al-Raḥmān Bint al-Shāṭiʾ. Cairo: Dār al-Maʿārif, 1397/1977 [7th ed.].

al-Maqrīzī, *Khiṭaṭ* = Taqī al-Dīn Aḥmad b. ʿAlī al-Maqrīzī, *al-Mawāʿiẓ wa-l-iʿtibār bi-dhikr al-khiṭaṭ wa-l-āthār*. Beirut (al-Shiyāḥ): Maktabat Iḥyāʾ al-ʿUlūm, 1959 [3 vols.].

al-Marwazī, *Ikhtilāf* = Abū ʿAbdallāh Muḥammad b. Naṣr al-Marwazī, *Ikhtilāf al-fuqahāʾ*. Ed. Muḥammad Ṭāhir Ḥakīm. Riyadh: Maktabat Aḍwāʾ al-Salaf, 1420/2000.

al-Marzūqī, *Sharḥ* = Abū ʿAlī Aḥmad b. Muḥammad al-Marzūqī, *Sharḥ Dīwān al-Ḥamāsa*. Eds. Aḥmad Amīn, ʿAbd al-Salām Hārūn. Cairo: Maṭbaʿat Lajnat al-Taʾlīf wa-l-Tarjama wa-l-Nashr, 1387-88/1967–68 [4 vols.].

al-Masʿūdī, *Murūj* = Abū l-Ḥasan ʿAlī b. al-Ḥusayn b. ʿAlī al-Masʿūdī, *Murūj al-dhahab wa-maʿādin al-jawhar*. Beirut: al-Sharika al-ʿĀlamiyya li-l-Kitāb, 1990 [2nd ed.] [2 vols.].

al-Māwardī, *Aḥkām* = Abū l-Ḥasan ʿAlī b. Muḥammad b. Ḥabīb al-Māwardī, *al-Aḥkām al-sulṭāniyya wa-l-wilāyāt al-dīniyya*. Ed. Khālid Rashīd al-Jamīlī. Baghdad: al-Maktaba al-ʿĀlamiyya, 1409/1989.

al-Maydānī, *Amthāl* = Abū l-Faḍl Aḥmad b. Muḥammad al-Nīsābūrī al-Maydānī, *Majmaʿ al-amthāl*. Ed. Naʿīm Ḥusayn Zarzūr. Beirut: Dār al-Kutub al-ʿIlmiyya, 1408/1988 [2 vols.].

Miskawayh, *Tajārib* = Abū ʿAlī Aḥmad b. Muḥammad Miskawayh, *Tajārib al-umam*. Ed. H. F. Amedroz. Baghdad: Maktabat al-Muthannā, 1332/1914 [2 vols.].

al-Munajjim, *Ākām* = Isḥāq b. al-Ḥusayn al-Munajjim, *Ākām al-murjān fī dhikr al-madāʾin al-mashhūra fī kull makān*. Ed. Fahmī Saʿd. Beirut: ʿĀlam al-Kutub, 1408/1988.

al-Muqaddasī, *Taqāsīm* = Abū ʿAbdallāh Muḥammad b. Aḥmad al-Muqaddasī al-Bishārī, *Aḥsan al-taqāsīm fī maʿrifat al-aqālīm*. Ed. M. J. de Goeje. Leiden: E. J. Brill, 1877.

al-Nadīm, *Fihrist* = Abū l-Faraj Muḥammad b. Isḥāq al-Nadīm, *Kitāb al-fihrist*. Ed. Riḍā Tajaddud. Tehran: Marvi Offset Printing, n.d. [1393/1973?].

al-Nafzāwī, *Rawḍ* = Sīdī Muḥammad b. Muḥammad al-Nafzāwī, *al-Rawḍ al-ʿāṭir fī nuzhat al-khāṭir*. Tunis: Maktabat al-Manār, n.d.

al-Naḥḥās, *Ṣināʿa* = Abū Jaʿfar Aḥmad b. Muḥammad b. Ismāʿīl al-Naḥḥās, *Ṣināʿat al-kuttāb*. Ed. Badr Aḥmad Ḍayf. Beirut: Dār al-ʿUlūm al-ʿArabiyya, 1410/1990.

al-Nawawī, *Fatāwī* = Muḥyī l-Dīn Abū Zakariyyā b. Sharaf al-Nawawī, *Fatāwī al-Imām al-Nawawī*. Ed. Maḥmūd al-Arnāʾūṭ. Damascus: Dār al-Fikr, 1419/1999.

al-Nuwayrī, *Nihāya* = Shihāb al-Dīn Aḥmad b. ʿAbd al-Wahhāb al-Nuwayrī, *Nihāyat al-arab fī funūn al-adab*. Cairo: Dār al-Kutub al-Miṣriyya, 1347/1929 [5 vols., 10 parts].

al-Qalqashandī, *Ṣubḥ* = Abū l-ʿAbbās Aḥmad b. ʿAlī al-Qalqashandī, *Ṣubḥ al-aʿshā fī ṣināʿat al-inshāʾ*. Cairo: Dār al-Kutub al-Khidīwiyya, 1331–18/1913–19 [14 vols.].

al-Qāriʾ, *Sharḥ* = Abū l-Ḥasan ʿAlī b. Sulṭān Muḥammad al-Qāriʾ al-Harawī, *Sharḥ al-Imām ʿAlī al-Qāriʾ ʿalā Kitāb alfāẓ al-kufr li-l-ʿAllāma Badr al-Rashīd*. Ed. al-Ṭayyib b. ʿUmar al-Ḥusayn al-Shinqīṭī. Riyadh: Dār al-Faḍīla, 1423/2002.

al-Qazwīnī, *Īḍāḥ* = Jalāl al-Dīn Abū ʿAbdallāh Muḥammad al-Khaṭīb al-Qazwīnī, *al-Īḍāḥ fī ʿulūm al-balāgha*. Ed. Muḥammad ʿAbd al-Munʿim Khafājī. Cairo (?): Maktabat al-Kulliyyāt al-Azhariyya, n.d. [2nd ed.] [6 vols.].

al-Rāghib, *Muḥāḍarāt* = al-Rāghib al-Iṣbahānī Abū l-Qāsim Ḥasan b. Muḥammad, *Muḥāḍarāt al-udabāʾ wa-muḥāwarāt al-shuʿarāʾ wal-bulaghāʾ*. Ed. Riyāḍ ʿAbd al-Ḥamīd Murād. Beirut: Dār Ṣādir, 1425/2004. [5 vols.].

al-Ṣafadī, *Tawshīḥ* = Ṣalāḥ al-Dīn Khalīl b. Aybak al-Ṣafadī, *Tawshīʿ al-tawshīḥ*. Ed. Albert Ḥabīb Muṭlaq. Beirut: Dār al-Thaqāfa, 1966.

al-Sakhāwī, *Iʿlān* = Shams al-Dīn Muḥammad al-Sakhāwī, *al-Iʿlān bi-l-tawbīkh li-man dhamma l-tārīkh*. Ed. F. Rosenthal. Beirut: Dār al-Kutub al-ʿIlmiyya, n.d.

al-Samʿānī, *Adab* = Abū Saʿd ʿAbd al-Karīm b. Muḥammad al-Samʿānī, *Adab al-imlāʾ wal-istimlāʾ*. Ed. Max Weisweiler. Leiden: E. J. Brill, 1952.

al-Samʿānī, *Ansāb* = Abū Saʿd ʿAbd al-Karīm b. Muḥammad al-Samʿānī, *Kitāb al-ansāb*. Ed. ʿAbdallāh ʿUmar al-Bārūdī. Beirut: Dār al-Jinān, 1408/1988 [5 vols.].

al-Samarqandī, *Fatāwā* = Abū l-Layth Naṣr b. Muḥammad b. Ibrāhīm al-Samarqandī, *Fatāwā l-nawāzil*. Ed. al-Sayyid Yūsuf Aḥmad. Beirut: Dār al-Kutub al-ʿIlmiyya, 1425/2004.

al-Shāfiʿī, *Umm* = Muḥammad b. Idrīs al-Shāfiʿī, *Kitāb al-Umm*. Ed. Rifʿat Fawzī ʿAbd al-Muṭṭalib. al-Manṣūra: Dār al-Wafāʾ li-l-Ṭibāʿa wa-l-Nashr wa-l-Tawzīʿ, 1429/2008 [5th ed.]. 11 vols.

al-Shahrastānī, *Milal* = Abū l-Fatḥ Muḥammad b. ʿAbd al-Karīm al-Shahrastānī, *al-Milal wa-l-niḥal*. Ed. Muḥammad Sayyid Kīlānī. Beirut: Dār al-Maʿrifa li-l-Ṭibāʿa wa-l-Nashr, 1395/1975 [2nd ed.]. 2 vols.

al-Shāṭibī, *Ifādāt* = Abū Isḥāq Ibrāhīm b. Mūsā al-Shāṭibī, *al-Ifādāt wa-l-inshādāt*. Ed. Muḥammad Abū l-Ajfān. Beirut: Muʾassasat al-Risāla, 1403/1983.

al-Shayzarī, *Nihāya* = ʿAbd al-Raḥmān b. Naṣr al-Shayzarī, *Kitāb nihāyat al-rutba fī ṭalab al-ḥisba*. Ed. al-Sayyid al-Bāz al-ʿArīnī. Cairo: Maṭbaʿat Lajnat al-Taʾlīf wa-l-Tarjama wa-l-Nashr, 1365/1946.

al-Shinqīṭī, *Wasīṭ* = Aḥmad b. al-Amīn al-Shinqīṭī, *al-Wasīṭ fī tarājim udabāʾ Shinqīṭ*. Ed. Fuʾād Sayyid. Cairo: Maṭbaʿat al-Khānjī, 1409/1989 [4th ed.].

al-Ṣūlī, *Adab* = Abū Bakr Muḥammad b. Yaḥyā al-Ṣūlī, *Adab al-kuttāb*. Ed. Muḥammad Bahja al-Atharī. Cairo: al-Maṭbaʿa al-Salafiyya, 1341 AH.

al-Ṣūlī, *Akhbār* = Abū Bakr Muḥammad b. Yaḥyā al-Ṣūlī, *Akhbār Abī Tammām*. Eds. Khalīl Maḥmūd ʿAsākir, Muḥammad ʿAbduh ʿAzzām, Naẓīr al-Islām al-Hindī. Cairo: Lajnat al-Taʾlīf wa-l-Tarjama wa-l-Nashr, 1356/1937.

al-Suyūṭī, *Ḥāwī* = Jalāl al-Dīn ʿAbd al-Raḥmān b. Abī Bakr al-Suyūṭī, *al-Ḥāwī li-l-fatāwī*. Ed. ʿAbd al-Laṭīf Ḥasan ʿAbd al-Raḥmān. Beirut: Dār al-Kutub al-ʿIlmiyya, 1421/2000. 2 vols.

al-Suyūṭī, *Mustaẓraf* = Jalāl al-Dīn ʿAbd al-Raḥmān b. Abī Bakr al-Suyūṭī, *al-Mustaẓraf min akhbār al-jawārī*. Ed. Ṣalāḥ al-Dīn al-Munajjid. Beirut: Dār al-Kitāb al-Jadīd, 1976 [2nd ed.].

al-Suyūṭī, *Tuḥfa* = Jalāl al-Dīn ʿAbd al-Raḥmān b. Abī Bakr al-Suyūṭī, *Kitāb tuḥfat al-ẓurafāʾ bi-asmāʾ al-khulafāʾ*. Ed. Maḥmūd Ḥasan Naṣṣār. Beirut: Dār al-Jīl, 1409/1989.

al-Ṭabarī, *Ikhtilāf* = Abū Jaʿfar Muḥammad b. Jarīr al-Ṭabarī, *Kitāb ikhtilāf al-fuqahāʾ*. Ed. Friedrich Kern. Beirut: Dār al-Kutub al-ʿIlmiyya, n.d. [2nd ed.] 2 parts in one volume.

al-Ṭabarī, *Tārīkh* = Abū Jaʿfar Muḥammad b. Jarīr al-Ṭabarī, *Tārīkh al-umam wa-l-mulūk*. Ed. Nawāf al-Jarrāḥ. Beirut: Dār Ṣādir, 1424/2003 [6 vols.].

al-Ṭabarsī, *Makārim* = Raḍī al-Dīn Abū Naṣr al-Ḥasan al-Ṭabarsī, *Makārim al-akhlāq*. Ed. Muḥammad al-Ḥusayn al-Aʿlamī. Beirut: Muʾassasat al-Aʿlamī li-l-Maṭbūʿāt, 1392/1972.

al-Tanūkhī, *Nishwār* = ʿAlī al-Muḥassin b. ʿAlī al-Tanūkhī, *Nishwār al-muḥāḍara wa-akhbār al-mudhākara*. Ed. ʿAbbūd al-Shāljī. Beirut: Dār Ṣādir, 1391–93/1971–73 [8 vols.].

al-Tawḥīdī, *Akhlāq* = Abū Ḥayyān ʿAlī b. Muḥammad al-Tawḥīdī, *Akhlāq al-wazīrayn*. Ed. Muḥammad b. Ṭāwīt al-Ṭanjī. Beirut: Dār Ṣādir, 1412/1992.

al-Tawḥīdī, *Baṣāʾir* = Abū Ḥayyān ʿAlī b. Muḥammad al-Tawḥīdī, *al-Baṣāʾir wa-l-dhakhāʾir*. Ed. Wadād al-Qāḍī. Beirut: Dār Ṣādir, 1408/1988 [6 vols., 9 parts].

al-Tawḥīdī, *Imtāʿ* = Abū Ḥayyān ʿAlī b. Muḥammad al-Tawḥīdī, *Kitāb al-imtāʿ wa-l-muʾānasa*. Ed. Khalīl al-Manṣūr. Beirut: Dār al-Kutub al-ʿIlmiyya, 1417/1997.

al-Tawḥīdī, *Muqābasāt* = Abū Ḥayyān ʿAlī b. Muḥammad al-Tawḥīdī, *al-Muqābasāt*. Ed. Ḥasan al-Sandūbī. Cairo: al-Maṭbaʿa al-Raḥmāniyya, 1347/1929.

al-Tawḥīdī [attr.], *Risāla* = Abū Ḥayyān ʿAlī b. Muḥammad al-Tawḥīdī, *al-Risāla al-baghdādiyya*. Ed. ʿAbbūd al-Shāljī. Beirut: Maṭbaʿat Dār al-Kutub, 1400/1980 [attributed to al-Tawḥīdī, the book's real author is Abū l-Muṭahhar al-Azdī].

al-Thaʿālibī, *Iʿjāz* = Abū Manṣūr ʿAbd al-Malik b. Muḥammad al-Thaʿālibī, *al-Iʿjāz wa-l-ījāz*. Beirut: Dār al-Rāʾid al-ʿArabī, 1403/1983 [1st ed. 1897].

al-Thaʿālibī, *Iqtibās* = Abū Manṣūr ʿAbd al-Malik b. Muḥammad al-Thaʿālibī, *al-Iqtibās min al-Qurʾān al-karīm*. Ed. Ibtisām Marhūn al-Ṣaffār. al-Manṣūra: Dār al-Wafāʾ li-l-Ṭibāʿa wa-l-Nashr wa-l-Tawzīʿ, 1412/1992. 2 vols.

al-Thaʿālibī, *Khāṣṣ* = Abū Manṣūr ʿAbd al-Malik b. Muḥammad al-Thaʿālibī, *Kitāb khāṣṣ al-khāṣṣ*. Ed. Ḥasan al-Amīn. Beirut: Dār Maktabat al-Ḥayāt, n.d.

al-Thaʿālibī, *Laṭāʾif* = Abū Manṣūr ʿAbd al-Malik b. Muḥammad al-Thaʿālibī, *Kitāb laṭāʾif al-ẓurafāʾ min ṭabaqāt al-fuḍalāʾ*. Facsimile edition of the Leiden MS, ed. Qāsim al-Sāmarrāʾī. Leiden: E. J. Brill, 1978.

al-Thaʿālibī, *Nathr* = Abū Manṣūr ʿAbd al-Malik b. Muḥammad al-Thaʿālibī, *Nathr al-naẓm wa-ḥall al-ʿaqd.* Ed. Aḥmad ʿAbd al-Fattāḥ Tammām. Beirut: Muʾassasat al-Kutub al-Thaqāfiyya, 1410/1990.

al-Thaʿālibī, *Tatimma* = Abū Manṣūr ʿAbd al-Malik b. Muḥammad al-Thaʿālibī, *Tatimmat al-Yatīma.* Ed. ʿAbbās Iqbāl. Tehran: Maṭbaʿat Fardīn, 1353 A. H. [2 parts].

al-Thaʿālibī, *Thimār* = Abū Manṣūr ʿAbd al-Malik b. Muḥammad al-Thaʿālibī, *Thimār al-qulūb fī l-muḍāf wa-l-mansūb.* Ed. Ibrāhīm Ṣāliḥ. Damascus: Dār al-Bashāʾir, 1414/1994 [2 vols.].

al-Thaʿālibī, *Yatīma* = Abū Manṣūr ʿAbd al-Malik b. Muḥammad al-Thaʿālibī, *Yatīmat al-dahr fī maḥāsin ahl al-ʿaṣr.* Ed. Muḥammad Muḥyī l-Dīn ʿAbd al-Ḥamīd [?]. Beirut: Dār al-Kutub al-ʿIlmiyya, 1399/1979 [4 vols.].

al-Ṭūsī, *Nihāya* = ʿImād al-Dīn Abū Jaʿfar Muḥammad b. al-Ḥasan b. ʿAlī al-Ṭūsī, *al-Nihāya fī mujarrad al-fiqh wa-l-fatāwā.* Ed. Muḥammad Taqī Dānishpazhūh. Tehran: Chāpkhāna-yi Dānishgāh, 1342–3 A. H. 2 vols.

al-ʿUmarī, *Masālik* = Shihāb al-Dīn Aḥmad b. Yaḥyā al-ʿUmarī, *Masālik al-abṣār fī mamālik al-amṣār.* Facsimile edition, ed. Fuat Sezgin. Frankfurt: Goethe-Universität, 1408–09/1988–9 [24 vols., 47 parts].

al-Walwālijī, *Fatāwī* = Abū l-Fatḥ Ẓahīr al-Dīn ʿAbd al-Rashīd b. Abī Ḥanīfa al-Walwālijī, *al-Fatāwī al-walwālijiyya.* Ed. Miqdād b. Mūsā Furaywī. Beirut: Dār al-Kutub al-ʿIlmiyya, 1424/2003. 5 vols.

al-Wansharīsī, *Miʿyār* = Abū l-ʿAbbās Aḥmad b. Yaḥyā al-Wansharīsī, *al-Miʿyār al-muʿrib wa-l-jāmiʿ al-mughrib ʿan fatāwī ahl Ifrīqiyya wa-l-Andalus wa-l-Maghrib.* Eds. Muḥammad Ḥajjī et al. Rabat: Wizārat al-Awqāf wa-l-Shuʾūn al-Islāmiyya, 1401/1981. 13 vols.

al-Washshāʾ, *Muwashshā* = Abū l-Ṭayyib Muḥammad b. Isḥāq b. Yaḥyā al-Washshāʾ, *al-Muwashshā (al-Ẓarf wa-l-ẓurafāʾ).* Beirut: Dār Ṣādir, n.d.

al-Yaḥṣubī, *Ilmāʿ* = ʿIyāḍ b. Mūsā al-Yaḥṣubī, *al-Ilmāʿ ilā maʿrifat uṣūl al-riwāya wa-taqyīd al-samāʿ.* Ed. Aḥmad Ṣaqr. Cairo, Tunis: Dār al-Turāth, al-Maktaba al-ʿAtīqa; 1398/1978.

Yāqūt, *Buldān* = Shihāb al-Dīn Abū ʿAbdallāh Yāqūt b. ʿAbdallāh al-Ḥamawī, *Muʿjam al-buldān.* Beirut: Dār Iḥyāʾ al-Turāth al-ʿArabī, n.d. [5 vols.].

Yāqūt, *Udabāʾ* = Shihāb al-Dīn Abū ʿAbdallāh Yāqūt b. ʿAbdallāh al-Ḥamawī, *Muʿjam al-udabāʾ.* Ed. Iḥsān ʿAbbās. Beirut: Dār al-Gharb al-Islāmī, 1993 [7 vols.].

al-Zajjājī, *Amālī* = Abū l-Qāsim ʿAbd al-Raḥmān b. Isḥāq al-Zajjājī, *Kitāb al-amālī l-wusṭā.* Ed. Aḥmad b. al-Amīn al-Shinqīṭī. Cairo: Maṭbaʿat al-Saʿāda, 1324 A. H.

al-Zawzanī, *Ḥamāsa* = Abū Muḥammad ʿAbdallāh b. Muḥammad al-ʿAbdulkānī al-Zawzanī, *Ḥamāsat al-ẓurafāʾ min ashʿār al-muḥdathīn wa-l-qudamāʾ.* Ed. Muḥammad Jabbār al-Muʿaybid. Baghdad: Dār al-Ḥurriyya li-l-Ṭibāʿa, 1978 [3 vols.].

al-Zubaydī, *Laḥn* = Abū Bakr Muḥammad b. al-Ḥasan al-Zubaydī, *Laḥn al-ʿawāmm.* Ed. Ramaḍān ʿAbd al-Tawwāb. Cairo: Dār al-ʿUrūba, 1964.

al-Zubaydī, *Ṭabaqāt* = Abū Bakr Muḥammad b. al-Ḥasan al-Zubaydī, *Ṭabaqāt al-naḥwiyyīn wa-l-lughawiyyīn.* Ed. Muḥammad Abū l-Faḍl Ibrāhīm. Cairo: Maktabat al-Khānjī, 1373/1954.

Secondary Sources

Abu-Lughod, Lila (1989): 'Zones of Theory in the Anthropology of the Arab World.' *Annual Review of Anthropology* 18: 267–306.

Abu-Lughod, Lila (1990): 'Shifting politics in Bedouin love poetry.' *Lutz, Abu-Lughod* (eds.): 24–45.

Abu-Lughod, Lila (1999): *Veiled Sentiments. Honor and Poetry in a Bedouin Society.* Berkeley, Los Angeles, London: University of California Press [1st ed. 1986].

Al-Shahi, Ahmed (1986): 'Pride and Vilification. Two Tribal Viewpoints.' *Themes from Northern Sudan.* London: Ithaca Press: 68–90.

al-Alūsī, ʿĀdil Muḥyī l-Dīn (1987): *al-Raʾy al-ʿāmm fī l-qarn al-thālith al-hijrī.* Baghdad: Dār al-Shuʾūn al-Thaqāfiyya al-ʿĀmma.

Ammann, Ludwig (1993): *Vorbild und Vernunft. Die Regelung von Lachen und Scherzen im mittelalterlichen Islam.* Hildesheim etc.: Georg Olms Verlag.

Arazi, Albert (1979): 'Abū Nuwās fut-il šuʿūbite?' *Arabica* 26: 1–61.

ʿArnīṭa, Yusrā Jawhariyya (1997): *al-Funūn al-shaʿbiyya fī Filasṭīn.* Abu Dhabi: al-Majmaʿ al-Thaqāfī [3rd ed.].

Asad, Talal (1986): *The Idea of an Anthropology of Islam.* Washington, D. C.: Center for Contemporary Arab Studies (Georgetown University).

al-ʿAskar, ʿAbd al-Muḥsin b. ʿAbd al-ʿAzīz (1425 A. H.), *al-Iqtibās, anwāʿuhu wa-aḥkāmuhu: Dirāsa sharʿiyya balāghiyya fī l-iqtibās min al-Qurʾān wa-l-ḥadīth.* Riyadh: Maktabat Dār al-Minhāj.

al-ʿAsrī, Muḥammad ʿAbd al-Wāḥid (2001): 'Risālat ʿAbd al-Masīḥ al-Kindī ilā ʿAbdallāh al-Hāshimī: al-ghayriyya al-dīniyya fī l-mujādala l-naṣrāniyya li-l-islām.' *al-Ṣūra* (Tanger) 3 (3): 6–20.

ʿAṭwān, Ḥusayn (n.d.): *al-Zandaqa wal-shuʿūbiyya fī l-ʿaṣr al-ʿabbāsī al-awwal.* Beirut: Dār al-Jīl.

ʿAwīs, Muḥammad (1977): *al-Mujtamaʿ al-ʿabbāsī min khilāl kitābāt al-Jāḥiẓ.* Cairo: Dār al-Thaqāfa li-l-Ṭibāʿa wa-l-Nashr.

al-ʿAẓma, ʿAzīz (1991): *al-ʿArab wa-l-barābira, al-muslimūn wa-l-ḥaḍārāt al-ukhrā.* London: Riad El-Rayyes Books.

Ball, Donald W. (1970): 'The Problematics of Respectability.' *Douglas* (ed.): 326–371.

Ballas, S.; Snir, R. (1998): *Studies in Canonical and Popular Arabic Literature.* Toronto: York Press Ltd.

Banton, Michael (ed.) (1966): *The Social Anthropology of Complex Societies.* London: Tavistock Publications.

Banton, Michael (1969): *Roles. An Introduction to the Study of Social Relations.* London: Tavistock Publications [1st ed. 1965].

Barth, Fredrik (1983): *Sohar. Culture and Society in an Omani Town.* Baltimore, London: The Johns Hopkins University Press.

Bauer, Thomas (1996): 'Raffinement und Frömmigkeit: Säkulare Poesie islamischer Religionsgelehrter der später Abbasidenzeit.' *Asiatische Studien* 50: 275–95.

Bauer, Thomas (1998): *Liebe und Liebesdichtung in der arabischen Welt des 9. und 10. Jahrhunderts. Eine literatur- und mentalitätsgeschichtliche Studie des arabischen Ġazal.* Wiesbaden: Harrassowitz Verlag.

Bauman, Richard; Sherzer, Joel (eds.) (1974): *Explorations in the Ethnography of Speaking.* London, New York: Cambridge University Press.

Beaumont, Daniel (1993): 'A Mighty and Never Ending Affair: Comic Anecdote and Story in Medieval Arabic Literature.' *JAL* 24: 139-159.

Beeston, A. F. L. et al. (eds.) (1983): *The Cambridge History of Arabic Literature. Vol. I: Arabic Literature to the End of the Umayyad Period.* Cambridge: Cambridge University Press.

Ben Cheneb, Mohammed (1922): *Abû Dolâma. Poète bouffon de la Cour des premiers Califes abbassides.* Algiers: Jules Cabonel.

Benedict, Burton (1966): 'Sociological Characteristics of Small Territories and their Implications for Economic Development.' *Banton* (ed.): 23–35.

Berkey, Jonathan P. (1995): 'Tradition, Innovation and the Social Construction of Knowledge in the Medieval Islamic Middle East.' *Past and Present* 146: 38–65.

Berkey, Jonathan P. (2001): *Popular Preaching and Religious Authority in the Medieval Islamic Near East.* Seattle, London: University of Washington Press.

Binay, Sara (2006), *Die Figur des Beduinen in der arabischen Literatur. 9. – 12. Jahrhundert.* Wiesbaden: Dr. Ludwig Reichert Verlag.

Blachère, R. (1930): 'Un pionnier de la culture arabe orientale en Espagne: Ṣāʿid de Bagdad.' *Hespéris* 10: 15–36.

Bonebakker, Seeger A. (1967): 'Reflections on the *Kitāb al-Badīʿ* of Ibn al-Muʿtazz.' *Atti del Terzo Congresso di Studi Arabi e Islamici, Ravello 1–6 Settembre 1966.* Naples: Instituto Universitario Orientale: 191–209.

Borg, Gert (2000): 'Lust and Carnal Desire: Obscenities Attributed to Arab Women.' *Arabic and Middle Eastern Literatures* 3, 2: 149-64.

Borg, Gert; de Moor, Ed (eds.) (2001): *Orientations. Representations of the Divine in Arabic Poetry.* Amsterdam, Atlanta: Editions Rodopi.

Bosworth, Clifford Edmund (1976): *The Mediaeval Islamic Underworld. The Banū Sāsān in Arabic Society and Literature.* Leiden: E. J. Brill [2 vols.].

Bosworth, C. Edmund (1994): 'Abū Ḥafṣ ʿUmar al-Kirmānī and the Rise of the Barmakids.' *BSOAS* 57: 268–282.

Bouhdiba, Abdelwahab (2004): *Sexuality in Islam.* Tr. Alan Sheridan. London: Saqi Books.

Bray, Julia (ed.) (2006): *Writing and Representation in Medieval Islam. Muslim Horizons.* London, New York: Routledge.

Brunner, Rainer et al. (eds.) (2002): *Islamstudien ohne Ende. Festschrift für Werner Ende zum 65. Geburtstag.* Würzburg: Ergon Verlag (in commission for the Deutsche Morgenländische Gesellschaft).

Bulliet, Richard W. (1972): *The Patricians of Nishapur. A Study in Medieval Islamic Social History.* Cambridge, Mass.: Harvard University Press.

Cachia, Pierre (1995): 'Freedom from Clerical Control: The Portrayal of Men of Religion in Modern Arabic Literature.' *JAL* 26: 175–185.

Cahen, Claude (1958-59): 'Mouvements populaires et autonomisme urbain dans l'Asie Musulmane du Moyen Age.' *Arabica* 5: 225–250; 6: 25–56, 233–265.

Calder, Norman (2000): 'The Limits of Islamic Orthodoxy.' *Daftary* (ed.): 66–85.

Calero Secall, María Isabel (2001), 'El proceso de Ibn al-Jaṭīb.' *Al-Qanṭara* 22: 421–49.

Casajus, Dominique (1987): 'Parole retenue et parole dangereuse chez les Touaregs Kel Ferwan.' *Journal des Africanistes* 57: 97–107.

Caton, Steve C. (1990): *"Peaks of Yemen I Summon". Poetry as Cultural Practice in a North Yemeni Tribe.* Berkeley, Los Angeles, London: University of California Press.

Chanfrault, Bernard (1996): 'Jeḥa (Djoḥa) en Tunisie: de la tradition au modernisme. Approche socio-historique de l'anecdote orale.' *RMMM* 77–78: 51–59.

Chejne, Anwar G. (1965): 'The Boon-Companion in Early ʿAbbāsid Times.' *JAOS* 85: 327–335.

Clinard, Marshall B. (1965): *Sociology of Deviant Behavior.* New York etc.: Holt, Rinehart and Winston.

Conermann, Stephan; von Hees, Syrinx (eds.) (2007), *Islamwissenschaft als Kulturwissenschaft I. Historische Anthropologie. Ansätze und Möglichkeiten.* Hamburg: EB-Verlag.

Cook, Michael (2000), *Commanding Right and Forbidding Wrong in Islamic Thought.* Cambridge: Cambridge University Press.

Cooperson, Michael (2001), 'Two Abbasid trials: Aḥmad Ibn Ḥanbal and Ḥunayn b. Isḥāq.' *Al-Qanṭara* 22: 375–93.

Cooperson, Michael (2005), 'Probability, Plausibility, and "Spiritual Communication" in Classical Arabic Biography.' *Kennedy* (ed.): 69–83.

Crone, Patricia; Moreh, Shmuel tr. (2000), *The Book of Strangers. Medieval Arabic Graffiti on the Theme of Nostalgia.* Princeton: Markus Wiener Publishers.

Daftary, Farhad (ed.) (2000): *Intellectual Traditions in Islam.* London, New York: I. B. Tauris.

Davies, Christie (1987): 'Language, identity and ethnic jokes about stupidity.' *International Journal of the Sociology of Language* 65: 39–52.

De Jong, Frederick (ed.) (1993): *Verse and the Fair Sex. Studies in Arabic Poetry and in the Representation of Women in Arabic Literature.* Utrecht: M. Th. Houtsma Stichting.

Denzin, Norman K. (1970): 'Rules of Conduct and the Study of Deviant Behavior: Some Notes on the Social Relationship.' *Douglas* (ed.): 120–159.

Dépaule, Jean-Charles (1997): 'A propos de salles de réception dans l'Orient arabe.' *Taïeb et al* (eds.): 15–26.

Douglas, Mary (1968): 'The Social Control of Cognition: Some Factors in Joke Perception.' *Man* (N.S.) 3: 361–376.

Douglas, Jack D. (1970): 'Deviance and Respectability: The Social Construction of Moral Meanings.' *Douglas* (ed.): 3–30.

Douglas, Jack D. (ed.) (1970): *Deviance and Respectability. The Social Construction of Moral Meanings.* New York, London: Basic Books.

Drory, Rina (1996): 'The Abbasid Construction of the Jāhiliyya: Cultural Authority in the making.' *SI* 83: 33–49.

Dubois, Nicole (2003), 'Introduction: the concept of norm.' *Dubois* (ed.): 1–16.

Dubois, Nicole ed. (2003), *A Sociocognitive Approach to Social Norms.* London, New York: Routledge.

Dubois, Nicole; Beauvois, Jean-Léon (2003), 'Conclusion: Some bases for a sociocognitive approach to judgment norms.' *Dubois* (ed.): 231–46.

Eickelman, Dale F. (1989): *The Middle East. An Anthropological Approach.* Englewood Cliffs, N. J.: Prentice-Hall [1st ed. 1981].

El-Outmani, Ismail (1995): 'Introduction to Arabic "carnivalised" literature.' Concepción Vázquez de Benito, Miguel Angel Manzano Rodríguez (eds.), *Actas XVI Congreso UEAI.* Salamanca: Agencia Español de Cooperación Internacional, Consejo Superior de Investigaciones Científicas: 165–178.

El-Rouayheb, Khaled (2005): *Before Homosexuality in the Arab-Islamic World, 1500–1800.* Chicago, London: The University of Chicago Press.

el-Zein, Abdul-Hamid (1977): 'Beyond Ideology and Theology: The Search for the Anthropology of Islam.' *Annual Review of Anthropology* 6: 227–254.

Enderwitz, Susanne (1989), 'Du Fatā au Ẓarīf, ou comment on se distingue?' *Arabica* 36, 2; 125–42.

Feuerstein, G.; al-Marzooq, S. (1978): 'The Omani *xanīth.*' *Man* (N.S.) 13: 665–667.

Fierro, M. Isabel (1990): 'Andalusian "Fatāwā" on Blasphemy.' *Annales Islamologiques* 25: 103–117.

Fierro, M. (1994): 'El Proceso contra Ibn Ḥāṭim al-Ṭulayṭulī (años 457/1064–464/1072).' *Estudios Onomástico-Biográficos de al-Andalus* 6: 187–215.

Fierro, Maribel (2001), 'Religious dissension in al-Andalus: ways of exclusion and inclusion.' *Al-Qanṭara* 22: 463–87.

Fofana [Fawfānā], Adamu (1425 A. H. [2004–5]), *al-Aḥkām al-mutarattiba ʿalā l-fisq fī l-fiqh al-islāmī.* Riyadh: Maktabat Dār al-Minhāj. 2 vols.

Foley, William A. (1997): *Anthropological Linguistics. An Introduction.* Oxford: Blackwell Publishers.

Freedman, Jim (1977): 'Joking, affinity and the exchange of ritual services among the Kiga of northern Rwanda: an essay on joking relationship theory.' *Man* (N.S.) 12: 154–165.

García Gómez, Emilio (1940): 'Convencionalismo e insinceridad en la poesía árabe.' *Al-Andalus* 5: 31–43.

García Gómez, Emilio (1981): 'Un vejamen de Tarifa y Algeciras (traducción de Ṭurfat aẓ-ẓarīf fī ahl al-Jazīra wa-Ṭarīf).' *SI* 53: 5–26.

Gellner, Ernest (1981): *Muslim Society.* Cambridge: Cambridge University Press.

Ghazi, Mhammed Ferid (1959): 'Un groupe social: "Les Raffinés" (Ẓurafāʾ).' *SI* 11: 39–71.

Gilliot, Claude (2000), 'Un florilège coranique: le *Iqtibās min al-Qur'ān* de Abū Manṣūr al-Ṯaʿālibī (*ob.* 430/*init.* 3 oct. 1038 ou 429).' *Arabica* 47: 488–500.

Goode, William J. (1960): 'Norm Commitment and Conformity to Role-Status Obligations.' *The American Journal of Sociology* 66: 246–258.

Gruendler, Beatrice (2003): *Medieval Arabic Praise Poetry. Ibn al-Rūmī and the Patron's Redemption.* London, New York: RoutledgeCurzon.

Gruendler, Beatrice (2005a), 'Meeting the Patron: An *Akhbār* Type and Its Implications for *Muḥdath* Poetry.' *Günther* (ed.): 59–88.

Gruendler, Beatrice (2005b), 'Verse and Taxes: The Function of Poetry in Selected Literary *Akhbār* of the Third/Ninth Century.' *Kennedy* (ed.): 85–124.

Günther, Sebastian (ed.) (2005): *Ideas, Images, and Methods of Portrayal. Insights into Classical Arabic Literature and Islam.* Leiden, Boston: Brill.

Haeri, Niloofar (2000): 'Form and Ideology: Arabic Socioliguistics and Beyond.' *Annual Review of Anthropology* 29: 61–87.

Hallaq, Wael B. (1986): 'On the Authoritativeness of Sunni Consensus.' *IJMES* 18: 427–454.

Hamdan, Omar; Schmidtke, Sabine (2008), 'Qāḍī ʿAbd al-Jabbār al-Hamadhānī (d. 415/1025): *On the Promise and Threat.* An Edition of a Fragment of the *Kitāb al-Mughnī fī Abwāb al-Tawḥīd wa al-ʿAdl* Preserved in the Firkovitch-Collection, St. Petersburg.' *MIDEO* 27: 37–117.

Hammoudi, Abdellah (1993): *The Victim and Its Masks. An Essay on Sacrifice and Masquerade in the Maghreb.* Transl. Paula Wissing. Chicago, London: The University of Chicago Press.

Hamori, A. (1969): 'Examples of Convention in the Poetry of Abū Nuwās.' *SI* 30: 5–26.

Hámori, András (1999), 'The Silken Horsecloths Shed Their Tears.' *Arabic and Middle Eastern Literatures* 2: 43–59.

Handelman, Don; Kapferer, Bruce (1972): 'Forms of Joking Activity: A Comparative Approach.' *AA* 74: 484–517.

Hartung, Jan-Peter (2007), 'Wider die Schmach: Eine historisch-anthropologische Untersuchung von "Beleidigung" in einigen muslimischen Kontexten.' *Conermann, von Hees* (eds.): 107–37.

Herzfeld, Michael (1980): 'Honour and Shame: Problems in the Comparative Analysis of Moral Systems.' *Man* (N.S.) 15: 339–351.

Hillelson, S. (1935): *Sudan Arabic Texts. With Translation and Glossary.* Cambridge: Cambridge University Press.

Hirsch, Susan F. (1998): *Pronouncing and Persevering. Gender and the Discourses of Disputing in an African Islamic Court.* Chicago, London: University of Chicago Press.

Howard, C. G. (1921): *Shuwa Arabic Stories. With an Introduction and Vocabulary.* Oxford: Oxford University Press.

Hoyland, Robert G. (2006), 'History, fiction and authorship in the first centuries of Islam.' *Bray* (ed.): 16–46.

Hymes, Dell (1974): 'Ways of Speaking.' *Bauman, Sherzer* (eds.): 433–451.

Ibrahim, Abdullahi Ali (1994): *Assaulting with Words. Popular Discourse and the Bridle of* Sharīʿah. Evanston, Ill.: Northwestern University Press.

Ingham, Bruce (1976): 'Regional and social factors in the dialect geography of southern Iraq and Khūzistān.' *BSOAS* 39: 62–82.

Ingrams, W. H. (1933): *Abu Nuwas in Life and in Legend.* Port-Louis (Mauritius): La Typographie Moderne M. Gaud et Cie.

Irvine, Judith T. (1979): 'Formality and Informality in Communicative Events.' *AA* 81: 773–790.

[JAL Symposium] (1994): 'Revelry and Remorse: A Poem of Abū Nuwās.' *JAL* 25: 116–134.

Jargy, Simon (1970): *La poésie populaire traditionelle chantée au Proche-Orient arabe. I: Les textes. Avec une introduction critique.* Paris, The Hague: Mouton.

Jones, Alan (1991): 'Final *Taḍmīn* in the poems of Abū Nuwās.' Alan Jones (ed.), *Arabicus Felix: Luminosus Britannicus. Essays in Honour of A. F. L. Beeston on his Eightieth Birthday.* Reading: Ithaca Press: 61–73.

Jourdan, François (1983): *La Tradition des sept dormants. Une rencontre entre chrétiens et musulmans.* Paris: Maisonneuve et Larose.

Kayyāl, Munīr (n.d.): *Ramaḍān wa-taqālīduhu l-dimashqiyya.* Damascus: Dār al-Ḥayāt.

Kennedy, Philip F. (ed.) (2005): *On Fiction and* Adab *in Medieval Arabic Literature*. Wiesbaden: Harrassowitz Verlag.
al-Khāqānī, ʿAlī (1381/1962): *Funūn al-adab al-shaʿbī*. Baghdad: Maṭbaʿat al-Azhar.
Khayati, Mustapha (1989): 'Brèves remarques sur le poème libertaire "As-Sabr Lillah..." et son auteur.' *RMMM* 51: 137–142.
Kilpatrick, Hilary (1997): 'Abū l-Farağ's Profiles of Poets. A 4th/10th Century Essay at the History and Sociology of Arabic Literature.' *Arabica* 54: 94–128.
Kilpatrick, Hilary (2003): 'Monasteries Through Muslim Eyes: The *Diyārāt* Books.' *Thomas* (ed.): 19–37.
Knappert, J. (1961): 'The figure of the Prophet Muhammad according to the popular literature of the Islamic people.' *Swahili* 32: 24–31.
Knappert, Jan (1970): 'Social and moral concepts in Swahili Islamic Literature.' *Africa* 40: 125–136.
Knappert, Jan (1978): *Myths and Legends of the Swahili*. London, Nairobi etc.: Heinemann [reprint of the 1970 ed.].
Kopf, L. (1956): 'Religious Influences on Mediaeval Arabic Philology.' *SI* 5: 33–59.
Kraemer, Joel L. (1986): *Humanism in the Renaissance of Islam. The Cultural Revival during the Buyid Age*. Leiden: E. J. Brill.
Kruse, Hans (1984), 'Takfīr und ğihād bei den Zaiditen des Jemen.' *Die Welt des Islams* (N.S.) 23: 424–57.
Lagrange, Frédéric (2006), 'L'obscénité du vizir.' *Arabica* 53, 1: 54–107.
Lambert, Jean (1997): 'Le *magyal* yéménite: perole, jeux et roles dans l›espace social masculin.' *Taïeb et al* (eds.): 27–50.
Lane, Edward William (1895): *An Account of the Manners and Customs of the Modern Egyptians*. The Hague, London: East-West Publications.
Lange, Christian; Fierro, Maribel (eds.) (2009): *Public Violence in Islamic Societies: Power, Discipline, and the Construction of the Public Sphere, 7th–19th Centuries CE*. Edinburgh: Edinburgh University Press.
Lapidus, Ira M. (1975): 'The Separation of State and Religion in the Development of Early Islamic Society.' *IJMES* 6: 363–385.
Larzul, Sylvette (1996): 'Un récit comique des *Mille et une nuits*: l'"Histoire d'Abu l-Hasan, ou le dormeur éveillé".' *RMMM* 77–78: 29–39.
Lentin, Jérôme (2005–9): 'Middle Arabic.' *Versteegh et al.* (eds.): III, 215–24.
Lindholm, Charles (1995): 'The new Middle Eastern ethnography.' *JRAI* (N.S.) 1: 805–820.
Lloyd, G. E. R. (1990): *Demystifying Mentalities*. Cambridge etc.: Cambridge University Press.
Lutz, Catherine A.; Abu-Lughod, Lila (eds.) (1990): *Language and the politics of emotion*. Cambridge, Paris etc.: Cambridge University Press, Editions de la Maison des Sciences de l'Homme.
Mahdi, Muhsin (2000): 'The Rational Tradition in Islam.' *Daftary* (ed.): 43–65.
al-Majdhūb, al-Bashīr (1408/1988): *al-Ẓarf wa-l-ẓurafāʾ bi-l-Ḥijāz fī l-ʿaṣr al-umawī*. Tunis: Dār al-Turkī li-l-Nashr.
Marçais, Philippe (1954): *Textes arabes de Djidjelli*. Algiers: Presses Universitaires de France.
Marçais, W.; Guiga, Abderrahman (1925): *Textes arabes de Takroûna*. Paris: Imprimerie Nationale.
Marcus, Abraham (1986): 'Privacy in Eighteenth-Century Aleppo: The Limits of Cultural Ideals.' *IJMES* 18: 165–183.
Marzolph, Ulrich (1992), *Arabia Ridens. Die humoristische Kurzprosa der frühen adab-Literatur im internationalen Traditionsgeflecht*. Frankfurt am Main: Vittorio Klostermann. 2 vols.
Marzolph, Ulrich (2000), 'The Qoran and Jocular Literature.' *Arabica* 47, 3: 478–87.
al-Marzūqī, Muḥammad (1967): *al-Adab al-shaʿbī fī Tūnis*. Tunis: al-Dār al-Tūnisiyya li-l-Nashr.
McCarthy, R. J.; Raffouli, Faraj (1965): *Spoken Arabic of Baghdad. Part Two (A): Anthology of Texts*. Beirut: Librairie Orientale.

Meisami, Julie Scott (1993): 'Arabic *Mujūn* Poetry: The Literary Dimension.' *De Jong* (ed.): 8–30.
Meisami, Julie Scott; Starkey, Paul (eds.) (1998): *Encyclopedia of Arabic Literature*. London: Routledge.
Messick, Brinkley (1993): *The Calligraphic State. Textual Domination and History in a Muslim Society*. Berkeley, Los Angeles, London: University of California Press.
Mezziane, Mohammed (2008), `Sodomie et masculinité chez les juristes musulmans du IXe au XIe siècle.' *Arabica* 55: 276–306.
Michalak-Pikulska, B.; Pikulski A. (eds.) (2006): *Authority, Privacy and the Public Order in Islam. Proceedings of the 22nd Congress of the Union Europenne des Arabisants et Islamisants*. Leuven, Paris, Dudley MA: Uitgeverij Peeters.
Miliani, Hadj (1997): '"Mots de passe et sujets de mise": adresses et dédicaces dans la culture populaire en Algérie.' *Taïeb et al* (eds.): 119–131.
Mkelle, Burhan (1976): 'Religious concepts in the formation of Swahili expressions.' *Kiswahili* 46 (2): 41–46.
Molina, Luis (2003): 'Levántate, David.' *al-Qanṭara* 24: 217–221.
Montgomery, James E. (1996): 'For the Love of a Christian Boy: A Song by Abū Nuwās.' *JAL* 27: 115–124.
Mottahedeh, Roy P. (1980): *Loyalty and Leadership in an Early Islamic Society*. Princeton, N. J.: Princeton University Press.
Pellat, Charles (1953): *Le milieu baṣrien et la formation de Ǧāḥiẓ*. Paris: Adrien-Maisonneuve.
Pellat, Ch. (1963): 'Seriousness and Humour in Early Islam.' *Islamic Studies* 2: 353–362.
Piamenta, Moshe (1979): *Islam in Everyday Arabic Speech*. Leiden: E. J. Brill.
Pouzet, Louis (1991): *Damas au VIIe/XIIIe s. Vie et structures religieuses dans une métropole islamique*. Beirut: Dar el Machreq Sarl Editeurs.
al-Qishṭaynī, Khālid (1992): *al-Sukhriyya al-siyāsiyya al-ʿarabiyya*.Transl. Kamāl al-Yāzijī. London: Dār al-Sāqī [2nd ed.].
Radcliffe-Brown, A. R. (1940): 'On Joking Relationships.' *Africa* 13: 195–210.
Redissi, Hamadi (1998): *Les politiques en Islam. Le Prophète, le Roi et le Savant*. Paris: L'Harmattan.
Reinink, G. J.; Vanstiphout, H. L. J. (ed.) (1991): *Dispute Poems and Dialogues in the Ancient and Mediaeval Near East. Forms and Types of Literary Debates in Semitic and Related Literatures*. Leuven: Departement Oriëntalistiek, Uitgeverij Peeters.
Rescher, O. (1919): 'Studien über den Inhalt von 1001 Nacht.' *Der Islam* 9: 1–94.
Rosen, Lawrence (1984): *Bargaining for Reality. The Construction of Social Relations in a Muslim Community*. Chicago, London: The University of Chicago Press.
Rosenthal, Franz (1956): *Humor in Early Islam*. Leiden: E. J. Brill.
Rowson, Everett K. (1991), 'The Effeminates of Early Medina.' *JAOS* 111: 671–93.
Rowson, E. K. (1998), 'Mujūn.' *Meisami, Starkey* (eds.): II, 546–8.
Rowson, Everett K.; Wright, J. W. (eds.) (1997): *Homoeroticism in Classical Arabic Literature*. New York: Columbia University Press.
Rubiera Mata, María Jesús (1992): *Literatura hispanoárabe*. Madrid: Editorial MAPFRE.
Sadan, Joseph (1983): *al-Adab al-ʿarabī al-hāzil wa-nawādir al-thuqalāʾ*. Tel Aviv, Acre: Saruji Press.
Sadan, Joseph (1998): '*Hārūn al-Rashīd and the Brewer*. Preliminary Remarks on the *Adab* of the Elite versus *Ḥikāyāt*.' *Ballas, Snir* (eds.): 1–22.
Salzman, Philip Carl (1978): 'The Study of 'Complex Society' in the Middle East: A Review Essay.' *IJMES* 9: 539–557.
Sanni, Amidu (1998): *The Arabic Theory of Prosification and Versification. On* Ḥall *and* Naẓm *in Arabic Theoretical Discourse*. Beirut: Franz Steiner Verlag.
Schippers, Arie (2001): 'Humorous Approach of the Divine in the Poetry of al-Andalus: The Case of Ibn Sahl.' *Borg, de Moor* (eds.): 119–135.

Schmidtke, Sabine (1999): 'Homoeroticism and homosexuality in Islam: a review article.' *BSOAS* 62: 260–266.

Serjeant, R. B. (1951): *South Arabian Poetry. I: Prose and Poetry from Ḥaḍramawt.* London: Taylor's Foreign Press.

al-Shakʿa, Muṣṭafā (1983): *al-Adab al-andalusī, mawḍūʿātuhu wa-funūnuhu.* Beirut: Dār al-ʿIlm li-l-Malāyīn [5th ed.].

Sheikh, Sauda (1994): 'Yanayoudhi kuyaona. Mafumbo na Vijembe Vya Kiswahili.' *Afrikanistische Arbeitspapiere (Universität zu Köln)* 1: 7–11.

Shepherd, Gill (1978a): 'Transsexualism in Oman?' *Man* (N.S.) 13: 133–134.

Shepherd, Gill (1978b): 'The Omani *xanīth.*' *Man* (N.S.) 13: 663–665.

Sherif, Muzafer (1936), *The Psychology of Social Norms.* New York, London: Harper and Brothers Publishers.

Sherzer, Joel (1987): 'A Discourse-Centered Approach to Language and Culture.' *AA* 89: 295–309.

Shoshan, Boaz (1991): 'High Culture and Popular Culture in Medieval Islam.' *SI* 73: 67–107.

Shoshan, Boaz (1993): *Popular culture in medieval Cairo.* Cambridge etc.: Cambridge University Press.

Snouck Hurgronje, C. (1931): *Mekka in the Latter Part of the 19th Century.* Transl. J. H. Monahan. Leiden, London: E. J. Brill, Luzac and Co.

Sonneck, C. (1904): *Chants arabes du Maghreb. Etude sur le dialecte et la poésie populaire de l'Afrique du Nord.* Paris: Librairie Orientale [2 vols.].

Sowayan, Saad Abdullah (1985): *Nabaṭi Poetry. The Oral Poetry of Arabia.* Berkeley, Los Angeles, London: University of California Press.

Sperl, Stefan (1989): *Mannerism in Arabic poetry. A structural analysis of selected texts (3rd century AH/9th century AD–5th century AH/11th century AD).* Cambridge etc.: Cambridge University Press.

Sprachman, Paul (1995), *Suppressed Persian. An Anthology of Forbidden Literature.* Costa Mesa, CA: Mazda Publishers.

Sprachman, Paul (1997): '*Le beau garçon sans merci*: The Homoerotic Tale in Arabic and Persian.' *Rowson, Wright* (eds.): 192–209.

Stambouli, F.; Zghal, A. (1976): 'Urban life in pre-colonial North Africa.' *British Journal of Sociology* 27: 1–20.

Stewart, Devin J. (1996): 'Popular Shiism in Medieval Egypt: Vestiges of Islamic Sectarian Polemics in Egyptian Arabic.' *SI* 84: 35–66.

Szombathy, Zoltan (2004), 'Ridiculing the Learned: Jokes about the Scholarly Class in Mediaeval Arabic Literature.' *Al-Qanṭara* 25: 93–117.

Szombathy, Zoltan (2005), 'Some Notes on a Poetic Convention.' *Alifbâ – Studi Arabo-Islamici e Mediterranei* 19: 115–125.

Szombathy, Zoltan (2006), 'On Wit and Elegance: The Arabic Concept of *Ẓarf.*' *Michalak-Pikulska, Pikulski* (eds.): 101–19.

Szombathy, Zoltan (2007), 'Freedom of Expression and Censorship in Mediaeval Arabic Literature.' *Journal of Arabic and Islamic Studies* 7: 1–24.

Szombathy, Zoltan (2009), 'Actions Speak Louder than Words: Reactions to Lampoons and Abusive Poetry in Mediaeval Arabic Society.' *Lange, Fierro* (eds.): 87–116.

Taïeb, Hannah Davis; Bekkar, Rabia; David, Jean-Claude (eds.) (1997): *Espaces publics, paroles publiques au Maghreb et au Machrek.* Paris: L'Harmattan.

Testé, Benoit (2003), 'Conformity and deviance.' *Dubois* (ed.): 17–37.

Thesiger, Wilfred (1967): *The Marsh Arabs.* London: Penguin Books.

Thomas, David (ed.) (2003): *Christians at the Heart of Islamic Rule. Church Life and Scholarship in ʿAbbasid Iraq.* Leiden, Boston: Brill.

Toorawa, Shawkat M. (2005): 'Defining *Adab* by (re)defining the *Adīb*: Ibn Abī Ṭāhir Ṭayfūr and storytelling.' *Kennedy* (ed.): 287–308.

Torrey, Charles C. (1911): 'Al-Aṣmaʿī's Fuḥūlat aš-Šuʿarāʾ.' *ZDMG* 65: 487–516.

Uld Abbāh, Muḥammad al-Mukhtār (1987): *al-Shiʿr wa-l-shuʿarāʾ fī Mūrītāniyā*. Tunis: al-Sharika al-Tūnisiyya li-l-Tawzīʿ.

Vajda, G. (1938): 'Les zindīqs en pays d'Islam au début de la période abbaside.' *Rivista degli Studi Orientali* 17: 173–229.

van Gelder, Geert Jan (1988), *The Bad and the Ugly. Attitudes towards Invective Poetry (*Hijāʾ*) in Classical Arabic Literature*. Leiden etc.: E.J. Brill.

van Gelder, G. J. H. (1992): 'Mixtures of Jest and Earnest in Classical Arabic Literature.' *JAL* 23: 83–108, 169–190.

van Gelder, Geert Jan (2002–3): 'Forbidden Firebrands: Frivolous *Iqtibās* (Quotation from the Qurʾān) According to Medieval Arab Critics.' *QSA* 20–21: 3–16.

van Nieuwkerk, Karin (2002), *"A Trade like Any Other". Female Singers and Dancers in Egypt*. Austin: University of Texas Press [4th paperback ed.].

Versteegh, C. H. M. et al. (eds.) (2005–9), *Encyclopedia of Arabic Language and Linguistics*. Leiden: E. J. Brill. 5 vols.

Virolle-Souibès, Marie (1989): 'Le Raï entre résistance et récupération.' *Revue du Musulman et de la Méditerranée* 51: 47–62.

vom Bruck, Gabriele (1996): 'Being worthy of protection. The dialectics of gender attributes in Yemen.' *Social Anthropology* 4: 145–162.

von Grunebaum, Gustave E. (1944): 'The Concept of Plagiarism in Arabic Theory.' *Journal of Near Eastern Studies* 3: 234–253.

von Hees, Syrinx (2007): 'Historische Anthropologie in der Islamwissenschaft.' In *Conermann, von Hees* (eds.): 21–35.

Wagner, Ewald (2008): *Abū Nuwās in der Nebenüberlieferung. Dem Dichter zugeschriebene Gedichte und Verse*. Wiesbaden: Harrassowitz Verlag.

Walther, Wiebke (2002): ' *"Fa-qad yaḏhabu bi-ʾl-hazli ʾḍ-ḍağarū"*. Scherze der Gebildeten in Nağaf in der ersten Hälfte des 20. Jahrhunderts.' *Brunner et al.* (eds.): 501–15.

al-Wardī, ʿAlī (1965): *Dirāsa fī ṭabīʿat al-mujtamaʿ al-ʿirāqī*. Baghdad: Maṭbaʿat al-ʿĀnī.

Weipert, Reinhard (2009): *Altarabischer Sprachwitz: Abū ʿAlqama und die Kunst, sich kompliziert auszudrücken*. Munich: Verlag C. H. Beck.

Westermarck, Edward (1930): *Wit and Wisdom in Morocco. A Study of Native Proverbs*. London: Routledge.

Wikan, Unni (1977): 'Man becomes woman: transsexualism in Oman as a key to gender roles.' *Man* (N.S.) 12: 304–319.

Wolf, Eric R. (1966): 'Kinship, Friendship, and Patron-Client Relations in Complex Societies.' *Banton* (ed.): 1–22.

Wright, J. W. (1997): 'Masculine Allusion and the Structure of Satire in Early ʿAbbāsid Poetry.' *Rowson, Wright* (eds.): 1–23.

Yassin, Mahmoud Aziz F. (1978): 'Kuwaiti Arabic Idioms.' *BSOAS* 41: 67–72.

Zubaidi, A.M. (1983), 'The impact of the Qurʾān and Ḥadīth on medieval Arabic literature.' *Beeston et al.* (eds.): 322–43.

Index

Page numbers in italics refer to footnotes

al-ʿAbbās b. al-Aḥnaf, 273
Abbasid period, ix, 19, 31, 49, 56, 73, 110, 115–8, 120, 125, 131, 147, 162, 165, 167, 178, 208, 226, 268–9, 271, 291–2, *170*
ʿAbd al-Jabbār al-Hamadhānī, 185
ʿAbdallāh b. Jaʿfar b. Abī Ṭālib, 262
ʿAbd al-Malik b. Ṣāliḥ, 201
ʿAbd al-Raḥmān b. Ḥassān b. Thābit, 262
ʿAbd al-Sayyid b. Jakar, *256*
al-Ābī, Abū Manṣūr, 234–5
ablution, see *wuḍūʾ*, 15, 87
Abraham, 55, 61, *56*, *57–8*, *197*
Abū Aḥmad b. Abī Bakr al-Kātib, *94*
Abū ʿAlī b. al-Rashīd, *174*
Abū ʿAlqama, also see jokes on grammarians, 101, 150
Abū l-ʿAtāhiya, 224, *39*, *217*
Abū l-ʿAynāʾ, 63, 142, 268
Abū Bakr (caliph), 84, *24*
Abū Bakr al-Ẓāhirī, *207*
Abū Dulaf, 119
Abū Dulāma, 123, 178, 297, *124*, *168*, *274*
Abū l-Faraj al-Iṣfahānī, 271, *205*
Abū Firās al-Ḥamdānī, 18–9
Abū Ḥanīfa, 189, *10*, *24*, *205*, *300*
Abū l-Ḥārith Jummayn, 53, 110
Abū Hiffān, 66, 263, *257*
Abū l-Hindī, *200*
Abū Ḥukayma, 121
Abū l-ʿIbar, 234, *274*
Abū ʿIṣma, 205
Abū l-Jahm b. Sayf, 275–6
Abū Khāzim, 206–7
Abu-Lughod, Lila, 248, 259, *261*
Abū Māḍī, Īliyā, *254*
Abū Nukhayla, 129, *173*
Abū Nuwās, al-Ḥasan b. Hāniʾ al-Ḥakamī, 47, 66, 68, 178–9,205, 269, 270, 288, 293, 297, 298, *118*
– as homosexual, 38, 69, 88, 89, 96, 99, 138–9, 294–5, *12*, *135*, *137*, *165*, *225*
– as poet, ix, 54, 55, 88, 107, 110, 112, 115, 125–6, 127, 131, 138–9, 202, 209, 212, 214, 221, 224, 253–4, 278, 292, 304, 305–6, *37*, *49*, *73*, *75*, *82*, *90*, *191*, *194*, *199*, *225*, *283–4*
– as protagonist of anecdotes, 38, 82, 93, 99
figure of – in folklore, 55, 253–4, *162*
popularity of his works, 124, 162–3, 169, 173, 202, 204, 209, 214, 235, 238–9, 244, 263–4, 286, *270*
Abū l-Rabīʿ b. ʿAbdallāh, 96
Abū Sahl b. Nawbakht, 38
Abū Ṭalḥa al-Ḥadhdhāʾ, 74
Abū Tammām, 131, 172, 175–6, 209, 212, 276, *82*
Abū ʿUbayda, *118*
Abū ʿUmar al-Azdī, 9, 202, 203, 205, *219–20*
Abū l-Yanbaghī, 148
Abū Yūsuf, *285*
Abyssinians, 49
adab, 145–6, 201, 259–60, 264, 265, *233*
– collections, 27, 36–7, 56, 119, 140, 201, 304, *196*, *272*, *273*
ʿadāla, see testimony
Adam, 53, 54, *299–300*
adhān,
parodies of –, 85–6, *86–7*
ʿādhil, ʿādhila, 40, 86, 112, 138–9, 165, 306, *199–200*
al-Adhruʿī, 192
ʿAdī al-Hakkārī, *162*
ʿAḍud al-Dawla, 278, *133*
adultery, see *zināʾ*,
ʿĀʾisha, 84, 119, *85*
ajwiba muskita, see quick repartee
akhbār, 6, 241–2, 283, *153*
Akhbār al-ẓirāf wa-l-mutamājinīn, 204
al-Akhfash al-Awsaṭ, 34
Akhlāq al-wazīrayn, 171, 235
al-Akhṭal, *110*
akhyār, *261*
ʿAkk, 30
ʿAlam al-Dīn Aḥmad, *262*
Aleppo, 8, 240, 277–8, *133*, *165*
ʿAlī b. Abī Ṭālib, *27–8*, *84*, *198*
ʿAlī b. ʿĪsā (vizier), 145, 202
Almohad dynasty, 223, *239*
alms tax, see *zakāt*
al-Alūsī, al-Muʾayyad, *220*
al-Aʿmash,73, *201*
al-Amīn (caliph), 171, 173, 263–4, *225*
conflict between – and al-Maʾmūn, *173*
ʿĀmir Zurūmī, *135*
ʿāmma, 20–9, 232
– and education, 22, 32
– and wealth, 21–2
attitudes of – to *mujūn*, 159–66, 253–8
disdain towards the –, 21, 23–9
etymology of –, *28*

mobs among the –, 163–4, *224*
Ammann, Ludwig, *41*
amorous poetry, 56, 76, 78, 79–80, 81, 95, 97, 105, 129–30, 132, 136, 192–4, 204, 206–7, 208, 210–1, 217, 224, 233, 284, 286, 292, 305–6, *20*, *135*, *191*, *203*, *225*, *257*, *261*, *283–4*, *295*
al-amr bi-l-maʿrūf wa-l-nahy ʿan al-munkar, 39, 162, 199–200, *3*
al-Andalus, 59, 122, 193, 226, 233, 238–40, 246, 286, *104*, *120*, *137*, *151*, *223*, *235*
anecdotes, 16, 27, 37–8, 61, 77, 92, 101, 108–9, 119, 137, 151, 161, 162, 204, 243, 252, 256, 261, 306, *42*, *153*, *229*, *284*
al-Anṭākī, al-Ḥusayn b. Samaydaʿ, 277
anthologies, also see *adab* collections, 36–7, 44, 51, 155, 213–4, 218, 235–6, 238–9, 245, 266, 283, 304, 305, *124*, *233*
anthropology, xii–xiii, 4–5, 248, 250
Antichrist, 101–2
Antioch, 277
ʿaqd, see versification
al-Aqṭaʿ al-Kūfī, 70
Arabia, 19, 68, 83, 115–8, 127, 166, *57*, *205*, *241*, *267*
Arabic, also see diglossia,
Classical –, 33–4, 47, 141, 149, 168
dialects of –, 50, 55, 110, 238, *255*, *265*
dialectal features in written – texts, 32–3, 35, 55, 141, 143–4, 225, 229–30, 253–8, 307, *31*, *71*, *75–6*, *148*, *149*
Middle –, *31*
use of Classical – in mundane contexts, 150–3
al-Aʿraj, Aḥmad al-Qaysī al-Qurṭubī, *152*
argot, see slang
arkān al-dīn, 85–97
aṣābiʿ Zaynab, 120
Asad, Talal, 249, 250
al-Asʿad b. Muqrib, 239
al-Asadī, 22
ʿaṣā Mūsā, also see Moses, 52–3, *57*
al-Aʿshā, 202, 212
Ashʿab, 74, 231
aṣḥāb al-kahf, see Seven Sleepers
ashqiyāʾ, *261*
ashrāf, 22, 204, 242, *23*
al-ʿAskarī, Abū Hilāl al-Ḥasan, 151
al-Aṣmaʿī, 61, 263
al-Atharī, Muḥammad Bahja, 245
aṭlāl motif, 125–6, 127, 306, *291*
al-ʿAttābī, 28
avarice, 24, 120, 261–2, *208*
Avicenna, *226*
Awlād ʿAlī, *261*
al-Awqaṣ al-Makhzūmī, 205
al-Awzāʿī, 15
ʿayyārūn, *26*
Ayyūbid dynasty, 55
Azāriqa, see Khārijites,86, *28*, *288*
al-Azharī, Abū Manṣūr Muḥammad, 40
al-ʿAzīz b. Ṣalāḥ al-Dīn, 55, 240

Bāb al-Shām, 28
Bāb al-Ṭāq, 292, *12*, *199*
al-Babbaghāʾ, Abū l-Faraj, 58
bacchic poetry, also see *khamriyyāt*, 86, 87, 107, 110, 111–2, 136, 217, 233, 234, 286, 304, *132*, *173*, *199*, *233*, *283–4*
backgammon, 16, *187*
badhāʾa, see obscenity
Badr, *83*
Badr al-Rashīd Muḥammad b. Ismāʿīl, 183, 185
Baghdad, 11, 25, 63, 79, 82, 84, 110, 143, 163–4, 175, 205, 230, 232, 235–6, 238, 251, 254, 256, 257, 279, 283, 292, 299, *12*, *57*, *64*, *68*, *98*, *148*, *170*, *199*, *203*, *216*
– as epitome of urbane culture, 240–2, 244
Baghdadian Epistle, see *al-Risāla al-baghdādiyya*
baghīḍ, 199–200, 202–3, 207, *151*
Bahāʾ al-Dawla, 169
al-Bākharzī, Abū l-Ḥasan ʿAlī, *135*, *214*
Bakhtin, Mikhail, 289
bāla, *145*, *267*
al-Baladī, ʿUbaydallāh b. Aḥmad, *111*
Balāghāt al-nisāʾ, 134, *245*
Ball, Donald W., *288*
al-Ballūṭī, Mundhir b. Saʿīd, 17
banning of books, 216–8, *236*
Banū Hilāl, 244
Banū Sulaym, 244
Banū ʿUdhra, 62, 129–30
al-Bāqillānī, 195
barāmika, *130*
al-Barbahārī, 164, 198
bārid, 202, 203
Barmakid family, *218*
al-Baṣāʾir wa-l-dhakhāʾir, *272*
Basra, 47, 292, *226*, *257*
al-Baṭāʾiḥī, Murajjā b. Battāh, 226
al-Battī, Abū Jaʿfar, 226
al-Battī, Aḥmad, 169
Bauer, Thomas, 144, 238–9, *136*, *262*
al-Bayhaqī, Ibrāhīm b. Muḥammad, 32
bazmāward, 110
beans, *197*
Beaumont, Daniel, *154*
Bedouin, also see protagonists of *mujūn* texts, 23, 31, 35, 62, 67, 154, 158, 230–1, 243–4, *272*
caricatures of – heritage, 118–21, 125–9, 306
– code of behaviour, also see *murūʾa*, 8, 17, 114, 115–8, 122, 190, *261*
– cultural heritage, 114, 115, 129–30, 208–9, 211, 253, 266, 284, 286, 292
– dress, 128
beggars, 35, 143, 256, *4*, *272*
Berbers, *12*, *230*, *289*
Berkey, Jonathan P., 5, *199*

bestiality, 127, 148
Bible, 49, 53
bid^ca, 14, 80, 251, *21*, *199*
anti-- treatises, 6, 161, 229, *36*, *70*
Bilmawn, *148*, *289*
Bilqīs, 55
al-Binṣ, Abū Naṣr, *205*
al-Bīrūnī, Abū l-Rayḥān, 293
blasphemy, 35, 103–5, 161, 185–7, 193, 222–4, 227–8, 229, 232, 284, *162*, *191*, *230*, *293*
boon-companion, 169, 173, 174, 177, 241, 263–4, *19*, *22*, *136*, *280*, *281*, *296*
Borg, Gert, 133
Bouhdiba, Abdelwahab, 159, *41*
Bourdieu, Pierre, 259
boys,
– as objects of longing, 10–2, 38, 56, 65, 69, 81, 86, 88, 89, 96, 98–9, 107, 131, 134–40, 173, 175–6, 192, 193, 239, 292, 293, 306, 307, *257*, *294–5*
– as preferable to women, 137–40, 264, 305, *126*
bridewealth, see *mahr*
Buhlūl, 231
buhtān, see lying
al-Buḥturī, 142, *275*
Bukhārā, 123
al-Bukhārī, *76*
al-Būshanjī, 153
al-Buṣrawī, Abū l-Ḥasan Muḥammad, 254
al-Bustī, Abū l-Fatḥ, *76*
Buyid period, 4, 9, 23, 26, 51, 63, 70, 82, 84, 104, 115, 124, 126, 128, 138, 145, 151, 160, 164, 168, 170, 205, 230, 234, 256, 278, 283, *57*, *135*, *199*
Byzantines, 108, 277, 282

Cairo, 237, 244, *201*
call to prayer, see *adhān*
calumny, see *qadhf*
Carmathians, 58
carnival, 288–9, *148*
carnivalised literature, 289
case endings, also see Arabic, 50, *151*
'censorship', 216–22, 227–8, 232–3, 243, 244–6
Central Asia, 31
Chad, 49
chess, 16, *148*, *187*, *300*
Christianity, Christians, xi, 35, 49, 73, 81–2, 146, 246, 306, *60*, *112*, *217*
circumcision, 45, *7*
cities, also see urban population, 115, 123, 127–8, 158, 240–1, 243–4, 251, 279, *10*
– and countryside, 29–31
'commanding right and forbidding wrong', see *al-amr bi-l-ma^crūf wa-l-nahy ^can al-munkar*
commoners, common people, see ^cāmma
convention, 52, 118, 123, 125, 291–5, 297, 298, 304
Cook, Michael, *3*
Cordoba, 17, 241
court jesters, 274, *168*
cowardice, 118–20
crime, criminals, *4*, *10*, *199*
Crone, Patricia, *6*, *111*, *158*
cupbearer, see *sāqī*
cynicism, 38, 67, 109–10, 130, 131, 133, 210, 266, *283*

al-Dabbās, Abū Tammām, 213, *276*
dābbat al-arḍ, 101
al-Dajjāl, see Antichrist,
al-Dalāl, 172
Damādh, Abū Ghassān, *233*
Damascus, 67, *89*, *92*, *164*, *174*, *244*, *256*
dance, 16, 130, 186, 206, 289, *219*
ḍarb mathal, *210*
David, 53
Daylam, 35, 59, 84, 230
decadence, 5, 170
Denzin, Norman K., *300*
derision, see *istihzā'*
descendants of the Prophet, see *ashrāf*
deserted camping-ground, see *aṭlāl* motif
al-Dhahabī, *262*
Di^cbil al-Khuzā^cī, *226*
diglossia, 31–4, *3*
discretion, 11, 12, 134, 174–5, 224, 280, 284–6, 308, *132*, *146*, *173*, *188*, *189*
divine law, see *sharī^ca*
divorce, 65–6, 182, 230, *189*
dīwān, 202, 208
double entendre, 75, 141–2, 307
Douglas, Jack D., 279
Douglas, Mary, 292
dress, 7
drinking parties, also see private situations, 8, 20, 25, 81–2, 130, 169, 173, 174, 176, 188, 201–2, 257, 263–4, 280, 292, 298, *21–2*, *86*, *146*
drunkenness, also see wine, 44, 205, *88*, *148*, *173*
Druzes, *23*
Durrat al-tāj min shi^cr Ibn al-Ḥajjāj, *235–6*
dūshāb, *29*

eating, 22, 28, 153, *189*
effeminate men, see *mukhannath*,
Egypt, 7, 55, 239–40, 244, 289, *16*, *31*, *64*, *130*, *146*, *226*, *236*, *245*, *261*
elegy, 105, 124, *218*, *235*
élite, see *khāṣṣa*
'empty talk', 16
ephebes, see boys
epigones, 236, 292, *238*
eschatology, also see Paradise, Hell, 97–102
everyday culture, 6, 15, 21, 45
execution, also see punishment, 79, 220, 222–7, 274, *80*, *87*, *164*, *170*, *216*, *218*, *280*
expiatory verses, 233
extramarital affairs, see *zinā*

fāḥisha, 40, 192
faḥl, *119*
Fakhr al-Mulk, 169
fālūdhaj, 53, 121
al-Farazdaq, *111*
fasting, also see Ramadan, 45, 90–3, 306, *79*, *193*
fatwā, 77–8, 186, 194, 306, 307, *196*, *203*, *285*
– collections, 6, 161, 167, 182–3, 193
fiction, fictionality, 6, 37–8, 63, 101, *183*
Fierro, Maribel, *223*
fiqh, 15, 106, 181–98, 219–20, 222, 252, 285, 288, *199–200*
– as source of motifs in *mujūn* literature, 76–81, 100
– manuals, 6, 13, 44, 161, 167, 181, 182–3, 185, *10*
fiqhiyyāt, 76
al-Firāsī, ʿAbd al-Raḥmān, *38*
fisq, 40, 106, 182, 187–9, 287–8, *199–200*
– and testifying in court, 188–9, *184–5*
overt –, 285
fityān, 299, *10*, *26*
folk epics, *193*
folk tales, *16*, *20*, *148*
food, also see eating, 29, 93, 120
fornication, see *zinā*
al-Fuḍayl b. ʿIyāḍ, 15
fuḥsh, see obscenity
fuqahāʾ, see jurisprudents
furūʿ, 114
futuwwa, see *fityān*

Gabriel, 161
gambling, *16*, *63*, *199*, *300*
genealogy, 120, *152*
al-Gharīḍ, 30, *100*
ghawāzī, *130*
ghazal, also see amorous poetry
al-Ghazālī, Abū Ḥāmid, 7, 191–2, 287, *17–8*, *28*, *109*, *285*
Ghazi, F. M., *266*, *268*
ghība, see gossip
ghilmān, see boys
gluttony, also see eating, food, 53, 120–1, 307
Gog and Magog, *102*
Goode, William J., 295–6
gossip, 171, 191, 206, 285, *133*, *187*
grammar, also see *naḥw*, 22, 101, 150–3, 256, 283
grammatical terms as sexual innuendoes, 141–2, 307
grammatical gender, *65*
use of feminine – among effeminates, *12*
use of masculine – in poetry, 136, 194
greengrocers, 24, 29

ḥadd, also see punishment, 79–80, 198, *173*
ḥadīths, 14–5, 46, 97, 181–2, 197, 205, 239, 285, *11*, *16*, *28*, *78*, *80*, *152*, *185*
– as source of *mujūn* motifs, 48, 68–75, 161, 200, *51*, *64*, *66*
– condemning sodomy, *10*
ḥadīth criticism, 75–6
pseudo- –, 73–5
Ḥaḍramawt, *244*
ḥajj, see pilgrimage
al-Ḥajjāj b. Yūsuf al-Thaqafī, 17, 83
ḥajr, see tutelage, 189
ḥalāl, also see *fiqh*, 78, 276, 288, *193*, *299–300*
ḥall, see prosification
al-Ḥallāj, Manṣūr, 38, *216*
al-Ḥamāsa al-maghribiyya, 238–9
al-Ḥamdānī, 275
al-Ḥamdūnī, 93, 123, *149*
Ḥāmid b. al-ʿAbbās, 145
Ḥammād ʿAjrad, 147, *131–2*, *226*
Ḥammād al-Rāwiya, *108*, *208*
ḥammām, see public baths, 198
Hammoudi, Abdellah, *289*
Ḥamza b. ʿAbd al-Muṭṭalib, 83, 85
Ḥamza al-Iṣbahānī, 305–6, *293*
Ḥanafite school, 81, 100, 103, 182–3, 185, 186, 188, 190, 193, 196, 197, 199, *15*, *191*, *192*, *200*, *285*, *288*
Ḥanbalite school, 70, 163–4, 183, 190, 191–2, 194, 195, 197, 204, *15*, *185*, *188*, *203*
ḥarām, also see *fiqh*, 78, 79, 192, 194, 288, *299–300*
al-Ḥarbī, Ibrāhīm,77
al-Ḥārithī, Yaḥyā b. Ziyād,100
Hārūn al-Rashīd (caliph), 24, 275, *149*, *170*, *217*, *218*
Hārūt and Mārūt, *102*
al-Ḥasan al-Baṣrī, *203*
al-Hāshimī, Yāsīn, *142*
Hāshimite family, 277, *22*
hawā, 16
Ḥayṣ-Bayṣ, *233*
al-Haytamī, Abū l-ʿAbbās Aḥmad, 183, 192, 195–6, *182*, *191*
al-Ḥaẓīrī, Saʿd, *257*
hazl, also see jesting, 18, 169, 183, 194, 212–3, 272, 284, 308
Hell, 28, 85, 92, 98, 102, 112, 306, *62*, *97*, *194*
Hell's Angels, *300*
heresy, see *zandaqa*
heroism, 117–8, 291, 292, *125*
parodies of –, 118–20, 306, 307
hijāʾ, 140, 147, 149, 179, 187, 190, 192, 194, 217, 224–7, 233, 283, 304, 306, 307, *129*, *214*
hijāʾ Ramaḍān, see Ramadan
Hijaz, 68, *118*, *205*, *241*
ḥilm, see self-restraint
Ḥimṣ, *12*, *242*
Hind bt. ʿUtba, 85
al-Ḥīra, 24
ḥisba, see *muḥtasib*
al-Ḥizāmī, Abū Muḥammad, *208*
holidays, see ʿīd
homicide, 79, *80*
homoeroticism, 10, 12, 132, 134
homosexuality, see *liwāṭ*, *ubna*

honour, 3, 36, 41, 113, 116–7, 121, 135, 225–6, 259, 272, 280, *165*, *179*, *208*
houris, 98–9
Hoyland, Robert, 37–8
Ḥubbā, 231
humour, also see jesting, x, 13–20, 35, 46, 51–2, 69, 100, 160, 192, 266, 273–4, 289–90, *60*, *88*, *101*, *144*, *151*, *168*, *211*
humourless bores, see *thaqīl*
al-Ḥurr al-ʿĀmilī, *135*
al-Ḥusayn b. ʿAlī b. Abī Ṭālib, 7, 83
al-Ḥusayn b. al-Ḍaḥḥāk, 270
Hymes, Dell, *298*
hyperbole,
excessive –, 103–5, 192, 193, 227–8
– in praise poetry, 102–5, 190, 192, 194, 283, 284
hypocrisy, 173, 281–2, *219–20*

Ibāḍites, *15*, *285*
ibāḥatī, *299–300*
Iberian peninsula, see al-Andalus
Ibn ʿAbbās, 15, 74
Ibn ʿAbd Rabbihi, *233*
Ibn Abī Karīma, 123
Ibn Abī Maryam al-Madanī, *170*
Ibn Abī Ṭāhir Ṭayfūr, 22, 133–4, *245*
Ibn al-ʿAmīd, Abū l-Faḍl, 171, *170*
Ibn ʿAqīl, 195, *188*
Ibn ʿAtīq, 119
Ibn Baydakīn al-Turkumānī, 70, 190, 191, *109*, *162*
Ibn Bint Abī Nūḥ, Abū ʿĪsā, *137*
Ibn Bulbul, Ismāʿīl, *222–3*
Ibn al-Dawraqī, *226*
Ibn Diḥya al-Balansī, *214*
Ibn Furāt, Abū l-Fatḥ, 276
Ibn al-Habbāriyya, Abū Yaʿlā Muḥammad, 109, 168–9
Ibn al-Ḥajjāj, 93, 270, 297
– as poet, 133, 169, 254
popularity of his works, 124, 169, 235–6, *214*, *284*
Ibn Hāniʾ al-Andalusī, *194*
Ibn Harma, *173*
Ibn Ḥijja al-Ḥamawī, 196
Ibn Hindū, Abū l-Faraj ʿAlī, 138
Ibn Hubayra, 221
Ibn al-Jawālīqī, Abū Bakr, *151*
Ibn al-Jaṣṣāṣ, 9, 232, *22*
Ibn al-Jawzī, 27, 84, 204
Ibn Khafāja, 122
Ibn al-Khaṭīb, Lisān al-Dīn, *223*
Ibn Lankak, *257*
Ibn Manẓūr, 40
Ibn Maʿrūf, 206
Ibn Miftāḥ, Abū l-Ḥasan, *216–7*
Ibn Mishkān, Abū Naṣr, 170
Ibn al-Mubārak, 242
Ibn Mufliḥ al-Maqdisī, 183, 192, 193, *185*, *188*, *203*
Ibn Mujāhid, 203, 282
Ibn Mujāwir, Najm al-Dīn, 239–40
Ibn Munādhir, Muḥammad, 73, 165–6, 271
Ibn al-Munajjim, Abū Muḥammad, *137*
Ibn Mundhir al-Baṭalyawsī, 239–40
Ibn al-Muʿtazz, 119, 218, 259, *131*, *137*, *162*, *214*
Ibn al-Muzarraʿ, Muhalhil al-ʿAbdī, *162*, *293*
Ibn Qirān, Abū l-Fatḥ, 233
Ibn Qurayʿa, 206
Ibn Quzmān, 59, 238, 255, *86*
Ibn Rashīq al-Qayrawānī, 55, 72, 272–3
Ibn al-Rāwandī, 229
Ibn Rushayd al-Fihrī al-Sabtī, 193
Ibn Sahl al-Andalusī, *56*
Ibn Saʿīd al-Andalusī, 239
Ibn Shabāba, *202*
Ibn Shannabūdh, *163*
Ibn Sharaf, 55
Ibn Shibl, *11*
Ibn Shukhayṣ, *120*
Ibn Sīda, 40
Ibn Sīrīn, Muḥammad, 203
Ibn Sukkara, 236
Ibn Surayj, *207*
Ibn Tammār al-Wāsiṭī, *167*
Ibn Taymiyya, 190, 197
Ibn Wahb, al-Ḥasan, 105
Ibn Wahb, Saʿīd, 232–3
Ibn Yāsmīn al-Ishbīlī, *137*
Ibn al-Zayyāt, Muḥammad b. ʿAbd al-Malik, 175–6
Ibrahim, Abdullahi Ali, *259*
ʿīd, 45, 77, 91, 93, *170*, *284*
ʿidda, 80
ideals,
– versus actual behaviour, 1–12, 114, 117–8, 128–9, 144–6, 166, 190, 191, 197, 200, 210–1, 258–9, 280, 284–5, *268*, *296*
al-Īdhajī, Abū ʿAlī al-Ḥasan, 147
ʿidhār, 69, 136, 307
al-Ifrīqī, Abū l-Ḥasan Muḥammad, *111*
īhām, see double entendre, 60, 75–6, 141–2, 307
iʿjāz al-Qurʾān, see Quran
ʿIkrima, 74
al-Iʿlām bi-qawāṭiʿ al-islām, 183
illiteracy, also see literacy, 4, 23, 30, 32, 47, 57, 65–6, 76, 84, 159–62, 237, *33*, *256–7*
ʿilm al-rijāl, see *ḥadīth* criticism
ʿImād al-Dīn al-Iṣbahānī, 245
imam, 38, 67, 89, 104, 165–6, 172, 189, *202*, *222*, *300*
'immorality', see *fisq*
impotence, see sex
imprisonment, also see punishment, 173, 194, 220–2, *217*, *224*
Imruʾ al-Qays, 126–7, 129, 212, 284
informality, also see private situations, 187, 190, 281–4, 301
informants, xii–xiii, 5, *4*, *146*
inheritance, 80, 139

innovations, see *bid'a*
intention, 41, 185–6, 212–3
invective poetry, see *hijā'*
iqtibās, 168, 209–10
  – as a legal issue, 182, 194–6, 190–1
  frivolous –, 51–68, 97, 98, 113–4, 160, 162, 172, 200, 306, 307, *239*
  – from *ḥadīths*, 68–71
  serious –, 47–51, *93*, *102*
Iran, 31, 153, 230, *122*, *128*, *245*, *280*
Iraq, 30, 55, 83, 84, 123, 128, 143, 199, 205, 226, 254, *7*, *10*, *12*, *23*, *29*, *41*, *105*, *135*, *142*, *147–8*, *261*, *265*, *267*
  – as centre of civilisation, 240–2
Isfahan, 241
Islam,
  – and norms, 180–1, 190, 284–5
  ethic of –, 16, 26, 63, 190, 287–8
  jesting treatment of –, 51–102, 105–12, 153–4
  'pillars' of –, see *arkān al-dīn*
  role of – in everyday life, 45–6
  unity and variety in –, 5–6, 81, 237–8, 248–51, *7*
Ismāʿīlites, see Shiʿism
isnād, 72, 134
  parodistic –, 72–5, 254, 306, 307
istiḥlāl, 288
istihzā', 183, *191*
istikhfāf, 184
istishhād, *210*
ʿIyāḍ al-Yaḥṣubī, 184, 194

Jacob, 53, 59
Jaʿfar b. Abī Ṭālib, 83
Jaʿfar al-Ṣādiq, *203*
al-Jāḥiẓ, 4, 6, 147, 154, 210, 260, 261–2, 270–1, *77*, *128*, *135*, *139*, *152*, *170*, *211*, *255*
Jaḥshawayh, *137*
Jamāl al-Mulk al-ʿAbsī, 217
al-Jammāz, 131, 169, 267–8, *80*, *126*, *225*
Janān, *294–5*
Janissaries, 22
jār, 116
al-jarḥ wa-l-ta'dīl, see *ḥadīth* criticism
al-Jaṣṣāṣ, *188*
Jawanqā, ʿAlī b. al-Haytham, *152*
jesting, 40, 41, 102, 212–3, 222, 284, 308, *51*
  apologia of –, 197–8, 211
  – being culture-specific, 52, 61, 75–6
  condemnation of –, 15, 18, 183–4, 190, 194, *187*, *219*
  frivolous – in front of rulers, 20, 172–9, 275–9, *170*, *281*
  relative value of –, 13–20, 260
Jesus Christ, 39, 53, 101, *54*
Jews, 35, 59, 73, 111, *60*, *272*
jidd, also see seriousness, 18, 183, 212, 272, 284
jihād, 80
jinn, 59
Job, 53, 194, *57*
jokes, also see anecdotes
  – on grammarians, 101, 150–3, 307, *255*
  scholarly –, 63, 69, 70, 100, 141–3, 152–3, 203–4, *54*
joking relationship, 290
Jonah, 53, *57*
Joseph, 53, 59, 67, 133, *57*
al-Jubbā'ī, Abū Hāshim, 185
Judaism, see Jews
judges, also see *qāḍīs*, 15, 17, 99, 167, 169, 189, 205–7, 219–20, 221, *11*, *149*, *172*
Juḥā, 231–2, 307
al-Jurāwī, Aḥmad, 238
jurisprudents, jurists, also see *fiqh*, 10, 15, 22, 26, 73, 77–8, 81, 180–207, 239, 241, 285, 288, *4*, *169*, *208*

Kaʿba, 83, 87, 95–6, 107, *28*, *214*
kabīra, see sin
kadhib, see lying
Kāfūr al-Ikhshīdī, *226*
kalām, see theology
kalām al-rijāl, *20*
Karbalā', *83*, *84*
al-Karkh, 84, 126
Kathīr b. Samālīq al-Wakīl, 213
Kenya, *12*, *262*
al-Khabbāz al-Baladī, *256*
Khalaf al-Aḥmar, 152–3
khanīth, *12*
khamr, see wine
khamriyyāt, 286, *132*, *284*
al-Khāqānī, Abū ʿAlī, 24
al-Khārakī, 271, 292
Kharīdat al-qaṣr, 245, *214*
Khārijites, 86, *28*, *288*
al-Khashshāb, ʿAbdallāh, 256, *208*
khāṣṣa, xii, 3, 4–5, 13, 34, 57, 129, 252, 258–9, 269, 271–2, *167*, *198*, *209*
  criteria of belonging to –, 21–2, 26
  defining –, 21–3, 158–9, *181*
al-Khaṣṣāf, Abū Bakr Aḥmad, 188
al-Khaṭīb al-Baghdādī, 23
al-Khawārizmī, Abū Bakr, 272
al-Khawlānī, Yaʿmur, *80*
al-Khubzaruzzī, Naṣr b. Aḥmad, *256–7*, *295*
Khurāsān, 25, 129, 276
kijembe, *145*
killjoys, see *baghīḍ*
Kilpatrick, Hilary, *31*
kināya, 187
Kishtainy, Khalid, *245*
Kitāb al-aghānī, 89, *100*, *205*, *220*
Kitāb al-badī', 259–60
Kitāb al-bukhalā', 261–2, *154*
Kitāb faḍl al-surm 'alā l-fam, *149*
Kitāb al-imtāʿ wa-l-mu'ānasa, 37, 235, 305, 306–7
Kitāb al-khaḍkhaḍa fī jald 'Umayra, *149*

Kitāb al-saḥḥāqāt wa-l-baghghā'īn, *149*
Kitāb tafḍīl al-satihīn ʿalā l-ḥariḥīn wa-l-lāṭa ʿalā l-jammāshīn, *139*
Kraemer, Joel, 41, *287*
al-Kūfa, 47, 165, *15*, *208*
kufr, see unbelief
kufriyyāt, 214
Kurds, 26, *108*, *162*
Kushājim, 121
kuttāb, 24, 158–9, 180, 269
attitudes of – to *mujūn*, 207–14, 269

al-Lādhiqiyya, *223*
laghw, see 'empty talk'
Lagrange, Frédéric, 214
al-Lakhmī, *189*
lampoons, see *hijā'*
land, see metaphor
Lane, Edward, 7, *146*, *244*, *245*
Larzul, Sylvette, *257*
laughter, 15–7, 20, 191, *14*, *188*, *197–8*
– as ritually polluting, 15
Laylat al-Qadr, 94
legal schools, see *madhhab*, and also see the names of individual legal schools
lesbianism, 307, *11*, *149*
Lévy-Bruhl, Lucien, *xii*
libertines, libertinism, see *mujūn*
Lindholm, Charles, *251*
Lisān al-ʿarab, 272, *77*
literacy, 3–4, 22, 43, 47, 157, 159, 180, 207, 253, 272, *73–4*, *168*
littérateurs, also see *udabā'*, xiii, 17, 33, 47, 131, 167, 207–14, 216, 238, 241, 256, 257, *196*, *223*
liwāṭ, 9–12, 165, 284, 294–5, *208*, *257*, *268*
active role in –, 135–6
– as theme of *mujūn* literature, 38, 98–9, 132, 134–40, 244, 270
passive role in –, also see *ubna*, 11–2, 137, 141, 307
Luqmān, 53
lute, 30, 86, 231
lying, 103, 183, 191, 192, 193, 194

al-Maʿarrī, Abū l-ʿAlā', 102, 213, *194*, *270*
al-Madā'inī, Aḥmad b. Muḥammad, 153
Maʿdān, *7*
madhhab, 81, 160, 237, *76–7*
al-madhhab al-kalāmī, 76
madīḥ, see panegyric
madrasa, 45
Maghreb, 55, 71, 244
mujūn in the –, 238–40, *38*, *88*, *92*, *167*, *220–1*, *229*
Maghrebi people, 33, 71, 72
stereotypes of –, 71, 238–40
al-Mahdī (caliph), 24, 108, 173, 223, 271, 277
Maḥmūd b. Sabuktakīn, 170, 175
mahr, 80
majlis, 20, 174, 177, *15*, *257*
majlis al-uns, see private situations
makārim al-akhlāq, 201
al-Makhzūmī, Abū Ghilāla, 123
makrūh, 78–9, 194, 195, *189*
male prostitutes, also see *mukhannath*, 11, 35, 307, *12*, *95*, *242*, *262*, *272*
Mālik (guardian of Hell), 98, *194*
Mālikite school, 81, 184, 193–4, *15*, *189*, *300*
Malikshāh, 62
Mamlūk period, *164*, *262*
al-Ma'mūn (caliph), 20, 24–5, 99, 169, *11*, *173*, *174*
Manicheanism, *223*
al-Manṣūr (caliph), 24, 129, *100*, *173*, *227*
al-Manṭiqī, Abū ʿAlī, *86*
al-manzila bayna l-manzilatayn, *199–200*
maqāma, 142, 244, *77*, *89*, *147*, *193*, *284*
Marcus, Abraham, 7–8
Mardāwīj, 59
Marques, J. M., *300*
'Marsh Arabs', see *Maʿdān*
martyrdom, *80*
Marzolph, Ulrich, *38*, *42*, *51*
mastūr, see *satr*
masturbation, 148, *149*
al-Masʿūdī, Abū l-Ḥasan ʿAlī, 28
Mauritania, *20*
al-mawlid, 45
mawwāl, *mawwāliyā*, 254–5, *135*, *142*
maysir, 63
Mecca, 30, 49, 66, 87, 96–7, 130, 213, *8*, *11*, *85*, *92*, *104*, *228*, *241*
Medina, 101, 102, *12*, *85*, *137*, *187*, *241*
Meisami, Julie Scott, 159, 304, *295*
mentality, xii
Messiah, 102
Messick, Brinkley, *250*
metaphor, 33, 50–1, 52–3, 56, 87, 88, 94–5, 95–6, 97–9, 194, 307, *72*, *78*, *84*, *91*
land as – of homosexual intercourse, 138, *139*
sea as – of heterosexual intercourse, 138, *139*
Mīkālī family, *122*
Miliani, Hadj, *281*
misspelling, see *taṣḥīf*
mizāḥ, also see jesting, 192
etymology of –, *17–8*
Mongol invasion, 240, 244
Montgomery, James E., *162*
moral entrepreneurs, also see norms, 160, 288, 289
Moreh, Samuel, *6*
Morocco, 96, 279, *16*, *88*, *146*, *148*, *297*
Moses, 54, 55, *56*, *58*, *62*, *66*
Mosul, *11*, *257*
Mottahedeh, Roy, 3, 205
muʿadhdhar, see ʿidhār
Muʿāwiya (caliph), 25, 62
muezzin, see *adhān*

al-Mufaḍḍal b. ʿAbd al-Razzāq, 62
Mufākharat al-jawārī wa-l-ghilmān, *139*
al-Mufarrijī, Abū ʿAbdallāh, 147
mufti, also see *fatwā*, 186, 189
Muḥāḍarāt al-udabāʾ, 305, 307
al-Muhallabī, 168, 206, *26*
Muḥammad (prophet), 14, 22, 68, 70, 72, 104, 105, 107, 197, 202, 228, 229, 242, *16*, *63*, *83*, *290*
  insulting –, 106, 184, 186–7, 194, 222, 246, *164*, *213*, *221*
  jesting about –, 13, 71, 161, 191, *162*, *221*
muḥdath, see poetry
muḥtasib, 201, 236, *192*
al-Muʿizz b. Bādīs, 55
mujāhara, see discretion
Muʿjam al-udabāʾ, *152*
mujūn,
  – and discretion, 12, 41, 134, 174–9, 284–6, 308, *173*
  – and *ghazal*, 105, 130, 284, 304, 305, *283–4*, *295*
  – and norms, xi–xii, 35–6, 105–6, 114, 156–7, 196, 248–302
  – and subversiveness, 284–90
  – and the commoners, 34–5, 159–66, 252–8
  – and the *kuttāb*, 207–14, 269
  – and the political élite, 166–80
  – and the religious élite, 180–207
  – as behaviour, 37–9, 110, 186–9, 198, 258–9
  – as deviance, 155–6, 300–1
  – as genre, ix, 36–7, 283–4, 304
  – as literature, ix, 36–7
  – as social role, 295–302
  – as urban phenomenon, 35, 157–8, 237, 243–4
  conventionalisation of –, 290–4
  definition of –, 34–42, 105–12, 303–9
  dictionary meaning of –, 40-1
  fluidity of the boundaries of –, 105–6, 303–5, 309
  historical themes in –, 83–5
  impact of popular culture on –, 252–7
  – in recent times, 242–6
  offensiveness of –, 301–2, 307–8
  popularity of –, 159–246
  profitability of –, 233–6
  reception of –, 155–246
  regional differences in reception of –, 237–42
  religious themes in –, 60–112
  'sincerity' of –, 36, 293–5
  social context of –, 13
  token disapproval of –, 214, 245
  'unworthy' topics in –, 121–4
  use of dialectal words in –, 32–3, 253–6, *67*
mujūniyyāt, see *mujūn* as genre
mukaffirāt, see expiatory verses
mukhannath, 11, 102, 137, 172, 231, 262, 266, 272, 307, *11–2*, *170*
mumaḥḥiṣāt, see expiatory verses
Muʾmin b. Saʿīd, *59*
Munkar and Nakīr, 98, *102*
al-Muqtadir (caliph), 24, 145, 275–6, *33*
al-Muqtafī (caliph), 23, *220*, *254*
murūʾa, 18, 116–7, *23*, *188*, *285*
Mūsā al-Kāẓim, *235*
al-Muṣʿabī, Isḥāq b. Ibrāhīm, 20
muṣādara, *276*
musaḥḥirūn, *92*
Musaylima, 84
music, 16, 122, 130, 175, 186, 187–8, 206, 219, 231, *78*, *132*, *173*
Muslim b. al-Walīd, 121
al-Mustaḍīʾ (caliph), 104
al-Mustanjid (caliph), 168, *208*
Muʾta, *83*
al-Muʿtaḍid (caliph), 25, 176, 232, *164*, *222–3*, *280*
al-Mutanabbī, Abū l-Ṭayyib, 104–5, 118, 212, 213, 292, *162–3*, *194*, *226*
al-Muʿtaṣim (caliph), 32, *257*
al-Mutawakkil (caliph), *83*, *234*, *275*
Muʿtazilism, Muʿtazilites, also see theology, 25, 177, 185, 229, *76*, *189–90*, *199–200*
Muṭīʿ b. Iyās, 271, *131–2*, *137*, *165*, *220*, *224*, *225*
al-Muwashshā, 268, 269
muwashshaḥ, 111, 255
Muzabbid, 68, 101–2, 231
mysticism, see Sufism

Nabateans, see *nabaṭī*
nabaṭī, also see peasantry, 30–1, 35
nabīdh, 81, 100, 160, 299, *188*, *300*
Nadel, S. F., 296–7
nadīm, see boon-companion
al-Nafzāwī, 235, *75*
naḥw, 141–2, 150–3
al-Najafī, Ḥusayn Qassām, *254*
al-Najjār, Ḥusayn, 154
al-Namarī, Manṣūr, *201*
al-Nāshiʾ, ʿAlī b. ʿAbdallāh, 39, 292, *256*
al-Nāṣir (Cordoban ruler), 17
Naṣr b. Aḥmad al-Sāmānī, *227*
Nasreddin Hoca, 231
Nathr al-durr, 234–5
nāṭif, *77*
al-Nāṭiq, Abū Ṭālib, 185
nawādir, see anecdotes
al-Nawawī, 195
Nawbakht family, *293*
Nawfal b. Musāḥiq, 78–9
Nawrūz, 289
Nazhūn al-Gharnāṭiyya, 59
al-Naẓẓām, Ibrāhīm, *76*, *199–200*
Newcomb, T. H., *296*
nifāq, see hypocrisy
al-Nimayrī, Jaʿfar, *259*
Nishwār al-muḥāḍara, *135*
niyya, see intention
Niẓām al-Mulk, 104, 168

normative behaviour, see norms
norms,
– as different from values, 1–2, 12–3, 46
breaches of –, 8–12, 35–6, 40–1, 111–2, 156, 248, 308–9
changes in –, 114, 237, 245–6
conformity to –, 167, 215–6, 279–80, *300*
definition of –, 1–2, 196
difference in – for old and young, 259–60
expectations of conformity to –, 106, 156, 237, 245–6, 258–9, *175*
– in the descriptive sense, 2, 46
– in the prescriptive sense, 2, 7–8, 46
transgression versus questioning of –, 285–8
validity of –, 2, 7–8, 12, 279–80, 281–2, 284–5, 289
North Africa, see Maghreb

oaths, 161, 182, 185, 191, 230
obscenity,
controversies concerning –, 191, 193, 210, *196*
– in *mujūn* literature, x, 35, 71, 79, 90, 110, 115, 124, 127, 135, 140, 151, 160, 169, 205, 218, 231, 235, 244–5, 254, 267, 305, 307, *63–4, 94, 95, 129, 139, 174, 208, 214, 275, 284, 292*
Oman, *12, 28, 146*
orality, 4, 33–4, 253, *252*
role of – in *mujūn* literature, 37, 43–4, 63, 101, 161–2, 243, 283, *126, 149*
oral remarks as source of written *mujūn*, 37–9, 44, 55, 74, 92–3, 119, 139–40, 142, 149, 253–8, *80, 104, 199*
Ottoman period, *135, 209, 269*

panegyric, 19, 96, 102–5, 127, 178, 192, 193, 194, 213, 221, 227–8, 273, 275, 278, 283–4, *226*
Paradise, 69, 97–101, 112, 224, 231, *194*
parasites, 122–3
parody, 118–9, 125–7, 130, 150–4, 306, *291*
importance of – in *mujūn* literature, 75, 306
– of *isnād*, 72–5, 254, 306, 307
– of theological discourse, 76, 154
– of Sufi discourse, 153–4
paronomasia, also see double entendre, 141–4
peasantry, also see rural population, 3, 4, 30, 35, 157, 253, 266
Pellat, Charles, 243, *17*
Perfumed Garden, see *al-Rawḍ al-ʿāṭir*
Persian language, 24, 34, 61, 143, 306, *53, 86, 87, 149, 169, 284*
Darī dialect of –, 24
Persians, 31, 96, 129, 187, 289, *174*
Pharaoh, 52, 53
philosophy, 76, 154
pilgrimage, also see Mecca, 95–7, 104, 213, *28, 85*
plague, 67–8
poetic personae, 117–8, 291
'sincerity' of –, 36, 292–5
poetry, 19–20, 48–9, 64, 102–5, 216–7, 254–5, 283–4, 290–1, 305–6
– and piety, 232–3, 287–8, 294
– as a legal issue, 181–2, 184–5, 190–6
– being like any other type of discourse, 182, 184–5, 192
developments in *muḥdath* poetry, 118, 125–8, 290–2
evaluations of 'modern' –, 208–12, 238
police, 20, *173*
popular culture, also see ʿāmma, 23, 249, 252–8
'old' and 'new' folklore within –, 252–3
Potiphar, 59, 67, 133
prayer, 15, 29, 32, 66, 70, 77, 85–90, 92, 110, 126, 165–6, 178, 192
– as metaphor of anal intercourse, 88
buffoonery at –, 89, 172, 191
wilful neglect of –, 36, 187, 288
preachers, 4, 163, 164, 191, 198, 205
popular –, 27, 28, 57, 85, 89
prestige, 13, 41, 258, 301, *181*
privacy, 8, 174–5, 284–5, *285–6*
private situations, also see privacy
ambiguity of –, 175–9
– as typical setting of *mujūn*, 37, 146–7, 169, 178–9, 206, 257, 282–4, *171, 173*
separation of – and public ones, 146, 174–9, 206, 258, 280–1, *260*
prophets, 36, 53–6, 59, 70, 104–5, 133, 194
false –, 84, 229, *83, 290*
'prophetic medicine', see *al-ṭibb al-nabawī*
prose, 61–4, 73, 192, 195, *42, 65, 138, 210, 284*
relative value of –, 19–20
prosification, 49
prostitution, 8, 11–2, *79, 199*
– as theme of literature, 130–1, 307, *149*
protagonists of *mujūn* texts, 229–32
Bedouins as –, 62, 67, 230–1
commoners as –, 229–30
fictitious –, 229, 231–2
grammarians as –, 101, 150–1
historical personalities as –, 229, 232
ignoramuses as –, 229–31
jurisprudents as –, 70, 73, 77–8
proverbs, 49, 55, 95, 119, 162, 271, 306, *10, 16, 17, 50, 54, 124, 128, 142, 255*
prudery, 9, 210–1, 245, *34*
public baths, 110, 198, 219, *210*
publicity, also see discretion,
– of homosexual relationships, 10–1, 134–5, 137
– of *mujūn*, 174–7, 280–1, 285
public opinion, 23–6, 28–9, 165–6
public situations, 175–7, 258, 275, *170*
eating as –, 28
punishment, 10, 186–7, 215–7, 274, 277–8, 288, *11–2, 174, 280, 290*
discretionary –, 194, 195, 198, 226, *173*
– for *hijāʾ* and political criticism, 179, 217–8, 220–7

– for *mujūn* works, 172, 179, 215–9, 222–7, 264
qadhf, 79, 186–7, 191
qāḍīs, 9, 15, 25, 76, 147, 180, 203, 226, *4, 11, 22, 140, 174, 219–20*
stereotyping of – as not overly pious, 205–7
al-Qāhir (caliph), 175
qahqaha, see laughter
al-Qāri᾿ al-Harawī, Nūr al-Dīn ᶜAlī, 185
al-Qarṭājannī, Ḥāzim, *255*
qaṣīda, 19, 125–7, 193, 208, 306, *291*
qāt, *201*
al-Qaynī, Abū l-Ṭamaḥān, 111
al-Qazwīnī, Jalāl al-Dīn Muḥammad, 33
qibla, 87, 95
qiṣāṣ, *80*
qiyāma, see resurrection
quick repartee, 266–8, 306, 307
– as important part of ẓarf, 266–8, 274, 275–7
effeminates as good at –, 102, 231, 266
Qumm, 242
Quran, 15, 25, 31–2, 46, 47–68, 71, 92, 104, 114, 145, 181–2, 183, 184, 187, 199, 230, 264, 277, *16, 20, 112, 163, 197, 203, 217, 222, 226, 270, 294, 300*
– as source of motifs in *mujūn*, 51–68, 80, 93, 94, 97–9, 100–2, 108–9, 138–9, 170, 172, 184, 239, 264, *33, 82, 133, 161–2, 230, 272, 300*
inimitability of the –, 39, 47, 83, 107, 228
memorising the –, 45, 47, 65–6, 69, 180
quotation from the –, see *iqtibās*,
Quranic school, 22, 45, 306
Quran readers, 35, 108
quṣṣāṣ, see preachers
Quṭrabbul, 206

al-Rabīᶜ b. Yūnus, *224*
Rabīᶜa b. Thābit al-Raqqī, 88
al-Rāḍī (caliph), 21, 164
Raḍī al-Dīn Hibatallāh b. al-Ḥasan, 130, *208*
al-Rāghib al-Iṣbahānī, 305
raï music, *78, 132, 142*
Rajā᾿ b. al-Ḍaḥḥāk, 148
Ramadan, 45, 90–4, 192, 282, *79, 193*
lampooning –, 90–3, 306
al-Rāmhurmuzī, Abū l-Ḥasan al-Ṣā᾿igh, 293, *90*
Raqᶜ al-libās wa-kashf al-iltibās fī ḍarb al-mathal min al-Qur᾿ān wa-l-iqtibās, *194*
al-Raqāshī, 119
al-Rawḍ al-ᶜāṭir, 66, 74–5, 235, *71, 149, 167*
al-Rayy, 24, 177, *208*
Reconquista, 246, 289
refinement, see ẓarf
religious élite, see ᶜulamā᾿
repentance, 109, 186, 232–3
– as an accepted possibility in *mujūn*, 233, 287–8, 294
partial –, *189*
rejection of –, 189, *217, 285*
reproacher, see ᶜādhil, ᶜādhila
respectability, 18, 113, 268, 273, 280, *151, 201*
resurrection, 53, 98, 101–2
retaliation, see *qiṣāṣ*
ribā, see usury
Riḍwān, 98, *194*
riots, 26, 163–4
al-Risāla al-baghdādiyya, 82, *57, 148*
Risāla fī l-alfāẓ al-mukaffirāt, 183
Risālat al-ghufrān, 102
rithā᾿, see elegy
Rosen, Lawrence, 279, *297*
Rowson, Everett K., *37, 41*
Rubāṭāb, *16, 20, 261*
al-Rūdhrāwarī, Abū Shujāᶜ, 23
rural population, also see peasantry, 3, 4, 7, 19, 29–31, 35, 45, 157–8, 237, 243–4, 253, 266, *12, 128*

Ṣaᶜāyda, *31*
al-Saᶜdī, *149*
al-Saffāḥ (caliph), 178
safīh, 189
ṣaghīra, see sin
ṣāḥib al-ghilmān, *138*
al-Ṣāḥib Ismāᶜīl b. ᶜAbbād, 24, 26, 70, 92, 107, 124, 145–6, 171, 177, 180, 272, *105, 174*
ṣāḥib al-nisā᾿, *138*
ṣāḥib al-zanādiqa, also see *zandaqa*, 223
saḥir, *261*
Said, Edward, 250
al-Sājī, Abū Manṣūr, 21
al-Sājī, Zakariyyā, 204
al-Salāmī, 278
Ṣāliḥ (prophet), 54
Salm al-Khāsir, 39
samāᶜ, see singing,
al-Samarqandī, Abū l-Layth, 182, *15, 22*
Sāmarrā, 142, *295*
sāqī, 136
Ṣarīᶜ al-Dilā᾿, *236*
Ṣarīᶜ al-Fālūdhaj, 121
Ṣarīᶜ al-Ghawānī, see Muslim b. al-Walīd
al-Sarī al-Raffā᾿, *257*
Satan, 27, 39, *15, 51*
satr, also see discretion, privacy, 280
sawād, *sawādī*, see peasantry,
sawālif, *19–20*
al-Ṣaydalānī, ᶜUthmān, 77
al-Ṣaymarī, Abū l-ᶜAnbas, *139, 149, 275*
scatology, also see *sukhf*, 41, 124, 148, 149, 160, 161, 235, 307
sea, see metaphor
secretaries, also see *kuttāb*, 4, 19, 24, 158–9, 180, 237, 252, 269, *267, 278*
secular,
distinction between religious and –, 44, 45, 113–4, *262*
Sefrou, 279, *297*
self-censorship, 227–33

self-restraint, 144, 145
Seljuk dynasty, 62
Seljuk period, 51, 84, 104, 130, 141, 168, 213, 217, 244, 245, *86*, *126*, *199*, *208*, *257*, *265*, *276*
seriousness, 35, 40, 48, 102, 128, 152, 160–1, 169, 177, 182, 183–6, 195, 211, 212–3, 283–4, 290, *129*, *131*, *201*, *273*, *292*
  relative value of –, 12–3, 18–20, 122, 153, 190, 212–3, 234–5, 260, 272
sermons, 32, 48, 49, 57, 88, 164
  mock –, 28, 89–90, 112, 132, 137–8, 191, 306
Serôdio, R. G., *300*
Seven Sleepers, 53, 55
Seville, *240*
sex, 8–12, 113, 186, 280, 284, 285, *146*, *188*, *199*, *268*, *288*
  – as subject of *mujūn*, 41, 44, 53, 65, 70, 127, 129–40, 148–9, 177, 244, 264, 292, 305, 307, *79*, *86*, *90*, *111*, *126*, *167*, *174*, *214*, *245*
  casual attitudes to –, 130–2, 134, 135–6
  sexual impotence, 121, 307
  sexual innuendoes, 53, 65, 69, 74–5, 87, 88, 99, 141–2, 187, 190
sexual segregation, 3
al-Shaʿbī, 73, 306, *203*
Shāfiʿite school, 7, 182–3, 184–5, 189, 191–3, 195–6, 287–8, 293, *14*, *188*, *194*, *285*, *300*
al-Shahrazūrī, Ibn al-Ṣalāḥ, 287–8
shalandī, 277–8
sharaf, see honour
sharīʿa, 14, 15, 44, 113, 186–9, 191–6, 214, 249, *78*, *173*, *208*, *259*, *299–300*
al-Sharīf al-Raḍī, also see *ashrāf*, 235
Shawwāl, 93
al-Shayzarī, *236*
Sheba, 55
Shiʿism, Shiʿites, 81, 163, 164, *86*, *198*, *218*, *236*
  Ismāʿīlite –, 58
  Twelver –, 23, 26, 84, 189, 194, *41*, *235*, *242*
  Zaydite –, 185, *216–7*
al-Shīrajī, Abū Muḥammad, 73
Shiraz, 240, *169*
Shuʿba, 73
al-Shurūṭī, Abū l-Maʿālī, *257*
shuṭṭār, *10*
shuʿūbiyya, 128, *125*
Ṣiffīn, 83, *84*
al-Sijistānī, Abū Ḥātim, 154
sikbāj, *121*
sin, 10, 14, 63, 111, 135, 165, 189, 199, 211–2, 233, 280, 281–2, 285, 287–8, 306, *191*, *200*, *217*, *299–300*
  major –, 15, 106, *68*
  minor –, 15, 106
singing, 16, 33, 39, 53, 78, 93, 95, 130, 175, 188, 205, 219, 228, 262, , *80*, *132*, *173*, *220*,
ṣirāṭ, 98
ṣīṣiyya, *135*
slang, also see Arabic, 43–4, 63, 79, 82, 254, 256, *98*
slaves, slavery, 10–1, 79–80, 131, 175–6, 180, 182, 230, *135*
slave-girls, 8, 39, 95, 133, 193, 207, 219, *54*, *149*, *294–5*
Snouck Hurgronje, C., 66, *8*
social role, 295–302
  – and status, 296
sodomy, see *liwāṭ*
Solomon, 53, 57, 59, 170, *54*
source material,
  biases of –, 3–4, 20–1
  problems of using –, 3–8, 37, 243, *33*
  types of –, 6–7, 36–7
spongers, see ṭufaylī
status, 258–9, 296
stories, also see *akhbār*, anecdotes, 6, 52–3, 59, *20*, *38*, *57*, *153*, *188*
al-Subkī, Bahāʾ al-Dīn, 195
Sudan, *16*, *20*, *89*, *101*, *259*, *261*, *267*
al-Suddī, 267
Sufism, Sufis, 4, 38, *10*, *16*, *109*, *152*, *162*, *203*, *216*
  typical discourse of –, 153–4
Ṣufriyya, see Khārijites
Sufyān b. ʿUyayna, 73, 204
sujūd, see prayer
sukhf, also see obscenity, 110, 115, 118, 124, 148–9, 169, 188, 235–6, 307, *77*, *284*
al-Sulamī, Abū Ḥafṣ ʿUmar, 223
Sulaymān b. ʿAbd al-Malik (caliph), *68*
al-Ṣūlī, Abū Bakr, 209, 255, *137*, *152*, *235*, *294*
ṣuʿlūk poets, 117
sunna, 103, *21*
Sunnites, 7, 23, 81, 84, 163, 185, *242*
sūqa, see ʿāmma
al-Suyūṭī, Jalāl al-Dīn, 48, 195, 210, *194*, *196*
Swahili, *88*, *145*, *162–3*, *267*
Syria, 33, 229, 240, *23*, *84*, *223*

ṭabāhija, 74
Ṭabaqāt al-shuʿarāʾ, 165
al-Ṭabarī, 163–4, 173
tadbīr, 182
taʾdīb, see *taʿzīr*,
taḍmīn, 143, *210*
al-Ṭāhir al-Jazarī, *10–1*
Tāj al-Ruʾasāʾ Nasīb b. al-Mūṣalāyā, 62
Talbīs Iblīs, 204
tamaththul, *210*
Tamīm b. Mufarrij al-Ṭāʾī, *86*
Tamīm b. al-Muʿizz, 72
al-Tamīmī, Muḥammad b. Ḥafṣ, *205*
al-Tanūkhī, 206, 232, *4*, *22*, *86*
tarāwīḥ, also see Ramadan, 92
taʿrīḍ, 187
taṣḥīf, 168

taverns, 35, 81, 178, 254, 257, 292
ṭawāf, 95
al-Tawḥīdī, Abū Ḥayyān, 24, 26, 36–7, 92, 107, 171, 211, 235, 255, 305, *148*, *174*
tawjīh, see double entendre
tawriya, see double entendre
tayammum, 87
ta'zīr, also see punishment, 226
taẓlīm Allāh, 184
testimony, 188–9, 219–20, *187–8*, *220*, *221*, *285*
al-Tha'ālibī, Abū Manṣūr, 57, 204, 210, 241, 269, *214*, *272*
Tha'lab, Abū l-'Abbās, 151
al-Thamānīnī, 22
thaqīl, 56, 202, *240*
theology, 6, 47, 82, 177, 201
  – as source of literary motifs, 76, *77*
  parodies of typical discourse of –, 76, 154
Thumāma b. Ashras, 25
al-ṭibb al-nabawī, 71
Tihāma, 30
tikka, 133
Touareg, *145*
traders, 21, 22, 24, 159, 299
transgression, 1, 41, 287, 303, 308
Trinity, 82
Trumpet of Judgement Day, 98
ṭufaylī, *66*
Tunis, *38*, *64*, *92*, *167*, *220–1*, *229*
Turks, 108
al-Ṭūsī, Abū Ja'far Muḥammad, 26, 189, 194
al-Tustarī, Sahl, *27*
tutelage, 189
Ṭuways, 262

'Ubayd-i Zākānī, 61, *169*
ubna, *137*
udabā', 152, 207
'udhrite love, 129–30, 210–1
Uḥud, *83*
'Ukbarā, 205, 206
'ulamā', 10, 15–7, 82, 159, 180–207, 215
  easygoing attitudes among –, 185–6, 197, 202–7
  heterogeneity of –, 167, 181, 196–7, 249
  influence of –, 180–1, 198–9, 269
  intolerant attitudes among –, 16–7, 190–2, 197, 202–3
  role of – in determining norms, 196, 260
'Ulayya bt. al-Mahdī, 108
'Umar b. Abī Rabī'a, 97, 130, *208*, *283*
'Umar b. al-Khaṭṭāb (caliph), *83*
Umayyad period, 17, 30, 114, 115, 130, 172, 205, 241, 262, 264, *117–8*, *129*, *132*, *170*, *171*
umma, 46, 250
unbelief, 14, 106, 110–1, 182–6, 190–1, 196, 201, 212, 214, 288, 294, *90*, *105*, *187*, *193*, *200*, *216–7*
underclass, 4, 143, 256
Upper Egypt, *31*
urban population, 4, 29–30, 115, 127–8, 243–4, 253, *7*, *181*
al-Usṭurlābī, *235–6*
uṣūl, 114
usury, 276
'Uthmān al-Khayyāṭ, 90
'Uthmān al-Warrāq, 28

values, 1–2, 12–3
  alternative –, 258–65
  situational –, 279–84
  value judgements, 13–32
  value scales, 260–1
verbal duels, 267, *138*
versification, 48–9
Victorian attitudes, 129, 245
Wagner, Ewald, *235*
Wahb b. Sulaymān, 124
al-Wajīh, 283
Wāliba b. al-Ḥubāb, 173, 270, *135*
al-Walīd b. Yazīd (caliph), 67–8, 83, 171, 270, *132*, *175*
al-Wallāda, *257*
al-Walwālijī, 193, *188*, *200*
al-Wansharīsī, Abū l-'Abbās, 193
waqf, 67
war, 18, 80, 83, 119, 246
al-Wasāṭa bayna l-zunāt wa-l-lāṭa, 138–9
al-Washshā', 18, *203*
  anachronistic views of –, *268*
al-Wāsiṭ, 123, *220*, *256*
al-Wāsiṭī, Abū l-Fatḥ Hibatallāh, *220*
'waste of time', 15–6, 190, 192
  jesting as –, 14
al-Wāthiq (caliph), 175, *227*
al-Wa'wā' al-Dimashqī, *256*
weavers, 29, 77
al-wildān al-mukhalladūn, 98–9
wine, also see bacchic poetry, boon-companion, 8, 36, 41, 44, 63, 73, 74, 80, 81, 82, 86, 100, 107, 109, 111–2, 119, 126, 132, 136, 160, 169, 173–4, 175, 178, 187, 193, 198, 201, 202, 206, 263, 280, 285, 286, 288, 289, 292, 299, 300, *146*, *176*, *188*, *219–20*, *245*
wit, see ẓarf
women, 3, 7, 8–9, 65–6, 192–4, 199, 217, 266, 281, *188*, *259*, *261*, *288*
  – as libertines, 133–4, 20, 231, *11*, *148*, *149*, *245*
  – as preferable to boys, 305, *138*, *139*
  – as topic of *mujūn*, 129–34, 54, 55, 66, 70, 79, 88, 110, 242, 307, *71*, *92*, *294–5*
wuḍū', 87

Yaḥyā b. Aktham, 25, 169, 180, 205, *172*
  – as notorious pederast, 99, *11*, *140*
Yāqūt al-Ḥamawī, 17, 21, 22, *89*, *122*
Yatīmat al-dahr, *214*
Yazīd I (caliph), 7, 111

Yazīd b. ʿAbd al-Malik (caliph), *139*
Yazīd b. Hārūn, 73
al-Yazīdī, al-Faḍl, 142
Yemen, 30, *20, 32, 76, 145, 152, 198, 201, 244, 259, 267*
Yūsuf Idrīs, *89*

zabāniya, 98
Ẓabyat al-Wādī, *132*
Zādmihr, 95
al-Zaʿfarānī, Abū l-Qāsim, *128*
al-Zāhira palace, *104*
Ẓāhiriyya school, 81
zajal, 238, 254–5, *86*
zakāt,
  metaphorical usages of the term –, 94–5, 307
zandaqa, 165, 186–7, 223–4, 271, *226, 287, 299–300*
zaqqūm, 98
ẓarf, 29, 262, 264, 265–79, *299*
  – and piety, 270–1, 282, *233*
  close association of – with *mujūn*, 241, 268–73, 293, 301
  constituents of –, 266–73, 274
  definition of –, 265–6
  English terms corresponding to –, 265
al-Zawāwī, Muḥammad ʿAwāna, *167*
Zenāta, see Berbers
zinā, 8, 36, 129–34, 186
zindīq, see *zandaqa*,
Zīrid dynasty, 55, 72
Ziryāb, *240*
Ziyārid dynasty, 59
Zoroastrianism, Zoroastrians, xi, 81, 306, *82*
zuhdiyyāt, 49
zumāward, see *bazmāward*
ẓurafāʾ, see ẓarf